Conversational Interaction in Second Language Acquisition:
A Collection of Empirical Studies

Published in this series

Conversational Interaction in Second Language Acquisition:

A Collection of Empirical Studies

Edited by
ALISON MACKEY

OXFORD
UNIVERSITY PRESS

OXFORD

UNIVERSITY PRESS

Great Clarendon Street, Oxford OX2 6DP

Oxford University Press is a department of the University of Oxford.
It furthers the University's objective of excellence in research, scholarship,
and education by publishing worldwide in

Oxford New York

Auckland Cape Town Dar es Salaam Hong Kong Karachi
Kuala Lumpur Madrid Melbourne Mexico City Nairobi
New Delhi Shanghai Taipei Toronto

With offices in

Argentina Austria Brazil Chile Czech Republic France Greece
Guatemala Hungary Italy Japan Poland Portugal Singapore
South Korea Switzerland Thailand Turkey Ukraine Vietnam

OXFORD and OXFORD ENGLISH are registered trade marks of
Oxford University Press in the UK and in certain other countries

ISBN: 978 0 19 442249 9

Printed in Spain by Ungraf S.L.

Contents

Acknowledgements

I am very grateful to many people who have assisted me with aspects of this edited collection. First, Rod Ellis encouraged my idea for a state of the art collection on interaction and suggested Oxford University Press, where it immediately found a home. Cristina Whitecross, Simon Murison-Bowie, and Jane Magrane at Oxford were a pleasure to work with, and their professional assistance throughout the project was inspiring. Critical to the quality of the book were the reviewers: Jenefer Philp, who read the whole volume, Lourdes Ortega, who reviewed the meta-analysis in the Epilogue, and numerous other anonymous evaluators, who took the time to provide careful, detailed, and insightful comments on particular chapters and sections. Next, I would like to thank several talented and dedicated Georgetown University Ph.D. students who provided invaluable help at various stages in the editing process, in particular, Jaemyung Goo, as well as Rebecca Sachs and Mika Hama. Also, each of the contributors to this collection deserves special thanks for their strenuous efforts in providing chapters that are significant and timely, as well as for the comments several of them made on the content and organization of the book. I also want to express gratitude to my colleagues at Georgetown University who investigate and teach on a wide range of aspects of second language acquisition, bilingualism, and applied linguistics in a number of departments, collectively creating a stimulating working environment. After almost a decade at Georgetown, I still feel privileged to work for an institution which values scholarship and provides support for that precious and important commodity: time to work on research. I would also like to thank Teresa Pica and Michael H. Long, for their crucial encouragement and support as I started on this research path. I conclude with heartfelt thanks to my family for their unwavering support for me as I worked on this project. The result, in the end, is a volume that I believe makes a valuable and significant contribution to the field of second language acquisition.

Introduction

The role of conversational interaction in second language acquisition

ALISON MACKEY

Background

There has been an extraordinary amount of progress in research in the field of second language acquisition (SLA) in recent years. While there is still no universally accepted theory of second language acquisition, a growing body of empirical findings has led researchers in a variety of sub-areas to expand their horizons by taking a more interdisciplinary view. For example, some researchers have begun to explore the learner-internal cognitive mechanisms that impact second language (L2) learning; others are documenting the importance of social and cultural factors, and still others are investigating innate linguistic universals. The ultimate goal is to integrate different perspectives and sources of information into one complete theory. However, the current division of SLA research into discrete areas of focus is practical, since it provides a means for tackling the enormous task of accounting for the multitude of variables which impact the L2 learning process. It also reflects researchers' particular preoccupations: some are primarily interested in SLA as a means of learning more about the human brain, for instance, while others are more concerned with L2 learning as an educational or social process. Different approaches have identified particular phenomena as more or less theoretically interesting and relevant to the task of explaining SLA. While this has both originated from and led to disagreements about basic issues (for example, the role of a learner's first language, the nature of L2 knowledge, the interfaces between explicit and implicit knowledge, the role of language production, and so on), at the same time, it makes for stimulating debates and collaborations.

Interaction research, in particular, has reached an exciting stage in its development. Having carved out an initial area of inquiry, it has now come to the point where researchers are contemplating the scope of the area, leading to questions which are qualitatively different from what they used to be. For example, the early research in the late 1970s and early 1980s was propelled by Hatch's (1978) proposal that, fundamentally, 'language learning evolves out of learning how to carry on conversations, out of learning how to communicate' (ibid.: 63), as well as by Long's (1981) work which suggested that 'participation in conversation with native speakers, made possible through modification of interaction, is the necessary and sufficient condition for SLA' (ibid.: 275). Also influential at the time was Krashen's (1978) Input Hypothesis, which argued that adult SLA was driven primarily by exposure to sufficient amounts of comprehensible input, such that the comprehension of language at a level slightly more advanced than a learner's current level led automatically to acquisition. While Krashen's ideas have often been criticized for lack of specificity, they nonetheless represent significant first steps in exploring relationships between input and acquisition which are still being investigated today. Following on the idea of input that is comprehensible and the potential value of interaction, Long (1983) suggested that if conversational adjustments in interaction help make input more comprehensible, and this is facilitative of L2 learning, then the linguistic and conversational adjustments that occur during interaction may promote language learning. These important claims, known as Long's 'Interaction Hypothesis' led to a great deal of work, including many early research efforts focused on demonstrating links between interaction and language comprehension. One major qualitative difference between early interaction research and interaction research today is that, having found relationships between specific interactional processes and learning outcomes, researchers are able to be increasingly precise in their questions regarding *how* interaction creates opportunities for learning.

One of the earliest studies to move away from the research goals of the 1980s and toward a focus on L2 development from interaction was Mackey's (1995, 1999) investigation of the link between interaction and L2 learning. This relatively small-scale study involved five groups of adult ESL learners and explored the relationship between interaction (and the influence of developmental readiness) and the development of question formation in English. Some of the learners engaged in communicative tasks, interacting with native speakers; others received pre-modified input from a native speaker (NS) interlocutor, and others simply observed the interactions without participating actively. Pienemann and Johnston's (1987) well-established developmental sequence for question formation was used to analyze the learners' production of question forms in pre- and post-tests. Whereas most of the developmentally-ready learners who had engaged in active interactions showed stage progression, the other groups did not demonstrate unambiguous evidence of development. This early study was followed by a number of similar inquiries into interaction and learning, by a range of researchers working in different contexts, and has since led the field to view learners' active negotiation for meaning in the process of communication as a vehicle for L2 learning. In Long's (1996) updated version of the Interaction Hypothesis, he maintains that interaction, while not sufficient for SLA, is highly beneficial, because it 'connects input, internal learner capacities, particularly selective attention, and output in productive ways' (pp. 451–2). Conceptualizations of the important constructs that are part of the current Interaction Hypothesis will be described and exemplified next.

To date, more than forty published empirical studies have investigated the relationship between interaction and L2 learning, with most of them providing some measure of support for claims that interaction benefits learning. Indeed, research advancements in this area have gone so far as to lead Gass and Mackey (2006) to argue that the Interaction Hypothesis shows signs of progression toward a theory. They contend that, in its current version, the Interaction Hypothesis 'includes elements of a hypothesis (an idea that needs to be tested about a single phenomenon), elements of a model (a description of processes or a set of processes of a phenomenon), as well as elements of a theory (a set of statements about natural phenomena that explains why these phenomena occur the way they do)' (ibid.: 174). As Table o.1 below illustrates, studies of interaction have been carried out in a range of different classroom and laboratory settings, with participants from a wide range of L1 backgrounds and ages, including children, adolescents, younger adults, and older adults. Although most studies have focused on syntactic or morphological features of L2s, some have examined lexical learning, and a variety of L2s have been the learning targets (most commonly English, Japanese, and Spanish). Interestingly, there has been very little interaction research to date that has focused on the acquisition of phonological features or pragmatics, although there is no reason to suspect that these areas would not be impacted by interaction. Many studies have measured L2 development using pre- and post-tests, while others have focused on learning opportunities or learner uptake, making the assumption or argument that they are developmentally helpful. The meta-analysis presented in the final chapter (Mackey and Goo this volume) sheds more light on the collective knowledge obtained from these studies.

Study[a]	Interactional focus Linguistic focus Participants
Developmental (for example, employing pre- and post-tests)	

a Classroom contexts	Doughty and Varela (1998)	Corrective recasts Past tense ESL, adolescents
	R. Ellis (this volume)	Recasts, metalinguistic feedback Past tense, comparative '–er' ESL, adults
	R. Ellis and He (1999)	Modified input, modified output Vocabulary (nouns) ESL, adults
	R. Ellis, Loewen, and Erlam (2006)	Recasts, metalinguistic feedback Past tense ESL, adults
	R. Ellis, Tanaka, and Yamazaki (1994)	Negotiation of meaning Vocabulary (nouns) EFL, adolescents
	Havranek and Cesnik (2001); Havranek (2002)	Recasts, elicitations, explicit corrections Grammar, lexicon, pronunciation EFL, range of ages
	Loewen (2005)	Focus-on-form episodes, uptake Grammar, vocabulary, pronunciation ESL, adults
	Loewen and Philp (2006)	Recasts, elicitation, metalinguistic feedback Grammar, vocabulary, pronunciation ESL, adults
	Lyster (2004)	Prompts, recasts Grammatical gender French immersion, children
	Mackey (2006a)	Interactional feedback, noticing Questions, plurals, past tense ESL, adults
	Muranoi (2000)	Interaction enhancement (recasts, requests for repetition) Articles EFL, adults
	Sheen (this volume)	Recasts, metalinguistic feedback Articles ESL, adults
	Soler (2002)	LREs, mediating strategies Pragmatics (requests) EFL, adults
	Swain and Lapkin (1998, 2002)	LREs Lexicon, form, discourse French immersion, adolescents
	Tocalli-Beller and Swain (this volume)	LREs, languaging Vocabulary (multiple meanings) ESL, adults

	Study	Interactional focus Linguistic focus Participants
b Laboratory contexts	Adams (this volume)	Feedback Questions, past tense, locative prepositions ESL, adults
	Ayoun (2001)	Recasts, models (written/computerized) Verb tense (*passé composé, imparfait*) French FL, adults
	de la Fuente (2002, 2003)	Negotiation, pushed output Vocabulary (nouns) Spanish FL, adults
	Egi (this volume)	Recasts, learners' interpretations Morphosyntax, lexicon Japanese FL, adults
	R. Ellis and Heimbach (1997)	Negotiation of meaning Vocabulary (nouns) ESL, children
	Gass and Alvarez Torres (2005)	Input, interaction Gender agreement, *estar* + location, vocabulary Spanish FL, adults
	Gass and Varonis (1994)	Interaction Subsequent task success (comprehension, production) ESL, adults
	Han (2002b)	Recasts Past tense ESL, adults
	Ishida (2004)	Recasts Aspectual form (*–te –i(ru)*) Japanese FL, adults
	Iwashita (2003)	Recasts, negotiation, models Verb morpheme (*–te* form), locative construction Japanese FL, adults
	Jeon (this volume)	Interaction Morphosyntax (relative clauses, honorific agreement), lexis (nouns and verbs) Korean FL, adults
	Leeman (2003)	Recasts Gender and number agreement Spanish FL, adults
	Linnell (1995)	Negotiation Syntax ESL, adults
	Loewen and Nabei (this volume)	Metalinguistic feedback, recasts, elicitation Questions EFL, adults

Study	Interactional focus Linguistic focus Participants
Long, Inagaki, and Ortega (1998)	Recasts, models Adjective ordering, locative construction, object topicalization, adverb placement Japanese FL, Spanish FL, adults
Mackey (1999)	Interaction Questions ESL, adults
Mackey and Oliver (2002)	Interactional feedback (recasts, negotiation) Questions ESL, children
Mackey and Philp (1998)	Recasts, learners' responses Questions ESL, adults
Mackey, Philp, Egi, Fujii, and Tatsumi (2002)	Recasts, noticing Questions ESL, adults
Mackey and Silver (2005)	Interactional feedback (recasts, negotiation) Questions ESL, children
McDonough (2005)	Negative feedback (clarification requests, repetitions), modified output Questions EFL, adults
McDonough (this volume)	Interactional feedback (recasts, clarification requests) Past tense (activity verbs) EFL, adults
McDonough and Mackey (2006)	Recasts, responses (repetitions, primed production) Questions EFL, adults
Nobuyoshi and Ellis (1993)	Modified output, clarification requests Past tense EFL, adults
Philp (2003)	Recasts Questions ESL, adults
Sachs and Suh (this volume)	Recasts (computer-mediated), attention/awareness Sequence of tenses EFL, adults
Sagarra (this volume)	Recasts (computer-delivered), modified output Gender and number agreement Spanish FL, adults

Study	Interactional focus Linguistic focus Participants
Silver (2000)	Interaction, negotiation Questions ESL, adults
Trofimovich, Ammar, and Gatbonton (this volume)	Recasts (computer-delivered), noticing Morphosyntax (possessive determiners), lexis (verbs) ESL, adults
Van den Branden (1997)	Negotiation, modified output Vocabulary range, amount of output, syntactic complexity and accuracy Dutch SL, children

Descriptive (for example, investigating learner uptake)

a Classroom
  contexts
	R. Ellis, Basturkmen, and Loewen
	(2001a, 2001b)
		Focus-on-form episodes
		Grammar, vocabulary, spelling, discourse,
		   pronunciation
		ESL, adults

	Kim and Han (this volume)	Recasts, learners' interpretations Morphology, syntax, lexis, phonology EFL, adults
	Lochtman (2002)	Explicit corrections, recasts, initiations to self-correct No specific linguistic focus German FL, adolescents
	Loewen (2004)	Focus-on-form episodes Grammar, vocabulary, pronunciation ESL, adults
	Lyster (1998b)	Recasts, repetitions Grammar, lexis, phonology French immersion, children

	Lyster (1998c)	Negotiation of form (clarification requests,
		   elicitations, metalinguistic feedback,
		   repetitions), recasts, explicit corrections
		Grammar, lexis, phonology
		French immersion, children

	Lyster and Mori (2006)	Recasts, prompts, explicit feedback Grammar, lexis, phonology French immersion, Japanese immersion, children

	Lyster and Ranta (1997)	Negotiation of form (clarification requests,
		   elicitations, metalinguistic feedback,
		   repetitions), recasts, explicit corrections
		Grammar, lexis, phonology
		French immersion, children

Study	Interactional focus Linguistic focus Participants
Mackey (2002)[b]	Learners' perceptions about interactional processes (comprehensible input, pushed output, hypothesis testing, feedback) No specific linguistic focus ESL, adults
Ohta (2000)	Recasts Variety of forms Japanese FL, adults
Oliver (2000)	Negative feedback (negotiation, recasts) Grammar, pronunciation ESL, children and adults
Oliver and Mackey (2003)	Feedback (negotiation, recasts, explicit feedback), modified output, interactional context No specific linguistic focus ESL, children
Panova and Lyster (2002)	Recasts, translations, clarification requests, metalinguistic feedback, elicitations, explicit corrections, repetitions Grammar, lexis, phonology ESL, adults
Pica, Kang, and Sauro (2006)	Interactional modifications, attentional processes Articles, determiners, pronouns, connectors, verbal morphology, modals ESL, adults
Storch (2002)	Interaction patterns/roles, LREs Articles, prepositions, verb morphology, vocabulary ESL, adults
Williams (1999, 2001)	LREs Lexis, grammar/morphosyntax ESL, adults
b Laboratory contexts	
Braidi (2002)	Recasts Morphosyntax ESL, adults
Carpenter, Jeon, MacGregor, and Mackey (2006)	Recasts, repetitions, learners' perceptions Morphosyntax, lexis, phonology ESL, adults
Gass and Lewis (this volume)	Recasts, negotiation, learners' perceptions Morphosyntax, phonology, lexis, semantics Italian FL, adults

Study	Interactional focus Linguistic focus Participants
Mackey, Gass, and McDonough (2000)	Recasts, negotiation, learners' perceptions Morphosyntax, phonology, lexis, semantics ESL, Italian FL, adults
Mackey, Oliver, and Leeman (2003)	Negative feedback (recasts, clarification requests, confirmation checks), modified output No specific linguistic focus ESL, children and adults
McDonough (2006)	Interaction (syntactic priming) Dative constructions ESL, adults
Oliver (1995, 1998, 2002)	Negotiation for meaning No specific linguistic focus ESL, children
Pica, Holliday, Lewis, Berducci, and Newman (1991)	Modified output No specific linguistic focus ESL, adults
Pica, Holliday, Lewis, and Morgenthaler (1989)	Negotiation, comprehensible output No specific linguistic focus ESL, adults
Polio, Gass, and Chapin (2006)	Recasts, negotiation, output, NS perceptions Morphosyntax, lexis, phonology ESL, adults
Ross-Feldman (this volume)	LREs (incidence and resolution) No specific linguistic focus ESL, adolescents and adults
Sato and Lyster (this volume)	LREs, feedback (elicitations, reformulations), modified output, learners' perceptions No specific linguistic focus EFL, adults
Shehadeh (1999, 2001, 2003)	Modified output, hypothesis testing Morphosyntax, lexis, phonology ESL, adults
Tarone and Bigelow (this volume)	Recasts Questions ESL, adolescents and adults

[a] The terminological differences and overlap that appear in this table (for example, 'lexis' versus 'vocabulary', 'LREs' versus 'focus-on-form episodes', 'children' versus 'adolescents' versus 'adults') reflect the terminology used by the authors
[b] Conducted in both classroom and laboratory contexts

Table 0.1 Empirical investigations of interaction, recasts, and L2 development

As mentioned above, the establishment of a clear link between interaction and L2 learning has encouraged current researchers to expand their horizons. The focus of inquiry being addressed from many different angles is no longer 'Does interaction impact learning?' Rather, researchers are currently asking, 'How does interaction create opportunities for learning?' 'What are the relationships among interactional feedback, learner-internal cognitive processes, and L2 learning outcomes?' and 'What aspects of language does interaction impact?' This means not only an expansion of what is typically classified as interaction research, but also an increasing amount of inter- and intradisciplinary collaboration as researchers work towards a more comprehensive overall account of second language acquisition. In part, connections to other research areas are also resulting in the adoption of increasingly sophisticated methodological approaches, as discussed in some detail in several of the articles making up the 2006 special issue of the journal *Studies in Second Language Acquisition*, which focused on pushing the methodological boundaries in interaction research (Mackey 2006b).

The robust and carefully designed empirical studies collected in this book have the common goal of shedding light on our understanding of how interactional processes drive L2 learning. While some chapters fall squarely within the traditional foci of interaction work, others articulate the Interaction Hypothesis with other hypotheses, such as Swain's (1985, 1995, 2005) output hypothesis, Schmidt's (1990, 1995, 2001) noticing hypothesis, and sociolinguistic concerns within SLA, each of which will be discussed in more detail below.

The book is divided into three parts, with Part One exploring some of the ways in which different types of learners and their interlocutors might influence the opportunities for learning generated through interaction. Learners may, of course, be distinguished along a number of dimensions, and research in second language acquisition has identified a select set of variables as being particularly relevant, including age, motivation, gender, L1, past language learning experiences, proficiency, memory, and language aptitude. The collection of research in this book begins with a study of how learners create and take advantages of opportunities for language development through conversations with each other (Adams). The next chapter considers the role of the gender of learners in interactional structure (Ross-Feldman), followed by a study of heritage and non-heritage learners' perceptions of interaction in the third chapter (Gass and Lewis). Next, some of the possible constraints on the benefits of interaction are discussed and illustrated in one of the first studies to examine the impact of alphabetic print literacy on interaction in SLA, more precisely, literacy as a variable in exploring how recasts are processed (Tarone and Bigelow). In the penultimate chapter in this section, learners' modifications of linguistic output are examined, both in the context of interactions with other learners and in the context of interactions with native speakers (Sato and Lyster). Finally, in the last chapter, the learning opportunities that can be generated through humor in interaction are explored (Tocalli-Beller and Swain). In sum, each chapter explores the influence of a different factor on learning outcomes, and, taken together, these studies provide a kaleidoscope of perspectives on the nature of interaction in relation to language learning. The research points also to the complexity of interaction: the pairing of learners with other learners rather than with native speakers may afford different kinds of learning opportunities; different gender pairings can affect outcomes for certain tasks; heritage learners may perceive the focus of interactional feedback more accurately, and at times quite differently, from non-heritage learners in some cases; literacy appears to impact our thinking and perceptions such that less literate adult language learners may process oral language differently from literate language learners. Finally, learning opportunities appear to differ qualitatively according to the relative knowledge of participants, with different levels of expertise possibly resulting in different experiences and ways of collaborating.

In Part Two of the book, several learner-internal processes believed to mediate the relationship between interaction and L2 development are explored. Chapters in this section include, first, two studies that investigate how learners' working memory capacities dictate what they can notice, process, and learn during interaction, together with a consideration of how learners' aptitude, attitudes, and grammatical sensitivity may be related to learning (Trofimovich, Ammar, and Gatbonton; Sagarra). Two chapters explore the role of learners' and instructors' perceptions about conversational interaction and feedback in their L2 learning processes (Egi; Kim and Han). The remaining chapter in this section examines learners' reports of awareness of interactional feedback and investigates how different levels of awareness may be related to learning outcomes (Sachs and Suh). All in all, Part 2 reflects the current state of SLA interactionist literature concerning feedback and learner-internal processes. At the same time, given that all five chapters in this section deal with recasts, they are likely to appeal to a somewhat specialized audience. Although the studies represent a very thought-provoking collection of research on learner-internal processes, as well as a significant contribution to the literature to date, it is also clear that studies of interaction are moving beyond a focus on recasts alone. It may not be necessary to compare different feedback types with each other; after all, no-one is suggesting that only one type is effective or that learners' interlocutors should provide one sort of feedback exclusively. However, it is important to ascertain what it is about various types of feedback that makes them effective, to keep in mind that particular interactional features may work both individually and in concert with others, and to realize that recasts are only one of many types of feedback provided to learners. These are points to which we return in the final chapter of the book.

Part Three consists of direct tests of whether and how linguistic development might be associated with conversational interaction, looking at different sorts of interactional feedback and their relative effectiveness at promoting the development of different sorts of knowledge. The first two chapters, for instance, examine recasts, as well as metalinguistic information (Sheen) and clarification requests (McDonough) in terms of their impact upon learning. The next chapter examines the differential effects of implicit and explicit feedback on two different grammatical forms (Ellis), and the following one explores the relationship between different feedback types and implicit and explicit L2 knowledge (Loewen and Nabei). This is followed by a chapter which investigates the linguistic scope of the interaction hypothesis (Jeon), asking what the impact of interaction is when a wider range of forms and languages are studied than has traditionally been the case. The book concludes with a meta-analysis of the interaction literature to date, including, where possible, the studies reported in this book (Mackey and Goo). Once again in Part 3, while the primary emphasis on corrective feedback reflects the focus of current research, there are growing indications that researchers are looking beyond recasts and metalinguistic feedback to other aspects of collaborative interaction, including, for example, learners' own linguistic production and the role of modified output.

The questions addressed in these chapters, while still far from being answered, reflect the field's increasing interest in exploring and connecting some of the 'messier' variables involved in the process of learning language through interaction. That being the case, before moving on to the interesting empirical studies contained within this book, it is important to prepare a foundation for understanding the assumptions and major constructs that are explored in the chapters that follow. The examples below, taken directly from chapters in this book, are intended to illustrate some of the principal tenets of the Interaction Hypothesis. Although the authors labeled their participants according to the various foci of their studies (for example, heritage and non-heritage learners, native speakers and non-native speakers, students and teachers, males and females, etc.), the terms 'learner' and 'interlocutor' will be used for consistency in this introduction.

How does interaction create opportunities for learning?

Focusing on input and output through negotiation for meaning

As mentioned above, early interaction researchers set out to examine the ways in which interaction could be modified by native speakers in order to make linguistic input more comprehensible for non-native speakers. Long (1983), in particular, identified a variety of interactional modifications employed with the goals of avoiding communication breakdowns and repairing discourse when necessary, including tendencies on the part of native speakers to accept unintentional topic switches, check comprehension and request clarification, tolerate ambiguity, use a slow pace and stress key words, and repeat utterances, among other things. Later, other researchers, including Pica (1994a, 1996) and Gass (1997), laid out arguments for the benefits of negotiation, pointing out that, through processes of repetition, segmentation, and rewording, inter-action can serve to draw learners' attention to form-meaning relationships and provide them with additional time to focus on encoding meaning. It has also been proposed that negotiation can help learners to notice mismatches between the input and their own interlanguage—an initial step in L2 develop-ment. These issues are discussed further in Gass and Mackey's contribution to VanPatten and Williams' (2006) book on theories in SLA.

In Example 1, from data presented by Jeon in Chapter 16 of this book (p. 390–1), we see a learner and a native speaker of Korean negotiating over a lexical item in Korean. The learner does not initially understand the native speaker's use of the word *cemcangi* ('fortuneteller'), but is able to obtain a definition by asking about its meaning through a clarification request.

Example 1	Negotiation over a lexical item (in response to comprehension difficulty)
Interlocutor	*Cemcangi–nun eti isseyo?*
	Fortuneteller–TOP where be–Q?
	'Where is a fortuneteller?'
Learner	*Cemcang?*
Interlocutor	*Cemcangi.*
Learner	*Cemcangi mwe–eyyo?* ← CLARIFICATION REQUEST
	Fortuneteller what–Q?
	'What is a fortuneteller?'
Interlocutor	*Cemcangi–nun milay–lul malhyecwu–nun*
	Fortuneteller–TOP future–ACC tell–give–REL
	salam i– eyyo.
	person be–DEC.
	'Cemcangi is the person who tells you the future.'

During negotiation for meaning, both learners and their interlocutors may request clarification. When learners express a lack of comprehension, as in the example above, they may receive modified input, which can be better tuned to their level of understanding and which might be developmentally useful. When interlocutors express a lack of comprehension, their clarifica-tion requests often prompt learners to modify their output until (sometimes) an acceptable level of understanding is reached. Gass and Lewis (Chapter 3, p. 85) provide an example of a learner of Italian interacting with a near-native speaker of Italian who initially has trouble understanding the learner's use of the word *certo* ('certain'). The Italian-speaking interlocutor provides clarification requests in the form of repetitions (*Certo?* and *Abierto?*) along with a recast (*Aperto*), and, after a slight detour into Spanish, the learner eventually produces the correct word for 'open' in Italian.

Example 2	Clarification requests and modified output
Learner	*Non è certo.*
	Is not certain.

Interlocutor	*Certo?*
	Certain?
Learner	*Um, oh, è abierto.*
	Um, oh is 'abierto.' (Spanish)
Interlocutor	*Abierto? Aperto?*
	'Abierto?' Open?
Learner	*Aperto, sì.*
	Open, yes.

When L2 learners are prompted in some way to modify their linguistic output, particularly after they have received feedback from an interlocutor indicating that an original utterance has not been understood, this may provide them with the impetus to focus more carefully on the form of their utterances, so as to make them more comprehensible. So, negotiation for meaning might be helpful both for its role in helping learners to focus on input and output.

Noticing the gap through feedback

Current theoretical and empirical work has suggested that an important source of interactional benefits is feedback—that is, the reactive information that learners receive regarding the linguistic and communicative success or failure of their utterances. A number of interaction studies have shown interactional feedback to be associated with L2 learning (for example, see the review in Mackey and Gass 2006), and research has recently shifted to a focus on understanding the specific contributions of not only the types, but also the components, of feedback. Clarification requests, confirmation checks, repetitions, and recasts occurring during interaction may serve as forms of implicit feedback. However, feedback may also consist of more explicit corrections and metalinguistic explanations. Example 3 below, from Ellis (Chapter 14, p. 349), shows an interaction in which a native speaker provides a learner with feedback in the form of explicit metalinguistic information.

Example 3	Explicit feedback from a native speaker
Learner	He kiss her
Native speaker	Kiss—you need past tense.
Learner	He kissed

These sorts of explicit corrections do not take place only between learners and native speakers. Data from Adams (Chapter 1, p. 40) demonstrate that learners talking to each other can provide explicit feedback as well.

Example 4	Explicit feedback from a learner
Learner 1	the man prepare for traveling
Learner 2	E–D
Learner 1	E–D he prepared

It has been proposed that feedback may lead to L2 development through helping to make problematic aspects of learners' interlanguage salient and giving them additional opportunities to focus on their production or comprehension, possibly promoting awareness of L1 strategies that do not work in processing the L2. Feedback may also be facilitative of SLA in allowing learners to subdivide complex production tasks into more manageable ones, to the effect that they are able to perform them better than they might have done otherwise.

Recasts represent a form of feedback that is proving to be a particularly fertile area of investigation in the quest to increase our understanding of interactional processes in SLA. Much current research has been devoted to investigating various characteristics of recasts and their relationship to L2 development. Recasts, which were discussed and studied in the first language literature before being investigated in the L2 literature (see, for example, Farrar 1992 or Saxton 1997), are typically defined as more targetlike versions of learners' incorrect utterances, which do not change their meanings. That is, recasts are interactional moves through which learners are provided with linguistically more targetlike reformulations of what they have just said. A recast does not necessarily involve the repetition of a learner's entire utterance. It may be a segmented version, focusing only on one problem area, or it may include additional elaborations not present in the original propositional content. Either way, a recast is semantically contingent upon a learner's utterance and usually temporally juxtaposed with it. This juxtaposition, and the salience it might create, is part of what Long (1996, 2006) identifies as contributing to the psycholinguistic rationale for the effectiveness of recasts. Long points out that one advantage of recasts as implicit feedback is the fact that the informational content contained in them is already contextualized; the interlocutors can probably be assumed to share an attentional focus, and learners may have attentional resources available to focus on form due to the fact that they already understand the intended meaning of the original message.

At the same time, while negotiation for meaning requires learner involvement, recasts themselves do not always make such participatory demands. Lyster (1998b, 1998c) has pointed out that reformulations of learners' language sometimes occur following grammatical utterances as well as ungramatical ones, and, based on his research in immersion classrooms, he has argued that a recast may be perceived as responding to the content rather than the form of an utterance, or as an optional and alternative way of saying the same thing. In Example 5 below, from data presented by Egi (Chapter 10, p. 258), a learner's retrospective comments suggest that he did not, in fact, recognize his interlocutor's response as corrective. The native speaker of Japanese in this example recasts part of the learner's non-targetlike utterance (changing *sanpyakyu doru* to *sanbyaku doru*, meaning 'three hundred dollars'), but she embeds this within a larger evaluative comment which simultaneously indicates that the learner's meaning has been communicated successfully. In recalling this interaction, the learner focuses on the semantic content of his interlocutor's utterance without mentioning the change in form.

Example 5	Recast interpreted as evaluative comment
Learner	**Jisho o sansatsu kaimashita. **Sanpyakyu** doru desu.*
	dictionary ACC three–classifier buy–past 300 dollar COP
	(He) bought dictionaries. They were 300 dollars.
Interlocutor	*Sanbyaku doru! Takai desu nee.* ← RECAST
	300 dollar expensive COP PAR
	300 dollars? (They) are expensive, aren't they?
Recall	She [the NS] thought 300 dollars was too expensive. But dictionaries can be quite expensive, particularly good Japanese dictionaries.

As other data from Kim and Han (Chapter 11, p. 283) suggest, it is not uncommon for learners to appear to interpret recasts as simple confirmations of their utterances. In Example 6, the learner's utterance lacks the plural ('feeling'), which the interlocutor provides in the recast, but the learner's retrospective comments imply that this correction has not been recognized as such.

Example 6	Recast interpreted as confirmation of meaning
Learner	I did not know I hurt her feeling.
Interlocutor	You hurt her feelings.
Learner	Yes, but I didn't know.
Recall	I thought he repeated what I had said to confirm.

At other times, even when a corrective intention has been recognized, the learner is not able to pinpoint the source(s) of difficulty, particularly when there are multiple changes. Example 7, also from Kim and Han's chapter (p. 283), illustrates this.

Example 7	Recast recognized as generally but not specifically corrective
Learner	We don't know the truth until we tried it itself.
Interlocutor	We don't know the truth until we have tried it ourselves.
Learner	Right.
Recall	Well, I thought what I said was grammatically incorrect. But … well … I didn't know where was wrong.

Taking this line of investigation beyond learner perceptions to the question of L2 development, Egi's examination of learners' performance on individualized post-tests (a tool being used by an increasing number of researchers; see also Swain and Lapkin 1998; Swain 2001a; Williams 2001; Nabei and Swain 2002; Loewen 2005; Loewen and Philp 2006; Adams this volume) provides evidence that recasts may not be developmentally effective when learners interpret them as being focused on the communication of meaning. In Example 8 (from Chapter 10, p. 264), a learner interprets a recast (targeting his oversuppliance of the locative particle *ni*) as a confirmation which 'sounds right'; he does not seem to make an overt comparison of form between the native-speaking interlocutor's utterance and his own. When Egi traces the learner's use of this form from pre- to post- to delayed post-test, she finds that errors continue to occur.

Example 8	Lack of evidence of development following a recast interpreted as confirmation of meaning
Learner	*Onna no hito futari desu. *Futari ni imasu.* woman GEN person two people COP. Two people LOC exist [They] are two women. There are two women.
Interlocutor	*Otoko no hito ga sannin to, onna no hito ga futari imasu.* man GEN person SUB three people and woman GEN person SUB two people exist There are three men and two women, aren't there.
Recall	I was just talking about the people in the store. Just trying to picture them and talk about it. You confirmed what I said, and I was like, sure, sounds right.

Immediate post-test

Learner **Otoko no hito ga futari ni imasu.*
men GEN person SUB two people LOC exist
There are two men.

Delayed post-test

Learner **Otoko no hito desu. Eeto, futari ni imasu.*
men GEN person COP um two people LOC exist
They are men. There are two [men].

Examples 9 and 10 from Loewen and Nabei (Chapter 15 p. 367) and Kim and Han (Chapter 11, p. 281), respectively, illustrate another feature of recasts: namely, the fact that they are not always followed by clearly appropriate opportunities for learners to respond. After providing the correct forms, the native speakers in these examples immediately move on to continue the conversations, thereby obviating any need for the learners to produce reformulated versions of their original utterances (i.e. modified output). In Example 9, the recast targets the learner's question formation, while in Example 10, a prepositional phrase is reformulated, changing the learner's attempt ('about the Jazz') to the more targetlike 'with Jazz'. In neither case would it be particularly fitting, pragmatically speaking, for the learner to respond by rephrasing his original utterance.

Example 9	Recast with no opportunity for modified output
Learner	Er how many people in your picture?
Interlocutor	How many people are there in my picture? Er three people.

Example 10	Recast with no opportunity for modified output
Learner	It means that I am not familiar about the Jazz?

Interlocutor	No, it does not mean you're not familiar with Jazz.
	It means you're familiar with Jazz, but you don't like it.
	You tried that, but you don't like it.
Learner	Oh, I see.

By alleviating the need for a response, it is possible that a recast provides a learner with the opportunity to hear (or read) a correct form, without any communicative pressure to respond. Indeed, this may be one of the sources of the effectiveness of recasts. Recasts allow interlocutors to provide more targetlike language without disrupting the flow of communication and often without making demands on the learner. In this way, some argue, recasts may facilitate the process of making connections between forms and meanings. Perhaps even more noteworthy is the fact that, regardless of responses and regardless of perceptions, interactional recasts have been implicated in L2 learning in a number of studies. As several researchers, including Mackey and Philp (1998), have pointed out, one cannot assume that learners will make overt acknowledgments of all the feedback they receive, and the benefits of feedback may take time to appear, showing up only on delayed measures of L2 development, or even as delayed responses during interaction (McDonough and Mackey 2006). Thus, it may be a mistake to equate learners' immediate responses, or the lack thereof, with learning. Apparent contradictions, such as those suggested by the data and findings presented here, make it particularly important to explore which specific characteristics of feedback are most strongly associated with their effectiveness.

As the chapters in this volume demonstrate, researchers are currently engaged in precisely this task, exploring not only different interactional contexts and features, but also which learner-internal characteristics appear to facilitate development in particular circumstances. For recasts, one characteristic that has been identified as potentially helpful is segmentation, as shown below in an example from Ellis (Chapter 14, p. 348). In this sequence, the recast is relatively explicit, focusing specifically on the non-targetlike part of the learner's utterance. In response, the learner modifies his original form, changing 'follow' to 'followed'.

Example 11	Partial recast with modified output
Learner	... they saw and they follow follow follow him
Interlocutor	Followed
Learner	Followed him and attacked him.

It has also been proposed that recasts can profitably be accompanied by overt prosodic cues as to their corrective nature. The next example, from Gass and Lewis (Chapter 3, p. 84), is reminiscent of Doughty and Varela's (1998) operationalization of corrective recasts, in which an interlocutor repeats a non-targetlike form with rising intonation and then follows it with the correct form. In this interaction, the learner modifies her output to be in line with the interlocutor's pronunciation.

Example 12   Partial repetition and recast followed by modified output
Learner   *Er, a sinestra i fiori …*
                   Er, to the left the flowers …
Interlocutor   *A sinestra?*
                   To the left?
Learner   *Um, è il pane*
                   Um, is the bread
Interlocutor   *A sinestra? Oh, a sinistra.*
                   To the left? Oh, to the left.
Learner   *A sinistra.*
                   To the left.

Even when not segmented or marked prosodically, however, recasts can lead to more targetlike responses. In the example below, from McDonough (Chapter 13, p. 332), the learner modifies her output in response to a recast which contains essentially her entire original utterance.

Example 13   Recast with modified output
Learner   But she was never come back
Interlocutor   She never came back?
Learner   Never came back he was very sad

Besides the influence of feedback characteristics, it has been pointed out that learners' expectations in a given context may also be important variables in the recognition and use of feedback (Sheen 2004). One phenomenon that has recently been receiving increased attention in studies of interaction is learners' own requests for feedback. Sometimes, independently of an error or a breakdown in communication, learners and their interlocutors may turn to a focus on the linguistic aspects of their interaction. These episodes fall under the larger rubric of what have been called language-related episodes (Kowal and Swain 1994; Swain and Lapkin 1998, 2002; Williams 1999) or form-focused or 'focus on form' episodes (R. Ellis, Basturkmen, and Loewen 2001b). A language-related episode (LRE) is said to occur whenever attention is drawn to language in terms of linguistic form in the context of meaningful communication. In the LRE below, an example from Ross-Feldman's chapter on gender differences in interaction (Chapter 2, p. 61), Learner 1 realizes that she does not know the name for a particular object. Providing a description of the object, she asks her partner explicitly for help; the question is resolved, and the learners move on with their task.

Example 14   Language-related episode
Learner 1   How can I say that? Ay. I don't remember, but I know the
                   name. It's go whoo and you can make juice.
Learner 2   Ah, blender?
Learner 1   Blender! Yes, blender. Where do you have the blender?

Whether learners remember or retain linguistic forms better when they have specifically requested help in expressing their intended meanings is a question currently being addressed in interaction research.

Testing hypotheses and automatizing language production through modifications of output

We have already discussed the question of how learners may benefit from the linguistic information they *receive* in feedback. Similarly, the process of rephrasing or reformulating one's original utterance, that is *producing* 'modified output', is believed to benefit L2 development through its role in stretching learners' linguistic abilities, testing hypotheses, and automatizing production. As Swain (1995) puts it, this sort of language production 'stimulate[s] learners to move from the semantic, open-ended non-deterministic, strategic processing prevalent in comprehension, to the complete grammatical processing needed for accurate production' (ibid.: 128). Example 15 below, taken from McDonough's chapter on the emergence of simple past activity verbs (Chapter 13, p. 332), illustrates an instance of modified output in which a learner reformulates his initial utterance in response to feedback about its apparent lack of comprehensibility. That is, after receiving a clarification request ('Huh?'), the learner appears to realize that his utterance was problematic in some way and modifies his linguistic output. In this case, the process involves reformulating and expanding upon the second part of the original utterance (i.e. changing 'go' to 'went', adding the (non-targetlike) preposition 'to', and adding the phrase 'with my friends').

> *Example 15*   Clarification request and modified output
> **Learner**   I got home about eight and after I go swimming
> **Interlocutor** Huh?
> **Learner**   I went to swimming with my friends

In addition to encouraging learners to focus on the form of their utterances, the process of producing modified output is believed to serve other functions as well. According to Swain (1995, 2005), these include promoting fluency and automaticity, providing opportunities for hypothesis testing, and drawing learners' attention to their linguistic problems. With respect to 'noticing the gap', as a learner's perception of a deficiency in his or her L2 knowledge is sometimes called, the idea is that if learners develop awareness about what they still need to know, they may become more attuned to relevant forms in subsequent linguistic input. Particular grammatical structures in the input may thus become more salient, creating a context for L2 learning. The examples below illustrate these phenomena.

In Example 16, from data presented by Adams (Chapter 1, pp. 48–9), two learners are working together to write a story based on a set of pictures. Learner 1 expresses uncertainty as to the correct past tense form of the verb 'arrive' and, in a language-related episode involving hypothesis testing, asks his partner repeatedly which of several alternatives is the right one. Unfortunately, at the end of this interaction sequence, Learner 1 seems to resolve to use the non-targetlike form that Learner 2 apparently prefers. However, he does seem to question the form several times before using it. Post-test evidence would be needed before we could conclude that he did or did not give up the correct form.

Example 16   Language-related episode with hypothesis testing

Learner 1	John arrive, arrove, arrove or arrive?
Learner 2	arrove is in past
Learner 1	arrove airport. Or arrived
Learner 2	arrove, is in past
Learner 1	I mean arrove or arrived
Learner 2	arroved the airplane
Learner 1	arrived or arrove?
Learner 2	arrove
Learner 1	arrove the airport at 8:30 am

An example from Tarone and Bigelow's chapter (Chapter 4, pp. 116–7) provides an interesting illustration of a learner apparently noticing the gap and producing modified output. In this interaction sequence, the learner seems not to know the word 'jar', which would be helpful in expressing his desired meaning. He uses the word 'barrel' instead at first; however, as the authors point out, upon hearing his interlocutor say the word 'jar', he is able to fill a lexical gap in his original utterance. As the interaction proceeds, the learner also seems to be rehearsing the new term he has heard. It should be noted that their study seems more concerned with linguistic segments. This was clearly evidenced among their low literate learners. As can be seen in the example, their low literate learners had a much easier time with vocabulary, suprasegmentals, and stress.

Example 17   Noticing the gap and modified output of vocabulary

Learner	OK (pause) what is barrel, what is, what is the thing in it? What is there? Is it, is there pennies in it?
Interlocutor	Yeah. Um, again. Are pennies in the jar?
Learner	Is, are the penny in the jar?
Interlocutor	Yes. And, um,
Learner	(whispers) jar
Interlocutor	you know she's a waitress, so she gets tips,
Learner	OK
Interlocutor	at the diner,
Learner	mhm
Interlocutor	and every day she puts her tips in a jar.
Learner	oh. (pause) (xxx xxx)
Interlocutor	Here's the jar.
Learner	A jar?

Tarone and Bigelow also report that this learner then uses the term 'jar' spontaneously twenty-two turns later ('Oh. Oh. Is this jar have, this jar, is this jar full of money?'), suggesting that it may be a new lexical item in his database. This resonates well with McDonough and Mackey's (2006) findings, which indicate that learners' ability to use the language provided in feedback productively during subsequent interaction, even many turns after the feedback exchange, is predictive of L2 learning.

When discussing the presumed benefits of modified output (for example, a learner's use of a new vocabulary item), it is important to keep in mind that many researchers claim that there are benefits regardless of whether the modified output is more, less, or equally as grammatical as the learner's first utterance. This is because one of the claims is that the process of modifying one's output is as important as the product. In an example of modified output, from Sato and Lyster (Chapter 5, p. 132), the learner does not modify her utterance in the direction of the feedback that is provided, and there are no retrospective comments to examine for hypothesis testing and noticing the gap. Nonetheless, it is possible to speculate about what might be happening in the interaction.

> *Example 18*   Modified output without incorporation of feedback
> **Learner**   Umm ..., I think the [pʌnk], the tire is [pʌnk].
> **Interlocutor**   Punctured?
> **Learner**   Break break.

Sato and Lyster explain that this learner's modification of her original utterance may be meant as an expansion or explanation of it. They note that the learner (a native speaker of Japanese) may be testing the hypothesis that the English word for 'flat tire' is similar to its Japanese rendering in katakana, [pʌnkú]. The native speaker provides the correct form, 'punctured', in a clarification request that serves also as a recast. However, instead of incorporating the feedback, the learner continues with a different word. Interaction researchers might argue that regardless of whether the interlocutor's utterance ('punctured') serves as intake, this interactional sequence may act to disconfirm the learner's hypothesis that [pʌnk] is an appropriate English word for 'flat tire', and it might sensitize her to the correct form in future input.

In Example 19, from Ross-Feldman (Chapter 2, pp. 73–4), another instance in which a learner does not immediately incorporate a lexical item, it seems likely that Learner 2 has internalized at least some of the information that his interlocutor (another learner) has provided. Although Learner 2 does not specifically use the (possibly imprecise) word 'bucket' suggested by Learner 1, the learners are able to resolve this minor communication difficulty to the extent that they can move on with the spot-the-difference task they are engaged in.

> *Example 19*   No overt incorporation of a lexical item
> **Learner 1**   In your picture is, uh, a red bucket on the table?

Learner 2	What, what do you mean? Bucket?
Learner 1	OK. Bucket is box, like box. The box like you carry your, your, for the picnic thing.
Learner 2	Oh, I can see, uh, box. Next to the, the table.

At other times, interlocutors' intentions in providing feedback seem actually to be misinterpreted by learners. In the following example, from classroom data provided by Sheen (Chapter 12, p. 319), a learner modifies his output, but not in the area which the interlocutor has intended to target with her feedback.

Example 20	Modified output of a form not targeted by feedback
Learner	So he took a snake home (note: snake has been mentioned previously)
Interlocutor	OK, he took THE snake home? The boy took THE SNAKE.
Learner	Yes, snack /snak/ snake /sneik/ home

In this case, the target of the feedback is the article 'a', with the interlocutor most likely intending to let the learner know that 'the' would be a better choice. A retrospective interview with this learner revealed that he thought his pronunciation was at fault, and Sheen explains that since articles lack salience, they may not be especially amenable to feedback through recasts. Indeed, while the learner's modified output here may facilitate certain aspects of his L2 development, it is not clear that it will have any effect on the particular form targeted. At the same time, salience is certainly not the only factor in learning (Leeman 2003), and even when learners do produce forms provided with emphasis in feedback, it is not always clear whether they are simply parroting what their interlocutor has said. The interaction below, from Tarone and Bigelow (Chapter 4, pp. 113–4), provides a rather extreme example of this.

Example 21	Modified output
Learner	What he sit on, what he SIT on, or whatever?
Interlocutor	What is he sitting on?
Learner	Mhm.
Interlocutor	What is he sitting on? Again. Repeat.
Learner	What he sitting on?
Interlocutor	What IS he sitting on?
Learner	Oh. What he sitting on?
Interlocutor	What IS he sitting on?
Learner	What IS he sitting on?

It is only after multiple recasts and repeated prosodic emphasis that the learner in this example supplies the required auxiliary in his final utterance. At first, backchanneling ('Mhm') suggests that he is treating the interlocutor's feedback as a confirmation of meaning (as discussed above in the section on recasts). Only later does he shift his focus to the form of his utterance and, even then, he does not initially incorporate the modification. Tarone and Bigelow point out that the learner's apparent success in the last line ('What IS he sitting on?') does not seem to involve changes in his competence; he produces the same type of error a few turns later, when he asks, 'What this girl, reading?' Still, he does reformulate his utterance more readily this time, as shown in Example 22 (from Chapter 4, p. 114).

Example 22   Modified output
Learner   What this girl, reading?
Interlocutor   What IS this girl reading?
Learner   What is, is this girl reading?

In sum, as these examples from the chapters in this volume illustrate, inter-action often involves feedback and modifications to input and/or output as interlocutors attempt to redress the misunderstandings which are sometimes caused by problems with language use. The above examples also demonstrate how interaction is usually tailored to individual learners' particular strengths, weaknesses, and communicative needs, eliciting and providing language that may be progressively more attuned to their stages of development. It is important to be open to the idea that, even if learners do not perceive feedback as providing information about grammaticality, and even if they do not have a sufficient command of the L2 to modify their utterances, or choose not to modify them for some other reason, interactional feedback might still be associated with some sort of interlanguage change. Gass (2003) explains, for example, that even if a learner does not produce modified output in direct response to feedback, the feedback 'may serve as a "priming device" or an initial step "setting the stage for learning"' (ibid.: 235). As interaction researchers turn to more fine-tuned characterizations of interactional proc-esses and individual learner differences to find out how interaction works, it is becoming increasingly clear that there is more than one route to L2 develop-ment through interaction. Learners appear to perceive feedback differently depending on the feedback type, the relevant area of language (morphosyntax, lexis, phonology), and possibly the specific target of the feedback (Mackey, Gass, and McDonough 2000). To date, there is no claim that one or more of the interactional processes 'work better' than any of the others, although it does seem likely that processes such as negotiation for meaning, feedback, and modified output may be differentially effective for various aspects of language, learner characteristics, contexts, and task demands. Indeed, the vast majority of research in this area suggests that these developmentally helpful interactional processes may work in concert or in unique ways.

What are the relationships among interactional feedback, learner-internal cognitive processes, and learning outcomes?

Claims about attention, awareness, and noticing are frequently made in the context of research on feedback, output, and negotiation for meaning in general. According to Schmidt (1990, 1993, 1995, 2001), learners must be consciously aware of linguistic input in order for it to be internalized; thus, learning cannot be dissociated from awareness. Differentiating between higher and lower levels of awareness, Schmidt claims that awareness at the lower level, which he calls noticing, is necessary for language learning, while awareness at the higher level, which he associates with understanding, may be facilitative but is not necessary for SLA. Other models along these lines (for example, Robinson 1995, 2001, 2003 and Philp's 2003 application) consider noticing to involve awareness and rehearsal processes, explaining that only input which receives focal attention and is encoded in working memory can subsequently be transferred to long-term memory. Rehearsal mechanisms (maintenance or elaborative rehearsal) are key players in noticing and higher levels of awareness since they are primarily in charge of sending information stored in short-term memory to long-term memory (Robinson 2003). These claims are controversial, however. An alternative perspective, presented by Tomlin and Villa (1994), divides attention into three components—alertness, orientation, and detection—and advocates a disassociation between learning and awareness, contending instead that the detection of linguistic input (without awareness) is the crucial attentional function for L2 learning to take place. Leow (1998) operationalized Tomlin and Villa's functional model of attention and found a superior role for detection, as compared to alertness and orientation, in learner performance. Nevertheless, Truscott's (1998) critical review of all such claims points out how difficult it is to empirically test them; Leow's work (1998) has also discussed and problematized the operation of noticing, and Simard and Wong (2001) have also pointed out problematic issues with modeling attention.

In any event, most interaction researchers point to the importance of learners' cognitive processes, regardless of the specific model or approach. In fact, interaction research to date has typically made little reference to particular models of attention, awareness, and noticing. Rather, these terms have been used in a general (and often seemingly interchangeable) way in claims about the utility of interaction. For example, Long (1996) describes the importance in interaction of 'internal learner capacities, particularly selective attention' (pp. 451–2). Mackey, Gass, and McDonough (2000) likewise argue 'it is assumed that, through interaction, some aspects of attention may become focused on the parts of their language that deviate from target language norms' (ibid.: 473). N. Ellis (1999, 2002) maintains that interaction can alert learners to potential gaps in their interlanguage, which they can then address by paying attention to input. Swain's (1998) claims about the noticing function of output and Pica's (1994b) suggestions about the noticing of input are similarly non-specific. This brings to mind also how non-specific the claims about 'meaning' are in relation to negotiation for meaning. As some researchers are beginning to point out, there is little reference in interaction research to a model or theory of meaning, and in fact, we may not all be using the same criteria by which to code meaning (Hauser 2005). As the interaction field matures and consolidates, researchers are beginning to focus on the desirability of formulating claims about the role of attention in interaction-driven learning in more testable ways. For this reason, several of the authors in the present collection of studies operationalize learners' 'noticing' or 'awareness' in relation to their particular research questions. A variety of perspectives are considered and a variety of approaches are taken. Quite a few authors, for instance, employ introspective methodologies, exploring learners' awareness and interpretations of feedback through the comments they make in stimulated recall protocols (Gass and Lewis; Egi; Kim and Han), exit questionnaires (Sheen), and concurrent verbal reports (Sachs and Suh). Tarone and Bigelow discuss the ability to notice negative feedback on linguistic segments among learners at different levels of literacy and operationalize noticing as uptake during interaction, while Trofimovich, Ammar, and Gatbonton use tests of executive cognitive functioning to measure learners' attentional control and working memory capacities in relation to the effectiveness of feedback.

In summary then, the studies in this collection raise new questions, bring methodological innovations, and suggest important directions for future investigations. As such, both individually and collectively, they make a significant contribution to the state of the art in interaction research.

PART ONE
Participants and learning opportunities in interaction

Do second language learners benefit from interacting with each other?

REBECCA ADAMS

Introduction

As the Introduction to this volume points out, the developmental benefits of second language feedback have been clearly demonstrated empirically (Gass and Varonis 1984, 1985b, 1989; Varonis and Gass 1985a; R. Ellis, Tanaka, and Yamazaki 1994; R. Ellis and He 1999; Mackey 1999; Silver 2000; Swain and Lapkin 2001, 2002; Mackey and Oliver 2002). Despite this body of work, for classroom language learners, especially those in a foreign language context, the majority of their second language interactions may occur with other learners. Relatively little research has examined the benefits of interactions between learners for promoting language development. Some studies have investigated the characteristics of learner–learner interactions and compared native speaker–learner interactions with learner–learner interactions (Gass and Varonis 1984, 1985a, 1989; Swain 1995; Pica, Lincoln-Porter, Paninos, and Linnell 1996; Oliver 1998). These studies have indicated that in learner–learner interactions, learners receive comprehensible input, opportunities to negotiate for meaning and receive others' feedback, and opportunities to produce modified output (Gass and Varonis 1985b, 1989; Pica *et al.* 1996; García-Mayo and Pica 2000; Mackey, Oliver, and Leeman 2003; García-Mayo 2005). These studies also indicate that interactions between learners differ significantly from interactions between learners and native speakers in terms of the input provided (Pica *et al.* 1996), opportunities to produce output (Bruton and Samuda 1980), and the provision of feedback (Pica *et al.* 1996; Mackey *et al.* 2003). Both quantitative and qualitative differences between native speaker–learner and learner–learner interactions demonstrate that interactional benefits from learner–learner interactions cannot be assumed; rather, empirical evidence is required to determine whether learner–learner interactions promote learning.

Learner–learner interactions and feedback

In learner–learner interactions, as in native speaker–learner interactions, feedback can take many forms, from implicit feedback such as recasts (for example, Leeman 2003) or negotiation for meaning signals (for example, Varonis and Gass 1985b; Gass and Varonis 1989) to relatively explicit feedback moves such as overt focus on form (for example, Williams 1999, 2001). The use of feedback has been documented in learner–learner interactions between adults as well as children (Oliver 1995; Mackey *et al.* 2003). Such studies provide empirical evidence that learners are able to provide and respond to feedback moves from other learners. Gass and Varonis (1985a, 1989) described multiple incidents of learners calling other learners' attention to their errors. They also found that learners very rarely replaced their interlocutors' correct forms with incorrect forms. However, feedback given by learners in interactions seems to differ in interesting ways from feedback provided by native speakers. Pica (1992) found that learners may not employ as many types of correction strategies as native speakers and may rely on segmentation of their interlocutors' non-targetlike forms to draw their attention to the error. While segmentation may provide implicit negative evidence that a form is incorrect, it does not provide the positive evidence a learner may need to align his interlanguage (IL) grammar with the target.

Bruton and Samuda (1980) observed adult ESL learners in an intensive English program to determine whether the learners would correct one another and how their corrections compared with teacher-provided corrections. They found that the learners did correct one another, and that learner–learner corrections were targeted at linguistic forms similar to those often corrected by teachers in the classroom. They also found that learners employed several different correction strategies, including offering alternatives, asking repair questions, and rejecting non-targetlike utterances. However, Bruton and Samuda found that learners did not always correct each other's errors, even when the errors caused misunderstanding; they hypothesized that learners were often not immediately aware that communication had broken down, and so were not always conscious of the need for correction. Analysis indicated that the discourse which came between the original error and the learners' recognition of a resulting communicative breakdown may have at times prevented the learners from pinpointing the original error that led to this breakdown. They did not discuss the treatment of errors that do not lead to communicative breakdowns, so it is not known whether learners received feedback on non-targetlike utterances that did not impede communication.

Bruton and Samuda also did not examine data of the teachers' treatment of errors, asserting that the teacher and learner roles in error treatment must be considered differently in learner-centered tasks. They imply that learners can only be responsible for correcting 'product-centered' errors. The implication for the classroom is that the teacher may need to maintain responsibility for providing certain types of feedback. In terms of second language acquisition

(SLA) theory, these findings also suggest that learner interlocutors may not be able to give certain types of feedback, which could influence the way that learning occurs.

In a study similar to Bruton and Samuda's, Porter (1986) compared native speaker–learner and learner–learner interactions to investigate the quality of input and interaction as well as the incidence of feedback. She found that native speakers corrected their own and the learners' errors more consistently. However, error correction was rare in both conditions. Native speakers corrected only eight per cent of learner errors; learners corrected only 1.5 per cent of each other's errors. Error correction was rarely explicit in either condition. Additionally, native speakers did not miscorrect errors; learners' miscorrections, while rare, did occur in her data. Similar to Bruton and Samuda (1980), Porter's findings suggest that learner–learner interactions may not provide sufficient opportunities for learners to receive feedback on their IL output.

These findings are reinforced by a study of native speaker–learner and learner–learner interactions carried out among advanced level Spanish L1 participants in an EFL context (García-Mayo and Pica 2000). These researchers found that in learner–learner interactions, self-correction occurred far more frequently than other-correction, and learners did not correct many L2 errors. Again, this indicates that learner–learner interactions may represent a relatively less rich environment for the provision of feedback. Typical non-corrected errors included consistent pronoun omission, misplacement of adverbs, and lexical imprecision. The researchers hypothesized that these errors may have been overlooked because they were unlikely to lead to a breakdown in communication.

While feedback may occur more frequently and be more varied in native speaker–learner interactions, further investigation of feedback strategies has uncovered advantages for learner-provided feedback. Mackey *et al.* (2003) compared the feedback provided in native speaker–learner and learner–learner dyads. They also examined the effect of interlocutor age on the provision of feedback. In the study, 48 dyads (evenly composed of adults and children and of native speaker–learner and learner–learner dyads) participated in a task-based interaction. The researchers based their analysis on the first 100 utterances for each dyad, and compared the different dyad types in terms of whether feedback was provided, whether the learner had an opportunity to modify their non-targetlike utterance, and whether the learner incorporated the feedback.

The researchers found that adult native speakers provided significantly more feedback than learners, but that the learners were more likely than the native speakers to give their interlocutor an opportunity to incorporate the feedback. This is similar to Bruton and Samuda's (1980) finding that feedback from learners is more likely to include prompts for negotiation than feedback from native speakers. In each case, the researchers found that learners are less likely to simply correct forms and move on with the conversation, but are more likely than native speakers to allow for uptake or further discussion of forms. They also found that among the child dyads, learners were more likely to produce modified output in response to feedback from learners than from native speakers. Mackey *et al.*'s (2003) findings indicate that important differences exist in the provision and use of feedback between native speaker–learner and learner–learner dyads. The possibility that these differences may ultimately affect the rate or path of language development over time remains to be researched. As the researchers explain,

> While we did not investigate the developmental effects of feedback in the current study, our results do show that participation in task-based interaction can provide exposure to feedback in theoretically sufficient amounts, and they offer support for claims that feedback may be one important benefit of interaction
> (Mackey *et al.* 2003: 56).

Also, Mackey *et al.* examined only the provision and use of feedback following non-targetlike utterances, while Porter's (1986) data indicated that learners did occasionally miscorrect targetlike utterances. It is possible that interlocutor behavior in response to targetlike utterances could differ between native speaker–learner and learner–learner dyads, and this could have implications for language development.

Learner interaction and negotiation for meaning

Research on negotiation for meaning has also indicated that learners can recognize and use implicit negative feedback. However, native speaker–learner and learner–learner interactions may differ with respect to both the quantity of negotiation sequences and the variation in negotiation moves. Varonis and Gass (1985b), for example, compared the use of non-comprehension exchanges for native speaker–native speaker, native speaker–learner, and learner–learner dyads composed of adult ESL students. The most significant difference among groups in their study was the quantity of non-understanding sequences. They found that in native speaker–native speaker exchanges, non-comprehension sequences occurred extremely rarely, more often in native speaker–learner exchanges, and most often in learner–learner exchanges. Varonis and Gass hypothesize that the lack of shared background knowledge in these conversations more often necessitated repair sequences. This interpretation was reinforced by Gass and Varonis's (1989) findings that learners used more negotiation sequences under conditions where there was a mismatch between learners in either proficiency or native language.

Varonis and Gass (1985b) further hypothesized that for learner–learner conversations, the face-threat was minimized by the participants' equal status as language learners. As Varonis and Gass point out, if we accept negotiation as a site for second language learning, the increased incidence of negotiation in learner–learner interactions should be accompanied by increased opportunities for second language development. However, this conclusion rests on the assumptions that learning occurs merely because negotiation has occurred and that all negotiation is equal. It is possible that the impact of negotiation on learning may vary according to the context of the interaction. For example, it is possible that negotiation with native speakers may be more likely to lead to learning of forms than negotiation with other non-native speakers.

In addition to differences in quantity of negotiation moves, native speaker–learner interactions may differ from learner–learner interactions in the types of negotiation moves used. Some of this variation is motivated by different purposes for negotiation moves. While for native speakers, negotiation moves mainly involve repeating, simplifying, or expanding the input (Gass and Varonis 1984, 1985b; Varonis and Gass 1985a); for learners negotiation of meaning can also serve as attempts to make their speech more targetlike to be comprehensible for their interlocutor, either other learners or native speakers (Swain and Lapkin 1998; Silver 2000; Swain and Lapkin 2001, 2002; McDonough 2005). In Pica *et al.*'s (1996) study of native speaker–learner and learner–learner interactions involving L1 Japanese ESL learners, differences were found in the quality, rather than the quantity, of feedback moves. Both groups in the study produced similar amounts of feedback. However, the learners were significantly more likely to use segmentation (segmenting, rather than reformulating utterances) as a feedback strategy than the native speakers. The researchers hypothesized that the use of segmentation as a feedback strategy allowed the learners to focus their interlocutor on the area of comprehension breakdown; however, Pica *et al.* also note that segmentation is a limited form of feedback compared with the variety used by native speaker interlocutors. While learner–learner interactions may provide a site for feedback to occur, the restricted set of feedback types may not provide evidence appropriate to learner developmental needs. While research indicates that negotiation for meaning may be quite frequent in learner–learner interactions, there remains little evidence of its effectiveness in promoting learning.

Learner–learner interaction and attention to form

Research on learners' collaborative attention to form in interaction has indicated that learner–learner interactions provide a context for learners to receive feedback on the targetlikeness of their output. Williams (1999) examined learner–learner discourse of four dyads of learners in classroom activities in four different levels of an ESL program to determine whether learners overtly attended to form, measured by the occurrence of language-related episodes (LREs). She found that learners engaged in task-based, dyadic interactions tended to discuss form, but the occurrence of LREs was influenced by both the learners' proficiency level and the activity they were engaged in. Higher proficiency learners produced almost twice as many LREs as lower proficiency learners. Williams hypothesizes that this could be due to their focus; lower-level learners may be focusing so much on simply conveying a message that they do not naturally attend to form, while more proficient learners may be more able to attend to form in spontaneous talk. The nature of the learning activity also influenced learner use of LREs; learners were more likely to attend to form when engaged in activities such as correcting grammar homework than when conversing freely with one another.

In a follow-up study with the eight learners from her 1999 study, Williams (2001) tested the learners on the forms they had discussed in the LREs. She found that learners retained many of the forms they had discussed with each other and with their teachers. Higher proficiency learners tended to retain more forms than lower proficiency learners, and forms discussed in episodes in which the learners had involved the teacher were more often remembered than those discussed among learners. Overall, Williams' (2001) research lends support to the effectiveness of classroom interaction for promoting the use of feedback strategies that can lead to formal learning. However, these data again seem to indicate that learners benefit more from discussing form with a native speaker than with another learner.

In summary, empirical research has indicated that the use of feedback in learner–learner interactions differs from that in native speaker–learner interactions in ways that may be significant for language acquisition. Negotiation for meaning (Varonis and Gass 1985b), and opportunities to modify output following feedback (Varonis and Gass 1985b; Mackey *et al.* 2003) may occur more frequently in learner–learner interactions. However, learners are also more likely to use fewer feedback strategies (Pica *et al.* 1996), and may miscorrect each other's errors and correct statements (Porter 1986). All of these differences make it likely that learning facilitated by native speaker–learner interactions is not equivalent to learning facilitated by learner–learner interaction. It can therefore not be assumed that the demonstrated benefits of native speaker–learner interactions apply to learner–learner interactions as well. Rather, empirical investigation is required to determine whether learning results from learner–learner interactions. Since learner–learner interactions make up the majority of interactions in classroom settings, and may be a significant source of feedback for second language learners, it is important to investigate whether learning is facilitated by learner–learner interactions. To this end, the current study addresses the following research question: Does feedback in learner–learner interactions promote the learning of second language forms?

Method

Participants

The participants in this study were 25 ESL learners in an adult community education center in the United States. The center, supported by government grants, was founded to provide affordable ESL instruction to speakers of minority languages in a large US city. The learners at the school are representative of the major immigrant populations in the eastern United States. They were all enrolled in intermediate classes and were placed at the intermediate level through in-house oral and written tests of reading, writing, oral communication, and grammar. The participants ranged in age from 21–62, represented a variety of L1 backgrounds, and were enrolled in ESL classes in order to enhance their career opportunities in the US. While most had studied English in their home countries, all learners indicated that they had had very limited exposure to English before coming to the US. At the time of the study, they had resided in the US for an average of 3.5 years. Most of the participants were working in the community, but often in environments where their own L1s were predominantly spoken. In this way, these learners were similar to many adult immigrants in English-speaking countries who study in community education programs and in some ways different from the relatively more educated and economically advantaged students found in university intensive English programs, who form the typical population of many SLA studies. Figure 1.1 summarizes important learner characteristics.

Age (mean)		35 years	
Length of residence (mean)		3.58 years	
Gender	male	8	
	female	17	
L1 background		13	Spanish
		4	Mandarin
		2	French
		2	Vietnamese
		1	Amharic
		1	Korean
		1	Russian
		1	Bengali

Figure 1.1 Learner characteristics

As can be seen from Figure 1.1, there were significantly more women than men and a higher proportion of Spanish speakers than learners from other language groups. These group characteristics were unavoidable because intact classes were used. While the use of intact classes limited the possibility of tightly controlling learner characteristics in the experiment, it also increased the similarity of the research participants and context to the real world.

Linguistic targets

In studies of feedback in native speaker–learner interaction, interlocutor training of native speakers is commonly used to make the provision of feedback more uniform. In this study, since both interlocutors in each dyad were research participants, interlocutor training would have disrupted the findings. Avoiding interlocutor training makes it more difficult to target specific forms in order to measure and compare development among participants. In order to both adequately describe the development arising from feedback in learner–learner interactions and to allow for comparison among participants, this study made use of tasks developed to target specific forms. (See, for example, Mackey 1999.) Three different linguistic targets were selected: a syntactic structure (question formation), a morphosyntactic structure (past tense form—both regular and irregular), and a lexical/morphological structure (locative preposition collocations). In addition, incidental feedback on lexical items related to the tasks was considered.

These three target structures were chosen to maximize the possibility of accurately characterizing any effects of feedback in learner–learner interactions on second language development. The three structures differ in terms of the linguistic systems they draw on. Question forms are multi-word structures; producing targetlike question forms requires the control of multiple syntactic movements as well as the morphosyntactic competence necessary for the use and marking of auxiliaries. Past tense draws more heavily on morphology, requiring learners to consider the grammatical coding of the semantic meaning of past time. The locative constructions targeted here (for example, 'next to', 'to the right of') require lexical knowledge for choosing the correct word to encode the spatial relationship as well as formal knowledge of the particles associated with native-like morphosyntactic use. Because feedback may be more effective for learning certain forms (for example, Williams and Evans 1998; Jeon this volume), forms that draw on different areas of linguistic competence were chosen. Research on feedback has also indicated that heightened salience may be a particularly important aspect of feedback in general (Leeman 2003), so linguistic targets with different levels of perceptual salience were selected (for example, Brown 1973; Pica 1984b; Goldschneider and DeKeyser 2001), ranging from multi-word question utterances to single phoneme, semantically redundant, past tense morphological markings.

Design

The study made use of tailor-made post-tests in order to investigate learning associated with feedback in learner–learner interactions. Learners participated in three interaction sessions with other learners. Each session consisted of three tasks, one targeted at each of the three target structures. These sessions were conducted over one week. Five days following the final interaction session, learners completed a tailor-made post-test with items individually designed to assess learning of the forms they received feedback on during the interaction sessions. The interactive tasks and the tailor-made post-tests are described in more detail below. Figure 1.2 provides a representation of the research design.

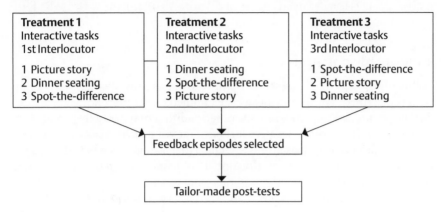

Figure 1.2 Research design

Treatment tasks

The tasks were all adapted from commercial ESL textbooks or resource books (Ur 1981, 1988) or from other research tasks (R. Ellis 2001; Swain and Lapkin 2001). While each task was designed to elicit the linguistic targets, the communication of meaning was primary to task completion. More information about the task types is provided in Figure 1.3 below.

Task	Structure	Description
Dinner seating	Locative Prepositions	Learners were given a picture of a table and chairs and a description of seating preferences and needed to determine who should sit where. The dyad was instructed to come to a consensus about the best seating plan, then fill out a worksheet describing where people were sitting.
Picture story	Past tense	Learners were each given one half of a picture story (eight pictures in total). Learners needed to figure out what the story was, and collaboratively write the story by filling in a worksheet.
Spot-the-difference	Questions	Learners were each given one of two very similar pictures. They were instructed to ask each other questions to determine what the differences between the pictures were.

Figure 1.3 Treatment task

The range of tasks was representative both of the sorts of activities done in dyads or groups in task-based second language classrooms (Foster 1998; Swain and Lapkin 1998; Mackey *et al.* 2003) and representative of the types of tasks typically employed in studies of interaction in learner–learner and native speaker–learner dyads (Gass and Varonis 1984, 1985a, 1989; R. Ellis *et al.* 1994; Pica *et al.* 1996; Mackey 1999; Mackey *et al.* 2003).

Tailor-made post-tests

Following the task-based treatments, the recordings of the dyadic interactions were transcribed. The transcripts were examined for the presence of feedback. For the purpose of this study, a wide range of different types of feedback were coded, including implicit negative feedback moves such as recasts or negotiation for meaning, as well as more explicit feedback episodes where discussion of form was initiated by an interlocutor. This definition of feedback episodes is similar to those used by other interactional researchers, including R. Ellis, Basturkmen, and Loewen (2001a, 2001b, 2002) and Williams (1999, 2001). Based on the feedback episodes, individual test items were created for each learner. Written, rather than oral, tailor-made post-tests were used in this research because of logistical constraints associated with working with intact classes. Two types of items (acceptability judgment items and picture labeling items) were used. The acceptability judgment items were used to test learning in grammar-focused episodes, while picture labeling items were used to test learning in vocabulary-focused episodes. An example of a grammar-focused episode and a description of the corresponding test item appears as Example 1 and an example of a vocabulary-focused episode and a description of the corresponding test items appears as Example 2. (All examples come from data collected for the current study.)

> *Example 1*   Learner 1 and Learner 2 are collaboratively writing out a picture story about a man traveling by air.
>
> **Learner 1**   he was pick up the bag.
> **Learner 2**   he was picking up the bag
> **Learner 1**   he was
> **Learner 2**   picking
> **Learner 1**   picking up

Learner 1's tailor-made post-test included an item asking him to judge the acceptability of the sentence 'Kim was pick up the bag yesterday'.

> *Example 2*   Learner 1 and Learner 2 are working on a spot-the-difference task. They were instructed to ask each other questions to uncover at least ten differences between the two questions.
>
> **Learner 1**   does you picture have bulletin board? Bulletin board?
> **Learner 2**   does it?
> **Learner 1**   this one this is not like a bulletin board
> **Learner 2**   maybe

Learner 1   does your does your picture has papers on the board wood?
Learner 2   yes
Learner 2's tailor-made post-test included an item that required him to
label a picture of a bulletin board.

Feedback episodes, as exemplified above, typically lasted over multiple
turns and were often highly collaborative. The boundaries of the feedback
episodes were measured in terms of the item discussed, rather than in terms
of individual feedback moves (such as a recast or a clarification request).
Because these moves often occurred within the same feedback episode (as in
Example 2, which includes a comprehension check, a repetition, and explicit
discussion of form), it would not be possible to determine whether one of
those moves, or all of them together, promoted learning. Therefore, feedback
episodes were defined as the interactional turns involved in discussing a
particular form (such as 'bulletin board' in Example 2).

In order to produce tests of similar length, nine individual acceptability
judgment items and three to five picture labeling items were created for each
learner. The items created did not reflect the total number of feedback episodes
in the data. Rather, efforts were made to base tailor-made post-test items on
feedback episodes where there was evidence that the feedback addressed a
knowledge gap or confusion on the part of the learner, rather than a performance error. For this, longer feedback episodes that spanned multiple turns and
included different feedback moves (such as those in Examples 1 and 2) were
included rather than shorter feedback episodes such as confirmation checks.
More importantly, for grammatical errors, care was taken to only include
items in the acceptability judgment tests that represented repeated errors.
The tailor-made post-tests only included items for past tense and locative
errors that were the target of multiple feedback episodes. Items were created
for each of the three structures targeted by the tasks, and there was a fairly
equal distribution of items for each structure. Vocabulary items were also
assessed through the use of tailor-made post-tests. They were tested through
picture labeling. If the learner used an alternate vocabulary term, the item
was discarded, and not considered for the subsequent data analysis. For
example, several learners participated in feedback episodes over the lexical
item 'waitress'. They were asked to label a picture of a waitress as part of
their tailor-made post-tests. If a learner used an alternate lexical item that
was not used in the feedback episode, such as 'server', the item was removed
from the analysis so that alternate terms that were not the target of feedback
in interactions would not influence the results.

Coding

The results of the tailor-made post-tests were analyzed with respect to the
original interactions for evidence of learning. For instance, in Example 3, the
learners are working on a past tense picture story task about a man packing

his suitcase and going to the airport. In a clear past tense context, Learner 1 fails to use past tense morphology on the verb 'prepare'. Learner 2 provides explicit feedback on the form, which Learner 1 incorporates in his following utterance. Based on this episode (and because Learner 1 omitted past tense marking more than one time), an acceptability judgment item was written for Learner 1's tailor-made post-test.

Example 3
Learner 1   the man prepare for traveling
Learner 2   E-D
Learner 1   E-D he prepared

Tailor-made post-test for Learner 1
The man <u>prepare</u> for traveling yesterday.
Yes   (No)

Learner 1 correctly rejected this ungrammatical use of past tense, and underlined the verb to indicate that it was the source of the error. This was considered evidence that some type of learning had occurred. In other instances, there did not seem to be a connection between feedback episodes and learning. In Example 4, the learners are engaged in the same task as above, this time describing a picture of a man entering an airport. In this example, Learner 1's initial utterance contains a past tense error; instead of past tense marking, the learner has used a present tense copula. Learner 2 provides a recast to the correct 'arrived', which Learner 1 uptakes in the following turn. Learner 2 gives further reinforcement in the following turn. Based on this interaction, and because Learner 1 had made similar past tense errors prior to this episode, an acceptability judgment test item on the past tense of 'arrive' was created for Learner 1's tailor-made post-test.

Example 4
Learner 1   he is arrive or
Learner 2   arrived, arrived yeah
Learner 1   he's arrived
Learner 2   11am it's okay 11am, write 11am arrived, arrived yes arrived
                no write arrive arrived
Learner 1   oh, oh

Tailor-made post-test for Learner 1
At 9:00 pm last night, he is arrive to the place.
(Yes)   No

As can be seen, Learner 1 incorrectly accepted the non-targetlike item, based on his original utterance. This was considered evidence that learning had not occurred.

All tailor-made post-test items were coded in this manner, according to the targeted structure (past tense, questions, locatives, or vocabulary) and according to whether or not there was evidence of learning. An independent coder examined 20 per cent of the data, and 95 per cent intercoder reliability was found. Because this coding was relatively low inference, this was considered sufficient for one coder to code the remaining data.

Results

For each learner, the percentage of items that evidenced learning for each item type was calculated. Table 1.1 displays the results by structure. (Individual results can be found in the Appendix.)

	Questions	Past tense	Locatives	Vocabulary	Total
Total items	62	69	66	37	234
Mean correct (per cent)	58	75	44	51	59
Standard deviation (per cent)	37	29	33	32	16

Table 1.1 Tailor-made post-tests: descriptive statistics

As can be seen from Table 1.1, there were moderate to high rates of learning for all structures included in the tailor-made post-tests. Overall, there was evidence of learning for more than half, 59 per cent, of the items tested. The distribution of learning for the four tested structures is illustrated in Figure 1.4 below.

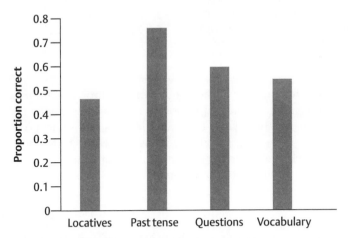

Figure 1.4 Learning on tailor-made post-tests

Evidence of learning occurred most often on past tense items. Evidence of learning was less frequent on the other three item types. It should also be noted that there were large standard deviations for learning on each of the forms. These indicate that the feedback episodes were more helpful for some students than for others, as illustrated in Table 1.2.

Learner #	L1	Locatives		Past Tense		Questions		Vocabulary	
		N	% TL	N	% TL	N	% TL	N	% TL
1	Spanish	2	50%	3	67%	3	0%	1	0%
2	Bengali	4	25%	3	100%	1	0%	0	N/A
3	Amharic	3	100%	2	50%	3	33%	2	0%
4	Spanish	2	100%	2	50%	3	0%	2	100%
5	Spanish	3	33%	2	50%	4	75%	2	50%
6	Spanish	2	0%	4	50%	3	33%	1	100%
7	Spanish	2	0%	6	33%	1	100%	0	N/A
8	Mandarin	3	0%	3	100%	3	67%	1	100%
9	Vietnamese	5	80%	2	100%	3	67%	2	100%
10	Spanish	3	67%	4	100%	1	100%	0	N/A
11	Spanish	2	50%	1	100%	3	100%	1	100%
12	Mandarin	0	N/A	0	N/A	3	67%	2	0%
13	Mandarin	4	50%	2	100%	2	0%	2	100%
14	French	2	50%	5	80%	1	100%	2	50%
15	Spanish	5	20%	2	0%	2	100%	1	100%
16	Spanish	0	N/A	4	100%	3	33%	1	0%
17	Spanish	2	50%	4	50%	2	50%	3	0%
18	Spanish	2	50%	2	50%	4	100%	3	33%
19	Russian	3	33%	3	100%	2	50%	1	100%
20	Korean	3	33%	2	100%	3	67%	0	N/A
21	Mandarin	4	25%	3	100%	3	100%	0	N/A
22	Vietnamese	2	100%	3	100%	3	100%	4	75%
23	Spanish	2	100%	2	100%	2	50%	3	33%
24	French	2	50%	3	100%	3	67%	1	0%
25	Spanish	4	0%	2	50%	1	0%	2	50%

Table 1.2 Individual results

As the table illustrates, for each form, the number of items for which there was evidence of learning ranged from 0–4 for locatives, past tense, and questions, and from 0–3 for vocabulary. Of the 25 students in this study, none demonstrated evidence of learning for all the items across the four target structures, and only two learners (learners 11 and 22) demonstrated learning for all the items across three of the four target structures.

Discussion

This study addressed the question: Does feedback in learner–learner interactions promote the learning of second language forms?

The analysis of the results indicates that feedback episodes in learner–learner interactions did lead to learning of forms. Overall, nearly 60 per cent of the feedback episodes included in the tailor-made post-tests evidenced learning. Considering that even relatively long feedback episodes only represent a few seconds of spoken interaction, this is quite a high rate of learning, especially when the unique characteristics of learner–learner interactions are considered. Indeed, this is quite similar to findings of other studies that use tailor-made post-tests to measure learning in classroom settings. For example, in Loewen's (2003a) study of learning from incidental focus on form between teachers and students in ESL classrooms, tailor-made post-testing revealed that when learners and teachers engaged in feedback episodes, learners overall learnt around 50 per cent of the forms discussed. In an analysis based on a subset of this data, Loewen and Philp (2006) found that learners evidenced learning on 53 per cent of the recast episodes and 75 per cent of the elicitation episodes that arose in classroom interactions with teachers. The findings of the current study may indicate that feedback episodes in learner–learner interactions and in native speaker–learner interactions are similar in their effectiveness in facilitating learning, at least when measured through tailor-made post-tests.

These findings are particularly interesting when compared with the research directly testing the Interaction Hypothesis, including studies by R. Ellis and He (1999), Gass and Varonis (1989), and Mackey (1999). In each of these studies, like the current one, the participants engaged in dyadic task-based interactions where they received interactional feedback from their interlocutor. The tasks in these studies were designed to promote learning of targeted linguistic items, and learning from interaction was measured in terms of learning the targeted structures. The difference, of course, is that in this study, learners interacted with other learners, rather than with native speakers. The analysis of results in this study, similar to that of the studies involving native speakers, indicated that participation in interaction promoted second language learning. While differences in the methods of measurement preclude direct comparisons, these findings provide evidence that interaction between learners, like interaction between learners and native speakers, is beneficial for second language development.

These high rates of accuracy on the tailor-made post-tests, however, should be considered with respect to the nature of second language learning. The items tested stemmed from specific errors that were the focus of feedback episodes during interactional sessions. They indicate that the feedback was successful in promoting learning of a specific item, but not necessarily that this learning led to restructuring of the linguistic system. For example, evidence of learning from the tailor-made post-test indicates that the feedback episodes examined promoted the learning of specific past tense forms, but it cannot be assumed that the feedback episodes examined here provoked revision of the past tense system overall. This distinction might best be conceptualized through a dual-mechanism model of language acquisition. Some researchers (for example, Skehan 1998; Hulstijn 2002) have hypothesized that language learning involves two mechanisms; namely, learning occurs both as the learning of specific items (also referred to as exemplars (Hulstijn 2002; R. Ellis 2003) or tokens (Skehan 1998)), and as the learning of linguistic rules or systems. As discussed in the introduction to this book, principles of connectionism (N. Ellis 1998) have been applied to these theories, considering system or rule learning as building and strengthening associations among exemplars. Learning, therefore, occurs when the learner is able to make associations through exposure to repeated patterns. To build and modify linguistic systems, items are gradually added to the system, and connections among them are built. Learners acquire, for example, the ability to correctly mark past tense as they acquire and strengthen associations between the lexical items and forms that express past tense. There may be a connection between feedback episodes, such as those examined here, and this type of learning. N. Ellis (2002) points out that learners need opportunities to relate form and meaning in order for the associations to be built. Gass and Mackey (2002) hypothesize that this may explain why learning occurs from interaction. They explain that 'through interaction, forms in the input are often repeated, rephrased, and segmented (Pica 1994a), thereby providing learners with a greater likelihood of making appropriate form-function connections' (ibid.: 251). As Gass and Mackey point out, receiving feedback in an interactional setting may additionally enhance the salience of these connections (Leeman 2003), so feedback episodes may provide individual opportunities for learners to acquire exemplars and test associations.

The short time-frame of this study (the three treatments and tailor-made post-testing all took place within a week) reduce the likelihood of associations being built or tested during this time-frame. However, there is evidence that the structures in question at least became more salient for the learners during the study. Examples 5–8 are taken from the past tense task in different treatments for the same learner (Learner 1). In these examples, Learner 1 seems to become increasingly aware of past tense marking in obligatory contexts. Example 5 occurs soon after the dyad began to write out the picture story. Learner 1's omission of past tense marking is explicitly pointed out by his interlocutor.

Example 5
Learner 1   ok so they call each other
Learner 2   oh no no no no just use past tense or use past
Learner 1   oh past tense yeah
Learner 2   they called each other, ok you can just write called

In Example 6, Learner 1 again receives negative feedback (this time implicit) from his interlocutor on the omission of past tense marking. Again, the learners are engaged in collaboratively writing out a picture story for which they have been given a past tense time-frame. In the story, a character at the completion of a journey discovers that he has accidentally exchanged suitcases with another passenger.

Example 6
Learner 1   the man opened the suitcase and he find the suitcase
Learner 2   find got a a mistake
Learner 1   got a a mistake

Learner 2 yes, yes, yes, yes, yes, man, the man opened, opened the suitcases, case, period. Suitcase
Learner 1 and
Learner 2 And he found he found that's found that's F-F-O-U-N-D

Learner 1's initial utterance here includes both a correctly marked past tense verb form ('opened') and an incorrect omission of past tense marking ('find'). His interlocutor's first concern here is correcting the meaning of the utterance, by pointing out that the character in question did not find his suitcase at that point, but rather found out that he had the wrong suitcase. After Learner 1 agrees with the semantic correction, Learner 2 provides feedback on the omission of past tense marking, by recasting the phrase 'and he find' to the targetlike 'and he found', repeating the recast, and then supplying the correct spelling. Acceptability judgment items were written for Learner 1 based on both Examples 5 and 6, and in both cases Learner 1 correctly rejected the non-targetlike sentences, providing evidence that the feedback episodes may have promoted learning of these items. However, in the final treatment, Learner 1 also shows evidence of greater awareness of the need for past tense verb marking in past tense contexts. In Example 7, as in the previous two, Learner 1 and his interlocutor are engaged in collaboratively writing a story from pictures.

Example 7
Learner 1 He walking, he want
Learner 3 He want to pass the
Learner 1 He walked the street a restaurant no is past tense you should write this one is here is past tense

As in the previous examples, Learner 1 omits past tense marking when it's needed. However, when his interlocutor begins to build on his non-target-like utterance, Learner 1 provides explicit feedback including metalinguistic information to indicate that past tense marking is needed. This is the first time that Learner 1 initiates discussion of a past tense error. Similarly, in Example 8 (also from the final treatment) Learner 1 provides his interlocutor with implicit negative feedback on her omission of past tense in an obligatory context.

Example 8
Learner 3 like the night because he don't look good. He remind, remembers,
Learner 1 He remind, remind something
Learner 3 remind
Learner 1 reminded

As in Example 7, Learner 1 here seems to pay more attention to the use of past tense marking during this task than he did in the first treatment. While it is clearly not reasonable, based on these examples, to assert that Learner 1 has built up new past tense representations, these data do indicate that, by the final treatment, Learner 1 is focusing explicitly on the use of past tense marking, where no such focus is seen in previous treatments. This may suggest that the use of past tense marking on verbs, at least in this particular task, has become salient to Learner 1 during the course of the treatments, and it is likely that the implicit and explicit feedback he received from his earlier interlocutors on his omission of past tense marking influenced this.

Hulstijn (2002) refers to this view of linguistic knowledge and language learning as both associative and rule-based. Learning is both acquiring exemplars, or tokens, and setting connections to create productive linguistic 'rules'. The tailor-made post-tests assessed whether learners had learnt exemplars: specific forms they had considered in feedback episodes. These results imply that the interactional feedback promoted the learning of exemplars. N. Ellis (2005) explains that repeated exposure to exemplars promotes the development of the associations.

This may point to a possible advantage for native speaker–learner interaction, particularly in instructed settings, over learner–learner interactions. As discussed in the method section, it is difficult to train learner interlocutors to focus on any specific form. Likewise, it is difficult for learner interlocutors to focus the feedback they give on any specific linguistic system. However, for instructed settings, it may be this very training that makes the interaction effective for promoting subsequent learning. If a substantial volume of exemplars is necessary to develop associations and build rule-based systems, it is possible that a trained native speaker interlocutor, perhaps in a pedagogical setting using tasks that elicit a targeted structure, is better able to provide focused feedback necessary for building rule-based knowledge. Additionally, as Mackey (2006a) has pointed out, such interlocutor training might make explicit what normally occurs implicitly in non-prepared interaction. Indeed, Mackey explains that, 'the implicit nature of interactional feedback is one of its key elements' (ibid.: 376). Training interlocutors to provide consistent feedback on a focused set of errors may influence both the salience of the form and the explicitness of the feedback. While the study reported in this chapter indicates that learner interactional feedback may be equally effective as native speaker feedback in promoting exemplar learning, this does not necessarily mean that native speaker and learner interlocutors are equally effective at promoting system-learning.

As discussed in the coding section, not every instance of interactional feedback resulted in learning. Overall, there was considerable variation with respect to the number of items learnt by each learner. The large standard deviations (ranging from 29 per cent to 37 per cent for the four structures included) indicate that for some learners, the feedback episodes were much more beneficial in promoting learning than for other learners. One possible reason for this may relate to the types of feedback moves used in the feedback episodes. As discussed above, the feedback episodes on a single item often included multiple feedback moves. While this may have enhanced the salience of the feedback episodes, it also makes it impossible to determine which types of feedback moves most promoted learning for each structure. A study with a larger sample size might allow researchers to determine whether specific types of feedback moves within feedback episodes are related to learning of different forms. It is additionally possible that interactional feedback in general is more effective in promoting learning for some learners than others. In both classroom settings and native speaker–learner interactions in laboratory settings (Mackey, Gass, and McDonough 2000), learners have been shown to vary in their perceptions of interactional feedback. It is possible that some learners are more likely to perceive interactional feedback as feedback, which could have implications for subsequent learning. The role of perceptions as well as other individual differences and their relation to the recognition and effectiveness of interactional feedback remain to be clarified.

These data indicate that feedback episodes were connected to subsequent learning. However, there was substantial variation in learning rates on the different linguistic targets included in this study. While not the focus of the study, a *post hoc* analysis was carried out to determine whether learning was more likely to occur on some targets than others. These data were submitted to paired-sample *t*-tests using the Bonferroni adjustment, which allows for multiple comparisons within a data set. The results of this analysis are presented in Table 1.3.

		Past tense	Questions	Vocabulary
Locatives	*t*	3.83	1.29	0.76
	df	26	26	21
	p	0.00	0.21	0.46
Past tense	*t*		1.99	1.59
	df		27	22
	p		0.06	0.13
Questions	*t*			0.05
	df			23
	p			0.96

Table 1.3 Tailor-made post-tests: analysis

There was only one significant difference: between locatives and past tense. Learners were significantly more likely to evidence learning when past tense was the topic of the feedback episode than when it was locatives. The remaining contrasts are not significant, which indicates that learning was equally likely on all of them. These data recall Loschky's (1994) findings on interaction among L1 English learners of Japanese. In Loschky's study, learners who received the opportunity to engage in interaction and negotiation for meaning had higher levels of comprehension, but did not retain the locatives significantly better than the other two groups. This is an unusual study, in that it is one of the only studies that has not found developmental benefits for interaction. It is particularly interesting in light of two studies on vocabulary learning through interaction, R. Ellis and He (1999) and R. Ellis *et al.* (1994). The treatments in both of these studies were quite similar to those of Loschky's study, but clear benefits of interaction were found both for comprehension and for acquisition. R. Ellis *et al.* (1994) suggest that the difference here might be the linguistic targets in each study. R. Ellis *et al.* (1994) and R. Ellis and He (1999) examined the interaction-based acquisition of English lexical items, while Loschky (1994) studied the acquisition of Japanese locatives. This raises the possibility that interaction may be more effective in promoting learning of some forms than others. In Williams and Evans' (1998) classroom study on focus on form, the researchers made a similar point about the effectiveness of interactional feedback episodes. They also postulated that the effectiveness of feedback for promoting learning may be related to the specific form targeted. (See also Jeon, this volume.) The findings of the current study indicate that this is as likely to be true for feedback in learner–learner interactions as it is in native speaker–learner interactions. In both cases, the rate of learning following interactional feedback seems to be related to the linguistic form.

Finally, it is important to remember that in learner–learner interaction, 'learning' promoted by feedback episodes may not necessarily be learning targetlike forms. Research has established that learners provide each other with non-targetlike input (Pica 1992) and that, while learner provision of feedback is generally low, there is always the possibility of miscorrections. While the pedagogical literature has often advised teachers not to be concerned about learners learning each other's errors (Bruton and Samuda 1980; Long and Porter 1985; Richards 1990; Richards and Rodgers 2001), and while previous research literature has shown that miscorrections may not necessarily lead to mislearning (for example, Gass and Varonis 1989), some of the tailor-made post-test results from the current study indicate that learners may learn each other's errors, particularly when attention is called to them. The tailor-made post-test items were designed to test learning from any LREs. In many LREs, like Examples 1 and 2, the learners jointly resolved to use a targetlike form in their spoken and written output. However, in others, LREs ended in a collaborative decision to use a non-targetlike form. Several of these were tested in the tailor-made post-tests, as in Example 9 below:

Example 9	Learner 1 and Learner 2 are collaboratively writing a picture story. They are writing a description of a picture of a man walking into an airport.
Learner 1	John arrive, arrove, arrove or arrive?
Learner 2	arrove is in past
Learner 1	arrove airport. Or arrived
Learner 2	arrove, is in past
Learner 1	I mean arrove or arrived

Learner 2   arroved the airplane
Learner 1   arrived or arrove?
Learner 2   arrove
Learner 1   arrove the airport at 8:30 am
Tailor-made post-test for Learner 1
John arrove at the airport last night.
(Yes)   No

In this example, Learner 1 seems initially uncertain of the correct past tense form for the verb 'arrive', questioning whether an unmarked version 'arrive' or an incorrectly marked version 'arrove' was the correct form. Learner 2 offers an explicit grammatical comment, incorrectly asserting that 'arrove' is the correct past tense form. Learner 1 continues to question this, asking whether 'arrived' is the correct past tense form. Learner 2 corrects this, repeating that 'arrove' is the correct form, as the verb is in the past. Following several turns, Learner 1 finally agrees with Learner 2 and writes the incorrect form 'arrove' in the story. It seems that Learner 1 is initially unsure of the correct past tense form for 'arrive', and has an incorrect form reinforced by his partner. While Learner 1 seems uncertain at the beginning of the LRE, he is willing to incorporate the incorrect form at the end of the discussion. He was presented with this sentence as grammatical on an acceptability judgment item on the tailor-made post-test. As can be seen, he incorrectly accepted 'arrove' as targetlike past tense usage. Because of his initial uncertainty, it is not possible to assert that Learner 2 taught Learner 1 this non-targetlike form. However, it seems likely that this interaction at least reinforced the error. Fewer than 20 episodes of incorrectly resolved LREs were included in the study; however, slightly more than half of these were learnt. The current data does not indicate that episodes like this are pervasive in learner–learner interactions; it also does not indicate that learning from miscorrections (or indeed any feedback in the study) influences the course of interlanguage development over the long-term. However, it does imply that the learning of errors is at least possible in learner–learner interactions. The overall findings of this study suggest that learners can acquire forms presented in feedback episodes with their peers. If miscorrections occur, this learning may not always occur in the direction of the target.

This phenomenon, however, does demonstrate the complexity of learner–learner interactions, and the ways that they are distinct from native speaker–learner interactions. While this research, like previous studies, demonstrates that learner–learner interactions differ in significant ways from native speaker–learner interactions, it also demonstrates that learner–learner interactions can promote learning. While these types of interactions are not equivalent, they are similar in providing opportunities for learners to acquire new second language forms.

Limitations

The items for the tailor-made post-tests emerged naturally from the learners' interactions, so no pre-testing was possible for the tailor-made post-tests. Therefore, it is not possible to determine whether the learners did not know the correct linguistic forms before the interactions. It is possible that some forms were known, and the errors made stemmed not from the interlanguage representations, but rather from the communicative pressure of completing an interactive task with another learner, and should be considered mistakes rather than true errors. Additionally, the testing involved significantly less communicative pressure than the treatments. This may have allowed learners to tap into explicit knowledge more on the tailor-made post-tests than in the interactions, making the knowledge base expressed in the tailor-made post-tests to a degree divergent from that in the interactions. It is also possible that some errors discussed in the treatments occurred due to coping with communicative pressure, rather than due to actual gaps in interlanguage competence. As mentioned above, efforts were made to create items for forms discussed in feedback episodes that addressed actual gaps in the learners' L2 knowledge, rather than feedback episodes that seemed to confirm previous knowledge or that stemmed from communicative pressure in the interaction. For example, only errors that occurred more than once were included, and errors that were self-corrected were excluded. However, it is indeed rarely possible, regardless of the type of linguistic data, to determine precisely what learners actually do and do not know. It is, therefore, important to interpret these results with caution.

It is also important to recognize that the learner sample in this study was quite small and that while there were several L1s represented in the sample, a clear majority of learners were native speakers of Spanish. It is unclear to what extent these findings on the effectiveness of learner–learner interactional feedback apply to learners from other backgrounds in other learning contexts. Child learners, for example, have been shown to use different patterns in the provision and use of feedback than adult learners (Mackey *et al.* 2003), and may not benefit from interactional feedback from each other in the same way. Further research is needed to investigate the effectiveness of learner feedback in other learning contexts. Additionally, as discussed previously, further research would be required to determine whether the learning of these exemplars would eventually result directly in strengthened associations for the overall system (as a connectionist perspective would predict, for example, N. Ellis 1996) or whether the item learning and rule learning would only be weakly related (as a dual mechanism perspective (for example, Hulstijn 2002) would predict). A longer-term study, involving more treatments and several tailor-made tests might allow researchers to determine whether learning of multiple exemplars leads to rule learning.

Conclusion

In terms of second language acquisition theory, this study lends direct empirical support for the effectiveness of learner feedback in promoting second language learning. This raises the possibility that the benefits of native speaker–learner interactions may also apply to learner–learner interactions. Differences in the quantity and quality of interactional feedback described in previous descriptive research (Bruton and Samuda 1980; Pica *et al.* 1996; Mackey *et al.* 2003) do not mean that learner feedback does not promote learning. It is important to remember, however, that demonstrating that learner feedback can promote learning does not imply that learner feedback is equivalent to native speaker feedback for developmental purposes. Further investigation is required to determine whether feedback in learner–learner interactions is as effective as feedback in native speaker interactions for promoting learning. If it is less effective, in-depth analysis of the connection between learner characteristics, feedback moves, and target forms might help explain any differences.

Additional implications relate to current understanding of second language pedagogy. As noted earlier in this study, for many non-native speakers, the majority of second language interactions may occur with other second language learners. This is usually the case for foreign language learners, who may have very limited access to native speakers in their home country, but it is also often the case among second language learners, such as those who participated in this study, who may live and work with other members of their first language group. Since many language learners have restricted access to native speakers of the target language, these findings are important because they affirm that second language interactions among learners may promote learning. As well, these findings lend support for classroom practices that promote group- and pair-work. Methodologies such as task-based language teaching that can promote focus on form in the context of meaningful communicative practice provide opportunities for learners to provide feedback to their interlocutors. These data indicate that such opportunities can promote second language learning. Overall, the study demonstrates the learner–learner interactions can promote second language learning, suggesting that the benefits of interaction are not limited to the native speaker–learner context.

2

Interaction in the L2 classroom: does gender influence learning opportunities?

LAUREN ROSS-FELDMAN

Introduction

A substantial body of research on language and gender has documented differences between the ways that males and females use language (c.f., West and Garcia 1988; Tannen 1990; Holmes 1994, 1998; Cameron 2003). However, the role of gender in second language acquisition (SLA) 'continues to be under-theorized and under-researched' (Piller and Pavlenko 2001: 1). Because many important differences between male and female speech have been identified in conversational interactions between native speakers (for example, Aries 1976; Bohn and Stutman 1983; West and Garcia 1988; Tannen 1990; Holmes 1994, 1998; Eckert 1998), one area of SLA in which the role of gender might be particularly relevant is in research conducted within the framework of the Interaction Hypothesis (Long 1996). As detailed in the Introduction to this volume, such research has indicated that conversational interaction can promote second language acquisition. Interaction may influence learning by providing learners with opportunities to receive input, produce output, and, through receiving feedback on the comprehensibility and grammaticality of their own language production, to notice the differences between their interlanguage and the target language. While it has been acknowledged that 'input or interactional modifications [may] differ across classes, genders, and cultures' (Long 1996: 421), most research in second language acquisition has not considered the ways in which the gender of the participants, or of their interlocutors, might influence second language interactions. In summary, because the Interaction Hypothesis postulates that conversational interaction is a site for second language learning, differences between males and females in these interactions may influence language learning through interaction. The purpose of the current study is to investigate the influence of learner gender on L2 task-based interactions and the language learning opportunities that arise in the course of such interactions.

Gender differences in native speaker language use

Researchers of native language conversational interaction have consistently found gender differences in interactional patterns and styles. Tannen's (1990) study of the discourse of same-sex friendships, for example, found that across age groups, males and females acted differently from each other when conversing with a same-sex friend. Males and females differed in the amount and type of talk they engaged in, with females generally talking more overall and discussing fewer topics than males, who discussed many topics briefly. Tannen also found that males' discussions were more abstract and focused on less personal issues than females' discussions.

Differences between males and females have been found in mixed-gender settings as well. As an example, in one study of undergraduate students, Aries (1976) found that males in her study discussed a wider range of topics in the mixed-gender groups than in male-only groups; the females, on the other hand, restricted their topics and conversational style in groups with males. She concludes from these data that the 'mixed group setting seems to benefit men more than women by allowing men more variation in their interpersonal style' (Aries 1976: 15). Bohn and Stutman (1983) found similar results, concluding that males control conversational interactions and females allow this control by making statements that indicate solidarity and agreement with the males. These findings are reinforced by West and Garcia's (1988) study of topic transitions in conversations between men and women; they found that men initiated the majority of topic changes, especially what they referred to as 'unilateral' or unwarranted topic changes. In their data, it appeared that, in changing the topic of conversation, men curtailed women's topic development and failed to follow up on what women were discussing. Holmes (1994: 161) also found in her research that females were more supportive of males' conversation than males were of females: 'while the men had the benefit of attentive, responsive and encouraging listeners, the women received relatively little support for their contributions, and were given less encouragement to continue when they did speak'. It seems that in these contexts, when males and females interact with each other, males have more opportunities to participate in and control conversations than do females. If this is true in second language interactions as well, it could influence the language learning opportunities that are available to males and females.

An important factor in interaction is the interlocutor; research has demonstrated that not only do males and females differ from each other in conversational interaction, but that individuals of both genders alter their use of interactional elements based on the gender of their conversational partner. Aries (1976) noted not only that males spoke more than females, but that both male and female participants directed more conversation to males than to females. Additional research pointing to interlocutor effects was conducted by Holmes (1998) in a study of compliment giving. She found that women both gave (68 per cent) and received (74 per cent) the vast majority of compliments. While men were unlikely to give or receive compliments, they were much more likely to give a compliment to a female (23 per cent) than to a male (nine per cent) and to receive a compliment from a female (17 per cent) than a male (nine per cent). Thus even within a linguistic behavior as gender-differentiated as compliment giving, both the gender of the speaker and the gender of the listener influence native speaker language use. When investigating the effect of gender on interaction, then, it is important to consider not only the gender of the participants, but also how participants might change the way they interact depending on the gender of their interactional partners.

Despite research that has found differences in language use between males and females, it is important to keep in mind that the influence of gender on interaction might vary depending on the participants' ethnic groups, social classes (Henley 1995; Reid, Haritos, Kelly, and Holland 1995; Aries 1996), and cultures (Melzi and Fernandez 2004), and of course there is individual variation within a given society or culture (Kimmel 2004). Individuals may vary in the extent to which they display gender-differentiated behavior, being affected by their own and their interlocutors' age, race, and class, as well as their relationship to their interlocutor, and characteristics of the interaction, including the task they are completing, the setting of the interaction, the topic of conversation, and the length of the interaction (Aries 1996). It is also possible that gender differences apparent in interactions in one language may not exist in interactions in a second language.

To pursue this possibility, Itakura (2001) examined the conversations of 16 male and 20 female native speakers of Japanese. Participants engaged in approximately ten-minute mixed-gender conversations in both English and Japanese, with the same conversational partner in each language. Aside from their gender, male and female participants were otherwise similar—in age, social position, and education—and did not have hierarchical working relationships with each other. Itakura examined topic nomination and development and found that males were less dominant in their L2, English, than in their L1, Japanese. She suggests that whether an individual has a self-oriented or an other-oriented conversational style may play a role in whether conversational dominance translates from the L1 to the L2. Self-oriented speakers pursue topics that are of interest to them while other-oriented speakers develop topics more collaboratively with their conversational partners; because self-oriented styles may 'require an ability to produce longer and more complex sentences or skills to maintain coherence' (Itakura 2001: 130), they may be less easily transferred from the L1 to the L2. Therefore, when speakers' conversational dominance results from a self-oriented style, as was the case with many of the male participants in Itakura's study, they may not be able to display the same sort of dominance in the L2.

The research on native language conversational interaction reviewed here has found that, depending on the context and the individuals involved, there may be differences in interactional style between males and females, and these differences cannot be assumed to automatically transfer from the L1 to the

L2. Empirical research is needed to document any gender differences in L2 interaction. Any such differences may be especially important if they affect opportunities for language learning that arise from conversational interaction. The following section reviews research that has been conducted in the area of gender and second language interaction.

Gender in L2 interaction

A small body of L2 interaction research has examined the influence of learner gender on negotiation for meaning, pointing to possible gender differences in second language interactions (Gass and Varonis 1985a, 1986; Pica, Holliday, Lewis, and Morgenthaler 1989; Pica, Holliday, Lewis, Berducci, and Newman 1991; Kasanga 1996; Oliver 2002). When examining the interactions of dyads composed of adult language learners, Gass and Varonis (1986) found that the most negotiation occurred in male–female dyads, followed by male–male dyads and then female–female dyads. Oliver (2002), the only researcher to examine the effect of gender on interactions between child language learners, found no significant differences between male–male and female–female dyads composed of child learners. When looking at individual learner language production, studies have suggested that both males and females negotiate more in mixed-gender pairings than in matched-gender pairings (Gass and Varonis 1986), males indicate non-understanding with a greater frequency than females (Gass and Varonis 1985a; Kasanga 1996), and in mixed-gender pairings, males dominate in both the amount of talk and the performance of the task (Gass and Varonis 1986). In interactions between learners and native speakers, no significant differences were found for the incidence of negotiation in different types of dyads (Pica *et al.* 1991), but when looking at individuals, female native speakers (NSs) were found to negotiate more with male learners than with female learners (Pica *et al.* 1989; Pica *et al.* 1991) and female learners were found to negotiate more with female NSs than with male NSs (Pica *et al.* 1991). There were no significant differences for males, either learners or native speakers. This raises the possibility that female language learners might be more sensitive to the influence of gender than male learners.

However, much remains unknown about the influence of gender on second language interaction. In studies that compared mixed- and matched-gender dyads, such as those conducted by Gass and Varonis (1985a, 1986), Pica *et al.* (1989), and Pica *et al.* (1991), different learners interacted under each condition. In other words, learners interacted in only one condition, either mixed- or matched-gender, with direct comparisons being made between these separate groups. Researchers assumed that this meant individuals' interactions were influenced by their interlocutors' gender, but this provides only indirect evidence of such interlocutor effects. Only by directly comparing individual learners' use of interactional features in each type of dyad can we begin to make claims about the effect of interlocutor gender in L2 interaction.

These studies also involved small numbers of participants, further increasing the possibility that differences could be due to individual styles, rather than gender-related behavior. Additionally, these studies did not consider the influence of gender on the use of interactional features such as language-related episodes.

Language-related episodes in classroom interaction

As discussed in the introduction to this volume, one of the key features of interaction is that it provides learners with an opportunity to attend to matters of linguistic form in the context of meaningful communication. These occasions when learners make use of interactional features to attend to the linguistic elements of their communication have been alternately referred to as form-focused episodes (Ellis, Basturkmen, and Loewen 2001a, 2001b; Basturkmen, Loewen, and Ellis 2002; Loewen 2003b, 2004) or language-related episodes, or LREs (Kowal and Swain 1994; Swain and Lapkin 1998, 2001, 2002; Williams 1999, 2001; Lapkin, Swain, and Smith 2002). LREs occur when learners, in the context of meaningful communication, focus on matters of language form and meaning. This includes '*all* interaction in which learners draw attention to form, that is, those that focus on form in the context of meaningful communication as well as those that are set apart from such communication and simply revolve around questions of form itself' (Williams 1999: 595). As Williams' definition makes clear, LREs occur when a learner has a question about the forms being used in the task, whether or not a communication breakdown has taken place.

As Swain (1995, 2005) discusses in her Output Hypothesis, producing language gives learners opportunities to notice the difference between their interlanguage and the target, to test their hypotheses about how the target language works, and to consciously reflect on their learning. All of these processes are present when learners interact during LREs. Because the interaction that occurs as a result of engaging in LREs has been targeted as a site where L2 development may occur (Swain and Lapkin 1998, 2001, 2002; Williams 1999, 2001; Ellis *et al.* 2001a, 2001b; Loewen 2004; Adams this volume), any effect for gender on the incidence and resolution of LREs might differentially influence the language learning opportunities available to male and female learners as a result of engaging in interaction.

The possibility that LREs might be influenced by learner gender is strong. While LREs have been found to occur relatively frequently in classroom contexts (Swain and Lapkin 1998, 2001, 2002; Williams 1999, 2001; Ellis *et al.* 2001a, 2001b; Loewen 2003b, 2004), the incidence of LREs is not constant, but rather varies according to several factors, including learner proficiency, learning activity (Williams 1999), and the cultural background of the learners (Loewen 2004). Other possible influences include the learning context as well as learner characteristics such as age and prior instruction in L2 grammar (Loewen 2004). If the incidence of LREs can be influenced by these characteristics, it is possible that they are also influenced by the gender of the learners participating in the interaction. Research reviewed in the previous section indicated that gender may influence the incidence of negotiation for meaning; this strengthens the possibility that LREs, as another element of interaction, may also be influenced by learner gender. Differences between males and females in the incidence and resolution of LREs may therefore be related to the developmental benefits learners glean from these interactions. The current study investigates the incidence and resolution of LREs in learner–learner interactions, with the goal of shedding some light on ultimate learning possibilities for males and females engaging in task-based interactions.

Research question

The current study analyzes interactions by males and females in mixed- and matched-gender dyads in an effort to determine to what extent and under what conditions learner gender influences the incidence of language-related episodes. The following research question was generated: Does learner gender influence the incidence of language-related episodes (LREs) in task-based dyadic interactions? If so, how?

Method

Participants

The participants for this study were L1 Spanish learners in an adult English language-learning center in a US urban area ($n = 64$; 32 males and 32 females). All participants were enrolled in intermediate level intensive English courses (level three of a four-level program), with placement in these classes having been determined through in-house tests of oral and written English ability.

Participants ranged in age from 16–53. They came to the United States between the ages of 15 and 47, and at the time of the study, had been in the United States for between six months and 18 years. Participants had studied English for between two months and 12.3 years at the data collection site, other US language programs, and in their home countries. The majority of language-learning experiences took place in the United States; those participants who provided details reported that English study in their native countries was minimal and consisted of one to three hours per week in primary and/or secondary school.

The characteristics of these participants are presented on the following page in Table 2.1. As can be seen in the table, independent sample *t*-tests revealed that there were no significant differences between males and females on any descriptive characteristics, increasing the likelihood that any differences found can be attributed to gender differences, rather than to differences in age, age of arrival in the US, length of residence in the US, or amount of English study.

Characteristic	Years	Males		Females		Independent samples t-tests
Age	Mean	29.25		31.62		$t(62)=-1.11, p=.27$
	Range	16–49		21–53		
Age of arrival	Mean	24.62		26.69		$t(62)=-1.13, p=.26$
	Range	15–47		16–40		
Length of residence	Mean	4.70		4.99		$t(62)=-0.28, p=.78$
	Range	0.67–18		0.50–13		
English study (years)	Mean	2.28		2.08		$t(62)=0.37, p=.71$
	Range	0.25–12.3		0.17–9.42		
Country of origin		24	El Salvador	17	El Salvador	
		2	Ecuador	5	Colombia	
		2	Peru	2	Bolivia	
		1	Colombia	2	Guatemala	
		1	Guatemala	2	Honduras	
		1	Honduras	2	Uruguay	
		1	Mexico	1	Dominican Republic	
				1	Ecuador	

Table 2.1 Participant characteristics

Participants of both genders came from mainly central and northern South America, with the majority of participants coming from El Salvador. It is true, of course, that Latin America is a large area, with 'immense variations in the economic, political, demographic, social and cultural characteristics of its constituent countries' (Chant and Craske 2003: 2) and that variation related to gender exists within these countries, including issues such as gender identity and typical gender roles (Gutmann 1997a, 1997b). Language use by Latinos, like other groups, can be 'complex and intertwined with a myriad of social variables' (Gonzalez Velasquez 1995: 422). However, efforts were made to restrict participant origin to as small a geographic region as possible in order to limit any potential mediating effects of different cultures on the effect of gender in interaction.

Design

The study employed a repeated-measures design, in which each participant interacted in both mixed- and matched-gender dyads (Figure 2.1). This approach was chosen to ensure that results reflect actual differences between interactions, rather than individual differences other than gender among participants. Participants, in dyads, completed three tasks on each of two separate days. In order to ensure that results from all pairs were comparable, and that any differences were due to gender rather than task-ordering effects, all dyads completed the tasks in the same order (first, the picture difference task, followed by the picture placement task, and finally the picture story task), and the instructions for each version of the task remained constant. Gender pairings were counterbalanced, as was the version of the task the participants completed. On the first day, participants were paired with either a person of the same gender or a person of a different gender. On the second day, participants interacted with a person of a different gender than their first partner. All interactions were audio-recorded and transcribed.

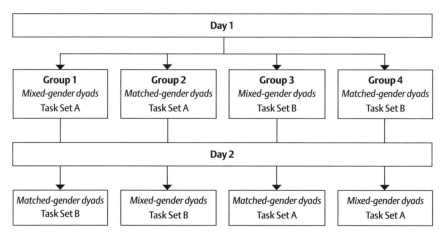

Figure 2.1 Design

Materials

Three tasks were chosen for this study: picture differences, picture placement, and picture story. A description of each task, as well as its features, including the type of task (Pica, Kanagy, and Falodun 1993), the flow of information (either one-way—from one participant to the other—or two-way—between the two participants), the exchange of information (required or optional), and the outcome of the task (either 'closed', meaning there is a pre-determined outcome, or 'open', meaning that the outcome is not pre-determined), is included in Table 2.2 on the next page. (For more on tasks, task features, and their effects on interaction, see R. Ellis 2000, 2003.) These tasks are similar to those readily available in commercial ESL textbooks. Two versions of each task were prepared.

Coding

Three aspects of LREs were examined: the incidence of LREs, whether LREs were resolved, and whether the resolutions were targetlike.

As Williams (1999) pointed out, language-related episodes include both those discussions that occur as a meaningful part of the larger interaction

Task	Description	Type	Flow of information	Exchange of information	Outcome
Picture differences	Without showing each other their pictures, learners must work together to identify ten differences between the pictures	Information gap	Two-way	Required	Closed
Picture placement	Without showing each other their pictures, learners must help each other place the missing objects in their pictures of a kitchen in order to make their kitchens identical.	Information gap	One-way repeated	Required	Closed
Picture story	Learners work together to arrange eight pictures in the correct order to tell a story and then write the story.	Decision-making	Two-way	Optional	Closed

Table 2.2 Treatment tasks

and those that momentarily break from the conversation to attend to matters of linguistic form. This may include instances of students asking for glosses of individual words or phrases or asking for specific feedback on linguistic form. In Example 1, below, the learners discuss the placement of the adjective 'more' while writing a story as part of the picture story task. This and all examples are from the current study.

Example 1	(LRE)
Male learner	Sleeping for two …
Female learner	For two
Male learner	More, two minutes. Two more minutes or two minutes more?
Female learner	Two more minutes.
Male learner	Two more minutes. All right.

LREs were coded as 'resolved' if learners decided on the answer to their question, as in Example 2, below, in which learners are completing the picture placement task. Female learner 1 is trying to remember the word for 'blender' (line 1) so that she can ask her interlocutor where to place it in her kitchen.

Example 2	(LRE: resolved)
Female learner 1	How can I say that? Ay. I don't remember, but I know the name. It's go woo and you can make juice.
Female learner 2	Ah, blender?
Female learner 1	Blender! Yes, blender. Where do you have the blender?

LREs were coded as 'not resolved' if learners did not decide on an answer to their question, as in Example 3, below, in which Male learner 1 never finds out the name of the playground equipment. As is apparent in this example, it was often possible to continue the task (here, the picture differences task) without resolving the issue raised in the LRE; in this case, Male learner 1's description of the playground equipment is detailed enough to allow his conversational partner to know that he doesn't have the object in his picture, even though neither learner knows the name of the object.

> *Example 3*   (LRE: not resolved)
> **Male learner 1**   How it's called, uh, the, the round thing where the, the, the children are playing? You know how they ...
> **Male learner 2**   In my picture, I don't have it.
> **Male learner 1**   Uh, your picture doesn't have, wow. Okay.

If LREs were resolved, the resolution was coded as being either targetlike or non-targetlike. In Examples 1 and 2, above, the resolutions were more targetlike; an example of a resolution that was not targetlike is provided from the picture story task in Example 4, below, in which Male learner 2 provides a non-targetlike spelling for 'ticket' (line 2).

> *Example 4*   (Resolved LRE: non-targetlike)
> **Male learner 1**   How you spell ticket?
> **Male learner 2**   t-i-k-e-t.

Inter-rater reliability

Forty-eight task-based interactions (sixteen dyads × three tasks), equaling 22.22 per cent of the data, were coded by an independent rater. The decisions of the researcher and the independent rater were submitted to a correlation analysis (Brown 1988); the coefficient was 0.94. This was considered sufficiently high for the researcher to independently code the remainder of the data.

Analysis

Studies of gender and second language interaction have analyzed the influence of gender in varied ways; however, none of them has directly compared the same learners' interactions in mixed- and matched-gender dyads. Such a comparison is needed to make claims about how the different contexts influence interaction.

Therefore, for each feature examined, the current study undertook three separate analyses in order to address the research question. First, following Gass and Varonis (1986), Oliver (2002), Pica *et al.* (1991), and Pica *et al.* (1989), the interactions of dyads as a unit were analyzed. In this analysis, a three-way comparison was made among the interactions produced by each dyad type: male–male, female–female, and male–female. Second, following Gass and Varonis (1985a, 1986), Kasanga (1996), and Pica *et al.* (1991), the interactions of learners in mixed-gender dyads were examined. In this analysis, the language production of male learners interacting in male–female dyads was compared to the interaction of their female interlocutors. Finally, in order to directly compare the condition of interacting in mixed-gender dyads with the condition of interacting in matched-gender dyads, individual learner language production in each condition was examined. In this analysis, learners' language production when interacting in mixed-gender dyads was compared to *their own* language production when interacting in matched-gender dyads.

Learners were allowed ten minutes to complete each task; however, because dyads used different amounts of the allotted time, in order to make the analysis of interactions uniform across tasks, the total incidence of LREs was analyzed as a proportion of LREs to the total turns taken by the learners to complete the task. Thus the total number of LREs for each dyad or individual was divided by the total number of turns taken by the dyad or individual in the task. When analyzing individual language production, the participant who first questioned the language being used was coded as initiating the LRE.

Results

Incidence of LREs

Comparing interactions in different types of dyads

To make comparisons among the interactions produced in the three types of dyads (male–male, female–female, and male–female), interactions from the dyad as a whole were considered. The LREs produced in each of the three types of dyads were compared using repeated-measures analyses of variance (ANOVAs). When ANOVAs found significant differences, *post hoc* Tukey tests, the appropriate analysis when all pairwise comparisons are of interest, were employed to locate the significant contrasts.

The incidence of LREs across dyad type in each task (Figure 2.2) was fairly uniform, with the exception of the picture story task, in which male–male dyads engaged in fewer LREs per turn than female–female and male–female dyads. Despite the differences on the picture story task, dyad type was not found to be significant ($F=1.39$, $df=2$, $p=0.26$), meaning that the incidence of LREs did not vary according to whether the dyad was comprised of two males, two females, or a male and a female. However, because the incidence of LREs in male–male dyads on the picture story task seemed to be different from the incidence of LREs in female–female and male–female dyads in the picture story task, two independent sample t-tests were run to compare the incidence of LREs by male–male dyads on the picture story task with that of female–female dyads and male–female dyads, respectively. The differences between dyad types closely approached significance: male–male dyads were found to have fewer LREs on the picture story task than both female–female dyads, $t(34)$=-1.99, p=0.055, and male–female dyads, $t(54)$=-1.96, p=0.056. These data indicate a strong trend of male–male dyads having a lower incidence of LREs on the picture story task.

The task learners were engaged in seemed to have an effect on the incidence of LREs: participants engaged in language-related episodes most often on the picture story task, followed by the picture placement task, and the picture differences task. According to repeated-measures ANOVAs, task was a significant factor (F=48.22, df=2, p=0.00), meaning that there were significantly different proportions of LREs on different tasks. *Post hoc* Tukey tests performed on the significant finding for task reveal that there were more LREs on the picture story task than on the picture placement (p=0.00) or picture differences (p=0.00) tasks, and there were more LREs on the picture placement task than on the picture differences task (p=0.00). The interaction between task and dyad type was not significant (F=1.98, df=4, p=0.10).

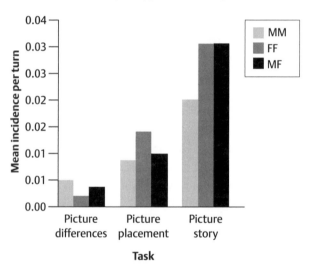

Figure 2.2 Language-related episodes in each dyad type

Comparing the interactions of males and females in mixed-gender dyads

In order to compare the interactions of males and females in mixed-gender dyads, individuals' contributions to the interactions were examined separately. LREs initiated by males and LREs initiated by females were compared using repeated-measures ANOVAs, with *post hoc* Tukey tests used to pinpoint the source of significant findings.

When examining the incidence of LREs initiated by males and females in mixed-gender dyads (Figure 2.3) two trends are apparent: (1) females consistently initiated more LREs than males, and (2) participants of both genders initiated more LREs on the picture placement task than on the picture differences task, and more on the picture story task than on either of the other two tasks. Despite the differences between males and females on each task, repeated-measures ANOVAs reveal that gender was not a significant factor ($F=3.00$, $df=1$, $p=0.09$), meaning there was no difference between the incidence of LREs initiated by males and females. Task was a significant factor ($F=31.28$, $df=2$, $p=0.00$); *post hoc* Tukeys performed on the significant finding for task reveal that, as in the analysis of dyads, there were more LREs on the picture story task than on the picture placement ($p=0.00$) or picture differences ($p=0.00$) tasks, and there were more LREs on the picture placement task than on the picture differences task ($p=0.00$). The interaction between task and dyad type was not significant ($F=2.42$, $df=2$, $p=0.09$).

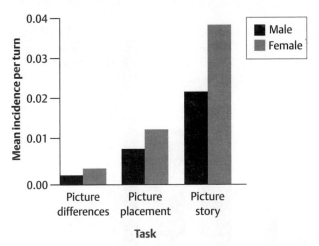

Figure 2.3 LREs initiated by participants in mixed-gender dyads

Examining changes in learners' interactions from mixed-gender dyads to matched-gender dyads

In order to directly test the assumption made by earlier research that learners' interactional experiences are different in mixed-gender dyads and matched-gender dyads, learners' interactions in both types of dyads were compared. The LREs produced by each participant in mixed-gender dyads were compared to the interactions produced by each participant in matched-gender dyads using paired-samples *t*-tests. A different type of analysis was required in this case because while the first two investigations were of differences *between* groups (first, the three types of dyads and second, males and females), the current examination is of *within* group differences (how males' interactions in mixed-gender dyads compared to their own interaction in matched-gender dyads, and the same for female participants).

Figure 2.4 is a graphical representation of the incidence of LREs by males and females in mixed- and matched-gender dyads on each task. The figure shows that males generally initiated quantitatively more LREs in matched-gender dyads than in mixed-gender dyads, although this trend was reversed on the picture story task, in which males initiated more LREs in mixed-gender dyads. Females also generally initiated more LREs in matched-gender dyads than in mixed-gender dyads, although there were slightly more LREs initiated by females in mixed-gender dyads than matched-gender dyads on the picture story task. However, according to paired-samples t-tests, none of these differences between mixed- and matched-gender dyads were significant, for males (picture differences: $t(31)=-1.02$, $p=0.32$, picture placement: $t(31)=-0.43$, $p=0.67$, picture story: $t(31)=1.44$, $p=0.16$) or for females (picture differences: $t(31)=0.67$, $p=0.50$, picture placement: $t(31)=-0.36$, $p=0.72$, picture story: $t(31)=0.57$, $p=0.57$).

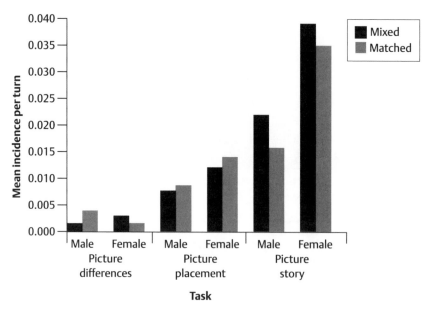

Figure 2.4 *LREs by participants in mixed- and matched-gender dyads*

LRE resolutions

Comparing interactions in different types of dyads

Each LRE initiated by a participant in the task-based interactions was coded as either resolved or not resolved; resolved LREs were further coded as to whether they were resolved in a targetlike manner. Figure 2.5 displays the per cent of total LREs produced that were resolved in a targetlike manner, resolved in a non-targetlike manner, and not resolved. With the exception of male–male dyads on the picture differences task, who resolved 50 per cent of their LREs, across dyad type and task LREs were more often resolved than not (ranging from 62 per cent to 96 per cent resolved—targetlike and non-targetlike—versus four per cent to 38 per cent unresolved). There are not enough data to run repeated-measures ANOVAs comparing the proportion of resolved LREs across dyad type and task. While it is possible to run a one-way ANOVA comparing the types of dyads on all tasks, the nearly identical proportions of resolved LREs across dyad types on the picture placement and picture story tasks preclude the likelihood of a significant finding for gender type. A one-way ANOVA comparing the proportion of resolved LREs on the picture differences task was run to determine if there were any significant differences among the dyad types in resolving LREs on this task; the results of the ANOVA ($F(2,18)=0.56, p=0.58$) indicate that there were not.

The numbers for the targetlikeness of LRE resolutions were too low to conduct inferential statistics, but the descriptive statistics strongly suggest no differences among the dyad types.

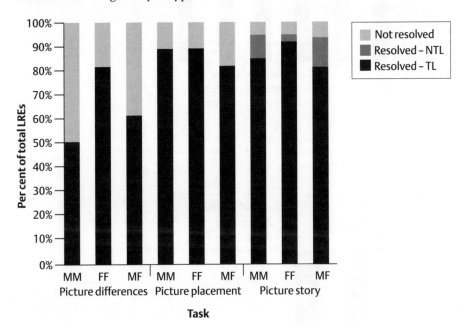

Figure 2.5 LRE resolutions in each dyad type

Comparing the interactions of males and females in mixed-gender dyads

Figure 2.6 shows the per cent of total LREs produced by males and females in mixed-gender dyads that were resolved in a targetlike manner, resolved in a non-targetlike manner, and not resolved. It is apparent that when males and females worked together in mixed-gender dyads, LREs initiated by males were resolved more often than LREs initiated by females. Because there were not enough data to run repeated-measures ANOVAs, the data for all tasks were combined (Figure 2.7), and a one-way ANOVA was run to compare these combined data for resolved LREs initiated by males and females on all

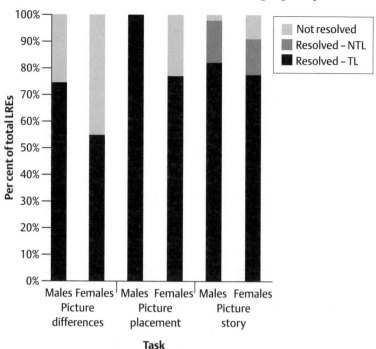

Figure 2.6 Resolutions of LREs initiated by participants in mixed-gender dyads

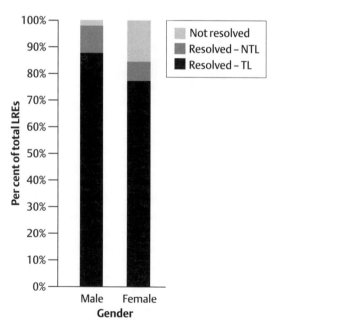

Figure 2.7 Resolutions of LREs initiated by participants in mixed-gender dyads on all tasks

tasks. This ANOVA showed that the difference is significant: LREs initiated by males were significantly more likely to be resolved than LREs initiated by females ($F(1,49)=4.42, p=0.04$).

When males and females worked together in mixed-gender dyads, LREs initiated by participants of both genders were overwhelmingly resolved in a targetlike manner, and when they were resolved in a non-targetlike manner (which only occurred in the picture story task), LREs initiated by males and females were resolved in a non-targetlike manner in nearly identical proportions (9.6 per cent for males and 8.6 per cent for females).

Examining changes in learners' interactions from mixed-gender dyads to matched-gender dyads

Figure 2.8 presents the per cent of total LREs initiated by males in mixed- and matched-gender dyads that were resolved in a targetlike manner, resolved in a non-targetlike manner, and not resolved; Figure 2.9 presents the same data for LREs initiated by females. (Data are not presented for the picture differences task because the numbers were so small that statistical tests could not be run.) There was a trend for LREs initiated by males to be resolved more often in mixed-gender dyads than in matched-gender dyads, and for LREs initiated by females to be resolved more often in matched-gender dyads than in mixed-gender dyads. These differences were not significant for either gender on the picture placement task (males: $t(3)=1.73, p=0.18$, females: $t(7)= -0.67, p=0.53$) or for males on the picture story task ($t(12)=1.00, p=0.33$). The difference for females on the picture story task approached significance ($t(20)=-1.83, p=0.08$).

LREs were equally likely to be resolved in a targetlike manner for males and females in mixed- and matched-gender dyads on the picture placement task, but in the picture story task, LREs initiated by males were resolved in a targetlike manner more often in mixed-gender dyads than in matched-gender dyads, and females' LREs were more likely to be resolved in a targetlike manner in matched-gender dyads. This trend was not, however, significant (males $t(12)=0.18, p=0.86$, females $t(20)=-1.18, p=0.25$).

Summary of findings

The gender composition of the dyad influenced the incidence of LREs only on the picture story task, on which male–male dyads engaged in fewer LREs than either female–female or male–female dyads. In mixed-gender dyads, LREs initiated by males were resolved significantly more often than LREs initiated by females. Whether participants interacted in mixed- or matched-gender dyads did not significantly influence the incidence of LREs initiated by males or females, or the likelihood that those LREs would be resolved, and when resolved, be resolved in a targetlike manner. While there were trends for LREs initiated by both males and females to be resolved more frequently

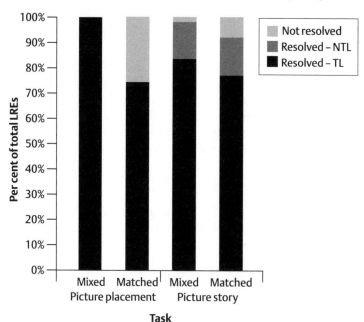

Figure 2.8 Resolutions of LREs initiated by males in mixed- and matched-gender dyads

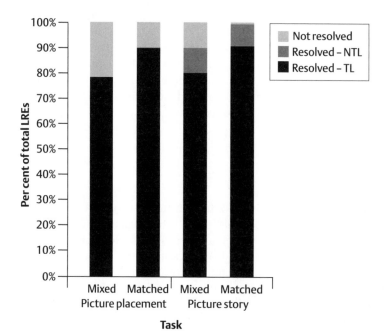

Figure 2.9 Resolutions of LREs initiated by females in mixed- and matched-gender dyads

and in a more targetlike manner when they worked with females, these trends were not significant.

Task influenced the incidence of LREs, with dyads engaging in significantly more LREs on the picture story task than on either of the other two tasks. When males and females worked together, they initiated significantly more LREs on the picture story task than on the picture placement task, and more on the picture placement task than the picture differences task.

Discussion

The findings of this study indicate that the gender of the learners participating in task-based interactions, as well as the task they are engaged in, influences the interactional patterns in terms of the incidence and resolution of language-related episodes.

When comparing the incidence of LREs in the three types of dyads (male–male, female–female, male–female), it was found that, on the picture story task, male–male dyads engaged in fewer LREs than either female–female or male–female dyads. Both of these latter two types of dyads have female participants; this is similar both to a conclusion drawn by Aries (1976: 14) that 'the presence of women change[d] the all-male style of interacting' and to Holmes' (1994) finding that females were more effective conversational partners than males. The current study suggests that working with a female in a certain type of task-based activity may have drawn learners' attention more to formal linguistic properties of the interaction; alternatively, it is possible that learners noticed form equally in mixed- and matched-gender pairs, but were more likely to articulate what they noticed when working with a female interlocutor.

This is especially interesting given the related finding that, in mixed-gender dyads, LREs initiated by males were resolved more often than LREs initiated by females. Below are two LREs from the same male–female dyad. In the first episode (Example 5), the Male learner asks the Female learner for the definition of a word (line 2), which she provides (line 3).

Example 5	(Male-initiated LRE: resolved)
Female learner	Okay. Okay, um the dishrag, dishrag is …
Male learner	Dishrag?
Female learner	Dishrag, is the fabric, the fabric that you use for clean, for drying the dish.
Male learner	Ah, okay. Where is?

In the second episode (Example 6), the Female learner is looking for the correct word to describe how the people in the story are exchanging their bags (line 1); her male partner, however, continues building the story without answering her question (lines 2 and 4), despite her second attempt to get her question addressed (line 3).

Example 6   (Female-initiated LRE: not resolved)
Female learner   Interchange their bags. What is the word? I don't know.
Male learner   After that they…
Female learner   Their bags.
Male learner   They went to the cafeteria and drink cup of coffee.

Work by Fishman (1978) found that in native language interactions between men and women, topics initiated by women were often abandoned, while topics initiated by men rarely were. Fishman concluded that 'women do the work necessary for interaction to occur smoothly. But men control what will be produced as reality by the interaction' (Fishman 1978: 405). West and Garcia (1988) found similar results, with the men in their study responsible for 64 per cent of topic changes in their database overall, and 100 per cent of 'unilateral' or unwarranted topic changes. Men

> initiated unilateral changes following women's 'passed turns,' and they initiated them in the course of women's turns-in-progress; they initiated them in the midst of ongoing topic development, and they initiated them in ways that curtailed such development. But perhaps most importantly, men initiated seemingly unilateral topic changes that permitted them to *refrain from other conversational activities*
> (West and Garcia 1988: 568; emphasis in original).

including following up on topics pursued by their female conversational partners. The language discussed in an LRE can be considered similar to a topic of conversation in some respects, in that one learner raises an issue about the target language and the other learner has the option to either join in the discussion or move on with the task at hand. It is therefore interesting that, similar to previous research findings on language and gender, topics (i.e. LREs) raised by males in this study were resolved more often than those raised by females. As Holmes and Marra (2004) point out, actions such as attending to others' needs, which Fishman and West and Garcia found that women did but men did not, is 'stereotypically 'feminine' […]. It is support work, oriented to people's face needs, to preserving their relationships with others and their dignity and self-esteem' (Holmes and Marra 2004: 391). It may be that when males and females worked together in task-based dyadic interactions, the females took on this supportive role, and were more willing to follow males' LREs through to their resolutions than males were willing to resolve females' questions about language use. Example 1, on page 61, concerning the placement of the adjective 'more' is an example of this. While the male learner tries to decide whether 'two more minutes' or 'two minutes more' is the more targetlike utterance, his female interlocutor offers supportive turns and helps him to a (targetlike) conclusion. This is an important finding because of the research linking LREs to potential language learning (Swain and Lapkin 1998, 2001, 2002; Williams 1999, 2001; Ellis *et al.* 2001a, 2001b; Loewen 2004; Adams this volume). In fact, research by Williams (2001) found that when learners resolved their LREs, they nearly always provided the correct answer on the relevant post-test item. If males' LREs are being resolved more often than females', this may lead to a situation in which males have more opportunities to learn from the interaction than females.

When looking at differences in learners' use of LREs between their interaction in mixed-gender dyads and their interaction in matched-gender dyads, there were no significant findings. There was, however, a trend for LREs initiated by males to be resolved more frequently and in a more targetlike manner in mixed-gender dyads, and those initiated by females to be resolved more frequently and in a more targetlike manner on matched-gender dyads. The fact that the descriptive statistics pointed to gender differences but inferential statistics found differences that only approached significance may be due to the large standard deviations in the data. This variation may be a reflection of the great deal of variation within genders, as research in the field of language and gender would lead us to expect: 'there is variation within each [gender] group and overlap between the two' (Cameron 2003: 189). It is therefore important to keep in mind that a learner's gender and the gender of his or her interlocutor may affect different learners differently. It cannot be assumed that every learner will be similarly influenced by gender; many factors contribute to the salience of gender for individual learners, including the context of the interaction.

In the current study, one context examined was task, with the finding that both gender differences and LREs were differentially apparent on the three tasks. A strong effect for task is in line with previous research (for example, Williams 1999; Gass, Mackey, and Ross-Feldman 2005) finding effects for tasks in mediating the incidence of interactional features. In the current study, the most LREs were initiated on the picture story task, followed by the picture placement task, and finally the picture differences task. This may be related to the learners' perceptions of the objectives of the activity, a suggestion originated by Williams (1999).

Participants were told that the goal of the picture differences task was to find ten differences between their pictures. Because they did not have to write anything, or even use specific terminology to describe the objects in their picture, accomplishing this goal may not have led to much focus on language as an object; rather, learners were using language as a tool to complete the task. Example 7, below, is typical of the LREs learners engaged in while completing the picture differences task. In this LRE, Male learner 2 is trying to find out what the word 'bucket' means, so that he can figure out if there is a difference between his picture and his partner's picture. Male learner 1 explains the meaning of the word (or rather, what he means by it), and the two are able to move on with the task.

Example 7   (LRE: picture differences task)
Male learner 1   In your picture is, uh, a red bucket on the table?
Male learner 2   What, what do you mean? Bucket?

Male learner 1   OK. Bucket is box, like box. The box like you carry your, your, for the picnic thing.

Male learner 2   Oh, I can see, uh, box. Next to the, the table.

The learners were able to achieve the goal of the task, finding differences between their pictures, without a great deal of focus on language other than when it impeded communication.

In the picture placement task, like the picture differences task, much of the linguistically oriented interaction focused on vocabulary. However, because the outcome of this task was more 'closed' than in the picture differences task—with a finite number of items to place rather than a larger pool of differences from which to find ten—and because each learner was provided with vocabulary words (in the form of labels) for the five items he had to help his partner place in her picture, learners may have felt compelled to use the specific words provided. Example 8, in which the Female learner is looking for the name of the item she needs to place in her kitchen ('dustpan'), typifies these LREs.

Example 8   (LRE: picture placement task)

Female learner   I don't know the name, you know the name to the, when you broom the floor and you put the trash. What is the name?

Male learner   Dustpan. Dustpan.

Female learner   Dustpan?

Male learner   Uh-huh.

It may be the fact that the attention of both learners was directed to a limited number of specific objects, or that they were each provided with half of the vocabulary words, that the incidence of LREs was higher in this task than in the picture differences task. In other words, while in the picture differences task learners just needed to understand each other, but not necessarily use the correct vocabulary term (which, in Example 7, would have been 'picnic basket'), in the picture placement task learners were concerned not only with understanding each other, but also in using the correct words for the items.

Finally, on the picture story task, learners had to both speak and write to create a story. It seems that having to write the story may have focused their attention on matters of language use, both lexis and form, perhaps because, as Williams (1999) suggested, they perceived this activity as having a language-oriented goal, i.e. writing. While LREs that focused on lexical issues, like those found on the other two tasks, were common (as in Example 9, below), this was the only task that successfully turned learners' attention to matters of morphosyntax (as in Example 10, on the following page).

Example 9   (LRE: picture story task—lexis)

Female learner   What is going on, the clock is going beep-beep-beep-beep?

Male learner   It's, yeah, alarm ring.

Example 10   (LRE: picture story task—morphosyntax)
Female learner 1   His suitcase he find.
Female learner 2   He found.
Female learner 1   In the past is find.
Female learner 2   Found
Female learner 1   Found
Female learner 2   He found the lady.

In addition to the effect of learner perception of the goal of the activity, it is likely that the success of the picture story task in focusing learners' attention on language as an object (as demonstrated by the fact that this task had the highest number of LREs) is due to the writing aspect of the task. Research has indicated that the addition of a writing component to communicative tasks increases the attention to form (Adams 2006); this may be evidence that, when engaged in collaborative writing tasks, learners may be willing to step away from the interaction and discuss matters of form even when not troubled by a breakdown in communication (Storch 1998, 2001).

Interestingly, the effect of learner gender on interaction was different in different tasks. The most significant effects for gender were found when learners were interacting while completing the picture story task. A possible explanation lies in the numbers. Because there were significantly more LREs on the picture story task, there was more opportunity for gender differences to emerge. The relatively lower numbers of LREs on the other two tasks decreased the likelihood of demonstrating a statistically significant difference. Another possible explanation, however, relates to the characteristics of the task itself. As the only task in which the exchange of information between learners was optional, because all of the information was shared between the two learners, the picture story task is the one in which it is most likely that the participation of the two learners is unequal. Gender differences may be more likely to arise in contexts in which interactants are not equal (Coates 1993; Galliano 2003); thus if one learner took greater control of the task than the other (for example, in deciding the order of the pictures, in writing the story, in making the decisions about correct language use), this would set up a situation in which gender differences would be likely to emerge. Regardless of the source of differential gender effects on different tasks, it is clear that tasks and task types should be carefully chosen not only to elicit the kinds of interactions desired, but also with an awareness that a variety of tasks and task types are needed to investigate the role of gender in second language interaction.

The current findings raise the possibility that males have more opportunities to learn the target language when they are working in mixed-gender dyads (because their LREs are more likely to be resolved in this context), while females have more opportunities in matched-gender dyads. These findings correspond to some of the research by Aries and Holmes in native language interaction discussed previously. Aries (1976) concluded from her study of conversational interaction in mixed- and matched-gender dyads that the mixed-gender context was beneficial for males, giving them opportunities that were not available to them in matched-gender contexts; however, the same mixed-gender context was more restrictive for females than the matched-gender context, limiting their interactional opportunities. Holmes (1994: 161) found that 'female language learners provide an ideal context for their conversational partners. In mixed-sex interaction, however, they are clearly receiving less than their fair share of conversational encouragement'. These findings are also in line with research in education finding that mixed-gender learning contexts are not as beneficial to females as are matched-gender contexts (for example, Sadker and Sadker 1994).

Combined with the findings from mixed-gender dyads, then, this may point to a situation in which males are advantaged in mixed-gender dyads, because of the increased attention to and resolved questions about matters of language use, but females are advantaged in matched-gender dyads, because their questions about language use are more likely to be resolved, and possibly in a more targetlike manner, when they work with other females. As a result, the learning that results from language-related episodes may be affected by gender as well. Given that, in this study, both males and females engaged in more LREs with females than with males, learners' opportunities to focus on form and learn from those interactions are greater when they work with a female interlocutor. The related finding that, in mixed-gender dyads, LREs initiated by males were more likely to be resolved than LREs initiated by females, and the trend for LREs initiated by learners of both genders to be resolved more often and in a more targetlike manner when interacting with females than with males, strengthens the possibility that the learning resulting from LREs may be influenced by the gender composition of the dyad, with males having more opportunities to learn in mixed-gender dyads and females having greater language-learning opportunities in matched-gender dyads.

Limitations

The current study examined interactions on three tasks. Future research should include more and different tasks and task types in order to more fully explore how task and gender interrelate. This is particularly important because the tasks used in the current study differ somewhat from the tasks used in earlier studies of gender and L2 interaction, with the current tasks being relatively more structured. Given that gender differences appeared more on some tasks than on others, research on how task characteristics mediate the influence of gender on L2 interaction is vital. It is possible that certain task types are better suited to matched-gender dyads, and others to mixed, and also possible that tasks may differ in the extent to which they reveal gender differences. Additionally, further research on how males and females collaborate when writing in tasks might clarify why the findings for gender effects were so much stronger on the picture story task than on the other two tasks. Related to this finding is the idea that the relative equality of learners with respect to their requirements for participating in the task may mitigate the effect of gender, as the picture story task differed from the other two not only in the addition of the writing element but also in that the exchange of information in this task was optional rather than required.

This study was a descriptive study of gender and second language learner interactions, and measures of development were not included. While previous research has implicated the interactional features investigated here in second language learning (Swain and Lapkin 1998, 2001, 2002; Williams 1999, 2001; Ellis *et al.* 2001a, 2001b; Loewen 2004; Adams this volume) further research is needed to determine whether the actual learning that results from interaction is influenced by learner or interlocutor gender.

Conclusion

The gender of both learners and their interlocutors has the potential to influence the incidence of language-related episodes in task-based interaction between learners. Interestingly, both males and females seem to be advantaged by working with female language learners. Researchers should be aware of this when designing their studies, and care should be taken in the classroom setting to ensure that both males and females have opportunities to interact with their female classmates.

Finally, researchers of language and gender might criticize this study for equating gender with biological sex for the purpose of analysis. However, as Holmes and Meyerhoff (2003:9) point out, we can argue about whether people ought to see male and female as a natural and essential distinction, and we can point to evidence showing that all social categories leak. However, that has not changed the fact that gender as a social category matters. There is extensive evidence to suggest that gender is a crucial component of people's social world. Certainly more in-depth research is required in order to develop a fuller and richer picture of what gender means to language learners, how it is enacted in the classroom environment, and how gender influences learners' interactions and resulting language learning. 'We cannot change society quickly enough to benefit our students, but we can manipulate the classroom environment' (Holmes 1994: 161). This study is a first step on the road to a fuller understanding of gender and second language interaction, and to providing teachers with the tools to help mediate the effects of gender in their L2 classrooms.

3

Perceptions about interactional feedback: differences between heritage language learners and non-heritage language learners

SUSAN M. GASS and KIM LEWIS

Introduction

Since the 1980s, second language acquisition (*SLA*) researchers have been investigating the effects of conversational interaction on learners' language. The Interaction Hypothesis (Long 1996) suggests that interactions involving those learning a second language may promote language development. The connection between interaction and learning may be based on two factors. First, interaction focuses the learner's attention on non-targetlike forms. Second, when the learner notices the gap between the non-target form and the target form (Schmidt and Frota 1986), this is 'a step towards change' (Mackey, Gass, and McDonough 2000: 473). Thus, it is well-established that through interaction, which includes feedback on erroneous forms, learners' attention is drawn to erroneous forms and they are pushed to make modifications. This is exemplified in Figure 3.1. As discussed in the Introduction to this volume, interaction includes negotiation as well as recasts and, importantly, includes feedback, or some indication that there has been a problem with the message. An indication of a problem, in turn, focuses attention on the problem area and allows learners to notice the problem, with, in ideal conditions, learning being the result.

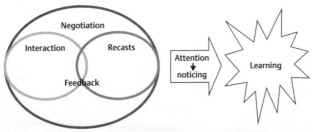

Figure 3.1 Graphic representation of interaction (adapted and reproduced with the kind permission of John Benjamins Publishing Company, Amsterdam/Philadelphia (www.benjamins.com) from S. M. Gass and A. Mackey in press. 'Input, interaction and output: an overview'. AILA Review 19: 3–17)

As noted above, for interaction to promote language development, learners must actually notice an erroneous form and recognize that it is erroneous. Therefore, some researchers claim that attention is crucial for learning to take place (Schmidt 1990, 1993, 1995; Long 1996; Gass 1997). If noticing is a significant part of learning, then the way that a learner perceives the input, and particularly feedback, is also important for language development.

The current study builds upon the research by Mackey, Gass, and McDonough (2000) in which they investigated how learners perceive interactional feedback. Their study involved ten learners of English as a second language (ESL) and seven learners of Italian as a foreign language (IFL). Briefly, in that study, most participants were able to perceive lexical, semantic, and phonological feedback accurately, that is, in the way the feedback was intended by the interlocutor, but they were not as successful at perceiving morphosyntactic feedback. There were, however, differences between the two groups, notably in their perceptions about phonological feedback. There was a relatively high degree of accuracy in perceptions for the ESL learners across morphosyntactic, phonological, and lexical feedback (52.1 per cent), but not for the IFL learners (37.1 per cent). Mackey *et al.* speculated that the results for the IFL group, with particular regard to pronunciation, may have been skewed given that there were heritage language learners (defined below) as well as true foreign language learners in that group. For example, there were fewer episodes of phonological feedback for the Italian learners than for the English learners possibly because that group included heritage learners who rarely have difficulties with pronunciation; in fact, in instances where there is prolonged use of the home language, their phonology may be almost the same as that of native speakers (Campbell and Rosenthal 2000). Mackey *et al.*'s (2000) inclusion of heritage language participants was incidental, thereby not allowing them to make definitive statements about differences between heritage and non-heritage learners. The study reported on in this paper is an attempt to further that research with a specific emphasis on the differences between those two groups with regard to their interactional involvement. To our knowledge, this is the first study investigating differences between heritage and non-heritage learners conducted within an interactionist framework.

In general, heritage speakers are individuals who are living in a second language environment, but who were raised in a home where a language other than the second language is spoken. Fishman (2001), whose interests do not relate to language learning, but to language maintenance, defines heritage language as referring to languages that 'have a particular family relevance to the learners' (2001: 81). More germane to the issues in this chapter is Valdés' characterization of a heritage language learner as someone who is 'raised in a home where a non-English language is spoken, who speaks or at least understands the language, and who is to some degree bilingual in that language and in English (2001a: 38)'.

Heritage language learners have knowledge of two languages (the home language and the language of the environment/school) and they are usually dominant in the second language. We recognize that this is an oversimplification as there is a wide range of heritage speakers, including those who were born in the second language environment and those who came to the second language environment during their school years. Another consideration is the amount of input in the home, ranging from only the heritage language spoken in the home (with perhaps parents only speaking the heritage language) to those situations in which the heritage language is spoken sporadically.

Heritage learners generally do not become bilingual speakers because they do not continue to speak the heritage language as much as they speak the language of the non-home environment. In some cases, they may not have heard or spoken the heritage language since they were very young because their families switch to the language of the environment. Heritage language learners form a heterogeneous group, since their experiences of the language may be very different. Some learners may have been raised by parents who only spoke the heritage language. However, when they went to school, English may have become their dominant language. Other learners may have only received very limited input of the heritage language in the home while they were very young. Nonetheless, it is generally accepted that the nature of language learning for heritage language learners differs from the language learning process of non-heritage language learners (Valdés 1995, 2001b; Campbell and Rosenthal 2000). As a result, heritage speakers often possess a subtly different knowledge base of the heritage language than true L2 learners of that language. In addition, they often differ from monolingual speakers of their heritage language. However, only a few studies have investigated the linguistic differences between heritage language and non-heritage language learners (for example, Nagasawa 1995; Polinsky 1995, 2000, in press; Ke 1998; Carreira 2002; Montrul 2002, 2004). The overall objective of the current study is to increase our understanding of how language learning may be dissimilar for heritage language learners and non-heritage language learners. The first goal is to examine whether heritage language learners perceive feedback in the same ways as non-heritage learners. The second goal is to investigate whether these two groups of learners perceive feedback on different parts of language in a diverse manner as suggested by Mackey *et al.* (2000).

This study replicates Mackey, Gass, and McDonough's 2000 study with different participant groups: a group of non-heritage language learners and a group of heritage language learners, thereby extending our understanding of what heritage language learners bring to the process of learning a second language. The main goal is to compare the perceptions about feedback in each of the two groups. Thus, the research questions guiding this study are the following:

1 Do heritage language learners and non-heritage language learners perceive phonological, lexical, and semantic feedback more accurately than they perceive morphosyntactic feedback?

2 Do heritage language learners and non-heritage language learners differ with regard to the accuracy of their perceptions?

The first research question asks whether interactional patterns of heritage language learners are like those of the non-heritage language learners from the Mackey *et al.* study. The second research question aims to find any further similarities or differences in perception about feedback between the two groups.

Method

Participants

Thirteen IFL learners participated in this study: seven non-heritage language learners and six heritage language learners. The participants were all recruited from undergraduate classes in Italian at a large mid-western university in the United States. They were classified at the beginning or lower-intermediate level by their programs. The data from two of the six heritage learners were from the original study by Mackey, Gass, and McDonough (2000). All remaining data were collected for this study. In Table 3.1 is the background information on the non-heritage language learners. All the participants were of a similar age, were from English-speaking homes, and had studied Italian for at least two years. Five participants in this group had spent approximately six weeks in Italy, usually for a study-abroad program. All but one of the participants had studied languages related to Italian such as Spanish and French.

Participant	Gender	Years of Italian study	Other languages studied	Time spent in Italy
KC	F	4	French, Spanish	Six weeks, study abroad
MK	M	2	French	Ten days, travel Six weeks, study abroad
MA	F	2	None	Three-week visit with Italian host family
MP	F	2	Spanish	None
SH	F	2	Spanish, French, Portuguese	None
LM	F	3	Spanish	Six weeks, study abroad One week, travel
MS	F	2	Spanish	Six weeks, study abroad One week, travel

Table 3.1 Background information: non-heritage learners (all from English-speaking homes)

Participant	Gender	Years of Italian study	Other languages studied	Heritage background	Time spent in Italy
MD	M	2	Spanish	Grandparents spoke some Italian	None
RV	F	1	Spanish	Parents spoke Italian at home until age four	Five visits to family: visits ranged from 12 days to two months
AV	M	3	Spanish	Parents spoke Italian at home until age six	Six visits to family
AW	F	1	Spanish	Maternal grandmother spoke Italian	Three visits to Italy: two for travel, ranging from four days to three weeks; one for study abroad for two months
MA	F	3	Spanish	Spent time in Italy with family	38 weeks
DC	M	2	Unavailable		12 weeks

Table 3.2 Background information: heritage learners

Table 3.2 provides the background information on the six heritage learners. As can be seen, the heritage language participants in this study had different experiences with Italian when they were young children. For example, participant MD had received very little Italian language input as a child. His grandparents spoke some Italian to him, but not his parents. As an adult, MD only had experience of the Italian language in his college classes and he had never visited Italy. On the other hand, participant RV had been exposed to Italian to a greater extent. Until the age of four, her parents had used Italian in the home. She had also visited family in Italy five times on trips ranging from 12 days to two months. Participant AV had received the most extensive language input. His parents had spoken Italian to him at home until he was six years old and he had visited family in Italy on six different occasions. The heritage language learners were of a similar age and all of them had also studied Spanish.

Procedure

The data collection procedure followed that laid out by Mackey *et al.* (2000). The participants took part in a task-based interaction (a spot-the-difference task) with an interlocutor who was a near-native speaker of Italian. Each participant had a picture that was similar to the picture given to the interviewer. The learner was asked to describe the picture and the goal was for the learner and the interviewer to find the differences between the two pictures. During the task, the interviewer gave the learner feedback on non-targetlike utterances whenever it seemed appropriate and natural to do so. More details on the types of feedback given are provided in the next section. The task-based activity was video-taped by another researcher.

Stimulated recall methodology was used to gather data on the learners' perceptions about the feedback that they received (Gass and Mackey 2000). Immediately following the activity, the video-tape was replayed for the learner. An interviewer, who had not participated in the data-collection task, paused the video-tape after feedback episodes and asked the learner to describe the thoughts that he or she had at the time that the interaction took place. The participants were given clear instructions to think back to the time of the interaction. The learners were also able to stop the video-tape themselves in order to recall what they were thinking. These recall sessions were conducted in English, the dominant language of the learners, and audio-taped. This introspective method was designed to elicit information from the learners about their original perceptions about the feedback.

Analysis

Two types of data were analyzed, the interactional feedback episodes and the stimulated-recall comments related to those episodes. The feedback episodes were coded into four categories: phonological, morphosyntactic, lexical, and semantic. Within each category, we included both negotiation and recasts. We return to this distinction below. An example of each type follows. Example 1 shows a phonological feedback episode. All examples in this chapter are from data collected for the current study.

> *Example 1*   Phonological episode
> Non-heritage learner (NHL)
> Interlocutor (I)
> NHL   *Er, a sinestra i fiori ...*
>   Er, to the left the flowers ...
> I   *A sinestra?*
>   To the left?
> NHL   *Um, è il pane*
>   Um, is the bread
> I   *A sinestra? Oh, a sinistra.*
>   To the left? Oh, to the left.
> NHL   *A sinistra.*
>   To the left.

The learner pronounced the word *sinistra* (left) incorrectly as *sinestra*. The interviewer first repeated the non-targetlike form and then provided the correct pronunciation. Example 2 illustrates a morphosyntactic episode.

Example 2 Morphosyntactic episode
Heritage learner (HL)
HL *E poi, sopra di bottiglie, ci sono due ...*
    And then, above of bottles, there are two ...
I *Sopra che cosa?*
    Above what?

In this case, the learner follows the preposition *sopra* (above), with an unnecessary preposition *di*. The interlocutor repeats the preposition without the second preposition.

Feedback was categorized as lexical when it was focused on vocabulary issues, as shown in Example 3.

Example 3 Lexical episode
HL *Un piccolo, um, candel, candelabra, no, cand ... lite?*
    A small, um, candel, candelabra, no, cand ... lite (nonword).
I *Una candela?*
    A candle?
HL *Sì, sì, candela.*
    Yes, yes, candle.

The learner tries to find a way to refer to the candle in the picture, and the interlocutor provides the lexical item in Italian. The exchange in Example 4 was also counted as a lexical feedback episode. The learner uses a Spanish word *abierto* (open) instead of the Italian word *aperto*, which is provided by the interviewer following the non-heritage language learner's use of the Spanish word.

Example 4 Lexial episode (Spanish)
NHL *Non è certo.*
    Is not certain.
I *Certo?*
    Certain?
NHL *Um, oh, è abierto.*
    Um, oh is 'abierto'. (Spanish)
I *Abierto? Aperto?*
    'Abierto?' Open?
NHL *Aperto, sì.*
    Open, yes.

The last type of episode was categorized as semantic as illustrated by Example 5. In this case, the learner's utterance was correct in terms of phonology, lexis, and morphosyntax, but the interviewer gives feedback to confirm meaning and to clarify what was said.

Example 5   Semantic episode
NHL   *Tazze, sì.*
   Cups, yes.
I   *Sì, anch'io.*
   Yes, me too.
NHL   *Quattro tazze in tutto.*
   Four cups in total.
I   *Ah, ci sono quattro tazze?*
   Ah, there are four cups?
NHL   *Sì, sì.*
   Yes, yes.

In Example 5, the non-heritage language speaker states that there are four cups in the picture. The interviewer rephrases the statement, but there is no corrective feedback provided. Instead, the feedback clarifies what the learner had just said.

Based on the audio-taped stimulated recall sessions, the participants' comments were categorized as being about phonology, morphosyntax, lexis, semantics, or having no content. Recall comments classified as phonology indicated that the learner was aware of a pronunciation problem, as in Example 6.

Example 6   Phonology
HL   *Due, per il vino, come la bottiglie?* (pronounced with hard 'g')
   Two, for the wine, like the (f.sg.) bottle (f.pl.)?
I   *Bottiglia.* (pronounced with soft 'g')
   Bottle.
Recall   ... then she corrected me 'cause I pronounced it wrong. And I was like, yes, yes, yes. Like once she said it, I was definite that was what I was talking about.

Example 7 is categorized as morphosyntax because the learner comments on grammatical error.

Example 7   Morphosyntax
NHL   *La pane.*
   The (f) bread (m).
I   *La, la pane?*
   The, the (f) bread (m)?
NHL   *Il pane.*
   The (m) bread (m)?
I   *Il pane.*
   The (m) bread (m).
Recall   I thought that *pane* was feminine because it ends in 'e' and I was just, automatically assuming.

Comments related to vocabulary difficulties were categorized as lexis, such as Example 8. Here the learner discusses the meaning of specific words.

Example 8   Lexis
HL   *Um, la ventana   sono chuiso*
       Um, the 'ventana' (f.sg.) are closed (m.sg.).
I   *La ventana.   Ventana?*
       The 'ventana'. 'Ventana?'
HL   *Sì.*
       Yes.
I   *La finestra?*
       The window?
HL   *Finestra, sì.*
       Window, yes.
Recall   I didn't think anything of it until she corrected me that I had said 'window' in Spanish instead of Italian.

When the recall comments were related to more general issues of meaning, they were categorized as semantic. In such cases, participants explained that they were trying to express an idea or indicated concern about whether they had conveyed their meaning accurately. Two examples are given below in Examples 9 and 10.

Example 9   Semantics
HL   *Okay. Um ... due tazze(f. pl.) sono alta (f. sg.), più alta (f. sg.).*
       Okay. Um ... two cups are high, higher.
I   *Le tazze sono più alte (f. pl.). Più alte di che cosa?*
       The cups are higher. Higher than what?
Recall   I was trying to say that they were higher up and I knew I was saying that they were tall, but I was hoping that she would get what I was trying to say.

Example 10   Semantics
I   *È normale la tua scopa?*
       Is your broom (f) normal?
NHL   *Er ...*
       Er ...
I   *La mia è molto corta. La tua è normale? È una scopa normale?*
       Mine (f) is very short. Is yours (f) normal? Is it a normal broom (f)?
NHL   *Um, è forse più lungo.*
       Um, it is perhaps more long (m).
I   *Lungo? È lunga?*
       Long (m)? Is it long (f)?
Recall   I was concerned because I didn't know if a push broom was a normal broom. So I didn't know if like she had a different type of broom.

In some cases, the recall comments did not fit into any of the four categories described above. These comments were either unrelated to the interaction or were related to task-based concerns. These types of comments, illustrated in Examples 11 and 12, were classified as 'no content.'

Example 11   No content
HL   *E poi a destra di tavolo c'è ...*
         And then to the right of table there is ...
I   *A destra di ...?*
         To the right of ...?
HL   *Tavolo. Tavolo.*
         Table. Table.
Recall   She didn't hear me.

Example 12   No content
NHL   *Non è fiori. Ma, um ...*
         It's not flowers. But, um ...
I   *Una pianta?*
         A plant?
NHL   *Pianta?*
         Plant?
I   *Sì, sì, anch'io. E una candela?*
         Yes, yes, me too. And a candle?
Recall   I was just trying to find another difference. I was like, 'Oh, gosh'.

In Example 11 the recall comment is not related to the preceding feedback episode and in Example 12 the comment is related to the task of finding the difference between the two pictures.

The data yielded a total of 186 feedback episodes and recall comments: 99 in the non-heritage language learner data and 87 in the heritage language learner data. A second rater coded one third of the data, and the two raters were in agreement 87 per cent of the time. In the cases where the raters did not agree, the data were discussed and agreement was reached on the appropriate coding.

Results and discussion

The analysis follows that of Mackey *et al.* (2000). The first analysis provides information on the range of data, both on the content of the feedback episodes and the content of the stimulated recall comments. Table 3.3 and Figures 3.2 and 3.3 illustrate the linguistic content of the 186 feedback episodes for the two groups of participants, non-heritage language learners and heritage language learners. As can be seen in Table 3.3 and Figures 3.2 and 3.3, the most common type of feedback episode with non-heritage language learners was lexical (51.5 per cent), while the second most common type was related to morphosyntax (26.3 per cent). Phonological and semantic feedback occurred at about the same rate (12.1 per cent and 10.1 per cent respectively). The heritage language group was similar to the non-heritage language group in that the most common type of feedback for heritage language learners was also related to lexis (43.7 per cent). However, there were also differences between the two groups. With the heritage language learners the second most common type of feedback was related to semantics (31.0 per cent) which occurred approximately three times more often than with the non-heritage language learners. Morphosyntactic feedback episodes were the third most common type (14.9 per cent). The phonological feedback episodes appear to be similar to the non-heritage language group (10.3 per cent).

Episode types	Non-heritage learners (99 total episodes)		Heritage learners (87 total episodes)	
	Number	Percentage	Number	Percentage
Phonological	12	12.1	9	10.3
Morphosyntactic	26	26.3	13	14.9
Lexical	51	51.5	38	43.7
Semantic	10	10.1	27	31.0

Table 3.3 Linguistic content of feedback episodes

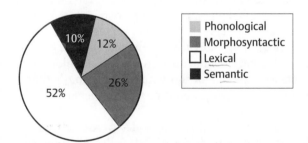

Figure 3.2 Linguistic content of non-heritage learners (99 total episodes)

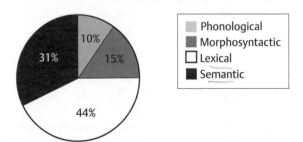

Figure 3.3 Linguistic content of heritage learners (87 total episodes)

We turn now to the stimulated recall comments. The linguistic content of the stimulated recall comments is shown in Table 3.4.

Comment types	Non-heritage learners (99 total comments)		Heritage learners (87 total comments)	
	Number	Percentage	Number	Percentage
Phonological	11	11.0	5	5.7
Morphosyntactic	9	9.0	2	2.3
Lexical	56	56.6	44	50.6
Semantic	3	3.0	29	33.3
No content	20	20.2	7	8.0

Table 3.4 Linguistic content of stimulated recall comments

The non-heritage language learners were most likely to comment on lexical issues (56.6 per cent). However, 20.2 per cent of the time the non-heritage language learners' comments were not related to the feedback episode at all (coded 'no content'), suggesting that they were often unaware of the focus of the feedback. The heritage language learners also commented most often on lexis (50.6 per cent); however, they were less likely to make unrelated comments, producing 'no content' comments only 8.0 per cent of the time. The heritage language learners commented on semantics approximately ten times more often than the non-heritage learners (33.3 per cent versus 3.0 per cent). Both groups commented on phonology more than on morphosyntax: 5.7 per cent of the heritage language learners' comments were about phonology and 2.3 per cent of the comments were about morphosyntax; for the non-heritage learners 11 per cent of the comments were about phonology versus 9.0 per cent about morphosyntax.

The learners' perceptions about the feedback episodes were analyzed by comparing the feedback episode type with the stimulated recall comment that followed. Research question 1 asked about the difference in accuracy between perceptions of morphosyntactic feedback on the one hand and phonological, lexical, and semantic feedback on the other. As can be seen in Table 3.5 and Figure 3.4, the answer to this research question is that there is a difference. With the exception of the non-heritage learners' perception of semantic feedback and the heritage learners' perception of phonology, in all cases, accurate perception of feedback was in the 65–90 percentage range. On the other hand, accurate morphosyntactic perception was in the 15–35 percentage range. We return to the phonology issue below.

Research question 2 asked about differences in accuracy of perception of feedback by the heritage and non-heritage learners. As in the Mackey *et al.* study, accuracy refers to the match between the content of the stimulated recall comments and the content of the feedback given. In what follows we consider the four feedback categories analyzed in this study: phonological, morphosyntactic, lexical, and semantic.

We turn first to phonological feedback episodes. The learners' perceptions about these feedback episodes are shown in Table 3.6.

Perception types	Non-heritage learners (percentage)	Heritage learners (percentage)
Phonological	66.7	45.0
Lexical	78.4	89.5
Semantic	10.0	70.4
Morphosyntactic	34.6	15.4

Table 3.5 Accuracy of perceptions

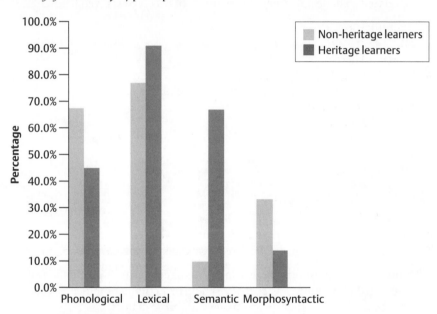

Figure 3.4 Accuracy of perceptions

Perception types	Non-heritage learners (12 total comments)		Heritage learners (9 total comments)	
	Number	Percentage	Number	Percentage
Phonological	8	66.7	5	45.0
Morphosyntactic	0	0	0	0
Lexical	2	16.7	0	0
Semantic	0	0	2	22.2
No content	2	16.7	2	22.2

Table 3.6 Learners' perceptions of phonological feedback

As can be seen in Table 3.6, the non-heritage language participants showed a high rate of accuracy in their perception about phonological feedback, accurately perceiving this type of feedback 66.7 per cent of the time. These results are similar to those for one group of learners from the Mackey *et al.* study in which the ESL learners perceived phonological feedback accurately 60 per cent of the time. However, the IFL learners in that study only perceived phonological feedback accurately 21.4 per cent of the time. In this study if the learners did not perceive that the feedback was related to phonology, they were most likely to think that the feedback was related to lexis (16.7 per cent of the time). Almost 17 per cent of the time learners provided a comment irrelevant to the feedback. Nine episodes of phonological feedback took place with the heritage language learners, five of which occurred with the same learner. Furthermore, the phonological feedback episodes with that learner were related to dialectal issues. An example of this type is given below.

> *Example 13*
> HL   ... *c'è sta, er, pane.*
>   There is, er, bread.
> I   *Pane. Il ...C'è, c'è pane, sì.*
>   Bread. The ... There is, there is bread, yes.
> HL   *Un cortello.*
>   A knife.
> I   *Un ...?*
>   A ...?
> HL   *Cortello.*
>   Knife.
> I   *Cortello? Coltello?*
>   Knife? Knife?
> Recall Um, I wasn't thinking anything until she corrected my
>   pronunciation and realized I was speaking Calabrese.

The interviewer questions the heritage language learner's pronunciation of the word *coltello* ('knife') as *cortello*. The recall comment indicates that the learner became aware that he was using Calabrese dialect.

As noted above, heritage language learners often come to the learning context with excellent pronunciation, and they are undoubtedly aware of this. The fact that very few non-dialect related phonological episodes occurred with the heritage language learners provides some evidence that these learners do not have the same phonological difficulties as non-heritage language learners. In our data only a small number of phonological feedback episodes occur with heritage language learners suggesting that the issues raised in these episodes are not the same as those that are raised with non-heritage language learners. It is perhaps because of the heritage learners' knowledge that few phonological problems exist that 22.2 per cent of the phonological episodes were perceived as something other than phonological feedback (semantic) and 22.2 per cent prompted 'no content' comments; this was not the case for the non-heritage learners who never interpreted phonological feedback as semantic feedback and who provided 'no content' comments 16.7 per cent of the time. This corroborates the findings of Mackey *et al.* (2000).

Table 3.7 shows the learners' perceptions about morphosyntactic feedback. Unlike the results for the phonological feedback, the learners' perceptions of morphosyntactic feedback were far less accurate. This finding is similar to that of the previous study (Mackey *et al.* 2000) in which the ESL learners perceived morphosyntactic feedback accurately only 13 per cent of the time and the IFL learners only 24 per cent of the time.

Perception types	Non-heritage learners (26 total comments)		Heritage learners (13 total comments)	
	Number	Percentage	Number	Percentage
Phonological	1	3.8	0	0
Morphosyntactic	9	34.6	2	15.4
Lexical	9	34.6	2	15.4
Semantic	2	7.7	5	38.5
No content	5	19.2	4	30.8

Table 3.7 Learners' perceptions of morphosyntactic feedback

The non-heritage language learners only perceived morphosyntactic feedback accurately 34.6 per cent of the time. When the feedback was morphosyntactic in nature, the learners were likely to comment on lexis (34.6 per cent of the time), or to make unrelated comments (19.2 per cent of the time). The heritage language learners were only accurate in their perception about morphosyntactic feedback 15.4 per cent of the time, about half as frequently as the non-heritage learners. With this type of feedback the heritage language learners were more likely than the non-heritage language learners to make unrelated comments (30.8 per cent of the time) suggesting that they may be even less aware of morphosyntactic feedback. The heritage language learners were again more likely to make comments related to semantics (38.5 per cent) than the non-heritage language learners (7.7 per cent).

Perception types	Non-heritage learners (51 total comments)		Heritage learners (38 total comments)	
	Number	Percentage	Number	Percentage
Phonological	0	0	0	0
Morphosyntactic	0	0	0	0
Lexical	40	78.4	34	89.5
Semantic	0	0	3	7.9
No content	11	21.6	1	2.6

Table 3.8 Learners' perceptions of lexical feedback

The learners' perceptions about lexical feedback are shown in Table 3.8. As in the Mackey *et al.* study, the non-heritage language learners achieved a high rate of accuracy in terms of their perceptions about lexical feedback (78.4 per cent of the time). Table 3.8 also shows that when the non-heritage language learners did not perceive lexical feedback accurately, they always made unrelated comments (21.6 per cent of the time).

The heritage language data in Table 3.8 shows a similarly high rate of accuracy for the perception about lexical feedback, with the learners perceiving this type of feedback correctly 89.5 per cent of the time. However, the heritage language learners were less likely to make unrelated comments (only 2.6 per cent of the time) and were more likely to make a comment related to semantics (7.9 per cent of the time). This suggests that heritage language learners may be more focused on semantic and lexical issues when engaged in interaction. It should also be noted that some of the lexical issues that were raised in feedback episodes with heritage language learners were related to their home language/dialect, as was found in the lexical feedback episodes, as illustrated in Example 14 and Example 13 earlier.

Example 14

HL	*Con il pane, i fiori.*
	With the bread, the flowers.
I	*Fiori. Va bene, anch'io.*
	Flowers. Good, me too.
HL	*Anche, la stúfa.*
	Also, the stove.
I	*Stúfa?*
	Stove?
HL	*Dove si cucina.*
	Where you cook.
Recall	We call it *stúfa* in my family. So and when she said *forno*—I mean the *forno* is in the backyard where you make the pizza with the, the fire. So I, I was like man, I don't know how to speak regular Italian.

In this example, the heritage language learner uses the word *stúfa* to refer to the stove in the picture. The interviewer questions this word, so the learner explains by saying, 'Where you cook'. At this point, the learner makes a recall comment comparing two possible words for 'stove', *stúfa* and *forno*, one in dialect and one in Italian. When the interaction continues (not shown here) the interviewer provides the word *forno*, but the learner explains that in his family the word *stúfa* would be used for an indoor kitchen stove. The heritage language learner clearly recognizes that the feedback is related to lexis, but the episode focuses on a dialect or home language issue.

The learners' perceptions about semantic feedback are shown in Table 3.9.

Perception types	Non-heritage learners (10 total comments)		Heritage learners (27 total comments)	
	Number	Percentage	Number	Percentage
Phonological	1	10.0	0	0
Morphosyntactic	0	0	0	0
Lexical	5	50.0	8	29.6
Semantic	1	10.0	19	70.4
No content	3	30.0	0	0

Table 3.9 Learners' perceptions of semantic feedback

The non-heritage language learners usually perceived semantic feedback inaccurately; in fact, they were only accurate 10.0 per cent of the time. They were very likely to comment on lexis (50.0 per cent) or to make unrelated comments (30.0 per cent). The heritage language learners show a noticeably different pattern of perception about semantic feedback. Although they did not perceive this type of feedback as accurately as they perceived lexical feedback, they were accurate in their perceptions about semantics 70.4 per cent of the time. Like the non-heritage language learners, when they were not accurate, they often commented on lexis (29.6 per cent). In contrast, the heritage language learners never made a 'no content' comment following semantic feedback indicating their awareness that some form of feedback had been provided. Examples 15 and 16 below are taken from two different heritage language learner transcripts illustrating accurate perception about semantic feedback.

Example 15
HL   *Nient'altro.*
      Nothing else.
I   *Nient' altro?*
      Nothing else?
HL   *Nient' altro. Solo piatti e cafè.*
      Nothing else. Only plates and coffee.
I   *Ah, va bene.*
      Ah, good.
Recall   Just further clarification. And then when, I thought I confused her because maybe I clarified too much when I said *nient'altro* (nothing else). Maybe she thought there was nothing else in the whole kitchen.

Example 16
I   *E che altro c'è?*
      And what else is there?
HL   *Er, due bicchieri.*
      Er, two glasses.
I   *Due bicchieri?*
      Two glasses?

HL   *Sì.*
        Yes.
Recall   Just we were discussing what was in the cabinet.

In both examples, the heritage language learner's recall comment shows his/her clear perception that the interviewer was clarifying what s/he had said. However, the heritage language learners' tendency to focus on semantics sometimes seemed to cause a misperception about the feedback given. We noted above, with regard to the way heritage language learners perceived lexical feedback, in several cases learners seemed to think that lexical feedback was actually related to semantic issues. In Example 17, the heritage language learner explains that there are two cups on the table and 'something for coffee'. The interviewer suggests that the object is for tea and the learner agrees with this. Therefore, the interviewer provides the word *teièra* (teapot).

Example 17
HL   *Anche, il tavolo er, due tazze e anche qualcosa per il cafè.*
        Also, the table er, two cups and also something for coffee.
I   *O il tè.*
        Or tea.
HL   *O il tè. Sì ...*
        Or tea. Yes.
I   *Una teièra.*
        A teapot.
HL   *Sì.*
        Yes.
Recall   She knew exactly what I meant.

The heritage language learner's recall comment does not relate to the vocabulary item 'teapot', but focuses on the fact that the interviewer 'knew exactly what I meant'. In Example 18, a different heritage language learner uses the the word *aberto*, which appears to be a mix of the Spanish word *abierto* (open) and the Italian word *aperto* (open). The interviewer gives feedback on this word by using a questioning tone while saying the Spanish word *abierto*.

Example 18
HL   *Um. La finestra è aberto.*
        Um. The window is 'aberto'.
I   *Abierto?*
        'Abierto?' (Spanish)
HL   *Abierto.*
        'Abierto'.
I   *Abierto.*
        'Abierto'.
HL   *Sì.*
        Yes.

Recall   And then right about there I was hoping she wasn't thinking the
window was actually open.

Although the interviewer questions the words *aberto* and *abierto* several
times, the heritage language learner's recall comment is not related to lexis.
Instead, his comment indicates that he was concerned about whether he had
conveyed his meaning successfully.

A final point to make with regard to these data relates to the feedback types
in these data. The study employed a task-based interaction with feedback not
being controlled. In other words, the goal was to make the task as natural
as possible. We did, nonetheless, perform a *post hoc* analysis to determine if
there were different feedback types given to different parts of the grammar
and to the two groups. To undertake this analysis, we categorized the feedback into two types: negotiation (including prompts) and recasts. There were
only a few instances where both were used together and these will not be dealt
with here. These results are presented in Table 3.10. For both groups of learners, there are more negotiations than recasts although the percentages differ
slightly between them. As can be seen, there are similarities with regard to the
relative order of negotiation, the most for lexical feedback, second highest
when there is semantic feedback, and least for phonological and morphological feedback. It is in the category of recasts, where there are differences: for
non-heritage learners, recasts occurred most often with morphosyntactic
feedback, second most frequently with phonological feedback, and third with
lexical feedback (none with semantic feedback); for the heritage learners, the
picture was slightly different with as many instances of recasts occurring with
lexical as with morphosyntactic feedback.

| | Negotiation | | | | Recast | | | |
| | Non-heritage learners | | Heritage learners | | Non-heritage learners | | Heritage learners | |
	Number	Percentage	Number	Percentage	Number	Percentage	Number	Percentage
Phonology	5	7.6	5	7.5	7	22.6	4	22.2
Morphosyntax	5	7.6	5	7.5	20	64.5	7	38.9
Lexical	47	71.2	31	46.3	4	12.9	7	38.9
Semantic	9	13.6	27	31	0	0	0	0
Grand total	66		68		31		18	

Table 3.10 Feedback types

General discussion

The results of this study are generally confirmatory of Mackey *et al.*'s (2000) findings and, more germane to the present chapter, also indicate subtle yet interesting differences between non-heritage language learners and heritage language learners. Mackey *et al.* (2000) found that ESL and IFL learners perceive phonological, lexical, and semantic feedback more accurately than they perceive morphosyntactic feedback. The current study showed that both non-heritage language learners and heritage language learners perceive phonological and lexical feedback much more accurately than morphosyntactic feedback. However, perceptions about semantic feedback differed between the two groups. The non-heritage language learners were generally not accurate in terms of their perceptions about semantic feedback, but the heritage language learners perceived semantic feedback accurately approximately 70 per cent of the time, as seen in Table 3.9.

It was noted in the previous study that fewer episodes of phonological feedback take place with heritage language learners. These results confirm this finding and also indicate that phonological feedback episodes that do occur with heritage language learners may be centered on dialectal issues, unlike phonological feedback given to non-heritage language learners.

In general, the heritage language learners appeared to be more focused on semantic issues than the non-heritage language learners were. The heritage language learners sometimes perceived both phonological feedback and lexical feedback as being related to semantics; however, the non-heritage language learners did not demonstrate this pattern in terms of their perception. The heritage language learners were less likely to make 'no content' recall comments following lexical and semantic feedback than the non-heritage language learners suggesting that they may be generally more aware of these types of feedback. On the other hand, the heritage language learners were more likely to make 'no content' recall comments following a morphosyntactic feedback episode. This result suggests that heritage language learners may be even less aware of morphosyntactic feedback than non-heritage language learners; however, it should be kept in mind that the total number of morphosyntactic feedback episodes with heritage language learners was very low.

The heritage language learners in this study had a variety of different experiences, but despite these differences in their backgrounds, they showed the same patterns in their perceptions about feedback. This suggests that even minimal exposure to a heritage language as a child might impact the nature of a learner's language learning experiences later in life.

We interpret these results to indicate that, in general, heritage language learners are more focused on semantic issues when engaged in conversational interaction. They perceived semantic feedback more accurately and also attributed other sorts of feedback to semantics rather than the intended target. This suggests a greater focus on meaning as opposed to linguistic form.

Similarly, the data indicated that heritage language learners pay less attention to morphosyntactic feedback, either interpreting it as semantic feedback or not being aware of it at all. The emphasis placed on semantics by heritage language learners, seen in their interpretation of non-semantic feedback (i.e. phonological, lexical, morphosyntactic) as semantic feedback (an average of 22.8 per cent for heritage language learners across these three feedback types versus 4.6 per cent for non-heritage learners) could be due to their experience with the heritage language. They are likely to regard language as a form of real communication whereas learners who acquire language only in a classroom setting may treat the language more as an intellectual exercise.

Conclusion

There are, of course, limitations to the interpretations of the current study. First is the limited number of participants and, hence, limited number of tokens in all categories of analysis. Second is the range of exposure to the heritage language amongst the participants. This, of course, is typical of all research on heritage language learning, but is more pronounced with heritage languages where migration occurred many years ago. In such instances, as is the case with Italian, the learners themselves are not first generation and, hence, the language in the home is often limited. Third, we do not know to what extent the results relate to different feedback types between the two groups (see Table 3.10) given that this was not a variable controlled for in this study. This is clearly an area for future research.

With these caveats aside, this study has shown that both non-heritage language learners and heritage language learners are able to perceive lexical and phonological feedback more accurately than morphosyntactic feedback. However, there are distinct differences between the two groups of learners, the primary one being the focus on semantics. Many educators argue that different classes should be provided for heritage language learners since they have different needs. Although educators and researchers are aware that language acquisition is not the same for heritage language learners as non-heritage language learners, there is currently little understanding of how the acquisition process differs between the two groups. This study sheds some light on how perceptions about interactional feedback may be different in the case of heritage language learners, thus providing some explanations of how their language learning experiences differ. However, further research is needed to increase our understanding of how adult heritage language learners acquire, or reacquire, the language they were exposed to as a child.

4

Alphabetic print literacy and oral language processing in SLA

ELAINE TARONE and MARTHA BIGELOW

Introduction

This paper explores the relationship between learners' degree of alphabetic print literacy and one aspect of oral second language acquisition (SLA): learners' recall of oral recasts of their errors in oral second language (L2) interrogative production. Most current theories of SLA state that L2 learners must be aware, at some level, of linguistic segments to acquire an L2. Schmidt (2001: 30) argues that regardless of the learning domain (i.e. phonology, pragmatics, syntax), 'attention must be specifically focused and not just global'. Schmidt and others have sought to demonstrate that when learners are exposed to L2 input, they are able to select only portions of the input that they can subsequently convert into intake. It is this portion of the input that is 'noticed'. 'Noticing', which is a particular level of attention, is defined as a conscious focus on 'elements of the surface structure of utterances in the input' (Schmidt 2001: 5) and does not assume metalinguistic awareness. Schmidt (personal communication) adds that noticing is something an individual does during online language processing, within working memory. We cannot directly observe 'noticing'. However, we believe that accurate uptake logically requires that the speaker notice the gap in form between their original utterance (and its intended meaning) and the recast. Therefore, throughout this chapter we infer that noticing has taken place when the learner modifies production (producing 'uptake') following corrective feedback in the form of a recast, as in:

Abukar (male, 15 yrs. old)	OK, Where, they?	(ungrammatical trigger)
MB (researcher)	Where are they?	(recast)
Abukar	Where are they?	(accurate recall/uptake)

This chapter aims to examine the nature of 'noticing' of recasts when L2 learners have low alphabetic print literacy. The term 'literacy' can include many types of oral and print-based abilities; it is used narrowly here to describe the ability to decode or encode alphabetic print. The results of this effort lead us to ask: Does a learner's literacy level affect the degree to which they notice corrective feedback on L2 form?

Research on linguistic awareness of illiterate adults

Noticing and awareness of language form have been the subject of investigation in SLA and fields related to SLA. Several L1 studies show that illiterate adults significantly differ from literate adults in their awareness of linguistic segments—including phonemes, syllables and words—in explicit oral processing tasks (Tarone and Bigelow 2005). The evidence for the impact of alphabetic literacy on phonemic awareness is particularly strong. One early study, for example, showed that illiterate adults could not delete or add a phoneme at the beginning of a non-word, while literate adults matched to them for sociocultural background could easily perform the same task (Morais, Cary, Alegría, and Bertelson 1979). Subsequent studies have shed additional light on the nature of oral language processing differences between literate and illiterate adults. Adrian, Alegría, and Morais (1995), for example, found that illiterate participants did significantly worse than literate participants on all tests that required conscious awareness of *phonemes*: phoneme detection (as with phoneme deletion (for example, 'If we subtract [t] from the word [tal], we have …?'), and as with phoneme reversal (for example, 'How would you say [los] backwards?' Answer: [sol]). Literacy also affected awareness of *syllables*, though to a somewhat lesser extent. Syllable tasks were significantly more difficult for illiterate than for literate participants: these were a syllable deletion task ('If we subtract [de] from the word [kade], we have …?') and a syllable reversal task ('Say [taro] backwards.' Answer: [rota]). And, finally, literacy affected the learners' ability to manipulate *words* in oral tasks, such as tasks requiring them to reverse words—for example, changing word order, and so manipulating syntax. Literacy did not seem to affect performance in oral tasks that did not require the ability to segment speech into linguistic units like phonemes, syllables, and words. For example, there was no impact of literacy on a phonetic discrimination task (for example, '*ta-sa*: same or different?') or a rhyme detection task (for example, '*mepu-pepu*: rhyme or not?'). The authors conclude that linguistic awareness—the ability to segment speech, and particularly the ability to do so on the basis of phonemes—is highly affected by degree of alphabetic literacy. Similarly, Reis and Castro-Caldas (1997), in a study of matched groups of illiterate and literate women in Portugal, found significant differences in their ability to do 'metalinguistic' as opposed to semantic processing of oral language. For example, the illiterate participants had a harder time than literate ones in repeating pseudo-words (permissible phonological sequences that have no semantic meaning) and performing *phonological* fluency tasks (for example, 'You have one minute to say all the words you can think of that begin with /p/.'). There was no difference between the groups in their ability to repeat meaningful words, or to perform *semantic* fluency tasks (for example, 'You have one minute to say all the names of animals you can think of.').

How does alphabetic literacy affect processing of oral language? Reis and Castro-Caldas (1997) propose that it creates a tool used in short-term memory for oral language processing:

> Learning to match graphemes and phonemes is learning an operation in which units of auditory verbal information heard in temporal sequence are matched to units of visual verbal information, which is spatially arranged. This type of treatment of auditory verbal information modulates a strategy in which a visual-graphic meaning is given to units that are smaller than words, and thus independent of their semantic representation. ... The awareness of phonology ... allows us to play with written symbols (which can be transcoded to sounds) to form pseudo-plausible words, independently of semantics. Therefore learning to read and write introduces into the system qualitatively new strategies for dealing with oral language; that is, conscious phonological processing, visual formal lexical representation, and all the associations that these strategies allow (1997: 445).

Brain activation research by the same research team (Castro-Caldas, Petersson, Reis, Stone-Elander, and Ingvar 1998) has recorded the physical impact of alphabetic print literacy on the functional organization of the adult brain. Positron Emission Topography and statistical parametric mapping were used in a brain activation study that compared word and pseudo-word repetition by literate and illiterate adults. Results showed that repetition of real words by both groups activated similar parts of the brain, but the repetition of pseudo-words activated different neural structures in the brains of illiterate and literate participants, and was more difficult for illiterates. Literate participants' accuracy rate in repeating pseudo-words was 84 per cent, while the illiterate participants' accuracy rate was 33 per cent. Referring to Rumelhart and McClelland's (1986) parallel distributed processing model, the researchers propose that all their participants used three different parallel strategies for repeating verbal material (semantic, lexical, and phonological), but that the phonological strategy used by their literate participants has been altered by the addition of a 'visuographic dimension' that improves their ability to repeat verbal material. Illiterate participants do not have access to this tool, and so rely much more heavily on semantic or lexical strategies for oral language processing.

Some might suggest that, in these and other studies on explicit oral language processing, the results could be due to educational level, intelligence, or social class, rather than alphabetic print literacy itself. To address this possibility, and also to explore the influence of a non-alphabetic as opposed to an alphabetic print script, Read, Zhang, Nie, and Ding (1986) studied two comparable groups of adult Chinese participants, both of them equally well educated and living in a similar communities. One group had become literate only in Chinese logographic characters, as they had been educated in schools that had not yet adopted the Chinese alphabetic print script (Hanyu Pinyin). The second group, comparable to the first in level of education, age, and social group, had become literate in *both* the logographic and the alphabetic script. Their differential exposure to an alphabetic print script was an accident of history and social change, and not to any differences in their level of education, cognitive ability, or their social situation. Both groups were asked to perform oral tasks in Chinese similar to those we have just reviewed. As in all the other studies, when asked to add or delete initial consonants or repeat pseudo-words, the adults who had alphabetic print literacy significantly outperformed those who did not. The authors conclude that the ability to segment oral language develops *as a consequence* of the process of learning to read and write in a print script which is alphabetical—that is, one that represents phonemes with visual symbols.

These conclusions are extremely important for all research on oral language processing. It is widely agreed that there is a strong positive correlation between phonological awareness (the ability to segment oral language into phonemes and to manipulate these) and alphabetic literacy. However, it is commonly assumed that it is phonological awareness that precedes, and so causes, successful alphabetic print literacy. In fact, the findings of these cognitive psychologists suggest that it is exactly the opposite: it is literacy in an alphabetic script that leads to this kind of phonological awareness. These studies provide strong evidence, supporting the claims of Olson (2002 and elsewhere), that the oral and written language systems interact in the human mind, and that the addition of alphabetic print literacy alters the way the brain functions in processing oral language. Learning to match phonemes and graphemes adds a visual dimension to the internal representation system for spoken language, and this in turn enables literate adults to use a kind of oral metalinguistic processing that illiterate adults struggle with.

At the same time, we need to know more about the strategies that are used to process oral language by adults who are either literate only in a logographic script or who are illiterate. How do such learners structure their short-term memory for oral language? What kinds of oral language tasks are easy for them, but hard for alphabetically literate adults? As Lourdes Ortega (personal communication) puts it, we need a better understanding of the possible 'cognitive advantages of the non-alphabetic mind'.

Illiterate adults acquiring second languages

The research just reviewed, although relating to the participants' processing of native languages, should be of intense interest to researchers interested in the role of attention and awareness in SLA. The studies we have cited above, showing significant differences in oral native language processing on the part of adults who lack alphabetic print literacy, make it imperative that we explicitly include and identify similar learners in our studies of SLA. Put bluntly, our SLA theories may only explain the processes and outcomes of literate L2 learners. Is interactional feedback designed to promote 'noticing' beneficial for all L2 learners, or only beneficial for literate learners? If illiterate learners do not attend to form in the same way or to the same degree, how do they acquire L2s? Does lack of alphabetic print literacy affect their oral L2 learning outcomes, and if so, how? The ability of SLA research to contribute to the fields of cognition, literacy, and L2 teaching will clearly be affected by our answers to such questions.

The Somali literacy study

In this chapter we summarize quantitative results originally reported in Bigelow, delMas, Hansen, and Tarone (2006), and for the first time, report qualitatively on the data from one participant gathered in this same study. This is the only SLA study we know of that explicitly examines the role of alphabetic print literacy as a variable in the acquisition of oral skills among adolescents or adults. This study documents the impact of literacy level on adolescent and adult Somali learners' ability to use recasts to repair their errors in English question formation. It is important to understand the quantitative data reported in Bigelow *et al.* in order to contextualize the qualitative data presented in this chapter. Therefore, we first briefly summarize quantitative results showing significant differences between a group of low literate and a group of moderately literate learners (fully reported in Bigelow *et al.* 2006 and Tarone, Bigelow and Hansen forthcoming). However, this analysis does not help us understand in detail how low literacy manifests itself in a learner's oral performance. Therefore, the detailed qualitative analysis of one of the low literate participants' attempts to recall recasts of his erroneous questions is provided in this paper. We use the qualitative and the quantitative data to explore the impact of alphabetic print literacy on adult learners' processing of linguistic elements in oral second language input, and consider the implications of our findings for SLA theory.

Quantitative results on oral recast processing by less literate L2 learners

Bigelow *et al.* (2006) present a partial replication of Jenefer Philp's (2003) study of literate and highly educated adults' ability to recall (repeat) a recast on grammatically incorrect interrogative formations. The replication aims to expand the participant pool in SLA studies to include individuals who were explicitly identified as having a high incidence of low alphabetic print literacy. Philp's study was a suitable choice for replication with a low literate population because, as in other interaction studies, her procedures used the oral modalities. Philp's focus on learners' ability to recall oral recasts of different lengths and numbers of changes was also interesting because we thought that this ability might differ in our population, given the heavy use of memory strategies in their daily lives (as opposed to list making, or note taking which are things literate adults may do routinely). The research questions in Bigelow *et al.* mirrored those of Philp (2003) but integrated learner literacy level as an additional variable. The questions were:

1 Is the ability to recall a recast related to the literacy level of the learner?
2 Is the ability to recall a recast related to the length of the recast? Do learners at higher literacy levels recall these better than lower literacy learners?
3 Is the ability to recall a recast related to the number of changes made by the recast? Do learners at higher literacy levels recall these better than lower literacy learners?

Like the study we replicated, we did not address acquisition over time. L1 and L2 literacy levels of the participants were determined through administration of English and Somali versions of the Native Language Literacy Screening Device, developed in New York by the Hudson River Center for Program Development. This tool is designed for practitioners to establish students' relative comfort with reading and writing in their native language for the purpose of informing placement into ESL classes. We used the tool with a rating scale to rate literacy level, which then served to group participants in a low literacy group and a moderate literacy group. (See Bigelow *et al.* (forthcoming) for a description of this literacy measure and the rating rubric used with it.)

Participants

The participants in the study were eight L1 Somali speakers between the ages of 15–27 who were living in the US. They were selected because their scores on the English and Somali literacy measures were either among the highest or the lowest in the initial set of 35 participants. As a group, they had lower literacy levels than the college students in Philp's (2003) study. These participants reported being in the United States from three to seven years. They were typical of Somali refugees of their age group in that they had experienced interrupted schooling and many years in refugee camps before settling in the US. The implication of this fact for the study was that even the four Somalis who scored the highest on our literacy measures were still not literate at the level of peers of comparable age without interrupted schooling. (By the same token, the four Somalis scoring the lowest in literacy were still not entirely illiterate, as the participants were in the cognitive psychology studies cited earlier.) They had all attended US public schools and therefore had been exposed to print. Most of the participants reported engaging with print in out-of-school activities such as study of the Qur'an.

The four participants who scored the highest in terms of literacy level reported that they all had literate and educated adults in their lives who had taught them how to read and write in Somali. They also reported seeking out print materials in Somali including, for example, the local Somali newspaper and books in Somali from the public library. One participant shared the fact that she tried to teach her friends how to read and write in Somali. Another told the researcher with pride that she and all of her siblings could read and write Somali because family members had taught them. These participants tackled the simple literacy tasks in English and Somali with confidence and ease.

None of the four participants with the lowest scores on the literacy measures reported any native language literacy support in their backgrounds. Likewise, none of these participants reported any L1 or L2 print materials in their homes. All but one participant could decode some written text on the tests, but their attempts to read in English and Somali were characterized by a lack of fluency, pointing at and reading words one by one, sounding words out, and the use of much sub-vocalization as a strategy to aid in their comprehension of the text. Three of the four participants in this group declined to attempt to write in Somali on the test. If alphabetic print literacy is a tool for cognitive processing, the less literate group had little mastery of that tool.

The developmental stage of English acquisition of all the participants was the same. Like Philp (2003), we established the developmental stage of our participants according to whether they could produce non-formulaic interrogatives of a given stage in at least two different contexts. Using this criterion, all of the participants were determined to be at stage 5. (See also Young-Scholten, Ijuin, and Vainikka 2005 for an alternative measure of second language development.) They produced between 6 and 28 spontaneous and accurate stage 5 questions. Their speech production was fluent and colloquial, and their interactions contained very few breakdowns in communication. Indeed, these adolescent and young adult participants often showed strong pragmatic skills; they routinely initiated small talk with the adult researchers that was unrelated to the tasks (for example, 'You teach like how to read and how to write?'), and backchanneled consistently throughout the conversation (for example, 'oh', 'yeah', 'mhm'). The following extract exemplifies their ability to nominate conversational topics, echo the interlocutors' turns, and give compliments. The exchange arose after a few seconds of silence while the researcher was switching materials between tasks:

Example 1 (Faadumo: female, 18 years old, KH: researcher)
01 **Faadumo** How many children you have? PERSONAL QUESTION
02 **KH** One.
03 **Faadumo** Just <u>one</u>. One daughter? What's her name? (echo, follow up question)
04 **KH** Sarah.
05 **Faadumo** Sarah. That's beautiful name. ECHO, COMPLIMENT
06 **KH** Yea, I like that name too. She's 27.

Methodology

The methodology used in this study was descriptive and quantitative. It involved engaging participants in four interactive spot-the-difference tasks, six interactive story completion tasks, a Somali literacy test, and an English literacy test. (See also Tarone, Bigelow, and Hansen forthcoming; Tarone, Bigelow, and Swierzbin in press; Hansen 2005 for information on other types of data collected in this experiment.) The tasks were all administered as in Philp (2003), with the intention of eliciting questions from participants representing the range of stages of acquisition (Pienemann and Johnston 1987; Pienemann, Johnston, and Brindley 1988). Stage was determined by participants' ability to produce two non-formulaic instances in two distinct contexts, the same criteria used in numerous other studies (for example, Mackey and Philp 1998; Mackey 1999; Spada and Lightbown 1999). While Philp's participants represented a range of stages, in the present study all the Somali participants selected had achieved stage 5. For this reason, the relationship between stage and ability to recall a recast was not considered in Bigelow *et al.* (2006). To understand whether there were any proficiency-related differences between participants, two experienced SPEAK test raters rated speech samples from the data collection. SPEAK scores ranged from 30–50, with scores evenly balanced between the moderate- and low-literate groups. Proficiency on the SPEAK test was statistically unrelated to ability to recall recasts, leaving the focus of this study on the relationship between literacy and recast recall.

As in Philp (2003), the participants' trigger utterances were categorized according to stage and the researcher's recasts were coded for length ('long' was six or more morphemes; 'short' was five or fewer morphemes) and number of changes. Participant recall of the recast was categorized as 'correct', 'modified', or 'no recall'. 'Correct' meant the recall of the question form exactly matched that of the recast:

> **Trigger**   What she is doing?
> **Recast**   What is she doing?
> **Recall**   What is she doing?

The recall was judged 'modified' if only some of the changes modeled in the recast were made:

> **Trigger**   He surprised?
> **Recast**   Is he surprised?
> **Recall**   Is he is surprised?

'No recall' meant none of the target changes were recalled:

> **Trigger**   What color?
> **Recast**   What color is it?
> **Recall**   What colorrrrr

Exact permutation tests (Efron and Tibshirani 1993; Good 2001) were used to evaluate the significance of the results. A detailed description and rationale for the use of exact permutation tests is provided in Bigelow *et al.* (2006). This significance measure is appropriate for small sample sizes that do not meet requirements for the underlying distribution for the test statistic required by standard parametric statistical analyses.

Results

Results of permutation analysis showed that the average recall of all 'correct' recasts by the moderate literacy group, while higher than that of the low literacy group, was not significantly higher, though it was close ($p=.057$). When participants' 'correct' and 'modified' recalls were combined, permutation analysis did show a significant difference between the two literacy groups; the more literate group recalled recasts in correct or modified form significantly more often than the less literate group ($p=.043$).

Correct recall

| Recast type | Mean group literacy level | | |
	Low literacy 1 to 6*	Moderate literacy 8 or 9	*p*-value**
All recasts	.633	.779	.057
Long recasts	.676	.751	.214
Short recasts	.657	.844	.086
1 change to recasts	.533	.597	.243
2+ changes to recasts	.429	.723	.143

Correct or modified recall

| Recast type | Mean group literacy level | | |
	Low literacy 1 to 6*	Moderate literacy 8 or 9	*p*-value**
All recasts	.852	.928	.043
Long recasts	.827	.907	.086
Short recasts	.851	.974	.071
1 change to recasts	.849	.909	.114
2+ changes to recasts	.820	1.000	.014

*Range of literacy measure 1–9   **All *p*-values are one-tailed

Table 4.1 Mean proportion of recalls under two criteria by group literacy level. Adapted from Bigelow et al. (2006)

A variety of analyses reported in Bigelow *et al.* (2006) showed no difference between recall of short versus long recasts for the two literacy groups. The average proportion of recast recall was significantly greater for the moderate literacy group than for the low literacy group. While the proportion of 'correct' recall of recasts with two or more changes to the trigger versus one change was not significantly different between the low- and moderate-literacy groups, when 'correct' or 'modified' recall were examined together, the difference between the two literacy groups was statistically significant ($p=.014$).

Discussion

The quantitative study establishes that degree of alphabetic print literacy is significantly related to L2 participants' recall of oral recasts of their errors in oral interrogative production. These results are entirely consistent with the evidence provided in cognitive psychology and brain research that oral metalinguistic processing is significantly impacted by alphabetic print literacy. This study establishes for the first time that this impact is not limited to oral L1 processing, but also extends to oral L2 processing. It thus establishes the relevance of this strand of literacy and oral language processing research for SLA.

Our findings differ in interesting ways from Philp's (2003) findings for more educated and literate participants. Stage of acquisition and proficiency level were controlled in our study, and so could not have caused the significant differences we found. In contrast to Philp (2003), the length of the recast was not a factor for our participants. It is possible that less literate participants use semantic strategies for processing recasts that are not affected by length (as measured by morpheme count) in the way that metalinguistic strategies are. Length may only be a factor for alphabetically literate learners who rely on visual morphosyntactic strategies to process oral language. Some might argue that even the short recasts were so difficult for the Somali participants that increased length made no difference; however, this seems unlikely given the stage of development of the participants. The overall ability of the Somali participants to recall a recast was not significantly related to the number of changes made by the recast, while it was in Philp's study. Participants in Philp's study were able to recall more recasts with one change than with two or more changes. However, number of changes was not significantly related to recall for the Somali learners as a group. Within the Somali participant pool, the moderate literacy group was somewhat better able to produce correct or modified recalls for recasts with two or more changes than the less literate group was. Here again, it is possible that language processing strategies used by less literate learners are less affected by differences in number of changes in linguistic segments, but more research is needed. For example, do illiterate or low literate learners use semantic language processing strategies that are more sophisticated and effective than those used by alphabetically literate learners?

The most substantial finding of this study was that literacy level was significantly related to the ability to recall oral recasts (when 'correct' and 'modified' recasts are collapsed) of the learners' erroneous L2 question formation. Less literate learners did not recall oral recasts on question forms as well as more literate learners.

Limitations

Bigelow *et al.* (2006) was not longitudinal and so it could not establish whether, or how, literacy level was tied to acquisition. The participant sample was small. Future studies with larger pools of participants with different native language backgrounds and different target languages would allow the use of more traditional inferential statistics and the ability to make stronger claims about the role of literacy in L2 oral skills. All the participants were at least partially alphabetically literate; future studies should include participants who are completely alphabetic print illiterate, and should include measures of linguistic and phonological awareness, such as phoneme deletion and reversal tasks. The study focused only on the facilitative impact of alphabetic literacy. Future studies should also document more precisely the oral processing strengths of less literate learners, such as rhyming as well as oral pragmatic skills. Finally, this analysis provides no detailed information on the language produced by the participants in response to recasts. A more fine-grained analysis is needed.

Qualitative analysis of a low literate learner's processing of oral recasts

In this section, in order to better understand the results from Bigelow *et al.*, we will examine in more depth how one of the less literate participants responds to recasts. We will call this participant Abukar.

Learner background

Abukar was a 9th grade male student from a large urban school in the Midwest of the United States. He was 15 years old at the time of the study. Abukar was typical among Somali immigrant adolescents in that the years when he should have been in school were eclipsed by the Somali civil war and subsequent refugee processing time in refugee camps. Abukar had been in a refugee camp for four years. At the time of the study, he had been in the United States for four and a half years—which is the total amount of formal education that he had had. Like the other participants, he had attained a stage 5 proficiency level; he had produced more than six spontaneous and accurate stage 5 questions, that is, questions with subject/aux inversion. The population of his current school was almost entirely African American and Somali. Outside of school, Abukar reported studying the Qur'an daily and learning words in Arabic and Oromo. He said he spoke both English and Somali every day in and out of school. His English seemed to reflect the urban vernacular he was exposed to and his dress had a hip-hop aesthetic common among adolescents in this metropolitan area.

Nature of the tasks

In doing the English literacy test, Abukar experienced a good deal of difficulty. As he did the reading section of the test, he used much sub-vocalization, sounding out words in order to comprehend the text. The following is what he wrote on the English literacy test in response to the prompt: 'Tell us why you want to learn English or anything else you would like to tell us'.

Example 2
I like play sports, like differen sport basketball, baseball, football.
I like to learn, my farati [favorite] subject is math gym and reading.

While this writing sample is very minimal, it is entirely comprehensible with impressively accurate spelling, given his literacy level. The Somali literacy test, however, was markedly harder for Abukar than the English test. Abukar responded in English to the questions on the Somali literacy test and did not attempt the paragraph in Somali with the same instructions as above. He decoded Somali text slowly, and again with much sub-vocalization.

As described above, Abukar was asked to perform several oral tasks in which the researcher provided recasts of his questions when they were grammatically inaccurate. He was instructed to repeat each recast. Correct repetitions are assumed to provide us with evidence that he has noticed the correct form, has compared it to his incorrect initial utterance, and has incorporated the correction into his reformulation ('uptake'). Nelson (1987) and Saxton (1997) refer to this process as cognitive comparison. Cognitive comparison requires the ability to hold both the initial erroneous question and the corrective recast in short-term memory long enough for the individual to examine the initial utterance against the negative evidence. These comparisons should ultimately result in the incorporation of the correct form or rule into Abukar's long-term memory—that is, the formation of a new rule in the learner's interlanguage. Levelt's (1989, 1992) model of speech processing offers a very useful explanation of how linguistic input can be converted into intake, and may shed light on Abukar's response to corrective feedback. The process, according to Levelt, requires more than just attending to the 'surface elements' of the input, as Schmidt (2001) claims. The process begins when the learner perceives the input via acoustic decoding. Acoustically processed input moves into the short-term store and can undergo comprehension or learning processes. During comprehension, the input is parsed by processes that use multiple types of knowledge, both semantic and metalinguistic, as resources. At this point, restructuring of the mental representation of interlanguage knowledge is engaged. New form–meaning mappings are created and existing mappings are refined so that cognitive comparisons and other internal representations can be made. It is this kind of cognitive process that L2 learners are assumed to engage in when they focus on linguistic form (Long 1991; Long and Robinson 1998; Doughty 2001) in oral interaction, as in recasts or negotiation of form, or a pedagogical intervention such as the myriad of focus on form techniques available (Doughty and Williams 1998). We wonder, however, if Abukar is able to efficiently process recasts and produce targetlike reformulations with minimal literacy as a tool to aid in cognitive processing.

In performing the tasks, Abukar's errors in question formation involved failure to invert subject and auxiliary in present progressive or copula, as in Examples 3 and 4, and use of a bare verb unmarked for tense, as in Example 5:

> *Example 3*
> **Abukar**   … what, what he is looking?

> *Example 4*
> **Abukar**   Why he is mad?

> *Example 5*
> **Abukar**   … why he come this room?

There are times when the researcher must make a choice about how to formulate the recast based on the context of the participant's utterance. For example, in the case of errors like those in Example 5, the researcher could choose to recast the question either in the present progressive ('Why is he coming …?') or simple past ('Why did he come?').

The data presented in the next section show a number of ways Abukar is using or not using the recast protocol to notice inversion for question formation in English. On the one hand, he seems to show very little ability to notice the inversion highlighted in the recasts, although in other instances he is able to use the recasts to modify his production. As with other learners, Abukar's performance is variable.

Form-focused recasts

There are multiple examples in the transcript of Abukar's apparent failure to modify his output in response to the researcher's repeated recasts of forms in his erroneous questions. While he did spontaneously produce some stage 5 questions, many of his questions in these tasks did not include subject/aux inversion. Thus, many of the recasts modeled subject/aux inversion. However, Abukar had difficulty accurately repeating these recasts. Early in the session, for example, we find this episode:

> *Example 6*
> 01 **Abukar**   What he sit on, what he SIT on, or whatever?
> 02 **MB**   What is he sitting on?
> 03 **Abukar**   Mhm.
> 04 **MB**   What is he sitting on? Again. Repeat.
> 05 **Abukar**   What he sitting on?
> 06 **MB**   What IS he sitting on?

07 **Abukar**   Oh. What he sitting on?
08 **MB**   What IS he sitting on?
09 **Abukar**   What IS he sitting on?

In line one, Abukar uses the bare verb 'sit' and in line two he receives a recast in present progressive, where he must notice an inserted aux 'is' and an inserted 'ing' on the verb. In line three, he simply backchannels, which suggests that he has not noticed the change in form, but rather treats the recast as a semantic confirmation check. Asked to explicitly repeat in line four, Abukar produces in line five a progressive question without an auxiliary; he has inserted the 'ing' but not the 'is'. This change suggests that he is now trying to focus on form rather than meaning. Again receiving the recast with the auxiliary in line six, he again repeats without the auxiliary in line seven. Perhaps he has been able to retain only a part of the recast in short-term memory and has not noticed the insertion of the auxiliary form. Only when the recast is provided for the third time with the inserted auxiliary form stressed does he insert a stressed auxiliary form in a correct question in line nine. This suggests that only then has he noticed the inserted aux form, performed a cognitive comparison, and inserted the aux himself. The sequence in Example 6 above suggests to us that Abukar focuses first on meaning—on the semantics of the exchange—and has difficulty shifting to a focus on form. In then trying to focus on form, he appears to have difficulty holding the forms in short-term memory for the process of cognitive comparison to take place. The correct aux form 'is' must be provided repeatedly in four sequential recasts, in line two, line four, line six, and line eight, and each repetition seems to become more explicit. His success in line nine, retaining the inserted aux 'is' form in short-term memory for cognitive comparison and inserting it correctly, does not seem to result in any transfer to long-term memory, for in Example 7 we see, only three turns later, that he produces exactly the same error: a failure to insert an 'is' auxiliary with the '–ing' participle in his question:

Example 7
01 **Abukar**   What this girl, reading?
02 **MB**   What IS this girl reading?
03 **Abukar**   What is, is this girl reading?

Nevertheless, here the uptake from the recasts occurs immediately. Abukar does produce a present participle, which he was able to correct on the first try in Example 6. The previous recasts may have had an influence on his immediate performance.

Such repeated provisions of recasts, with repeated failure of uptake, are common in Abukar's data. It seems that Abukar often *tries* to focus on form in processing the corrective input in this task; he just does not always perceive the correction. Here is another example, again with a bare verb and present progressive recast, from the middle of one of the story completion tasks:

Example 8
01 **Abukar**   Oh. What he try to write down?
02 **MB**   What IS he trying to write down?
03 **Abukar**   What he's, he's try to write down?
04 **MB**   What IS he trying
05 **Abukar**   What he is t, try to, write down?

Abukar's apparent failure to notice the inversion of subject and aux is particularly interesting, in light of the difficulty that illiterate participants in the cognitive psychology experiments had inverting words and syllables. Even at the very end of the story completion task, Abukar continues to omit aux in question formation, and requires repeated recasts of this error before he produces a correct recall.

Example 9
01 **Abukar**   What he thinking about, what he thinking?
02 **MB**   What is he thinking?
03 **Abukar**   What is he is thinking?
04 **MB**   What IS he thinking?
05 **Abukar**   What IS he thinking?

Even here, at the very end of the interaction, after numerous recasts of this same error, there is evidence that Abukar may have difficulty noticing first the required aux and then its inversion with the subject. Here at the end of the task, he certainly does not seem to have this new form in long-term memory. That is, he has apparently not acquired a categorical rule for this form. An alternative to this interpretation is that he does notice the change, but is unable to alter his output accordingly; that is, the problem may not be with noticing as much as it is with uptake. It is hard to know how to choose between these two interpretations in this case. A third possibility is that Abukar may have acquired a stable variable rule, with one variant ('be') being standard and the other ('be'-deletion) non-standard. (See Preston 2002).

Abukar's apparent preference for semantic cognitive processing in these examples, and his extended difficulty in noticing inserted linguistic forms in these recast questions are consistent with Castro-Caldas *et al.*'s (1998) view that a limited 'visuographic dimension' demonstrably restricts the ability to use phonological strategies in short-term memory. Abukar may not be able to represent linguistic segments with visual symbols in short-term memory in order to make the required cognitive comparisons. If so, there is no long-term change in Abukar's performance, and also, we assume, no change in the interlanguage grammar.

Abukar often seems to realize that his production is flawed, but is unable to repair according to the input offered by the recast. In the following exchange, for example, which occurs just a minute after the exchange in Example 6, he alters stress placement rather than performing a subject/copula inversion.

Example 10

01 **Abukar**   Why he is mad? Why [he], he is mad?
02 **MB**   [yeah]
03 **MB**   Why IS he mad?
04 **Abukar**   Why HE is mad? Why
05 **MB**   Why IS he mad?
06 **Abukar**   Why IS he mad? Why is, [is he]…

In line one, Abukar produces an uninverted subject/copula question; in line three he receives a recast with the subject and verb correctly inverted, with stress on the copula, which is now in second position. In line four, Abukar produces exactly the same uninverted word order he originally produced, but now he stresses the word in second position, which unfortunately is a pronoun. The form he seems to have noticed is *second position stress* rather than inversion in word order. His difficulties seem analogous to those that illiterate participants had inverting syllables and words in the cognitive psychology literature. In line five, the researcher provides exactly the same recast again, and this time, in line six, Abukar successfully inverts subject and verb, retaining second position stress. But it has again required several repetitions of the recast to achieve success in the process.

Vocabulary recasts

We have argued above that, although he tries to focus on form, Abukar has difficulty doing so; he seems to rely primarily on semantic processing strategies. This strategy relates to Castro-Caldas *et al.*'s (1998) findings that illiterate participants have better access to semantic and lexical strategies than to phonological strategies. We would predict that Abukar might have much less difficulty processing new lexis provided by recasts. And indeed, Abukar does process new lexical items provided in recasts more successfully—that is, he seems to be able to use new words without requiring the repeated recasts that are typical of his response to syntactic recasts. Mackey, Gass, and McDonough (2000) found that literate learners also noticed lexical items more readily than morphosyntactic items. We have already noted that semantic language processing seems to be unaffected by literacy; thus we would expect lexical processing and noticing to be high for both literate and illiterate learners. Abukar's ability to use this feedback more successfully may signal that he is engaging a different process. Filling a lexical gap in his initial utterance appears to be easier than inverting subject and auxiliary. At one point it becomes clear that Abukar does not know the word 'jar', which he needs in order to ask his question:

Example 11

01 **Abukar**   OK (pause) what is barrel, what is, what is the thing in it?
02   What is there? Is it, is there pennies in it?
03 **MB**   Yeah. Um, again. Are pennies in the jar?

04 **Abukar**   Is, are the penny in the jar?
05 **MB**   Yes. And, um,
06 **Abukar**   (whispers) jar
07 **MB**   you know she's a waitress, so she gets tips,
08 **Abukar**   OK
09 **MB**   at the diner,
10 **Abukar**   mhm
11 **MB**   and every day she puts her tips in a jar.
12 **Abukar**   Oh. (pause) (xxx xxx)
13 **MB**   Here's the jar.
14 **Abukar**   A jar?

In line one Abukar uses a communication strategy (see, for example, Tarone 1980), producing 'barrel' in approximation to the word he does not know, which is 'jar'. In line three, the researcher supplies the word 'jar', and in line four Abukar immediately recalls the recast 'jar' accurately. Interestingly, he then does more: he repeats the word 'jar' to himself in line six; in Vygotskian terms, he engages in private speech to rehearse the new word. Such rehearsal has been claimed to help move the new term from short-term memory to long-term memory (for example, Ohta 2001; Tarone 2000). It is interesting that we observed no evidence of this kind of rehearsal in his processing of syntactic recasts. Abukar hears the new word again as the researcher answers his question in line 11, hesitates in line 12, and receives an explicit recast again in line 13, with uptake in line 14. Twenty-two turns later, as shown below in Example 12, Abukar spontaneously uses the new word in a new question, suggesting that it is now in long-term memory; possibly he has 'acquired' it:

Example 12
Abukar   Oh. Oh. Is this jar have, this jar, is this jar full of money?

The process Abukar demonstrates in recalling this recast lexical item and spontaneously producing it later is much more successful than his processing of recast linguistic units.

To sum up: we have seen in Examples 6 through 10 that recasts targeting aux insertion and subject/aux and subject/copula inversion in interrogatives must be repeated several times before Abukar successfully recalls them. Although initially this failure often seems to derive from his focus on meaning, it continues when he is clearly and explicitly trying to focus on form. Though he appears to have great difficulty with recasts of morphosyntactic forms in his questions, he seems to have virtually no difficulty with using the interaction with the researcher to fill lexical gaps that occur in those same questions. His difficulties seem restricted to the processing of corrective input on segmental form rather than suprasegmentals like stress or semantic content.

Discussion of qualitative analysis

The recasts provided in this study as interactional interventions were intended to promote Abukar's noticing of his non-target question formations in English, in the context of his meaningful interactions. We would argue that the potential of the recasts in our study to promote noticing was bolstered by the fact that the recasts focused on a single form (questions in English) and resulted in a great deal of input on the same forms—an input flood (Sharwood Smith 1993). As in other recast studies, however, the first use of a recast was often interpreted by the learner, not as corrective feedback, but as a confirmation check regarding the semantic meaning of the initial utterance (for example, Lyster 1998a, 1998b).

Abukar's interaction manifests very little noticing of the difference between linguistic segments in his own production and those provided in the recast. Even when focused explicitly on the targeted linguistic form, Abukar shows little evidence in his production of the sort of cognitive comparison that recasts are supposed to produce in short-term memory. Abukar's ability to repeat linguistic segments, particularly verbal material devoid of semantic content as the aux is in these examples, is poor: the processing he is able to perform appears unequal to the task of noticing aux insertion and subject/aux inversion. We suggest that his ability to retain representations of both his own interrogative forms and those provided in recasts in short-term memory, and to compare these, is impaired by his low literacy level.

Though longitudinal data might have shown otherwise, there is little evidence of learning of syntactic forms as the interaction itself unfolds; Abukar makes the same error repeatedly over the course of the interaction. At the end of the interaction, in Example 9, he still seems to experience the same problems inserting the aux 'is' into his questions as he does at the beginning in Example 6. Even when Abukar's focus on the aux form results in successful uptake in one instance, aux placement does not seem to generalize to the next instance. We contrasted these syntactic failures with his success in noticing, rehearsing, and spontaneously producing a new lexical item, postulating that his use of semantic and lexical processing strategies was much more effective than his apparent use of the form-focused processing strategies required for cognitive comparison of semantically empty linguistic units.

We stress that Abukar had reached stage five of question formation, in that he had met the accepted criterion of being able to correctly use aux insertion and inversion in at least two non-formulaic instances in two distinct contexts. And yet in the examples given above, he showed a robust inability to produce aux insertion and inversion in response to repeated recasts, even when trying very hard to repair his utterance. The literature does not suggest that this kind of pattern—a pattern of failure to recall repeated recasts of appropriate stage level morphosyntactic forms—occurs *to the same extent* with more literate learners. Nor do we believe that Abukar was unique in exhibiting this pattern; indeed, local teachers describe this pattern to us as a distinguishing feature of learners with minimal print literacy.

Limitations

This in-depth qualitative analysis of the interlanguage of one learner does not involve many different types of data, elicited and unelicited, or provide data over time that would permit an analysis of acquisition, rather than an analysis of only the immediate performance. This limitation makes it very difficult to draw definitive conclusions about the effects of recasts on language development for the learner or the role literacy has to play in the acquisition of second language oral skills. But this analysis is coupled with the quantitative findings reported in Bigelow *et al.* (2006); as such it suggests a promising direction for future study.

Conclusion

Our quantitative and qualitative research results show that interactional feedback in the form of recasts had very little impact on the ability of low literate learners to produce targeted linguistic segments correctly. The lower the literacy level of the learner, the less likely it was that learners would recall, either correctly or with some modification, the provided recasts. This occurred despite the apparent appropriateness of input level, the multiple repetitions of the same corrective feedback, and persistent effort on the part of the learner to repair his utterances.

How can we reconcile these research results with the central theme of this book, which is to examine the link between interactional feedback and L2 learning? In our research, we examined the processing of oral corrective feedback by low literate learners, and we found little evidence of a link between the interactional linguistic feedback they received and either immediate recall or eventual L2 learning. We believe that this research could have major implications for future SLA research on noticing and literacy.

Our research suggests that the ability to consciously attend to and analyze oral L2 input in terms of segmental linguistic units may depend on prior alphabetic print literacy. Low literate adults and adolescents, essentially unstudied by SLA researchers thus far, use strategies for oral language processing that cause them significant difficulty doing tasks that require form-focused processing strategies involving the manipulation of linguistic segments. Our results suggest that L2 learners with low literacy may find it difficult to use recasts as a way to discover what is non-target about their interlanguage. Perhaps it is alphabetic literacy that affords the ability to attend to 'surface elements' in the input. Perhaps learners with less literacy require an intervention that directs their attention to the target form at a higher level of awareness than recasts. Alternatively, perhaps they require as-yet-unidentified methods of intervention that capitalize on the as-yet-unidentified 'cognitive advantages of the non-alphabetic mind'.

It is clear that the low literate participants in this study are acquiring massive amounts of linguistic oral skill regardless of their relative inability to benefit from recasts. One possibility is that illiterate and low literate L2 learners achieve proficiency in rather different areas of the L2, based upon their use of 'non-alphabetic' oral language processing strategies. They may acquire less academic language or complex syntax, but show more sophistication in social registers. The low literate learners in our study have clearly acquired some L2 forms and abilities and not others, using the language processing strategies they have. For example, they have clearly acquired a functioning set of English linguistic forms and use these systematically. That interlanguage system is solid: indeed, it seems resistant to corrective feedback in certain areas. In addition, the low literate learners in our study use their interlanguage effectively; they are highly skilled in the area of pragmatic and sociolinguistic competence. We have already pointed out the impressive fluency and pragmatic L2 skills of this population. But what about their linguistic competence? Does literacy level affect metalinguistic awareness of L2 in contexts other than the noticing of recasts? If so, are illiterate and low literate learners prevented by their lack of alphabetic literacy from using metalinguistic strategies to acquire certain of the more complex linguistic forms of the L2?

Research on first language acquisition suggests that native language children must first have alphabetic literacy before they are able to acquire a defined set of more complex syntactic structures which characterize the written language (Ravid and Tolchinsky 2002). In this view, while a set of simple syntactic structures is acquirable without alphabetic print literacy, there is a set of more complex syntactic structures (such as those identified by Biber (1988) and Biber *et al.* (2002) as characterizing the use of language for literacy) that may not be acquired until after several years of literate experience. One possibility in SLA is that some L2 forms may be easily acquirable without alphabetic literacy, but others, possibly more complex syntactic structures such as relative clauses, may require metalinguistic cognitive comparison using the tool of visuographic representation. Such a relationship might mean that while illiterate or low literate L2 learners could become quite fluent in the use of a set of simple syntactic structures, and learn to use semantic and lexical strategies in a sophisticated way to achieve pragmatic and sociolinguistic goals, they might still not acquire some of the more complex syntactic structures that are most frequent in written language. Some of the syntactic structures useful for linguistic literacy in the L2 might, in the end, require prior alphabetic print literacy. Thus, it is important to add the variable of literacy level to the range of already established learner-internal factors (for example, proficiency, aptitude, readiness) that are accounted for by SLA theories.

It is urgent that we forge an SLA research agenda that can address these and related possibilities. We must study the oral SLA of low literate and illiterate learners. Such an agenda is important for L2 studies on attention and awareness, for SLA theory construction, and for our ability to improve L2 pedagogy for the large numbers of adolescent and adult L2 learners, both in the US and abroad, who lack alphabetic print literacy skills.

5

Modified output of Japanese EFL learners: variable effects of interlocutor versus feedback types

MASATOSHI SATO and ROY LYSTER

Introduction

As discussed in the Introduction to this volume, negotiated interaction plays a key role in driving second language (L2) development forward. According to Long's (1996) Interaction Hypothesis, this is because both positive evidence and negative evidence are made available 'by the NS [native speaker] or more competent interlocutor' (1996: 451) to L2 learners during interaction. Interaction also provides learners with opportunities to control the input to some extent, as they ask their interlocutors to modify their speech in ways that make the input more accessible and more likely to be integrated into the learners' developing interlanguage system (Pica 1994a; Long 1996; Gass 1997). In addition, interaction enables learners to test their hypotheses as it provides them with crucial information about their communicative success (Long 1977) along with important opportunities for modifying or repro-cessing non-target output (Swain 1985, 1995; Pica, Holliday, Lewis, and Morgenthaler 1989; Shehadeh 2003).

Research on interaction takes on many forms, allowing researchers to investigate the nature and effects of interaction between learners and NSs of the target language in laboratory settings, or between learners and teachers in classroom settings, or between learners and other learners in either labora-tory or classroom settings. A considerable amount of research supporting the role of interaction has investigated learner–NS dyads (Brock, Crookes, Day, and Long 1986; Gass and Varonis 1994; Oliver 1995; Lin and Hedgcock 1996; Van den Branden 1997; Mackey and Philp 1998; Braidi 2002; Philp 2003), examining various conversational moves used to solve problems in message comprehensibility, such as clarification requests, confirmation checks (including recasts and repetition), and comprehension checks. Findings have generally confirmed that these conversational moves provide learners and their interlocutors with useful strategies for facilitating comprehension (Pica, Young, and Doughty 1987). There is also evidence that conversational moves such as clarification requests (Nobuyoshi and Ellis 1993; McDonough 2005) and recasts (Mackey and Philp 1998) benefit L2 development. (See table on page 4 in the Introduction to this volume.)

In addition, a growing number of studies of learner–learner dyads have been conducted in L2 classrooms, some of which have shown that when L2 learners work collaboratively to complete tasks with a linguistic focus they are able to use 'meta-talk' in which 'learners use language to reflect on language use' (Swain 1998: 68) and to negotiate areas of language difficulty. (See also Donato 1994; Kowal and Swain 1994, 1997; Swain and Lapkin 1998, 2001, 2002.) Other research has shown that even during communication tasks, learners' negotiation of meaning may often include learner-generated attention to form (Williams 1999; McDonough and Mackey 2000; Foster and Ohta 2005). Storch (2002) found that some types of dyads are more successful than others (see also Foster 1998; Iwashita 2001), concluding that 'learners, when working in pairs, can scaffold each other's performance, yet such scaffolding is more likely to occur when pairs interact in a certain pattern: either collaborative or expert/novice' (2002: 147). Many studies of dyadic interaction in classroom settings claim an important role for teachers to intervene in timely ways that draw attention to wrong hypotheses and non-target output (Swain 1998; Williams 1999; Samuda 2001). Teacher–student interaction has itself been the focus of a number of interaction studies, documenting the ways in which teachers provide feedback to students and how students respond (Lyster and Ranta 1997; Mori 2000; Ellis, Basturkmen, and Loewen 2002; Havranek 2002; Lyster and Mori 2006).

Of particular relevance for the present study is research designed to compare learner–learner dyads with learner–NS dyads during communication tasks (Varonis and Gass 1985a; Pica, Lincoln-Porter, Paninos, and Linnell 1996; Shehadeh 1999, 2001, 2003; Futaba 2001; Mackey, Oliver, and Leeman 2003). Although one might predict more learning opportunities to occur during learner–NS interaction, results of some of these studies revealed instead that, while learners are exposed to more grammatical input during learner–NS interaction, interactional moves hypothesized to facilitate L2 development may occur more frequently during learner–learner interaction. Because L2 learners negotiated more when interacting with other learners than with a NS in their study, Varonis and Gass (1985a) concluded that communication breakdowns in learner–learner dyads must be negotiated before the exchange of information can proceed, whereas the inequality in the status of the participants in learner–NS dyads discourages negotiation and results in a greater tendency for conversation to proceed without negotiation (see also Gass and Varonis 1985a, 1989). More recently, investigating negotiation triggered by inaccuracy rather than incomprehensibility, Mackey *et al.* (2003) compared learner–learner and learner–NS dyads, and also focused on differences between child and adult dyads. Interestingly, in the case of adult interaction, they found that NSs provided significantly more feedback than learners, but that the type of feedback provided by learners created more opportunities for modified output than feedback provided by NSs, although there were no significant differences in the amount of modified output actually produced by learners in learner–learner versus learner–NS dyads.

While the research on interaction has been predominantly conducted in L2 settings, the present study investigates the interactional patterns of Japanese learners of English as a foreign language (EFL). In Japan, English is a compulsory subject throughout junior high and high school, and the many students who pursue post-secondary education in Japan typically continue taking English classes. The linguistic environment of EFL learners in Japan, however, lacks sufficient exposure to the target language (Robinson, Sawyer, and Ross 2001), and the socio-educational environment does not encourage students to speak up in classrooms, because of the hierarchical relationship between students and teachers in which teachers are considered as authorities and classrooms are teacher-centred (Kess 1996; Lee 1999). Thus, despite the length of time of English education in Japan, students generally end up as non-fluent speakers, having been exposed for the most part to grammar-translation methods of instruction, but are often considered good readers and writers. Drawing on Berns' (1990) discussion of second versus foreign language learning, Block (2003) summarizes the EFL context in Japan as follows:

> learning the English language is seen … as a way of communicating with the 'West' (symbolized most often by the US), and … therefore is tied up with more abstract questions about national identity and Japan's place in the world. In addition, until recently, there has been little emphasis in language classrooms on speaking skills and this has led to millions of EFL students with a high degree of linguistic competence but lacking communication skills in English
> (Block 2003: 49).

It is interesting in such a context to explore the feasibility of implementing communication tasks and the extent to which they provide learners with opportunities to practice their oral skills and to proceduralize their relatively well-established declarative knowledge developed primarily through grammar-translation methods. (See, for example, DeKeyser 1998; Skehan 1998.)

The present study contributes to research on interaction by comparing interactional patterns of learner–learner and learner–NS dyads in a distinctively foreign language setting. We focus in particular on learners' production of modified output during task completion and whether this differs depending on their interlocutor. The few studies to date that have explored different interactional moves in learner–learner versus learner–NS dyads analyzed both learners and NSs alike as providers of input, feedback, and modified output. In the present study, we analyze learners' interactional moves as an independent variable by including twice as many learner–NS dyads as learner–learner dyads to permit comparisons of interactional moves used by learners in two different types of dyad. This particular research design lets us explore how differently learners interact depending on whether their interlocutor is another learner or a NS. In addition, through use of retrospective stimulated recall sessions, we investigate how learners' perceptions of their interlocutor influence their use of specific interactional moves. Our three research questions (RQs) are:

1   What differences, if any, appear in the types of feedback to which learners are exposed during learner–learner and learner–NS interaction?
2   In response to feedback, do learners in learner–learner dyads modify their output more or less frequently than learners in learner–NS dyads?
3   Do learners' perceptions affect the way they interact? If so, how?

Method

Participants

Participants were eight Japanese learners (three males and five females) of EFL and four NSs (four males). The learner participants were randomly selected from among 151 18–19-year-old students attending required freshman EFL classes at a university in Japan. A questionnaire was distributed to all 151 students by which the samples for the study were chosen. The questionnaire was designed to ensure a relatively homogenous sample of typical Japanese EFL learners who had neither spent a significant amount of time nor studied in an English-speaking country. These learners had demonstrated solid grammatical knowledge, having passed two entrance examinations for admission to their university. The examinations assess reading, writing, and listening skills, but not speaking ability. We looked at such learners in this context because we were particularly interested in how they use their grammatical knowledge in oral production in a foreign language context.

Of the four NSs who participated in the present study, all were university students whose ages ranged from 21–23-years-old; three were from Australia and one was from Canada. Their length of stay in Japan ranged from two to four years; they had thus been in Japan long enough to experience general speaking abilities of Japanese English learners. None of the NSs had any formal training in or experience of teaching English. By virtue of not being trained teachers, NSs in the present study were similar in background to the Assistant Language Teachers normally involved in the Japanese Exchange and Teaching (JET) program sponsored by the Ministry of Education, Culture, Sports, Science, and Technology (MEXT). Assistant Language Teachers have usually just graduated from undergraduate colleges, because, as stated in the eligibility criteria, the MEXT recruits younger people holding a bachelor's degree, but without necessarily any teaching experience. Thus, although the present study was not conducted in a classroom setting, the NS participants were similar in background to the Assistant Language Teachers that Japanese students are likely to interact with in their EFL classrooms.

Task

The two-way information exchange tasks employed in the present study were jigsaw tasks in which both participants in a dyad hold the same amount of information so that they have to provide their interlocutor with accurate descriptions of the pictures to complete the task. For each task in the present study, participants each held three pictures and described them to their interlocutor. Therefore, there were six pictures in total with clues indicating the timeline of an event. Gathering the information that they obtained from each other, they worked together to put the six pictures in chronological order. Thus, it was expected that there would be a two-way flow of request and suppliance of the information, without only one interlocutor talking and dominating the conversation. (See Pica, Kanagy, and Falodun 1993.) During the tasks, participants each sat on a chair facing each other at a table without any partition. They were asked to complete the task in English without looking at each other's pictures.

Procedures

To compare learners' interactional moves in learner–learner dyads with those in learner–NS dyads, the participants were paired in four learner–learner dyads and eight learner–NS dyads. Each of the four learners who interacted with each other had a different NS interlocutor, thus meeting conditions for statistical analyses of matched pairs. To facilitate data collection, learners were randomly assigned to one of two groups. Group 1 included four learners who interacted in learner–learner dyads at Time 1 and then in learner–NS dyads at Time 2. Group 2 included four learners who interacted in learner–NS dyads at Time 1 and then in learner–learner dyads at Time 2. (See Table 5.1.) Two similar two-way information gap tasks were used so that each participant completed different tasks at Times 1 and 2. This design was intended to decrease both interlocutor and task familiarity effects. The conversations, which varied from 20–30 minutes, were recorded with digital audio recorders.

	Time 1 Task 1	→	Time 2 Task 2	
Group 1	Learner 1 ↔ Learner 2		Learner 1 ↔ NS1	Learner 3 ↔ NS3
	Learner 3 ↔ Learner 4		Learner 2 ↔ NS2	Learner 4 ↔ NS4
Group 2	Learner 5 ↔ NS1 Learner 7 ↔ NS3		Learner 5 ↔ Learner 6	
	Learner 6 ↔ NS2 Learner 8 ↔ NS4		Learner 7 ↔ Learner 8	

Table 5.1 Composition of learner–learner and learner–NS dyads at Times 1 and 2

During the two days following task completion, this chapter's first author transcribed the oral interaction data, and then conducted a retrospective stimulated recall session with each participant, during which participants were asked what linguistic features they noticed, why they acted in certain ways, and what their perceptions were while engaging in the task. Adapting procedures used by Mackey, Gass, and McDonough (2000), the researcher had participants listen to the audio recordings of their oral interaction as he asked questions about specific language exchanges and about their perceptions. Participants were also encouraged to ask the researcher to stop the recording at any time and comment on whatever they noticed in the conversation.

The stimulated recall procedure used in the present study was based on Ericsson and Simon's (1984) criteria and Gass and Mackey's (2000) suggestions for using retrospective data analysis. (See also Mackey 2002.) Stimulated recall was used for two reasons. First, it was used to understand learners' perceptions of having either a learner or a NS as their interlocutor, and thus why they interacted as they did. Second, this method was employed to make the coding procedure of the transcriptions more reliable. The participants were asked about ambiguous utterances that were difficult to interpret solely from the recordings. The stimulated recall sessions were conducted in Japanese and lasted approximately one hour for each participant; excerpts discussed later in this chapter appear in English translation.

Coding

To code the interaction data, LREs were identified in which participants either negotiated for meaning or exchanged conversation that started with grammatically inaccurate utterances. A language-related episode (LRE) in the present study shares features with Williams' (1999: 595) definition: 'discourse in which the learners talk or ask about language, or question, implicitly or explicitly, their own language use or that of others'. (See also Swain and Lapkin 1998.) Swain and Lapkin (2001: 104) explain that LREs 'entail discussion of meaning or form, but may emphasize one of these more than the other'. In the present study, we identified LREs in which an interlocutor gives feedback to the speaker reacting to message comprehensibility and/or grammatical accuracy unintentionally or intentionally, and the speaker responds to the feedback implicitly or explicitly. Adapting coding schemes used by Varonis and Gass (1985b; see also Shehadeh 1999, 2001, 2003) and by Pica *et al.* (1996), we coded LREs as a sequence of three interactional moves: triggers, feedback, and responses. Table 5.2 identifies these three coding categories and their component subcategories used to analyze LREs in the present study.

Triggers

- Trigger stemming from incomprehensibility
- Trigger stemming from inaccuracy

Feedback

- Elicitation
  - Clarification request
  - Confirmation request without modification of trigger
  - Non-verbal signal
- Reformulation
  - Recast
  - Confirmation request with modification of trigger

Responses

- Modified output
  - Modification of trigger with incorporation of feedback
  - Modification of trigger without incorporation of feedback
- Non-modified output
  - Repetition of trigger
  - Acknowledgement
  - Topic continuation
  - Inability to respond
  - Ignore feedback

Table 5.2   Coding categories for interactional moves in language-related episodes

Triggers

LREs were initiated by one of two types of trigger, stemming from either incomprehensibility or inaccuracy. Triggers stemming from incomprehensibility involved communication breakdowns resulting from a problem with message comprehensibility. Triggers stemming from inaccuracy contained errors in form that did not impede comprehensibility but led nonetheless to a language-related episode. Cases where an utterance contained one or more grammatical errors and the message was not understood by the interlocutor were still coded as communication breakdowns. Finally, cases where communication breakdowns or grammatically inaccurate utterances did not lead to an LRE were classified as abandonment.

Feedback

Feedback was identified as interactional moves that immediately followed either type of trigger and that were of one of two types: elicitation or reformulation. Examples of feedback and other moves provided henceforth are from data collected for the present study along with pseudonyms for all learner participants.

Elicitation feedback

Elicitation feedback generally requests clarification or confirmation without providing correct reformulations of the erroneous utterance contained in the trigger.

Clarification requests are utterances with rising intonation 'designed to elicit clarification of the interlocutor's preceding utterance(s)' (Long 1983: 137). In Excerpt 1, Mariko intends to say 'man' but utters an incomprehensible utterance with a phonological error. To solve this communication breakdown, the NS gives feedback in the form of a clarification request.

> *Excerpt 1*
> **Mariko**   In B … maybe they finished cleaning. And in the garage there
>   are a [mʌn].
> **NS**   Sorry?

Confirmation request without modification of trigger is a move used to confirm an interlocutor's incomprehensible and/or inaccurate utterance without modifying it. This move may include 'literal repetitions of the trigger, or parts of it' (Van den Branden 1997: 606) and also includes elaboration that does not directly modify the error. In Excerpt 2, Shigeo tries to say that the man in the picture is in the midst of cleaning, but instead chooses to use 'on the way', an expression that the NS repeats with rising intonation.

> *Excerpt 2*
> **Shigeo**   A is … on the way he clean the his garage.
> **NS**   On the way?

Non-verbal signals include frowning and interjections such as 'Umm …' and 'Ah …' (Van den Branden 1997), and are used by participants to show difficulty understanding their interlocutor. Because the interactions were not video-taped, non-verbal signals were difficult to identify and so were coded as such only when followed by a response. In Excerpt 3, Taka uses silence as a non-verbal signal that was considered as elicitation feedback because it was in turn followed by Mayumi's modified output.

> *Excerpt 3*
> **Mayumi**   I think I have one picture that is … that picture is … he is
>   annoyed?
> **Taka**   (silence)

Reformulation feedback

Reformulation feedback provides correct target forms either through recasts or confirmation requests that modify the trigger.

Recasts reformulate erroneous utterances, minus the error (Lyster and Ranta 1997). Confirmation requests with rising intonation that reformulate erroneous utterances were coded as recasts in the present study. In Excerpt 4, Taka makes a grammatical error that is comprehensible and is followed by a recast.

Excerpt 4
Taka Three children, B picture, in the B picture, they didn't got on bus.
NS Yeah, yeah. Three children didn't get on the bus.

Confirmation requests with modification of trigger modify incomprehensible and/or inaccurate utterances. This move may include provision of alternatives, but was distinguished from a recast in that it does not directly provide more comprehensible or accurate forms, similar to 'noncorrective recasts' in Farrar's (1992) study of mother-child interaction. In Excerpt 5, Mayumi makes a morphosyntactic error which generated negotiation. To confirm Mayumi's message, the NS modifies Mayumi's utterance and provides a clue to repair the grammatical error indirectly.

Excerpt 5
Mayumi B picture, three children getting the bus.
NS Like they are walking on the bus now?

Responses
Responses are interactional moves following feedback that were first classified as either (a) modified output or (b) non-modified output, and then classified as one of seven subcategories.

Modified output
Modified output refers to learners' repair moves that contain more comprehensible and/or accurate versions of their initial erroneous utterances.
    Modification of trigger with incorporation of feedback This is a response that directly includes either a full or partial repetition of the feedback, modifying the erroneous utterance contained in the trigger. In Excerpt 6, although the NS gives a clarification request first, he provides the correct version of the incomprehensible utterance in the same turn. Responding to this reformulation feedback, Mariko successfully modifies her phonological error by incorporating the feedback.

Excerpt 6
Mariko And she is carrying the ... [tricaikəl].
NS The what? Sorry? Tricycle?
Mariko Tricycle!

Modification of trigger without incorporation of feedback This is a response that does not incorporate the feedback, yet modifies the initial incomprehensible and/or inaccurate utterance in the trigger. This may be an expansion or an explanation of the trigger. In Excerpt 7, Mayumi tries to explain that the bus in the picture gets a flat tire. Because the Japanese rendering of 'flat tire' is [pʌnkú] in katakana (a syllabic form of writing in Japanese used to transliterate non-Japanese words), she guesses that the English word would be similar and tests her hypothesis. In response, the NS provides the correct form, but Mayumi does not incorporate the feedback; instead she tries another way of describing the picture to solve the problem.

Excerpt 7
Mayumi   Umm ..., I think the [pʌnk], the tire is [pʌnk].
NS   Punctured?
Mayumi   Break break.

Non-modified output

Repetition of trigger This is a response that repeats the trigger and is still incomprehensible and/or inaccurate. In Excerpt 8, the NS gives a clarification request because he does not understand Mariko. In response, Mariko simply repeats the word that generated negotiation.

Excerpt 8
Mariko   She is hanging the ... snow shovel. Snow shovel.
NS   Sorry?
Mariko   Snow shovel.

Acknowledgement is a response that confirms or negates the feedback when the interactant has an opportunity to modify the error. In Excerpt 9, Shigeo makes a morphosyntactic error. Daisuke provides the correct version of the error in the form of a recast. Although Shigeo has an opportunity to modify his initial erroneous utterance here, he chooses to acknowledge what his interlocutor said.

Excerpt 9
Shigeo   B, three children, I said first, was pushed out another ... by
                another three children. Another children getting on the bus, at
                last.
Daisuke   I think... I imagine ... I think in the C picture, they are waiting
                six children. And in the B picture, three children interrupted.
                So *the other three children* can't ride.
Shigeo   Yes yes.

Topic continuation In this move, an interactant either chooses to continue or switch the topic or does not have an opportunity to react to the feedback. In Excerpt 10, although the NS recasts Shigeo's morphological error, there is no opportunity for Shigeo to modify his erroneous utterance. It is pragmatically more appropriate to answer his interlocutor's question than to modify his error by incorporating the recast.

Excerpt 10
Shigeo   And he *clean* his garage.
NS   *Cleans* his garage. OK. In B, is the garage clean or messy?
Shigeo   Clean.

Inability to respond This is a response that shows difficulty to react to the feedback. In Excerpt 11, the NS does not understand Taka's utterance and requests clarification of the message by using a recast. However, Taka does not understand the recast so he tries to stop the conversation to create time to reformulate his utterance.

Excerpt 11
Taka   A picture, A picture is ah ... [10 second pause] bus drive, bus ... going bus.
NS   Bus is driving?
Taka   Ah ... wait.

Ignore feedback This is a response that does not react to the request in the feedback. In Excerpt 12, Atsuko notices that she heard an unfamiliar word and tries to negotiate for mutual understanding. However, the NS does not try to explain the word 'tow truck' and instead switches the conversation to a new topic.

Excerpt 12
NS   The car is stopped on the side of the road, and somebody is fixing the car. And ... there is a tow truck coming.
Atsuko   Tow truck? Tow?
NS   Alright. OK. Forget it.

Inter-rater reliability

The first author coded all the data according to the preceding categories, then trained another researcher, who was also a native speaker of Japanese with native-like proficiency in English, to code data according to these same categories. Following training sessions, the second rater independently coded a randomly selected subsample of 15 per cent of the transcriptions to ensure the reliability of the coding procedure. This test of inter-rater reliability yielded a simple percentage agreement level of 93 per cent.

Results

Because four learner–learner dyads and eight learner–NS dyads participated in the present study, the complete data set comprises interactional moves of eight learners interacting with another learner and the same eight learners interacting with a NS. The audio-taped conversations of the eight learner–NS dyads and four learner–learner dyads yielded six hours of interaction data that were transcribed then coded according to the categories identified in the previous section. Specifically, learner utterances that initiated LREs as a result of either incomprehensibility or inaccuracy were coded as triggers. As displayed in Table 5.3, the database consists of a total of 205 language-related episodes, which were generated for the most part by incomprehensibility rather than inaccuracy and which occurred with similar frequency in both types of dyad. Thus, learners engaged in a proportionally similar number of LREs, triggered primarily by incomprehensibility, whether they interacted with NSs or with each other.

Trigger	Learner–NS dyads	Learner–learner dyads	Total
Incomprehensibility	80	65	145
Inaccuracy	43	17	60
Total	**123**	**82**	**205**

Table 5.3 Number of language-related episodes

Statistical comparisons, using *t*-tests for matched samples with an alpha level of .05, were conducted in order to answer RQs 1 and 2 concerning differences in feedback and responses provided in learner–learner versus learner–NS dyads. For the analysis of interactional moves within one type of dyad, numbers of occurrences were compared. To investigate differences between the two types of dyads, proportions of an interactional move in each type of dyad were compared.

The stimulated recall sessions were also audio-taped, yielding eight hours of interaction between the researcher and each of the eight learner partici- pants. These data too were transcribed and then used primarily to interpret the quantitative results and to answer RQ3 about how learners' perceptions of their interlocutor affected interactional patterns. These qualitative results are reported in the discussion section.

Analysis of feedback

To answer RQ1, comparisons were made of feedback types provided by NSs and by learners, as presented in Table 5.4 and displayed graphically in Figure 5.1. For this analysis, because the samples were not matched pairs, a *t*-test for equal variance was employed to reveal quantitative differences in feedback types provided to learners either by a NS or another learner. Of the NSs' feedback moves, 41 per cent were elicitation, whereas 66 per cent of the learn- ers' feedback moves were elicitation. The proportion of elicitation feedback relative to total amount of feedback was compared and this difference was statistically significant. Thus, learners provided each other with a signifi- cantly higher proportion of elicitation feedback than NSs did. This result, at the same time, indicates that NSs provided learners with significantly more reformulation feedback than did other learners.

The difference between the two types of feedback was also analyzed by comparing occurrences of elicitation and reformulation. NSs gave feedback in the form of elicitation 51 times and in the form of reformulation 72 times, a difference that was not significant. In contrast, there was a significant dif- ference between elicitation and reformulation in learners' feedback. Of 82 feedback moves provided by learners, 54 were elicitation moves and 28 were reformulation moves. Thus, learners provided feedback in the form of elicita- tion significantly more frequently than reformulation.

	NSs		Learners	
	n	Percentage	n	Percentage
Elicitation	51	41$_a$	54$_c$	66$_a$
Reformulation	72	59$_b$	28$_c$	34$_b$
Total (feedback)	123	100	82	100

Pairs having the same subscript differ significantly at $p < .05$

Table 5.4 Learners versus native speakers as feedback providers

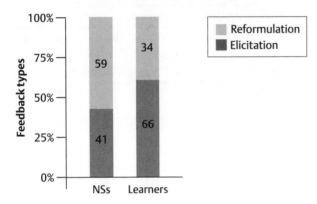

Figure 5.1 Feedback types provided by NSs and learners

Analysis of responses

To answer RQ2, the proportions of modified output following each type of feedback were compared to reveal what type of feedback was more likely to lead to modified output. (See Table 5.5.) The results revealed that when the proportion of modified output generated by elicitation moves was compared with the modified output generated by reformulation, there were no significant differences. In learner–NS dyads, 25 per cent of the NSs' elicitation moves and 29 per cent of the NSs' reformulation moves led to learners' modified output. In learner–learner dyads, 51 per cent of the elicitation moves and 48 per cent of the reformulation moves led to modified output. These results suggest that type of feedback does not affect the amount of modified output produced by learners in either learner–learner or learner–NS dyads.

	Elicitation		Reformulation	
	n	Percentage	n	Percentage
Learner–NS dyads	13	25	21	29
Learner–learner dyads	28	51	13	48

Table 5.5 Modified output following elicitation versus reformulation

Table 5.6 shows the comparison between the amount of modified output and non-modified output and the comparison of these responses in learner–NS dyads versus learner–learner dyads. The amount of modified output and non-modified output and their proportions are divided following the two types of feedback. This analysis shows how the interlocutor variable (learner or NS) affects the way learners modify their initial erroneous utterances. These comparisons are displayed graphically in Figure 5.2.

	Learner–NS dyads				Learner–learner dyads			
	Elicitation		Reformulation		Elicitation		Reformulation	
	n	Percentage	n	Percentage	n	Percentage	n	Percentage
MO	13_a	25_c	21_b	29_d	28	51_c	13	48_d
Non-MO	38_a	75	51_b	71	27	49	14	52
Total (Responses)	51	100	72	100	55	100	27	100

MO = Modified output; Non-MO = Non-modified output
Pairs having the same subscript differ significantly at $p < .05$

Table 5.6 Relationships between response types and feedback types across dyad types

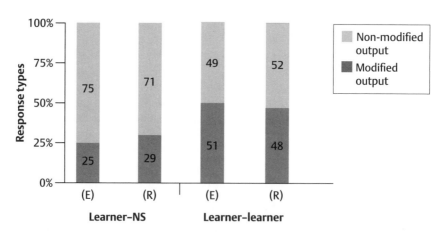

Figure 5.2 Response types (modified and non-modified output) after elicitation (E) and reformulation (R) across dyad types

The results revealed that, following feedback from NSs, a significantly higher proportion of learner responses contained non-modified output than modified output, both after elicitation and after reformulation. Specifically, of the 51 triggers that led to elicitation feedback from NSs, learners modified 13 and 38 were non-modified output. Of the 72 responses following reformulation, 21 contained modified output and 51 were non-modified output. Thus, learners tended not to modify their output in response to either type of feedback in learner–NS dyads. In contrast, these comparisons did not reach significance in learner–learner dyads. When learners interacted with other learners, following elicitation feedback, 28 of their responses were modified output and 27 were non-modified output; following reformulation feedback, 13 of their responses were modified output and 14 were non-modified output. Therefore, in learner–learner dyads, there were no significant differences in the amount of modified versus non-modified output following either type of feedback. A comparison of the proportions of modified output generated by each type of feedback in learner–NS dyads and in learner–learner dyads confirmed that learners modified their output significantly more when they interacted with other learners than when they interacted with NSs following both elicitation (25 per cent in learner–NS dyads versus 51 per cent in learner–learner dyads) and reformulation (29 per cent in learner–NS dyads versus 48 per cent in learner–learner dyads).

A further comparison combining both types of feedback confirmed that the amount of modified output was significantly less than non-modified output in learner–NS dyads but similar in learner–learner dyads (see Table 5.7). Specifically, of the 123 feedback moves in learner–NS dyads 34 (28 per cent) led to modified output and 89 (72 per cent) led to non-modified output. In learner–learner dyads, however, no significant difference was found when instances of modified output and non-modified output were compared. In addition, analysis of the proportion of modified output relative to total amount of responses in the two types of dyads confirmed that the proportion of modified output was significantly higher in learner–learner dyads (50 per cent) than in learner–NS dyads (28 per cent).

	Learner–NS dyads		Learner–learner dyads	
	n	Percentage	n	Percentage
MO	34_a	28_b	41	50_b
Non-MO	89_a	72	41	50
Total (Responses)	123	100	82	100

MO = Modified output; Non-MO = Non-modified output
Pairs having the same subscript differ significantly at $p < .05$

Table 5.7 Modified output and non-modified output across dyad types

Discussion

RQ1 asked about differences in the types of feedback that learners are exposed to in learner–learner versus learner–NS dyads. Within-dyad comparisons showed that learners provided one another with significantly more elicitation feedback than reformulation. Between-dyad comparisons showed that learners provided one another with significantly more elicitation feedback than did NSs, who in turn provided learners with significantly more reformulation feedback.

RQ2 asked about differences in the amount of modified output produced by learners in learner–learner versus learner–NS dyads. Results revealed that learners modified their output significantly more in learner–learner dyads than in learner–NS dyads, irrespective of feedback type (i.e. both elicitation and reformulation led to similar amounts of modified output).

RQ3 asked how learners' perceptions of their interlocutor affect interactional patterns. To answer this question and to explain the quantitative results used to answer RQs 1 and 2, we refer to the qualitative data from stimulated recall sessions.

Why did learners tend to provide more elicitation than reformulation feedback, whereas the opposite pattern was adopted by NSs? That feedback provided by NSs contained more reformulations than elicitations reflects the observation that NSs could actually guess what their interlocutors wanted to say, similar to the guessing ability of the teachers described by Musumeci (1996) and Pica (2002). In learner–learner dyads, learners were also able at times to guess one another's meaning, mainly because of their shared L1. That is, there were cases where learners succeeded in conveying a message by employing katakana, which triggered LREs in learner–NS dyads but not in learner–learner dyads. However, of greater influence on feedback type than their shared L1 was their comfort level with one another, which led to more elicitations than reformulations. Learners reported that they felt much more comfortable in learner–learner dyads asking questions about incomprehensible utterances, because they felt less pressure and thus perceived a non-threatening environment for negotiation. (See also Gass and Varonis 1989.) For instance, Daisuke reported that he felt under pressure when interacting with his NS interlocutor:

Excerpt 13
I knew that my partner was a perfect speaker so I felt pressure to speak English to him. Sometimes I could not say what I wanted to say. I was totally relying on him. Well, I think I could lead the conversation when I was doing the task with Shigeo.

Other learners reported similar perceptions of NSs as 'perfect' speakers, explaining that they did not have to or did not want to ask questions when they interacted with NSs, because the NS interlocutors were good at understanding their 'poor' English. In fact, it was observed that apparent communication breakdowns were frequently abandoned and thus did not lead to language-related episodes. Some learners reported feeling unable to ask questions of their NS interlocutor, even when they were inclined to clarify a message. For example, Aya reported having negative feelings of regret and frustration while she was engaging in the task with her NS interlocutor:

Excerpt 14
When I was talking with my native-speaker partner, I was always thinking that I would be sorry if I wouldn't be able to understand him. I was so concentrating on listening to what he was saying so that when I was going to say something it was too late. Topics have already been switched to another topic all the time.

Although these perceptions did not result in learners giving quantitatively more interactional feedback in learner–learner dyads than in learner–NS dyads (c.f., Varonis and Gass 1985b; Porter 1986; Pica *et al.* 1996; Futaba 2001), they provide helpful insights into why and how different types of feedback and responses were used in learner–learner and learner–NS dyads.

Why did learners produce significantly more modified output after feedback provided by other learners than after feedback provided by NSs? All learner participants in the present study reported that they had more time to plan what they were going to say when they were interacting with another learner, and this arguably provided ideal conditions for the production of modified output (Mehnert 1998). Atsuko, for example, reported that, whereas she had time to think when she was doing the task with her learner interlocutor, she was struggling with communicating with her NS interlocutor:

Excerpt 15
I really wanted to use body language to explain to him what I wanted to say when I was doing the task with my native-speaker partner. When I was communicating with Risa, however, I thought like I had time to think so why don't I take time before I say something.

Learners also reported that the NSs' ability to guess their message obviated the need for them to modify their output. Mariko described this ability as follows:

Excerpt 16
I don't know why but I feel that native speakers are good at guessing what we want to say in English. Let's say I am speaking with a foreigner who is learning Japanese. I think I could understand him better than anyone whose first language is not Japanese.

In addition, in the case of elicitation feedback learners reported that, even when they were aware that they were asked a question, they did not perceive it as a request for them to modify their initial utterance. They reported that it seemed unnecessary to modify their initial utterances despite the elicitation feedback, because the conversation kept on going smoothly anyway. Because elicitation feedback frequently led to reformulation through multiple exchanges, it was both feasible and appropriate for learners to simply acknowledge the feedback or continue the conversation by the time they received the reformulation feedback. In addition, all the participants reported that they felt that they could get more information in learner–NS dyads. Thus, when learners interacted with NSs, they frequently achieved implicit mutual agreement that let them move on without any modification moves from the learner side.

The finding that there was minimal modified output following reformulation feedback provided by NSs supports previous research showing that reformulation feedback does not lead to modified output very effectively in dyadic interaction (Pica *et al.* 1989) nor in some classroom settings (Lyster and Ranta 1997; Panova and Lyster 2002; Tsang 2004), but does in others (Ellis, Basturkmen, and Loewen 2001a; see comparative studies by Sheen 2004 and Lyster and Mori 2006). In the case of elicitation feedback, a number of studies have reported that feedback such as clarification requests is more likely than reformulation to lead to modification of learner utterances, both in dyadic interaction (Pica *et al.* 1989) and in classroom interaction (Lyster and Ranta 1997). In the present study, however, the quantitative analyses revealed two important findings: first, elicitation feedback did not lead to more modified output than did reformulation in either type of dyad; second, learners modified their output significantly more in learner–learner dyads responding to both types of feedback. Therefore, the probability of learners' modification of their initial incomprehensible and/or inaccurate utterances was determined more by whom they interacted with than by what types of feedback they received.

The finding that the interlocutor variable played a more significant role than the feedback variable in terms of production of modified output differs from results of Van den Branden's (1997) study, which demonstrated that, for L2 learners of Dutch in a school setting where Dutch was the primary language of instruction, modified output was determined more by types of feedback than by the interlocutor. In the present study with post-secondary EFL learners in Japan, the learners' perceptions revealed through retrospective recall help to explain these different findings. First, learners felt less pressure when they interacted with other learners; second, they felt that they had more time in learner–learner dyads to plan what they were going to say; third, they believed that their NS interlocutors were capable of guessing the meanings of their utterances; and fourth, they felt much more comfortable communicating with their learner interlocutor when they engaged in the task. Mayumi's comment seems to illustrate all of these perceptions:

Excerpt 17
My native-speaker partner was giving me very specific questions so I was answering his questions all the time. Plus, I could have more information when I was working with him, so it was much easier to complete the task compared to when I was working with Taka. I think I was a listener when I was communicating with my native-speaker partner, and I was a speaker when I was working with Taka.

Thus, what made the interlocutor variable have greater influence than the feedback variable on interactional patterns seems to be related to social relationships between the interlocutors. (See Storch 2001.) In the present study, as seen in Mayumi's reflection above, it was found that NSs played a dominant role throughout the task even though a two-way information exchange task was employed to avoid dominant/passive relationships. In contrast, when learners interacted with each other, they succeeded in creating a forum for working collaboratively together to complete the task (see Foster and Ohta 2005). In response to each other's feedback, learners tried to make their output more comprehensible by generating and assessing alternatives. (See Swain and Lapkin 1998.) It seems that, in the present study, this strength of learner–learner interaction, in addition to the learners' different perceptions of their two interlocutors, overrode the differential effects of different types of feedback.

Conclusion and limitations

The present study investigated how Japanese EFL learners interact differently in learner–learner and learner–NS dyads during a communicative task. Results showed that opportunities for learners to negotiate meaning were proportionally similar in both types of dyad, but that learners provided one another with significantly more elicitation feedback than NSs did, and that learners modified their output significantly more in learner–learner dyads than in learner–NS dyads. Significant differences between learner–learner and learner–NS dyads in the amount of modified output produced by learners emerged not as a result of different feedback types but rather as a result of whether the interlocutor was another learner or a NS. These findings indicate that, if we consider that modified output is likely to positively affect target language development, learners in this research context tend to employ more beneficial interactional moves when they interact with each other rather than with NSs. In the follow-up retrospective recall sessions, the learners helped to explain these quantitative findings by acknowledging that whether their interlocutor was a NS or another learner affected their interaction. Specifically, they expressed being under pressure and more passive during interaction with a NS, generally taking advantage of what they perceived as the NSs' ability to guess their meaning. In contrast, they felt more comfortable when they interacted with other learners and more willing to ask questions about language.

The finding that learners modified their output proportionally more in learner–learner dyads than in learner–NS dyads supports the claim that tasks involving learner–learner interaction, if indeed modification moves are facilitative of L2 development, should be integrated into classroom activities as an important source of learning, especially for improving speaking abilities. (See edited volumes by Crookes and Gass 1993a, 1993b; Bygate, Skehan, and Swain 2001.) The present study showed that the NSs, who were not trained L2 teachers, were so adept at guessing L2 learners' meaning during communicative tasks that they did not push learners beyond their use of interlanguage forms. Yet it is precisely this pattern of learner–NS interaction that is most prevalent in EFL classrooms in Japan where JET-sponsored Assistant Language Teachers are typically assigned this role. In classroom settings, therefore, drawing on learners, such as the Japanese EFL learners in the present study, as interlocutors of the target language and as feedback providers has considerable potential that merits further research into its effects on continued L2 development. More specifically, the findings of the present study put into question a typical EFL teaching environment where NSs are considered as the best learning source, and point to a need for comparative studies of trained language teachers (including non-native teachers) and untrained native-speaking instructors interacting with classroom learners.

The 205 LREs generated by eight learners interacting with another learner and the same eight learners interacting with a NS were sufficient to permit statistical analyses in the present study, but limit nonetheless the generalizability of the findings. Another limitation of the present study is the absence of any measures of L2 development. Although peer interaction has considerable potential for providing learners with important L2 learning opportunities, research has yet to provide strong empirical evidence that learner–learner interaction pushes L2 development forward. Classroom research has shown experimentally that interactional feedback from teachers benefits L2 development (Doughty and Varela 1998; Lyster 2004; Ammar and Spada 2006) and also that students can benefit from collaborating together in language-focused tasks (Swain and Lapkin 2002). Further research is required, however, to demonstrate experimentally the effects on L2 development of learner–learner interaction during communicative tasks, by identifying the types of L2 skills and features that classroom learners actually learn from one another. The present study provides good incentive for pursuing such research insofar as it discredits the higher-status role typically reserved for NSs as ideal interlocutors. The Japanese EFL learners in the present study actively elicited modified output from each other more than NSs did (see also Mackey *et al.* 2003), and they also produced more modified output while interacting together than with NSs. These findings contribute further support for undermining the unequal power relations that L2 learners are reported to experience relative to NSs (Peirce 1995; Pavlenko 2002) and that are exacerbated through the pervasive use of negative-status labels such as 'non-native speakers' and 'limited-English proficient learners'.

6

Riddles and puns in the ESL classroom: adults talk to learn

AGUSTINA TOCALLI-BELLER
and MERRILL SWAIN

Introduction

The concept of interaction plays a significant role in theorizing about the process of second language learning (for example, Pica 1994a; Gass 1997) and interest in the role of interaction in second language learning has become a significant aspect of the research agenda of the field. From a Vygotskian sociocultural theory of mind perspective, learning occurs *in* the interaction, not as a result of it (Donato 1994, 2000; Lantolf and Appel 1994; Swain 1997, 2000a, 2000b, 2001a, 2001b; Swain and Lapkin 1998; Lantolf 2000a, 2000b; Swain, Brooks, and Tocalli-Beller 2002). A few recent studies (Lantolf 1997; Sullivan 2000a, 2000b; Broner and Tarone 2001; Bell 2002; Beltz 2002) have investigated the role that playing with language has in such interaction and thus in second language learning. With the exception of Lucas (2005), these studies have been restricted to an examination of spontaneous language play and most of them have disregarded the humorous effect this form of language may have on language learning.

Vygotsky (1978) emphasized the importance of play in child development. For him, play is a site for learning which leads to development. To quote:

> [P]lay is in advance of development, for in this manner children begin to acquire the motivation, skills, and attitudes necessary for their social participation. During preschool and school years the conceptual abilities of children are stretched through play. In play a child is always above his average age, above his daily behavior, in play it is as though he were a head taller than himself
> (Vygotsky 1987: 129).

Vygotsky (1987, original 1926) argued that play is not an 'accidental whim, a pastime, but an important vital necessity' (ibid.: 88) and that nearly all of our (adult) most fundamental and most characteristic reactions have their origin and develop 'in the course of the games we play as children' (ibid.: 89). Vygotsky argued that play and work are not polar opposites but that they in fact share 'the same psychological nature' because 'games are the natural form of work in children ... as preparation for [their] life in the future' (ibid.: 93). Play then entails more than having fun, joy and/or pleasure. Moreover, even though play and games are leading activities of children and move forward their development, they continue to promote development in adulthood even though they may no longer be the leading activity of adult life.

Cicogna, Danesi, and Mollica (1992) argue that adults seem to derive great pleasure from playing with words and language, as evidenced by the inclusion of crossword puzzles, plays on words, and puns in most daily newspapers and by the amount of space puzzle magazines and books occupy on book shelves. In spite of the fact that there have been some attempts in second language pedagogy to include play and problem-solving games in the curriculum (Mollica 1976, 1979; Omaggio 1982; Danesi 1989, 2002, 2003; Cicogna *et al.* 1992; Danesi and Mollica 1994), it can be said that the experimental literature considering the learning efficacy of such an element is not extensive. As Danesi (2003) points out,

> [V]ery little has been done in the way of giving the topic of ludic tech-
> niques thorough empirical treatment. Two clear factors have nevertheless
> emerged from the sketchy literature and from anecdotal evidence. First,
> such techniques seem to be supportive of language acquisition processes.
> Second, for such techniques to be effective, they must be designed with
> specific instructional/learning objectives in mind
> (ibid.: 112).

Furthermore, Danesi (ibid: 112) notes that 'rarely has anyone ventured to design a syllabus, or teaching system, aimed at making the whole SLT [second language teaching] process ludic in orientation'. To date, second language acquisition studies that investigated language play in language learning explored the topic from different, yet somewhat overlapping, perspectives. Language play has been studied as a social, ludic phenomenon (Cook 1996, 1997, 2000; Sullivan 2000a, 2000b) as a form of private speech (Saville-Troike 1988; Lantolf 1997, 2000a) and as an enhancement of sociolinguistic competence (Broner and Tarone 2001; Tarone 2002). What all views of language play have in common is the manipulation of both the form and the meaning of the linguistic item, though one can take precedence over the other depending on the instance of language play.

The data in this chapter come from an in-depth study carried out on the intentional inclusion of humorous language play in a second language cur-riculum (Tocalli-Beller 2005). We provide examples of peer–peer interactions as learners unravel the meaning of puns and riddles. Over time and together, the students work out the meaning of the puns and riddles by talking to each other, sharing their expertise or previous knowledge and providing the neces-sary feedback so that later, on their own, they can define the meaning of key words and understand the basis of the humor. The students' languaging—

which includes feedback the learners give each other (sometimes using the teacher or a dictionary as a resource) and the co-construction of meaning—is, it is argued, a source of second language learning. In this study, we are able to show how the students move from no knowledge of the 'semantic triggers' (what is needed to 'get' the riddle or pun), to being able to define the triggers and use them in a sentence, and even explain the riddle or pun to others. This is done by tracing what happens in the collaborative dialogue (languaging) of the students using a pre-test/post-test/delayed post-test design. Through such a design, and by making use of microgenetic analyses of the on-task interactions, we trace how learners moved from non-comprehension to spontaneous use mediated by their dialogue *about* language.

Theoretical background

Languaging: an aspect of second language learning 'in flight'

All learning is mediated by semiotic tools. An important mediational tool is language. Within the input–interaction–output model (Block 2003), language is viewed as a conveyer of a fixed message. However, in a Vygotskian sociocultural theoretical perspective, language is seen to have a second function: it serves as a cognitive tool—a tool of the mind. In this sense, language is an activity of the mind which mediates cognitive functioning by compelling the speaker to push thinking into the meanings created by the culture that are encoded in language. It is in the dialectic between meaning and contextual needs that sense is created and thinking completed. This activity has been conceptualized as 'languaging' (Swain in press) to indicate (1) language is an activity (a process), not an object (a product) (Swain 2005); (2) that the activity of speaking and writing (the activity of producing language) have key functions in externalizing cognition, manipulating it, and internalizing it; (3) that individuals are agents in the developmental processes which are realized in interaction. So, by observing and analyzing speaking as it mediates thinking, we can observe learning in progress. (Vygotsky 1978; 1986; Wertsch 1985; Donato 1994; Lantolf 2000b; Swain 2000b). In this way, speaking makes cognitive activity visible as language knowledge is co-constructed in language use.

Second language learning research informed by a sociocultural theory of mind situates second language learning in the dialogic interactions between learners and learners, learners and themselves, and learners and the artifacts available in their world, for example books, computers, etc. This dialogic interaction—languaging—is one source of learning. Among other things, the concept of languaging allows us to recognize that knowledge is constructed and co-constructed through its use (Swain 2000b). The knowledge that is constructed may be about mathematics, biology, etc., and it may also be about a second language as in the case of the ESL learners in this study.

Languaging takes place when individuals encounter a cognitive (or affective) problem and solve it by interacting with others, the self, or a cultural artifact. A microgenetic analysis of languaging allows us, in the words of Vygotsky (1978), to 'grasp the process in flight' (ibid.: 68) 'from its social origins through historical processes to task completion, the term 'historic' referring to the duration of the activity from its origin and its evolution to its end' (Platt and Brooks 2002: 373–4).

Humor in everyday speech

Carter (2004) and Carter and McCarthy (2004) present excerpts from their corpus of adult native speaker interaction in the UK and Ireland which involve and evolve from linguistic creativity. The researchers include 'playing with language forms to entertain others' (Carter and McCarthy 2004: 64) among the purposes of linguistic creativity in everyday language. Analyses of the corpus reveal a number of characteristic features of spoken discourse. In the words of Carter:

> [First], that ordinary, everyday language is far from being either everyday or ordinary (on the contrary, it is pervasively 'artful'); second, that verbal play with language is often undertaken for humorous purposes, serving in part to bring people closer together and member-shipping them inclusively; third, that this kind of linguistic creativity and inventiveness is almost always contextually embedded in so far as it depends on the social relations which obtain between participants ...; that it is a *frequent*, not exceptional feature of ordinary, everyday language use and that it is not an uncommon but a *common* practice to share pleasure, align viewpoints and create convergence in and through language and to do so often by means of creative play with language
> (2004: 108).

Friendly joking is a salient element in social discourse. In the words of Norrick (1993: 193), 'joking around is a natural part of friendly conversation, because we talk to enjoy ourselves'. Nerlich and Clarke (2001) also present examples of everyday discourse and note 'how much people play with multiple meanings in their daily linguistic interactions and how much of their linguistic interaction is structured by the play with multiple meanings' (ibid.: 2).

Coupland (2000) demonstrates that small talk and casual conversation of varying types are endemic even in professional settings; the CANCODE corpus in Carter (2004) and Carter and McCarthy (2004) support this claim. Block (2003) argues that the marginalization of ludic talk, that is, of humorous and playful uses of language by SLA researchers has resulted in a lack of attention to what is variably known as 'small talk' (Coupland 2000) or 'casual conversation' (Eggins and Slade 1997). These discourses should not be regarded as purposeless or peripheral. On the contrary, 'small talk' or 'casual conversation' should be considered as part of the foundation of 'the establishment, maintenance and strengthening of social ties' (Block 2003: 71).

The ubiquity of language play in talk indicates that playing with language is indeed part of what 'would normally be held to be part of a native speaker's competence in a particular language' (Lyons 1996: 24). Furthermore, Cook (1997, 2000) argued that '[k]nowing a language, and being able to function in communities which use the language, entails being able to understand and produce play with it, making this ability a necessary part of advanced proficiency' (2000: 150). Notwithstanding this, much of the current focus on classroom interaction and task-design disregards this kind of speech. With the exception of a few studies (Lantolf 1997; Sullivan 2000a, 2000b; Broner and Tarone 2001), scant attention has been paid to the role and impact of language play in second language learning.

Humor in task-based interaction

Tasks are considered to be the back-bone of the input–interaction–output model (Block 2003) and have become a topic of research in the field of SLA (for example, Bygate, Skehan, and Swain 2001; R. Ellis 2003). In general, researchers agree that tasks are designed to promote the natural and authentic use of language that focuses on meaning rather than on form (Nunan 1989; Skehan 1998). Skehan identifies different task-based activities for language learning:
1 completing one another's family trees;
2 agreeing on advice to give to the writer of a letter to an agony aunt;
3 discovering whether one's paths will cross (out of school) in the next week;
4 *solving a riddle* [emphasis added];
5 leaving a message on someone's answering machine
  (1998: 95–6).
To date, however, no studies have looked into the potential of riddles and puns as language learning tasks.

According to Long (1985), tasks reflect real-world activities, which are after all 'the hundred and one things people *do* in everyday life, at work, at play, and in between' (ibid.: 89). A good deal of current second language pedagogical research, however, directs its attention towards the sort of interaction found in what people do 'at work' and turns away from what people do 'at play', that is when interaction happens in a friendly, relaxed, leisure-type of context. In other words, second language pedagogical research focuses on the simulation of the conversations students might engage in when doing more transactional and goal-oriented activities such as the tasks exemplified by Long (1985), be it making an airline or hotel reservation, borrowing a library book, giving a street direction, etc.

With this focus on conversations that are work-based, transactional, and practical came an emphasis on meaning rather than on form. As Swain and

Lapkin (2001) put it: '[w]ith a few exceptions ... definitions of communicative tasks emphasize the importance of a focus on meaning.' However, they argue that an alternative view 'is that a task can still be considered communicative even if learners focus quite explicitly on form' (ibid.: 100). Moreover, Cook (1997) argues that a great deal of adult speech is form-oriented. He notes that although adult language is usually conceived as 'doing things [and] making meaning' (ibid.: 228).

> many conversations between friends and intimates contain little informa-
> tion, and may be regarded as instances of play and banter. These
> discourses are not ... 'task-based'. They are language for enjoyment, for
> the self, for its own sake. And they are often fantasies—not about the real
> world, but about a fictional one in which there are no practical outcomes
> (ibid.: 231).

In his recent book on task-based learning, R. Ellis (2003) distinguishes unfocused production tasks from focused communicative ones. The former are designed to elicit samples of learner production and are not targeted for students to use a specific linguistic feature. Focused communicative tasks, however, are designed to elicit attention to and use of specific features. Within focused communicative tasks, R. Ellis distinguishes three types: (1) structure-based approach tasks, (2) comprehension tasks (enriched input tasks and interpretation tasks), and (3) consciousness-raising tasks. Ellis considers the first two to make use of implicit learning processes. Consciousness-raising tasks, on the contrary, are intended to cater primarily to explicit learning processes and thus are designed to attract attention to language and develop awareness since these processes promote language learning through logic, reasoning, and problem-solving. Furthermore, whereas structure-based and comprehension tasks are built around content of a general nature (for example, stories, pictures of objects, opinions about someone you like), con-sciousness-raising tasks make language itself the content (R. Ellis 2003). For the present study, to understand the riddles and puns, the students inevitably had to focus on certain words or idiomatic expressions if the humor were to be understood. In this way, the riddles and puns (the language play pieces) 'isolate[d] a specific linguistic feature for focused attention' (R. Ellis 2003: 234) and thus catered for explicit learning as a consciousness-raising task requires.

Understanding and using second language humor

Humor is a highly valued art and practice across societies. In western socie-ties, humor is an essential element of everyday interaction and of socialization (Boxer and Cortés-Conde 1997). The theory of humor most commonly linked to classroom pedagogy is the cognitive-perceptual theory (Vizmuller-Zocco 1992). This theory assumes that humor results from playful situations, more specifically, when 'the perceiver meets with an incongruity (usually in the form of a punch line or a cartoon) and then is motivated to resolve the incongruity either by retrieval of information in the joke or from his/her own storehouse of information' (Suls 1983: 42). From these situations, two characteristics of the rational human being arise: problem-solving and amusement. The former is manifested by explaining the incongruity and the latter is precisely the enjoyment of becoming aware of the incongruity, that is, of noticing 'something which clashes with our mental patterns and expectations' (Morreall 1989: 1).

There are different classifications of types of humor. Schmitz (2002) organizes humorous discourse into three groups: (1) universal or reality-based humor, (2) culture-based humor, and (3) linguistic or word-based humor. The present study focuses on linguistic or word-based humor, a recurrent type of humor and, more often than not, one that is difficult for second language speakers to comprehend, even when their proficiency in the language is high. The difficulty in understanding this type of humor usually lies in the use of a word or expression referred to as 'the semantic script-switch trigger' (Raskin 1985) or simply 'the trigger' (Nash 1985). The *semantic-trigger*, as we call it in this study, is the key element to understanding the language and humor at play because it is the 'centre of energy, some word or phrase in which the whole matter of the joke is fused, and from which its powers radiates' (Nash 1985: 7).

The use and understanding of second language humor constitute two major challenges for second language learners as they require sophisticated linguistic, social, and cultural competence (Bell 2002). For many learners of English, both the forms and functions of humor differ from those of their first language and culture, making the understanding and use of humor all the more problematic for them. Second language humor has therefore earned the reputation of being 'unteachable' (and even unnecessary and frivolous), prompting second language teachers to shun its inclusion in the curriculum. Yet, as we have seen, life is imbued with humor and students are bound to encounter it.

Method

The research site

The data were collected in an ESL non-credit eight-week course of the English Conversation Program of a North American university. The focus of the English Conversation Program lies primarily in developing fluency and accuracy in oral English communication. A new course within the English Conversation Program, entitled Understanding English Culture and Humor had the purpose of achieving this goal through a humor-based curriculum. The course was designed and taught by the first author of this chapter. Just like all the courses, this new course took place for two hours each week.

The students who enrolled in the course were international graduate students seeking opportunities to speak English outside their current academic environments and therefore who volunteered to participate in the study. The proficiency levels varied and their backgrounds and interests were also different. Table 6.1 presents some background information about the students in the present study. During the research, all students in the course (nine students) worked together in self-selected pairs/trios, as well as engaged in whole-class activities. All tests were done individually.

Research questions

Two research questions are addressed in this study:
1 When asked to solve riddles and/or puns (pieces of language play) collaboratively, do students 'language' about language form and meaning?
2 Is their languaging a source of second language learning?

Data collection procedure

This research involved two cycles of data collection, which took place sequentially during the whole course, as shown in Table 6.2. All students participated in both cycles though not with the same partner(s). Additionally, at the beginning of the course a background questionnaire was administered, and an interview and survey were administered at the end of cycle 1. Also, two weeks after the course ended, a dyad-specific post-test was administered which consisted of the post-tests from cycle 1 and cycle 2. A basic cycle consisted of the administration of the following stages:

Stage 1 a pre-test, which was the same for all student dyads, was administered. It included the semantic triggers that were key to understanding all the language play pieces, i.e. riddles and puns that were used in the study.

Stage 2 a language play task in which the dyads worked on their own set of language play pieces. Completion of Stage 2 meant that dyads (or trios where applicable) had discussed and tried to understand all language play pieces in the set that they were given. Even though each language play set had different language play pieces for each pair/trio, sets were similar in terms of the nature of the semantic triggers as well as the number of pieces. Dyads were allowed to use the *The Longman Dictionary of Contemporary English* as a reference tool to help them solve the language play pieces. All dyads were video- and audio-taped in order to (a) identify dyad-specific items to include in the post-tests, (b) conduct a stimulated recall session with each pair of students (to gain introspective data of the students on-task), and (c) transcribe and analyze the students' on-task talk.

	Don	Kim	Tom	John	Eric
TOEFL score**	563	N/A	500	633	647
Degree of study	MA Medicine	Visiting student	BS Computing	MA Engineering	MA Engineering
Nationality	Russian	Korean	Chinese	Chinese	Chinese
L1	Russian	Korean	Mandarin	Cantonese	Cantonese
Other languages	—	—	—	—	—
Residence in Canada	8 months	1 year	1 year	1.5 years	2 months
Residence in other L2 countries	—	—	—	—	2 months in USA
ESL instruction in Canada	—	—	3 months	—	—
EFL instruction at home	7 years	No instruction	8 years	15 years	10 years

Table 6.1 Information on the participants of the Understanding English Culture and Humor course

	Harry	Will	Lisa	Helen*
TOEFL score**	587	647	647	637
Degree of study	MA Computing	MA Business	Special student	MA Genetics
Nationality	Iranian	Chinese	Swedish	Chinese
L1	Persian	Mandarin	Swedish	Cantonese
Other languages	—	—	Danish/French/ German	—
Residence in Canada	1.6 years	1.5 years	7 months	1.5 years
Residence in other L2 countries	—	—	—	—
ESL instruction in Canada	1 month	—	—	1.5 years
EFL instruction at home	4 years	8 years	10 years	15 years +

* All names are pseudonyms   **These are self-reported scores

Table 6.1 (continued)

Stage 3 a language play post-test, which was dyad-specific (tailor-made), was administered two to four days after the students completed the set of language play pieces. This post-test included items consisting of the semantic triggers of the language play set of the dyad plus any other words/expressions that the students talked about during the language play task that helped them understand the language at play.

Stage 4 a stimulated recall session occurred two to four days after doing the language play task. During the stimulated recall, the student dyads watched the tape of themselves doing their language play set. We stopped the video at relevant features in their language production so that the students could explain their thoughts about why they stopped at, discussed, explained, and/or repeated such features. The stimulated recall interviews were audio-taped and the dialogues that took place were transcribed for analysis.

Stage 5 a class activity, which was intended to engage the entire class in real-life playful and humorous joke-telling. Each dyad told and explained their language play pieces to the class in whatever order they chose.

Stage 6 a class activity post-test, which was equivalent to the pre-test but only included those semantic triggers which were discussed in the class activity in order to analyze the learning that happened during class. There had not been enough time for students to tell and explain all their language play pieces during the class activity.

The design of the tests

To establish whether the languaging about the language play pieces was a source of second language learning, and thus address the second research question, a pre-test/post-test/delayed post-test design was adopted. Due to the nature of the language play pieces, much of the languaging was centered around the meanings of the semantic triggers. For this reason, we chose Wesche and Paribakht's (1996) Vocabulary Knowledge Scale as the testing instrument. The Vocabulary Knowledge Scale was designed to assess levels of familiarity with given words by eliciting both self-reported and demonstrated knowledge of individual words in a written mode. 'The scale ratings range from complete unfamiliarity, through recognition of the word or some idea of its meaning, to the ability to use the word with grammatical and semantic accuracy in a sentence' (Wesche and Paribakht 1996: 29).

Wesche and Paribakht acknowledge that the Vocabulary Knowledge Scale does not tap knowledge of *different* meanings of the same word and call for an extension of the scale to explore this aspect of lexical knowledge (1996: 33). For this study we therefore provided this extension because puns and riddles entail different meanings of the same word. We adjusted the test to incorporate knowledge about more than one meaning of the target word and thus the scale was extended by repeating lines three and four of the original scale. This repetition allowed students to define and/or illustrate in a sentence another meaning of the semantic trigger in question (if applicable). Table 6.3

presents the adaptation of the original Vocabulary Knowledge Scale used in the present study.

Cycle 1				
Week 1 Feb. 21	**Week 2** Feb. 28	**2–4 days** **later**	**Week 3** March 7	**Week 4** March 14
Class time	*Class time*	*Outside class time*	*Class time*	*Class time*
• Introduction to the course • Background questionnaire • Other activities *Pre-test* (20 min.)	• LP task • LP task survey	• LP post-test • Stimulated recall	• Class activity (2 hours) • Class activity survey	• CA post-test • Other activities *Outside class time* • **Interviews**

Cycle 2						
Week 5 March 21	**Week 6** March 28	**2–4 days** **later**	**Week 7** April 4	**Week 8** April 11	**Week 9**	**Week 10** April 25
Outside class time • Interviews *Class time* • Other activities *Pre-test* (20 min.)	*Class time* • LP task	*Outside class time* • LP post-test • Stimulated recall	*Class time* • Class activity (2 hours)	*Class time* • CA post-test • Other activities • Conclusion to the course		*Outside class time* • Delayed post-test

LP Task: Language Play Task   CA: Class Activity

Table 6.2 Research design and data collection schedule

Self-report categories
a I don't remember having seen this word before
b I have seen this word before, but I don't remember what it means
c I know this word. It means _____(synonym and/or definition)
d I can use this word in a sentence _____
If applicable also complete sections e and f
e I know this word also means _____
f I can use this word in a sentence _____

Table 6.3 Vocabulary Knowledge Scale: self-report categories (adapted from Wesche and Paribakht, 1996)

The contents of each of the tests varied as outlined in the data collection procedure section above. Furthermore, some tests were the same for the whole class and some were dyad-specific depending on the stages of data-collection. (See Data Collection Procedure above.)

Unlike the original Vocabulary Knowledge Scale, the scoring of the adapted scale in the present study includes 'no answer' and 'wrong answer' as possible scores. (See Table 6.4.) For Wesche and Paribakht (1996), a category (c) may lead to a score of 2 even if the synonym and/or definition are wrong. In our scoring scheme the synonym or definition had to be correct. Also, in the Wesche and Paribakht scoring scheme, if knowledge of the meaning of the word is shown in category (d) but the word is not appropriately used in a sentence, a score of 3 (instead of 4) is given. In our scoring scheme, however, category (d) responses had to be semantically and grammatically accurate (but only with respect to the word or expression at issue). Thus, once a wrong answer was given (no matter at what stage), the item was counted as wrong and thus learning (or lack of it) could be accurately traced. Therefore, logically, in our scheme, categories (c) and (d) had to be correct to get full points. For example, in our scoring scheme, a score of 4 was given for Eric's 'The door was ajar so the thief come* in' where 'ajar' was the semantic trigger.

Possible Score	Meaning of Scores
0	No answer
✗	Wrong answer
1	The word is not familiar at all
2	The word is familiar but the meaning is unknown
3	A correct synonym and/or definition is given
4	The word is used with semantic appropriateness and grammatical accuracy in a sentence.

Table 6.4 Vocabulary Knowledge Scale scoring categories: meaning of scores

Unit of analysis: language-related episodes

The students' languaging from stages 2, 4, and 5 was transcribed and coded for language-related episodes (LREs). As defined by Swain and Lapkin (2001), an LRE is any part of the dialogue where learners talk about the language they are producing or produced, question or reflect on their language use (and/or knowledge), or correct themselves or others. For this research, the following LREs have been distinguished in order to capture different types of talk prompted by the puns or riddles and their impact on language learning:

a *Meaning LREs*
Students focus on understanding words or expressions (many of which were semantic triggers) they do not know, or understanding new meaning(s) of a word/expression they already knew.
b *Form LREs*
Students focus on formal features of the semantic triggers or other linguistic items (for example, suffix, prefix, spelling, etc.).

c *Metatalk LREs*
Students use metalinguistic terms (for example, noun, adjective, verb, etc.) to understand and/or explain the reasoning behind the pun or riddle.

Data analysis and findings

Quantitative analyses: impact on learning

As noted previously, this study encompassed two cycles of data collection which were methodologically equivalent. Thus the study allows for a comparison of learning across cycles that the use of language play activities had throughout the stages of data collection. Table 6.5 describes the specifics for each cycle in terms of: (a) the number of language play pieces in each set, (b) the average number of linguistic items about which languaging occurred per set, (c) the average number of minutes per language play set, (d) the average number of words spoken per language play piece, and (e) the average number of turns taken per LP piece.

Cycle specifics						
		# LP pieces	# language items focused on	# minutes per set	# words spoken per LP piece	# turns per LP piece
Cycle 1						
9 students	Mean	7	14	28	454	41
	SD	0	2	8	293	26
Cycle 2						
8 students*	Mean	9	16	39	535	44
	SD	0	3	10	297	25

*One student, who missed some of the most important stages of data collection, is not counted in Cycle 2

LP: Language play

Table 6.5 Cycle 1 and Cycle 2: information about the language play tasks

As shown in Table 6.5, in the first cycle students took about half an hour on average to complete their language play sets of seven pieces, and in the second cycle they took about ten minutes more on average to complete nine pieces. In each set, students focused on an average of between 14 and 16 linguistic items (including the semantic triggers), which accounted for much of the peer–peer interaction. When the students began to try to understand each language play piece, they often found the humor incomprehensible. Through languaging of an average length of 41–44 turns per piece, students came to understand the language and humor involved by providing feedback to each other and reflecting on and discussing the language used to solve the linguistic puzzle at hand. This focus on, and discussion about, language was operationalized by all three types of LREs. In each stage of data collection, LREs were identified for both qualitative and quantitative purposes. As indicated in Table 6.6, meaning-based LREs were the most frequent in every stage of data collection. This is mainly due to the fact that most of the source of the humor lay in the use of different meanings of the ST. Overall, the two cycles were similar suggesting the non-uniqueness of the patterns displayed in Tables 6.5 and 6.6.

	Stages of data collection											
	LP set				Stimulated recall				Class activity			
	Type of LRE (percentage)				Type of LRE (percentage)				Type of LRE (percentage)			
	⊃	Form	Mean	Meta-talk	⊃	Form	Mean	Meta-talk	⊃	Form	Mean	Meta-talk
Cycle 1												
Mean	29	12	68	20	21	12	68	21	37	28	52	20
SD	10	6	10	12	4	8	22	15	6	8	10	10
Cycle 2												
Mean	57	21	60	19	33	11	57	32	32	19	50	32
SD	16	7	12	5	16	8	7	7	9	12	13	7

Table 6.6 LRE count across stages of data collection

Tables 6.7 and 6.8 show the pre-test and post-test results for each participant for cycles 1 and 2 respectively. For each test item, a student response was considered correct if they could do (c) and/or (d) in the adapted Vocabulary Knowledge Scale, that is, define another meaning of the semantic trigger and/ or illustrate it in a sentence. (See Table 6.3 above.) If they knew the second meaning for a word, this was treated as a separate item and was considered correct if they could do (e) and/or (f). For each student, a percentage correct was calculated by dividing the number of correct items by their total number of items. Recall that each dyad's post-tests were specific to the dyad. (See description of Stages 3 and 6 under data collection procedures.)

As Table 6.7 and Table 6.8 indicate, results from both cycles indicate that considerable learning took place between the pre-test and the language play post-test. The language play post-test was followed by two other stages, the stimulated recall and the class activity, both of which allowed for further languaging and learning. The results from the delayed post-test which took place two weeks after the end of the course indicate that the learning which had taken place earlier was sustained. Note that for cycle 1, the delayed post-test results are based on languaging that took place at least six weeks prior to the administration of the test.

Students	N*	Week 1	Week 2	2–4 days later		Week 3	Week 4	—	Week 10
	STs and other items	Pre-test	LP task	LP Post-test	SR	CA	CA Post-test	—	Delayed Post-test
Lisa	12	67		100			100		92
Helen		50		100			100		100
Harry	15	27		100			93		100
Will		13		73			87		80
Don	15	33		100			100		100
Tim		27		80			80		93
Kim		33		60			n.a.		67
Eric	12	53		93			100		100
John		53		93			100		100
Mean		40		88			95		92
SD		17		15			8		12

* N is the total of semantic triggers (ST) plus those words/expressions that were also discussed in the language play task and were repeated in the discussions of the stimulated recall (SR) and the class activity (CA)

Note that Kim was absent for the class activity and class activity post-test

Table 6.7 Cycle 1 pre-test and post-test results (in percentages) across all stages

Qualitative analyses: microgenetic analyses of learning

In this section, we present two examples of how the learning unfolded over time for two dyads through a microgenetic analysis that illustrates the patterns described above. The characteristics of the two examples are summarized in Table 6.9. So as to be maximally illustrative of the whole data set, an example from each cycle of data collection is given (a pun and a riddle respectively). We show students whose expertise in relation to their partner's is different (i.e. expert + novice; novice + novice) in order to see the learning that can take place for students with different proficiency levels and language knowledge. Expertise is defined as having knowledge about the semantic trigger of the language play piece. One of the semantic triggers (lean) was homonymous/polysemous and thus two different meanings were at play as indicated below the semantic trigger in column D of Table 6.9. If one of the students knew the meaning (or one of the meanings of the semantic trigger), it is represented in column E as (+1). If s/he did not know the meaning, it is represented by (-1). Column F summarizes the type and number of language

Students	N*	Week 5	Week 6	2–4 days later		Week 7	Week 8	Week 9	Week 10
	STs and other items	Pre-test	LP task	LP Post-test	SR	CA	CA Post-test	—	Delayed Post-test
Don	13	15		77			100		100
Eric		31		92			100		92
Tim	7	29		57			100		100
Lisa		71		100			100		100
Harry	6	67		100			100		100
John		67		100			100		100
Helen	9	22		89			100		100
Kim		22		67			89		100
Mean		41		85			98		99
SD		24		17			4		3

*N is the total of semantic triggers (ST) plus those words/expressions that were also discussed in the language play task and were repeated in the discussions of the stimulated recall (SR) and the class activity (CA)

Table 6.8 Cycle 2 pre-test and post-test results (in percentages) across all stages

A	B	C	D	E	F			
Example	Type of LP	Cycle	ST + # of meanings at play	Pairs of students + expertise distribution	# of LRE*			
					Type of LRE	LP	SR	CA
1	Pun	1	lean 2	Helen & Lisa (+1)(+1)	Form			2
					Meaning	2	2	4
					Meta-talk			1
2	Riddle	2	ajar 1	Don & Eric (-1)(-1)	Form	1	1	1
					Meaning	1	2	4
					Meta-talk	1	2	1

LP: Language play; LRE: Language-related episode; SR: Stimulated recall; CA: Class activity; ST: Semantic trigger

*These are the total number of LREs generated by the semantic trigger but for space reasons, not all of them are reproduced in Tables 6.10 and 6.12

Table 6.9 Information about the two language play pieces selected for microgenetic analysis

related episodes that the dyad produced across the stages of data collection that relate to the semantic trigger.

Tables 6.10 and 6.12 provide a microgenetic presentation of the languaging that the two student pairs produced that relate to the semantic trigger. Due to space limitations only parts of their dialogue are presented. Missing lines are represented by (…) in the excerpts. The transcription conventions we used are shown in the Appendix. In our discussion of these tables, we refer the reader to the corresponding turns which are in bold type for easy reference.

In Tables 6.10 through 6.13, the number of meanings known (3 on the vocabulary knowledge scale) and/or used correctly in a sentence (4 on the LREs Vocabulary Knowledge Scale) in the pre-test and post-tests is shown in bold type.

Microgenetic analysis of 'lean': Lisa and Helen

As shown in Table 6.10, in Cycle 1 Lisa and Helen discussed a pun that featured two meanings of the word 'lean'. Lisa knew one meaning and Helen knew the other. This knowledge of different meanings marked separate expertises at the outset of the task and therefore each person in the pair was able to help the other one learn another meaning for the same word.

During the LP task, Lisa and Helen explained one meaning to each other (turns 11–18). They then checked the dictionary which corroborated what they had said. Because each of them knew one meaning for 'lean' and both meanings needed to be understood in order to understand the pun, they were careful to explain the meaning the other needed to understand. This is a clear example of how expertise shifts in peer–peer learning.

Four days later, Lisa and Helen completed the language play post-test making sure that the new meanings they had learnt were included and illustrated with a sentence. At the time of the stimulated recall four days later, Helen enthusiastically pointed out how Lisa's explanation made her understand the new meaning and thus the overall joke (turn 15). Lisa had already stated that she liked and found useful the role of 'the expert' and repeats this in turn 17 in response to the researcher's question. She said that she found it useful for herself because she needed to search for English words and explain them. Thus exposure to the trigger and the opportunity provided in the stimulated recall to talk about it again was another source of learning and helped to sustain the meaning learnt (Swain 2006).

Lisa and Helen's learning proved to be sustained over the longer term. Seven weeks after the whole class activity, when they last discussed the meanings of 'lean', they still remembered the new meanings discussed initially in the language play task.

By the time of the class activity three days after the stimulated recall, both Lisa and Helen were the 'experts' for that joke and as such, they helped their classmates understand the meanings of 'lean' that were at play in the pun. Interestingly, each of them explained the one meaning they did not know

ST	'lean'	
Pair	**Lisa**	**Helen**
Pre-test **Week 1**	No fat. The girl was very lean. (+1)	Stand against. He leans on against the wall. (+1)
LP piece	Waiter, I'd like a corned beef sandwich, and make it lean. Yes, sir! In which direction?	

LP task **Week 2**		
	11 H	I don't understand what is lean.
	12 L	Uh ... lean can mean uh not fat, not fatty.
	13 H	Oh. And also uh ... you lean on something. That direction or that direction.
	14 L	Oh, lean against the wall?
	15 H	Yeah. And lean is not fat?
	16 L	Yeah.
	17 H	There is no fat in the meat.
	18 L	Yes, I think so [they check the dictionary]
	19 H	xx
	20 L	Yes.
	21 H	Lean meat does not have much fat on it. OK, I got it!

LP **Post-test** **4 days later**	Not fat at all. I want some lean meat in my sandwich. To bend over. When I lean on a wall, I don't stand entirely on my feet. (+2)	Meat without fat. Stand against. He is sick, so he leans against the wall. (+2)

SR **4 days later**		
	9 H	I didn't know the other meaning of lean.
	10 R	Which meaning did you know?
	11 H	I just know to stand against. Not the other meaning of it.
	12 R	Um-hum. And what was the other meaning?
	13 H	It means without fat.
	14 R	OK. Excellent. And that's something that Lisa explained very well. **Did it help to get that explanation?**
	15 H	Yeah, yeah! [laughs].
	16 R	[to L] And you said that it also helped to explain things?
	17 L	Yes, it does because I need to search my mind to English words and explain it.

Class activity **Week 3**		
	538 **Helen**	The lean is l-e-a-n.
	539 **Eric**	Oh, make it 'lean'.
	540 **Harry**	Oh, the same joke in Persian (...)
	550 **Helen**	Lean. One meaning means that it's x, I mean, that is not fat. Is not fat. (...)
	553 **Eric**	And what's the other meaning for lean?
	554 **Tim**	Lean is, you know ...
	555 **Eric**	Lean the first meaning is
	556 **Lisa**	Leaning against the wall.
	557 **Tim**	Yeah, yeah.
	558 **Harry**	Yeah.
	559 **Eric**	OH, yeah! Leaning against the wall. OK.
	560 **Tim**	Another is, another is -
	561 **Eric**	-without fat. Without fat.
	562 **Tim**	Without fat?
	563 **Eric**	Yeah.
	564 **Helen**	Yeah.
	565 **Don**	It means without fat.

CA **Post-test** **Week 4**	*Not fatty (food).* *The meat on the sandwich must be lean.* *To take support on a wall.* *The man was leaning at the wall, waiting.* (+2)	Not fat. *Stand against.* (+2)
Delayed **post-test** **Week 10**	*Not fat.* *Not standing straight.* (+2)	*Without fat.* *To be against.* (+2)

See appendix for transcription conventions

Table 6.10 Microgenetic analysis for 'lean'

before the language play task (turns 550 and 556). Their explanations mediated the learning of the rest of the class as shown in Table 6.11. Except for John, the students initially knew either one meaning for 'lean' or none at all. However, after Lisa and Helen explained the joke to the other students in the class during the whole class activity, all students learnt a new meaning and were able to demonstrate this knowledge on the post-test given seven days later in week 4 (Stage 6).

	Week 1 – Pre-test	Week 3	Week 4 – CA Post-test
Don	I have seen this word but I don't know what it means. (–2)		a **Lie down against. Could you lean it in this way?** b **Without fat. Please, may I have the lean part?** (+2)
Eric	**The beef is so lean that I like to taste. (+1)**		a **The singer leaned against the wall and sang.** b **The beef is lean.** (+2)
Harry	**Not straight. The tree is leaning back. (+1)**		a **Bend. He falls asleep when he leans back.** b **Thin, less fat. I prefer lean meat. (+2)**
John	a **Thin. He is quite lean.** b **You in support from sthg. He leans against the wall.** (+2)		a **Thin. I like lean meat.** b **Depend against. He is leaning against the wall.** (+2)
Kim	A part of boy		N/A (Absent from CA).
Tim	I have seen this word but I don't know what it means. (–2)		a **Free of fat.** b **Bend.** (+2)
Will	**Thin. I just help them implement lean manufacturing. (+1)**		a **Non-fat.** b **Turn, bend.** (+2)

Class activity: Lisa and Helen's explanation.

See appendix for transcription conventions

Table 6.11 'Lean': pre-test and post-test results for the class

Microgenetic analysis of 'ajar': Don and Eric

In Cycle 2, Don and Eric worked on a riddle that helped them learn the meaning of the word 'ajar', a word they had never seen before as they indicated on the pre-test. When Don and Eric read the answer to the riddle (a-jar) they focused on the word 'jar'. In the following turns (244–248), they first defined this word and said:

244   E Jar. Jar means what? Jar is a bar, right? [takes the dictionary]
245   D No, no. 'When it's a-jar'.
246   E I think is bar. You can see here [reads from the dictionary] 'A round glass container'.
       Oh, no, no, no. It's a bottle.
247   D A round glass ...? [Pause. They both read the entry] It's container, right?
248   E Yeah. Container.

Once they understood the word jar, they began to wonder what the connection with door was (turns 254–257) as Table 6.12 shows. Since they indicated being 'stuck' (turn 260) and did not seem to notice the hyphen in the riddle script of 'a-jar' as a hint, the teacher pointed this out (turns 258–262). This help, the only instance of teacher support in the language play pieces of Cycle 2, offered Don and Eric a solution, and through their further languaging, we are able to see learning 'take flight'.

With the help of the dictionary definition (turn 264) and the discussion they had in which they contrasted ajar to open (turns 281–282), Eric and John reached an understanding collaboratively of the word and demonstrated their newly acquired knowledge in the language play post-test three days after working on their set.

In the stimulated recall, three days after the language play post-test, Don and Eric made it clear that originally they had not understood the word ajar:

257   E This [riddle] is a very difficult one because the -
258   D - we didn't know the word ajar.

Eric pointed to an actual door in the classroom that was actually ajar (turn 267). Later on, in their own meta-interlanguage, they were able to point out how 'ajar', if divided, becomes an article (a) and a noun (jar) and means something different (turns 473–477). The learning of this new word proved to be long-term for Don and Eric as in the delayed post-test, 3 weeks after they discussed it for the last time, they were able to illustrate 'ajar' in two good examples.

In the whole-class activity, Don and Eric engaged their classmates in a useful discussion: there was an explicit focus on form (turn 944), a sentence that illustrated the meaning of ajar clearly (turn 947) and an attempt to transfer knowledge (turns 968–973). In this latter instance of languaging they made it clear that ajar is only used for door. All students included door in their examples for the class activity post-test demonstrating that learning had taken place during the peer–peer discussions of the class activity (Table 6.13).

ST	'ajar'	
Pair	**Don**	**Eric**
Pre-test **Week 5**	I don't remember having seen this word before. (-1)	I don't remember having seen this word before. (-1)
LP piece	When is a door not a door? When it is ajar.	

LP task Week 6		
254	E	Jar means a container. But this has something to do with door?
255	D	Jar. So what's the second meaning? Jar.
256	E	x-x.
257	D	[whispers something] [reading from the dictionary but it's indecipherable speech].
258	T	Is everything OK here?
259	E	[not very convincingly] Yes.
260	D	Yeah. We are stuck here. [as T points out at ajar as one word] Ajar!
261	T	This is one word, right?
262	E	Ah!!
263	D	Wow! [they start laughing]
264	E	[checks the dictionary] It's here. 'A door that is ajar is slightly open'. See here!
265	D	Ajar.
266	E	'See picture at open' [looks it up] I see!
267	D	So what's?
268	E	Ajar is open.
269	D	An open x like this. (...)
277	D	So this is not a door. This is a jar
278	E	Because if it is widely open, if it is xx. If it is a small opening, it is called ajar.
279	D	Ajar.
280	E	Ajar.
281	D	If it's open what is it? If it is whole open?
282	E	If it is whole open it is just open.

LP **Post-test** **3 days later**	A door which is opened a little bit It's ajar here. (+1)	The door was ajar at night so the thief come in. (+1)

SR 3 days later		
267	E	[pointing to the door] Can I say that now the door is ajar?
268	R	Excellent. It is ajar! (...)
269	E	A jar means a, one jar. [he moves his hands to show that they are different words]
270	D	One jar.
271	E	Yes, one jar.
272	D	One jar.
273	E	Yes, one jar. So if it is connect it has only one meaning, right? It's half open.

Class activity Week 7		
944	Don	A-j-a-r. Like a little bit open. [H and L start laughing]
945	Tim	What's ajar? Means open a little bit.
946	Don	Open. A little bit open.
947	Eric	Yeah. In a sentence: At night and because the door is ajar so the thieves coming <u>and take the money.</u>
948	Tim	Oh, yeah. Ah-ha.(...)
968	Harry	And can you leave the window ajar?
969	Helen	Yes, I think.
970	Eric	No. Ajar is for the door.
971	Lisa	So something to be ajar needs to be hung here and be able to go like this [swings her hand]
972	Eric	No ajar is only used for
973	Tim & Helen	<u>Door.</u>

CA **Post-test** **Week 8**	Not well closed door. Please leave it ajar. (+1)	I leave the door ajar. (+1)
Delayed **post-test** **Week 10**	A door than not quite close. Don't close! Please leave it ajar! (+1)	The door is ajar so the child won't be afraid during sleep. (+1)

See appendix for transcription conventions

Table 6.12 Microgenetic analysis for 'ajar'

	Week 5 – Pre-test	Week 7	Week 8 – CA Post-test
Harry	I have seen this word before but I don't know what it means. (−1)		Half open/half close. Please let the door ajar. (+1)
Helen	I have seen this word before but I don't know what it means. (−1)		Open slightly. The door is ajar. (+1)
John	I have seen this word before but I don't know what it means. (−1)	Don and Eric's explanation	Door slight open. Keep door ajar. (+1)
Kim	I have seen this word before but I don't know what it means. (−1)		Open a door slightly. (+1)
Lisa	I have seen this word before but I don't know what it means. (−1)		A door slightly open. Leave the door ajar, please. I want to see the light. (+1)
Tim	I have seen this word before but I don't know what it means. (−1)		A door open a lit bit. (+1)

See appendix for transcription conventions

Table 6.13 'Ajar': pre-test and post-test results for the class

In summary, peer–peer interaction as a site for learning was the focus of this study. The learners' languaging, when analyzed at the micro-level demonstrated how the peer–peer talk allowed students to move from no comprehension to comprehension and production. As shown in each microgenetic analysis of learning, even when expertise varied among students, the students' languaging constructed new knowledge. In these data we see that the source of learning was interaction mediated by the students' languaging. The post-tests were done individually, demonstrating that learning had taken place. Languaging mediated the comprehension of both the humor and the language involved in the language play. We believe this study negates the criticism of sociocultural theory-based studies made by R. Ellis (2003) and Mitchell and Myles (1998) that researchers have not shown evidence of learning, especially in the long term (R. Ellis and Barkhuizen 2005).

To understand instances of language play, the students needed to discover the incongruity involved. To do this they had to understand 'the normal' and the deviation from it—what Crystal (1998: 1) refers to as 'bending and breaking' the rules. Students needed to operate within two linguistic worlds at once, the normal and the abnormal, trading them off against each other to understand the language and appreciate the humor involved in its playful use. Languaging mediated this cognitively complex process.

Once the students reached this understanding, they usually laughed and said things such as 'I got it!', 'Oh, yeah!', 'Ah-ha!'. The fact that laughter occurred may signal other phenomena besides having a 'fun' time and interpreting the activity as ludic. Though laughter can signal embarrassment at not knowing something, shyness, and avoidance, etc. (see Markee 2000: 290 for descriptions on laughter tokens in actual conversations), in this study laughter was also a sign of release at solving a kind of mental conflict. The language play pieces represented 'a kind of puzzle which when solved enables learners to discover for themselves how a linguistic feature works' (R. Ellis 2003: 163).

Pedagogical implications: the importance of being humorous

As the students themselves reported in the interviews, they would not have been able to understand the humor and language involved were it not for the help of a partner and the discussion they had. Therefore, these problem-solving and knowledge-building dialogues (i.e. the students' languaging), became sites for learning as shown in the comparison between the pre-test and post-test results.

Tim provided a reason why language play and humor were conducive to long-term learning. In the interview he said that a good joke is 'inspiration to remember. Because you think of it and you can remember it forever. If you think a lot about this word, you will remember it forever'. The language play activities presented an intellectual challenge to the students, who were pushed to think about language on two different levels: the normal level, and the abnormal or playful level in which words and expressions do things that they do not normally do. The playful context and the need to resolve the inherent incongruity of the humor pushed students to think about language and notice gaps in their knowledge which had to be filled if the pun or riddle were to make sense. This problem-solving process, mediated by language, helped students to make new connections. As John explained:

> I think that is a common problem with the international students because we speak our own languages. We have connections between our language and English. But we don't have connection with the English word and the English word. Or even with the two meanings of the same word but we never connect them together, you know. They have a bridge English to Chinese and then Chinese to English. You have a direct connection. That's why for something like that we know both meanings but we never think 'Oh, you can put together to make fun with that'.

Furthermore, Kim said that she had 'learnt more English. (…) And I understand the deep meaning of the same word'. Learning the 'deep meaning' (i.e. understanding the different meanings of a word and/or its possible grammatical functions) was something that Don and John also pointed out was a result of their struggle with understanding puns and riddles:

You know, now I think in clear words and something much more deeper. (Don)

Now I know 'stuffed' has two meanings for, you know, the kind of food. Another 'stuffed' is like toy. Like stuffed bear or something like that. But I have never connected these two meanings together. (John)

We have argued that a comprehensive view of second language communicative performance should include the ludic/playful and humorous functions of language. Making jokes and being witty and creative with language presupposes a reasonably high level of second language performance. Yet, many second language learners, despite their high proficiency, do not feel comfortable and/or capable of understanding and using the genres of language play and humor. Such students, like the ones in this study, had received L2 instruction, but the genres of language play and humor were neglected in the L2 curriculum. This is likely because, as Block (2003: 73–4) argues, many second language acquisition researchers and teachers following the input–interaction–output model:

> have managed to get themselves in a quandary: they want a conceptualisation of what people do with language that is grounded in the real world, but they do not seem willing to take on the fact that in the real world, there is play as well as work.

Moreover, when there is work there is also the establishment, maintenance, and strengthening of social ties. Such social processes have, as argued by Carter and McCarthy (2004), many instances of linguistic creativity in the form of language play and humor. It follows then that allowing students to only participate in tasks that will evoke transactional communication and information exchange, will not equip them completely for socialization and participation in the second language community. Furthermore, one of the students in an earlier pilot study, Mark, reported: 'I told the jock [joke] to my fellow student and he laughed so I think that I am not so bad jocks [joke] teller', a quote which shows that he is confident about the use of L2 in actual social interaction and that he felt pleased with himself for being able to engage in real-life humorous discourse.

In light of the findings of this study, it can be said that the examination of language-based aspects of humor is a rewarding area of study for second language learners and researchers. By investigating linguistic humor, students not only understand examples of humor, but they also learn new language and can gain insights into how the second language and culture work, and become equipped to tell jokes, riddles, or puns to others if they wish to do so. The students gained the opportunity to participate in the play as well as the work of their second language. The inclusion of humor in the L2 curriculum can be a daunting and intimidating task for both second language teachers and students. However, as noted above, much humor is deeply embedded in language, which prompts Medgyes (2002: 5) to suggest that '[w]e can use the language to make humor accessible for students and, conversely, use humor to make language accessible'. Furthermore, teachers can explain culturally appropriate responses to puns and riddles.

The greatest pedagogical challenge lies in finding material exemplifying language play that suits the specific needs of the students. The data from this study suggest that it may also be a question of allowing students time for playful manipulation of language, and providing discussion time with peers to work out the 'linguistic puzzle' by themselves.

Appendix

Transcription conventions

Layout	Turns are numbered consecutively.
	Indented turn: overlapping speech
-	Incomplete utterances
.	Turn completed
?!	Interrogative or exclamatory intention
CAPS	Emphasis
italics	Acquired knowledge
underlying	Overlapping speech
[ ]	Comments/clarification and/or descriptions of relevant behaviour
[=]	Glossary
' '	Utterances read from text
xx	Indecipherable speech
( )	Unclear speech but which is most likely what is written inside the brackets
R	Researcher
Other initials	Students

PART TWO

Feedback, learner-internal processes, and perceptions in interaction

7

How effective are recasts? The role of attention, memory, and analytical ability

PAVEL TROFIMOVICH, AHLEM AMMAR, and ELIZABETH GATBONTON

Introduction

Language is a complex cognitive skill, and its complete mastery requires extended amounts of experience and practice. (For review, see Tomasello 1998.) Learning a second (or subsequent) language is clearly no exception. Indeed, second language (L2) learners' speech and writing are often characterized by a great number of errors (Lightbown and Spada 1990; 1994). These errors reveal the complex nature of L2 learning and suggest that many learners may fall short of native-like L2 mastery (DeKeyser 2000), often notwithstanding what are believed to be the 'optimal' conditions for L2 development: availability of comprehensible input and an emphasis on the communication of meaning (Long 1996; Gass 2003). Why are some learners unable to take advantage of their exposure to often rich, contextualized, and meaningful input? In the study reported in this chapter, we sought to explain learners' difficulties in L2 learning in terms of individual differences, those related to learners' attention, memory, and language aptitude. To this end, we examined the role of four cognitive processing factors—phonological memory, working memory, attention control, and analytical ability—in determining the effectiveness of recasts. Our goal was to examine the extent to which individual differences influence learners' ability to notice and benefit from recasts.

Recasts and L2 development

Defined as discourse moves that 'rephrase [a learner's] utterance by changing one or more sentence components [...] while still referring to its central meanings' (Long 1996: 434), recasts are believed to promote L2 development in the context of meaningful interaction. As argued by Long in his discussion of the Interaction Hypothesis (Long 1996), recasts are considered to be effective in promoting L2 development because they (as well as other types of interactional feedback) often occur in reaction to communication breakdowns in L2 interaction. In such cases, recasts are believed to offer learners both negative feedback (by reformulating a non-target utterance) and positive input (by modeling the intended targetlike utterance) about their problematic production (Leeman 2003). Recasts appear to promote L2 development, at least in part, because they draw learners' attention to the discrepancy (the 'gap') between the target linguistic system and the learners' own conception of it (Rutherford and Sharwood Smith 1985; Schmidt 1990; 2001; Long 1991), precisely at the time when learners are negotiating for meaning. Often described as an ideal interactional feedback technique (Long 2006, but see Lyster 1998b), recasts are appealing because, first, they are implicit and unobtrusive (i.e. they highlight the error without breaking the flow of communication) and, second, they are learner-centered (i.e. their use is contingent on the meaning that the learner is trying to communicate). In fact, recasts appear to be one of the most common interactional moves documented in both L1 discourse (Hirsch-Pasek, Treiman, and Schneiderman 1984; Demetras, Post, and Snow 1986) and in L2 communication (Lyster and Ranta 1997; Braidi 2002).

One question central to the Interaction Hypothesis pertains to investigating the effectiveness of recasts in promoting L2 development. To date, two approaches have largely been used to answer this question. The first approach has been to document the extent to which learners notice recasts. Measuring the 'noticeability' of recasts is important because the outcomes of interactional modification, triggered by recasts, might crucially depend on learners' noticing either the negative feedback or the positive input (or perhaps both) available in recasts. (See Leeman 2003 for further details on this issue.) Several studies have looked at the noticeability of recasts, measuring this construct in terms of learners' modified responses (incorporations) following recasts (Mackey and Philp 1998; Braidi 2002), learners' retrospective recall (Mackey, Gass, and McDonough 2000; Mackey, Philp, Egi, Fujii, and Tatsumi 2002), cued immediate recall (Philp 2003), and their online visually cued discrimination accuracy (Ammar, Trofimovich, and Gatbonton 2006). The second approach to investigating the effectiveness of recasts has been to examine either the immediate or delayed benefits of recasting for learners' accuracy in the context of L2 interaction. The studies that have used this approach overall have documented positive effects of recasting on L2 development (Doughty and Varela 1998; Long, Inagaki, and Ortega 1998; Mackey and Philp 1998; Leeman 2003; Ammar and Spada 2006).

The effectiveness of recasts, however, appears to be qualified by several factors. One factor is the linguistic structure targeted by recasts. Thus, for example, learners (particularly those at a low proficiency level) have been shown to notice fewer morphosyntactic than lexical errors targeted by recasts (Mackey *et al.* 2000; Ammar *et al.* 2006) and to benefit more from recasts targeting some L2 structures than others (Long *et al.* 1998). Another factor is the learners' L2 proficiency level. For example, high and intermediate proficiency learners appear more likely than low proficiency learners to notice recasts (Philp 2003) and to modify their production in response to them (Mackey and Philp 1998; Ammar and Spada 2006). More importantly for the purposes of this study, learners' ability to notice recasts also appears to depend on their phonological and working memory, the only cognitive factors investigated to date in the context of L2 interaction. Mackey *et al.* (2002) showed that learners with larger working and phonological memory spans tend to be more likely to notice recasts than learners with smaller spans. No study known to us has to date examined whether cognitive (processing) factors, those related to learners' attention, memory, and language aptitude, also influence learners' ability to benefit from recasts.

Taken together, the findings reported above reveal possible constraints on the effectiveness of recasts, thereby suggesting some limitations of recasting as an interactional feedback technique. More importantly, these findings underscore the importance of research into the effectiveness of recasts as a function of individual differences, not only differences in learners' age (Mackey and Oliver 2002) and proficiency (Philp 2003) but also possibly those in learners' attention, memory, and language aptitude. This research agenda is compatible with recent calls to relate L2 development to cognitive processes underlying it. (For a review, see Robinson 2002a.) The purpose of the study reported in this chapter was therefore to investigate the extent to which learners notice and benefit from recasts as a function of four cognitive factors: phonological memory, working memory, attention control, and analytical ability.

Cognitive factors and recasts

The choice of the factors investigated here in relation to learners' ability to notice and benefit from recasts was prompted by their likely involvement in L2 learning, particularly in the context of oral interaction. In his information-processing model, Skehan (2002) describes several L2 acquisition stages and identifies the cognitive processing skills required at each stage. According to Skehan, *noticing* (Stage 1) calls for skills in auditory speech segmentation, attention management, working memory, and phonemic coding. In turn, *pattern identification* (Stage 2) draws on working memory skills and grammatical sensitivity (analytical ability). If learners' processing of recasts entails the ability to notice, identify, and compare patterns of language, then the skills associated with the noticing and pattern identification processing should determine the degree to which learners can notice and ultimately benefit from recasts.

How can the cognitive factors underlying the noticing and pattern identification stages in Skehan's framework—working memory, phonological memory, analytical ability, and attention control—influence the degree to which recasts are noticed and used? The first of these factors, working memory, underlies an individual's ability to simultaneously process and store verbal information relevant to the processing task at hand. (For a review, see Miyake and Friedman 1998.) In previous research, working memory has been shown to relate to learners' performance on tests of L2 grammar, vocabulary, and reading (Harrington and Sawyer 1992) as well as to learners' oral ability (Geva and Ryan 1993). In the context of L2 interaction, working memory may delimit the amount of verbal information learners can simultaneously attend to, thus defining the extent to which recasts are registered (Mackey *et al.* 2002), processed, and ultimately acted upon.

The second factor, phonological memory, refers to an individual's capacity to retain spoken sequences temporarily in a short-term memory store. This capacity is usually associated with the 'phonological loop', a subcomponent of the human working memory system responsible for temporary storage of verbal-acoustic information. (For a review, see Baddeley, Gathercole, and Papagno 1998.) Phonological memory has been found to be a strong predictor of learners' ability to repeat (Service 1992) and eventually learn (Gathercole and Baddeley 1990) new words, suggesting that there is a causal relationship between phonological memory and L2 vocabulary learning. Other evidence has implicated phonological memory in L2 grammar development as well. O'Brien, Segalowitz, Collentine, and Freed (2006), for example, demonstrated that phonological memory explained 16 per cent of the unique variance in L2 Spanish learners' use of grammar in spoken narratives. (See also N. Ellis and Sinclair 1996.) In the context of L2 interaction, phonological memory may influence the degree to which learners are able to encode and retain, in their short-term phonological memory store, the information available in recasts and to make this information available for further analysis.

The third factor, analytical ability, typically describes an individual's sensitivity to grammatical structure. (See Skehan 2002 for a review.) Several studies have to date reported associations between analytical ability and L2 development. Harley and Hart (1997) found that analytical ability was significantly associated with adolescent learners' L2 proficiency measures, including morphosyntactic accuracy rates. Similarly, Ranta (2002) and DeKeyser (2000) both reported a link between morphosyntactic development and analytical ability in younger and older learners, respectively. If analytical ability has a role to play in L2 interaction, it likely defines learners' capacity to identify and focus on the structural properties of their own speech and the speech addressed to them (for example, in the form of a recast). This capacity may affect learners' success in noticing the elements targeted by a recast and, ultimately, in benefiting from this information.

The final factor examined here in relation to learners' ability to notice and benefit from recasts is attention control, or the ability to efficiently allocate attention among different aspects of language or different cognitive processing tasks. (For a general review, see Schmidt 2001.) As a cognitive construct, attention control involves a number of functions associated with a variety of neurobiological structures (Posner 1995). When applied to language, attention control may refer to enhanced processing of the linguistic stimuli that are relevant to the task at hand and to inhibited processing of the stimuli that are irrelevant to it (Eviatar 1998). Attention control may also refer to an individual's ability to shift attention efficiently among different sets of linguistic relationships (Talmy 1996). In one study that established a link between linguistic attention control and L2 proficiency, Segalowitz and Frenkiel-Fishman (2005) showed that English-French bilinguals' ability to efficiently allocate attention between two sets of linguistic targets (temporal versus causal) in their L2 explained 32 per cent of the unique variance in these same bilinguals' French (L2) proficiency (defined as efficient lexical access). In other words, these bilinguals' ability to efficiently switch attention among several aspects of their L2 had an independent contribution to predicting the same bilinguals' L2 proficiency. In the context of L2 interaction, attention control may influence how well learners can attend to different aspects of linguistic information available in a recast or how well learners can switch their attention among different cognitive tasks in which they are (nearly) simultaneously engaged (for example, perceiving a recast and subsequently encoding their own message). In either case, efficient attention control should lead to learners' ability to notice and benefit from recasts.

The present study

To examine whether learners' ability to notice and benefit from recasts depends on individual differences in learners' working memory, phonological memory, analytical ability, and attention control, we tested Francophone learners of English as a second language (ESL) on several tasks. First, the learners performed an online picture description task. In this task, they described simple drawings whose descriptions elicited a particular feature of the L2 (described below). They heard corrective feedback (recast) about each description, indicated whether they noticed the feature targeted by the recast, and described each drawing again. Because learners' ability to notice and benefit from recasts might be related to the type of L2 feature targeted by a recast (Mackey *et al.* 2000), we used three types of L2 features as targets: morphosyntactic (English possessive determiners), lexical (intransitive verbs), or both (transitive verbs followed by a possessive determiner/noun combination). Because it is important to assess the effectiveness of recasts as a function of when learners receive it (Mackey and Philp 1998), we tested learners immediately after the recast was heard (in the immediate turn) and after a 2–12 minute delay. Following the treatment and tests, the learners then completed four more tests: (1) a test of phonological memory measuring phonemic coding skills, (2) a test of working memory measuring the executive function of working memory, (3) a test of attention control measuring executive attention management, and (4) a test of analytical ability measuring grammatical sensitivity.

Because phonological memory, working memory, analytical ability, and attention control are complex cognitive constructs, representing a cluster of different processing skills (see Robinson 2002a for a review), we hypothesized that learners with relatively larger phonological memory, more extensive working memory spans, more efficient attention control, and stronger analytical ability would be more likely to notice the feature targeted by the recasts, and to use the recast form in subsequent picture descriptions than learners with weaker attention, memory, and analytical ability skills. The assumption was that learners with weaker attention, memory, and analytical ability would have difficulties in processing and encoding incoming information in the recasts in memory, in efficiently switching their attention among different aspects of language or among several cognitive tasks (for example, perceiving a message and encoding their own message), and in focusing on the structural properties of their own speech and the speech addressed to them.

Method

Participants

no control group w/ no recasts?

The participants in this study were 32 adult Francophones (24 females, eight males) residing in Québec (mean age: 30.4, range: 19–54). All were native speakers of French who were born and raised in monolingual French homes in France (four) or in Québec (28). All had received primary and secondary education in French and all reported using French as the only home language. With the exception of three, whose first exposure to English occurred in their early 20s or 30s, the participants started learning English as children at an average age of 9.7 as part of primary ESL instruction in Québec, and had studied English on average 45 minutes per week in elementary school, 75 minutes per week in high school, and 180 minutes per week in junior college. Prior to testing, the participants (henceforth, the learners) estimated their daily use of French and English on a 0–100 per cent scale. These self-ratings indicated that the learners on an average daily basis used French 86 per cent of the time (range: 50–100, $SD = 5.3$) and English the other 14 per cent of the time (range: 0–80, $SD = 3.2$).

A speaking task was administered to obtain a measure of the learners' L2 proficiency. In this task, the learners spoke extemporaneously for about two minutes in English in response to a simple prompt ('Talk about one frightening experience in your life.'). The learners were recorded using a Sony TCM-200DV portable recorder; their speech was later transcribed. Three measures were derived from the recorded samples. Speech rate, a fluency measure, was calculated by dividing the number of uttered words by the total duration of the sample, which included pauses and hesitations, yielding a speech rate ratio (words per second). Durations were measured to the nearest millisecond from the display of digital speech-analysis software (*CoolEdit 2000*). Proportions of lexicosemantic and morphosyntactic errors were the two accuracy measures, computed by dividing the number of words containing an error of each type by the total number of words in the sample. Errors in sentence structure, morphology, and syntax (for example, article use, word order, tense/aspect) were classified as morphosyntactic errors. Inappropriately used lexical items (including French words) were classified as lexical errors.

Results of these analyses revealed that the learners on average produced 24 words (18 per cent) containing errors (*SD*: 19.4; range: 4–77) and spoke at an average rate of 1.5 words per second (*SD*: .60; range: .53–2.82). Of the total number of words containing errors, 11 words (seven per cent) on average contained morphosyntactic errors (*SD*: 8.31; range: 1–36), 13 words (11 per cent) contained lexicosemantic errors (*SD*: 13.04; range: 1–52). The accuracy scores (number of words with each error type over the total number of words) ranged from .02–.14 (*SD* = .03) for morphosyntactic errors and from 0–.48 (*SD* = .12) for lexicosemantic errors. These accuracy scores suggested that the learners represented a range of L2 ability levels.

Tasks

The testing, which lasted approximately 90 minutes, was conducted individually in a quiet location using a personal computer. The researcher, a French–English bilingual, gave testing instructions in French. The learners performed several tasks (described in detail below). A schematic representation of the tasks used appears in Figure 7.1.

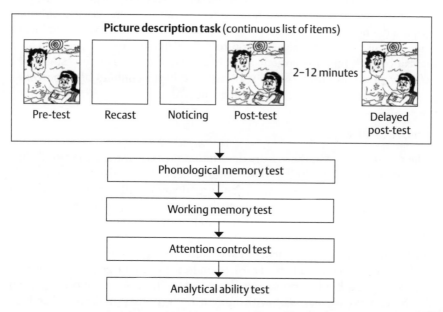

Figure 7.1 Schematic representation of the tasks used in this study

Picture description

Operationalization

Recasts are defined as reformulations of learners' non-targetlike utterances that are contingent on learners' errors (Long 1996; Mackey and Philp 1998). However, the design of the running picture description task used in this study required that the learners receive digitally recorded native speaker responses after all of the learners' picture descriptions, which ranged in accuracy from 4–85 per cent correct ($SD = 22$). Thus, for example, if the learners made an error in their picture description (*'He is scratching the back'), the response ('Yeah, he is scratching his back') 'acted' as a recast targeting an erroneous production. However, if the learners produced the expected picture description accurately ('He is scratching his back'), the response was effectively a repetition of their targetlike production. To ensure that the results of this study are comparable to previously reported findings (c.f., Mackey and Philp 1998), in the critical analyses conducted as part of this study (i.e. analyses of recast noticeability), we distinguished between the provided native speaker responses that were 'true' recasts and those that were repetitions. In other words, the data reported below were computed for each individual learner, where appropriate, as proportions based on the total number of that learner's *non-target utterances* only. By definition, then, the responses given to learners in these cases (in reply to their non-target utterances) were recasts. Although recasts defined in this way may not fully generalize to reactive, spontaneous language use in the course of person-to-person interaction (a point which we revisit below), this conceptualization of recasts allowed us to investigate the effectiveness and noticeability of recasts within the confines of a controlled laboratory-based language processing study.

Task materials

The materials used in the picture description task consisted of 96 simple line drawings depicting members of two families, each consisting of one male and one female child, their parents and grandparents, all engaged in ordinary daily activities such as playing, eating, brushing teeth, etc. Of these 96 drawings, 48 were designated as experimental drawings and 48 as distractors. The 48 critical items were constructed by pairing each experimental drawing with a question-recast sequence. There were three types of linguistic targets: 24 grammar targets, 12 lexical targets, and 12 'mixed' targets. The grammar targets elicited English possessive determiners ('his', 'her'; henceforth PDs) in the context of their use with human body parts ('his head', 'her leg') and with kin-different animate nouns ('his mother', 'her brother'), with 12 items in each set ('He is washing his face', 'She is talking to her brother'). These contexts represented the cases of PD use that are most problematic for Francophone learners of English (White 1998). PDs agree in gender and number with the determined noun (*sa mère* ['his mother'], *sa* = fem.) in French (Grevisse 1993). By contrast, in English they agree with the possessor ('his mother', 'his' = masc.) and are invariant in the number and gender of the noun they determine (Quirk, Greenbaum, Leech, and Svarvik 1972). The 12 lexical targets elicited English intransitive verbs ('She is yawning'). The 12 'mixed' targets elicited English transitive verbs (lexical targets) in conjunction with PDs (grammar targets) used with human body parts ('He is scratching his back'). The three linguistic targets and sample question-recast sequences used with each target appear in Table 7.1. The distractors were comparable line drawings that elicited English transitive verbs ('She is reading a book') and English PDs used with kin-same animate nouns ('He is playing with his brother'), a context in which PD use in English and French overlaps.

Item type	Materials	
	Question	Recast
Grammar (body parts)	What is he washing?	Yeah, he is washing his face.
Grammar (kin-different)	Who is she talking to?	Yeah, she is talking to her brother.
Lexical	What is she doing?	Yeah, she is yawning.
Mixed	What is he doing?	Yeah, he is scratching his back.
Distractor (kin-same)	Who is she playing with?	

Table 7.1 Sample item materials used in the picture description task

Task procedure

The questions and recasts associated with each drawing were digitally recorded by a male native English speaker. Each of the 48 critical items (drawings and sound files), 48 distractors, and 24 repeated critical items (discussed below) were organized in a continuous randomized list of four–event sequences, presented using the DMDX software developed by K. I. Forster and J. C. Forster at the University of Arizona. There were four such randomized 120-item experimental lists to which learners were assigned randomly. (See Figure 7.2 for a schematic representation of a sample sequence. The example depicted in Figure 7.2 illustrates a four–event sequence for a kin-different grammar target.)

The first event in each sequence was a *pre-test*. Here the learners saw a drawing and, approximately 2.5 seconds after it appeared on the screen, heard a question about the drawing ('Who is he swimming with?') to which they had to respond using a simple sentence, which could be either correct ('He is swimming with his daughter') or incorrect (*'He is swimming with her daughter'). The drawing was displayed for five seconds. The second event was a *recast*. Here the learners heard the expected picture description ('He is swimming with his daughter'). The third event was *noticing*. Here the learners were prompted to indicate, by saying 'yes' or 'no', whether they noticed any difference between their own original description and the description played back to them ('Did you notice any difference? Please say yes or no'). The fourth event was a *post-test* in which the learners saw the same drawing again and heard the same question to which they had to respond again using a simple sentence.

The final event in each sequence was a *delayed post-test*. Twenty-four critical items (six items randomly selected from each linguistic target set, resulting in 24 unique items in each of the four 120-item lists) were designated to be repeated and used as delayed post-test. These items (drawings and sound files) appeared again after at least four but no more than 24 intervening items (i.e. with a 2–12 minute delay, on average) following their original presentation. Here the learners saw the drawing and described it in response to the question heard (Figure 7.2). Both the post-test and the delayed post-test were included to examine the extent to which the learners were able to 'act' on their noticing of the recast heard, that is, to be able to use the correct form provided in the reformulation. The 48 distractors, representing picture descriptions not followed by a recast and a noticing question, were randomly inserted between critical items.

Figure 7.2 Schematic representation of a sample sequence in the picture description task

Prior to testing, the learners were familiarized with the family relationships of the characters depicted in the drawings. All learners were able to pass a simple test in which they were asked to name the relationships ('brother', 'mother', etc.) among the family members. The learners were then informed that they were taking part in a picture description experiment. Their task was to give a one-sentence description of each drawing in response to the auditorily presented question and, for the critical items, to indicate (by saying 'yes' or 'no') whether they noticed any difference between their picture descriptions and those that they had just heard. The learners initiated each subsequent trial by pressing the space bar on the computer keyboard. The entire session was recorded (using a Sony TCM-200DV portable recorder) and later analyzed.

Data coding

Four measures were derived for each learner in the picture description task. Three were measures of production accuracy, defined for each learner as the proportion of correctly produced linguistic targets of the same type (grammar, lexical, mixed). These scores were calculated separately for the drawings presented in pre-tests, post-tests, and delayed post-tests. A picture description was scored as '1' if the learner produced the correct PD-noun combination (in response to grammar targets), the verb (in response to lexical targets), or both (in response to mixed targets), and was scored as '0' if the learner failed to do so. Errors unrelated to the linguistic targets were disregarded. A score of '0.5' was assigned to a picture description (in response to mixed targets) if the learner produced correctly only the verb or the PD-noun combination, but not both ('He is cleaning his teeth' or 'He is brushing the teeth' in place of 'He is brushing his teeth'). The fourth measure was the proportion of noticing, computed by dividing, for each learner, the number of correctly detected non-target descriptions by the total number of non-target descriptions. Non-target descriptions were defined as those that mismatched the provided description by the linguistic target only (PD, verb, or both). In other words, the descriptions that mismatched the expected descriptions in any other way (i.e. by a form that was not targeted in this study or by *more than one* form) were not considered in the calculation of the noticing score. These descriptions were excluded because the noticing responses based on such descriptions could not be unambiguously attributed to accurate detection of the targeted error only. The proportions of non-target descriptions ranged between .15 and .96 (*SD* = .22) for individual learners.

Phonological memory

A serial non-word recognition task was used as a measure of phonological memory. A non-word recognition task, as opposed to widely used non-word repetition tasks or recall tasks involving words and non-words, appears to minimize lexical (vocabulary knowledge) influences on phonological memory, yielding a relatively accurate estimate of phonological memory. (For theoretical justifications, see Gathercole, Pickering, Hall, and Peaker 2001.) English non-words (i.e. non-words that adhered to English phonotactics) were used in this task to assess the learners' ability to encode and temporarily access auditory sequences in their L2. In this task, the learners judged whether two consecutively presented sequences of pronounceable English non-words were in the same or in a different order.

Task materials

The materials consisted of 160 one-syllable CVC non-words taken from Gathercole *et al.* (2001). The non-words were digitally recorded by a male native English speaker. They were organized into sequences of four, five, six, and seven items. There were four pairs of non-word sequences of four items, and eight pairs of non-word sequences of five, six, and seven items in each, for a total of 28 pairs of non-word sequences. All items within a sequence had a different vowel sound, and the consonant composition within each sequence was as distinctive as possible. Half of the sequence pairs of each length contained identical sequences. That is, the second sequence in each pair was identical to the first sequence (for example, 'loog jahl deech kerm meb ... loog jahl deech kerm meb', where ellipses indicate a short pause). The other half of the sequence pairs of each length contained different sequences. Although the items within the two sequences were identical, one pair of items was transposed in the second sequence, with the constraint that the first and last pair of items were never transposed (for example, 'lod tudge jick norb garm ... lod tudge norb jick garm'). This constraint reduced the salience of transposed items and encouraged the learners to process the complete stimulus sequence. The location of the transposed pair was varied randomly across sequence lengths.

Task procedure

The 28 non-word sequences were presented using speech presentation software (Smith 1997) over computer speakers, with the four four-item sequence pairs presented first, the eight five-item sequence pairs presented next, followed by the eight six-item sequence pairs and, finally, the eight seven-item sequence pairs. The non-words were presented at the rate of one item every 800 milliseconds, with a 1.5 second pause between the two sequences in each pair. Upon hearing each sequence pair, the learner indicated, by clicking one of the buttons labeled 'same order' and 'different order' on the computer screen, whether the two sequences were presented in the same or a different order. The learners had unlimited time to provide their judgment but were not permitted to replay the sequence or to change their response. Before testing, the learners were given two same and two different sequence pairs as practice. The number of correct responses (out of 28) was recorded and used as a measure of phonological memory.

Working memory

The learners' working memory was assessed using the Letter–Number Sequencing subtest from the Wechsler Adult Intelligence Scale—WAIS-III (Psychological Corporation 1997). Because this task, validated in both normal and brain-injured populations (Donders, Tulsky, and Zhu 2001), presumably requires the learners to manipulate information online, the task is sensitive to measuring the processing and executive aspects of working memory (Myerson, Emery, White, and Hale 2003). In this test, the learners heard a series of numbers and letters and then recalled the numbers in numerical order followed by the letters in alphabetical order. This task was administered in the learners' L1 (French) because working memory capacity likely represents a general (as opposed to language-specific) ability to simultaneously store and process incoming information (Osaka, Osaka, and Groner 1993).

Task materials and procedure

The stimuli consisted of French letters (A–Z) and digits (1–9), digitally recorded by a female native French speaker. The digits and letters were organized into sequences of two to eight items, with three sequences of each length, for a total of 21 sequences. The 21 letter–digit sequences were presented using speech presentation software (Smith 1997) over computer speakers. The three two-item sequences (one number, one letter) were presented first (for example, *L … deux* [two]), followed by the three sequences at each consecutive length, with the three eight-item sequences (four numbers, four letters) presented last (for example, *cinq* [five] … *H* … *neuf* [nine] … *S* … *deux* [two] … *N* … *huit* [eight] … *A*). The digits and letters were presented at the rate of approximately one per second. Upon hearing each sequence, the learner had to report the presented sequence orally first by naming the digits in ascending numerical order followed by the letters in alphabetical order. For example, the expected responses for the sample sequences given above were *deux … L* and *deux … cinq … huit … neuf … A … H … N … S*. The test continued until the learner failed to produce the correct response for all three trials of a given sequence length. The number of correct responses (out of 21) was recorded and used as a measure of working memory.

Attention control

Task materials and procedure

The Trail Making Test, originally designed as part of the US Army Individual Test Battery (1944), was used to estimate attention control. The test appears to provide a language-neutral estimate of an individual's ability to shift attention between two sets of stimuli (Lee, Cheung, Chan, and Chan 2000). The test consists of two parts and involves drawing a line to connect consecutive digits from 1 to 25 (1—2—3—4—5—6, etc.) in Part A and drawing a similar line to connect alternating digits and letters (1—A—2—B—3—C, etc.) in Part B. Assuming that the time it takes to complete a non-alternating digit sequence (Part A) provides the baseline for each individual's motor and visual control, the additional cost imposed on the individual by the alternating digit–letter sequence (Part B) provides a measure of this individual's executive control, or the ability to switch attention between two stimulus sequences. In other words, the difference in completion time between Part B and Part

A of the test is indicative of the individual's attentional control of switching between different stimuli (Corrigan and Hinkeldey 1987) and between different cognitive tasks (Arbuthnott and Frank 2000).

For all learners, Part B of the test followed Part A, each preceded by an eight-item practice session. The completion times for both parts of the test were measured using a digital stopwatch and were recorded in seconds, with the values rounded to the nearest one hundredth of a second. The difference in completion times between Part B and Part A of the test, which were moderately correlated ($r = .48$, $p = .005$), was used as a measure of attention control. A smaller score, corresponding to a smaller difference in completion time between Part B and Part A of the test, represented more efficient attention control.

Analytical ability

Task materials and procedure

Analytical ability was assessed using Part IV of the Modern Language Aptitude Test (Carroll and Sapon 1958, French translation). The French version of the test was used to obtain a measure of analytical ability that was independent of L2 knowledge. Part IV of the test assesses the ability to understand the function of words and phrases in sentences, a measure of what is often termed as sensitivity to grammatical structure or capacity to focus on the structural properties of linguistic input (Ranta 2002; Skehan 2002). In this test, the learners read 31 pairs of sentences (*Ottawa est la capitale du Canada* [Ottawa is the capital of Canada], *Elle aime aller pêcher en Gaspésie* [She likes to go fishing in Gaspésie]) and indicated, by circling the appropriate choice, which of the underlined words in the second sentence (*Elle*) performed the same grammatical function as the underlined word in the first (*Ottawa*). The number of correct responses (out of 31) was used as a measure of analytical ability.

Results

For all analyses reported below, the alpha level for significance was set at .05 and was adjusted for multiple comparisons, where appropriate, using the Bonferroni correction. The reported effect sizes are partial eta squared (η_p^2), calculated by dividing the effect sum of squares by the effect sum of squares plus the error sum of squares.

Noticeability of recasts

The learners' noticing scores for each set of linguistic targets (grammar, lexical, mixed) were submitted to a one-way repeated-measures analysis of variance (ANOVA), which yielded a significant F ratio, $F(2, 62) = 8.27$,

p <.001, η_p^2 = .21. Tests exploring the significant F ratio (Bonferroni corrected α = .017) revealed that the learners were statistically significantly more accurate at detecting a mismatch in lexical than in grammar targets following recasts (p < .001). There was also a tendency for the learners to be more accurate at detecting a mismatch in the mixed than in the grammar targets following recasts. This latter difference was, however, not significant after the Bonferroni correction (p = .032). These findings suggest that, when the learners made errors and then received recasts, they detected fewer morphosyntactic than lexical (verb) mismatches between their own descriptions and those provided to them. The learners' mean noticing accuracy is summarized in Table 7.2.

Target	Number of targets	Range of recasts received	Noticing accuracy	Range of noticing accuracy
Grammar	24	0–23	84.84 (19.31)	41–100
Lexical	12	4–12	96.94 (06.53)	73–100
Mixed	12	0–12	92.66 (12.62)	50–100

Table 7.2 Number of linguistic targets, ranges of recasts received, means and ranges of noticing accuracy (per cent correct) as a function of target (standard deviations appear in parentheses)

Effects of recasts

The learners' production accuracy was submitted to a two-way repeated-measures ANOVA with test (pre-test, post-test, delayed post-test) and target (grammar, lexical, mixed) as within-subjects factors. This analysis yielded significant main effects of test, $F(2, 62)$ = 186.30, p < .0001, η_p^2 = .86, and target, $F(2, 62)$ = 24.55, p < .0001, η_p^2 = .44, and a significant interaction, $F(4, 124)$ = 28.66, p < .0001, η_p^2 = .48. Tests of simple main effects conducted to explore the significant interaction (Bonferroni corrected α = .002) revealed that, for all targets (grammar, lexical, mixed), the learners were statistically significantly more accurate on the post-test than on the pre-test and the delayed post-test, and that they were statistically significantly more accurate on the delayed post-test than on the pre-test (all ps < .0001). This finding suggests that, regardless of the target, the learners overall benefited from a recast immediately after it was given (on the post-test) and sustained this benefit over a short delay (on the delayed post-test).

Tests of simple main effects also revealed that the obtained significant target × test interaction was due to different accuracy rates on the pre-test. On the pre-test, the learners were statistically significantly more accurate at producing grammar targets than they were at producing lexical and mixed targets. The learners were also statistically significantly more accurate at producing mixed targets than they were at producing lexical targets (ps < .0001). This finding suggests that prior to receiving a recast, the learners were more accurate at correctly using English PDs in their picture descriptions than they were at using verbs. This finding likely reflected the learners' initial unfamiliarity with the (relatively low-frequency) verbs used as lexical and mixed targets ('slide', 'scratch', 'pluck', 'parachute', 'barbecue', 'yawn', etc.). The learners' mean production accuracy is summarized in Table 7.3.

Target	Tests		
	Pre-test	Post-test	Delayed post-test
Grammar	71.50 (26.89)	88.63 (21.34)	80.11 (25.51)
Lexical	27.94 (17.25)	85.00 (18.32)	68.87 (31.08)
Mixed	42.59 (21.03)	86.87 (21.77)	66.25 (29.10)

Table 7.3 Mean accuracy (per cent correct) for picture description as a function of target (standard deviations appear in parentheses)

The preceding analyses indicated that the learners in this study were overall able to detect the corrective nature of feedback received and to benefit from such feedback targeting both lexical and morphosyntactic errors in their speech. However, the noticing and production data analyzed thus far were characterized by a large amount of individual variability (see *SD* values in Tables 7.2 and 7.3). Indeed, the individual learners' production accuracy (regardless of the target type) ranged from a minimum of 0 to a maximum of 100 per cent correct. Although the variation in noticing was smaller by far, these scores nevertheless spanned a 27–59 per cent range, from a low of 41 to a high of 100 per cent accurate detection of mismatched (erroneous) targets following recasts. The next analyses were therefore conducted to explain individual variability in the learners' ability to notice and benefit from recasts, using measures of phonological memory, working memory, attention control, and analytical ability as predictors.

Cognitive factors and the noticeability and effects of recasts

To explore the relationship between the learners' ability to notice and benefit from recasts and their individual differences in attention, memory, and language aptitude, zero-order correlations were computed between the learners' noticing and production scores, on the one hand, and their phonological memory, working memory, attention control, and analytical ability measures, on the other. Because a large number of correlations were computed, the alpha level for significance was adjusted using the Bonferroni correction. Summaries of these analyses for noticing and production appear in Table 7.4 and Table 7.5, respectively.

Target	Predictor variables			
	Phonological memory	Working memory	Attention control	Analytical ability
Grammar	-.03	.19	-.13	.22
Lexical	-.10	.16	-.32	.38
Mixed	-.34	-.06	-.30	.44

Table 7.4 Summary of correlation analyses between predictor variables and noticing scores as a function of target

The first set of correlation analyses explored the relationship between the learners' noticing scores and the four predictor factors (Bonferroni corrected $\alpha = .004$). As seen in Table 7.4, there were no significant associations between the learners' noticing scores and any of the four factors examined. This finding likely reflects the relative salience of the interactional feedback received (focused on all types of targets) in the context of the picture description task. This salience may have minimized the need for the learners to rely, in their processing of recasts, on attention, memory, and language aptitude in order to notice the targeted error. Another possibility is that the task used here to measure noticing did not draw heavily on the learners' processing resources; thus, it did not allow us to detect the influence of the examined cognitive (processing) factors on the learners' ability to notice recasts.

The next set of correlation analyses explored the relationship between the learners' production accuracy and the four predictor factors (Bonferroni corrected $\alpha = .0013$). These analyses revealed several findings. (See Table 7.5.) First, there was a relatively strong and significant negative association between the learners' attention control and their accuracy at producing targets on the pre-test (for grammar targets), on the post-test (for mixed targets), and on the delayed post-test (for all targets). That is, higher production accuracy was related to more flexible executive attention control, conceptualized as a lower cost (hence, negative correlation) incurred due to the alternation between digits and letters in Part B of the attention control test. Second, there was a relatively strong and significant positive association between the learners' analytical ability and their accuracy at producing grammar targets on the delayed post-test. That is, higher production accuracy on grammar targets was related to better analytical skills, conceptualized as the ability to focus on structural properties of language. Third, the associations between the learners' phonological and working memory and their production accuracy were weak and non-significant. Finally, significant associations were obtained (in large part) for production accuracy on the delayed post-test rather than on the post-test. This last finding is indicative of a greater demand on processing resources in situations when interactional feedback or other sources of positive and negative evidence are not available for immediate processing. Also, it is noteworthy that the four predictor factors were not correlated with one another ($ps > .06$), suggesting that the four cognitive dimensions measured in this study represented separable constructs. In addition, the four predictor factors were not correlated with any of the proficiency scores ($ps > .31$) obtained in a separate task (lexicosemantic and morphosyntactic accuracy scores, speech rate). This finding indicated that the four cognitive (processing) factors were associated only with the learners' accuracy rates in the picture description task and were not predictive of their overall L2 proficiency at the time of testing.

Target	Predictor variables			
	Phonological memory	Working memory	Attention control	Analytical ability
Pre-test				
Grammar	.30	.27	-.55**	.44
Lexical	.25	.12	-.17	.07
Mixed	.41	.26	-.44	.35
Post-test				
Grammar	.36	.34	-.51	.47
Lexical	.23	.38	-.37	.21
Mixed	.26	.48	-.66***	.45
Delayed post-test				
Grammar	.41	.28	-.60***	.55**
Lexical	.11	.22	-.55**	.20
Mixed	.24	.27	-.56**	.52

Asterisks identify correlation coefficients that remained significant after a Bonferroni correction ($\alpha = .0013$). **$p < .001$ ***$p < .0001$, two-tailed

Table 7.5 Summary of correlation analyses between predictor variables and picture description scores as a function of target and test

The final set of analyses, using step-wise multiple regression, was conducted to estimate the unique contributions of phonological memory, working memory, analytical ability, and attention control to predicting the learners' accuracy at producing grammar, lexical, and mixed targets on both the post-test and the delayed post-test. No such analyses were carried out to predict the learners' ability to notice the linguistic targets following recasts because there were no strong associations between noticing scores and the four predictor factors. (See Table 7.4.) In each analysis, the accuracy score (for each linguistic target and test) was used as the criterion measure, and the phonological memory, working memory, analytical ability, and attention control scores were entered separately as predictors, in decreasing order of their correlation with the criterion variable (entry criterion: $p \leq .05$). In each analysis, either the learners' morphosyntactic, or lexicosemantic accuracy scores, or both (based on the speaking test described earlier) were entered first, as a measure of L2 proficiency, in Step 1 of the analysis. Thus, the morphosyntactic accuracy score was entered in Step 1 of the analyses for the grammar targets. The lexicosemantic accuracy score was entered in Step 1 of the analyses for the lexical targets. Both the morphosyntactic and lexicosemantic scores were entered in Step 1 of the analyses for the mixed targets. Next, the four predictors were entered all together, in Step 2 of each analysis. This two-step procedure allowed for estimating the contribution of phonological memory, working memory, attention control, and analytical ability that was *independent* from the learners' individual differences in L2 proficiency.

The regression analyses using production accuracy on the post-test revealed that proficiency (measured by either the morphosyntactic, the lexicosemantic score, or both) explained 21–57 per cent of the unique variance (R^2) in production accuracy, Fs (1, 30) > 8.04, ps < .01. This contribution of proficiency was significant, ß range = - .46 – -.70, ps < .01. Attention control accounted for an additional 14–23 per cent of the unique variance in production accuracy for the grammar and mixed, Fs (2, 29) > 7.96, ps < .0025, but not lexical, targets. The contribution of attention control was also significant, ß range = - .40 – -.51, ps < .025. The proportion of the unique variance (R^2) explained by each predictor on the post-test is depicted in Figure 7.3. These results suggest that only attention control explained a significant amount of the learners' accuracy at producing linguistic targets, an amount that was over and above that attributable to L2 proficiency alone.

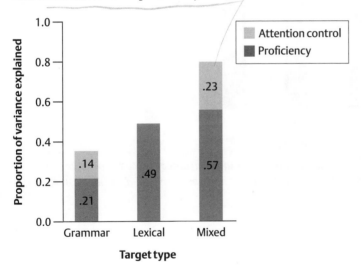

Figure 7.3 The proportion of the unique variance (R^2) explained by each of the predictor variables on the post-test as a function of linguistic target

The regression analyses using production accuracy on the delayed post-test revealed that proficiency (measured by either the morphosyntactic, the lexicosemantic score, or both) explained 19–45 per cent of the unique variance in production accuracy, Fs (1, 30) > 7.17, ps < .025. This contribution of proficiency was significant, ß range = - .444– -.61, ps < .025. Attention control accounted for an additional significant 17–23 per cent of the unique variance in production accuracy for the grammar, lexical, and mixed targets, Fs (2, 29) > 10.02, ps < .001, ß range = - .44 – -.51, ps < .0025. Moreover, analytical ability explained an additional significant 9 per cent, F (3, 28) = 10.20, p < .001, ß = .29, p < .05, while phonological memory an additional significant 8 per cent of the unique variance, F (4, 27) = 10.57, p < .001, ß = .35, p < .025, in production accuracy for the grammar targets only. The proportion of the unique variance (R^2) explained by each predictor on the delayed post-test is depicted in Figure 7.4. These results suggest that attention control, analytical ability, and phonological memory explained a significant amount of the learners' accuracy, mainly at producing grammar targets. Again, the contributions of these cognitive factors were independent of L2 proficiency.

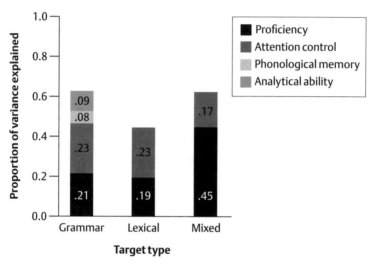

Figure 7.4 The proportion of the unique variance (R^2) explained by each of the predictor variables on the delayed post-test as a function of linguistic target

Discussion

Summary of findings

The goal of the study reported in this chapter was to investigate the noticeability and effectiveness of recasts as a function of learners' individual differences in phonological memory, working memory, analytical ability, and attention control. First, analyses of the learners' noticing scores (defined as the ability to detect the targeted error following a recast) revealed that, when the learners made errors and then received a recast, they were more likely to detect their lexical than their morphosyntactic errors. Second, analyses of the learners' accuracy in producing linguistic targets revealed that overall the learners benefited from the recasts received. Their production accuracy on the post-test and delayed post-test was superior to their accuracy on the pre-test. These two findings are in line with the results of previous studies that cited lower noticing rates for recasts targeting morphosyntactic than lexical errors (Mackey *et al.* 2000) and showed beneficial effects of recasts on learner accuracy (Mackey and Philp 1998; Ammar and Spada 2006; and the studies summarized in the introduction to this volume).

Further analyses, conducted to identify factors that influence learners' ability to notice and benefit from recasts, revealed several significant predictors of the learners' production accuracy, but not their noticing. In particular, the learners' morphosyntactic and lexicosemantic accuracy scores (proficiency measures established in a separate task) accounted for 19–57 per cent of the unique variance in the learners' accuracy of producing linguistic targets. That is, the higher proficiency learners in this study overall benefited from recasts more than the lower proficiency learners, suggesting that learners' existing knowledge of a particular form or the state of their 'readiness' to acquire it (or perhaps both) enhance the usefulness of recasts for them. In addition, measures of attention control, analytical ability, and phonological memory accounted for significant proportions of the unique variance in the learners' production accuracy. For example, the combined contribution of these three factors explained 40 per cent of the unique variance in the learners' ability to accurately produce grammar targets (English PDs) on the delayed post-test. This contribution was independent of L2 proficiency. That is, large phonological memory, efficient attention control, and strong analytical ability appear to be associated with learners' accurate production of L2 morphosyntax after hearing a recast. Each of these factors appears to have an independent effect on learners' ability to benefit from recasts. The *combined* influence of these factors on the usefulness of recasts is, however, unclear as the relationship *among* these complex cognitive constructs is not well understood. Nevertheless, these findings are consistent with the results of previous studies that cite greater benefits of recasts for higher than lower proficiency learners (Mackey and Philp 1998) and link working and phonological memory with the effectiveness of recasting (Mackey *et al.* 2002). Moreover, these findings go beyond previously reported results in suggesting that attention control and analytical ability are also central to the usefulness of recasts.

Cognitive factors and recasts

Before discussing the effect of cognitive factors on the effectiveness of recasts, it is important to address one finding of this study that seemingly contradicts previously reported data. In the only study that has, to date, examined the contributions of working and phonological memory to the noticeability of recasts, Mackey *et al.* (2002) reported that learners with larger working and phonological memory spans tended to be more likely to notice the error targeted by recasts than learners with smaller spans. By contrast, in this study, measures of working and phonological memory (or any other measure, for that matter) were not associated with noticing rates. Reasons for this discrepancy may be the different methodologies employed by the two studies to measure noticing (stimulated recall versus visually cued discrimination) or to the different measures of phonological and working memory used (non-word recall, listening span versus serial non-word recognition, letter–number sequencing). Perhaps a more plausible reason for this discrepancy lies in the relative salience and predictability of the corrective feedback in the two studies. In this study, recasts were frequent. Of the 120 picture descriptions, 48 were followed by a native speaker response, whether or not an error occurred. The feedback received in the context of a computerized task was therefore contextually prominent, perhaps more so than it would be in an interaction with a partner in a more naturalistic situation, for example, as used by Mackey *et al.* (asking questions about a picture). This salience and predictability of interactional feedback may have consequently made the task used to measure noticing less demanding, thereby minimizing the role of individual differences in learners' attention, memory, and language aptitude.

Although none of the cognitive factors examined here predicted the rate at which the learners noticed mismatched (erroneous) linguistic targets following recasts, the effect of individual differences on the learners' use of the information available in recasts was clear. Measures of attention control, phonological memory, and analytical ability explained up to 40 per cent of variance in L2 morphosyntactic accuracy (use of English PDs) and up to 23 per cent of variance in L2 lexical accuracy (use of English verbs), in excess of what was explained by L2 proficiency alone. Taken together, these findings show how cognitive constructs of attention, memory, and language aptitude 'shape' L2 interaction on a minute-by-minute basis in a simple task.

One cognitive factor that appears to determine the effectiveness of recasting is phonological memory. The finding of this study that phonological memory explained a modest (yet significant) proportion of variance in L2 morphosyntactic accuracy on the delayed post-test suggests that phonological memory is likely involved in L2 interaction at the level of L2 morphosyntax rather than at the level of L2 lexicon (c.f., Service 1992; N. Ellis and Sinclair 1996; O'Brien *et al.* 2006). Phonological memory might underlie learners' ability to encode and subsequently use, in the course of interaction, elements of L2 morphosyntax targeted by recasts. Because the effect of phonological memory on learners' production was detectable only on the delayed post-test, it is possible that phonological memory may play an essential role in shaping long-term benefits of interactional feedback. That is, individual differences in learners' phonological memory spans may be particularly predictive of learners' ability to benefit from recasts precisely at the time when the exact auditory percept of the spoken recast is no longer available. At this point, learners may need to rely on their phonological memory to maintain the form of the recast in their short-term memory to be able to analyze it for further processing. This role of phonological memory in interaction is likely akin to that proposed to mediate self-perception, or the ability to detect phonological errors in one's own speech (Baker and Trofimovich 2006). That is, phonological memory may ensure that learners maintain, in an active state, their own spoken utterances or those produced by others, thereby making these utterances available for subsequent storage or processing.

Another cognitive factor that likely determines the effectiveness of recasts is analytical ability. The finding of this study that analytical ability accounted for a modest (yet significant) proportion of variance in L2 morphosyntactic accuracy on the delayed post-test suggests that analytical ability may mediate the benefits of recasts for learners' use of L2 morphosyntax. Analytical ability likely determines learners' capacity to identify and focus on the structural properties of their own speech and the speech addressed to them. Thus, learners with stronger analytical skills may be more likely to engage in a 'deeper' processing of a recast and therefore undertake a more efficient analysis of its formal properties than learners with weaker analytical skills. Because the effect of analytical ability was detected in this study only on the delayed post-test, analytical ability may play a greater role in L2 interaction at the time when interactional feedback or other sources of negative (or positive) evidence are no longer available. In fact, this 'delayed' effect of analytical ability and phonological memory on the 'deployment' of L2 morphosyntax (Long 2006) is consistent with recent claims that learners' performance immediately following interactional feedback is not necessarily predictive of longer-term learning and that interactional feedback-driven learning is often delayed (Mackey and Philp 1998; Mackey 1999). As the results of this study suggested, after a mere 2–12 minutes following the presentation of a recast, learners are no longer as accurate at producing L2 morphosyntactic and lexical targets as they are at doing so immediately after a recast. (See Table 7.3.) More importantly, their performance after a short delay appears to be highly contingent on the available processing resources and conditional on learners' individual differences.

Last but not least, attention control or the ability to efficiently allocate attention among different aspects of language or different cognitive processing tasks appears to determine the effectiveness of recasts as well. The finding of this study that attention control predicted a large and significant amount of L2 morphosyntactic and lexical accuracy in learners' production is indicative of the contribution of attention control to L2 interaction and is consistent with previously documented effects of attention control on L2 proficiency (Segalowitz and Frenkiel-Fishman 2005). In a recent study, Taube-Schiff and Segalowitz (2005) clarified the nature of the link between L2 proficiency and attention control. They showed that, in fact, L2 proficiency is related to the ability to efficiently allocate attention among relational (grammaticized) aspects of the L2 (for example, spatial prepositions), but not among its non-relational (lexical) aspects (for example, nouns). In other words, high L2 proficiency appears to be associated with efficiency in shifting attention among grammaticized (morphosyntactic) elements of the L2. Whether or not L2 proficiency is related to efficient attention shifting among morphosyntactic or lexical aspects of the L2 (or both), the findings reported here suggest that accurate L2 use may be contingent on efficient attention control. In L2 interaction, attention control may characterize learners' ability to efficiently switch attention among different aspects of language or among different cognitive tasks, thereby determining learners' success in using interactional feedback.

Limitations and conclusions

The present study has several limitations that concern the nature of interactional feedback provided to the learners as part of a computerized task. As discussed earlier in this chapter, the online picture description task employed here required that native speaker responses be provided to the learners in response to all critical utterances, both targetlike and erroneous. To overcome this limitation, for our analyses of the noticeability of recasts we used only the data that were based on 'true' recasts, operationalized here as pre-recorded native speaker responses reformulating the learners' erroneous picture descriptions. It is likely, however, that the resulting noticing rates may have been 'inflated' by the additional positive evidence available to the learners through non-corrective repetitions following their targetlike picture descriptions. If indeed present, this additional contribution to noticing was, however, small, as the linguistic targets used in this study were seemingly already salient in a laboratory-based task containing a number of repeated items. Presumably, the presence of non-corrective repetitions may have also exaggerated the learners' production accuracy rates, thus potentially inflating the extent to which recasting was shown to be effective. Again, the likelihood of this was, however, small. First, it is unlikely that a few non-corrective repetitions would significantly affect already stable, targetlike performance. Second, the learners' existing knowledge of the linguistic targets was partialled out, as part of their L2 proficiency scores, in the regression analyses carried out to examine the production data. These reasons notwithstanding, the limitations outlined above warrant further investigation into the noticeability and effectiveness of recasts under circumstances that allow researchers to determine exactly *what* learners notice as they hear recasts and thus to isolate their corrective nature.

Situated within L2 interaction research, this study was conducted to explain learners' difficulties in L2 learning at the level of individual differences. More specifically, this study examined the role of four cognitive factors in determining learners' ability to notice and benefit from recasts, an interactional feedback technique that aims at promoting L2 development in the context of meaningful interaction. Results overall showed support for the involvement of three (phonological memory, attention control, analytical ability) of the four factors in determining the effectiveness of recasts, lending further evidence to previous claims that implicate attention, memory, and language aptitude factors in L2 development (Skehan 2002).

At a general level, the findings of this study contribute to an understanding of individual differences from a perspective that casts L2 learning as the development of flexible and fluent cognitive processing skills in an unpredictable, often changeable interactive environment. (See Segalowitz 1997 for more details on this view of individual differences.) Although the picture description task used here imposes far fewer (and perhaps different) demands on L2 learners than face-to-face interaction, in which interlocutors may go 'off topic' and may focus on a particular discourse or language feature unexpectedly, the cognitive skills involved in this task are likely representative of such an interaction. This study, however, is only a preliminary attempt to untangle the many factors determining the effectiveness of interactional feedback. It leaves unanswered many questions about, for example, the role of other, non-phonological, aspects of working memory in determining the noticeability and effectiveness of recasts (see Miyake and Friedman 1998) or about the role of individual difference factors in naturalistic face-to-face interaction. These and other questions remain to be explored in future research.

8

Textually enhanced recasts, learner awareness, and L2 outcomes in synchronous computer-mediated interaction

REBECCA SACHS and BO-RAM SUH

Introduction

The study described in this chapter brings the technique of textual enhancement into the context of synchronous computer-mediated communication (CMC), exploring the effectiveness of textually enhanced recasts for second language (L2) development in relation to learners' attentional processes during interaction. Despite disagreements in the literature regarding the necessity of awareness for second language learning (Tomlin and Villa 1994; Robinson 1995; Schmidt 1995, 2001), suggestions that awareness may be facilitative of SLA have been influential and are supported by empirical research (Leow 1997a, 2000; Rosa and O'Neill 1999; Rosa and Leow 2004b). In fact, much of the rationale behind research on input enhancement and focus on form in interaction builds upon ideas about the importance of directing selective attention to L2 stimuli which are perceptually non-salient or communicatively redundant. Although external attempts to manipulate the salience of linguistic forms do not guarantee their noticeability or internal salience to learners (Sharwood Smith 1991), it has been argued that attempts to enhance linguistic stimuli in ways that do induce their noticing and further processing may facilitate learning (Sharwood Smith 1993; Doughty and Long 2003b).

At present, the effectiveness of interaction with feedback for L2 development has been empirically demonstrated (see the Introduction to this volume for a summary), and researchers have recently shifted their focus to exploring in more detail how interaction works to impact learning. In relation to the current study, it is important to note, as Nicholas, Lightbown, and Spada (2001: 720) have pointed out, that implicit types of feedback such as recasts appear to have a greater impact on learning when 'it is clear to the learner that the recast is a reaction to the accuracy of the form, not the content, of the original utterance'. A common recommendation is that recasts be accompanied by overt prosodic cues (Doughty and Varela 1998) or presented in reduced or segmented form, adding stress for emphasis, to make it clear that they are corrective (Roberts 1995; Lyster 1998b). In support of this, Philp (2003) has reported that recasts appear to be more salient to learners when they are short and contain relatively few changes—a finding she links to working memory constraints. Moreover, Loewen and Philp (2006) recently found relationships between certain features of recasts and learners' accuracy on individualized post-tests; for example, features such as interrogative intonation, short length, and a relatively small number of changes predicted accurate test scores, leading the authors to argue that these characteristics were likely facilitative of comparisons between non-targetlike utterances and targetlike responses.

Long (2006) has proposed that future research on the effects of interactional feedback should be carried out in the written modality since the salience of targeted linguistic items can readily be manipulated there. Research on CALL has already provided several descriptive analyses of computer-based activities which are modeled to a certain extent on synchronous oral conversations, focusing on the language learners produce, the negotiations they engage in, and the feedback they receive (Chun 1994; Warschauer 1995; Blake 2000; Warschauer and Kern 2000). Separately, studies of textual enhancement have been carried out under assumptions similar to those discussed above—namely, that learners can profitably be encouraged to focus on form through attempts to render particular linguistic features more salient. In textual enhancement studies, however, learners are generally presented with the task of reading a passage for propositional content as opposed to communicating meaning with a live interlocutor, and linguistic input is manipulated by means of typographical as opposed to prosodic modifications. The current study brings together and extends these lines of investigation through visually enhancing the external salience of targeted linguistic forms in the context of written online computer-mediated interactions and evaluating learners' L2 development.

Still, before assuming that this technique will be effective, it is worth mentioning that the results of studies of textual enhancement in non-interactive written contexts have not been conclusive. Such studies have employed a variety of textual modifications, including changes in font style and character size, underlining, bolding, italicizing, highlighting with color, and various combinations of these. While a few (for example, Shook 1994; Jourdenais, Ota, Stauffer, Boyson, and Doughty 1995; Barcroft 2003) have found benefits for textual enhancement in terms of L2 outcomes, others (for example, Alanen 1995; Overstreet 1998; Shook 1999; Leow 2001; Leow *et al.* 2003; Wong 2003; Park 2004) have not found it to promote targetlike control of the linguistic elements under investigation to a greater extent than occurred in conditions without enhancement. Rather, textual enhancement in the latter set of studies has been shown to affect learners' ability to state explicit rules about targeted forms (Alanen 1995), to influence their recall of idea units (Wong 2003), and occasionally (Overstreet 1998)—though not always

(Leow 1997b, 2001; Leow *et al.* 2003)—to have negative effects on reading comprehension.

Researchers in this area have suggested a variety of possible reasons for this lack of consistency, including the communicative value (Wong 2003) and 'inherent' salience (Shook 1994, 1999; Leow *et al.* 2003) of the linguistic targets, some of which may not have been made salient enough by the enhancement (for example, the non-meaningful agreement markings in Wong 2003), and others of which may have been meaningful, salient, or familiar enough without highlighting (for example, the imperative verb forms in Leow 1997b, 2001, and the L1–L2 cognates in Leow *et al.* 2003). It has also been suggested that the specific ways in which targeted forms are visually enhanced may moderate the potential effects of treatment (Barcroft 2003; Wong 2003; Park 2004). Enhancement might lead learners to focus on pieces of informational content rather than linguistic form, for example, as may have been the case in Wong (2003). That study attempted to enhance the salience of agreement properties in French relative clauses by enlarging, bolding, and italicizing the articles of direct objects and the agreement markings on past participles; however, Wong reasons that since the relative clauses themselves were also underlined and the learners were informed that they would be asked to recall the content of what they had read, they may have been inclined to pay attention to the meanings of the clauses in their entirety rather than to their agreement properties *per se*.

Another consideration in interpreting the results of the textual enhancement studies may be the fact that the language and visual highlighting of these texts is always determined in advance; that is, it is not provided in response to language generated by the learners themselves. Part of the psycholinguistic rationale for the effectiveness of recasts has been argued to lie in the immediate contingency and juxtaposition of non-targetlike and targetlike utterances (Saxton 1997; Long, Inagaki, and Ortega 1998; Long 2006). This has not been present in the reading passages employed in textual enhancement experiments, but would seem to be important in light of hypotheses regarding the significance of interactional adjustments, individualized input, and learners' attentional processes for SLA (Long 1996; Gass and Mackey 2006). In fact, one of the reasons for the benefits of interaction may involve learners' focus on communicating their own messages. If feedback can be provided in a way that encourages them to attend to the more targetlike linguistic forms which can be used to convey their meanings, the contexts for learning created in this fashion may lead to L2 development.

Indeed, the theoretical construct of focus on form refers to when learners' attention is drawn to linguistic items 'as they arise incidentally in lessons whose overriding focus is on meaning or communication' (Long 1991: 45–6). It presupposes three main conditions: (1) that learners be engaged in attention to meaning when incidental attention to linguistic form occurs, triggered by a perceived problem in communication, (2) that the targeted form(s) be an integral part of the learners' communicative needs, and (3) that the drawing of attention takes into account the learners' ability to make use of the focus on form (Long 1991). Arguably, these conditions can be met by synchronous interactions (oral or written) in which reactive input, created through negotiation of meaning and recasts, is 'at least roughly tuned to learners' current processing capacity' (Doughty and Long 2003b: 66). The attention to form designed to occur in static textual enhancement, on the other hand, may not be as sensitive to learners' abilities or immediately and directly relevant to their communicative needs. Furthermore, when reading a text, learners are not participating in an active back-and-forth interaction in which they share an attentional focus with an interlocutor, already understand the propositional content of their own intended messages, and have a vested interest in witnessing the effects of their utterances, factors which Long (2006) identifies as contributing to the effectiveness of recasts. The study described in the present chapter was based on the idea that importing these features into the written mode might create a context in which textual enhancement could facilitate L2 development through making the forms targeted by feedback more salient.

It is, of course, an empirical question whether the findings of research on interactional feedback will hold for interactions in the written modality. Chapelle (1998) contends that many of the theories and methods from research on spoken interaction are applicable to uses of CALL technology, and Pelletieri (2000: 59) has argued that 'because synchronous [CMC] bears a striking resemblance to oral communication, it seems logical to assume that language practice through CMC will reap some of the same benefits for second language development as practice through oral interaction'. However, Chapelle (2001) has also pointed out that some of the major challenges in CALL research involve making task conditions practical, generalizable, and comparable to more traditional language learning tasks, and de la Fuente (2003) has cautioned that computer-mediated interaction creates a different communicative environment when compared with face-to-face interaction. For one thing, CMC is a text-based 'hybrid between text and oral communication' which involves a relative absence of non-verbal communication and different social dynamics in terms of interruptions and competition for turn-taking (ibid.: 51).

In fact, there is some evidence that beneficial interactional processes occur in CMC. For example, Blake (2000) has found that learners negotiate lexical meaning and modify their output in computer-mediated interactions, Pelletieri (2000) has observed that corrective feedback on morphosyntax is later incorporated by learners, and Salaberry (2000) has noted that learners monitor their language and correct themselves. Furthermore, whereas VanPatten (1989) has pointed out that language learners may have difficulty attending to both form and meaning given the limited capacity available for conscious attention in serial information processing (see also McLaughlin 1987), it has often been suggested that learners have more time in the written modality to plan their linguistic output, to process incoming information in relation to their own production, and to produce more complex language (Warschauer

1995; Choi 2000). In an expanded dual-mode replication of VanPatten (1989), Wong (2001) has shown that learners can attend to both form and meaning without impeding comprehension in the written modality.

Another challenge in CALL research is that it is not possible simply to assume that commonly accepted definitions of terms can be operationalized similarly across modalities. For instance, written recasts enhanced with textual highlighting may not be implicit enough to be categorized as recasts at all under strict definitions of the term, which require that recasts maintain a primary focus on meaning (Long 2006). At the same time, there are researchers who employ a more elastic definition of the term 'recasts', taking the position that characterizations of their various features (for example, additional prosodic cues to their corrective nature) can be helpful in exploring which qualities of feedback have the greatest impact on SLA (Loewen and Philp 2006). Under such broader definitions, research (for example, Choi 2000; Ayoun 2001) has shown that recasts are effective in the written modality as well.

In sum, several studies have demonstrated the effectiveness of interaction for L2 development, and there is some evidence indicating that this may carry over into the written modality. Research on interactional feedback has drawn much of its theoretical justification from ideas about learners' attentional processes and focus on form, assuming that these are especially important to encourage for the acquisition of non-salient linguistic structures. Researchers have suggested that with implicit forms of feedback such as recasts, it is important for learners to be aware of their corrective nature and to notice the more targetlike forms contained within them. While studies of textual enhancement have not always shown straightforwardly positive effects on L2 outcomes, there are reasons to hypothesize that the characteristics of individualized written interactions may create a favorable context for textually enhanced feedback. Visual highlighting may serve to make the changes in recasts more salient to learners, and the interactive juxtaposition of contingent feedback with the learners' own utterances may make the enhancement more meaningful.

With this as a foundation, there is one final issue to keep in mind: many studies whose hypotheses are based on the importance of attention have discussed learners' attentional processes without measuring them directly—a tendency which Leow (1999: 65) identifies as perhaps 'the most important shortcoming' of such research during the 1990s. In relation to this, Leow advises that process measures should be employed to provide a clearer picture of learners' 'potential levels or degrees of awareness while processing L2 forms' (1997a: 473). Given that some research employing introspective measures has shown textual enhancement to affect learners' mentioning of targeted linguistic structures and rules (Alanen 1995; Jourdenais *et al.* 1995), and given that learners' reports of awareness at the level of understanding (i.e. containing rules about targeted structures and/or reports of meta-awareness) have shown stronger associations with performance on L2 tasks than reports of awareness at the lower level of noticing or reports which do not show evidence of awareness (Robinson 1997; Leow 1997a, 2000; Rosa and O'Neill 1999; Rosa and Leow 2004a), verbal protocols may be an especially useful source of information in this context.

Concerns have been raised, however, regarding the reactivity of concurrent think-alouds, suggesting that the methodology may affect the very processes it is trying to measure (Stratman and Hamp-Lyons 1994; Jourdenais 2001). The few SLA studies that have addressed the issue empirically (Leow and Morgan-Short 2004; Bowles and Leow 2005; Sachs and Polio 2007) have produced conflicting findings; none the less, there is a measure of agreement that introspective techniques allow researchers to obtain information about learners' perceptions which would otherwise be inaccessible (Mackey, Gass, and McDonough 2000). In the context of the current study, assuming that learners should be able to verbalize their thoughts while typing, we reasoned that the written modality of CMC might allow us to investigate the relationships between learners' reported awareness in dyadic interactions with feedback and their subsequent L2 performance. At the same time, since researchers (for example, Leow and Morgan-Short 2004) have advised that SLA studies employing concurrent verbalization as a research tool should include a check for reactivity, we incorporate that concern here as a methodological question.

The present study employs written synchronous computer-mediated interactions in order to compare the efficacy of textually enhanced and unenhanced recasts of a targeted linguistic form for L2 development. To explore the role of learners' attentional processes in relation to the enhancement of recasts, the study also measures learners' reported levels of awareness of the linguistic target through concurrent think-aloud protocols, a methodological tool which is then checked for reactivity. The research questions are as follows:

1 Does the textual enhancement of recasts affect learners' subsequent accuracy in using a targeted form?
2 Does the textual enhancement of recasts affect the levels of awareness of the targeted form suggested by learners' verbal reports?
3 Is there a relationship between the levels of awareness of the targeted form suggested by learners' verbal reports and the learners' subsequent accuracy in using the form?

Method

Design

The experiment reported on in this chapter employed a pre-test–treatment– post-test design to examine the impact of textually enhanced recasts on learners' subsequent accuracy in using a targeted linguistic form: backshifting in reported speech. Participants were randomly assigned into groups which differed with respect to two variables: (1) whether the learners received textually enhanced or unenhanced recasts in task-based synchronous CMC and (2) whether or not they were asked to think aloud during the treatment. The pre- and post-tests were designed to assess the learners' ability to choose appropriate uses of backshifting in context in cloze passages and to produce it themselves in computer-mediated interactions. Verbal protocols were used to explore whether enhancement was related to the learners' reports of awareness during the treatments. Correlational analyses were also performed in order to investigate relationships between the learners' verbalizations and how well they performed on the post-tests. The procedure is described in more detail below.

Participants

The participants were 30 Korean EFL learners, ages 19–27, attending universities in Seoul, South Korea. There were 19 female participants and 11 males. Their English proficiency levels varied from intermediate to high-intermediate. As most of them had begun studying English in middle school (i.e. at around age 13), they had been studying English for between 6–13 years; however, apart from three participants who reported using English for about two or three hours per week, English use among these learners was limited to less than one hour per week, and only one participant had experience living in an English-speaking country. The majority had experience with other foreign languages, with 23 reporting at least basic abilities in Spanish, six in Chinese, three in French, three in German, two in Portuguese, one in Japanese, and one in Italian. Six participants had no experience with other languages. All participants were proficient enough typists and familiar enough with computers to be able to engage in online interactions in English. The native speaker (NS) interlocutor, who was also one of the researchers, was a 26-year-old American graduate student. She interacted with the participants over the computer from the United States while the other researcher, a 25-year-old Korean graduate student, oversaw the experiment in Korea.

Linguistic target

The linguistic structure targeted in this study involved sequencing of tenses in English—more specifically, the backshifting of verbs from the past to the past perfect in certain contexts of indirect reported speech. In English, when a reporting verb (for example, 'say', 'claim') in a matrix clause is in the past tense, words in the 'that'-clause complement often undergo a shift in perspective, such that the tense and/or aspect of the verbs are changed and deictic terms such as 'ago' and 'tomorrow' are changed to counterparts such as 'earlier' and 'the next day' (Celce-Murcia and Larsen-Freeman 1999: 690). Thus, for example, one might report an original utterance of 'We finished our paper two weeks ago' in the following ways:

<u>Simple present</u> (no backshifting):   They <u>say</u> that they **finished** two weeks ago.

<u>Present perfect</u> (no backshifting):   They <u>have said</u> that they **finished** two weeks ago.

<u>Simple past</u> (with backshifting):   They <u>said</u> that they **had finished** two weeks earlier.

This last configuration, with the matrix reporting verb ('said') in the past tense and the reported verb ('had finished') backshifted, was the type elicited and recast during the interactions and assessed on the pre- and post-tests of this study. Since such sentences are easily understandable even without the shift in perspective, the structure was considered to be relatively low in communicative value and was chosen following suggestions by Wong (2003) to the effect that such forms may be particularly amenable to textual enhancement. Based on VanPatten's (1996, 2000) model of input processing, Wong argues that learners generally try to understand the content of a message before focusing on how it is encoded linguistically; thus, their attention may need to be drawn more actively to forms low in communicative value. We also reasoned that backshifting would potentially be learnable through short-term interactive treatments with intensive feedback, given that the intermediate-level learners in our study could be expected to be familiar with the past perfect even if they were not familiar with its specific uses in backshifting. It should be noted that, while native speakers of English do not always backshift verbs in reported speech (common exceptions being when they wish to emphasize that events are still true or when they are reporting on utterances immediately after they have been said, for example), it was possible for the NS interlocutor to back-shift consistently and authentically during the interactions of this study since the experimental tasks were designed to avoid these sorts of exceptions.

Recasting and enhancement techniques

Recasts were operationalized as the NS interlocutor's more targetlike reformulations of the learners' non-targetlike language. A general attempt was made to preserve the meanings the learners expressed in the matrix and subordinate clause pairs which created contexts for backshifting; however, as will be discussed in more detail below, the recasts often included expansions on the learners' statements as well. As for the textual enhancement technique, efforts were made to ensure that the learners were not encouraged to focus solely on propositional content without attending to linguistic form (Wong 2003; Park 2004); that is, we tried to put the relevant verbs in focus by underlining the matrix verbs to indicate contexts of reported speech and by presenting the backshifted verbs in boldface. Example 1 is from an interaction with Participant 21 in the unenhanced recast condition, while Example 2 shows a textually enhanced recast with Participant 15.

Example 1   Unenhanced recast

P21   Pete revealed that ex-boss fired Lisa [*backshifting not supplied in obligatory context*]

R   Oh, he told Gary that their ex-boss had fired Lisa? [*unenhanced recast*]

P21   Coz of her unhonest

R   Aha! So Gary got clued in

P21   Yes he informed Gary

Example 2   Enhanced recast

P15   Yes but it is not true

R   Oh ... uh oh!

P15   But he says he received awards [*backshifting not supplied, non-obligatory context*]

R   When he <u>said</u> that he **had received** awards, was that a lie, too? [*enhanced recast with matrix verb underlined, backshifted verb presented in bold face*]

P15   It was a lie, too. He said that during the interview

It is important to note that the NS interlocutor (R) not only recasts the reported verbs in these examples ('fired' in Example 1, 'received' in Example 2), but also modifies other non-targetlike aspects of the learners' output (for example, adding the possessive 'their' in Example 1) and expands on the content (questioning the recipient of the news in Example 1 and asking, 'was that a lie, too?' in Example 2). This was typical of the recasting provided in both conditions. The recasts were invariably sentence-length, often involved more than one change, and were sometimes nested in interrogatives with more than one possible functional interpretation. Other common forms of recasts included evaluative or attitudinal components (for example, 'I bet she was surprised when ...'), questions to advance the storyline (for example, 'How did he react when she told him ...?'), and other efforts to create natural contexts for learners to attempt the linguistic target. These features likely served to intensify the problems of ambiguity (Lyster 1998b) and blame assignment (Pinker 1989) which are commonly argued to occur with implicit feedback. They also present differences from how recasts have been operationalized in other studies, where some researchers (though not all) have taken more precautions to maintain the meanings of learners' original utterances, modifying only the ungrammatical aspects (for example, Long, Inagaki, and Ortega 1998; Leeman 2003; Philp 2003). What this arguably means is that some of the functions of textual enhancement, if found to be effective in the context of this study, might be in providing cues to help learners recognize the corrective nature of recasts (Doughty and Varela 1998; Nicholas *et al.* 2001) and in allowing for comparability with the learners' own utterances (Loewen and Philp 2006).

Materials

Treatment

The framework for each participant's treatment was one of three guided story-retelling tasks, which were used to provide contexts for interactional feedback on backshifting. All of the stories dealt with the importance of not lying during a job interview (a topic also used in Park's (2004) textual enhancement study), and each included eight targets (four verbs with regular past participles, four with irregular). The participants were given 14 sequenced picture and vocabulary prompts, designed to elicit the targets along with six distractors and to keep the content discussed similar across the groups. Appendix A contains a sample story (A1), a sample picture prompt (A2), and a chart detailing the prompts, targets, and distractors for that story (A3). As will be discussed below, a portion of the pre- and post-testing involved the same sorts of story-retelling tasks, minus the recasting. The three stories were thus counterbalanced for order across the tests and treatment in case one proved to be more difficult to relate than the others.

During the treatment, each participant read a short story in their L1, Korean, then put it aside and was given a set of sequenced cards illustrating the main events of the story in pictorial form along with lexical items in English so that s/he could retell the story via one-on-one synchronous written CMC with a native speaker (NS) of English. This design was chosen largely to balance a degree of spontaneity against Long's (1996: 448) assertion that free conversation is 'notoriously poor as a context for driving IL [interlanguage] development' since free conversation allows learners to avoid areas of language that give them trouble. It also followed a precedent set in other studies; for instance, Choi (2000) used a very similar technique in her study of written recasting, and Ortega (1999) had participants listen to a taped L1 version of a story before retelling it orally in their L2—not only in order to constrain language and content to the extent possible, but also to reduce the cognitive load of the task. In the current study, the goal was to ensure that all of the target sentences would be attempted and that the learners would receive natural, contextualized recasts on the same forms regardless of experimental group assignment.

Another consideration was that the computer-mediated interactions should be similar not only to the sorts of oral communicative activities commonly used in classrooms and interaction research (such as information gap and narrative tasks), but also to the synchronous CMC tasks that learners might be assigned to perform in pairs in a computer laboratory. As mentioned above, research has demonstrated that L2 learners negotiate for meaning, modify their output, and incorporate feedback in such contexts (Blake 2000; Pelletieri 2000); the NS interlocutor in this study purposely asked questions to encourage the participants to explain aspects of the story which lent themselves to backshifting.

Tests

There were two types of pre- and post-tests, which were the same for all participants: (1) paper-based multiple-choice text completion tests, designed to assess the learners' ability to choose verbs backshifted to the past perfect in past tense contexts of reported speech, and (2) interactive computer-mediated tests, designed to assess the learners' ability to produce verbs backshifted to the past perfect in past tense contexts of reported speech. Two versions of the text completion test and three versions of the interactive story-retelling task were created so that their order could be counterbalanced across groups.

The two different dependent measures were chosen in light of important distinctions between implicit and explicit knowledge (R. Ellis 2005) and receptive and productive knowledge and control (Sharwood Smith 1993). Unspeeded tasks focusing on discrete items (such as the text completion tests here) may promote the use of explicit knowledge to a greater extent than tasks requiring more spontaneous online production (such as the computer-mediated interactions), and research has demonstrated the importance of employing more than one type of test to measure learners' gains. (See chapters in this volume by Ellis and by Loewen and Nabei.) Furthermore, it is important to measure recognition as well as production since relatively more receptive abilities may precede production skills.

The text completion tests were adapted from news stories, and possibly unfamiliar vocabulary words were glossed in Korean on the side. Ten of the blanks in each passage were targets, while ten were distractors (blanks requiring other verb tenses, articles, prepositions, and vocabulary items). The learners had four choices for each blank, and one point was given for each correct target response; thus, each learner was given a score out of ten points. An excerpt from one of the text completion passages is shown in Appendix B.

As mentioned above, the interactive production tests were carried out in almost exactly the same way as the computer-mediated treatment sessions, using story-retelling tasks. The only difference was that the NS interlocutor did not use the past perfect or recast the learners' non-targetlike forms during testing. In scoring these tests, a ratio was calculated for each participant, taking into account not only accurate suppliance of backshifting in obligatory contexts, but also non-targetlike attempts at backshifting and overuses of the past perfect in non-obligatory contexts, both of which might be taken to suggest incremental development. The formula, which we called Revised Targetlike Use (RTLU, from Pica's (1984a) TLU), was thus designed to be sensitive to emergence instead of simply to increases in accuracy; however, it did weight accurate Suppliance in Obligatory Contexts (SOC) more heavily than non-targetlike Misformations in Obligatory Contexts (MOC) and Suppliance in Non-Obligatory Contexts (SNOC):

$$\frac{(2 \times SOC) + (MOC) + (SNOC)}{\text{Obligatory Contexts}}$$

After a training session on two of the participants' interaction transcripts, both researchers coded a random sample of approximately 25 per cent of the interactions in order to ascertain the reliability of the coding method. (Examples of the coding can be seen in Examples 1 and 2 above.) Inter-rater agreement was calculated using Kappa and found to be above the level of .80 suggested by Davies *et al.* (1999) (κ = .90 for suppliance of backshifting; κ = .83 for creation of obligatory contexts). One of the researchers then coded the rest of the data, performing an intra-rater agreement check on 25 per cent of the data after an interval of three months (κ = .98 for backshifting, κ = .95 for obligatory contexts).

Procedure

All of the treatment and testing was carried out individually. Approximately two weeks before the interaction sessions, each participant took a text completion pre-test. Then, on the day of the treatment, each learner engaged in three story-retelling tasks. The first, without recasting, served as an interactive pre-test; the second, with recasting, served as the treatment; and the third, again without recasting, served as an interactive post-test. The participants were divided into four groups, which differed only in terms of what happened during the treatment (i.e. whether or not the forms in the recasts were textually enhanced [+/– E], and whether or not the participants were asked to think aloud [+/– TA]). Immediately after the interactive post-test, each participant took a text completion post-test and filled out a debriefing questionnaire (based on Rosa and Leow 2004a, and included as Appendix C), which probed into whether the learners had inferred anything about the purpose or linguistic focus of the experiment and whether they thought they had learnt anything. An overview of the procedure is shown in Figure 8.1.

One of two free instant messaging programs was used for the computer-mediated interactions, depending on its availability in the Korean universities' computer laboratories: *America Online Instant Messenger*™ (*AIM*®) or *MSN Messenger*. The programs are very similar in appearance and functionality; in both, interlocutors are able to type messages which then appear beneath the previous discourse on the screen. The window size is expandable, and it is possible to scroll back and re-read what has been typed.

The transcripts of the interactions were examined to confirm the similarity of the conditions apart from the planned differences in enhancement and thinking aloud, and no significant differences were found between the +E and –E conditions in terms of the mean number of recasts received ($t(28)$ = 1.581, p = .13), the amount of time spent in the interactive treatment ($t(28)$ = 0.856, p = .40), or the amount of time spent interacting overall ($t(28)$ = 1.737, p = .09). Likewise, the +TA and –TA conditions did not differ significantly in the number of recasts received ($t(28)$ = -.651, p = .52), the amount of time spent in the treatment (when they were also asked to think aloud)

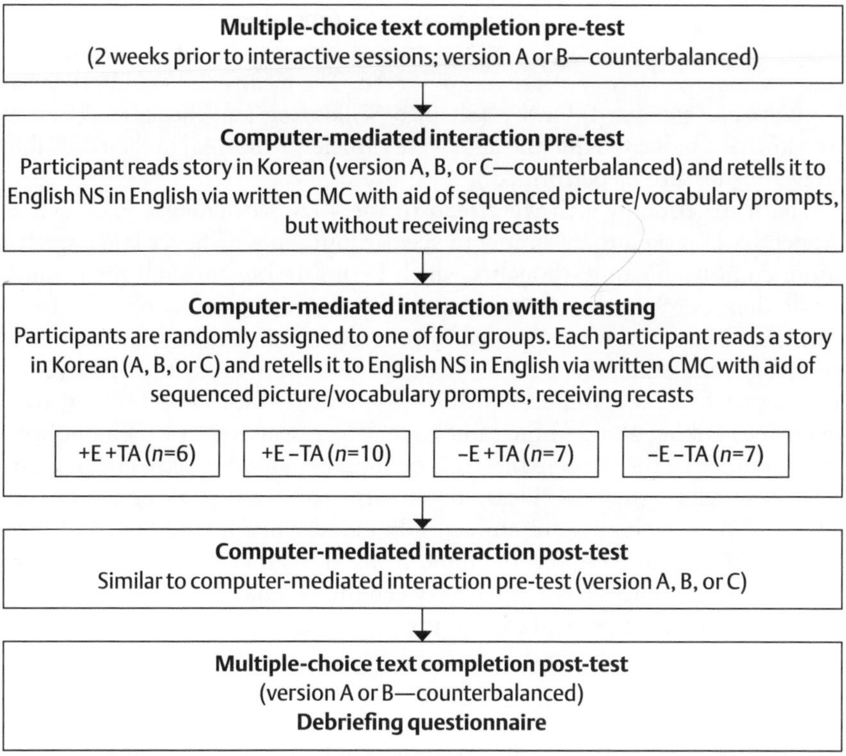

Multiple-choice text completion pre-test
(2 weeks prior to interactive sessions; version A or B—counterbalanced)

$\downarrow$

Computer-mediated interaction pre-test
Participant reads story in Korean (version A, B, or C—counterbalanced) and retells it to English NS in English via written CMC with aid of sequenced picture/vocabulary prompts, but without receiving recasts

$\downarrow$

Computer-mediated interaction with recasting
Participants are randomly assigned to one of four groups. Each participant reads a story in Korean (A, B, or C) and retells it to English NS in English via written CMC with aid of sequenced picture/vocabulary prompts, receiving recasts

+E +TA (*n*=6)	+E –TA (*n*=10)	–E +TA (*n*=7)	–E –TA (*n*=7)

$\downarrow$

Computer-mediated interaction post-test
Similar to computer-mediated interaction pre-test (version A, B, or C)

$\downarrow$

Multiple-choice text completion post-test
(version A or B—counterbalanced)
Debriefing questionnaire

Figure 8.1 Procedure

	Unenhanced recasts (–E)		**Enhanced recasts (+E)**		**Non-think-aloud (–TA)**		**Think-aloud (+TA)**	
	Mean	*SD*	**Mean**	*SD*	**Mean**	*SD*	**Mean**	*SD*
Number of recasts received	8.4	2.3	7.1	1.9	7.5	2.3	8.0	2.1
Time spent in treatment (in minutes)	28.9	6.4	26.8	6.6	27.7	6.0	27.9	7.3
Time spent interacting overall (in minutes)	86.4	17.8	75.5	16.7	79.7	17.3	81.9	19.0

Table 8.1 Time spent and number of recasts received in each experimental condition

$(t(28) = -.113, p = .91)$, or the amount of time spent interacting overall $(t(28) = -.330, p = .74)$. That is, in contrast to other research (Bowles and Leow 2005), no latency effect was observed. The means and standard deviations are presented in Table 8.1. (Shapiro-Wilk's tests and checks of skewness and kurtosis indicated that the data were sufficiently normal in their distributions for t-tests to be performed.)

The instructions which were read to the +TA participants (included as Appendix D) asked them simply to speak aloud, in whichever language felt more comfortable, any thoughts which naturally ran through their minds while they were engaged in retelling the second story (i.e. during the treatment). They were not encouraged to provide metalinguistic information or to justify their statements. As a warm-up, they were given the opportunity to interact for a few minutes with the NS interlocutor on a topic of their choosing, talking aloud at the same time. The researcher in Korea unobtrusively reminded the participants to keep thinking aloud if necessary, making brief comments, such as, 'Please don't forget to keep speaking aloud'. All of the +TA participants did, in fact, talk aloud while interacting, and their verbalization data were recorded and transcribed for coding purposes. No significant differences were found between the +E and –E groups in terms of number of verbalizations $(t(28) = 1.379 \, p = .20)$.

Coding of think-alouds

Schmidt has claimed that learner awareness of L2 form can be classified at the level of noticing (i.e. involving the perception of 'surface level phenomena and item learning' (1995: 29)) or at the higher level of understanding (i.e. involving a 'deeper level of abstraction' and 'system learning' (1995: 29)—that is, noticing plus some sort of metacognition, conscious insight, attempt to understand a form's significance, or analysis and comparison to what has been noticed on other occasions). As one example to illustrate the difference between noticing and understanding, Schmidt (1995: 30) states,

> Awareness that a target language speaker says, on a particular occasion, 'He goes to the beach a lot,' is an example of noticing. Being aware that *goes* is a form of *go* inflected for number agreement is understanding.

Our coding of the learners' verbalization data draws on insights both from Schmidt's ideas and from research by Leow (1997a), who has coded learners' concurrent think-aloud protocols according to three criteria for the presence of awareness. In the first category, [+ cognitive change (+CC), – meta-awareness (–MA), – morphological rule (–MR)], learners register L2 forms with awareness (i.e. produce them or make verbal or written corrections), but make no report of a subjective experience or verbalization of any rule. In the second, [+CC, +MA, –MR], learners report subjective experiences but do not verbalize any morphological rules, and in the third, [+CC, +MA, +MR], learners both report on subjective experiences and metalinguistically verbalize rules. The first category (which we will abbreviate as CC) is taken to represent awareness at the level of noticing, while the last two (abbreviated as MA and MR) are taken to represent awareness at the level of understanding.

In the present study, each verbalization related to an interaction turn was coded separately so that learners could be classified not only with respect to the highest levels of awareness they reached overall in their verbalizations with respect to the linguistic target, but also so that they could be compared in terms of the amount of awareness reports which they made at the various levels. An example of each coding level is presented in Table 8.2.

Turn in interaction	Corresponding verbalization	Coding
R Oh, I see, so she <u>told</u> Gary that she **had been** unhappy	P9 'She told Gary that she had been unhappy. Yes, she told to Gary.'	CC (<u>C</u>ognitive <u>C</u>hange, considered awareness at the level of noticing)
P9 And their ex-boss had fired because she was not honest	P9 'Anyway, ex-boss fired her, and their ex-boss was fired, have fired, had fired because she was not honest, NOT honest.'	MA (<u>M</u>eta-<u>A</u>wareness, considered awareness at the level of understanding)
P9 She said that she had quit last job	P9 'She said that she *the past perfect tense* had quit last job.' (Italicized portion spoken in Korean)	MR (<u>M</u>orphological <u>R</u>ule formation, considered awareness at the level of understanding)

Table 8.2 Examples of verbalization coding categories

In practice, the criteria used here for coding verbalizations at particular levels differ from those used in certain other applications of Leow's coding scheme (for example, Rosa and O'Neill 1999). In the current study, whenever participants verbalized their own written linguistic output or the researcher's input, this was taken to qualify as evidence of awareness at the level of noticing (CC)—that is, the perception of surface-level linguistic phenomena. However, when they stopped to repeat (part of) a turn, modifying their output, this sort of self-correction was considered to represent meta-awareness (MA) even if the learners did not explicitly make a separate statement to the effect that they were experiencing conscious insight regarding linguistic form. Any uses of specific metalinguistic terminology to identify the tense/aspect of a targeted form were coded as morphological rule formation (MR). Rosa and O'Neill (1999), in contrast, did not consider reading aloud to constitute a report of awareness at the level of noticing. In their study, noticing had to include evidence of focal attention being directed towards specific forms—for example: 'I'm looking at *hubiera ganado* and I'm thinking what tense is that?' and 'I guess I don't know the rule about using the participle with the past subjunctive, but I'll figure it out eventually' (ibid.: 530). It may thus be important to keep in mind, when interpreting and comparing our results with those of other research, that the examples from Rosa and O'Neill representing awareness at the level of noticing sometimes appear to involve analysis, metalinguistic terminology, and attempts to relate surface linguistic forms to other knowledge, illustrating more than the simple perception of surface features, whereas it is possible that our codings of CC involve less than Schmidt would intend to qualify as noticing.

In any event, the learners' verbalizations in the current study were transcribed (and translated when spoken in Korean), and, following a training session on 15 per cent of the data, another 15 per cent of the data were coded by both researchers. Inter-rater agreement was calculated using Kappa and found to be acceptable (κ = .85 for reported levels of awareness; κ = .92 for the identification of relevant target contexts). The remaining think-alouds were then coded by one of the researchers, who performed an intra-rater agreement check on 25 per cent of the data after an interval of three months (κ = .84 for reported levels of awareness; κ = 1.00 for the identification of relevant target contexts).

Results

To answer our first research question, which asked whether there was a relationship between textual enhancement of recasts and learners' subsequent accuracy with backshifting, t-tests were first performed to ascertain that there were no pre-test differences between the enhanced (+E) and unenhanced (-E) recast groups ($t(26)$ = 1.71, p = .10 for text completion; $t(28)$ = 0.32, p = .75 for production). The data of two participants who scored 90 per cent on the text completion pre-test were excluded from analyses of the text completion data due to possible ceiling effects. Repeated-measures ANOVAs were then conducted with treatment as the between-group factor, time (pre versus post) as the within-subjects factor, and text completion and production scores as the dependent variables (run separately). In both cases, a significant main effect was found for time ($F(1,26)$ = 6.492, p = .02* for text completion; $F(1,28)$ = 5.373, p = .03* for production), but there was no significant main effect for treatment ($F(1,26)$ = 2.518, p = .13 for text completion; $F(1,28)$ = 0.482, p = .49 for production) and no significant interaction effect ($F(1,26)$ = 0.274, p = .61 for text completion; $F(1,28)$ = 1.898, p = .18 for production).

For another perspective on the data, we examined effect sizes (η^2), which provide an estimate of the magnitude of treatment effects. Though the effect sizes for improvement over time were large (η^2 = 0.20 for text completion, η^2 = 0.16 for production), the effect sizes for the treatment and interaction effects were small to moderate (treatment: η^2 = 0.09 for text completion, η^2 = 0.02 for production; interaction: η^2 = 0.01 for text completion, η^2 = 0.06 for production). A *post hoc* power analysis showed that the observed power for the treatment and interaction effects ranged from 0.08 to 0.33 (well below the recommended level of 0.8), suggesting that the lack of statistically significant results may have been due to small sample size. The groups' mean pre- and post-test scores are presented in Table 8.3 and Figures 8.2 and 8.3.

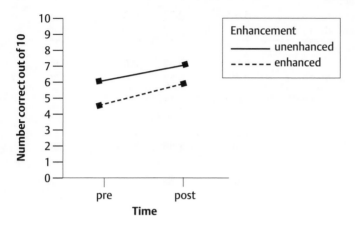

Figure 8.2 Text completion scores in the enhanced and unenhanced conditions

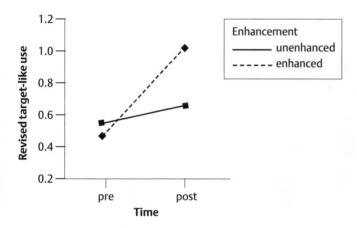

Figure 8.3 Interactive production scores in the enhanced and unenhanced conditions

For the second research question, regarding the relationship between enhancement and reported awareness, data came from the participants who had thought aloud during the treatment ($n = 13$). As shown in Figure 8.4, all of the learners in both the +E condition ($n = 6$) and the –E condition ($n = 7$) verbalized awareness at the level of noticing in target contexts (CC), and all of the +E participants also produced verbalizations which were coded as representing meta-awareness (MA). However, only three learners receiving

Condition	n	Pre-test mean	SD	Post-test mean	SD
Effectiveness of textual enhancement					
Text completion					
Unenhanced	13	5.92	2.33	6.85	2.70
Enhanced	15	4.40	2.38	5.80	2.40
Interactive production					
Unenhanced	14	0.54	0.42	0.68	0.68
Enhanced	16	0.48	0.58	1.02	0.96
Reactivity of concurrent verbalization					
Text completion					
Think-aloud	13	5.92	2.10	7.54	2.57
Non-think-aloud	15	4.40	2.56	5.20	2.04
Interactive production					
Think-aloud	13	.65	.52	.90	.61
Non-think-aloud	17	.39	.47	.83	1.00

Table 8.3 Mean pre- and post-test scores in the different experimental conditions

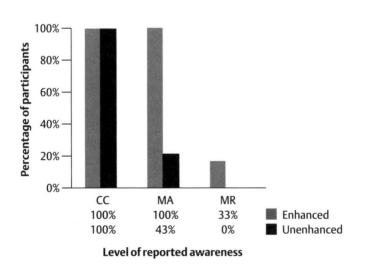

Figure 8.4 Percentages of participants in each group reporting awareness at the various levels in target contexts

unenhanced recasts produced verbalizations indicating meta-awareness. Furthermore, while two participants in the +E condition used metalinguistic terms regarding the target (MR), none of the –E learners did so. A Pearson's chi-square analysis revealed a significant difference between the +E and –E conditions with respect to the number of participants who reported awareness at the level of noticing (coded CC) versus at the level of understanding (coded MA or MR) as their highest level in target contexts ($\chi^2(1, 13) = 4.95$, $p = .03^*$).

In addition to examining the number of learners in each condition who verbalized awareness at the various levels in target contexts, we used Mann-Whitney U tests to compare the conditions with respect to the participants' relative *amounts* of such awareness reports. (Non-parametric tests were chosen because Shapiro-Wilk's tests and checks of skewness and kurtosis indicated non-normal distributions.) No significant between-group differences were found in terms of the learners' percentages of awareness reports at the lower level of noticing (mean rank +E: 5.25, –E: 8.50, $p = .13$) or in the number of times past perfect forms were used or mentioned (mean rank +E: 8.33, –E: 5.86, $p = .25$). However, there was a significant difference between the groups with respect to how much the participants reported awareness at the level of understanding in target contexts (mean rank +E: 9.33, –E: 5.00, $p = .04^*$); the participants receiving enhanced recasts tended to do so more. Table 8.4 presents the mean frequencies and percentages.

Condition	Mean number of past perfect verbalizations	Mean per cent of awareness reports at level of noticing	Mean per cent of awareness reports at level of understanding
Unenhanced	4.00	79.10	11.38
Enhanced	7.17	67.51	20.69

Table 8.4 Mean frequencies of verbalizing the target structure and percentages of reporting the levels of awareness in target contexts

In order to answer the third research question, concerning the relationships among learners' awareness reports and their subsequent accuracy with backshifting, non-parametric bivariate correlations (Spearman's rho) were run between frequencies of verbalizing at the various levels of awareness in target contexts and the learners' text completion and production scores. Table 8.5 illustrates the general trend which was found: higher levels of reported awareness tended to show stronger positive correlations with post-test scores. The strongest correlation was between production scores and reports using metalinguistic terminology (coded MR, morphological rule formation).

Post-test	Noticing	Meta-awareness	Morph. rule formation	Past perfect verbalized
Text completion (*n* = 13)	.16 (*p* = .60)	.17 (*p* = .57)	.32 (*p* = .29)	.29 (*p* = .34)
Interactive production (*n* = 13)	.15 (*p* = .62)	.46 (*p* = .12)	.54 (*p* = .06)	.47 (*p* = .11)

Table 8.5 Correlations between frequencies of reporting awareness in target contexts and post-test scores

Finally, in order to address the methodological concern that verbal protocols may be reactive as a research tool (Jourdenais 2001; Leow and Morgan-Short 2004; Bowles and Leow 2005; Sachs and Polio 2007), *t*-tests were first performed to ascertain that there were no significant pre-test differences between the think-aloud (+TA) and non-think-aloud (–TA) groups ($t(26)$ = -1.705, p = .10 on text completion; $t(28)$ = -1.408, p = .17 on production). Again, the text completion scores of two participants were excluded due to possible ceiling effects. Repeated-measures ANOVAs were then carried out with think-aloud status as the between-group factor, time (pre versus post) as the within-subjects factor, and text completion and production scores as dependent variables. These showed significant main effects for time ($F(1,26)$ = 7.163, p = .01*, η^2 = 0.22 for text completion; $F(1,28)$ = 5.070, p = .03*, η^2 = 0.15 for production) and a significant between-group effect on text completion ($F(1,26)$ = 6.478, p = .02*, η^2 = 0.20). However, there was no significant between-group effect on production ($F(1,28)$ = .629, p = .44, η^2 = 0.02), and the interaction effects were small and non-significant ($F(1,26)$ = .816, p = .38, η^2 = 0.03 for text completion; $F(1,28)$ = .356, p = .56, η^2 = 0.01 for production). The significant between-group main effect on text completion indicates that the +TA and –TA groups performed differently from each other regardless of time. In order to conclude that thinking aloud was reactive, however, it would have been necessary to find a significant interaction effect, indicating that the groups' trajectories from pre- to post-test had differed. This was not found. In light of these findings, strong conclusions regarding reactivity should not be inferred.

Discussion

This study set out to investigate three main questions in the context of computer-mediated interactions: (1) whether textual enhancement of a relatively non-salient and communicatively redundant targeted form—backshifting in indirect reported speech—would serve to increase the effectiveness of written recasts, impacting learners' subsequent accuracy in selecting and using the form, (2) whether textual enhancement would be associated with higher levels of reported learner awareness of the form, and (3) whether learners' reports of awareness at various levels would be associated with their subsequent accuracy with backshifting. We predicted that visual highlighting would affect learners' attentional processes regarding the targeted form and thereby affect their later uses of backshifting. The results did not completely bear out this prediction. In brief, while we found, as expected, that enhancement was related to reported awareness and that higher levels of reported awareness showed stronger correlations with post-test performance, we did not find a direct significant relationship between enhancement and post-test performance.

The fact that the participants made statistically significant improvements from pre- to post-test indicates that interaction with recasting and guided production opportunities was effective in this computer-mediated context, just as it has been found to be effective in oral interaction. This is an important finding. However, textual enhancement was not found to make a direct difference in the learners' L2 performance, a result consistent with the findings of several other studies (for example, Overstreet 1998; Shook 1999; Leow 2001; Leow *et al.* 2003; Wong 2003; Park 2004). At the same time, in contrast to the findings of Leow (2001) and Leow *et al.* (2003), learners' attentional processes were shown to be affected by the textual enhancement in our experiment. The simple fact of receiving unenhanced recasts in many cases did not lead learners to report meta-awareness of the specific form being targeted, but participants receiving enhanced recasts did tend to report awareness at higher levels in our study. These findings evoke, to a certain extent, the results of studies by Jourdenais *et al.* (1995) and Alanen (1995), in which enhancement apparently encouraged the participants to mention the targeted forms or to state more explicit rules about them.

Regarding the relationship between reported awareness and subsequent L2 performance, the correlational findings overall appear to support theorizing (for example, Schmidt 2001) and past research (for example, Leow 1997a; Rosa and O'Neill 1999; Rosa and Leow 2004a) showing that higher levels of reported awareness of a targeted form are associated with better L2 outcomes. Interestingly, when Leow *et al.* (2003) found a lack of effects for textual enhancement in their study, they were able to explain the findings by examining the relationships between the learners' reported awareness and their subsequent L2 performance. Calculating correlations separately for the different experimental conditions, they compared them statistically and found that the correlations between awareness and performance were similar regardless of whether or not the texts had been enhanced. With this in mind, we performed a *post hoc* analysis to determine whether there were differences between the +E and –E groups with respect to the strengths of correlations between frequencies of awareness reports and post-test scores.

The results, presented in Table 8.6, show that, in contrast to the findings of Leow *et al.* (2003), the correlations were stronger for the learners who had received enhanced recasts. (Since the two post-tests showed fairly similar trends, correlations with text completion scores will be discussed here for illustration purposes.) For instance, there appear to be differences in correlation strength not only for reports of meta-awareness ($r_s = .93, p = .01^*$ in the enhanced condition versus $r_s = .40, p = .37$ in the unenhanced condition), but also for reports at the level of noticing ($r_s = .77, p = .07$ in the enhanced condition versus $r_s = .14, p = .76$ in the unenhanced condition). Verbalizations of the past perfect in target contexts (at any level of awareness) likewise showed a strong significant positive relationship with post-test scores in the +E condition ($r_s = .94, p = .01^*$), in contrast to a weak non-significant relationship in the –E condition ($r_s = .12, p = .80$).

Post-test	Any level of awareness	Noticing (CC)	Meta-aware (MA)	Morph. rule (MR)	Past perfect verbalized
Unenhanced (n = 7)					
Text completion	.14 (p = .76)	.14 (p = .76)	.40 (p = .37)	n/a	.12 (p = .80)
Interactive production	-.30 (p = .51)	-.30 (p = .51)	.54 (p = .21)	n/a	-.29 (p = .52)
Enhanced (n = 6)					
Text completion	.94* (p = .01)	.77 (p = .07)	.93* (p = .01)	.84* (p = .04)	.94* (p = .01)
Interactive production	.84* (p = .04)	.83* (p = .04)	.73 (p = .10)	.74 (p = .10)	.97* (p<.01)

Table 8.6 Correlations between frequencies of reporting awareness in target contexts and post-treatment production scores, by condition

Considering the operationalizations in this study, where simply reading interactions aloud qualified as reporting awareness at the relatively low level of noticing, it might seem to make sense that the –E group showed weak correlations between reports coded CC and subsequent accuracy in backshifting. For interactive production post-test scores, in fact, the correlation with reports at this lower level of awareness was negative ($r_s = -.30, p = .51$). However, interestingly, the +E group showed strong positive correlations between reports of awareness at the level of noticing and accurate subsequent use of the target. Actually, the learners who received enhanced recasts displayed strong significant correlations between reports of awareness and performance regardless of the awareness-level coding. In addition to contributing to evidence that textual enhancement had some sort of effect in this study, these findings raise methodological questions related to the veridicality of think-alouds and the adequacy of the awareness coding scheme. That is, it seems plausible to speculate that the –E participants were not truly 'noticing', or that the +E participants were experiencing more than just 'noticing', when their verbalizations were coded as such.

The participants' answers on the debriefing questionnaire (Appendix C) also provide some qualitative evidence for differences between the +E and –E conditions in terms of learner awareness. Whereas in response to question three (i.e. 'Did you ever think that your interlocutor was focusing on something specific when she responded to you?'), only one learner (out of 14) in the

–E condition reported sensing that the NS interlocutor had been focusing on the correct use of verb tenses such as the past and past perfect, six participants (out of 16) in the +E condition did so. (It should be noted, however, that only two participants in the +E condition and one in the –E condition specifically proposed that the experiment may have been about reporting others' speech indirectly.)

As mentioned above, we tried in this study to ensure that our enhancement technique would lead learners to focus specifically on the linguistic target. Based on the verbalization data, in which the participants receiving enhanced recasts tended to report more awareness at higher levels in target contexts, it seems that the +E participants were more attuned to linguistic form. Still, the +E group did not demonstrate a greater ability to recognize appropriate uses of backshifting in context or to produce it themselves. It is possible to speculate about some of the potential reasons for this. One possibility, for instance, might be that the enhanced recasts were often successful in highlighting verb forms, but did not make it clear enough to the participants that their own uses of the past tense in past contexts of reported speech were non-targetlike. That is, without being given metalinguistic information explicitly outlining the rather abstract connection to that context, the +E learners may have been aware of the forms, and perhaps a bit more prone to using them, without picking up on the larger rule for backshifting. (See debriefing questionnaire.) Other studies have found that the effectiveness of corrective feedback and learners' perceptions of it depend at least in part on the target structure (Mackey *et al.* 2000; see also the chapters by Jeon and Ellis in this volume). If the NS interlocutor in the current study had instead been recasting and highlighting agreement morphology in a Romance language, for example, the learners might have understood more readily that the NS's version was the only correct one, as opposed to one of potentially many alternatives. Again, it is noteworthy here that in the conversational format of this computer-mediated task, the recasts often served as discourse moves confirming understanding of what the participants had said and were sometimes nested within further questions to move the story along. Even with the enhancement, it may not always have been clear to the learners that the recasts were implying something about the linguistic accuracy of their original utterances.

Another factor to consider is the potential role of individual differences in aptitude (Carroll 1990; Robinson 2002b, 2005). As Robinson (2005: 54) points out, 'where strengths in patterns of abilities, or aptitudes, match the processing demands of specific instructional sets ... such patterns of abilities additionally facilitate L2 learning'. However, it also appears to be the case that some learners can learn from a variety of pedagogic techniques, while others do not benefit much from any. In our study, it may be reasonable to interpret the results as suggesting that textual enhancement has a place in the learning process which is mediated by individual differences in cognitive abilities and propensities. Looking more closely at descriptive statistics of the learners' verbalizations in each group, we found, for example, that whereas the standard deviation for the percentage of reports coded as representing meta-awareness was 21 per cent in the –E condition, it was only six per cent in the +E condition. This might be taken to suggest that textual enhancement served in part as a sort of external equalizer on the +E group's attentional processes and that, while most participants in the –E group did not verbalize much meta-awareness of the target form, there were a few who managed to do so even without external manipulation. That is, in line with Robinson's (2002b, 2005) discussion of the aptitude complexes which may be drawn on in processing recasts, individual differences in processing speed, pattern recognition, grammatical sensitivity, and/or working memory capacity (Mackey *et al.* 2002) may have enabled learners with fast analytic abilities to notice the gap (Schmidt and Frota 1986), experience awareness of linguistic forms at higher levels, make cognitive comparisons (Nelson 1987), and improve, even (or particularly) in a more implicit treatment—thereby mitigating some of the potential effects we might otherwise have found for textual enhancement.

Limitations and future research

This study was able to utilize the methodological suggestions of several previous researchers in the areas of interaction and textual enhancement, addressing problems they had identified and taking advantage of their insights. Instead of having textual enhancement appear in fixed texts whose language was determined in advance, the current study involved individualized interactions which unfolded in real time, potentially incorporating some of the psycholinguistic rationale proposed for the effectiveness of recasts. As mentioned above, the scoring of learners' interactive production attempted to capture incremental development, and the method of enhancement attempted to focus closely on the linguistic target—backshifted verbs themselves, along with the reporting verbs which triggered backshifting.

Inevitably, there were some limitations to this study that should be addressed in future research. In order to have more confidence in the findings, data should be collected from a greater number of participants with lower levels of prior knowledge of the target. Given that short-term experiments providing a limited amount of exposure to targeted forms may underestimate the effectiveness of feedback or show a bias in favor of one type of treatment, future research should also increase the amount of interaction time and input exposure (Long 2006). Furthermore, it is important to keep in mind that the effects of interaction may not appear immediately (Gass 1997; Mackey 1999) and that recasts (with or without enhancement) might induce noticing and further processing of forms in future input, thereby facilitating subsequent learning. Future research could additionally investigate other target structures, examining whether they are efficiently learnable from recasts or whether metalinguistic information might be more effective, and making note of whether they tend to cause communication breakdowns requiring negotiation to redress or whether they are expendable in terms of informational content (Pica 1994a; Wong 2003).

As alluded to earlier, a more refined coding method for the think-alouds could be useful in investigating relationships between learner-internal processes and SLA. Additional measures of individual differences (for example, in cognitive variables such as working memory capacity and grammatical sensitivity, as well as in motivation, anxiety, strategies, prior knowledge, etc.) would also provide a richer picture of the factors mediating input and L2 outcomes. The study could also be extended by examining the immediate discourse contexts in which enhanced and unenhanced recasts were provided and coding for uptake and modified output in order to ascertain the more immediate impact of both recasts and enhancement. Learners' accuracy in using the targeted forms during the treatment could be inspected in light of their concurrent verbalizations as well (c.f., Camps 2003, who found that Spanish learners correctly identified the antecedents of 92 per cent of the pronouns they mentioned during a reading activity, compared to 69 per cent of those that were unmentioned).

In providing some additional information regarding participants' attentional processes, concurrent verbal protocols helped us to interpret our results in a way that would not have been possible based merely on test scores. Some of the participants in the present study mentioned that verbalizing their thoughts had been difficult or distracting, in line with concerns in the literature that concurrent think-alouds may be reactive as a research tool. However, the statistical tests we carried out did not lead us to conclude that thinking aloud had affected the learners' improvement from pre- to post-test. Keeping in mind that this is only one small study, of course, it would be worthwhile to investigate further whether and when learners can sometimes verbalize their thoughts without affecting an experiment's results and for which task types, linguistic forms, and learner characteristics think-alouds might constitute a non-reactive tool for SLA research.

Still-to-be-pursued avenues of research notwithstanding, what this study did find was that participating in one-on-one computer-mediated interactions with recasting of a targeted form leads to improvement and that, while one might not be able to expect an immediate and direct impact of textual enhancement in this context, it does appear to be associated with higher levels of reported awareness when learners think aloud. Enhancement in this study was found to influence learners' processing of the input, and the fact that reports of higher levels of awareness were associated with more accurate subsequent performance would seem to bolster the underlying rationale premised on attention. However, there is more to learning than simply becoming aware of linguistic forms; thus, the influence of individual differences in interaction with different pedagogical treatments merits further investigation, as does the learnability of different target forms from particular types of feedback.

Appendix A1

Story B: *Office Drama*

(English translation of Story B with targets indicated)

A woman named Lisa wanted to get a job in an office. The boss, Gary, wanted someone who was very organized, trustworthy, and responsible. Lisa was organized and fairly responsible, but she wasn't so trustworthy! During the interview, Lisa <u>said</u> that she **had quit** her last job. She <u>mentioned</u> that she **had been** unhappy about the number of hours in her workday. She also <u>claimed</u> that her boss **had** often **insulted** the employees. Gary believed her and decided it didn't make much sense to call her boss if he was such a terrible person. Lisa really impressed Gary in the interview, and he hired her.

Lisa was actually doing great on the job, but in an amazing coincidence, there was another employee, Pete, who used to work with Lisa at the same company! In a conversation with Gary, Pete accidentally <u>revealed</u> that his old boss **had fired** Lisa. That was hard for Gary to believe. But Pete <u>said</u> that, in fact, she **had lost** her job because of her dishonesty. Gary called Lisa's old boss and found out the truth. The next morning, Gary took Lisa aside and <u>told</u> her that he **had spoken** with Pete. First Lisa blamed Pete and <u>argued</u> that he **had lied**. But then Gary <u>revealed</u> that he **had called** her old boss. Lisa realized that she was in trouble and started to feel nervous. Of course, she lost her job that day, but she decided always to tell the truth in the future.

Appendix A2

Sample picture/vocabulary prompt from Story B: *Office Drama*

Appendix A3

Chart of vocabulary prompts and targets for Story B: *Office Drama*

Expected sentences for picture cards	Vocabulary prompts on picture cards	Reporting verb	Backshifting Regular	Backshifting Irregular
The boss Gary wanted someone who was organized, trustworthy, and responsible.	boss, Gary, want, organized, responsible, employee			
In the interview, Lisa *said* that she **had quit** her last job.	interview, Lisa, say, quit, last job	said		had quit
She *mentioned* that she **had been** unhappy about the number of hours in her workday.	mention, be, unhappy, number, hours	mentioned		had been
She also *claimed* that her boss **had** often **insulted** the employees.	claim, boss, insult, employees	claimed	had insulted	
Lisa really impressed Gary, and he hired her.	Lisa, impress, Gary, hire			
But another employee, Pete, was one of Lisa's old co-workers.	Pete, Lisa, previously, co-workers			
Pete accidentally *revealed* that their boss **had fired** Lisa.	Pete, reveal, ex-boss, fire, Lisa	revealed	had fired	
Pete *informed* Gary that Lisa **had lost** her job because of dishonesty.	Pete, inform Gary, Lisa, lose job, dishonesty	informed		had lost
Gary called her old boss and found out the truth.	Gary, call, ex-boss, find out, truth			
The next morning, Gary *told* Lisa that he **had spoken** with Pete.	Gary, tell, Lisa, speak with, Pete	told		had spoken
First Lisa blamed Pete and *argued* that he **had lied**.	Lisa, blame, argue, Pete, lie	argued	had lied	
But then Gary *revealed* that he **had called** her old boss.	Gary, reveal, call, ex-boss	revealed	had called	
Lisa realized that she was in trouble and started to feel nervous.	Lisa, realize, in trouble, start, feel, nervous			
Lisa lost her job, but she decided always to tell the truth in the future.	Lisa, lose job, decide, tell, truth, future			

Appendix B

Excerpt from multiple-choice text completion pre-test

(Form B: The mystery of the silent 'piano man')

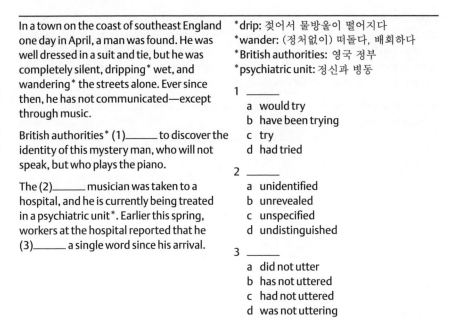

In a town on the coast of southeast England one day in April, a man was found. He was well dressed in a suit and tie, but he was completely silent, dripping* wet, and wandering* the streets alone. Ever since then, he has not communicated—except through music.

British authorities* (1)_____ to discover the identity of this mystery man, who will not speak, but who plays the piano.

The (2)_____ musician was taken to a hospital, and he is currently being treated in a psychiatric unit*. Earlier this spring, workers at the hospital reported that he (3)_____ a single word since his arrival.

*drip: 젖어서 물방울이 떨어지다
*wander: (정처없이) 떠돌다, 배회하다
*British authorities: 영국 정부
*psychiatric unit: 정신과 병동

1 _____
a would try
b have been trying
c try
d had tried

2 _____
a unidentified
b unrevealed
c unspecified
d undistinguished

3 _____
a did not utter
b has not uttered
c had not uttered
d was not uttering

Appendix C

Instructions and questions from debriefing questionnaire

(English translation—given to participants in Korean)

*Please read the following questions carefully and answer them in as much detail as possible. You have as much time as you need, but please **do not read ahead**. Please answer the questions **in order** and **do not go back**. Don't worry; this information will be confidential, and you are free to skip any of the questions if you would prefer not to answer.*

1 What do you think was the purpose of the experiment overall? (That is, besides just doing research on language learning, was there something specific you thought we might be studying?)

2 What do you think was the purpose of the interactions specifically?

3 Did you ever think that your interlocutor was focusing on something specific when she responded to you? If so, what do you think she was focusing on?

4 Did you learn anything in this study? Did you notice anything interesting about English? (for example, verbs, prepositions, vocabulary, etc.)

5 If you had to explain to a friend how to report what another person has said in English (for example, if you want to tell your friend Mi-Young what your other friend Wook-Jin said), could you give them some sort of a 'rule' that would help? If so, please write down that 'rule'.

Appendix D

Scripted think-aloud instructions

(English translation—explained to participants in Korean)

We're interested in finding out what you're thinking while you're interacting with Rebecca (your American interlocutor). So while you're telling this next story, we would like you to speak your thoughts out loud. That is, we would like you to say everything that you would normally say to yourself silently while you're thinking. Just pretend you're alone in the room speaking to yourself. You don't have to try to explain your thoughts or give any reasons for what you're thinking—just say whatever goes through your mind.

I'll use a tape recorder to record what you say, but it's not a test, so please don't worry about whether you're saying something correct or incorrect, and don't even worry about speaking in complete sentences. We're just interested in whatever thoughts you might normally have, the same way you would normally think them to yourself. You can speak in whichever language is more comfortable—Korean or English, or both.

You shouldn't try to talk to me as though it's a conversation. Actually, try to pretend I'm not here. I won't talk at all or answer any questions, but I might remind you to keep talking aloud if you are silent for a while. Do you understand what we'd like you to do?

First we'll practice without a tape recorder so that you feel comfortable. You can start typing to Rebecca and ask her about anything you're interested in. She'll type back, and you'll have a short free conversation for about 2–3 minutes. Think out loud while you're interacting so that you can practice. You can start whenever you're ready.

(When finished practicing): OK, do you have any questions? Just remember to keep talking the whole time and say whatever goes through your head while you are chatting with Rebecca. Are you ready to start telling the second story? I'll turn on the tape recorder now. Please start whenever you are ready.

9

From CALL to face-to-face interaction: the effect of computer-delivered recasts and working memory on L2 development

NURIA SAGARRA

Introduction

Two of the factors that account for the benefits of conversational interaction on L2 learning are the feedback that learners receive when they produce incorrect utterances and the consequent modifications they make to their output (see the Introduction to this volume for a review). While feedback can be explicit or implicit, Long (1996) suggests using implicit feedback, such as recasts, to promote attention to formal linguistic features without obstructing communication. The positive effects of recasts have been reported in classroom settings (Doughty and Varela 1998; Ohta 2000) and experimental ones (Mackey and Philp 1998; Leeman 2003) (see Long 2006 for a comprehensive review). However, development can be hindered by learners' tendency to perceive recasts as responses to content rather than as positive or negative evidence (Lyster and Ranta 1997; Lyster 1998c; Panova and Lyster 2002; for other findings, see Carpenter, Jeon, MacGregor, and Mackey 2006; Mackey 2007; Egi this volume; Kim and Han this volume).

To make the corrective intent of recasts more overt, teachers can use additional cues in the classroom, such as repeating learners' incorrect utterances and changing stress patterns and intonation (Doughty and Varela 1998). Unfortunately, the explicitness of these practices, while promoting the interpretation of recasts as corrections of grammatical errors, may threaten the goal of using language for communication in the classroom. One way to solve this problem may be to provide great amounts of overt feedback in a computer-assisted language learning (CALL) environment outside the classroom to facilitate L2 linguistic development. Current research indicates that feedback on grammatical errors during co-operative online exchanges is beneficial in directing learners' attention to the gaps that exist in their interlanguage grammar (Kitade 2000). However, a question that has not been answered, and one that is addressed in this study, is whether practice with computer-based corrective recasts in the absence of interaction can facilitate targetlike production in face-to-face interaction.

In particular, the present study examines the pedagogical value of performing tasks which are accompanied by individualized computer-delivered feedback focused on a target structure for the development of linguistic accuracy. In this study, the term 'recasts' refers to isolated corrective reformulations delivered via computer that immediately follow learners' incorrect utterances. While this definition of recasts does not correspond precisely to the use of recasts during face-to-face interaction, the goal of this study is to develop pedagogical, computer-based techniques that promote L2 development, rather than to expand the substantial body of research that examines the effect of 'natural' recasts on linguistic accuracy. Modified output, which has been used as a way to assess the noticing of recasts (McDonough 2005), is operationalized as the learners' incorporation of information provided by a recast into their response following that recast. The current study also takes recent research to the next step by exploring the extent to which learners' working memory capacities predict their L2 development from computer-delivered feedback.

Computer-delivered recasts

Some researchers (for example, R. Ellis, Basturkmen, and Loewen 2001a; Nicholas, Lightbown, and Spada 2001; Sheen 2004) have claimed that context modulates the efficacy of recasts. Learning in computer–enhanced contexts might be expected to promote learner awareness of form by making the corrective nature of recasts more salient to learners. Recent research suggests that synchronous computer-mediated communication not only promotes targetlike production, but also improves oral proficiency (see Payne and Ross 2005 and references therein). Synchronous computer-mediated communication is normally defined as learner–learner or learner–teacher simultaneous conversational exchanges that take place in virtual contexts, such as chatrooms. Two studies have examined the role of recasts supplied in synchronous settings: Choi (2000) and Sachs and Suh (this volume). In Choi's study, beginning L2 learners of English participated in two 30-minute chat sessions with the researcher. The task of the students was to provide L2 narrations of stories they had read in their native language. The recasts group received recasts immediately after they produced irregular past tense verbs incorrectly, but the control group did not receive any feedback. Results from a fill-in-the-blank post-test revealed that recasts promoted lexical learning and linguistic pattern generalization. Sachs and Suh divided participants into four groups: +/- enhancement, +/- think-aloud protocols. Findings from interactive story retellings and a recognition post-test indicated that recasts increased the learners' linguistic accuracy with backshifting in English indirect reported speech and that textual enhancement of the recasts affected the learners' awareness of the targeted form.

Castañeda (2005) notes that teachers provide more corrective feedback and more explicit correction in asynchronous contexts than in synchronous contexts, while providing more recasts in synchronous exchanges. Sotillo (2000) argues that asynchronous computer-mediated contexts (for example, bulletin boards, email) are more effective than synchronous ones. The systematic practice typical of asynchronous contexts facilitates the formation and testing of L2 hypotheses, general skill performance (Ericsson and Charness 1994), and L2 automaticity (see chapters by Hulstijn and Segalowitz in Doughty and Long 2003a). In an oft-cited study, Ayoun (2001) investigated the effect of computer-mediated recasts, modeling, and metalinguistic explanation on the learning of the *passé composé* and *imparfait* in L2 French. She found that all groups improved in their written production of both tenses, but recasts proved more beneficial than metalinguistic explanation, and equally beneficial as modeling, in learning the *passé composé* (although see Ayoun 2004, for evidence in favor of metalinguistic explanation). In another computer-mediated study, Sagarra (2004) investigated the effect of recasts, utterance rejection, and metalinguistic explanation on the production of L2 Spanish gender–number agreement. The results revealed that recasts and utterance rejection yielded better written production when preceded by metalinguistic explanation than when presented alone. In the absence of metalinguistic explanation, recasts were more beneficial than utterance rejection for written and oral production. These two studies suggest that metalinguistic explanation facilitates the written production of L2 forms (see also Nagata 1997; Heift 2001, 2004; Rosa and Leow 2004b), but that implicit feedback (in the form of recasts) is effective as well.

The results of synchronous and asynchronous studies show that recasts provided via computer can promote linguistic accuracy. It is noteworthy to highlight, however, that these CALL research findings are restricted to recasts delivered in the written mode, whereas recasts used during face-to-face interactions are always oral. The simultaneous manipulation of context (computer) and input mode (written) in these studies does not allow us to determine which variable promotes the efficacy of computer-delivered written recasts. The present study is innovative in investigating how computer-based recasts presented in the oral mode affect L2 development. Given that human sentence processing is highly attuned to attending to prosodic features in the input (Pynte and Colonna 2002), that interactional recasts are oral, and that oral input consumes more attentional resources than written input (Wong 2001), it is imperative to investigate whether the positive effects of computer-delivered recasts found in the written mode are also obtained in the oral mode and with students who exhibit lower working memory spans.

Working memory and second language acquisition

Working memory is 'the temporary storage and manipulation of information that is assumed to be necessary for a wide range of complex cognitive activities' (Baddeley 2003: 189). Single-resource capacity theories posit that processing and storage depend on and compete for a shared pool of limited resources that vary from person to person. These theories are divided into multiple-component (Baddeley 2003) and single-component (Just and Carpenter 1992) theories, and the two coincide on the existence of a central processor, whose main function is to minimize the possibility that a task will deplete a person's attentional resources. To accomplish this goal, this central executive filters the input (inhibitory control), allocates attention to the filtered input (selective attention), and controls what knowledge will be activated in long-term memory.

There is substantial evidence that working memory is associated with a myriad of L2 mechanisms, including processing (Miyake and Friedman 1998; Vos, Gunter, Schriefers, and Friederici 2001), lexical access (Kroll, Michael, Tokowicz, and Dufour 2002), comprehension (Harrington and Sawyer 1992; Walter 2004), production (speaking: Payne and Ross 2005; writing: Abu-Rabia 2003), and, most importantly for the current chapter, the noticing of recasts. For example, Mackey, Philp, Egi, Fujii, and Tatsumi (2002) investigated the relationship between working memory, noticing of interactional feedback, and L2 development of English question forms by low-proficiency English learners. The results indicated that working memory was associated with the learners' ability to notice interactional recasts and suggested that, although learners with lower working memory capacities might show evidence of L2 development initially, learners with higher working memory capacities may demonstrate development more in the longer term. In a more recent study, Trofimovich, Ammar, and Gatbonton (this volume) explored the roles of working memory, phonological memory, analytical ability, and attention control on targetlike production and the ability to notice corrective recasts. The findings from noticing prompts, immediate post-tests, and post-tests which were delayed for between 2–12 minutes suggested that the cognitive factors under investigation predicted production accuracy, but not the noticing of recasts. They explained the discrepancy between their findings and those obtained by Mackey, Philp *et al.* (2002) in terms of methodological differences. In another study, Mackey, Adams, Stafford, and Winke (2002) examined the association between working memory and the production of modified output. They reported that high-span learners modified their output following interactional feedback (clarification requests, repetitions with rising intonation, and recasts) more often than low-span learners, even though the correlation between working memory and modified output was moderate to low. The present study focuses on the relationship between working memory and learners' ability to benefit from computer-based oral recasts in developing linguistic accuracy and producing modified output.

The present study

As discussed earlier, it is difficult for L2 learners to interpret interactional recasts as corrections of grammatical errors. The present study takes a novel approach to this problem by using practice with oral recasts delivered via computer to facilitate the development of linguistic accuracy. In addition, this study examines how working memory interacts with the learners' ability to benefit from computer-delivered recasts in the development of a second language.

The first research question explores whether computer-delivered oral recasts can facilitate the development of linguistic accuracy in two types of tasks: written tests and face-to-face interactions. Gass, Mackey, and Ross-Feldman (2005) examined interaction in different tasks and contexts, and found that the type of task that the learners completed yielded greater differences in interactional patterns than the context in which the tasks were carried out (classroom or experimental). As mentioned above, computer-mediated tasks with L2 feedback have been shown to promote targetlike written production and oral proficiency; however, this research so far has been limited to written feedback. The current study investigates whether the positive effects of computer-delivered recasts also occur when recasts are provided in the oral mode, examining whether such effects are evident in written and oral outcomes.

The second research question explores the effect of computer-delivered oral recasts on the production of modified output. Modified output has been found to be one of the strongest predictors of learning (Loewen 2003b; McDonough 2005), potentially because it allows learners to reflect upon their errors, notice surface differences, and internalize linguistic information that is still stored in declarative memory. This is why modified output is believed to promote the development of linguistic accuracy even when learners' modified output is incorrect (Gass 1997; Swain 1995, 2005).

The last two research questions relate to the effect of working memory on learners' development of linguistic accuracy (research question 3) and their production of modified output (research question 4). Because working memory restricts how much input learners can process and store during interactional exchanges, it can also modulate their ability to process and register recasts (Mackey, Philp *et al.* 2002). This, in turn, may affect their use of recasts in making the changes in their interlanguage systems that will help them to develop linguistic accuracy.

To address these questions, 82 English learners of basic Spanish as an L2 were given tasks which involved completing L2 sentences with adjectives. When their answers were incorrect during the treatment, some participants listened to the correct constructions (recasts group), while others did not receive any feedback (control group). Recasts were not provided for correct utterances because, by definition, interactional recasts are supplied only after learner errors and because recasts following targetlike utterances would undermine the purpose of helping learners notice recasts as responses to form rather than to content. Development of linguistic accuracy was measured through delayed written tests and face-to-face interactions without feedback; the ability to produce modified output was assessed via an oral information gap task with feedback; and working memory was measured by means of a reading span test.

Method

Participants

Eighty-two native speakers of English enrolled in a first-semester under-graduate Spanish course at a large North American university were randomly assigned to the control or the recasts group. They volunteered to participate in the study in exchange for extra credit (for performing the written tests and working memory test) and a small monetary compensation (for the face-to-face interactions). In order to be included in the study, participants had to score at or below 25 per cent accuracy on a pre-test to control for previous knowledge of the target structure, and at or above 80 per cent accuracy on a vocabulary test and three written post-tests to ensure that lack of knowledge of the target nouns and adjectives did not affect the results. Because Spanish has four noun–adjective gender–number combinations for nouns carrying transparent gender (see next section), a 25 per cent cutoff guaranteed that the students had produced the target form correctly by chance less than 25 per cent of the time. The 80 per cent cutoff was motivated by L2 literature claiming that a form is acquired if it is produced accurately at least 80 per cent of the time (for example, Slabakova 2003). Participants also completed a debriefing questionnaire, and those with previous or current exposure to Spanish or another Romance language outside the course were excluded from the study. Students were also eliminated if they failed to complete all items of the vocabulary test, the pre-test, the treatment, the written post-tests, the working memory test, and the debriefing questionnaire. The final sample pool consisted of 65 participants: 35 in the recasts group and 30 in the control group. Some students did not participate in the oral face-to-face interaction tasks because they did not have time to meet with the researcher individually for one hour outside of class. Therefore, only 37 students took part in that part of the study: 19 in the recasts group and 18 in the control group.

Target structure

The choice of the Spanish noun–adjective agreement construction was motivated by its low perceptual salience, its limited communicative value, and by the lack of gender agreement in English, which means that this form generally goes unnoticed by learners (Harley 1998). In Spanish, adjectives must agree in gender and number with the nouns they modify, giving rise to four prototypical combinations: masculine singular endings with –o (*libro rojo* [red book]), masculine plural endings with –os (*libros rojos* [red books]), feminine singular endings with –a (*puerta roja* [red door]) and feminine plural endings with –as (*puertas rojas* [red doors]). Given that grammatical and semantic gender coincide in most animate nouns, only inanimate nouns were included in the study.

Materials and procedure

This empirical study was conducted in class, except for the treatment and the working memory test, which were carried out in a computer laboratory, and the face-to-face interaction tasks, which took place in a separate room. To avoid factors other than recasts influencing the results, participants did not complete any activities in class or outside of class which focused on noun–adjective agreement, and instructors did not provide any grammatical explanation or feedback about the target form until the end of data collection. Figure 9.1 displays an outline of the study.

Screening tests

During the second week of class, the students completed a consent form and attended a 50-minute PowerPoint presentation on the 32 target nouns (20 with transparent gender and 12 fillers with opaque gender) and the 16 target adjectives. The presentation was given in class by a researcher trained to provide all participants with the same input, practice, and format of adjectives (masculine singular). Four days after this vocabulary presentation, the participants completed a vocabulary screening test and a grammar screening test (also used as a pre-test). The vocabulary test was administered to confirm that the students had learnt the target nouns and adjectives prior to the treatment. This test required learners to match Spanish nouns like *puerta* to English nouns with pictures like 'door' ⊟, and to translate English adjectives like 'red' into Spanish (*rojo*).

The goal of the grammar screening test/pre-test was to exclude participants who were already familiar with the target structure, by asking them to fill in the blanks of sentences like *la puerta es* ____ (red) [the door is ____ (red)] with the appropriate adjective in Spanish (in this case, *roja* [red$_{feminine}$]). It included 64 sentences based on the 16 adjectives presented in class: 32 sentences with familiar nouns and 32 with new nouns. Familiar nouns consisted of nouns that were presented with adjectives in the treatment. New nouns never appeared in the treatment and were English cognates of similar frequency of occurrence, according to the *NTC's Dictionary of Spanish Cognates* (Nash 1997) and the *LEXESP, Léxico Informatizado de Español* (Sebastián-Gallés, Martí, Carreiras, and Cuetos 2000). Given the strict scoring criterion for learners to be included in the study (i.e. below 25 per cent correct on this test) and the fact that written production tends to be easier than oral production (Wong 2001), an oral pre-test was deemed unnecessary. The low scores on the written grammar test made it unlikely that the participants would have scored well on an oral pre-test; therefore, the written test was taken as a pre-test for the written post-tests and the oral face-to-face interaction post-tests.

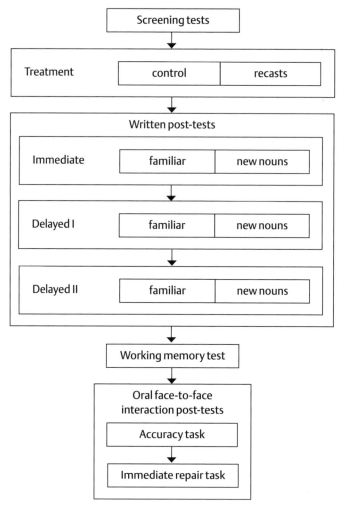

Figure 9.1 Experimental design

Treatment task

One week after the screening tests, the treatment and the first written post-test were carried out via computer in a 50-minute session. All participants filled in the blanks of 32 sentences like '*la puerta es* ____ (red)' [the door is ____ (red)] with the appropriate Spanish adjective (*roja* [red$_{feminine}$] in this case), submitted their response, read the prompt 'Move on to the next sentence', and began the process again with the following sentence. The control group did not receive any feedback on errors and was included in the study to separate the effect of recasts from simple exposure to input in the classroom. Participants in the recasts group were given headsets to listen to the correct construction (for example, *la puerta es roja* every time they produced an incorrect response. To prevent participants from moving on to the following sentence without listening to the targetlike reformulation, learners had to write down correctly English numeric codes which they heard after the recast.

The number and format of the sentences in the pre-test, the treatment, and the written post-tests were the same for the control and recasts groups. Sentences were balanced for gender and number, and the same noun–adjective combination did not appear more than once in the pre-test, the treatment, or any of the post-tests. The nouns and adjectives used in the treatment were the same ones that the participants had learnt in class during the first session of the experiment. Since there were 32 sentences in the treatment, each noun appeared once and each adjective twice. However, original and repeated adjectives did not appear close to each other because a Latin square divided the sentences into two blocks: the first contained 16 different adjectives and the second contained the repeated versions of the 16 adjectives of the first block.

Written post-tests

After the treatment, the participants completed written and oral post-tests based on the 16 target adjectives. The items on the post-tests were balanced for gender and number and included nouns that could not be accompanied by the same adjective more than once. The written post-tests followed the same fill-in-the-gap format previously used in the pre-test and the treatment in order to assess the effect of the treatment on familiar tasks. Familiar tasks can reduce cognitive load, facilitate focus on form (Swain and Lapkin 2001), and affect performance in interactional tasks (Gass, Mackey, and Ross-Feldman 2005).

The written post-tests included familiar nouns that had already appeared with adjectives in the treatment, as well as new nouns that had not appeared in the treatment and that were created following the criteria used in the grammar screening test. New exemplars were used to evaluate the learners' ability to generalize linguistic patterns. As shown in Figure 9.1, the learners carried out three 15-minute written post-tests. The first was administered immediately after the treatment, and the other two took place during two 50-minute sessions one week and one month after the treatment to evaluate the long-term effects of the treatment.

Oral face-to-face interaction post-tests

Two months after the treatment, participants completed two oral face-to-face interactional tasks: an oral post-test and an immediate repair task. Each of these two tasks contained 32 items: 16 were masculine nouns and 16 were feminine. In each case, 12 (six singular and six plural) had transparent gender, and four (two singular and two plural, acting like fillers) had opaque gender. Both tasks were administered in a single 50-minute session and consisted of oral information gap activities that required production of the targeted structure while maintaining a primary focus on meaning. The adjectives used in these tasks corresponded to the original 16 adjectives. The nouns had not appeared previously in the study, but had been covered in class and were displayed in posters on the wall for further reference (for example, *manzana* 🍎). Finally, participants completed five conversational distractor tasks and a language background questionnaire.

Before completing the face-to-face interaction tasks, the learners read a model dialogue in Spanish with a masculine singular noun. In the oral post-test, they were provided with pictures of the items needed by a department store in order to fill some of its empty shelves. Their task was to call an employee at the back of the store to see which items needed to be ordered from the main warehouse. For example, a student would see a picture of eight yellow apples and ask, *¿Tienes manzanas amarillas?* [Do you have yellow $_{\text{fem, pl}}$ apples$_{\text{fem, pl}}$?]. Then the researcher would respond, *Sí, tengo seis* [Yes, I have six], and the student would write '2' in the shopping list column next to the picture of the eight yellow apples. The participants did not receive any feedback on correct or incorrect responses.

The decision to include a task where participants received feedback on incorrect responses was guided by the use of modified output as a measure of uptake. (See Lyster 1998c, but see Mackey and Philp 1998, for an argument against equating learner repair and learning.) In the immediate repair task, participants saw a picture of an apartment and had to find out which objects had changed color after a remodeling. For example, a student saw a picture of a red lamp, and said *En mi foto, la lámpara es roja* [In my picture, the lamp$_{\text{fem, sing}}$ is red$_{\text{fem, sing}}$]. Then the researcher responded *En mi foto también* [In my picture too] or *En mi foto no* [In my picture no], and the student circled the lamp if the color was different. When a learner produced an utterance with incorrect noun–adjective agreement (for example, *En mi foto, la lámpara es rojo* [In my picture, the lamp$_{\text{fem, sing}}$ is red$_{\text{masc, sing}}$], the researcher responded with a recast, *La lámpara es roja* [the lamp$_{\text{fem, sing}}$ is red$_{\text{fem, sing}}$], paused to give the learner the opportunity to repair, and responded to the content specifying whether the object in the picture had changed color. No feedback was provided in response to other grammatical, lexical, or phonological errors.

Working memory test

The working memory test was carried out in a computer lab immediately after the last written post-test in order to avoid disrupting students and instructors with another experimental session in class and to include students who had completed all the tests but could not participate in the oral face-to-face interaction tasks. The working memory test was adapted from

Waters and Caplan's (1996) reading span test and required participants to read 80 sentences in English on a computer screen, one by one. Half of the sentences were semantically plausible and the remaining half were semantically implausible (for example, 'It was the cavity that extracted the dentist', with subject-object animacy inversion). Sentences were grouped into 20 sets of sentences, divided into five groups (span sizes two to six sentences) of four sets each. They were presented in English because most research suggests that working memory is language-independent (Osaka and Osaka 1992; Osaka, Osaka, and Groner 1993) and because the learners' low L2 proficiency level would affect the outcome of the test. For each set, the participants pressed a button to initiate the trial, looked at a 500-ms fixation sign (+) at the center of the screen, read a sentence silently, pressed a 'yes' or a 'no' button to indicate whether the sentence was semantically plausible, looked at another fixation sign, read another sentence, and repeated the cycle as many times as there were sentences in the set. At the end of the set, the word 'RECALL' appeared on the screen and participants wrote down the final word of each sentence within that set.

Scoring

Screening and testing tasks

Participants received one point for each correct answer on the screening and testing tasks. Responses corresponding to masculine singular nouns were not tabulated because L2 learners tend to use masculine singular as the default form (Dewaele and Véronique 2001; Finnemann 1992; White, Valenzuela, Kozlowska-Macgregor, and Yan-Kit 2004). As a result, the means of the pre-test, the written post-tests, and the oral face-to-face interaction tasks were based on a k of 12 for gender agreement (six feminine singular nouns + six feminine plural nouns) and 12 for number agreement (six masculine plural nouns + six feminine plural nouns). Statistical analyses for gender and number agreement were conducted separately because gender agreement has been found to be acquired later than number agreement (Finnemann 1992). Scores for familiar and new nouns were also calculated independently. Modified output included a complete or partial repetition of the corrected utterance, or any type of modification of the original incorrect utterance (since less than one per cent of the learners' changes involved lexical or phonological modifications, this by and large represented modifications of gender and number agreement). All of the dyads were recorded and transcribed, but the scoring for modified output was based only on the dyads where feedback was provided. Four researchers coded the data from these feedback dyads separately, and then they discussed their coding until they reached a consensus.

Working memory test

Working memory comprises the *simultaneous* processing and storage of information in cognitively complex tasks. On the working memory test, one point was given per sentence if the semantic plausibility judgment was accurate, the final word of the sentence was recalled correctly, and the reading time (RT) for the plausibility judgment was between 300 and 5000 ms and was not 2.5 standard deviations above or below the mean. Because the plausibility judgment measures processing and the recall evaluates storage, sentences with a correct recall and an incorrect plausibility judgment, or a correct plausibility judgment and an incorrect recall, were excluded from the total count. Reading times below 300 ms or above 5000 ms were not included because the average college student needs between 225 ms and 400 ms to process a single word (Rayner and Pollatsek 1989) and because allowing learners to read for as long as they liked would have jeopardized the complexity of the test. Finally, the mean RTs for plausible and implausible sentences were calculated separately to control for response bias—a learner's trend to answer 'yes' or 'no'.

Results

The means for the gender and number agreement scores are shown in Tables 9.1 and 9.2. Statistical analyses for the written post-tests and the oral face-to-face interaction tasks were conducted separately because only 35 of the 65 students who completed the written post-tests also participated in the oral tasks. The alpha level was set at .05 for all statistical analyses, and some degrees of freedom had decimals following the Huynh-Feldt's formula.

The means for reading span were 46.77 (control group) and 48.81 (recasts group) ($k = 80$). An independent samples t-test revealed that the difference was non-significant: $t(63) = .489, p > .05$ (Levene's $F = 2.036, p > .05$), suggesting that differences between the control and recasts groups did not result from one group having learners with higher reading spans than those in the other group.

Pre-test

To rule out linguistic differences among the groups prior to the treatment, two two-way repeated-measures ANOVAs with a 2 (group) × 2 (noun type) factorial design were conducted for the pre-test: one for gender (F_1) and one for number (F_2) agreement scores. The analyses revealed no significant differences for group [$F_1(1) = 2.353, p > .05; F_2(1) = 1.179, p > .05$], noun type (familiar, new) [$F_1(1) = 1.136, p > .05; F_2(1) = 3.490, p > .05$], or the interaction of group × noun type [$F_1(1) = 1.136, p > .05; F_2(1) = .267, p > .05$]. This indicates that the sample pool was homogeneous and that any differences observed in the testing tasks were caused by the treatment. To confirm the same for the group of students who participated in the oral face-to-face interaction

Test	Gender				Number			
	Control		Recasts		Control		Recasts	
	M	*SD*	*M*	*SD*	*M*	*SD*	*M*	*SD*
Pre-test								
Familiar nouns	0.20	0.22	0.00	0.00	0.23	0.83	0.45	1.11
New nouns	0.00	0.00	0.00	0.00	0.00	0.00	0.40	0.98
Immediate post-test								
Familiar nouns	0.07	3.65	9.78	4.75	1.00	1.23	11.14	3.21
New nouns	0.00	0.00	9.66	4.67	0.85	1.14	11.00	3.22
Delayed post-test I								
Familiar nouns	0.20	0.00	9.49	3.77	0.85	1.21	10.29	3.41
New nouns	0.10	4.03	9.37	3.75	0.77	1.09	10.00	3.42
Delayed post-test II								
Familiar nouns	0.83	1.66	8.91	4.56	1.77	2.17	9.71	4.07
New nouns	0.87	1.93	8.71	4.61	1.31	2.25	9.36	4.01

k = 12 for each score. Also, *n* = 30 for the control group and *n* = 35 for the recasts group

Table 9.1 Descriptive statistics for the pre-test and written post-tests

Test	Gender				Number			
	Control		Recasts		Control		Recasts	
	M	*SD*	*M*	*SD*	*M*	*SD*	*M*	*SD*
Pre-test								
Familiar nouns	0.07	0.37	0.00	0.00	0.28	0.83	0.53	1.01
New nouns	0.20	0.81	0.00	0.00	0.11	0.47	0.24	0.66
Oral post-test								
Immediate repair task	0.44	1.10	5.14	4.91	0.77	1.30	6.57	4.69
	0.78	1.78	7.64	3.88	3.08	2.78	9.53	2.15

k = 12 for each score. Also, *n* = 18 for the control group and *n* = 19 for the recasts group

Table 9.2 Descriptive statistics for the pre-test and oral face-to-face interaction tasks

tasks, two additional two-way repeated-measures ANOVAs were carried out for the scores of these participants on the pre-test: one for gender (F_1) and one for number (F_2) agreement scores. As expected, no significant differences were found for group $[F_1(1) = .747, p > .05; F_2(1) = .711, p > .05]$, noun type (familiar, new) $[F_1(1) = .361, p > .05; F_2(1) = 3.058, p > .05]$, or the interaction of group × noun type $[F_1(1) = .361, p > .05; F_2(1) = .234, p > .05]$.

Written post-tests

To examine the short- and long-term effects of computer-delivered recasts in the written post-tests, two 2 (group) × 3 (time: three post-tests) × 2 (noun type) repeated-measures ANCOVAs were performed with working memory as a covariate. The results revealed a significant main effect for group [$F_1(1)$ = 76.221, $p < .01$; $F_2(1)$ = 63.252, $p < .01$], and multiple contrast comparisons indicated that the recasts group was better than the control group in all post-tests (all $ps < .01$) (see Figures 9.2 and 9.3). The results also showed non-significant main effects for time [$F_1(1.32)$ = 1.416, $p > .05$; $F_2(1.31)$ = 1.318, $p > .05$] and for the interaction of time × group [$F_1(1.32)$ = 2.296, $p > .05$; $F_2(1.31)$ = 2.330, $p > .05$], demonstrating that the linguistic gains in the recasts group were maintained over time. Furthermore, learners in the recasts group were able to apply the gender–number agreement rule to new exemplars, judging by the non-significant main effect of noun type [$F_1(1)$ = .747, $p > .05$; $F_2(1)$ = 1.179, $p > .05$]. Also, the interactions of noun type × group [$F_1(1)$ = .488, $p > .05$; $F_2(1)$ = .308, $p > .05$], noun type × time [$F_1(1.29)$ = 1.188, $p > .05$; $F_2(1.60)$ = 2.738, $p > .05$], and noun type × time × group [$F_1(1.29)$ = .164, $p > .05$; $F_2(1.60)$ = 1.204, $p > .05$] were non-significant.

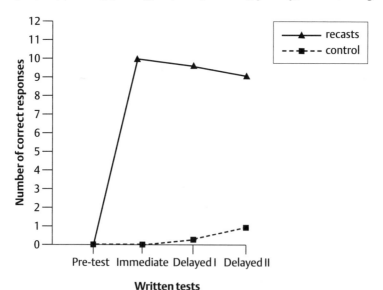

Written tests

The means of this figure are based on data for new nouns

Figure 9.2 Means of correct production of gender agreement in the written tests by group

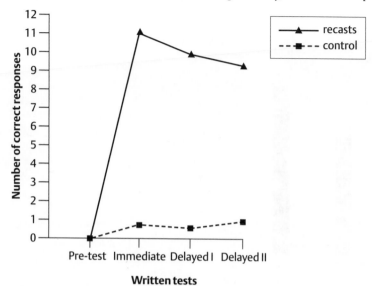

The means of this figure are based on data for new nouns

Figure 9.3 Means of correct production of number agreement in the written tests by group

In addition, there was a significant main effect for working memory [$F_1(1) = 11.311$, $p < .01$; $F_2(1) = 14.674$, $p < .01$]. Follow-up comparisons suggested that working memory was related to the performance of the recasts group in the three written tests (all $ps < .01$), but working memory was not associated with the performance of the control group (probably due to floor effects). Finally, the interactions of working memory × time [$F_1(1.32) = 1.407$, $p > .05$; $F_2(1.31) = 1.298$, $p > .05$], working memory × noun type [$F_1(1) = .352$, $p > .05$; $F_2(1) = .678$, $p > .05$], and working memory × time × noun type [$F_1(1.52) = .500$, $p > .05$; $F_2(1.29) = .592$, $p > .05$] were non-significant.

Oral face-to-face interaction tasks

To explore the long-term effect of computer-administered recasts on the development of grammatical accuracy during oral face-to-face interaction tasks, two 2 (group) × 2 (task) repeated-measures ANCOVAs were conducted with working memory entered as a covariate. The findings showed a significant main effect for group [$F_1(1) = 32.654$, $p < .01$; $F_2(1) = 60.404$, $p < .01$], and subsequent contrast comparisons indicated that the recasts group outperformed the control group in both tasks, all $ps < .01$ (see Figures 9.4 and 9.5). There was also a significant main effect for task [$F_1(1) = 2.56$, $p < .05$; $F_2(1) = 6.601$, $p < .05$], and follow-up comparisons revealed that the means of the immediate repair task were higher than those of the oral post-test (all

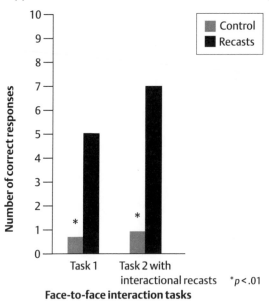

Figure 9.4 Mean of correct production of gender agreement in the face-to-face tasks

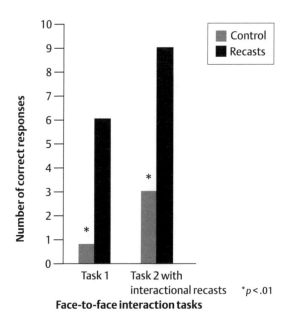

Figure 9.5 Mean of correct production of number agreement in the face-to-face tasks

*p*s < .05 except the control group for gender agreement scores, which was non-significant). It is likely that performance on the immediate repair task was higher because learners received feedback after they produced incorrect utterances. The control group improved in their production of targetlike number (*p* < .05) but not gender. As mentioned above, one way to explain these results is that plural is generally acquired before gender (Finnemann 1992). Another possibility is that the participants, Anglophone learners of a Romance language, were more sensitive to number because English and Spanish both mark plural with the suffix '–s', whereas English lacks gender agreement. The better performance scores of the control group on number than on gender agreement explains why there was a significant interaction of task × group [$F_1(4.93) = 9.124, p < .01$] for gender but not for number [$F_2(1) = .333, p > .05$].

In addition, there was a main effect for working memory [$F_1(1) = 16.279, p < .01; F_2(1) = 49.259, p < .01$], and follow-up comparisons showed that there was a relationship between working memory and the scores of the recasts group in the two face-to-face interaction tasks (all *p*s < .01), but not between working memory and the scores of the control group (again, probably due to floor effects). Lastly, the interaction of working memory × task was not significant [$F_1(1) = 1.143, p > .05; F_2(1) = 1.942, p > .05$].

The inferential statistics from the oral post-tests presented above speak to the effect of the treatment and working memory on the development of L2 linguistic accuracy. To examine the effect of computer-delivered recasts and working memory on the production of targetlike modified output, additional analyses were conducted to assess the performance of the recasts group on the immediate repair task (i.e. the task where participants received feedback when they produced incorrect utterances). Descriptive statistics indicated that learners who had been exposed to computer-delivered recasts modified their output 79.87 per cent of the time that they received feedback. Of every occurrence when they modified their output, learners made noun–adjective gender–number agreement changes 71.78 per cent of the time, noun–adjective number agreement changes 27.59 per cent of the time, lexical changes 0.63 per cent of the time, and phonological changes 0 per cent of the time. A one-way repeated-measures ANCOVA was conducted on gender and number targetlike modifications of the output with working memory as a covariate. The findings revealed a significant main effect for type of modification [$F(1) = 6.640, p < .05$], working memory [$F(1) = 15.230, p < .01$], and the interaction between the two [$F(1) = 13.022, p < .01$]. These results suggest that learners produced more targetlike modified output for number than for gender agreement, and follow-up comparisons indicated that working memory was related to the amount of targetlike modified output for gender and number agreement.

Discussion

The results of this study indicated that oral recasts administered via computer had an immediate and delayed positive effect on the development of grammatical accuracy in written tests and face-to-face interactions, as well as on the production of modified output following interactional recasts. Furthermore, working memory was found to predict learners' ability to benefit from computer-delivered recasts. A discussion of the findings for each of the four research questions is provided below.

The first research question investigated whether computer-delivered oral recasts can facilitate the development of linguistic accuracy in written tests and face-to-face interactions. The findings revealed that learners receiving computer-delivered recasts improved in their targetlike production of noun–adjective agreement in written tests and face-to-face interaction tasks. This result was obtained both for familiar and new nouns, indicating that learners were able to extrapolate the information from the treatment task not only to known lexical items but also to novel ones. These findings are in line with studies reporting a positive effect of recasts on the development of L2 grammatical accuracy in classroom settings (Doughty and Varela 1998; Ohta 2000), experimental settings (Mackey and Philp 1998; Leeman 2003), and computer-mediated contexts (Choi 2000; Ayoun 2001; Sagarra 2004; Sachs and Suh this volume). In addition, the benefits of computer-administered recasts were maintained over a period of two months, suggesting lasting effects of this feedback. Taken together, these findings provide empirical support for the use of computer-delivered recasts outside the classroom to promote L2 morphosyntactic development.

The second research question examined the effect of oral recasts delivered via a computer on the production of modified output. The results of this study reveal that computer-mediated oral recasts promote the production of modified output during later face-to-face interactions with recasts. This study stakes out new territory because it proposes that extensive and intensive practice with oral recasts supplied by a computer increases learners' production of targetlike modified output during oral human–human interaction. As mentioned earlier, Gass (1997) and Swain (1995, 2005) have claimed that modified output facilitates grammatical L2 development because it promotes noticing of target forms. While learner repair does not ensure learner intake, the former may increase the probability that the latter takes place, and this may explain why the amount of modified output learners produce has been found to correlate positively with linguistic accuracy and learning (Loewen 2003b; McDonough 2005). Although modified output can be correct or incorrect, it should be emphasized that the amount of targetlike modified output following interactional recasts was higher with the presence of preceding computer-delivered recasts (71.78 per cent for gender changes and 99.37 per cent for number changes) than it has been in their absence (for example,

51 per cent for targetlike changes and 28 per cent for repetitions of feedback in Mackey, Adams, Stafford, and Winke 2002).

The remaining two research questions of the study explored the relationships between working memory and the learners' ability to benefit from computer-delivered recasts in terms of linguistic accuracy and the production of modified output. The results showed that working memory was associated with the development of linguistic accuracy in written tests and face-to-face interaction tasks for the recasts group but not for the control group. In addition, working memory was related to the amount of targetlike modified output following interactional recasts. As mentioned earlier, the lack of a relationship between working memory and performance of the control group may have been due to this group's low scores on all the tests and tasks (floor effects).

The results of the present study can be compared with Mackey, Philp, Egi, Fujii, and Tatsumi's (2002) findings. In their study, working memory was related to the noticing of recasts and also seemed to be related to L2 development. However, they noted that the high-span learners in their study apparently needed more time than the low-span learners to show changes in their interlanguage system. Whereas all of the learners with low working memory showed development on the immediate post-test, only one of the learners with high working memory did so. On the delayed post-test, on the other hand, the trend appeared to be reversed, and more of the high-span learners showed development. Given the small number of participants in their study, the authors warn that these results are merely suggestive, but it is interesting to note that both their study and the present study (which employed a series of post-tests up to two months after the treatment) showed delayed effects. The same reasoning could explain why Trofimovich, Ammar, and Gatbonton (this volume) did not find an association between working memory and L2 development based on post-tests that were delayed by only 2–12 minutes.

The finding of the present study that working memory was related to the amount of production of targetlike modified output in the recasts group strengthens the results of Mackey, Adams *et al.* (2002) in two ways. First, it provides further evidence that the low to moderate correlations in Mackey, Adams *et al.* between working memory and modified output may have been affected by other factors, as the authors suggested. Second, it provides indirect support to the idea that the relationship between working memory and modified output can be extrapolated to L2 development, as learners in the present study still made changes to their output after interactional recasts two months after exposure to the treatment. While it is not clear whether the treatment, the presence of interactional recasts, or a combination of the two factors facilitated the production of modified output, the results of this study indicate that working memory promotes development of linguistic accuracy in an L2—which is the ultimate goal of using recasts.

Conclusion

In conclusion, the current research suggests that oral recasts provided via computer not only improve learners' development of grammatical accuracy in written tests and oral face-to-face interactions, but also promote the production of modified output following subsequent interactional recasts. Moreover, this study indicates that working memory constrains learners' ability to benefit from computer-delivered recasts in developing linguistic accuracy and producing modified output after interactional recasts. The computer-administered recasts in this study were presented in a controlled and overt format. Having established a relationship between computer-delivered oral recasts, working memory, L2 development, and the production of modified output, future studies should investigate whether the same associations are observed when computer-administered recasts are provided in a less controlled way (see for example Choi 2000; Sachs and Suh this volume). Additionally, the fact that working memory was related to the development of linguistic accuracy does not imply that other cognitive factors do or do not also predict these variables (Trofimovich, Ammar, and Gatbonton this volume). It is also important to note that the findings of this study apply to beginning learners in a foreign language context and, thus, do not speak to learners at other proficiency levels and learning settings. Bearing in mind these limitations, the present study makes a valuable contribution to L2 interactional research because it contributes to evidence of a relationship between working memory and L2 development and because it demonstrates the pedagogical value of computer-based oral recasts outside the classroom, thus potentially allowing teachers to strengthen the focus on communication in the classroom.

10

Recasts, learners' interpretations, and L2 development

TAKAKO EGI

Introduction

As discussed in the Introduction to this volume, research to date has documented the beneficial effects of recasts in second language acquisition (SLA). As we have learnt in the earlier chapters, recasts are multidimensional utterances that on the one hand, provide semantic information relevant to the conversation, and on the other hand, provide negative and positive evidence that may facilitate SLA. Although much of the current line of interactionist research examines how and under what conditions recasts bring about SLA, relatively little is known about which component of recasts is responsible for second language (L2) development.

There is considerable debate over how recasts contribute to SLA. Researchers have often attributed the benefits of recasts to the negative evidence they provide (for example, Farrar 1992; Oliver 1995, 2000; Long, Inagaki, and Ortega 1998). Negative evidence is claimed to facilitate SLA and perhaps be necessary for learning certain aspects of the L2 (White 1991; Trahey and White 1993; Long 1996). However, for negative evidence to become usable, Carroll (1995) argues that learners must recognize the corrective intent of feedback and identify their linguistic problems. However, some classroom studies suggest that this condition is not always met. Given the multidimensional, complex structure of recasts, some researchers have claimed that recasts are ambiguous, and thus learners do not always interpret them as teachers intend, that is, as corrections. Rather, they interpret recasts as alternative expressions or comments on content (Lyster and Ranta 1997; Lyster 1998a, 1998b; Panova and Lyster 2002). These researchers argue that this interpretation makes the negative evidence in recasts inaccessible to learners and thereby limits their developmental benefits. However, this claim requires empirical validation because it rests only on the observation that recasts often result in little learner uptake. That is, this claim still needs to be validated by empirical evidence indicating that recasts interpreted as comments on content or alternative expressions do not lead to *development*.

If learners do fail to notice negative evidence as some classroom researchers claim, any developmental benefits may be ascribed to the positive evidence component of recasts.

The view that recasts promote learning as sources of positive evidence is not new. It originated in the first language literature, where recasts have been defined as both corrective and non-corrective (for example, expansion of child's targetlike utterances). For instance, Morgan and Travis (1989) and Morgan, Bonamo, and Travis (1995) argue that recasts merely function as positive evidence that adds variety to children's language use. Some SLA researchers have also suggested that positive evidence in recasts is more important than negative evidence. For example, Leeman (2003), in a study that compared the effectiveness of negative and positive evidence in the learning of Spanish grammatical gender agreement, ascribed the primary benefits of recasts to enhanced positive evidence. In her study, 74 first-year learners of Spanish engaged in native speaker (NS)–non-native speaker (NNS) dyadic interactions in one of four conditions: implicit negative evidence, enhanced positive evidence, recasts, and control. The results indicated that learners who received recasts and enhanced positive evidence (through phonological stress) significantly outperformed the control group who received simple models. In contrast, the implicit negative evidence group did not show significant improvement compared to the control group. This finding led Leeman to conclude that the benefits of recasts are primarily due to enhanced positive evidence.

Despite research such as Leeman's, given the limited research base, the field has not found a firm answer to the debate over which component of recasts brings about SLA. The discussion may benefit from a construct of learner interpretations, which is an extension of the concept of noticing (Schmidt 1995, 2001). Noticing of recasts implies that learners have paid attention to recasts. However, it does not suggest that learners have noticed negative evidence in recasts, as suggested by R. Ellis and Sheen (2006). In fact, they may have interpreted recasts as sources of positive evidence, such as simple models, or as responses to content, such as confirmation. The construct of learner interpretations addresses the roles learners assign to the recasts they notice, that is, recasts as negative evidence, positive evidence, and/or responses to content. A better understanding of their roles from the learner's viewpoint may provide insight into the question of which component of recasts facilitates SLA. Thus far, little research has investigated whether there is any causal relationship between learners' interpretations of recasts and their developmental benefits. The current study empirically examines this under-researched question by tracing learners' morphosyntactic and lexical development in relation to their interpretations of recasts. The following section examines the potential mediating role that learners' interpretations play in SLA. It also discusses how the factor of linguistic targets might interact with the cognitive variable of learner interpretations.

Recasts, interpretations, and L2 development

Noticing has been identified as a critical factor that mediates L2 input and interaction-driven learning (Gass and Varonis 1994; Long 1996; Gass 1997). Previous research generally suggests that learners notice interactional feedback (for example, Mackey, Gass, and McDonough 2000; Philp 2003; Carpenter, Jeon, MacGregor, and Mackey 2006; Mackey 2006a). However, little research has empirically tested the direct link between noticing of feedback and L2 development.

To test this potential link, Nabei and Swain's (2002) case study traced an EFL learner's language development in relation to the aspects of input she noticed: meaning, language, and feedback. 'Attention to meaning' was operationalized as comments indicating the learner's 'understanding and reflection upon the content of discussion', while 'attention to language' was operationalized as comments 'made on aspects of language' (2002: 51). 'Noticing feedback' was operationalized as comments indicating that the learner interpreted recasts as corrections. The researchers video-taped a lesson and, within a week, administered an acceptability judgment test constructed based on recasts the learner received during the lesson. The test was followed by a stimulated recall interview where the learner reported her thoughts about classroom interactions. This procedure was repeated six times and concluded with a delayed post-test comprised of all the previously given test items. When the learner accurately interpreted recasts as corrections, she performed better on the immediate post-test (67 per cent) than when she attended to the content of class discussions (57 per cent) and linguistic form (47 per cent). However, the learner showed improvement in all categories on the delayed post-test, diminishing the mean differences found on the immediate post-test. Swain and Nabei speculated that the learner's heightened awareness from repeated stimulated recalls may have contributed to these findings. This methodological limitation made the long-term effects of learner interpretations inconclusive.

More recently, Mackey (2006a) empirically examined the relationship among 28 ESL learners' noticing of feedback, linguistic targets, and L2 development in a classroom context. 'Noticing of feedback' was operationalized as learners' awareness of the gap between their non-targetlike production and the targetlike form provided in recasts (i.e. interpretation of recasts as negative and positive evidence), as demonstrated by learner comments gathered through online learning journals, stimulated recall, and questionnaires. The results indicated a clear, positive relationship between learners' noticing and the learning of question forms, whereas for the other two linguistic targets, plurals and past tense, the results were less defined. The study suggests that learners' noticing of feedback and SLA potentially interact with linguistic targets. Further research in this area may provide cognitive accounts for why the learning of certain linguistic features is more amenable to the benefits of conversational interactions than other linguistic targets, as often reported in previous research (for example, Long *et al.* 1998; Iwashita 2003; Jeon this volume).

Given the limited research base in this area, further investigation is clearly needed to examine how learners' different interpretations of recasts may affect the learning of different linguistic targets. If recasts are less effective when learners interpret them as comments about content (i.e. when they do not attend to linguistic evidence), it may lend support to the Noticing Hypothesis, which ascribes a critical role to learners' noticing of form (Schmidt 1995, 2001). If learners do not report noticing negative evidence in recasts, then any developmental gains may be attributed to positive evidence (for example, Leeman 2003). In contrast, if failure to report noticing negative evidence impedes learning, it may support claims that negative evidence facilitates SLA (for example, White 1991; Trahey and White 1993; Long 1996). These questions are the subject of the investigation reported in this chapter. To examine which component of recasts promotes SLA, this study aims to answer the following research question.

Research question

Is there a relationship between learners' interpretations of recasts (as responses to content, negative evidence, and/or positive evidence) and their L2 development?

To answer this question, two hypotheses were tested. The first hypothesis was that learners will show more development when they interpret recasts as negative evidence and/or positive evidence than when they interpret recasts as responses to content (for example, Lyster and Ranta 1997; Schmidt 2001). The second hypothesis was that learners will show more development when they interpret recasts as positive evidence than when they interpret recasts as negative evidence (for example, Leeman 2003).

Method

Operationalizations

'Recasts' were relatively broadly operationalized as a NS's corrective reformulation of all or part of a problematic learner utterance. Researchers have suggested that some recasts are more marked than others due to such features as stress, intonation, and segmentation that signal the error to the learners (for example, Nicholas, Lightbown, and Spada 2001; Sheen 2006). The current study did not differentiate between more and less marked recasts that naturally occurred during interactions, nor did it manipulate learners' attention by using such attention-drawing techniques as repetition and phonological emphasis of the error. (See, for example, Doughty and Varela 1998.) An example of a recast is shown below. All data presented in this chapter come from the current study.

Example 1 Recast
NNS **Obaasan   o   kimasu.*   ← LEARNER ERROR
           grandmother **ACC** come
           (My) grandmother will come.

NS   *Obaasan   ga   kimasu ka?* ← RECAST
           grandmother **SUB** come   Q
           Will (your) grandmother come?

'Noticing of recasts' was operationalized as any verbal comment that indicated the learner had noticed, or paid attention, to the recast at the time. When the learner notices a recast, their attention may be oriented to particular aspect(s) of the recast. Noticing of recasts was subdivided into the following four categories that emerged from the analysis of the verbal report data: interpretations of recasts as (a) responses to content, (b) positive evidence, (c) negative evidence, and (d) negative + positive evidence, each of which will be described in the coding section below.

Participants

Forty-nine adult Japanese as a foreign language (JFL) learners (M: 23; F: 26), ages 18–41 (M = 26), participated in the experiment. The majority of them were English NSs (English, 43; Korean, 3; Chinese, 1; Spanish, 1; French, 1). They were recruited from high-beginning and intermediate Japanese language classes at universities and private language schools in the Washington, D.C. metropolitan area. The average length of prior Japanese instruction was 29 months (SD = 19). This proficiency level of learners were selected because they had acquired enough Japanese to carry out task-based activities and use the language productively but not always accurately, creating the necessary context for recasts to occur naturally. Three female NSs (the researcher and two research assistants), all of whom had JFL teaching experience, served as interlocutors in interactions and elicited learners' introspective comments. The assistants were trained in conducting task-based activities, providing interactional feedback, and eliciting learners' introspective comments.

Design

As shown in Figure 10.1, on Day 1 all learners engaged in a practice task, followed by the first treatment that consisted of a dyadic task-based interaction session. During the interaction, learners received recasts of their non-targetlike utterances from a NS. On Day 2, they participated in the second treatment session, immediately followed by the first post-test. The learning outcomes were analyzed in relation to the learners' introspective comments about recast episodes, gathered through immediate reports (n = 31) and stimulated recall (n = 18). Learners were randomly selected for either immediate reports or stimulated recall and provided their comments at different times (during the

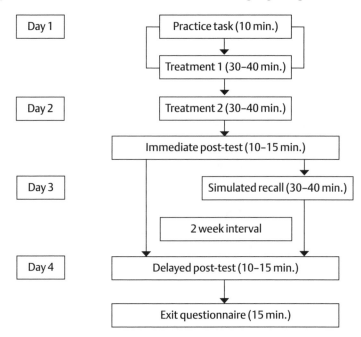

Figure 10.1 Experimental procedure and approximate times

treatment and after the immediate post-test, respectively) as will be explained later. Two weeks after the immediate post-test, all learners took the delayed post-test. At the end of the experiment, learners completed the exit question-naire designed to probe whether they received any external input on the test items. Each experimental instrument is described below.

Treatment materials

As shown in the procedure diagram, the treatment consisted of two NS–NNS conversational sessions. Learners completed two communicative tasks, a 'one-way picture description task' and a 'two-way spot-the-difference task', in each session. Two versions of each task type were developed. In task administration, the order of the task types was counterbalanced, whereas the order of the versions was randomized. In the one-way tasks, pictures showed a scene before and after a crime occurred. The learner held the pre-crime scene and described it in detail to the NS, who played the role of a police officer. In the two-way tasks, each member of a dyad had a similar but slightly different picture and asked each other questions in order to find out the differences between the pictures. A screen hid the pictures from the view of the partner to create an information gap context. During the interactions, the NS provided feedback mainly in the form of recasts on a wide variety of morphosyntactic and lexical errors.

Testing materials

The learners' L2 development was measured using tailor-made immediate and delayed post-tests, designed to test each learner's individual problem areas, following Swain and Lapkin (1998), Swain (2001a), Williams (2001), Nabei and Swain (2002), and Loewen (2005). The post-tests were oral picture description tasks developed based on the recasts each learner received of their morphosyntactic and lexical errors. Thus, both the number and target of test items were contingent upon the errors each learner produced and recasts provided for these errors during the treatment. Because each learner's pattern of errors was not entirely predictable, no formal pre-test was administered. Rather, recast episodes served a similar function to a pre-test, demonstrating either the learner's faulty knowledge or limited control of form.

Each learner was tested on the items for which he or she had received recasts using picture cards developed from the treatment tasks. To differentiate between the treatment and tests, tests were designed by first dividing the treatment tasks into smaller individual pictures. The pictures were further modified by removing, adding, and resizing elements. The NS interlocutor kept careful notes of the learner's errors and recasts during the treatment and selected appropriate cards based on the notes immediately after the second treatment. The selected cards were then shuffled with six distractor cards and presented to the learner for the tailor-made post-test. The same cards were used for the delayed post-test but presented in a different order. An example of a test item is shown in Example 2 below, where the learner was asked to describe a scene in which his use of a lexical item had been non-targetlike and a recast was supplied. By asking him to describe a similar scene, it was possible to test whether the learning of the lexical item had occurred after the recast was provided.

> *Example 2* Targeted item: *kashu* (singer)
> Recast episode
> NNS   *Piano no   *tonari wa,* **uta, uta**   **no**   **hito**   *ga imasu.*
>   piano GEN next TOP **song song GEN person** SUB exist
>   There is a singer by the piano.
>
> NS   *Suteeji no*   *ue*   *ni*   **kashu** *ga*   *iru*   *n*   *desu ka?* ← RECAST
>   stage   GEN above LOC **singer** SUB exist GEN COP Q
>   Is there a singer on the stage?
>
> Tailor-made post-test item developed based on the recast episode
> NS   (Presented the picture card.)
>   *Kono e*   *nitsuite hanashite kudasai.*
>   this picture about speak   please
>   Would you describe this picture?
>
> NNS   **Ano,* **uta, uta** *hito*   *desu. Utatteimasu.*
>   uh   **sing sing person** COP sing-progressive
>   Uh, [she] is a singer. [She] is singing.

Because there was no time to review the recordings before the test sessions, after the interaction data were transcribed, all test items and related recast episodes were carefully examined. Only test items (a) whose associated episodes involved clearly identifiable errors and (b) for which learner commentaries were obtained were selected for the analysis. Another selection criterion concerned external influences. On the exit questionnaire, each learner was presented with a list of the test items for that particular learner and asked to identify any items for which the learner received external input. To control for external influences, those items were eliminated from the learner's data. Of the total of 560 potential test items, 350 items were selected; for each learner, an average of seven test items was selected, ranging from 4–17.

Introspective measures

The learners' comments about recast episodes were gathered through immediate reports ($n = 31$) and stimulated recall ($n = 18$). As shown in Figure 10.1, during the practice task on Day 1, the 31 learners were trained in the immediate report procedure, while the remaining 18 learners completed the task without any intervention. Immediately before the stimulated recall interview, the 18 learners received training in the stimulated recall procedure using a video of this task interaction. The validity of recall data is an important consideration when addressing the role of learner interpretations in SLA. Immediate reports were used with a larger number of participants because their immediacy in recall elicitation was thought to allow information retrieval from short-term memory, which according to Ericsson and Simon (1993) is one of the foremost criteria for valid protocol data. The two techniques are described below.

Immediate reports

Following Egi (2004), each learner was instructed to verbalize thoughts he or she had during a 10–15 second long conversational turn, when cued by the NS, who knocked twice on the table. Prompts were provided immediately after (a) recasts of NNS errors on morphosyntactic and lexical items and (b) correct NNS responses (as distractors). To make recall elicitation less intrusive and predictable, recall was elicited after 10–20 per cent of the error and error-free turns in random order. This procedure has been found not to influence learners' task performance (for example, Egi 2004). When prompted, learners reported their thoughts in English without elaboration or reasoning. They were asked to talk aloud to themselves, rather than conversing with the NS. After the completion of one recall, the task activity resumed until the next knocking stimulus.

Stimulated recall

Following Gass and Mackey (2000), the NS interviewer elicited recall comments from each learner using a series of video clips from the treatment sessions as recall stimuli. As with the immediate report procedure, the video was paused after both (a) recasts of morphosyntactic and lexical errors and (b) correct NNS responses in random order. The treatment tasks were also presented to learners to facilitate recall of thoughts. The NS oriented them towards the time of the task interaction (for example, 'What were you thinking then?') and asked them to recall thoughts at that time in English without elaboration or reasoning. During the interview, the NS listened intently to the learner but avoided actively engaging in the conversation.

Coding

The verbal protocols were coded in terms of whether learners interpreted recasts as being about: (1) responses to content, (2) negative evidence, (3) positive evidence, or (4) negative + positive evidence, each of which is operationalized below. Examples for each category are shown in Table 10.1. Other comments that did not suggest learners' noticing of recasts were not considered in this study. Those comments included learners' reference to task interactions in general, issues irrelevant to the study, and not remembering any thoughts.

1 Responses to content: (a) comments that indicated the learner's interpretation that the NS recast was a comment on content (for example, confirmation, acknowledgement) or (b) comments that concerned the semantic content of the recast. The first example in Table 10.1 shows that the learner interpreted the NS recast of his non-targetlike utterance as a confirmation of meaning. In the second example, the learner received a recast of a non-targetlike numeral expression. His comment suggests he focused on the semantic content of the NS recast. However, he did seem to pay attention to this particular NS turn because his response was different from comments about interactions in general, for example, 'there are so many differences between our pictures. So far, we found five differences', which seemingly suggests that the learner did not pay attention to any particular NS turn. Those sorts of responses were disregarded in this study.

2 Negative evidence: comments which suggested that the learner recognized they had made an error and/or received a recast without a clear indication that the learner noticed the targetlike model in the recast. In the example, the learner reported that she had made an error and received feedback, however, the report does not explicitly suggest her awareness of the targetlike model in the recast.

3 Positive evidence: comments which indicated that the learner noticed the targetlike form in the recast without any report of having attended to negative evidence. As shown in the example, the learner's mention of the targetlike model (*haizara*, ashtray) suggests that he noticed the form. However, the learner did not report that he made an error or was corrected.

4 Negative + positive evidence: comments that indicated the learner not only (a) recognized that he or she had made an error and/or received a recast (i.e.

negative evidence) but also (b) noticed the targetlike model in the recast (i.e. positive evidence).

Interpretation Examples

Responses to content	a Comments on content

> **NNS** **Kokku ga imasu. Nanika niru?* **Yaku, n,　niru o　shimasu.**
> cook SUB exist something boil **bake mm boil ACC do**
> There is a cook. Boil? Bake, mm, [he is] boiling something.

> **NS**　*Kokku-san wa* **niteimasu**　　　*ka?* **Yaiteimasu**　　*ka?*　　← RECAST
>　Cook Mr. TOP **boil-progressive** Q　**bake-progressive** Q
>　Is the cook boiling or baking?

> Recall comment
> Y-san [the NS] confirmed if the cook was boiling or baking something.
> It could be either, but since I see something like water, maybe he is boiling something.
> I don't know.

> b Comments that concerned the semantic content of the recast
> **NNS** **Jisho　　o　　sansatsu　　　kaimashita.* **Sanpyakyu doru　desu.**
>　dictionary ACC three–classifier buy–past　**300**　　　dollar COP
>　(He) bought dictionaries. They were 300 dollars.

> **NS**　**Sanbyaku** *doru! Takai　　desu nee.*　　　　　　　← RECAST
>　**300**　　　dollar expensive COP PAR
>　300 dollars? (They) are expensive, aren't they?

> Recall comment
> She [the NS] thought 300 dollars was too expensive. But dictionaries can be quite
> expensive, particularly good Japanese dictionaries.

Negative evidence	

> **NNS** **X'mas da　kara,　　kutsu o　　katte kudasai.* **Ichi, ichikoo**　　*irimasu.*
>　X'mas COP because shoes ACC buy　please　**one one-classifier** need
>　Because [it's] X'mas, please buy shoes [as a gift]. She needs a pair of
>　shoes.

> **NS**　*X'mas ni　kutsu o　　**issoku**　　　hoshii n　desu ne?*　　← RECAST
>　X'mas for shoes ACC **one-classifier** want　GEN COP PAR
>　She wants a pair of shoes for X'mas?

> Recall comment
> I was having trouble there. I think she [the NS] corrected me.

Positive evidence	

> **NNS** **Watashi no e, teeburu no ue*　　*ni,* **tabako　no　osara** *ga arimasu.*
>　I GEN picture table　GEN above LOC **tobacco GEN dish** SUB exist.
>　In my picture, there is an ashtray on the table.

> **NS**　*Watashi no e　wa,* **haizara** *to　wain gurasu ga　arimasu.*　　← RECAST
>　I　GEN picture TOP **ashtray** and wine glass　SUB exist
>　In my picture, there is an ashtray and a wine glass.

> Recall comment
> She [the NS] said, in her picture, there is an ashtray and a wine glass, um, *haizara to*
> *wain gurasu.* My picture does not have a wine glass.

Negative + positive evidence	NNS	*Kodomo wa watashi ni asonde kudasai. Iimashita.*
		child TOP I **LOC** play please say-past
		The child said, 'please play with me.'
	NS	*Kono aoi fuku no kodomo? Boku to asonde to iimashita ka?* ← RECAST
		this blue clothes GEN child I **with** play COMP say-past Q
		The boy in blue? Did [he] say 'please play with me'?
	Recall comment	
		She [NS] helped me, and I realized I used *ni* instead of *to*. I should have used *to*.

Table 10.1 Interpretation categories and examples

A coding hierarchy was used in order to assign only one interpretation category to each recast episode: negative + positive evidence > negative or positive evidence > responses to content. Negative + positive evidence was ranked highest in the hierarchy because it was the most inclusive category, encompassing both negative and positive evidence. In contrast, responses to content were ranked the lowest among the four because any verbal reference to the linguistic targets of recasts disqualified a comment from being coded as focus on the semantic content. When a learner reported more than one type of interpretation in response to one recast episode, a coding category at a higher level overrode one at a lower level in the category assignment. Of the 307 recalled recast episodes, approximately six per cent of the recast episodes (18) were initially coded in more than one category. Approximately 25 per cent of the recall data was coded by two coders, with inter-coder reliability calculated as simple percentage agreement (97 per cent) and Cohen's Kappa (.97). Following Orwin (1994), the Kappa value of .97 was interpreted as highly reliable.

Scoring

On the post-tests, one point was awarded for targetlike production, and zero points for non-targetlike production. Targetlike production of lexical items was operationalized as correct suppliance of lexical items (for example, one point: *neko*, cat; zero points: **neku*). Targetlike production of morphosyntactic items was operationalized as correct suppliance of morphemes and/or formation of syntactic structures (for example, one point: *hon o **yondeiru** hito*, a person who is reading a book; zero points: **hon o **yomimasu no** hito*, non-targetlike production of the relative clause).

Two independent raters scored approximately 25 per cent of the randomly-selected tests, with high inter-rater reliability as measured by simple agreement percentage (98 per cent) and Pearson correlation coefficients (.999*, $p < .05$). When the raters disagreed on rating or coding, they discussed the discrepancy and recoded the data. Data for which they did not reach agreement after discussion were excluded from the analysis (two per cent of the test data and three per cent of the recall data).

Analysis procedure

As noted earlier, learners' non-targetlike knowledge or limited control of form was established on the basis of their non-targetlike production that triggered recasts. Of the 307 recalled recast episodes, 177 (57.65 per cent) to which learners reported one of the four types of interpretations (responses to content: 16.95; negative: 35.03; positive: 19.77; negative + positive: 28.25 per cent) were considered in this study. As discussed in the coding section above, recast episodes that learners did not report noticing were not considered because the goal of the study was to examine the relationship between the ways learners interpret recasts they *noticed* and subsequent learning. The effectiveness of these noticed recasts was assessed based on whether learners showed any improvement after receiving them, as demonstrated by targetlike production on the tailor-made post-tests. To examine the relationship between learners' interpretations and test performance, within each of the four interpretation categories, each learner's test scores were calculated as a percentage of the correctly answered items.

For the immediate post-test, each learner's test scores were submitted to a repeated-measures analysis of variance (ANOVA) to find out whether the mean scores between the interpretation categories differed significantly. This test excluded cases with missing values (i.e. learners who did not report all types of interpretations), resulting in nine learners for inferential statistics. Due to the small sample size, a non-parametric Friedman test was performed to complement the parametric repeated-measures ANOVA analysis. For both procedures, the alpha level was set at .05. To locate the source of statistical significant differences, a series of *post hoc* paired *t*-tests were conducted. Because multiple *t*-tests may increase the chance of Type 1 error, the alpha level was adjusted to .0083 using Bonferroni correction (Howell 1992).

For the delayed post-test, only descriptive statistics were performed due to the small sample size. The delayed post-test data from the 18 learners who experienced stimulated recall were excluded from the analysis due to a concern for the influence of stimulated recall on their performance. While there were no significant between-group differences on the immediate post-test, after the 18 learners participated in stimulated recall, they outperformed the learners who experienced immediate reports on the delayed post-test ($t(44) = -3.51$, $p = .00$, $Ms = 38.77$, 18.10, respectively), suggesting that the stimulated recall influenced their performance. Because the elimination of these learners from the delayed post-test data significantly decreased the sample size and precluded a reliable statistical analysis, only descriptive statistics were performed. Likewise, no inferential statistics were run for the analysis of the test items by linguistic type. All statistical analyses were conducted using SPSS Version 10.0.5 for Windows.

Results

The research question addressed whether there is a relationship between learners' interpretations of recasts (as responses to content, negative evidence, and/or positive evidence) and their L2 development. The section below first presents the analysis of the tailor-made items and then discusses the items by linguistic type (i.e. morphosyntax and lexis).

Test	Responses to content			Negative			Positive			Negative+Positive		
	n	M	SD	n	M	SD	n	M	SD	n	M	SD
Post-test	27	15.12	32.85	33	27.07	40.81	23	45.65	45.29	22	51.06	44.58
Delayed	21	8.33	24.15	22	12.88	30.83	18	23.15	38.41	14	29.76	37.08

n = the number of learners who reported the respective type of interpretation

Table 10.2 Summary of mean test scores for each interpretation category

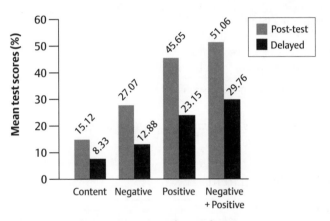

Figure 10.2 Mean test scores for each interpretation category

The descriptive statistics for learners' mean post-test scores by interpretation are presented in Table 10.2. Figure 10.2 graphically illustrates the mean scores by interpretation. There was a linear increase in the mean scores on the immediate post-test: responses to content (15.12 per cent), negative evidence (27.07 per cent), positive evidence (45.65 per cent), and negative + positive evidence (51.06 per cent). A similar trend was found on the delayed post-test (with a decrease in the mean scores in all interpretation categories). In short, on both the immediate and delayed post-tests, the learners' interpretation of recasts as negative + positive evidence led to the highest gains and that as responses to content led to the smallest gains.

Both the parametric repeated-measures ANOVA and non-parametric Friedman tests indicated that the mean differences on the immediate post-test were significant, $F_{(3, 24)} = 7.09$, $p = .00^*$ and $X^2_{(3)} = 12.39$, $p = .01^*$, respectively. In other words, the learners' performance was significantly different depending on how they interpreted recasts. To locate the source of these statistically significant differences, *post hoc* paired *t*-tests were conducted. As presented in Table 10.3, the learners performed significantly better in the short term when they interpreted recasts as positive evidence (p = .00*) or negative + positive evidence (p = .00*) compared to when they interpreted recasts as responses to content. The learners' interpretation of recasts as positive or negative + positive evidence also led to greater gains than their interpretation of recasts as negative evidence; however, the mean differences (p = .04, .02, respectively) were not statistically significant with the adjusted alpha level of .01. The test items were further analyzed in terms of the linguistic focus of the recasts, and these findings are discussed next.

Test	Pairs	df	t	p
Immediate post-test	Content < Negative	18	-0.27	.79
	Content < Positive	15	-4.30	.00*
	Content < Negative + Positive	14	-4.69	.00*
	Negative < Positive	14	-2.31	.04
	Negative < Negative + Positive	16	-2.57	.02
	Positive < Negative + Positive	15	-0.11	.92

X < Y indicates that the mean score for Y was greater than that for X
* p < .01

Table 10.3 Post hoc *paired* t-*tests for mean immediate post-test scores across the interpretation categories*

Morphosyntactic and lexical items

	Morphosyntax											
	Responses to content			Negative			Positive			Negative+Positive		
Test	n	M	SD	n	M	SD	n	M	SD	n	M	SD
Post-test	16	14.58	34.36	25	37.00	47.39	14	39.29	44.63	16	44.79	48.20
Delayed	12	8.33	28.87	17	14.71	34.30	10	10.00	21.08	11	25.76	40.39

	Lexis											
	Responses to content			Negative			Positive			Negative+Positive		
Test	n	M	SD	n	M	SD	n	M	SD	n	M	SD
Post-test	16	11.46	27.70	16	21.88	40.70	13	53.85	51.89	30	28.89	41.28
Delayed	12	11.11	29.59	8	12.50	35.36	12	33.33	49.24	24	25.69	36.03

n = the number of learners who reported the respective type of interpretation

Table 10.4 Summary of mean test scores by linguistic type

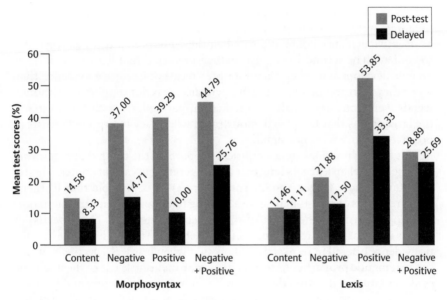

Figure 10.3 Mean test scores by linguistic type

As shown in Table 10.4 and Figure 10.3, the analysis of the morphosyntactic items also showed a linear increase in the mean scores; learners' interpretation of recasts as responses to content showed the lowest mean scores in both short-term (14.58 per cent) and longer-term (8.33 per cent) learning. For the lexical items, learners who interpreted recasts as being primarily about content indicated the smallest gains on both the immediate (11.46 per cent) and delayed (11.11 per cent) post-tests. Lexical learning was noticeably different from morphosyntactic learning in one way. Learners' interpretation of lexical recasts as positive evidence led to substantially greater learning (immediate, 53.85 per cent; delayed, 33.33 per cent) relative to the other ways in which learners interpreted recasts.

Discussion

Learners' interpretations and L2 development

This section discusses the findings in light of the research question that addressed the relationship between learners' interpretations of recasts and L2 development. The results lent partial support to the first hypothesis that when learners interpret recasts as negative evidence and/or positive evidence, the recasts are more developmentally beneficial than when learners interpret them as responses to content. The learners' interpretation of recasts as positive evidence alone or a combination of negative and positive evidence resulted in significantly greater short-term learning than did their interpretation of recasts as responses to content. However, contrary to the prediction, learning outcomes were not significantly greater when learners interpreted recasts only as negative evidence compared to when they interpreted them as responses to content. The second hypothesis, which predicted that learners will show greater development when they interpret recasts as positive evidence than when they interpret them as negative evidence, was not supported. Although trends were consistent with the prediction, particularly with lexical items, the larger gains that learners demonstrated when they interpreted recasts as positive evidence were not significant.

This finding provides some empirical support for the claim that recasts are less effective when learners interpret them as comments about content (Lyster and Ranta 1997; Lyster 1998a, 1998b, 2004). It is possible that learners' interpretations of recasts may serve a filtering function, perhaps through some focusing in terms of the target of their selective attention. The aspect(s) of recasts that learners attend to may in part determine the utility of the linguistic evidence offered in recasts. It is likely that when learners selectively attend to the semantic properties of recasts, they may make little use of the linguistic evidence contained within them, thereby limiting its developmental benefits. Example 3 below illustrates a typical example of learners' test performance when they interpreted recasts as responses to content.

> *Example 3*   Interpretation of a recast as a response to content and
> subsequent test performance
> NNS *Onna   no   hito   futari   desu. *Futari   ni   imasu.*
>   woman GEN person two people COP.   Two people LOC exist
>   [They] are two women. There are two women.
> NS   *Otoko no hito ga sannin to, onna no hito ga*
>   *futari imasu.*   ← RECAST
>   man GEN person SUB three people and woman GEN person SUB
>   two people exist
>   There are three men and two women, aren't there.
> Recall I was just talking about the people in the store. Just trying to picture
>   them and talk about it. You confirmed what I said, and I was like,
>   sure, sounds right.
> Immediate post-test
> NNS *Otoko no   hito   ga   futari   ni   imasu.*
>   men   GEN person SUB two people LOC exist
>   There are two men.
> Delayed post-test
> NNS *Otoko no   hito   desu. Eeto, futari   ni   imasu.*
>   men   GEN person COP um   two people LOC exist
>   They are men. There are two [men].

In Example 3, the NS provided a recast of the learner's non-targetlike oversuppliance of a locative particle *ni* before the existential verb (*imasu* there is/are). As the recall comment indicates, the learner interpreted the recast as a confirmation of meaning. On the immediate post-test, the learner repeated the same error, *otoko no hito ga futari **ni** imasu* there are two men. Also on the delayed post-test, the learner continued to produce the error. The pattern of test results illustrated by Example 3 was frequently observed when learners interpreted recasts as comments about content. Learners' attention to recasts did not seem conducive to learning when they failed to attend to the linguistic evidence.

The next question that needs to be addressed is whether learners' selective attention to the negative evidence or positive evidence component of recasts differentially impacts L2 learning. The descriptive findings of the current study evidenced a detectable, albeit non-significant, trend in support of Leeman (2003), who ascribed the benefits of recasts primarily to enhanced positive evidence. The learners' interpretation of recasts as positive evidence often resulted in superior performance than their interpretation of recasts as negative evidence. It is, however, premature to draw a conclusion about the relative effectiveness of negative and positive evidence based on the limited research base in this area. And it should be noted that in the current study, unlike Leeman's, learners showed the greatest improvements when they interpreted recasts as providing both negative and positive evidence. It is quite possible that the benefits of recasts cannot be simply attributed to one type of linguistic evidence, and careful consideration must be made to the acquisition processes involved in the learning of particular linguistic targets.

Lyster (2004) and Panova and Lyster (2002) argue that recasts, which contain both positive and negative evidence, may efficiently assist the internalization of new forms, while negotiation moves, which only offer negative evidence, may more effectively help increase learners' control over partially-internalized forms through pushed output processes (Swain 2005). The relative contributions of positive and negative evidence might vary according to the linguistic domains in question. (For a discussion of the effects of a combination of interactional modifications on different linguistic areas, see Jeon this volume.) Morphosyntactic learning may involve hypothesis testing and rule generalization, while lexical learning may primarily be driven by memorizing of targetlike examples as discussed by Schmidt (1995). In the current study, the benefits of noticing positive evidence were far more apparent in lexical learning than in morphosyntactic learning. Learners performed considerably better when they interpreted lexical recasts as positive evidence than when they interpreted them as negative evidence. This is demonstrated by large mean differences between the two interpretation categories in both the short-term (31.97 per cent) and long-term (20.83 per cent) learning. In lexical learning, learners' noticing of positive evidence may be more likely to result in immediate interlanguage changes than in morphosyntactic learning. Grammatical knowledge gained through hypothesis testing and rule generalization may be revised through repeated exposures to negative as well as positive data, gradually approximating the targetlike rules. In building such linguistic knowledge, both positive and negative evidence might be equally important. In the current study, learners performed similarly when they interpreted morphosyntactic recasts as negative evidence and when they interpreted them as positive evidence, as demonstrated by much smaller mean differences for both the short-term (2.29 per cent) and long-term (4.17 per cent) learning. In short, the benefits of recasts may not be simply attributable to a single type of linguistic evidence, and future research on the relative effectiveness of negative and positive evidence may benefit from more attention being paid to the acquisition processes involved in the learning of different linguistic items.

Limitations and future directions

As is commonly acknowledged, findings of the kind reported in this chapter cannot be generalized to other learners and learning environments without careful consideration. The participants of the study represented only a subset of JFL learners, who were educated adults with experience of formal language instruction. They were exposed to the L2 interaction in a controlled laboratory setting, the nature of which might be considerably different from a classroom setting (although see Gass, Mackey, and Ross-Feldman 2005). Given that it is mostly studies within classroom contexts which have led to suggestions that recasts are not useful when learners interpret them as comments on content, further empirical testing in classroom settings with different populations is clearly warranted to broaden the scope of the claim that learners' interpretations may affect the effectiveness of recasts.

The tailor-made post-tests employed in this study allowed testing of the learners' idiosyncratic, widely varied problem areas. However, tailor-made post-tests are not without problems. Because the errors learners would make were unpredictable, pre-testing was not possible. Instead, recast episodes were taken as evidence of faulty L2 knowledge or little control of form. It was therefore unclear whether an error represented a gap in the learner's knowledge or a performance error during oral production. Tailor-made post-tests are limited in clearly establishing learners' prior knowledge, making it difficult for researchers to identify the nature of learner errors. Pre-testing on pre-selected linguistic items may be more reliable in this respect because multiple opportunities to produce particular linguistic forms enhance reliability, allowing researchers to assess learners' prior knowledge with more confidence. Using a pre-post-test design on selected linguistic targets, continued research on the relationship between learners' interpretations and L2 development is currently underway.

One of the issues this study addressed was the relative contributions of negative and positive evidence. However, it should be noted that unlike Leeman (2003), the treatment in the current study did not empirically isolate linguistic evidence. Learners' failure to report one type of linguistic evidence does not, therefore, mean that they did not receive the linguistic evidence. Rather, the study intended to address the effectiveness of recasts when learners interpret them as providing certain linguistic evidence or comments on content. However, it is important to note that learners' reports of noticing one aspect of recasts do not mean that they did not notice other aspects. It is quite possible that they have noticed, but did not fully report their thoughts during recall. As with any introspective research, the recall data in this study inevitably contained this sort of under-reporting problem, and interpretation of data necessitated the researcher's inference. In addition, learners showed wide individual variations in their orientation of attention and subsequent learning. Some learners seemed to take an analytical approach to language learning, while some seemed to take a meaning-oriented approach. There was a trend that the former reported form-focused comments, while the latter reported meaning-focused comments. Often times, little correlation was found between their reports and test performance, suggesting that for some individuals, self-report data may not be a reliable predictor of subsequent learning. These individual differences contributed to large variations in the effects of learner interpretations on subsequent learning, as evidenced by large standard deviations. Another methodological limitation concerns the completeness of the recall database. It was not practically possible to elicit learners' reports about every recast episode. It is thus possible that the learners' post-test performance might have been better explained by recasts that were not recalled. Taken together, the results should be carefully interpreted with consideration for these inherent limitations of introspective research.

Conclusion

The present study has extended knowledge of cognitive processes involved in interaction-driven learning by shedding some light on the question of how learners' interpretations of recasts may mediate L2 acquisition processes. The study provides empirical support for the argument that recasts are of limited utility when learners interpret them as responses to content. Learners demonstrated significantly greater short-term learning when they interpreted recasts as positive evidence alone or a combination of negative and positive evidence than when they interpreted them as responses to content. However, as Mackey (2007) notes, 'the fact that learners sometimes fail to identify feedback as such does not necessarily imply that the feedback is not beneficial for learners'. Little is known about exactly how much feedback learners need to interpret as such in order to benefit from it, and it is a question that requires further empirical investigation. The study also suggests that the relative effectiveness of negative and positive evidence may be discussed more productively with attention to the types of linguistic knowledge to be learnt. In conclusion, the current study suggests that learners' interpretations of recasts undoubtedly serve a gate-keeping role, determining the extent to which learners may benefit from the linguistic evidence recasts offer.

11

Recasts in communicative EFL classes: do teacher intent and learner interpretation overlap?

JI-HYUN KIM and ZHAOHONG HAN

Introduction

Long's (1996) Interaction Hypothesis—that interaction ties input, output, corrective feedback, and selective attention together in a meaningful environment and thereby facilitates second language development—has served as a major theoretical framework for L2 empirical research over the last ten years. Its pedagogical corollary, focus on form, has, in particular, been a central object of investigation. Focus on form (Long 1991) refers to an overt yet incidental focus of learner attention to certain forms, naturally induced by communicative negotiation, and as such, can be realized in a variety of ways, including recasting (for example, A: 'He goes to school yesterday.' B: 'He went to school yesterday.'), which is the focus of this chapter.

Recent SLA literature has witnessed a proliferation of studies on recasts, a type of implicit feedback that simultaneously embodies positive and negative evidence (Leeman 2003). Researchers have both described and experimented with recasts as they naturally occur in classrooms or are contrived in laboratory settings. Collectively, these efforts have given rise to the understanding that the efficacy of recasts as a vehicle for corrective feedback depends largely on their interaction with external and internal factors. (For reviews, see Introduction to this volume; Nicholas, Lightbown, and Spada 2001; Braidi 2002; Long 2006; Loewen and Philp 2006.) It is understood, for example, that context—as an external factor—may predict the likelihood that a learner will attend to the corrective function of a given recast. (See, for example, R. Ellis, Basturkmen, and Loewen 2001a; Sheen 2004; Lyster and Mori 2005.) In the meantime, there is a growing awareness that learner internal factors, such as working memory, perception, readiness, L1 influence, and metalinguistic sensitivity, may curtail the desired effects of recasts, dependently or independently of the external factors.

What is noteworthy about this body of research, however, is that the two sets of factors have so far received unequal attention. On the one hand, numerous studies have been conducted to identify and manipulate external factors such as context, intensity, length, and scope, driven, often, by the assumption that the efficacy of recasts ensues from gaining control over these variables. On the other hand, there exists only a slim amount of research on learner internal factors. Consequently, little is known as to how learner-internal constraints may function to modulate the effectiveness of recasts (or corrective feedback in general, for that matter), even when external factors are conducive. Yet it is becoming increasingly clear that for most, if not all, quarters of SLA research, the line on learner perceptions needs to be pursued, continued, and substantiated. As Slimani-Rolls (2005) insightfully concludes from her recent study of classroom learner interaction mediated by different task setups, learner idiosyncrasy is 'a far more important phenomenon than commonality' (ibid.: 195).

In this chapter, we would like to contribute to the on-going discussion on learner perceptions about interactional feedback by reporting and discussing an empirical study we conducted in four EFL classes in Korea on the relationship between teachers' intent for recasts and learners' interpretation thereof, taking account of such variables as the type of teacher intent (communicative or corrective), the type of addressee (direct or indirect), the type of linguistic target (morphology, syntax, phonology, or lexis), and the form of recast (isolated declarative, isolated interrogative, integrated declarative, or integrated interrogative). In the sections that follow, we will offer a brief overview of the existing research by sampling four previously conducted studies, outline the variables that our study sought to investigate, describe the design of the study, report the results, and discuss key findings. We will conclude by summarizing the insights that emerged from the study and noting the methodological limitations of the study.

Empirical research on learner cognitive reactions

The term 'cognitive reactions', as used in this chapter, is used broadly, subsuming such terms that have appeared in the literature as learner response, view, perception, noticing, awareness, understanding, and interpretation in relation to corrective feedback generally, and recasts specifically. As noted above, the research on learner cognitive reactions is as yet scarce, and in fact, began only quite recently. In this section, we review four studies: Roberts (1995), Mackey, Gass, and McDonough (2000), Philp (2003), and Han (2001).

Roberts (1995) examined how much error correction students noticed and understood in a college-level, Japanese as a foreign language class where error correction was a key component of the teacher's pedagogy. Drawing on Schmidt's (1990) Noticing Hypothesis, Roberts hypothesized that 'the efficacy of error correction is directly related to the condition that the L2 learner not only recognizes that he/she is being corrected, but understands the nature of the correction' (1995: 167). For the study, he video-taped and transcribed a 50-minute class, and several days later, invited three students to individually view the video and note down any instance of teacher correction. The data, comprising mainly the transcript of the session and the students' analysis, were then respectively coded for error types, correction strategies (for example, recasts, repetition, and confirmation checks), the number of error corrections noted, and the number of error corrections understood. The results showed, among other things, that of a total of 92 instances of error correction, the students were, on average, able to identify 32 (35 per cent) and understood about 19 (21 per cent). Where recasts are concerned, they noticed approximately 25 of 65 recasts (38 per cent), and understood about 16 (25 per cent). One interesting finding from this study relates to the role played by proficiency: it appears that lower-proficiency learners are more apt than higher-proficiency learners at identifying error correction. Roberts conjectured that 'it may be that the less proficient students experience more correction than those who are more proficient and thus are more finely tuned to the teacher's error correction signals' (ibid.: 179). On the whole, he concluded:

> [S]tudents are only aware of corrective activity in the classroom a fraction of time and even when they are, it is not likely that they understand the nature of the error in many instances
> (ibid.: 180).

The study thus documented a discrepancy between teacher corrective feedback and learner perception, underscoring the latter as a source of limitations on the effectiveness of the former.

A similar, though not quite identical, finding is reported in Mackey *et al.* (2000). Motivated by the Interaction Hypothesis (Pica 1994a; Long 1996; Gass 1997), and in particular, the assertion that negotiated interaction directs learners' attention to particular aspects of language, Mackey *et al.* investigated learner perceptions about interactional feedback including recasts. Two specific concerns guided their data collection and analyses: (a) whether feedback was indeed perceived as such by learners; and (b) whether their perceptions of the target of the feedback were accurate. Ten learners of English as a second language (ESL) and seven learners of Italian as a foreign language (IFL) separately participated in a dyadic interactional task with native speakers. The interactions were video-taped and played back to the learners as a way to stimulate their recalls of thoughts at the time of the original interaction. (On the methodology of stimulated recall, see Gass and Mackey 2000.) The recall sessions were audio-recorded, from which episodes of interactional feedback and learners' comments were then extracted and coded for types of linguistic content. Tabulations of tokens of four types of recalls—morphosyntactic, phonological, semantic, and lexical—indicated that the participants had most often made remarks about lexis and least about morphosyntax. Further, tabulations of the linguistic target of the feedback episodes and of the accuracy rate of the learners' perceptions vis-à-vis these episodes revealed the following patterns:

For the ESL participants:

a Distribution of linguistic content of feedback episodes
   morphosyntactic (47 per cent) > phonological (41.5 per cent) > lexical
   (10.5 per cent)
b Correctness of perceptions
   lexical (83.3 per cent) > phonological (60 per cent) > morphosyntactic (13
   per cent)

For the IFL participants:

c Distribution of linguistic content of feedback episodes
   lexical (48 per cent) > morphosyntactic (31.5 per cent) > phonological (18
   per cent)
d Correctness of perceptions
   lexical (66 per cent) > morphosyntactic (24 per cent) > phonological (21.4
   per cent)
   (Mackey *et al.* 2000)

It appears, then, that overall and across the board, there is a discrepancy between feedback and perception, as reported in the Roberts (1995) study. In this case, not only did the learners' perceptions never fully match up with the feedback provided, but they differed also with respect to the linguistic target of the feedback—with grammar-oriented feedback (i.e. morphosyntactic) always trailing meaning-oriented feedback (i.e. lexical). Furthermore, according to the *post hoc* analyses of data from the ESL participants, morphosyntactic errors were mostly treated through recasts (92 per cent), which, as in Roberts (1995), nevertheless elicited a low rate of perception (<12 per cent) and of uptake (<16 per cent). Mackey *et al.* thereby deduced that 'using recasts to provide morphosyntactic feedback may have been suboptimal' (ibid.: 493; see also Gass and Lewis this volume).

Contrary, however, to this finding, Philp (2003) reported that participants in her study noticed over 60–70 per cent of recasts. Targeting one morpho-syntactic feature, viz., question formation, and using cued immediate recall as a measure of noticing, Philp collected and assessed the accuracy of recalls by 33 adult ESL learners while taking part in five sessions of dyadic task-based interaction with native speakers. The results showed *inter alia* that the participants' accuracy of noticing is significantly determined by their own cognitive resources, such as their current interlanguage knowledge and attentional capacity. The study thus highlights the selective nature of learner noticing of recasts (see also Mackey *et al.* 2000), and provides supporting evidence for a more generally noted bias in second language input processing (White 1987; VanPatten 1996; Gass 1997; Carroll 1999). Learners, that is, typically notice certain things in the input to the exclusion of others.

This processing bias can, in fact, be a function of a myriad of learner-internal constraints, not the least of which is the learner's knowledge of his/her L1. Han (2001) documents through a longitudinal case study how L1 influence may persistently misguide a learner's interpretation of corrective feedback. Participants in the study were (a) a female Thai speaker, Siri, who at the time of the study was attending a college-level intensive program in Norwegian as a Second Language, and (b) her teacher, a native speaker of Norwegian, who had had many years of practical experience. Han followed, over the course of one academic year, Siri's responses to the teacher's corrective feedback—mostly written recasts—on errors shown in her weekly essays. Of relevance to our purposes is that there was one particular construction in Siri's interlanguage which persisted over seven months irrespective of the teacher's repeated correction—16 recasts. An example appears in Example 1a and 1b.

Example 1a Siri
På genser si har ord. (4/11/94)
on sweater his has words

Example 1b Teacher
På genseren hans er det ord.
On his sweater there are words.
(Han 2001: 586)

Han's elicitation, through interviewing, of Siri's interpretation of the error corrections revealed that Siri, notwithstanding her repeated noticing, had consistently misinterpreted the teacher's recasts and misconstrued the contrast between the recast and her own sentence. When asked about Example 1a and 1b, for instance, she said both were acceptable with the only difference being that 1b carries emphasis and 1a does not. Thus, she was completely oblivious to the real difference that 1a contains a null subject and has the word order of AV$_{(null}$S)O, whereas 1b has AVSO. In summary, Siri's interpretation shed light on the persistence and resistance of this particular error in her production.

Further investigation of the nature of the error using elicitation tasks such as translation and grammaticality judgment demonstrated a full congruence between Siri's persistent and resistant behavior and her mental representation. But more important is that it tracked down the true driving force behind the interlanguage construction, namely, the implicit influence of, *inter alia*, a prevalent pragmatic word order licensed in the native language, Thai. (For a full discussion, see Han 2001.) Such influence shielded Siri from seeking alternative routes to processing the recasts (i.e. restructuring), and continuously biased her processing of the *det være* ('there be') construction, contained in the recasts and elsewhere (for example, in the textbook), as being equivalent to *ha* ('to have').

To sum up the existing research: there have only been a small number of studies on learner cognitive reactions to corrective feedback/recasts. Even so, these studies, collectively, lend themselves to a gradient of understanding. Beginning with the earliest attempt, Roberts's study, featuring a generic concern with the extent to which classroom learners recognize and understand teachers' corrective feedback, identified a broad discrepancy between the give and the take of feedback. This finding was subsequently confirmed and substantiated in later studies: Mackey *et al.*'s (2000) investigation of learners' perceptions about feedback led to the crucial finding that different linguistic contents mediated through recasts and/or negotiation embody varying saliency for learners, resulting, therefore, in differential perception and uptake. Philp (2003), exploring cued learner uptake of recasts, delimited learners' current interlanguage knowledge and working memory capacity as significant modulating variables that may affect the extent of noticing of recasts. Finally, through an in-depth, longitudinal analysis and diagnosis of an individual learner's responses to written recasts, Han (2001) established that the discrepancy between teacher feedback and learner interpretation thereof may also arise from L1 influence, and notably, that L1-inspired perception and behavior are not quite amenable to recasts (c.f., Selinker and Lakshmanan 1992; Mackey *et al.* 2000).

The existing studies have, thus, afforded some important insights into learners' cognitive reactions to corrective feedback/recasts. Clearly, however, this strand of research is limited, both in breadth and depth. In the study reported below, we considered two issues. The first issue relates to learners' interpretation of recasts in relation to teachers' underlying intent, and the second issue concerns learners' ability to recognize gaps or contrasts between teachers' recasts and the trigger utterances. On the latter issue, we were particularly interested in the role played by (a) the type of teacher intent (corrective or communicative), (b) the type of addressee (direct or indirect), (c) the type of linguistic target (morphology, syntax, phonology, or lexis), and (d) the form of recast (declarative or interrogative), each of which is described below. This study departs from the previous studies reviewed above in that it focuses exclusively on recasts and incorporates both students' and teachers' perceptions, hence providing the hitherto most comprehensive analysis of instructed learners' perceptions of recasts.

The type of teacher intent

According to Lyster (1998b; Lyster and Ranta 1997), in meaning-based classrooms, teachers often use recasts not only to indicate students' non-targetlike utterances, that is, for a corrective purpose, but also to sustain classroom interaction and maintain its coherence, that is, for a communicative purpose. There are, therefore, likely times when the two functions are conflated and confused in learners' minds, which may reduce the chances of recasts being noticed. However, to date, there has been no direct empirical research into teachers' underlying intent for recasts. Hence, little is known about whether corrective and communicative recasts differentially affect learners' noticing of gaps between their utterances and the recasts.

The type of addressee

In a classroom setting, learners not only directly receive recasts but also observe recasts directed to peers. According to Ohta (2000), students do seem to notice salient contrasts conveyed by the recasts that are directed to their peers. Nabei and Swain (2002), on the other hand, provide evidence suggesting that recasts are more accurately noticed by direct addressees than otherwise. The impact of recasts on indirect addressees, therefore, remains to be ascertained.

The type of linguistic target

It is now widely accepted that linguistic forms are not equal, and hence are differentially processed and acquired. (For discussion, see Hulstijn and DeGraaff 1994; VanPatten 1996; Han 2004; DeKeyser 2005.) In the literature on recasts, this has been demonstrated in studies by Long, Inagaki, and Ortega (1998), Iwashita (2003), Ellis (this volume), and Jeon (this volume), among others. Mackey *et al.* (2000) has shown, as discussed above, that learners' perceptions of recasts vary such that they are more accurate about lexical and phonological feedback than about morphosyntactic feedback. However, further investigation is warranted on the generalizability of this finding.

The form of recast

Recasts can take different forms, even though the majority of the studies tend not to differentiate them. Lyster was the first to perform a fine-grained analysis of recasts. In his 1998 study, for example, he distinguished between four different forms of recasts—the isolated declarative, the isolated interrogative, the incorporated declarative, and the incorporated interrogative—noting that in the immersion classrooms, isolated declarative recasts generated more uptake than recasts of any other form (c.f., Sheen 2004). But, again, does this finding generalize to other instructional settings?

Research questions

Guided by the above considerations, the following research questions were formulated:

1 To what extent do teacher intent and learner interpretation overlap?
2 To what extent do learners accurately recognize the gaps between the trigger utterances and the linguistic information contained in the recasts?
3 Is recognition of gaps affected by the type of teacher intent, the type of addressee, the type of linguistic target, and the form of recast?

Method

Context and participants

The study was conducted in four intermediate English as a Foreign Language (EFL) classes at a private institute in Seoul, Korea. The classes were taught by two native-speaking teachers of English, following a communicative methodology. The focus of the classes was on developing communicative skills through oral practice in everyday English, and the classroom interaction was meaning-oriented, guided by a theme-based textbook featuring activities such as role plays, interviews, and discussions.

Every week, the classes met for five sessions of 50 minutes. On the days the study was conducted, the class size ranged from 8–10 students. Detailed information is given in Table 11.1.

	Teacher 1		Teacher 2	
	Class 1	**Class 2**	**Class 3**	**Class 4**
Number of students	10 (7 females; 3 males)	9 (7 females; 2 males)	10 (8 females; 2 males)	8 (5 females; 3 males)
Level	Intermediate	Intermediate	Intermediate	Intermediate
Theme	Unfamiliar foods	Fear of unknown foods	Have you ever offended (or been offended by) someone?	The culture of money
Format of interaction	Teacher–student; student–student	Teacher–student; student–student	Teacher–student; student–student	Teacher–student; student–student

Table 11.1 Class information

The students, aged between 19 and 35, were placed into the intermediate level by their scores on the institute's placement test. Most of them had learnt English in traditional teacher-fronted classrooms in middle school and high school. None of them had lived in an English-speaking country. Twenty students, five from each class, who appeared to interact most often with the teachers, were invited to participate individually in a stimulated recall interview. The two teachers individually participated in a separate stimulated recall interview. Both of them were male, and had taught EFL for more than a year. Neither of them had any academic grounding in current theories of SLA.

The non-randomized selection of student participants was based on the following consideration: the methodology of stimulated recall, as applied in this context, is predicated on learners' output. In the present study we were interested in learners' concurrent thoughts on the recasts that were directed to others' output or to their own. If, by random selection, participants in the stimulated recall interview happened to be the ones who, during the class interaction, produced little output and hence received few recasts, the data would subsequently be inadequate for us to address our research question. We readily admit that the lack of randomization may compromise the generalizability of our findings, and a solution to the dilemma might lie in working with a much larger pool of class participants than the present study involved.

Design and procedure

Class selection

On the first and second days of the study, one of the researchers observed eight intermediate classes, out of which four were selected for the study on the grounds that the teachers frequently and primarily deployed recasts in their interactions with the students. As will be detailed in the section on coding, the recasts they used took an assortment of forms, performing communicative as well as corrective functions.

Recording of classroom interaction

Classes 1 and 2, taught by Teacher 1, were observed and video-taped on the third and fourth days of the study, and Classes 3 and 4, taught by Teacher 2, on the fifth and sixth days. In addition to video-taping, a wireless, clip-on microphone was attached to the teachers for audio-recording.

Stimulated recall interview with students

Twenty students individually watched the class video with the researcher. It is worth pointing out that although this happened immediately after the class, the fact that students had to wait their turn to be interviewed produced relative delays for some of them, the maximum delay being six hours. During each interview, the researcher, guided by the notes she had taken while observing the class and/or aided by the number indexes displayed on the recorder, paused the tape after every instance of a recast and asked the student to describe what s/he was thinking at the time the recast was given. As a distracter, the same question was also asked after a few episodes on other types of feedback (for example, clarification requests and explicit correction) and on teachers' questions that were irrelevant to the focus of the study. The student was also encouraged to pause the tape at any time as s/he wished, to add thoughts about any part of the class interaction. The interview was conducted in Korean so as to ensure that the students' recalls would not be obfuscated by their lack of L2 speaking ability. The interview was audio-taped and subsequently translated and transcribed in English. The average time taken for each interview was 73.5 minutes.

Stimulated recall interview with teachers

The interview with Teacher 1 was conducted by the same researcher on the fourth day of the study and with Teacher 2 on the sixth day. To minimize any conceivable priming effect, it was administered immediately after the second class taught by each teacher. During the interview, the teacher watched two video-tapes (i.e. one tape per class), and was asked to recall his thoughts at the time he provided the feedback. He, too, could pause the tape at any time, if he wanted to add any thoughts. The interviews, conducted in the teachers' native language, English, were audio-taped and transcribed. The interview with Teacher 1 took 137 minutes and 148 minutes with Teacher 2. Table 11.2 sums up the schedule of the study.

Day	Schedule	Time taken
Day 1	Class observation (4 intermediate classes)	200 minutes
Day 2	Class observation (4 intermediate classes)	200 minutes
Day 3	Observing and video-taping Class 1 (T1) →	50 minutes
	Stimulated recall interview with students in Class 1	330 minutes (S1: 77 mins.; S2: 65 mins.; S3: 64 mins.; S4: 60mins.; S5: 64 mins.)
Day 4	Observing and video-taping Class 2 (T1) →	50 minutes
	Stimulated recall interview with students in Class 2 →	395 minutes (S1: 85 mins.; S2: 72 mins.; S3: 79 mins. S4: 70 mins.; S5: 89 mins.)
	Stimulated recall interview with Teacher 1 about Classes 1 and 2	137 minutes
Day 5	Observing and video-taping Class 3 (T2) →	50 minutes
	Stimulated recall interview with students in Class 3	380 minutes (S1: 83 mins.; S2: 74 mins.; S3: 63 mins.; S4: 87 mins.; S5: 73 mins.)
Day 6	Observing and video-taping Class 4 (T2) →	50 minutes
	Stimulated recall interview with students in Class 4 →	365 minutes (S1: 89 mins.; S2: 72 mins.; S3: 78 mins.; S4: 60 mins.; S5: 66 mins.)
	Stimulated recall interview with Teacher 2 about Classes 3 and 4	148 minutes

Table 11.2 Day-to-day schedule

Coding

The data, comprising transcripts of recast episodes and the students' and teachers' recall comments, were subjected to three rounds of coding, according to (a) their complexity, (b) their linguistic content, and (c) their form and meaning. A recast was operationalized as either an isolated or expanded rephrasing of a student's erroneous utterance. A recast episode, following Nabei and Swain (2002), contained a sequence of one or more turns, involving at least one recast. It therefore began with a non-targetlike utterance which was then recast by a teacher, and ended with a student's utterance signalling either a response to the recast or topic continuation. Note that the episodes are culled from the class transcripts. As such, the last line of each episode is not co-terminous with the end of the interaction.

Recasts according to complexity

The recasts were first coded into simple or complex recasts, according to whether they involved one or more than one change. Examples are given in 2 and 3.

Example 2   A simple recast
Episode 26
S2.3   Yes, in Seoul ... we ordered it ... because we was very curious.
T1   We were very curious.
S2.3   We were very curious.

Example 3   A complex recast
Episode 22
S2.4   I can see their leg.
T1   I could see their legs.
S2.4   I could see.

In Example 2, Teacher 1 (T1) provided a simple recast of a non-targetlike utterance produced by Student 3 from Class 2 (S2.3), targeting only one error, namely, the lack of subject–verb agreement between 'we' and 'was'. By contrast, in Example 3, T1 provided a complex recast in response to the utterance of Student 4 of Class 2 (S2.4), targeting two errors, viz., an incorrect use of verb tense for 'can' and an omission of the plural '–s'.

Recasts according to linguistic content

A second round of coding was performed on the recasts according to their linguistic content, resulting in four categories: the morphological, the syntactic, the lexical, and the phonological.

Morphological recasts targeted errors concerning plurals, verb tense, subject-verb agreement, articles, and gerunds. In Example 4, the student used the word 'eat' in a non-targetlike way, which was recast by the teacher into 'eating', a gerund.

Example 4   Morphology
Episode 4
S1.5   We can know the taste after eat.
T1   We can know the taste after eating.
S1.5   After eating.

Syntactic recasts encompassed those that targeted errors concerning relativization, word order, sub-categorization, auxiliary verbs, modals, comparatives, passivization, reflexives, and question formation. In Example 5, S4.4 formed a question in a non-targetlike way such that he did not invert the subject 'you' and the auxiliary 'will', which triggered the recast from T2.

Example 5   Syntax
Episode 60
S4.4   How many people you will invite?
T2   How many people will I invite?
S4.4   Yes.

Lexical recasts targeted errors concerning choice of word, prepositions, collocations, and derivational affixes. In Example 6, T1 recast S2.9's word choice of 'eat' into 'drink'.

Example 6   Lexis
Episode 14
S2.9   Some Koreans eat deer's blood.
T1   Drink blood. What's that? Brain?
S2.9   Brain? No brain … umm … horn?

Phonological recasts targeted errors related to pronunciation. In Example 7, the student pronounced the word 'ingredient' in a non-targetlike way, which triggered the teacher's recast.

Example 7   Phonology
Episode 32
S2.4   It is very expensive ingredient /ingridint/
T1   Very expensive ingredient /ingridiənt/
S2.4   Ingredient /ingridiənt/

Recasts according to form and meaning

A third round of coding of the recasts focused on their form and meaning. Depending on whether it was declarative or interrogative and whether or not it carried additional meaning, a recast was classified into one of the four categories: the isolated declarative, the isolated interrogative, the incorporated declarative, or the incorporated interrogative (Lyster 1998b). The four categories are respectively illustrated and defined in Examples 8–11.

Example 8   An isolated declarative recast
Episode 57
S4.4   Everyone don't want to pay.
T2   Everyone doesn't want to pay.
S4.4   Doesn't want to

In Example 8, T2 reformulated part of S4.4's utterance with falling intonation and with no additional meaning.

Example 9   An isolated interrogative recast
Episode 7
S1.4   It sounds fish to me.
T1   Fishy?
S1.4   Yes.

In Example 9, T1 reformulated part of S1.4's utterance with rising intonation and no additional meaning.

Example 10   An incorporated declarative recast
Episode 6
S1.1   It means that I am not familiar about the Jazz?
T1   No, it does not mean you're not familiar with Jazz. It means you're familiar with Jazz, but you don't like it. You tried that, but you don't like it.
S1.1   Oh, I see.

In Example 10, T1 provided additional information by incorporating the correct reformulation of part of S1.1's utterance into a longer statement, and hence, with added meaning.

Example 11   An incorporated interrogative recast
Episode 8
S1.4   There is some famous restaurant.
T1   Where are the famous restaurants? Are they near Kang-Nam?
S1.4   Well, I don't know ... umm ... I know one ... near Yong-In.

In Example 11, T1 sought additional information by incorporating the correct reformulation of part of S1.4's utterance into a question.

Stimulated recall comments by teachers

The teachers' comments were coded into three categories: (a) corrective intent, (b) communicative intent, or (c) no comment. Category (c) concerns cases in which the teacher did not remember his original intent. Illustrations of categories (a) and (b) appear in Examples 12 and 13. In the interest of space, the teachers' comments are abridged to reflect what is the most relevant.

Example 12   Corrective intent
Episode 1
S1.3   I pick up the two.
T1   I picked up two.
S1.3   I picked up two.
T1's recall   I intended to correct two things: pick and the two.

Example 13   Communicative intent
Episode 2
S1.3   It is nineteen.
T1   Nineteenth?
S1.3   Yes.
T1's recall   I was not sure what she said.

In Example 12, S1.3 produced an utterance with two incorrect forms, viz., an incorrect verb tense form for 'pick' and the oversupplied article 'the'. T1 subsequently recast it, and as his recall shows, his intent was indeed to correct the errors. In Example 13, on the other hand, T1's underlying intent for the recast was communicative; that is, he recast S1.3's utterance, not because he wanted to correct an error, but because he wanted to be sure what the student had just said.

Concerning the above episode in Example 12, the editor of this volume raised the possibility that the corrective intent and the communicative intent might overlap. We believe that this is a separate empirical question, beyond the scope of the present study. Our coding here was based entirely on the teacher's comment in response to the prompt 'What were you thinking at the time you responded to the student?'

Stimulated recall comments by students

Two rounds of coding were performed on the students' comments. A schema of the coding categories is provided in Figure 11.1. The first round involved coding the comments as (a) no recognition of recast, (b) recognition of recast, or (c) no comment. Recognition was considered isomorphic with noticing, and following Schmidt (1990; 1994), it was operationalized as interpretative comments on the intent of the teacher's response to a student's utterance.

The no recognition of recast category contains instances of students failing to recognize the intent of the teacher's recast as well as cases in which students made irrelevant comments. As illustrated in Example 14, S3.2's original utterance lacked the obligatory plural marking of the noun 'feeling'. T2 reformulated the utterance, recasting 'feeling' into 'feelings'. S3.2's comment, however, indicates that she noticed T2's output but failed to recognize its corrective intent.

Example 14 No recognition of recast
Episode 42

S3.2	I did not know I hurt her feeling.
T2	You hurt her feelings.
S3.2	Yes, but I didn't know.
S3.2's recall	I thought he repeated what I had said to confirm.
(T2's recall	I thought she was not aware of my correction.)

The category of recognition of recast, as shown in Figure 11.1 and in Examples 15 and 16, consists of those cases where the student recognized a recast as error correction. Within this category, two sub-cases were further established: no recognition of gap and recognition of gap. The term 'gap' denotes the contrast between a recast and its trigger utterance. S1.1's recall in 15 illustrates no recognition of gap in which case the student knew that she was given correction but could not identify the locus of the problem in her own utterance, hence failing to recognize the contrast intended by the teacher. Example 16 illustrates recognition of gap in which case S1.2 not only knew that the teacher corrected her but also recognized the gap between the correction and her own utterance.

Example 15 No recognition of gap
Episode 5

S1.1	We don't know the truth until we tried it itself.
T1	We don't know the truth until we have tried it ourselves.
S1.1	Right.
S1.1's recall	Well, I thought what I said was grammatically incorrect. But ... well ... I didn't know where was wrong.
(T1's recall	I understood her, but the sentence was not quite correct.)

Example 16 Recognition of gap
Episode 9

S1.2	I am not adventurous of food.
T1	I am not adventurous with food.
S1.2	Adventurous with.
S1.2's recall	I was wrong. I said 'adventurous of'. I should have used 'with', not 'of'.
(T1's recall	I taught this expression before. I was glad she actually used this ... although it was not correctly used.)

The examples given so far are only of simple recasts. For the complex recasts, recognition of gap (see Figure 11.1) was sub-divided into two types: complete versus partial recognition of gap. An example is given in 17.

Example 17 Complete versus partial recognition of gap
Episode 50

S3.2	They are in their honeymoon.
T2	They were on their honeymoon?
S3.2	They were on their honeymoon.

S3.2's recall	He corrected me. I was not sure about using the preposition 'in'. Using prepositions properly is always tricky. And, I did not use the past tense.
S3.3's recall	He corrected her. She did not use the past tense.
(T2's recall	I thought the couple might have felt offended.)

In Example 17, S 3.2's original utterance contained two errors (line 1), that is, an incorrect use of verb tense for 'be' and an incorrect use of the preposition 'in'. Her recall comment shows that she recognized, fully, the gap between the teacher's recast and her own utterance. S3.3's recall, on the other hand, suggests partial recognition.

Example 18   No comment

This category contains the comments that express inability to recall anything in relation to a particular recast. Examples are 'I don't know' and 'I don't remember'.

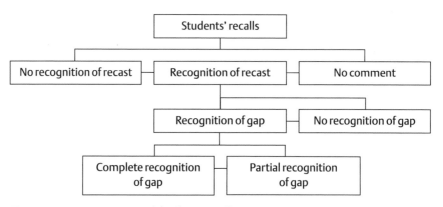

Figure 11.1 Categories of student recall comments

The second round of coding of the students' comments focused on the type of addressee. Two categories were identified: (a) direct addressees (i.e. students who were recipients of recasts) versus (b) indirect addressees (i.e. students who were observers of recasts). For example, S3.2 in Example 17 was a direct addressee, whereas S3.3 was an indirect addressee.

Inter-rater agreement

An independent rater and one of the researchers separately coded the classroom interactions and recall comments made by the students. We purposely employed the independent rater, who had little bearing to the data, to ensure reliability in the coding of these types of data that might at times appear ambiguous. The rater was given general information on the purpose of the study, participants, and so on. He then practiced coding the data with one of the researchers several times before doing it independently. The subsequent inter-rater agreement for simple versus complex recasts, the type of addressee, and the form of recast was 100 per cent, and for the type of linguistic target and recognition of recast, it was respectively 90 per cent and 97 per cent. The teachers' comments, on the other hand, because of their clear-cut nature, were coded by the researchers with 100 per cent inter-rater agreement.

Results

There were 68 recast episodes, distributed as follows: 14 from Teacher 1 of Class 1, 21 from Teacher 1 of Class 2, 17 from Teacher 2 of Class 3, and 16 from Teacher 2 of Class 4. Of the 68 recast episodes, there were 45 simple recasts (66 per cent) and 23 complex recasts (34 per cent). Together, the 20 students (i.e. five from each class) contributed 340 comments on the 68 episodes (70 on Teacher 1 of Class 1; 105 on Teacher 1 of Class 2; 85 on Teacher 2 of Class 3; and 80 on Teacher 2 of Class 4). Detailed results are organized and reported below according to the research questions.

To what extent do teacher intent and learner interpretation overlap?

Of the 68 recast episodes, as illustrated in Table 11.3, Teacher 1 and Teacher 2 provided 53 (78 per cent) recasts with corrective intent (hereafter, 'corrective recasts') and 14 (21 per cent) with communicative intent (hereafter, 'communicative recasts'). Further, of the 53 corrective recasts, 33 were simple and 20 complex. Eleven of the 14 communicative recasts were simple and three complex.

Type of intent	T1/Class 1 (N = 14)	T1/Class 2 (N = 21)	T2/Class 3 (N = 17)	T2/Class 4 (N = 16)	Total (N = 68)
Corrective	10 (71)	16 (76)	12 (71)	15 (94)	53 (78)
Communicative	4 (29)	5 (24)	4 (24)	1 (6)	14 (21)
No comment	0 (0)	0 (0)	1 (1)	0 (0)	1 (1)

T1 = Teacher 1; T2 = Teacher 2 ; percentages in parentheses

Table 11.3 Teacher intent for recasts

Results on the extent to which the students' interpretation overlaps with the teachers' intent were obtained through tabulating the instances of the students' (a) recognition of recast, (b) no recognition of recast, and (c) no comment. As shown in Table 11.4, among the simple recasts, the students recognized 69 per cent of the corrective recasts, missing 25 per cent of them. Of the complex recasts, on the other hand, they recognized 58 per cent of the corrective recasts, missing 37 per cent (37 of 100). Similarly, tabulations of

Learner recognition	Simple recast	Complex recast	Total
RR	114 (69)	58 (58)	172 (65)
NRR	42 (25)	37 (37)	79 (30)
NC	9 (6)	5 (5)	14 (5)
Total	165 (100)	100 (100)	265 (100)

RR = recognition of recast; NRR = no recognition of recast;
NC = no comment; percentages in parentheses

Table 11.4 Learner recognition of corrective recasts

Learner recognition	Simple recast	Complex recast	Total
RR	10 (18)	3 (20)	13 (19)
NRR	42 (76)	12 (80)	54 (77)
NC	3 (6)	0 (0)	3 (4)
Total	55 (100)	15 (100)	70 (100)

RR = recognition of recast; NRR = no recognition of recast;
NC = no comment; percentages in parentheses

Table 11.5 Learner recognition of communicative recasts

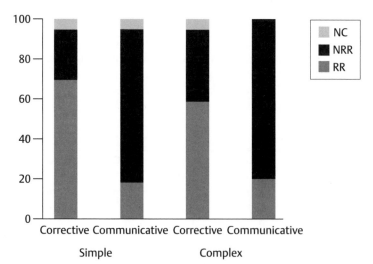

RR = recognition of gap; NRR = No recognition of recast; NC = no comment

Figure 11.2 Learner recognition of recasts by teacher intent

the communicative recasts yielded the results displayed in Table 11.5, which shows that for the simple recasts, 76 per cent of the communicative recasts were correctly interpreted as such and 18 per cent were misinterpreted as corrective. For the complex recasts, 80 per cent (12 of 15) of the communicative recasts were correctively interpreted as such and 20 per cent (3 of 15) were mistaken for corrective. Thus, there is a sizable overlap between the students' interpretation and the teachers' intent. The results from chi-square analyses confirmed a significant relationship between the two: $\chi^2 = 46.968$, $df = 1$, $p = .000$, and phi = .475 for the simple recasts; $\chi^2 = 8.838$, $df = 1$, $p = .003$, and phi = .283 for the complex recasts. Notice that this analysis did not include the no comment category, since 'no comment' equals neither 'no recognition' nor 'recognition'. An overall picture of the learners' recognition of the recasts with respect to the type of teacher intent is given in Figure 11.2.

The type of addressee and teacher corrective intent

Tabulations of the instances of direct and indirect addresses and of the corrective recasts yielded the results displayed in Table 11.6.

Learner recognition	Simple recast		Complex recast		
	DA	IDA	DA	IDA	Total
RR	22 (79)	92 (67)	13 (72)	45 (55)	172
NRR	6 (21)	36 (26)	5 (28)	32 (39)	79
NC	0	9 (7)	0	5 (6)	14
Total	28	137	18	82	265

DA = direct addressee; IDA = indirect addressee; RR = recognition of recast;
NRR = no recognition of recast; NC = no comment; percentages in parentheses

Table 11.6 Learner recognition of corrective recasts by type of addressee

As illustrated in Table 11.6, the recognition of corrective recasts by the direct addressees had an accuracy rate of 79 per cent for the simple recasts—in contrast with the accuracy rate of 67 per cent by the indirect addressees. For the complex recasts, the accuracy rate for the direct addressees was 72 per cent, and for the indirect addressees, 55 per cent. At first blush, these figures seem to suggest that the corrective recasts were better perceived by the direct addressees than by the indirect addressees. However, the chi-square statistic proves no significant relationship between the type of addressee and the corrective recasts ($\chi^2 = .524$, $df = 1$, $p = .465$, and phi = .058 for the simple recasts; $\chi^2 = 1.165$, $df = 1$, $p = .280$, and phi = .111 for the complex recasts), suggesting that the students perceived the teachers' corrective recasts more or less equally well, importantly, irrespective of whether they were the direct or indirect addressees.

To what extent do learners accurately recognize gaps between the trigger utterances and the recasts?

As illustrated in Table 11.7, of a total of 225 student recalls for the simple recasts, 110 (49 per cent) show accurate recognition of gaps (i.e. contrasts between the recasts and the trigger utterances), while 16 recalls (eight per cent) show no recognition of gaps, and 87 (37 per cent) show no recognition of recasts. For the complex recasts, as provided in Table 11.8, 46 of 115 (40 per cent) recalls involve accurate recognition of gaps, of which nine (eight per cent) show complete recognition of gaps and 37 (32 per cent) partial recognition. Moreover, 15 recalls (13 per cent) show no recognition of gaps, and 48 (43 per cent) no recognition of recasts. In sum, while the students demonstrated they were able to recognize gaps to some extent, they did not do as well with the complex recasts as with the simple recasts.

Learner recognition	T1/Class 1 (n = 40)	T1/Class 2 (n = 80)	T2/Class 3 (n = 55)	T2/Class 4 (n = 50)	Total (n = 225)
RG	20 (50)	41 (51)	26 (47)	23 (46)	110 (49)
NRG	0 (0)	3 (4)	4 (7)	9 (18)	16 (8)
NRR	15 (37)	31 (39)	24 (44)	17 (34)	87 (37)
NC	5 (13)	5 (6)	1 (2)	1 (2)	12 (6)

RG = recognition of gap; NRG = no recognition of gap; NRR = no recognition of recast; NC = no comment; percentages in parentheses

Table 11.7 Learner recognition of gap for simple recasts

Learner recognition		T1/Class 1 (n = 30)	T1/Class 2 (n = 25)	T2/Class 3 (n = 30)	T2/Class 4 (n = 30)	Total (n = 115)
RG	CRG	1 (3)	3 (12)	3 (10)	2 (7)	9 (8)
	PRG	8 (27)	9 (36)	15 (50)	5 (17)	37 (32)
NRG		3 (10)	4 (16)	3 (10)	5 (17)	15 (13)
NRR		15 (50)	8 (32)	9 (30)	17 (56)	49 (43)
NC		3 (10)	1 (4)	0 (0)	1 (3)	5 (5)

CRG = complete recognition of gap; PRG = partial recognition of gap; percentages in parentheses

Table 11.8 Learner recognition of gap for complex recasts

Is recognition of gaps affected by the type of teacher intent, the type of addressee, the type of linguistic target, and the form of recast?

The type of teacher intent

First, in the case of the simple recasts, the students recognized gaps in 98 out of 165 (59 per cent) corrective recasts, and ten out of 55 (18 per cent) communicative recasts. Given, as reported in the previous section, that there was a significant overlap between the teachers' underlying intent for recasts and the students' interpretation thereof, this result came as no surprise. Clearly, the students were better at recognizing gaps with the corrective recasts than with the communicative recasts. A chi-square statistic was computed, which proves significant interaction between the students' recognition of gaps and the type of teacher intent (χ^2 = 29.685, df = 1, p = .000, and phi = .378 for corrective recasts; χ^2 = 19.692, df = 1, p = .000, and phi = .615 for communicative recasts). Notice that in the computation, cases of no recognition of gap and no recognition of recast were collapsed into one category, since both involved no recognition of gaps.

Turning now to the complex recasts, the students were able to recognize gaps with 43 out of 100 (43 per cent) corrective recasts, of which only seven per cent featured complete recognition, the rest being partial (36 per cent). With the communicative recasts, on the other hand, 20 per cent of recognition was observed, of which 13 per cent showed complete recognition and seven per cent partial recognition. Although, as observed for the simple recasts, the students were better able to recognize gaps when the recasts were corrective in nature than when they were communicative, the results from the chi-square analysis, in which the categories of complete recognition and partial recognition were collapsed into one category, yielded no significant relationship between the students' recognition and the type of teacher intent for the complex recasts (χ^2 = 3.398, df =1, p = .065, and phi = .176 for communicative intent; χ^2 = .853, df = 1, p = .356, and phi =.095 for corrective intent). It, thus, appears that the extent to which the type of teacher intent affected the learners' recognition of gaps was modulated by the complexity of the recasts.

The type of addressee

For the simple recasts, the direct addressees demonstrated 53 per cent recognition of gaps (20 out of 38), and the indirect addressees 48 per cent. For the complex recasts, the recognition rate by the direct addressees was 53 per cent, of which there was 16 per cent complete recognition of gaps and 37 per cent partial recognition. The recognition rate by the indirect addressees was 38 per cent, of which six per cent was complete recognition and 31 per cent partial recognition. The results from chi-square analyses suggested no significant interaction between the type of addressee and the recognition of gaps for the simple (χ^2 = .018, df =1, p = .893, and phi = .009) or the complex recasts (χ^2 = 1.104, df = 1, p = .293, and phi = .100). In other words, the type of addressee did not affect the learners' recognition of gaps, regardless of the complexity of the recasts.

The type of linguistic target

Similar to the results reported elsewhere (see for example, Lyster and Ranta 1997; Mackey *et al.* 2000; Nabei and Swain 2002; Oliver 1995), the present study revealed that morphosyntactic problems triggered the most recasts, followed by lexical and phonological problems. In the case of the simple recasts, the phonological recasts led to recognition of gaps at a rate of 90 per cent, followed by the morphological recasts at 55 per cent, the lexical recasts at 48 per cent, and the syntactic recasts at 31 per cent. For the complex recasts, the recognition of gap rates were respectively 80 per cent for the phonological recasts, 38 per cent for the lexical recasts, 18 per cent for the morphological recasts, and 13 per cent for the syntactic recasts. Chi-square analyses, excluding the phonological recasts (too few to warrant inclusion), established a significant relationship between the students' recognition of gaps and the type of linguistic target for both the simple (χ^2 = 8.770, df = 2, p = .012, and phi = .213) and complex recasts (χ^2 = 10.862, df = 2, p = .004, and phi = .213). Put otherwise, irrespective of the complexity of the recasts, the type of linguistic target significantly affected the learners' recognition of gaps.

The form of recast

Tables 11.9 and 11.10 show the proportions of the students' recognition of gaps for the simple versus complex recasts delivered in four different forms: (a) the isolated declarative, (b) the isolated interrogative, (c) the incorporated declarative, and (d) the incorporated interrogative. As illustrated, the most frequently assumed form of recasts, irrespective of their complexity, is (a) (see also Lyster 1998b), followed in order by (b), (c), and (d). For the simple recasts, the students' recognition of gap rate was 74 per cent for (a), 35 per cent for (d), 29 per cent for (b), and ten per cent for (c). The results for the complex recasts were similar: 56 per cent for (a), split between 11 per cent complete recognition of gaps and 45 per cent partial recognition; 36 per cent for (b), with eight per cent complete recognition and 28 per cent partial recognition; ten per cent for (d), with o per cent complete recognition and ten per cent partial recognition; and o per cent for (c). Chi-square results confirmed a significant interaction between the students' recognition of gaps and the form of the recasts (χ^2 = 58.182, df = 3, p = .000, and phi = .523 for the simple recasts; χ^2 = 22.542, df = 3, p = .000, and phi = .453 for the complex recasts). Simply put, the form of the recasts, regardless of their complexity, significantly affected the learners' recognition of gaps.

Learner recognition	Iso D	Iso I	Ico D	Ico I	Total
RG	78 (74)	23 (29)	2 (10)	7 (35)	110
NRG	11 (10)	5 (6)	0 (0)	0 (0)	16
NRR	10 (10)	48 (60)	18 (90)	11 (55)	87
NC	6 (6)	4 (5)	0 (0)	2 (10)	12
Total	105 (100)	80 (100)	20 (100)	20 (100)	225

Iso D = isolated declarative recast; Iso I = isolated interrogative recast;
Ico D = incorporative declarative recast; Ico I = incorporative interrogative recast;
RG = recognition of gap; NRG = no recognition of gap; NRR = no recognition of recast;
NC = no comment; percentages in parentheses

Table 11.9 Learner recognition of gap by form of recast for simple recasts

Learner recognition		Iso D	Iso I	Ico D	Ico I	Total
RG	CRG	7 (11)	2 (8)	0 (0)	0 (0)	9
	PRG	29 (45)	7 (28)	0 (0)	1 (10)	37
NRG		9 (14)	3 (12)	3 (20)	0 (0)	15
NRR		16 (25)	12 (48)	12 (80)	9 (90)	49
NC		4 (6)	1 (4)	0 (0)	0 (0)	5
Total		65 (100)	25 (100)	15 (100)	10 (100)	115

Iso D = isolated declarative recast; Iso I = isolated interrogative recast;
Ico D = incorporative declarative recast; Ico I = incorporative interrogative recast;
CRG = complete recognition of gap; PRG = partial recognition of gap;
NRG = no recognition of gap; NRR = no recognition of recast; NC = no comment; percentages
in parentheses

Table 11.10 Learner recognition of gap by form of recast for complex recasts

Discussion

In summary, the results reported above indicated that:
1 There was a considerable overlap between the teachers' intent for recasts and the students' interpretation thereof.
2 Simple versus complex recasts had a differential impact on the students' recognition of gaps between the trigger utterances and the recasts.
3 The type of linguistic content of the recasts also differentially affected the students' recognition of gaps.
In what follows, we discuss each of the three main results in turn, in order to bring out further insights and provide for a deeper understanding of the nature of recasts and students' interpretation.

Concerning the first result, the teachers mostly had a corrective intent when providing recasts (78 per cent), a considerable portion of which were correctly interpreted by the students (69 per cent for the simple recasts, and

58 per cent for the complex recasts)—importantly, irrespective of whether they were receivers (direct addressees) or observers (indirect addressees). (See also Ohta 2000.) This rate was much higher than the 38 per cent reported by Roberts (1995), approaching the 60–70 per cent reported by Philp (2003). (See also Mackey *et al.* 2000; Carpenter *et al.* 2006.) The latter 'co-incidence' is interesting and worthy of note, given that a conspicuous difference exists between the present study and Philp's study. Philp experimented with one linguistic feature, whereas our study concerned multiple linguistic features. Previously, it has been demonstrated in several studies that the focus on a singular linguistic feature may prime learners to pay attention to the linguistic content of the recast (see, for example, Doughty and Varela 1998; Mackey and Philp 1998; Han 2002b), and the explanation sought was that a narrow focus creates salience for the linguistic content of the recast, which, in turn, facilitates the learner's noticing of it. In this light, then, the high rate of accurate perception found in Philp's study is not surprising. What is intriguing, though, is the similar rate of accurate perception shown in the present study where recasts targeted multiple linguistic features. That may have been because the teachers consistently used recasts, albeit in various forms, as an interactional strategy. Consistency, as Han (2002b) points out, is one of the conditions necessary for recasts to achieve efficacy. By the same token, the lack of such consistency as a result of the teachers using a variety of corrective strategies may account for the observed low rate of accurate perception in Roberts (1995). Finally, it is interesting to note that taken together, the perception rates offered by the three studies—one laboratory-based (Philp 2003) and two classroom-based (Roberts 1995 and the present study)—yield a minor role for context or setting, a generally accepted modulating variable on recasts (Pica 2002; Iwashita 2003; Oliver and Mackey 2003; Sheen 2004). Experimental research is necessary to tease out the effects of recast-internal versus recast–external variables.

The second main result from the present study relates to simple versus complex recasts which appeared to have had a differential impact on the recognition of gaps. The students were much better able to recognize gaps with the simple recasts than with the complex recasts (i.e. 59 per cent versus 40 per cent), a finding identifiable, again, with that from Philp (2003). Philp, it may be recalled, attributed this to limited cognitive resources on the learner's part. Future research should benefit from exploring the upper limit of the number of linguistic changes a recast may contain and that can be processed by learners.

The third main result from the present study concerns the role played by the type of linguistic target in learner recognition of gaps. There appears to be an inverse relationship, particularly for the complex recasts, between the frequency of the recasts and the recognition of gaps they evoked in the learners:

1 Frequency of recasts
   morphology > syntax > lexical > phonological

2 Recognition of gaps
  phonological > lexical > morphology > syntax

1 and 2 bear much resemblance to the findings from ESL data by Mackey *et al.* (2000; c.f., Oliver 1995). Mackey *et al.* attributed the lack of noticing of recasts addressing morphosyntactic problems to the fact that the latter rarely induced negotiation—unlike phonological or lexical problems—hence the lack of learner involvement. Negotiation, the researchers hypothesize, 'because it can require more learner involvement and hence ensure that some processing has taken place on the part of the learner, might result in a greater likelihood that learners' attention is focused on the language of the negotiation (Gass 1997)' (Mackey *et al.* 2000: 491). Their reasoning granted, we would like to suggest, however, an alternative explanation, namely that the lack of noticing may have been driven by learners' natural inclination for processing input for meaning (Harley 1993; VanPatten 1996; 2004; c.f., Han and Peverly 2007). Mackey *et al.* themselves, in fact, reported that 'In relation to morphosyntactic feedback, ESL learners were more likely to report that they were thinking about the semantic content of the morphosyntactic episodes (38 per cent) or not about the content at all (21 per cent)' (ibid.: 488).

As a further illustration of the learner bias for meaning when processing recasts, consider another episode from the current database:

Example 19
Episode 43
S3.3   It cause vio … violation.
T2   It causes violence.
S3.3   Violence
Recall
S3.3   I thought he corrected me. I said 'violation'. I meant to say 'violence' I guess.
S3.1   He said 'violation'. But, it was not the right word for the situation.
S3.2   Was he wrong? I thought so. I thought 'violation' and 'violence' had the same meaning. But they are not, are they?
S3.4   I thought the teacher corrected him. The word choice was not correct.
S3.5   'Violation' was not an appropriate word here.

In Example 19, S3.3's trigger utterance contained a morphological error, viz., an omission of the 3rd person singular '–s', and a lexical error, viz., an inappropriate word choice of 'violation'. Although both words were reformulated in T2's recast, none of the students, including S3.3 who was the direct addressee, recognized the recast of the morphological error while all of them nevertheless reported their recognition of the recast of the lexical error. It thus seems that in processing the recast, the students naturally channelled their attention towards the element that was the most meaningful to the communication at the time.

Also of interest to note here is that the recast in Example 19 is a complex one, and if we took account of the processing constraints that Philp (2003) and Han (2001) identified, it would follow that the difficulty in processing complex recasts might be underlain by any, or a combination, of these factors: (a) memory capacity, (b) current interlanguage knowledge, (c) L1 influence, and (d) meaning-primacy in input processing. Future experimental research may seek to isolate these factors to assess their individual contributions to the processing difficulty.

The present study provided strong corroborating evidence for a finding by Lyster (1998b), that is that recasts assuming the form of an isolated declarative statement were the most noticeable of all forms. (See, however, Long 2006.) Compare Example 20 with Example 21:

Example 20
Episode 3
S1.7   It's not my tasty.
T1   It's not your taste?
S1.7   Yes.

Example 21
Episode 26
S2.5   We was very curious.
T1   We were very curious.
S 2.5 We were very curious.

Students' recalls of Example 20 indicated that none of them had interpreted the recast as correction; rather, they had taken it to be a communicative confirmation check. In contrast, all the students (five out of five) who were prompted to recall Episode 26 (Example 21) had not only interpreted the recast as error correction but also accurately recognized the gap between S2.5's original utterance and the recast. Both recasts, as illustrated, were short but they differed in that one was provided in the form of an isolated declarative recast while the other had the form of an isolated interrogative recast. Naturally and logically, in a meaning-based environment, it would be the latter, because of its interrogative function, that would be more likely taken as communicative in nature (c.f., Brock, Crookes, Day, and Long 1986)—as opposed to corrective—than the former. This was confirmed in the present study inasmuch as 60 per cent of the simple recasts in an isolated interrogative form were not interpreted as correction, compared to merely ten per cent of the simple recasts in an isolated declarative form.

Similarly, recasts in an incorporated declarative form as well as an incorporated interrogative form are potentially ambiguous. Like isolated interrogative recasts, they often carry multiple meanings and functions beyond the meaning and function contained in the original utterance of the learner. In consequence, they are not easy to perceive for what they are. Philp (2003: 118) notes that 'recasts that are closer to the trigger utterance and that change the utterance in few ways ... may be of more benefit to learners'. Furthermore, recasts in either an incorporated declarative or an incorporated interrogative form tend to be long, and as such, they are less recognizable than shorter recasts. As Philp explains, 'Lengthy recasts (over five morphemes) may overload time limitations of phonological store and are difficult to retain in working memory ...' (ibid.: 117; c.f., Cowan 1988; N. Ellis and Sinclair 1996; Long 1996; Baddeley, Papagno, and Vallar 1998). Given these insights, it is appropriate to hypothesize for future research that morphosyntactic features carrying little communicative value (VanPatten 1996) may be more open to modification through simple recasts in an isolated declarative form than through any other form of recasts. Experimental research controlling both for the form of the recast and the communicative content of the morpho-syntactic feature may verify this hypothesis.

Conclusions and limitations

L2 Research on recasts has gained much strength and momentum since the late 1990s, significantly advancing the general understanding of the contribution of recasts to L2 acquisition; much, however, remains to be explored. One area that has consistently fallen short of close scrutiny concerns learners' cognitive reactions to recasts. The existing studies are, as yet, few, but each nevertheless has yielded important insights.

Building on those pioneer efforts, the present study focused in depth on four communicative EFL classes, and, employing the methodology of stimulated recall, examined both the students' and teachers' perceptions about recasts in general; more specifically, it examined the extent to which the students, as recipients or observers, were able to (a) differentiate the corrective versus communicative nature of the recasts as provided by their teachers, and (b) to recognize the gaps or contrasts between the trigger utterances and the recasts. In relation to the latter, the study also explored and examined the impact of four putative factors: the type of teacher intent, the type of addressee, the type of linguistic target, and the form of recast. As a result, the following insights emerged:

1 Students, recipients and observers alike, are by and large able to identify teachers' intent for recasts as corrective or communicative.
2 Corrective recasts, overall, fare better than communicative recasts in enabling students to recognize gaps between the recasts and the trigger utterances.
3 Simple recasts, on the whole, fare better than complex recasts in inducing students' recognition of gaps.
4 Complex recasts generally result more in partial than in complete recognition of gaps.
5 Teachers' intent for recasts (corrective or communicative) interacts with the complexity of the recasts (simple or complex) in modulating students' recognition of gaps.

6 Students' roles as recipients or observers of recasts do not affect their recognition of gaps—regardless of the complexity of the recasts.

7 The type of linguistic target (phonological, lexical, morphological, or syntactic) overrides the influence of the complexity of recasts in modulating students' recognition of gaps.

8 The form of recast (isolated declarative, isolated interrogative, incorporated declarative, or incorporated interrogative) overrides the influence of the complexity of recasts in modulating students' recognition of gaps.

Clearly, these insights should be subject to empirical verification. Follow-up research, it appears, may pursue multiple avenues. One is to replicate the present study in its entirety or in its component parts, but with different learner populations. Another avenue is, as suggested earlier, to break down the variables and conduct focused experiments on each of them. Alternatively, one may focus on one or two of the variables and conduct an in-depth investigation into the processes that drive any of their associated patterns. For instance, questions can be raised with regard to 2 above as to (a) what enabled the students to differentiate between corrective and communicative recasts, (b) what guided the teachers' decision to provide corrective versus communicative recasts, and so forth. For the benefit of any future, follow-up research, and by way of conclusion, we would now like to turn to the limitations of the study.

In hindsight, the design of the study suffered a number of weaknesses, the obvious ones being the small sample size, lack of control for individual differences among the participants, insufficient control for the length of delay experienced by participants in the stimulated recall interview, the non-longitudinal nature of the study, lack of randomization of participants, and the like. However, a less obvious but more germane and central problem might have lain in the methodology itself.

Due to the retrospective nature of stimulated recall, there is no guarantee that the thoughts elicited in the present study were entirely the thoughts the participants had at the time a recast was given; rather, it is likely that some of their comments were 'second thoughts' as a result of the participants (i.e. interviewees) being tasked with viewing the tape and commenting, a task-induced effect, so to speak.

Given that noticing is a momentary and fleeting experience (c.f., Tomlin and Villa 1994), there is arguably an *a priori* constraint on the extent to which it can be verbalized through stimulated recall—not to mention the *a posteriori* constraint imposed by the elapse of time, typically, hours and days. Thus, it is conceivable that all things being equal, what is verbalized on stimulated recall is not the thoughts accompanying the mental activity of noticing, but rather, a portion of what is noticed, that is, the outcome of noticing, which is a product rather than a process. This process of verbalizing a product can be further modulated by learners' working memory capacity, their general propensity to articulate a subjective experience, and so on, as many have recognized. (See, however, Tocalli-Beller and Swain this volume.)

Another potentially confounding issue, one that may further compound the nature of the recall comments, is that the stimulated recall process may afford a learning opportunity for the interviewee. Swain (2005), for example, spoke of the dual roles of stimulated recall: of being a research tool and a learning tool. It is therefore possible that the two roles could conflict such that, when employed as a research tool, the stimulated recall process might deflect the interviewee's thinking by triggering new recognition of the form in question. How, then, to tease the original thoughts apart from the new or secondary thoughts in the interviewee's comments is a thorny problem.

In short, given these potential threats to validity, appropriate caution must be exercised to avoid over-interpreting learners' recall comments and/or treating them as deterministic. In the meantime, finding methods to bolster stimulated recall becomes a compelling task confronting future research on learners' concurrent cognitive reactions to recasts (and corrective feedback in general, for that matter), as discussed in Mackey (2006a), if the goal of the research is to achieve validity, reliability, and generalizability.

PART THREE

Interactional feedback and linguistic development

12

The effects of corrective feedback, language aptitude, and learner attitudes on the acquisition of English articles

YOUNGHEE SHEEN

Introduction

This chapter addresses the effect of different types of corrective feedback on the acquisition of English articles and the extent to which individual differences might influence the effectiveness of corrective feedback. Corrective feedback is operationalized as a teacher's reactive move that invites learners to attend to the grammatical accuracy of something a learner has said. The two types of corrective feedback that are investigated are recasts and metalinguistic feedback. The individual difference factors are language aptitude and learners' attitudes towards error correction. The target structure is English definite and indefinite articles.

Corrective feedback is a demonstrably complex phenomenon. That is, corrective feedback in the classroom involves a complicated and dynamic process of human interaction encompassing linguistic, cognitive, psycholinguistic, and pragmatic choices by both the receiver (i.e. the learner) and the provider (i.e. the teacher or another learner). The extent to which we can generalize from previous research is uncertain since corrective feedback studies have differed considerably in terms of (1) how they were designed, (2) how corrective feedback was operationalized, and (3) how the effectiveness of corrective feedback was measured. (See Keck, Iberri-Shea, Tracy-Ventura and Wa-Mbaleka 2006, for a meta-analysis of interactional research.)

Recently, researchers' attention has been directed at theorizing and investigating the relative effectiveness of different types of oral corrective feedback (i.e. explicit versus implicit, input-providing versus prompts; see R. Ellis 2006). Since Lyster and Ranta's (1997) influential work on corrective feedback and their taxonomy of different types of corrective feedback, researchers have investigated the relationship between interactional feedback and (1) learner uptake (for example, R. Ellis, Basturkmen, and Loewen 2001a; Sheen 2004); (2) noticing (for example, Mackey, Gass, and McDonough 2000; Philp 2003); and (3) L2 learning (for example, Lyster 2004; Loewen 2005). Due to space constraints, the following review will focus on research relating to the two types of corrective feedback relevant to the current study: recasts and metalinguistic feedback.

Recasts

Research has consistently shown that recasts are by far the most frequent type of corrective feedback in and out of the classroom (Oliver 1995; Lyster and Ranta 1997; Braidi 2002; Sheen 2004). From a theoretical perspective, recasts are assumed to promote noticing of form while a focus on the meaning/message is maintained (Long 1996). In so doing, they may create the optimal condition for cognitive comparison (R. Ellis 1994a).

This line of argument draws heavily on Schmidt's (1990, 1995) notions of noticing and noticing the gap. However, whether recasts are effective in promoting noticing is a matter of dispute. Lyster and Ranta (1997), in their examination of elementary French immersion classrooms, found that recasts, the most frequently occurring corrective feedback type, were the least effective in producing learner uptake which may constitute evidence of noticing. In a follow-up study, Lyster (1998b) further suggested that recasts were too implicit for his young learners to notice their corrective function. Lyster posited they had difficulty in distinguishing between teacher utterances that were corrective in force (recasts) and utterances which were simple repetitions. He concluded that implicit recasts in an immersion classroom context may not function as negative evidence. Oliver and Mackey (2003) examined interactional feedback (including recasts) in child content-based ESL classrooms and found that the utility of recasts was much higher in an explicit instruction context than in a communicative context. They concluded that the pedagogical approach influenced the extent to which learners responded to recasts as corrective feedback.

However, recasts focusing intensively on a specific grammatical target are likely to be more noticeable than recasts targeting a variety of linguistic errors in the same period of time. Han (2002b) reported that six learners in a laboratory setting improved their use of English regular past tense over several months as a result of recasts directed repeatedly at this grammatical structure. Doughty and Varela's (1998) classroom study also found that intensive corrective recasts directed at past simple and past conditional tenses led to interlanguage development. The recasts in this study involved the teacher highlighting the error by repetition and then, if necessary, recasting with emphatic stress on the target form, and thus they were very explicit. The recasts in these two studies were probably noticeable to the learners, and this may have been why they were effective in promoting acquisition of the target features.

The majority of studies providing evidence of the acquisitional value of recasts have been carried out in laboratory settings (Long, Inagaki, and Ortega 1998; Mackey and Philp 1998; Han 2002b; Iwashita 2003; Ishida 2004). Evidence in favour of recasts in classroom settings has been much weaker, with two recent experimental classroom studies (Lyster 2004; R. Ellis *et al.* 2006) reporting either no effects or a limited effect of recasts on acquisition. The case for recasts of the more implicit kind serving as a facilitator of acquisition in a classroom context still needs to be demonstrated.

However, two non-experimental classroom-based studies do suggest that recasts can be effective. In a descriptive study of the relationship between recasts and learner uptake in the classroom, Sheen (2006) reported that more explicit recasts (for example, short recasts with few changes involving lexical or phonological errors) led to higher levels of learner uptake/repair. Also, Loewen and Philp (2006) examined the relationship between different characteristics of recasts and learning as measured in tailor-made tests and found that short, interrogative recasts targeting a single error were predictive of learning.

Metalinguistic feedback

Schmidt (2001) distinguished awareness as noticing from awareness as understanding. Noticing involves simply attending to exemplars of specific forms in the input (for example, English has 'a' and 'the' in noun phrases) whereas understanding entails knowing the abstract rule or principle that governs that aspect of language (for example, English uses 'a' before the first mention of a noun and 'the' before the second mention). Metalinguistic feedback, a form of explicit feedback common in form-focused instruction (Spada and Lightbown 1993), can be hypothesized to assist learners in developing awareness at both the level of noticing and understanding and thus may be especially effective in facilitating acquisition.

Several studies have found that explicit types of corrective feedback (including metalinguistic feedback) are more effective than implicit types of corrective feedback. For example, Carroll and Swain (1993) reported that an explicit correction group (where learners were told they had made an error and were given an explicit metalinguistic explanation) outperformed the groups that received other corrective feedback types, including recasts. In a later study, Carroll (2001) also found that this kind of explicit corrective feedback was more effective than recasts in helping learners to form linguistic generalizations. In these studies, explicit feedback was defined as 'any feedback that overtly states that a learner's output was not part of the language-to-be-learnt' (Carroll and Swain 1993: 361), whereas implicit feedback was used to refer to corrective feedback that consisted of confirmation checks, recasts, and requests for clarification.

These studies all took place in a laboratory, but similar results have been obtained in a number of classroom studies. R. Ellis, Loewen, and Erlam (2006) found that metalinguistic feedback (explicit corrective feedback) was superior to recasts (implicit corrective feedback) in promoting the acquisition of English regular past tense. Lyster (2004) examined the differential effects of recasts and other feedback types ('prompts' in his terms) in form-focused instruction directed at French gender assignment and found that the prompts, which included metalinguistic feedback, were more effective than recasts. The prompts in his study had one feature in common: they all encouraged self-repair (pushed output) from learners by withholding the correct forms. For this reason, Lyster argued that prompts work better than recasts, which provide the correct form but frequently do not result in learner repair. However, the distinction between recasts and prompts is conflated with another important distinction, namely the implicit versus explicit distinction. Thus, Lyster's metalinguistic feedback may have proved more facilitative of acquisition not because it elicited output from the learners, but because it provided explicit information about the target structure.

Another possibility is that metalinguistic feedback consisting of provision of the correct form together with grammatical information (i.e. direct metalinguistic feedback) will prove more effective than metalinguistic feedback consisting only of grammatical information (i.e. indirect metalinguistic feedback). Carroll and Swain's (1993) study of dative alternation lends support to this claim. This study found that direct metalinguistic feedback was superior to indirect metalinguistic feedback (and recasts) in the short-term.

Individual difference factors in corrective feedback research

This chapter defines individual differences (IDs) as the cognitive and psychological variables affecting how learners learn and how successful they are. Accordingly, the present study investigated two individual difference factors—language aptitude and learners' attitude towards error correction.

Despite the plethora of error correction studies, few studies have examined the effects of corrective feedback and individual difference factors. In relation to the current research, two studies are noteworthy. In his report of an interaction effect of corrective feedback and individual difference factors, DeKeyser (1993) found that students with high previous achievement, high language aptitude, and low anxiety benefited the most from error correction. Similarly, Havranek and Cesnik (2001) reported that corrective feedback was likely to be beneficial to learners who had a positive attitude towards error correction. These two studies, however, did not isolate different types of corrective feedback, nor did they investigate the interrelated effects of individual variables on the acquisition of specific linguistic structures.

A number of studies have demonstrated that language analytic ability (one component of language aptitude) predicts success in L2 learning (for example, Ehrman and Oxford 1995). Ranta (2002) claimed that this ability is likely to be involved in both implicit learning (i.e. the implicit analysis of naturalistic input) and explicit learning (i.e. the explicit analysis required by metalinguistic tasks). She also suggested that it is related to learners' metalinguistic knowledge. One possibility explored in the present study is that the mediating effect of language analytic ability will be evident in learning gains resulting from both implicit feedback (recasts) and explicit feedback (metalinguistic information) but will be greater in the case of the latter.

A number of researchers (for example, Krashen 1982; Truscott 1996) have warned of the negative affect resulting from correcting learners. However, research into learners' beliefs and attitudes has consistently shown that L2 learners desire to be corrected (for example, Cathcart and Olsen 1976; Chenoweth, Day, Chun, and Luppescu 1983). Most recently, Kim and Mathes (2001) reported that EFL students expressed a strong wish to be corrected and also that they preferred to be corrected explicitly. Thus, it is possible that learners' attitudes towards error correction mediate the effect of corrective feedback. For example, Havranek and Cesnik (2001) reported that the beneficial effect of error correction in general favoured those learners who were only slightly irritated and not embarrassed by correction.

In sum, few studies have systematically examined the extent to which the effect of different types of error correction is mediated by cognitive and affective factors. The study reported in this chapter is an attempt to fill this gap by comparing two types of corrective feedback (recasts versus metalinguistic correction) and investigating the extent to which language analytic ability and attitudes towards error correction mediate their effect on the acquisition of articles. The study seeks answers to the following three research questions:

1 Do recasts and metalinguistic correction have a differential effect on the acquisition of English articles?
2 To what extent does the learner's language aptitude mediate the effect of corrective feedback?
3 To what extent does the learner's attitude towards error correction mediate the effect of corrective feedback?

Method

Design

The study employed a quasi-experimental research design with a pre-test–treatment–post-test–delayed post-test structure, using intact ESL classrooms. The research also involved a correlational analysis of the relationship between the two individual learner variables (one cognitive, one affective) and criterion test scores in the post-tests and delayed post-tests, with a view to examining the moderating effects of these variables on the effects of the error correction treatment on the acquisition of English articles. Figure 12.1 illustrates the design of the research.

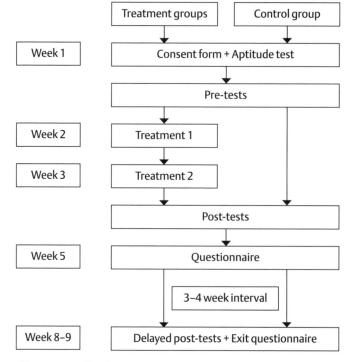

Figure 12.1 Design

Participants

The current study was conducted in six intact classes in the American Language Program (ALP) of a community college in the United States. The instructors were five native-speaking American teachers and their 99 intermediate level students (aged 20–51), representing various language and ethnic backgrounds (i.e. Chinese, Japanese, Korean, Spanish, Polish, Russian, Turkish). Most students held a college degree or were in the process of applying to college. Their length of residence in the US ranged from one year to five years. The class sizes ranged from 15 to 22. In the end, 80 students completed the aptitude test, pre-tests, post-tests, delayed post-tests and the questionnaire; 19 students with incomplete datasets were excluded from the sample. Out of a total of five intact classrooms, three groups were formed: one 'recasts' group (n = 26), one 'metalinguistic correction' group (n = 26), and one control group (n = 28).

The students in the sample were taking a combination of two to three courses in grammar, writing, reading, and speech (i.e. listening comprehension involving audio tapes and speaking), lasting for one hour and 20 minutes to three hours each session for the whole semester. The ALP program has four levels: Foundation, Level I, II, and III (the most advanced level). Prior to the current study, the researcher visited the site many times and observed and piloted a few instruments in several classes with different levels. All of the participating students came from level II.

Operationalizations

Recasts

Recasts were operationalized as a teacher's reformulation of a student's erroneous utterance, without changing the meaning of the student's original utterance, in the context of a communicative activity (Sheen 2006). The recasts could be full (see Example 1) or partial—where the teacher only reformulated the incorrect segment (i.e. phrase, word) of the learner's utterance, as in Example 2 below.

> *Example 1*
> **Student**   There was fox.
> **Teacher**   There was a fox.

> *Example 2*
> **Student**   He took snake back.
> **Teacher**   The snake.

Metalinguistic correction

Metalinguistic correction was operationalized as a teacher's provision of the correct form following an error, together with metalinguistic information. It should be noted that this operationalization of metalinguistic correction differs from 'metalinguistic feedback' as defined by other researchers (Lyster and Ranta 1997; Lyster 2004; R. Ellis *et al.* 2006), who excluded provision of the correct form. An example of metalinguistic correction used in the study is given below:

> *Example 3*
> **Student**   There was a fox. Fox was hungry.
> **Teacher**   The fox. You should use the definite article 'the' because you've already mentioned 'fox'.

Target structure

Articles were chosen as the target structure for the current study with a view to isolating the effect of error correction from any potential effect of grammar instruction in general. This decision was made after a series of discussions with the participating faculty members at the college, which revealed that (1) participating students were not explicitly taught articles during the semester and (2) articles, while constituting a structure where students commonly make errors, were infrequently corrected due to their non-salience and the complicated rule explanations required. English articles are considered to be a non-salient feature because misuse of articles rarely leads to communication breakdown (Master 2002). It was also thought likely that the intermediate learners investigated in the current study would know the linguistic forms 'a' and 'the', yet would typically not know or have full control over their functions.

While 'the' and 'a' belong to the top five most frequently occurring words in English according to the COBUILD corpus (Sinclair 1991), it has been well documented in the SLA literature (for example, Butler 2002; Liu and Gleason 2002; Master 2002) that learners have difficulty in learning articles because of their complex nature (i.e. both linguistic and pragmatic factors determine article use). For this reason, care was taken in the current study to focus the correction on errors involving just two major functions—'the' as anaphoric reference and 'a' as first mention, as in the following example:

When I found *a* red box in front of my house, *the* box blew up with a terrific explosion.

Corrective feedback treatment instruments and procedures

Narrative task instruments

There were two treatment sessions. Each session involved a narrative stimulus for the purpose of eliciting article errors from the learners, who were asked to retell each narrative to the class. The first narrative task involved an adapted Aesop's fable, *The Fox and the Crow*, as shown in Table 12.1. There were seven indefinite articles and seven definite articles in the story. The ALP faculty considered the task suitable for their intermediate level students, yet expected that the students would often make article errors.

There was once a crow who stole a piece of cheese from a kitchen window. She flew off with the cheese to a nearby tree. A fox saw what the crow had done, and he walked over to the tree. 'Oh, Mistress Crow, you have such lovely black feathers, such little feet, such a beautiful yellow beak, and such fine black eyes! You must have a beautiful voice. Would you please sing for me?' The crow felt very proud. She opened her beak and sang CAW-CAW-CAW-CAW. Of course the cheese fell down, and the fox ate the piece of cheese.

Table 12.1 The Fox and the Crow

The second story was constructed by the researcher with a view to making an interesting, yet simple story with easy vocabulary that afforded plentiful instances of the two functions of articles. There were seven indefinite articles and ten definite articles in the story. The story is shown in Table 12.2.

A boy bought a snake from a pet shop. He took the snake home. His mother screamed when she saw the snake. She told him to take the snake back to the pet shop but the owner refused to take the snake back. The boy put the snake in a box and left it on a seat in the park near his house. An old woman found the box. When she saw the snake she had a heart attack.

Table 12.2 The Pet Snake

Corrective feedback treatment procedures

Meetings with participating teachers were arranged several weeks before the corrective feedback treatments began. For the treatment groups, teachers were given research materials and were fully informed about the research procedures well in advance. The researcher and each teacher met 15 minutes prior to class and rehearsed how the teacher would provide feedback when the students retold the stories. For the corrective feedback treatment groups, a 15-minute rehearsal in the presence of the researcher took place, using the treatment narrative. After a series of email exchanges and rehearsals, the teachers said that they were familiar and very comfortable with the research procedures. The corrective feedback treatment was also piloted by the teachers and some changes made to the procedures.

The ensuing corrective feedback treatment took place in the five intact classes over a period of two weeks. The treatment involved the two narrative tasks in two treatment sessions. In each case a 30–40 minute narrative task was used to elicit article errors from the learners. Each session was audio-recorded with a clip-on microphone attached to the teacher. The procedures were as follows.

1 The teacher handed out the fable/parable to the students and told them that they were to read a short story and then tell the story themselves.
2 The teacher asked them to read the story silently.
3 The teacher discussed the moral of the story with the class.
4 The teacher then collected the stories and read the story aloud to refresh their memory as the students noted down the key words.
5 The teacher gave the students five minutes to practise telling the story in groups of three or four. Only one group was asked to tell the original story while other groups were asked to revise it by changing the names of people, animals and objects in the narrative (i.e. from 'boy' to 'girl' or from 'snake' to 'spider').
6 Each group retold the story (or a modified version of the story) to the entire class, with each individual in the group providing only one or two sentences before passing the speaker role to the next group member.
7 Whenever a student made an error in article usage, the teacher corrected the error using either a recast (in the recast group) or metalinguistic feedback (in the metalinguistic group).

Testing instruments and procedures

For each testing session (pre-test, post-test, and delayed post-test), three tests were administered: a speeded dictation test, a writing test, and an error correction test. In addition, an aptitude test was administered prior to the pre-test session.

Language analysis test

The instrument used to measure language analysis was based on an aptitude test developed by Istvan Otto and used previously by Schmitt, Dörnyei, Adolphs, and Durow (2003). The test consisted of 14 multiple-choice items. The learners were given a glossary consisting of words and sentences from an artificial language and their English translations. They were then given 14 English sentences and for each sentence were asked to choose the correct translation from the four choices provided. In order to make the correct choice the learners needed to analyze grammatical markers supplied in the glossary and apply these to the multiple-choice translations.

Speeded dictation test (eight minutes)

This test consisted of 14 items, each of which contained one or two sentences involving the use of indefinite and definite articles as shown in Example 4 below.

Example 4
I saw a movie last night. The movie made me sad.

Example 4 contains the two stimuli ('a movie' and 'the movie') to measure knowledge of the indefinite article 'a' and the definite article 'the'. The test was time pressured to limit learners' ability to draw on their explicit grammatical knowledge (R. Ellis 2005). Each item in the test had one or two stimuli involving article-obligatory contexts. The total number of article stimuli in the test involved nine indefinite and 12 definite articles.

In scoring this test, targetlike use (TLU) scores were calculated (Pica 1991). The TLU analysis measures learners' knowledge of articles by taking overuse of the target form into consideration. Articles were first scored for correct use in obligatory contexts. This score then became the numerator of a ratio whose denominator was the sum of the number of obligatory contexts for articles and the number of non-obligatory contexts in which articles were supplied inappropriately.

In taking this test, each student wrote the dictated sentences in a small notebook provided by the teacher. The researcher first explained the procedures to the students. Then the teacher read two sample sentences so that the students could familiarize themselves with the procedure. Each item was read at a normal speed and students were directed to write down one item per page as fast as they could and exactly as they heard it. Once the students turned to the next page for the next item, they were not allowed to return to the previous page. This prevented the students from consciously reworking what they had written.

Writing test (12 minutes)

This test was adapted from one of Muranoi's (2000) test instruments for English articles. The writing stimulus consisted of four sequential pictures and the students were asked to write a coherent story based on them. Word prompts next to each picture were included to elicit noun phrases involving article usage. For example, next to the first picture the word prompts were 'old man', 'paint', and 'picture', thereby encouraging the students to construct a sentence such as 'An old man wanted to paint a picture'.

In coding the writing data, the same scoring guidelines as for the dictation test were adopted, i.e. targetlike use (TLU) scores (Pica 1991). Using the TLU analysis, students' scores were calculated as percentages. The writing test guidelines for scoring were as follows: when it was not clear whether a noun phrase (NP) constituted an obligatory context for 'a' or 'the' based on the student's writing, the NP was not coded. Only suppliance/non-suppliance in unambiguous contexts was coded (i.e. the contexts where the researchers could definitely determine that 'a' or 'the' was needed). This meant that some possible errors were ignored. Examples of this procedure were as follows:

1 In the case of the word prompt 'park', both 'in the park' or 'in a park' were possible so NPs containing this word were excluded from coding. However, when neither article ('a' or 'the') was present in the NP, it was coded as non-suppliance.

2 In the case of the word prompts 'boy' and 'girl', when the student wrote, 'A boy and girl', only the first NP (i.e. 'a boy') was coded since it is not clear whether the student used the elision rule correctly. In a similar vein, when the student used 'the boy and girl' as second mention, only the first NP was coded. However, if the first NP was erroneous, either as first mention or second mention (i.e. 'boy and a girl', 'boy and girl'), each NP was included in the coding.

3 Any NP where a determiner and an article were co-present as in the following example, 'A boy and girl are look at the his picture' were excluded.

4 Articles in idiomatic phrases—i.e. 'all of a sudden', 'a few minutes', 'at the moment'—were also excluded.

Error correction test

This test consisted of 17 items. Each item contained two related statements, one of which was underlined and contained an error, which the learners were asked to correct in writing. The items were adapted from test instruments used in Liu and Gleason (2002) and Muranoi (2000). Four distracter items were included, involving the use of past tense, modal choice, and subject-verb agreement. Example 5 below is taken from the test, followed by the correct answer.

Example 5
I saw an interesting movie last night. *I forgot the name of movie.*
Answer: I forgot the name of the movie.

The error correction test was scored on a discrete item basis. One point was given for each correct suppliance of an article in the 14 obligatory contexts in the underlined sentences in the test. Excluding the distracters, 14 points was the perfect score for the test, and students' final scores were calculated as percentages. The students were given 15 minutes for this test.

Questionnaire

This was designed to examine learners' attitudes towards error correction. Nine items measured learners' feelings and beliefs about error correction. All the items used a six-point Likert scale ranging from 'strongly disagree' to 'strongly agree'. The following are examples of the questionnaire items used:

> The best way to learn English is when the teacher corrects my errors.
> It bothers me when the teacher corrects my errors.

Care was taken to preserve respondent anonymity. The participants were also reassured that their responses would remain confidential and would never be revealed to their teachers. The researcher explained key vocabulary and expressions and discussed a number of statements that might be difficult for the students to understand. The students were allowed to ask the researcher questions or use their dictionaries. Twenty minutes were given for administering the survey. Prior to collecting the questionnaires from the students, the researcher took care to ensure that they did not omit any items or produce more than one response for each item.

Exit questionnaire

A short questionnaire was administered immediately following the error correction test in the delayed post-test session. This exit questionnaire was designed to examine whether the students had become aware of the focus of the error correction treatments and tests. The two questions in the exit questionnaire were as follows:

1 Now that you have completed the story tasks and the tests, what do you think they were all about?
  a They were practicing and testing writing.
  b They were practicing and testing my grammar.
  c They were practicing and testing my general English skills.
  d They were practicing and testing my vocabulary.
2 Please write a sentence saying what you think you learnt from this.

Test reliability

Table 12.3 displays the results for test reliability. In the dictation and writing tests, a second researcher coded a sample of 25 per cent of the total data. The sample came equally from the pre-tests, post-tests, and delayed post-tests.

	Percentage agreement		Reliability coefficient (r)		
Test	Dictation	Writing	Error correction	Language analysis	Questionnaire
Pre-test	87.1	83.7	.84	.92	.79
Post-test 1	89.2	87.6	.83		
Post-test 2	92.1	89.8	.91		

Table 12.3 Reliability of tests

Results

Descriptive statistics for total test scores and for each of the individual tests are presented below. However, inferential statistics were calculated only for total test scores (i.e. average scores for the three tests). This is justified by the exploratory factor analysis presented in Table 12.4 below which shows a one-factor solution, with all three tests loading at .77 or higher. This factor accounted for 78.5 per cent of the total variance.

Component	Eigen value	Percentage of variance	Cumulative percentage	Test	Component 1
1	2.07	78.52	78.52	Dictation	.89
				Writing	.83
				Error correction	.77

Table 12.4 Principal component analysis of the three tests (pre-tests)

Tables 12.5 through 12.8 present the descriptive statistics for total scores as well as for the separate scores for the dictation test, writing test, and error correction test over the three testing periods: pre-test, post-test 1 and post-test 2. In the case of total scores the two experimental and control groups showed a gain from pre-test to post-test 1, but only the two experimental groups showed further gains from post-test 1 to post-test 2. Similar results were obtained for each of the separate tests. In the case of the error correction tests, however, gains were only evident in the metalinguistic group.

	Pre-test		Post-test 1		Post-test 2	
	M	SD	M	SD	M	SD
Recast group (n = 26)	46.3	15.0	52.6	15.5	54.0	16.4
Metalinguistic group (n = 26)	50.4	14.0	61.4	15.0	63.4	16.9
Control group (n = 28)	48.3	14.2	52.1	15.6	51.2	16.2

Table 12.5 Group means and standard deviations for total test scores

| | Pre-test | | Post-test 1 | | Post-test 2 | |
	M	SD	M	SD	M	SD
Recast group (n = 26)	55.0	20.0	66.4	17.7	67.1	19.8
Metalinguistic group (n = 26)	57.2	16.7	72.4	13.0	74.4	16.6
Control group (n = 28)	58.1	12.9	64.1	13.9	62.4	13.7

Table 12.6 Group means and standard deviations for the speeded dictation test

| | Pre-test | | Post-test 1 | | Post-test 2 | |
	M	SD	M	SD	M	SD
Recast group (n = 26)	51.7	16.3	58.7	20.6	61.2	16.8
Metalinguistic group (n = 26)	58.4	14.2	65.4	17.5	67.8	17.4
Control group (n = 28)	57.3	21.4	63.9	24.4	63.9	22.8

Table 12.7 Group means and standard deviations for the writing test

| | Pre-test | | Post-test 1 | | Post-test 2 | |
	M	SD	M	SD	M	SD
Recast group (n = 26)	32.1	21.5	32.7	22.8	33.8	22.4
Metalinguistic group (n = 26)	35.7	21.7	46.5	25.6	48.0	25.2
Control group (n = 28)	29.5	19.6	28.4	21.4	27.4	19.3

Table 12.8 Group means and standard deviations for the error correction test

Figure 12.2 provides a visual representation of the mean total test scores for the three testing periods for the two corrective feedback treatment groups and the control group. The figure confirms the initial impression: the total test scores for the two treatment groups rose over time whereas the control group's scores varied little from one test time to another. The figure also shows that the metalinguistic correction group outscored the recast group on both post-test 1 and post-test 2.

To establish whether the differences in the groups' scores on the pre-test were statistically significant, a one-way analysis of variance (ANOVA) was performed. This showed no statistically significant group differences among the three groups, $F(2, 77) = 1.54$, ns.

In order to examine whether the differences in group scores over time were statistically significant, a two-way repeated-measures ANOVA was performed with total scores as a dependent variable and with time (pre-test, post-test 1, post-test 2) and corrective feedback treatment as independent variables. Table 12.9 shows the results of the analysis.

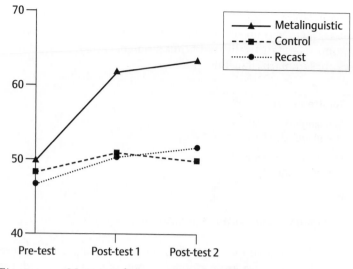

Figure 12.2 Mean total test scores versus time

One-way repeated-measures ANOVAs showed a significant effect for time; that is, all three groups' test scores increased from pre-test to post-test 1 and from pre-test to post-test 2.

Given that there were significant longitudinal gains for all the groups, the crucial analysis concerns whether there was a time × treatment interaction. As can be seen in Table 12.9, there was a significant time effect and time × treatment interaction, indicating that the groups performed differently from each other over time. One-way ANOVAs revealed significant group differences in both post-test 1, $F(2, 77) = 3.06$, $p = .05$ and post-test 2, $F(2, 77) = 4.01$, $p < .05$.

	Source	Df	F	p
Between students	Corrective feedback treatment (CFT)	2	2.41	.09
	Error	77	(645.6)	
Within students	Time	1.85	43.1	<.001
	Time × CFT	3.7	5.31	<.01
	Error	142.5	(37.5)	

Table 12.9 Repeated-measures ANOVA across the three treatments and the three testing periods

Tukey's *post hoc* pair-wise comparisons were used to isolate where the significant differences lay among the groups (with alpha level of .05). These analyses revealed that in the immediate post-test (i.e. post-test 1), the metalinguistic group performed better than both the recast group and the control group on total test scores. Also, in the delayed post-test (i.e. post-test

2), the metalinguistic group was superior to the other two groups on total test scores. However, there was no significant difference between the recast and the control group. The statistically significant differences that emerged from these analyses are summarized in Table 12.10.

	Total test scores
Post-test 1	Metalinguistic > Control*
	Metalinguistic > Recast*
Post-test 2	Metalinguistic > Control**
	Metalinguistic > Recast*

*$p<.05$ **$p<.01$

Table 12.10 Summary of statistically significant between-group differences

Table 12.11 displays the descriptive statistics for the language analysis test. The mean scores for the three groups ranged from 45.7 to 53.9, with the recast group being the highest and the control group the lowest. A one-way ANOVA revealed that these differences were not statistically significant, $F(2, 77) = 1.09$, ns.

Group	M	SD	Min	Max
Recast (n = 26)	53.9	16.8	21	79
Metalinguistic (n = 26)	52.8	21.7	14	100
Control (n = 28)	45.7	18.7	21	86

Table 12.11 Descriptive statistics for the language analysis test

Table 12.12 below displays the descriptive statistics for attitudes towards error and error correction. The instrument used to measure learners' attitudes was based on a Likert scale (1–6); thus, the mean scores for the three groups ranged from 4.57 to 4.73 with the metalinguistic group being the highest and the recast group the lowest. A one-way ANOVA revealed that these differences were not statistically significant, $F(2, 77) = 1.25$, ns.

Group	M	SD	Min	Max
Recast (n = 26)	4.57	.88	2	6
Metalinguistic (n = 26)	4.73	.64	3	6
Control (n = 28)	4.62	.90	2	6

Table 12.12 Descriptive statistics for attitudes towards error correction (using the Likert Scale)

Table 12.13 presents the results of two correlational analyses that investigated the relationship between the test gain score and (1) the language analysis score and (2) the score for attitudes towards error correction. Immediate gains were calculated by subtracting the pre-test scores from the post-test 1 scores. Delayed gains were computed by subtracting the pre-test scores from the post-test 2 scores.

In the case of the metalinguistic group, there was a significant positive association between the students' gain scores and their scores for the language analysis test. In contrast, no significant association was found in the recast group. The metalinguistic group yielded relatively high correlation coefficients ($r = .69$ and $r = .68$ for the immediate and delayed gain scores respectively), with the language analysis score accounting for nearly 50 per cent of the variance. In the control group there was a significant but much weaker association for the delayed gain scores.

The correlations between gain scores and attitude towards error correction were weaker, achieving significance only for immediate gain scores in the metalinguistic group. This group yielded a correlation coefficient ($r = .41$) with attitudes towards error correction accounting for 16 per cent of the variance in these scores. In other words, in comparison to language analytic ability, the learners' attitudes towards error correction correlated more weakly with immediate gains in the metalinguistic group.

Group	Score gains	Language analysis score (r)	Attitude towards error correction (r)
Recast (n = 26)	Immediate	−.13	.19
	Delayed	−.07	.17
Meta (n = 26)	Immediate	.69**	.41*
	Delayed	.68**	.26
Control (n = 28)	Immediate	.27	.14
	Delayed	.39*	.29

*$p < .05$ **$p < .01$

Table 12.13 Correlations between the gain scores and aptitude scores and attitudes towards error correction

Summary

The metalinguistic group outperformed both the recast and control groups whereas the recast group did not perform significantly better than the control group. In the metalinguistic group, there was a significant positive relationship between students' immediate and delayed gain scores on the one hand and their language analytic ability on the other. The immediate gains in the metalinguistic group were also positively correlated with learners' attitudes towards error correction. In contrast, the gain scores in the recast group were not significantly related to learners' ability for language analysis nor their reported feelings about error correction.

Discussion

The first research question concerned the relative effects of recasts and metalinguistic correction on the acquisition of the English definite and indefinite articles. The results presented in the preceding section show that in the immediate and delayed post-tests, the metalinguistic group outperformed both the control and the recast groups. There was no significant difference between the recast and the control group. It should be noted that there was an improvement in the control group as well as the experimental groups over time, suggesting there was a test practice effect. However, the metalinguistic correction group outperformed the recast and the control group, indicating that there was an effect for the error correction treatment over and above and test practice effect.

While both feedback types were input-providing in R. Ellis' (2006) categorization of corrective feedback, they were different in two major ways: the degree of explicitness and the nature of the input provided in the feedback. Metalinguistic correction is explicit whereas recasts are more implicit. Metalinguistic feedback also leads to a longer time-out from communicating and thus affords more time for noticing the corrected feature. What the results of this study show is that the more informative type of correction (metalinguistic feedback + provision of correct form) resulted in the acquisition of articles whereas simply providing learners with the correct form through recasts did not.

The positive effect of metalinguistic correction reported in the study can be explained in terms of Schmidt's (1995) two levels of awareness (i.e. noticing and understanding). According to Schmidt, 'noticing' is a crucial step towards acquisition while 'understanding' can lead to greater and deeper learning. It is not unreasonable to assume that understanding entails noticing while the reverse is not always true. It is, therefore, perhaps not so surprising that provision of the correct form together with metalinguistic feedback proved more effective than the recasts alone because it led to noticing and understanding of the underlying rule.

A similar result to this study was reported by Carroll and Swain (1993). Also, more recently, R. Ellis, Loewen, and Erlam (2006) found metalinguistic feedback superior to recasts in helping learners to acquire regular past tense. In their study, however, the stronger effect for the metalinguistic feedback was evident only in the delayed post-tests, whereas in the present study a beneficial effect was found in both immediate and delayed scores gains for the metalinguistic feedback. Both studies involved a relatively short treatment (one hour in total) and in both studies the target linguistic features were morphological and non-salient in nature.

However, the operationalizations of metalinguistic feedback differed. Whereas the metalinguistic feedback in R. Ellis *et al.* (2006) constituted an output prompt (Lyster 2004), consisting of a metalinguistic clue but without provision of the correct form, the metalinguistic feedback in the present study provided both the correct form and grammatical explanations. Simply providing learners with metalinguistic comments may 'prime' the learners but they need time to use the explicit information they obtain from the feedback to acquire the feature. On the other hand, providing learners with the correct form together with metalinguistic information affords both positive and negative evidence, which together appear to be sufficient to produce an immediate effect.

Recasts have been shown to be facilitative of learning when they target a single feature intensively (Doughty and Varela 1998; Long *et al.* 1998; Mackey and Philp 1998; Han 2002b). An important question, then, is why the recasts had no significant positive effects in the present study. Two explanations can be offered. First, the recast treatment used in this study was short. It can be argued that if recasts had been provided to the learners over a longer period of time, greater gains might have become evident. Second, it may be that the recasts involving article errors were not sufficiently salient for learners to notice their corrective function. These two limitations were not evident in previous studies (Doughty and Varela 1998; Han 2002b) that found recasts had a positive impact on learning.

Moreover, the choice of target structure (indefinite and definite articles distinguishing the first and second mention of a referent in NPs) probably does not constitute an ideal target feature for recasts in communicative tasks. Articles lack salience, even when attention is drawn to them by means of a recast; furthermore, perhaps because articles are inherently difficult to emphasize, or because teachers are not used to emphasizing them, the teachers in this study found themselves unable to do so consistently. Consider the following example taken from the current classroom data. Here the learner failed to perceive the corrective force of the teacher's recast. A *post hoc* interview with this learner revealed that he thought that his pronunciation was wrong.

> **Student**   So he took a snake home (note: snake has been mentioned before)
> **Teacher**   OK, he took THE snake home? The boy took THE SNAKE.
> **Student**   Yes, snack /snak/, snake /sneik/ home

Research has demonstrated that the noticing of the corrected feature in recasts depends largely on the linguistic feature that is being targeted (Mackey *et al.* 2000; Philp 2003; Egi 2005). As Slobin's (1973) operating principles suggest, some grammatical features are likely to be inherently more noticeable than others. The learners' responses to the exit questionnaire revealed that no one in the recast group recognized that articles were the target of the treatment and tests whereas more than half of the students in the metalinguistic group responded that the focus was on grammar and more than 35 per cent of the students in this group specifically identified articles as the focus of the instruction. In short, it seems clear that the corrections of the articles in the recasts were not attended to by the learners. Unless recasts of articles are enhanced in some way, they simply may not be attended to.

One might argue that the findings of this study do not demonstrate that the explicit type of corrective feedback had any effect on learners' implicit knowledge, as the tests used in the study did not clearly distinguish between explicit and implicit knowledge. Nevertheless, there are grounds for arguing that even if the knowledge imparted by the feedback was of the explicit kind, it would be of value to learners, if explicit knowledge can assist the subsequent development of implicit knowledge (R. Ellis 1994b; N. Ellis 2005). In support of this claim, it should be noted that R. Ellis *et al.* (2006) reported that the explicit feedback treatment in their study resulted in significant gains in implicit knowledge, but only in the delayed post-test.

The second research question asked whether the effects of the recasts and the metalinguistic correction were mediated by the learners' language analytic ability. In the recast group a near-zero correlation was found between language analytic ability and gain scores. This can be explained by the learners' lack of awareness of the target of the corrective feedback. Robinson (2001) reported a strong positive correlation between aptitude and awareness. Thus it is possible that the learners with high aptitude in the recast group did not benefit from recasts because they did not engage in any analysis. Recasts that occur as brief time-outs from communication and target a non-salient grammatical feature such as articles may not result in the conscious cognitive comparison which language analytic ability is likely to facilitate.

In the metalinguistic group, strong correlations between language analytic ability and both immediate and long-term gains were found. This makes sense. If language analysis is seen as a measure of learners' capacity to acquire explicit knowledge (in particular), it follows that analytical skills will be strongly related to gains resulting from metalinguistic correction. Those learners with strong analytical skills in the metalinguistic feedback group were more likely to have developed high levels of awareness and thus were better placed to relate the corrected form to the grammatical explanation in the metalinguistic feedback and to carry out the cognitive comparison needed to advance their interlanguages.

Though weak, a significant association between language aptitude and longer-term gain scores was found in the control group. This may simply reflect a positive relationship between language aptitude and learning in general (Dörnyei 2005). In this study the measure of article acquisition may have served as a proxy measure of general acquisition.

The third research question examined the extent to which learners' attitudes towards corrective feedback mediate the effectiveness of corrective feedback. The results show that there was a significant correlation between the learners' attitudes towards error correction and immediate gains in the metalinguistic group. That is, learners with a more positive attitude towards error correction performed better on the immediate post-tests than those with a less positive attitude. No relationship between attitudes and gain scores in the recast group was found. Again, a relationship between attitudes towards error correction and the effects of corrective feedback can only be expected if learners are aware they are being corrected, and this may not have occurred in the recast group. Finally, the fact that the cognitive variable (language analytic ability) was more strongly related to gains resulting from the corrective feedback than the affective variable (attitudes towards error correction) reflects the general finding in the SLA literature on individual differences regarding the relative effect of language aptitude as opposed to learner beliefs on learning (R. Ellis 1994a).

Conclusion

The findings reported in this chapter suggest that a moderate amount of recasts may not constitute an effective corrective feedback strategy in a classroom context, especially when the target structure is a non-salient one. As R. Ellis and Sheen (2006) point out, the claim that implicit recasts, which arise naturally from negotiation/incomprehension, create an optimal condition for acquisition (Long and Robinson 1998) needs to be shown empirically. While there are laboratory type studies that do show recasts work for acquisition (Mackey and Philp 1998; Han 2002b), this has not been convincingly demonstrated in classroom studies. In contrast, the current study suggests that metalinguistic feedback (especially if this is accompanied with provision of the correct form) can be effective.

It should be noted, however, that recasts can be made explicit depending on their characteristics and the teachers' and learners' orientation to form in a communicative context (Sheen 2006), which in turn influences learner noticing of recasts (Egi 2005). Loewen and Philp (2006) reported a significant positive relationship between recasts that were explicit and subsequent learning in a non-experimental classroom study. One can argue that for recasts to work for acquisition they must create the conditions that lead learners to notice the gap between their own production and the target forms, as in Doughty and Varela's (1998) study. What is needed next is a study that compares the effectiveness of *explicit* recasts and metalinguistic correction. Such a study may be able to show whether it is the explicitness of the feedback or the provision of metalinguistic information that matters.

Truscott (1996), one of the most vocal opponents of error correction in the classroom, acknowledges that corrective feedback may be beneficial to some learners under certain circumstances. However, despite the plethora of corrective feedback studies, few have explored the relationship between individual learner differences and the effects of different types of corrective feedback. The study presented in this chapter demonstrates that individual differences can affect learners' ability to take advantage of corrective feedback and points to the need to investigate other individual difference factors in corrective feedback studies.

The metalinguistic feedback investigated in this study constituted an input-providing type of feedback, and thus, unlike prompts, did not 'push' learners to modify their output, which has been hypothesized to promote learning

(Lyster 2004; Swain 1995). Thus, it remains a possibility that other types of corrective feedback leading to pushed output will be even more effective than the metalinguistic feedback.

The current study is limited in that the measures of acquisition did not include a measure of learners' unplanned oral production (for example, an oral elicited imitation test). While desirable, this was not possible at the site where the study was conducted, as it would have required individual testing. One could argue that the testing instruments employed in the current study, all of which involved the written medium, may have tapped the learners' use of their explicit knowledge, and thus may have favoured the metalinguistic feedback. Another limitation is that while including a control group that completed just the tests, the study lacked a comparison group that performed the narrative tasks minus corrective feedback. Lastly, this study focused on only two functions of English articles. Given the complex nature of articles, the findings of the study cannot be generalized to the acquisition of articles in general let alone to other grammatical features.

13

Interactional feedback and the emergence of simple past activity verbs in L2 English

KIM McDONOUGH

Introduction

One goal of interaction research is to compare the developmental outcomes associated with different types of interactional feedback (Havranek 2002; Lyster 2004; R. Ellis, Loewen, and Erlam 2006). This line of research is important in understanding how feedback might work to facilitate second language (L2) learning. For example, Lyster (2004) has suggested that prompts, which encourage learners to modify their output, may be more beneficial than recasts, which typically do not elicit learner responses. Similarly, R. Ellis and colleagues (R. Ellis *et al.* 2006) have reported that interactional feedback in the form of metalinguistic information followed by learner responses (which Lyster classifies as a type of prompt) had a greater impact on L2 learning than recasts. Finally, Havranek (2002) has suggested that interactional feedback which overtly directs learners' attention to form may be more effective than more implicit forms of feedback, such as recasts. Thus, the comparative research to date has indicated that interactional feedback which elicits learner responses and/or is overt, such as prompts, may be more effective than recasts. However, as Sheen (this volume) has pointed out, these types of interactional feedback differ from recasts in both their explicitness and learner responses. Consequently, it is difficult to determine whether their greater effectiveness when compared to recasts is due to the explicitness or the elicitation of learner responses (or both).

Situated in this line of interaction research, the current chapter reports the findings of an empirical study that compared the developmental outcomes associated with two types of interactional feedback: recasts and clarification requests. Whereas previous studies compared recasts with more explicit forms of interactional feedback, the focus of comparison here is between recasts and another implicit type of feedback. Although both recasts and clarification requests are generally considered to be more implicit, they differ in their elicitation of learner responses. Unlike recasts, which rarely elicit learners' responses, clarification requests typically 'push' learners to modify their output (Linnell 1995; Lyster and Ranta 1997; Lyster 1998c; Oliver 1995, 2000; Panova and Lyster 2002; Lyster 2004). The purpose of the current study is to investigate (a) whether recasts are associated with development despite infrequent learner responses, and (b) whether implicit feedback that does elicit responses (i.e. clarification requests) is more effective than recasts.

One challenge in interaction research is to select an appropriate linguistic target that is likely to be affected by interactional feedback. Previous interaction-development studies have targeted a variety of linguistic forms in English, with two frequent targets being question development (for example, Mackey 1999; Spada and Lightbown 1999; McDonough 2005; McDonough and Mackey 2006) and past tense verb forms (Sato 1986; Nobuyoshi and R. Ellis 1993; Doughty and Varela 1998; Takashima and R. Ellis 1999; Han 2002b; R. Ellis *et al.* 2006; Mackey 2007), in part due to the ease in eliciting these forms during communicative, task-based interaction. Once selected, the linguistic target needs to be operationalized in a way that reflects development as opposed to accuracy. As many researchers have pointed out (for example, Meisel, Clahsen, and Pienemann 1981; Pienemann 1998; Norris and Ortega 2004), there are several problems associated with taking accuracy in production of L2 forms as a reflection of interlanguage development.

While operationalizing development is relatively straightforward for ESL question development due to the availability of Pienemann and Johnston's (1987) developmental sequence for question formation, it is more challenging for past tense. However, researchers have identified a developmental progression for the emergence of past tense morphology based on the inherent lexical aspect associated with different verb classes and their predicates (Anderson 1991; Anderson and Shirai 1996; Bardovi-Harlig 1998, 1999, 2000). According to this developmental progression, achievement predicates (i.e. verbs that are dynamic, telic, and punctual) are most likely to be inflected for simple past morphology, followed by accomplishment predicates (i.e. verbs that are dynamic and telic but not punctual). Activity predicates (i.e. verbs that are dynamic, but neither punctual nor telic) are the least likely of all dynamic verbs to be marked for simple past morphology, and are most likely to occur in progressive forms. Finally, state predicates (i.e. verbs that are neither dynamic, punctual nor telic) are least likely to be marked for simple past morphology. Despite the availability of this predictive hierarchy, few interaction researchers have adopted this framework to assess the impact of interactional feedback on the emergence of past tense forms. (A notable exception is Ishida 2004, who tested the predictions of this framework with Japanese L2 learners.)

The current study adopted this predictive framework to compare the impact of recasts and clarification requests on the emergence of simple past activity verbs, which emerge later than achievement or accomplishment verbs. Prior to describing the details of the current study, a review of previous interaction research that has explored the relationship between interactional feedback and past tense follows. Although these studies have many methodological differences, their collective findings provide some support for a beneficial relationship between interactional feedback and learners' production of past tense forms.

Interactional feedback and past tense

As described in the introductory chapter, one of the earliest studies to examine the potential link between interaction and learners' production of past tense morphology was a longitudinal study carried out by Sato (1986), in which she described the interlanguage development of two Vietnamese boys. Although Sato found little evidence that interaction positively impacted their use of morphology to indicate of past time, she acknowledged that little interactional feedback specifically involving past time reference had occurred. Consequently, subsequent researchers have carried out experimental research that allows for greater control over the provision of interactional feedback, as exemplified in two studies by R. Ellis and colleagues (Nobuyoshi and R. Ellis 1993; Takashima and R. Ellis 1999). In both studies, the researchers investigated whether the provision of clarification requests during task-based interaction influenced learners' subsequent production of past tense verbs. In the first small-scale study, they reported that three learners who received clarification requests when they produced non-targetlike past time verbs subsequently had more accurate production than three learners who had not received any interactional feedback. However, this claim is difficult to evaluate due to the small-scale nature of the study, and the corresponding lack of inferential statistics. In the larger follow-up study, seven members of an intact EFL class received clarification requests when reporting an oral narrative to their classmates. Only three of those seven learners showed an immediate increase in their production of accurate past tense forms, and only one learner maintained the increase over time. Taken together, the findings of these two studies provide little empirical support for a positive relationship between interactional feedback in the form of clarification requests and learners' production of past tense forms.

Whereas R. Ellis and colleagues focused exclusively on interactional feedback in the form of clarification requests, Mackey (2006a) explored the relationships among different types of interactional feedback, learners' noticing of that feedback, and developmental outcomes for past tense (as well as plurals and questions). ESL learners ($n = 28$) in two classes carried out laboratory-based oral production tests and in-class treatment activities over a four-week period. One class of learners received interactional feedback in the form of negotiation, recasts, and combinations of negotiation plus recasts in response to their non-targetlike past tense usage while playing game-show activities with their teacher and a researcher. The other class played the same game-show activities but did not receive any interactional feedback. Few learners reported noticing the feedback they had received in response to their non-targetlike past time verbs, and only one learner who had received interactional feedback showed more accurate production of past tense forms on the post-test. However, as Mackey pointed out, little interactional feedback was provided in response to the learners' non-targetlike past tense usage, as compared to their non-targetlike plurals and questions.

Whereas the studies described previously have not established a strong relationship between interactional feedback and learners' production of past tense forms, two studies have reported some benefits for recasts (Doughty and Varela 1998; Han 2002b). In a classroom-based study, Doughty and Varela (1998) explored whether corrective recasts facilitated more accurate use of verbal morphology to indicate past time reference. Unlike previous researchers who focused on learners' accurate production only, Doughty and Varela also analyzed interlanguage forms, which they defined as verbs (a) with the correct form but the incorrect function or (b) with the incorrect form but the correct function. ESL learners ($n = 34$) enrolled in two content-based science classes completed oral and written science laboratory reports over a 14-week period. Half of the learners received corrective recasts from their teacher when they produced non-targetlike past time verbs. Corrective recasts were defined as repetition of the non-targetlike form with stress and rising intonation, followed by a recast with added stress on the reformulated verb forms, and an opportunity to repeat the recast. They reported that learners who received corrective recasts showed improvement in their oral and written production of both targetlike and interlanguage past tense forms. The more explicit nature of corrective recasts as opposed to the more implicit recasts typically found in naturalistic and classroom-based interaction may have facilitated the learners' improved production.

Han (2002b) also found that recasts had a positive impact on ESL learners' production of past tense verb forms. Over a two-month period, eight ESL learners participated in several test and treatment sessions in which they narrated stories from picture prompts orally and in writing. During the treatment sessions, the researcher provided half of the learners with recasts when they demonstrated tense inconsistency in their oral narratives. In other words, if a learner started the oral narrative using past tense but did not maintain consistent use of past tense morphology, then the researcher provided recasts. However, if a learner chose to narrate the story in present tense or used present tense to provide background information or to describe present time events, no recasts were provided. The test data was analyzed in terms of tense consistency, which was calculated as proportions of consistent usage for present and past tenses separately. The learners who received recasts demonstrated increased consistency in their use of past tenses in the oral and written narratives for both the immediate and delayed post-tests. Although the small-scale nature of the study necessarily precluded the use of inferential statistics, the findings suggest that recasts may help learners gain control over their past tense usage.

Finally, R. Ellis and colleagues (R. Ellis *et al.* 2006) compared the effects of different types of interactional feedback on learners' knowledge and elicited production of past tense verbs. ESL learners ($n = 34$) enrolled in three classes carried out two story narration tasks and several tests over a three-week period. One class received metalinguistic information and an opportunity to reformulate if they produced non-targetlike past tense forms while narrating their stories, while the second class received recasts and the third class did not receive any interactional feedback. The results of an oral imitation test indicated that the metalinguistic information group scored higher than the no feedback group and the recast group on the delayed post-test only. The results of a grammaticality judgment test indicated that the metalinguistic information group scored higher than the recast group on the delayed post-test only. The authors suggested that interactional feedback in the form of metalinguistic information may have been more effective than recasts because learners may be more likely to perceive it as overtly corrective. As they pointed out, the findings should be interpreted cautiously due to the small number of learners in each treatment condition.

To summarize the previous research, some studies have reported a positive relationship between learners' production of past tense forms and recasts (Doughty and Varela 1998; Han 2002b), while other studies have reported no benefits for recasts (R. Ellis and Sheen 2006). In addition, previous studies have found few positive effects for clarification requests (Nobuyoshi and R. Ellis 1993; Takashima and R. Ellis 1999) or combinations of different feedback moves (Sato 1986; Mackey 2006a). However, as pointed out previously, comparisons among these studies are hampered by differences in their participants, design, treatment activities, coding, and operationalization of development. For example, the studies that found a positive effect for recasts provided more explicit recasts (Doughty and Varela 1998) or implicit recasts over a longer period of time (Han 2002b) than the studies which reported no advantage for interactional feedback. In addition, some researchers operationalized development as consistent past tense usage (Han 2002b), while others defined it as accurate production of past tense verbs in past time contexts (such as Mackey 2006a). Consequently, more tightly controlled studies are necessary to clarify the relationship between different types of interactional feedback and learners' acquisition of past tense. The purpose of the current study was to compare the impact of two types of implicit interactional feedback—clarification requests and recasts—on the emergence of simple past activity verbs. The following research question was addressed: do clarification requests and recasts differentially impact the emergence of simple past activity verbs? The research question was investigated in a single study that consisted of two data collection phases. Both phases were situated in the same context and used identical research materials and procedures, but were separated by approximately two years.

Method

Participants

The EFL participants were 106 first-year university students enrolled in a bachelor's degree program in English at a large public university in northern Thailand. Since no objective measures of the learners' general proficiency or their knowledge of simple past forms were available, inclusion criteria were created based the participants' pre-test and treatment performance. In terms of their pre-test performance, two inclusion criteria were applied. First, learners had to produce simple past morphology with achievement and accomplishment verbs at a higher rate than they did for activity verbs, which was taken as an indication of their 'readiness' to acquire simple past activity verbs. Second, learners had to use simple past morphology with less than 70 per cent of the total past time activity verbs they produced on the pre-test in order to minimize possible ceiling effects. In terms of their treatment performance, two additional inclusion criteria were applied. First, learners had to produce at least six non-targetlike past time activity verbs during the treatment tasks, in order to ensure that they had opportunities to receive interactional feedback. Second, learners in the interactional feedback groups had to receive feedback for at least 20 per cent of their non-targetlike past time activity verbs to ensure that they were receiving a comparable quantity of feedback.

Application of the inclusion criteria resulted in the removal of 32 learners from the data set, 22 learners based on their pre-test performance and ten learners based on their treatment performance. The resulting participant pool consisted of 74 learners, 59 women and 15 men, who were all native speakers of Thai. Their ages ranged from 18–21 years, with an average of 18.3 years (SD = .79), and the length of their previous English study ranged from 8–14 years, with an average of 10.6 years (SD = 2.26). Only six learners reported having lived for longer than two weeks in a country where English was spoken as a native language or was used as a medium of communication. Although the maximum pre-test score had been set at 70 per cent to minimize ceiling effects, only 12 out of the 74 participants had scores above 60 per cent.

The native speaker participants included the researcher and 11 lecturers (seven women and four men) who were native speakers of American and British English. The lecturers were working in the English department at the same university where the learners were enrolled. They were recent graduates of bachelor's degree programs who intended to work in Thailand for one or two years before returning to their home countries. They met with the researcher individually or in small groups to discuss the purpose of the research study and to review the treatment tasks. During the meeting, they received information only about the type of interactional feedback that they were assigned to provide. They were asked to participate in task-based interaction with the learners and to focus on meaning, either (a) responding to the learners' non-targetlike past tense forms and usage with the type of feedback they had learnt about during the meeting or (b) providing no feedback. None of the learners or lecturers participated in both data collection phases.

Design

The study employed a pre-test–post-test design to examine the impact of interactional feedback on the emergence of simple past activity verbs. The learners were randomly assigned to receive interactional feedback in the form of clarification requests (in phase one) or recasts (in phase two), or to receive no interactional feedback in response to their non-targetlike (NTL) past tense forms and usage. Clarification requests were operationalized as open-ended requests for clarification, such as 'huh?' 'pardon?' 'what?' 'again?', as illustrated in Example 1.

Example 1	Clarification request	
Learner	and then one day one of his children uh name Ken	
NS	Ken?	
Learner	Ken	
NS	okay	
Learner	one day Ken uh go out to play	NTL USE: BASE FORM
NS	what?	CLARIFICATION REQUEST

The native speakers generally paused after clarification requests so that the learners could respond, as clarification requests are discourse moves that naturally elicit a response.

Recasts were operationalized as reformulations of the learners' utterances that repaired the learners' problematic form or usage while preserving meaning, as shown in Example 2.

Example 2	Recast	
Learner	I saw the beautiful girl	
NS	mhm	
Learner	and she was interested in me too	
NS	you were very handsome?	
Learner	uh I'm the only boy on this island so I go with her	NTL USE: BASE FORM
NS	you went with her?	RECAST

The native speakers either continued speaking after the recast or paused depending on which response they felt was contextually appropriate.

The learners in the no feedback group did not receive any interactional feedback involving their past time verbs. Instead, the native speakers ignored any problematic past tense forms or usage. The no feedback condition is illustrated in Example 3.

Example 3   No interactional feedback
Learner   I have a lot of happiest time in
              high school   NTL USE: BASE FORM
NS   Okay tell me about one
Learner   In high school I am studying
              at Prince Royal's College   NTL USE: PRESENT PROGRESSIVE
NS   Okay

The native speakers provided feedback in response to the learners' non-targetlike past tense forms and usage. While non-targetlike forms involved ungrammatical verb forms, such as 'he was come yesterday', non-targetlike usage involved grammatical verb forms used inappropriately in past time contexts, such as 'they come yesterday' (Bardovi-Harlig 1992).

Materials

The treatment materials were communicative activities in the form of two-way information exchange and information gap tasks that elicited contexts for past time verbs. They were adapted from commercial textbooks and resource books. Three sets of treatment materials were created, and each set consisted of two communicative activities that targeted past tense. The testing materials were communicative activities in the form of one-way information gap tasks that the learners carried out individually in a language laboratory. Each test contained a dream narration task that elicited contexts for past time verbs. The treatment and test materials also included two tasks that elicited question forms. (For complete information about the question data, see McDonough 2005 and McDonough and Mackey 2006.)

Procedure

Each learner completed an oral production pre-test in week one, participated in three treatment sessions during week two, and completed oral production post-tests in weeks three, six, and nine. The oral production tests were administered in a language laboratory using a pre-recorded audio-tape that gave instructions and controlled the amount of time for each activity. The learners were seated at individual carrels equipped with boom microphones. The treatment and test sessions took approximately 20 minutes to complete. Learners were randomly assigned to a treatment group (either clarification requests or no feedback in phase one, and either recasts or no feedback in phase two) and carried out communicative tasks with a native speaker over three sessions. During each session, the learner and the native speaker carried out activities that elicited past time verbs and created opportunities for feedback. As noted previously, the native speakers provided feedback in response to the learners' non-targetlike past tense forms and usage when it was contextually appropriate to do so. They did not manipulate the learners' opportunities to respond to the feedback, but allowed such opportunities to occur naturally as part of the activities. Except for the researcher, who participated in both data collection phases, the native speakers provided only one type of interactional feedback (or no interactional feedback at all) during the treatment tasks.

Measure of development

A conservative emergence criterion was used to assess the learners' production of simple past activity verbs. Emergence was operationalized as the production of simple past activity verbs that had not been produced on the pre-test. First, each unique simple past activity verb produced on the pre-test was identified. Next, each unique simple past activity verb produced on the post-tests was identified. Any activity verb that the learner had produced at the pre-test was removed from the list of activity verbs produced on the post-tests, as those forms already existed in the learner's interlanguage system prior to carrying out the treatment tasks. The final score was the total number of unique simple past activity verbs that each learner produced on all three post-tests combined. Because the analysis focused on types rather than tokens, narrative structure was not considered.

Analysis

The audio-tapes of the learners' test performance and treatment sessions with the native speakers were transcribed by the researcher and research assistants. First, the test and treatment data were analyzed to identify verbs produced in past time contexts. Following previous research (Bardovi-Harlig 1998; Lardiere 1998) the following ambiguous contexts were excluded from the analysis: (a) verbs without past tense morphology that could be interpreted as referring to either present or past time, (b) formulaic chunks with ambiguous temporal reference, (c) utterances that could be interpreted as reported speech or quotatives, (d) instances where past and non-past verb forms are identical, (e) verbs with non-syllabic past tense followed by homorganic stops, and (f) verbs that ended in consonant clusters followed by interdental fricatives.

Next, activity verbs in past time contexts were identified according to Vendler's (1967) aspectual classes using the tests summarized in Lee (2001). Following previous research (Anderson 1991; Bardovi-Harlig 1998; Lee 2001), activity verbs were defined as dynamic verbs without an inherent endpoint (telic) that involve some duration (punctual), such as 'write', 'read', 'play', 'sing', as shown in Example 4.

Example 4 Activity verbs
I had an idea that uh I should go to that hill so I *walk* alone in the forest
I *ran* very very fast to get away from that place
And after that I *dance* with my friends.

Activities differ from accomplishments in terms of telicity, as the latter have a specific end point (for example, 'write the letter', 'play the game', 'sing a song').

Next, the learners' activity verbs in past time contexts were coded in terms of their grammatical form, as simple past morphology supplied or absent. Errors in the formation of simple past tense morphology, such as the overgeneralization of regular past tense morphology to irregular verbs (for example, 'telled', 'woked', 'writed') were coded as supplied. Other past tense forms (such as past progressive and past perfect) was not included in the analysis, which was focused narrowly on the learners' production of simple past forms.

Finally, the learners' treatment task data were analyzed in terms of (a) the native speakers' provision of interactional feedback in the form of either clarification requests or recasts and (b) the learner's responses to that feedback. As shown in Example 5, responses to clarification requests were operationalized very narrowly as more targetlike reformulations of the originally non-target-like past time verbs.

	Example 5 Clarification request and response	
Learner	I got home about eight and after I go swimming	NTL USE: BASE FORM
NS	Huh?	CLARIFICATION REQUEST
Learner	I went to swimming with my friends	RESPONSE: SIMPLE PAST FORM

Responses to recasts were also operationalized narrowly, as repetitions of the reformulated past time verb provided in the recast, as illustrated in Example 6.

	Example 6 Recast and response	
Learner	After that he was waiting for her every day	
NS	Waiting and waiting mhm	
Learner	But she was never come back	NTL FORM
NS	She never came back?	RECAST
Learner	Never came back he was very sad	RESPONSE: SIMPLE PAST FORM

Responses that involved reformulations or repetitions of other linguistic structures were not included in the analysis. The total amount of interactional feedback received and the percentage of interactional feedback to total errors involving past time activity verbs were calculated. The total number of responses produced and the number of responses per interactional feedback were also calculated. In the case of recasts, the percentage of responses was based on the recasts which provided an opportunity for response only, since some recasts do not allow for a response (such as if the native speaker continues speaking).

Inter-rater reliability was calculated on a subset of the data (20 per cent) by comparing the researcher's coding to that of an independent rater. Simple percentage agreement with the researcher's coding was 96 per cent for the identification of verbs in past time contexts, 94 per cent for the identification of activity verbs, 100 per cent for the suppliance of simple past morphology, 99 per cent for the provision of interactional feedback, and 96 per cent for responses to interactional feedback. Alpha was set at .05 for all statistical tests.

Results

Description of the data set

In terms of the pre-test data, the learners in all three treatment groups produced a similar quantity of past time activity verbs with simple past morphology. As shown in Table 13.1, the clarification request group produced a mean of 35 per cent of their past time activity verbs with simple past morphology. The recast group produced a mean of 38 per cent of their past time activity verbs with simple past morphology while the mean for the learners in the no feedback group was 36 per cent. Learners in all three groups tended to use present and base forms with their past time activity verbs and rarely produced progressive forms. A Kruskal-Wallis test, a nonparametric ANOVA, indicated that there were no statistically significant differences in the learners' production of past time activity verbs with simple past morphology at the pre-test (Kruskal-Wallis $\chi^2 = .41, p > .05$).

For the treatment data, also shown in Table 13.1, the learners in all three groups produced a similar number of non-targetlike past time activity verbs while interacting with the native speakers. The clarification request group produced a mean of 14.05 ($SD = 6.37$) non-targetlike past time activity verbs, while the recast group produced 11.41 ($SD = 5.59$) and the no feedback group produced 10.58 ($SD = 5.02$). In terms of interactional feedback, the clarification request group received clarification request for 30 per cent of their non-targetlike past time activity verbs, while the recast group received recasts for 45 per cent of their non-targetlike past time activity verbs. Finally, in terms of responses to interactional feedback, the clarification request group reformulated their non-targetlike past time activity verbs following 31 per cent of the clarification requests, but the learners in the recast group repeated the reformulated past time verbs after only 15 per cent of the recasts. As planned, the no feedback group did not receive any clarification requests or recasts when they produced non-targetlike past time verbs, and therefore, had no opportunity to respond to feedback.

	Clarification request (*n* = 21)		Recasts (*n* = 27)		No interactional feedback (*n* = 26)	
	M	*SD*	*M*	*SD*	*M*	*SD*
Simple past activity verbs on the pre-test	35%	20.41	38%	19.32	36%	19.00
NTL past time activity verbs during interaction	14.05	6.37	11.41	5.59	10.58	5.02
NTL past time activity verbs receiving feedback	30%	12.36	45%	17.44	0	0
Feedback followed by learner response	31%	24.68	15%	27.15	0	0

Table 13.1 Overview of the data

Interactional feedback and the emergence of simple past activity verbs

The research question, which asked whether clarification requests and recasts differentially impact the emergence of simple past activity verbs, was addressed by examining the total number of unique simple past activity verbs produced by each learner. As described previously, an emergence criterion based on the total number of unique simple past activity verbs produced on all three post-tests was used to assess development. As shown in Table 13.2, learners in the clarification request group produced a mean of 6.48 (*SD* = 2.94) unique simple past activity verbs on all three post-tests, while the recast group produced a mean of 5.56 (*SD* = 3.03). In contrast, learners in the no feedback group produced a mean of 3.62 (*SD* = 1.33) unique simple past activity verbs. A Kruskal-Wallis test indicated that the difference in scores was significant.

	Sum	*M*	*SD*	χ^2	*p*
Clarification request group (*n* = 21)	141	6.71	2.90		
Recast group (*n* = 27)	150	5.56	3.03	18.47	.000
No feedback group (*n* = 26)	94	3.62	1.33		

Table 13.2 Unique simple past activity verbs

Individual Mann-Whitney tests, non-parametric independent-samples *t*-tests, were used to determine the location of significance. Alpha was reduced to .016 to account for possible Type I error by dividing the original alpha level of .05 by three (the number of individual comparisons). As shown in Table 13.3, the clarification request group produced significantly more unique simple past activity verbs than the no feedback group, with a large effect size (Cohen's

$d = 1.36$). The recast group also produced significantly more unique simple past activity verbs than the no feedback group, but with a smaller effect size (.83). Finally, the difference between the clarification request group and the recast group was not significant, and the effect size was smaller (.39).

	Mean rank	Mean rank	Z	p	d
Clarification request and no feedback	34.00	15.92	4.55	.000	1.36
Recast and no feedback	32.13	21.67	2.49	.013	.83
Clarification request and recast	27.40	22.24	1.28	.201	.39

Table 13.3 Pair-wise comparisons for simple past

To summarize the findings, both clarification requests and recasts facilitated the emergence of simple past activity verbs, and there was no statistically significant difference in their impact on development.

Discussion

The current study found that both clarification requests and recasts facilitated the emergence of simple past activity verbs. The findings confirm those of previous recast studies (Doughty and Varela 1998; Han 2002b), but contradict the findings of previous clarification request studies (Nobuyoshi and R. Ellis 1993; Takashima and R. Ellis 1999). Several differences between the current study and the previous clarification request studies may help account for the contradictory findings, such as the context (laboratory-based versus classroom-based), treatment task differences (information-exchange versus narratives), and the operationalization of development (emergence versus accuracy). In addition, the findings revealed no advantage for clarification requests over recasts, which differs from previous comparative studies that found prompts to be more effective than recasts (Lyster 2004). However, a prompt can occur in more explicit forms than the open-ended clarification requests exclusively targeted here, such as a metalinguistic hint, and the greater explicitness of some prompting techniques may help account for the different findings.

As mentioned in the introduction to this chapter, feedback that provides the targetlike form, such as a recast, may not encourage learners to modify their output. In contrast, feedback that indicates that a breakdown in the communication of meaning has occurred without providing the targetlike form, such as a clarification request, may elicit more responses. The current study provides additional evidence that clarification requests are more effective in eliciting learners' responses than recasts, as learners reformulated their past tense forms in response to 31 per cent of the clarification requests they received, but only 15 per cent of those recasts that created opportunities for response.

The response patterns associated with clarification requests and recasts are illustrated in Examples 7 and 8. During the treatment sessions, the learner in Example 7 produced 15 past time activity verbs without past morphology, and the native speakers provided clarification requests in response to 47 per cent of those utterances (7 out of 15). Following the native speakers' clarification requests, she typically reformulated her original utterances by producing the correct past tense form, as illustrated in Example 7.

Example 7	Clarification requests and responses	
Learner	And then the next day the police came to her house and knock	NTL USE: BASE FORM
NS	What?	CLARIFICATION REQUEST
Learner	Knocked	RESPONSE: SIMPLE PAST

Although the learner in Example 8 produced a similar number of non-targetlike past tense forms during the treatment sessions (18) and received a comparable quantity of interactional feedback in the form of recasts (9 out of 18 or 50 per cent), he rarely responded to those recasts by repeating the reformulated verb. Instead, he typically acknowledged the recast, as shown in Example 8.

Example 8	Recasts without responses	
Learner	After that she saw a mall	
NS	Mhm	
Learner	She go shopping	NTL USE: BASE FORM
NS	She went shopping?	RECAST
Learner	Yeah	RESPONSE: ACKNOWLEDGE

Despite their differing response patterns, both learners produced a similar number of unique simple past activity verbs on the post-tests. While the learner in Example 7 produced seven unique simple past activity verbs on the post-tests, the learner in Example 8 produced six unique simple past verbs. Thus the learner in Example 8 appears to have benefited from recasts even though he rarely responded to them by repeating the targeted past tense forms, which suggests that responses may not be necessary for recasts to work. Although some researchers have questioned whether the absence of learner responses may limit the effectiveness of recasts (Havranek 2002; Havranek and Cesnik 2001; Lyster 2004; R. Ellis *et al.* 2006), the current findings suggest a positive relationship between recasts and the emergence of simple past activity verbs despite infrequent responses. A similar dissociation between immediate responses and learning outcomes has been reported in other interactional feedback studies that explored the relationships among recasts, responses and L2 development (Mackey and Philp 1998; Loewen and Philp 2006; McDonough and Mackey 2006).

In this study, the impact of interactional feedback on the acquisition of past tense was investigated by narrowly focusing on the emergence of simple past activity verbs, which was motivated by the learners' predominant use of base and present forms in the pre-test data. However, as reported in previous aspect studies, progressive forms (Ø progressive, present progressive, and past progressive) associate robustly with activity verbs, and this association strengthens as proficiency increases (Bardovi-Harlig 1998, 2000; Bardovi-Harlig and Bergström 1996; Bardovi-Harlig and Reynolds 1995; R. Robison 1995). Thus an interesting question is whether interactional feedback also facilitated the emergence of progressive activity verbs. While using progressive forms in past time contexts often involves non-targetlike usage, particularly for Ø progressive (V + '–ing' with no auxiliary) and present progressive, it represents development as learners' reliance on the present and base forms decreases and they begin to distinguish lexical verb classes by using progressive forms. Consequently, a *post hoc* analysis was carried out to determine whether interactional feedback also facilitated the emergence of progressive activity verbs.

In the *post hoc* analysis, the total number of progressive forms used with past time activity verbs on all three post-tests was calculated. The activity verbs occurring in progressive forms on the post-tests were checked against the pre-test data to ensure that the forms did not exist in the learners' interlanguage systems prior to interacting with the native speakers. In addition, the post-test data was also checked to ensure that those verbs occurring in the progressive on the post-tests did not also occur in the simple past form. Thus, the final score represented the number of past time activity verbs that occurred in a progressive form that (a) did not appear in the progressive or simple past on the pre-test and (b) did not occur in the simple past on any post-test. The mean number of progressive activity verbs was 2.52 (SD = 1.33) for the clarification request group, 1.52 (SD = 1.31) for the recast group, and 1.38 (SD = 1.42) for the no feedback group.

A Kruskal-Wallis test indicated that the difference in scores was significant (Kruskal Wallis χ^2 = 10.18, p < .05), so additional pair-wise comparisons were calculated using individual Mann-Whitney tests with an adjusted alpha level of .016. The clarification request group had significantly more progressive activity verbs than the no feedback group [Z = 2.97, p < .05] and the recast group [Z = 2.56, p < .05], with large effect sizes (.83 and .76, respectively). However, there was no statistically significant difference between the recast and no feedback groups [Z = .54, p > .05]. Thus, the *post hoc* analysis indicated that only interactional feedback in the form of clarification requests facilitated the emergence of progressive activity verbs. While recasts facilitated the emergence of simple past activity verbs, they appeared to have no effect on the emergence of progressive forms. Taken together, the findings suggest that clarification requests may impact several forms across developmental stages simultaneously, whereas recasts may have a more concentrated impact on a single developmental feature. However, this suggestion should be considered speculative as the current study was not designed to investigate this claim rigorously.

In sum, the current study suggests interesting relationships among clarification requests, recasts, and the emergence of simple past and progressive activity verbs. As many researchers have suggested, recasts may have differential effects on different types of structures, and future research would profit from investigating a larger array of linguistic targets, as well as target languages (Gass, Svetics, and Lemelin 2003; Havranek and Cesnik 2001; Iwashita 2003; Leeman 2003; Ishida 2004). Interestingly, previous research carried out in this Thai EFL context (McDonough 2005; McDonough and Mackey 2006) similarly found that both clarification requests and recasts were associated with ESL question development. As noted in the Introduction to this volume, additional studies are needed to identify which linguistic structures in which languages are positively affected by interactional feedback, and to investigate the effectiveness of different types of feedback and learners' responses across a variety of instructional and naturalistic contexts. While several chapters in this book go some way towards addressing these questions, research in this area is still scarce. Methodological innovations in interaction research are needed to help researchers identify learners' cognitive processes in real time, thereby gaining further insight into the relationship between interactional feedback and development (Mackey 2006b). While the current study has provided some insight into the impact of clarification requests and recasts on the emergence of simple past and progressive activity verbs, many questions still need to be answered before we will have a clear understanding of how various types of interactional feedback impact development.

14

The differential effects of corrective feedback on two grammatical structures

ROD ELLIS

Implicit and explicit corrective feedback

The focus of the study reported in this chapter is implicit and explicit corrective feedback. In the case of implicit feedback there is no overt indicator that an error has been committed, whereas in explicit feedback there is. Implicit feedback often takes the form of *recasts*. (See the Introduction to this volume.) Explicit feedback can take several forms: it may draw attention to the *source of problem indicated* (for example, 'Not goed'), where only negative evidence is provided; it may provide *explicit correction* (for example, 'No, not goed—went.'), where the feedback clearly indicates that what the learner has said is incorrect and supplies the correct form, thus providing both positive and negative evidence; or it may offer *metalinguistic feedback* (for example, 'You need past tense.'), defined by Lyster and Ranta (1997) as 'comments, information or questions related to the well-formedness of the learner's utterance' (ibid.: 47), which again only provides negative evidence.

A number of studies have investigated the effects of these two types of feedback on second language (L2) acquisition. These studies demonstrate that both types of corrective feedback are effective in promoting acquisition of the grammatical structures targeted when the feedback is focused and intensive. A number of the studies (for example, Carroll and Swain 1993; Nagata 1993; Carroll 2001; Rosa and Leow 2004a) demonstrated that explicit feedback was more effective than implicit feedback. R. Ellis, Loewen, and Erlam's (2006) study of the effects of recasts and metalinguistic feedback on the acquisition of English past tense '–ed' also found that the explicit type of feedback was more effective than the implicit type. However, a number of other studies (for example, Kim and Mathes 2001; Sanz 2003) reported no difference. Only one study (Leeman 2003) found implicit corrective feedback more effective than explicit feedback. However, in this case the explicit feedback took the form of 'source of problem indicated' (i.e. there was no positive or metalinguistic evidence provided), as Leeman's study was primarily concerned with investigating the relative effects of salient positive evidence and just negative evidence on acquisition.

It is difficult to come to firm conclusions regarding the relative effectiveness of implicit and explicit corrective feedback on the basis of these studies for a number of reasons. First, the two types of feedback were not operationalized in the same way in all the studies. Implicit feedback was operationalized as recasts in most of the studies but recasts can vary enormously. (See the Introduction to this volume.) The explicit feedback also varied depending on whether it only indicated an error had been committed, provided a correction, or included metalinguistic information or some combination of these strategies. In future research, it would seem sensible to 'bias for best'—that is, to operationalize the two types of feedback in such a way as to have the greatest potential effect on acquisition. Therefore, in the study reported below, implicit corrective feedback was operationalized as recasts that were partial, declarative, focused on a single error, and involving a simple substitution and thus likely to be salient to the learners. Also, in accordance with Han's (2002b) recommendation, the recasts focused intensively on a single grammatical structure. Explicit feedback was operationalized as source of problem indicated together with metalinguistic information (but no provision of the correct form).

A second reason why the results of previous studies are difficult to interpret is the method of operationalizing and testing acquisition. Most of the studies did not include measures of implicit knowledge, a general failing in form-focused instruction studies (Doughty 2003). The kinds of tests they typically employed (i.e. grammaticality judgment tests, sentence completion, picture prompt tests, translation tests) clearly favoured the use of explicit knowledge as they did not require learners to access their linguistic knowledge rapidly online and had no communicative purpose. It is, therefore, perhaps not so surprising that, on balance, the studies found explicit corrective feedback to be the more effective. What is needed is a study that tests the effects of implicit and explicit feedback on both implicit and explicit L2 knowledge. The study reported below attempts this, using an oral imitation test to measure implicit knowledge and an untimed grammaticality judgment test and a metalinguistic test to measure explicit knowledge. The rationale for these measures is provided later in the section on Method.

Finally, the previous studies varied in their choice of target grammatical structure. Some of the studies investigated morphological features—for example, distinguishing nouns and verbs in Carroll (2001) or French grammatical gender in Lyster (2004)—while other studies examined syntactical features—for example, dative alternation in Carroll and Swain (1993) or clitic pronoun position in Spanish in Sanz (2003). It is not unreasonable to suppose that the effectiveness of the corrective feedback treatment will depend on the choice of the target structure. Pienemann (1998), for example, proposes that the order in which grammatical structures are acquired as implicit knowledge depends on the processing operations they involve. Many of the target structures investigated to date involved complex processing operations that some of the learners may not have been developmentally ready for. The structures also differed considerably in how easy they were to learn as explicit knowledge. For example, Spanish noun–adjective agreement (Leeman 2003) constitutes a relatively simple rule to understand whereas dative alternation is much more difficult. There is an obvious need to give careful consideration to the choice of target structure, bearing in mind both the developmental stage of the learners and the conceptual complexity of the structure chosen.

Choice of target structure

One way of investigating what effect the choice of target structure has on acquisition is to conduct a study involving two different structures. However, experimental corrective feedback studies to date have generally focused on a single target structure. An exception is Nagata (1993). This computer-based study investigated the effects of two types of explicit correction (source of problem indicated and metalinguistic explanation) on two different Japanese grammatical structures. The group receiving metalinguistic explanations made fewer errors in the post-test on one of the grammatical structures (particles) but there was no difference in the number of errors involving the other structure (verbal predicates) in a written achievement test. Nagata, however, was not primarily concerned with how feedback differentially affected the two structures and offered no discussion of the results pertaining to this.

In this section, therefore, I will consider a number of other experimental form-focused instruction studies that compared the effects of explicit/implicit instruction on the acquisition of simple and complex structures. However, the basis for distinguishing the simple and complex structures differed greatly. DeKeyser (1995), for example, distinguished them in terms of whether the rules for the structures were categorical (simple) or 'fuzzy' and prototypical (complex) whereas Robinson (1996) relied on the judgments of a number of 'experts'. The operationalizations of implicit and explicit instruction in these studies also differed. In some cases explicit instruction consisted only of metalinguistic explanations (Scott 1989) while in others it involved metalinguistic explanations accompanied by practice activities (de Graaff 1997). Also, differences were evident in the instruments used to measure learning. In general, though, these were of the metalinguistic judgment and constrained constructed response type (Norris and Ortega 2000). In fact, only one study (Scott 1989) included an oral measure likely to tap implicit knowledge. Given these differences, care needs to be taken in synthesizing the results. The following is a tentative list of conclusions:

1 In general, explicit instruction is more effective with simple rules. However, this may simply reflect the fact that the testing instruments only provided measures of explicit knowledge.

2 For complex rules the picture is mixed. In three studies (DeKeyser 1995; Robinson 1996; Ayoun 2001), the implicit instruction proved more effective. In two studies (Scott 1989; de Graaff 1997) the explicit instruction was more effective for learning complex structures.

3 In the one study that included an oral task more likely to tap implicit knowledge (Scott 1989), no difference was found in the effects of the two types of instruction.

Taken together, these studies suggest that the choice of target structure does influence the effectiveness of the instruction. The studies also point to the need to provide clear and explicit grounds for distinguishing the target structures to be investigated and also to design testing instruments that measure both implicit and explicit knowledge.

The two structures chosen for the present study were regular past tense '–ed' and comparative '–er'. Brief descriptions of these two structures are provided below followed by an account of typical learner errors. Then the rationale for the choice of the two structures is considered.

Regular past tense is formed in English by adding /id/, /d/ or /t/ to the base form of the verb, depending on whether the final phoneme in the base is an alveolar stop, a voiced sound other than /d/ or a voiceless sound other than /t/. In the study, however, learners were credited with marking a verb for past tense providing they produced some identifiable form of the '–ed' inflection (i.e. accuracy of pronunciation was not an issue).

In terms of Dulay, Burt and Krashen's (1982) surface structure taxonomy of L2 errors, typical learner errors in past tense '–ed' involve either omission or misformation. Omission is evident when learners use the verb's simple form (for example, 'ask') in place of the '–ed' form ('asked'). This is very common. Misformation occurs less frequently, as when learners substitute an alternative inflection for '–ed' (for example, 'asking').

The comparative structure investigated was:
noun X is (comparative adjective) than noun Y.

The form of the comparative adjective depends on prosody. A morphological form ('–er') is chosen when the adjective is monosyllabic (for example, 'faster') or bisyllabic ending in '–y' (for example, 'happier') or '–er' (for example, 'cleverer'). Otherwise a phrasal form (in the case of this study this was always 'more') is chosen (for example, 'more beautiful'). In a few cases both forms are possible (for example, 'oftener' and 'more often'). There are also a small number of suppletive forms (for example, 'better').

A variety of learner error types arise with the comparative: omission, double marking, regularization, and misformation. Omission occurs when learners omit '–er' or 'more' from the comparative adjective (for example, 'simple' instead or 'simpler'; 'famous' instead of 'more famous'). Double marking arises when learners use both '–er' and 'more' on the same adjective (for example, 'more smarter'). Regularization is evident when learners overuse the morphological marker with adjectives that require a phrasal marker (for example, 'beautifuler'). Finally, misrepresentation is seen when learners substitute a phrasal comparative marker for the morphological marker (for example, 'more smart').

Past tense '–ed' and the comparative were chosen with two principal conditions in mind. First, both structures needed to be potentially learnable as a result of intensive corrective feedback provided over a relatively short period of time (one hour). To ensure this, the structures needed to already be evident in the learners' production but not to the point where they had already demonstrated mastery. Given that the participants in the study were classified as 'lower intermediate' (see section on Participants below), it was reasonable to assume that this condition held. The results of the pre-test (reported later) supported this assumption. The second condition was that the two structures should be distinguishable in terms of their learning difficulty, i.e. one structure should be demonstrably easier than the other. The criteria used to establish this condition were as follows:

1 *Grammatical domain*

Whereas past tense '–ed' constitutes a purely morphological feature, the comparative is both morphological (i.e. there is phrasal or inflectional modification of the adjective) and syntactic (i.e. comparisons involve whole clause constructions).

2 *Input frequency*

While the input frequency of the two structures is likely to vary depending on the specific genres to which the learners are exposed, it is likely that overall past tense '–ed' occurs more frequently than comparative '–er'. This expectancy was borne out in an analysis of the two million-word Corpus of Spoken Professional American English, which resulted in 10,175 past tense '–ed' items and 4,818 comparative forms, a ratio of more than 2:1 in favour of past tense '–ed' (Michael Barlow, personal correspondence).

3 *Learnability*

According to Pienemann's (1998) Processability Theory, grammatical structures are acquired in an order that reflects a set of hierarchical processing operations. The two operations that govern past tense '–ed' and the comparative are, respectively, the category procedure and phrasal procedure. The category procedure differs from the phrasal procedure in that it does not involve any exchange of information from one sentence constituent to another. The '–ed' morphological marker of past time is attached to the verb in the learner's lexicon. That is, learners can access the past form of the verb without reference to any other constituent in the clause. The phrasal procedure allows diacritic features to be stored and unified between the head of a phrase and its modifiers. This procedure is required to enable learners to choose between the phrasal or morphological comparative adjective. In Pienemann's theory, the category procedure needs to be mastered before the phrasal procedure. For this reason, I hypothesize that past tense '–ed' will emerge before the comparative.

4 *Explicit knowledge*

The regular past tense rule is an easy rule to understand and thus learn as explicit knowledge; it states simply that '–ed' must be added to the simple form of the verb when referring to a completed action in the past. In contrast, the rule for the comparative is more complex as it must incorporate details of prosody (i.e. the syllabic structure of adjectives). Also, it requires explication of the syntactical patterns involving comparative sentences.

5 *Scope*

Hulstijn and de Graaff (1994) comment that 'the scope of a rule is said to be large or small when the rule covers more or fewer than 50 cases' (ibid.: 103). The scope of past tense '–ed' is clearly large. Ignoring morphophonemic variation, the '–ed' rule applies to every regular verb. The scope of the comparative is more difficult to assess. Clearly, both the morphological and phrasal markers occur in more than 50 cases but the numbers of suppletive and ambidextrous comparative adjectives are fewer than 50. Overall, the scope of the comparative rule can be said to be smaller than that of the past tense '–ed' rule.

6 *Reliability*

Hulstijn and de Graaff (1994) state that 'the reliability of a rule is said to be high or low when the rule applies in more or less than 90 per cent of all cases' (ibid.: 103). If 'cases' is taken to refer to 'all verbs' and 'all adjectives', then, clearly, neither the past tense '–ed' rule nor any of the comparative rules achieve the 90 per cent criterion. The '–ed' rule has low reliability because of the large number of irregular past tense forms in English. The rules for the use of '–er' and 'more' both apply to less than 90 per cent of all adjectives. In addition, they both have a number of exceptions even when they are applied to the subset of adjectives they are relevant to. In this latter respect, they contrast with the past tense '–ed' rule.

7 *Formal semantic redundancy*

Both past tense '–ed' and the comparative are formal semantic rules. That is, the morphological markers of these structures convey clear meanings. In both cases, the morphological markers are often redundant. Past time can be marked lexically by means of adverbs or can be inferred from context and frequently are in early L2 acquisition (Klein and Perdue 1992). Morphological and phrasal markers of comparatives are also frequently redundant as the structure of a sentence frequently makes it clear that a comparison is intended.

These criteria afford a mixed picture with regard to the relative learning difficulty of the two structures. In terms of grammatical domain, input frequency, learnability, explicit knowledge and scope, past tense '–ed' emerges as easier than the comparative. However, in terms of reliability and formal semantic complexity there is no obvious difference. Overall, however, these criteria do point to the comparative posing a greater learning burden than past tense '–ed', but not to such an extent as to negate the first selection principle, namely that both structures are learnable by the intended participants in the study. Table 14.1 summarizes the various claims made about the learning difficulty of the two structures.

Criterion	Past tense '–ed'	Comparative
1 Grammatical domain	Morphological	Morphological and syntactic
2 Input frequency	Relatively frequent	Relatively less frequent
3 Learnability	Category procedure (lexical morphology)	Phrasal procedure (phrasal information)
4 Explicit knowledge	Easy	More difficult
5 Scope	Large	Smaller
6 Reliability	Low	Low
7 Formal semantic redundancy	Often redundant	Often redundant
8 Experts' opinion	Easy	More difficult

Table 14.1 The learning difficulty of past tense '–ed' and the comparative

Research questions

The study reported below was motivated by the mixed results of previous studies of the effects of implicit and explicit feedback on acquisition and by a paucity of studies that have examined whether the effect of corrective feedback differs according to target structure. To this end three research questions were formulated:

1 Do recasts have a differential effect on the acquisition of English past tense '–ed' and comparative?
2 Does metalinguistic feedback have a differential effect on the acquisition of English past tense '–ed' and comparative '–er'?
3 To what extent does the effect of corrective feedback on the different grammatical structures differ according to type of feedback?

Method

Design

The effects of two types of oral corrective feedback (recasts and metalinguistic explanations) on the acquisition of two different grammatical structures (past tense '–ed' and comparative '–er') were investigated in a quasi-experimental study involving two experimental groups and a control group, which followed a normal course of instruction (i.e. did not complete the instructional tasks and did not receive any feedback). The basic design of the study is shown in Table 14.2. The three groups completed a pre-test, post-test 1 (immediately after the treatment was completed) and post-test 2 (approximately two weeks after post-test 1). The testing involved three instruments: an oral imitation test, an untimed grammaticality judgment test, and a metalinguistic knowledge test.

Group	Past tense '–ed'	Comparative
Group A (n = 12)	Recasts	Metalinguistic explanation
Group B (n = 12)	Metalinguistic explanation	Recasts
Group C (n = 10)	No treatment	No treatment

Table 14.2 Design of the study

Participants

The study was conducted in a private language school in New Zealand. Three classes of students (N = 34) were involved. The school classified all the students as 'lower intermediate' according to scores in a placement or a previous class achievement test. Information obtained from a background questionnaire showed that the majority of the students (i.e. 77 per cent) were of East Asian origin. Most of them had spent less than a year in New Zealand; the mean length of time spent in New Zealand was just over six months. The mean age of all participants was 25 years. The students indicated that they had been formally engaged in studying English for anywhere from 8 months to 13 years with the average length of time being seven years. Around 44 per cent of participants indicated that their studies had been mainly formal (grammar-oriented) in nature, while 30 per cent had received mainly informal instruction and the rest a mixture of both formal and informal instruction.

The teaching approach adopted by the school placed emphasis on developing communicative skills in English. Students received between three and five hours of English language instruction a day, for which they were enrolled as part-time or full-time students. Classes were arbitrarily assigned to become one of the two treatment options or the control group.

Instructional treatments

The instructional treatments for the two experimental groups lasted approximately one hour. They took the form of communicative tasks performed by the learners in a whole-class context. A researcher (acting as the teacher) provided corrective feedback either in the form of recasts or metalinguistic explanations whenever a participant made an error in a target structure. It is important to note that while the corrective feedback was directed at individual students, the tasks were designed to ensure that the attention of the whole class was focused as much as possible on the speaker at these times. The following description of the treatments will be in two parts: the tasks used to teach each grammatical structure and the corrective feedback provided.

Tasks

- *Past tense '–ed'*
  ### Task 1 (Day 1)
  Students were assigned to four groups of three. Each group was given the same picture sequence which narrated a short story and one of four different versions of a written account of the same story. Each version differed in minor ways from the others. Students were told that they would have only a couple of minutes to read the written account of the story and that they needed to read it carefully because they would be asked to retell it in as much detail as possible. They were not allowed to make any written notes. The stories were removed and replaced with the following list of verbs that students were told they would need in order to retell the story.

  visit live walk turn kill want follow attack laugh point
  stay watch

  Students were given about five minutes to plan the retelling of their story. They were told that they would not be able to use any prompts other than the picture sequence and verb list. The opening words of the story were written on the board, to clearly establish a context for past tense.

  Yesterday, Joe and Bill …

  Students were then asked to listen to each group's collective retelling of the story in order to identify what was different from their own story.

  ### Task 2 (Day 2)
  Students were once again assigned to groups of three. Each group was given a picture sequence depicting a 'day' in the life of one of two characters: Gavin or Peter. Each picture sequence was different. Pictures were chosen to depict actions that would require the use of verbs with regular past tense '–ed' forms. Students were given five minutes to prepare for recounting the day of either Gavin or Peter. Again, they were not allowed to take any written notes. Each group then gave an oral account to the rest of the class beginning with 'Yesterday Peter/Gavin had a day off'. Students who were listening were provided with an empty grid and pictures which they had to place on the grid in the appropriate sequence. One picture card did not fit and students had to identify which card was remaining.

- *Comparative*
  ### Task 1 (Day 1)
  Students were told that they were going to complete an activity to find out if their teacher was sexist or not. The meaning of the word sexist was explained to them. Students were then asked to think of three words describing men and women and to use these words to write sentences comparing the two sexes using these models:

Men are _____ women.
Women are _____ men.

They took it in turns to say aloud their sentence (they were discouraged from reading) and to address it to their normal teacher whose reaction to the statement they would record in a table as being 'sexist' or 'not sexist'. They subsequently addressed the same statements to the researcher/teacher to ascertain who was the more sexist. When students had used up all their statements they were shown a number of one syllable adjectives and two syllable adjectives ending in '–y' and asked to make up further statements. When enough statements had been addressed to the researcher/teacher (i.e. 15) and consensus had been reached about how sexist they were, individual students' opinions were canvassed as to whether their normal teacher or the teacher/researcher was more sexist.

Task 2 (Day 2)
Students were told that they were going to play a game. They were asked to think of someone in the class and to write down three adjectives describing that person. The one syllable and two syllable adjectives ending in '–y' that were shown to them in Task 1 were written on the board as options for them to choose from. They were then told to think of three statements comparing themselves to that person using this model:

He/she is _____ me.

Students then were asked to say their statements (without reading them) to the whole class. Their classmates had to guess who in the class was being described and compared to the speaker.

Corrective feedback

A second researcher sat in all lessons and kept a pen-and-paper record of each time a student made an error and whether it was corrected by the researcher/ teacher. The students received corrective feedback while they performed the tasks, as follows:

- Recasts
  The recasts were typically declarative and of the partial type and as such might be considered to lie at the explicit end of the implicit → explicit continuum for recasts (see Sheen 2006). However, they intruded minimally into the flow of the discourse. For example:

Student	… they saw and they follow follow follow him
Researcher	Followed
Student	Followed him and attacked him.

Student	Women are kind than men.
Researcher	Kinder.
Student	Kinder than women.

- Metalinguistic feedback
  For the past tense, the instructor first repeated the error and then supplied metalinguistic information. For the comparative, the researcher only provided metalinguistic information as it was assumed it was clear which item this referred to. For example:

Student	He kiss her
Researcher	Kiss—you need past tense.
Student	He kissed

Student	Men are clever than women.
Researcher	You need a comparative adjective.
Student	Men are cleverer.

Testing instruments and scoring/coding procedures

The immediate post-testing was completed the day following the second and last day of instruction and the delayed post-testing 12 days later. The tests were administered in the following order: untimed grammaticality judgment test, metalinguistic knowledge test, oral imitation test.

The oral imitation test (Erlam 2006) was intended to provide a measure of the learners' implicit knowledge, while the untimed grammaticality judgment test (ungrammatical sentences) and the metalinguistic test were designed to provide measures of learners' explicit knowledge. R. Ellis (2004, 2005) discusses the theoretical grounds for these claims. He argues that tests of implicit knowledge need to elicit use of language where the learners operate by 'feel', are pressured to perform in 'real time', are focused on meaning, and have little need to draw on metalinguistic knowledge. In contrast, tests of explicit knowledge need to elicit a test performance where the learners are encouraged to apply 'rules', are under no time pressure, are consciously focused on form, and have a need to apply metalinguistic knowledge. The oral imitation test was designed to satisfy the criteria for tests of implicit knowledge while the untimed grammaticality judgment test and the metalinguistic test were designed to meet the criteria for tests of explicit knowledge. The tests are described in detail below.

a *Oral imitation test*
  This test consisted of a set of 36 belief statements. Statements were grammatically correct ($n = 18$) or incorrect ($n = 18$). They consisted of 12 statements targeting simple past tense '–ed' (six grammatical and six ungrammatical), 12 targeting comparative adjectives (six grammatical and six ungrammatical) and 12 distractor items. Examples of the past tense '–ed' items were:

  Everyone liked the movie Star Wars.
  *An American invent Microsoft Word.

Examples of the comparative adjectives items were:

> Life was easier fifty years ago than today.
> *Asian people are tall than Americans.

Examples of the distractor items were:
> Young women like cigarettes and fast cars.
> *People worry about their children future.

The sentences in the pilot test were extensively piloted with a view to establishing whether the length of the sentences and the procedures described below were effective in ensuring that learners were not able to simply rote memorize the sentences for reproduction. It was clear that the test achieved this objective. In audio-recording the sentences, care was also taken to ensure that the target features (for example, past tense '–ed') were clearly articulated and thus available to be heard by the learners.

Each statement was presented orally one at a time, on an audio-tape, to test-takers who were required to first indicate on an answer sheet whether they agreed with, disagreed with, or were not sure about the statement. They were then asked to repeat the statement orally in 'correct' English. Pre-test training presented students with both grammatical and ungrammatical statements (not involving the two target structures) to practise with and they were given the correct responses to these items. Students' responses to all items were audio recorded. These were then analyzed to establish whether obligatory occasions for use of the target structure had been established. Errors in structures other than the target structure were not considered. Each imitated statement was allocated a score of either 1 (i.e. the grammatically correct target structure was correctly imitated or the grammatically incorrect target structure was corrected) or 0 (the target structure was avoided/the grammatically correct target structure was attempted but incorrectly imitated/the grammatically incorrect target structure was imitated but not corrected). If a learner self-corrected, then only the initial incorrect production was scored as it was felt that this would provide the better measure of learners' implicit knowledge. Scores were expressed as percentage correct. Three versions of the test were created for use over the three testing sessions; in each the same statements were used but presented in a different order. Reliability (Cronbach's alpha) for the pre-test was .779. For more information about the theoretical rationale for this test and its design see Erlam (2006).

b *Untimed grammaticality judgment test*
This was a pen-and-paper test consisting of 45 sentences. Fifteen sentences targeted past tense '–ed', and 15 sentences comparative adjectives, and 15 sentences other structures. Of each set of 15 sentences, seven were grammatically correct and eight grammatically incorrect. Sentences were randomly scrambled in different ways to create three versions of the test. Test-takers were required (1) to indicate whether each sentence was grammatically

correct or incorrect, (2) to indicate the degree of certainty of their judgment (as proposed by Sorace 1996) by typing in the box provided a score on a scale marked from 0 per cent to 100 per cent, and (3) to self-report whether they used 'rule' or 'feel' for each sentence. Students were given six sentences to practise on before beginning the test. Each item was presented on a new page and test-takers were told that they were not allowed to turn back to look at any part of the test they had already completed. For past tense '–ed', seven of the 15 statements presented the target structure in the context of new vocabulary and eight in the context of vocabulary included in the instruction. Learners' responses were scored as either correct (1 point) or incorrect (0 point). A total score was calculated and also separate scores for grammatical and ungrammatical test items. Reliability (Cronbach's alpha) for the pre-test was .63. Test-retest reliability (Pearson r) was calculated for the control group (n = 10) only. For the pre-test and post-test 1 it was .65 (p = .04) and for the pre-test and post-test 2 it was .74 (p = .01).

c *Metalinguistic knowledge test*
Students were presented with five sentences and told that they were ungrammatical. Two of the sentences contained errors in past tense '–ed' and three errors in comparative adjectives. The part of the sentence containing the error in each example was underlined. Students were asked to (1) correct the error, and (2) explain what was wrong with the sentence in English using their own words. They were shown two practice examples. As in the previous test each item was presented on a new page and test-takers were told that they were not allowed to turn back. Students were scored 1 point for correcting the error and 1 point for a correct explanation of the error. A percentage accuracy score was calculated for past tense '–ed' and for comparatives.

Results

Table 14.3 shows the focused tasks elicited roughly equal numbers of attempted use of the two target structures (i.e. 196 for past tense '–ed' and 216 for the comparative). However, the participants produced more incorrect utterances for past tense '–ed' (79) than for the comparative (46). In other words, the learners were more likely to get the comparative right than past tense '–ed'. Since feedback is contingent on learners' errors, the number of feedback moves directed at past tense '–ed' errors (67 for the recasts and metalinguistic groups combined) exceeded that directed at the comparative (41). It should be noted, however, that the percentages of erroneous past tense and comparative errors corrected by the researcher were similar (85 per cent and 93 per cent respectively). A final observation of interest is that the recast group received more feedback than the metalinguistic group for both structures.

Treatment groups	Past tense '-ed'			Comparative			Total feedback
	Correct	Incorrect	Feedback	Correct	Incorrect	Feedback	
Recast (*n* = 12)	45	49	42	74	24	22	66
Metalinguistic knowledge (*n* = 12)	72	30	25	96	22	19	44
Totals	117	79	67	170	46	41	110

Table 14.3   Numbers of target forms elicited and feedback moves

Tables 14.4, 14.5, and 14.6 show the descriptive statistics (means and standard deviations) for the oral imitation test, the untimed grammaticality judgment test, and the metalinguistic knowledge test. Scores for the grammatical and ungrammatical sentences in the oral imitation test and the untimed grammaticality judgment test are presented separately as the learners performed differently on these. Also, previous research (for example, Hedgcock 1993; R. Ellis 2005) has shown that learners apply different strategies with the two types of sentences. Specifically, the ungrammatical sentences in a grammaticality judgment test are more likely to tap learners' explicit knowledge. These statistics are considered first for the recast groups and then the metalinguistic groups. Finally, the differential effects of the two types of corrective feedback are examined.

a **Pre-test**

Group	Past tense '-ed'				Comparative '-er'			
	Grammatical		Ungrammatical		Grammatical		Ungrammatical	
	M	SD	M	SD	M	SD	M	SD
Recast	.278	.278	.194	.282	.751	.110	.264	.076
Meta	.444	.192	.333	.225	.505	.279	.140	.186
Control	.307	.207	.200	.253	.566	.238	.168	.193

b **Post-test 1**

Group	Past tense '-ed'				Comparative '-er'			
	Grammatical		Ungrammatical		Grammatical		Ungrammatical	
	M	SD	M	SD	M	SD	M	SD
Recast	.403	.279	.319	.240	.813	.157	.472	.406
Meta	.618	.257	.375	.267	.751	.219	.583	.337
Control	.417	.317	.217	.209	.745	.225	.260	.193

c **Post-test 2**

Group	Past tense '-ed'				Comparative '-er'			
	Grammatical		Ungrammatical		Grammatical		Ungrammatical	
	M	SD	M	SD	M	SD	M	SD
Recast	.514	.180	.375	.334	.848	.180	.639	.338
Meta	.736	.194	.653	.694	.831	.175	.639	.324
Control	.400	.211	.267	.196	.750	.179	.351	.264

Table 14.4   Descriptive statistics for the oral imitation test

a Pre-test

| Group | Past tense '-ed' | | | | Comparative '-er' | | | |
| | Grammatical | | Ungrammatical | | Grammatical | | Ungrammatical | |
	M	SD	M	SD	M	SD	M	SD
Recast	.714	.122	.854	.129	.738	.210	.855	.159
Meta	.738	.134	.844	.108	.773	.156	.689	.265
Control	.586	.247	.788	.145	.713	.136	.840	.165

b Post-test 1

| Group | Past tense '-ed' | | | | Comparative '-er' | | | |
| | Grammatical | | Ungrammatical | | Grammatical | | Ungrammatical | |
	M	SD	M	SD	M	SD	M	SD
Recast	.833	.147	.844	.152	.964	.090	.969	.107
Meta	.929	.144	.833	.154	.845	.188	.918	.133
Control	.786	.181	.813	.189	.873	.216	.860	.165

c Post-test 2

| Group | Past tense '-ed' | | | | Comparative '-er' | | | |
| | Grammatical | | Ungrammatical | | Grammatical | | Ungrammatical | |
	M	SD	M	SD	M	SD	M	SD
Recast	.784	.142	.813	.146	.929	.205	.918	.178
Meta	.941	.072	.844	.094	.894	.202	.968	.058
Control	.871	.142	.738	.190	.901	.097	.840	.203

Table 14.5 Descriptive statistics for the untimed grammaticality judgment test

Recast groups

In the oral imitation test, scores for the comparative were considerably higher than those for past tense '–ed'. Grammatical and ungrammatical sentence scores for both structures showed an increase over time with the most marked increase evident in the ungrammatical scores for the comparative. To establish whether the grammatical and ungrammatical scores for the two structures were significantly different a split plot ANOVA (SPANOVA) was employed. No significant differences for time/group interaction were found for either grammatical sentences ($df = 2$, $F = .792$, $p = .459$) or ungrammatical sentences ($df = 2$, $F = 1.026$, $p = .367$).

In the grammatical sentences in the untimed grammaticality judgment test, both recast groups showed an initial gain from pre-test to post-test 1 but a small subsequent decline in scores at post-test 2. This pattern was different for the ungrammatical sentences. Whereas the comparative recast group performed in much the same way as on the grammatical sentences, the past tense recast group showed a slight decline in scores from pre-test to post-test 1 and

a Pre-test

Group	Past tense '–ed'		Comparative '–er'	
	M	SD	M	SD
Recast	.958	.144	.667	.201
Meta	.833	.246	.667	.284
Control	.850	.241	.667	.272

b Post-test 1

Group	Past tense '–ed'		Comparative '–er'	
	M	SD	M	SD
Recast	.833	.326	.972	.096
Meta	.917	.194	.889	.296
Control	.900	.210	.667	.157

c Post-test 2

Group	Past tense '–ed'		Comparative '–er'	
	M	SD	M	SD
Recast	1.000	.000	.944	.130
Meta	.917	.194	1.000	.000
Control	.850	.337	.867	.172

Table 14.6 Descriptive statistics for the metalinguistic knowledge test

from post-test 1 to post-test 2. To establish whether the grammatical and ungrammatical post-test scores of the two structures were significantly different a SPANOVA was employed. No significant differences for time/group interaction were found for grammatical sentences ($df = 2$, $F = 1.976$, $p = .151$) or for ungrammatical sentences ($df = 2$, $F = 1.599$, $p = .214$).

In the metalinguistic knowledge test, the past tense group scored higher than the comparative group overall. The comparative group's scores increased, mainly from pre-test to post-test 1. No statistical test was computed as scores for the past tense '–ed' were close to 1 on the pre-test.

Metalinguistic groups

In the oral imitation test, grammatical item scores increased for both past tense '–ed' and for the comparative from pre-test to post-test 1 and from post-test 1 to post-test 2. In the case of the ungrammatical items, however, the results were somewhat different for the two structures. As Figure 14.1 shows, the comparative scores showed a sharp increase from pre-test to post-test 1 whereas the past tense scores increased only moderately. In contrast, the past tense scores rose sharply from post-test 1 to post-test 2 whereas the comparative scores hardly increased at all. A SPANOVA found no statistically significant difference in the time/group interaction for the grammatical items

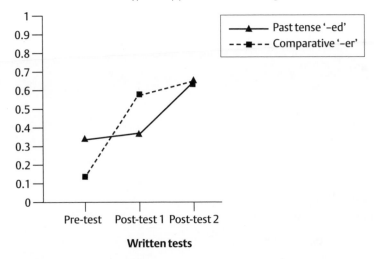

Figure 14.1 Oral imitation test—ungrammatical sentences (metalinguistic groups)

$(df = 2, F = .210, p = .812)$ but did find one for the ungrammatical sentences $(df = 2, F = 6.11, p = .005)$.

In the case of the grammatical sentences in the untimed grammaticality judgment test, the metalinguistic treatment benefited past tense '–ed' to a greater extent than the comparative. In particular, scores increased more strongly for past tense '–ed' from pre-test to post-test 1. Scores on the ungrammatical sentences showed a different pattern (see Figure 14.2) with the metalinguistic treatment having a stronger effect on the comparative. Indeed ungrammatical item scores for past tense '–ed' hardly changed. A SPANOVA found no significant time/group interaction for the grammatical sentences $(df = 2, F = 1.699, p = .195)$ but did find one for the ungrammatical items $(df = 2, F = 6.861, p = .003)$.

Finally, the metalinguistic groups' results for the metalinguistic knowledge showed greater gains for the comparative group than for the past tense '–ed' group, especially from post-test 1 to post test 2, although it must be noted that the past tense '–ed' scores were close to asymptote from the start. The interaction between time and group (the two structures) approached statistical significance on the SPANOVA multivariate test $(F = 3.23, p = .06)$.

The differential effect of the two types of corrective feedback

Separate SPANOVAs (2 structures × 3 groups × 3 testing times) were computed separately for the grammatical and ungrammatical sentences in the oral imitation test and the untimed grammaticality judgment test. Note that in this analysis the control group's scores were included. The tests of Between Subjects Means for the two structures taken together showed that there were

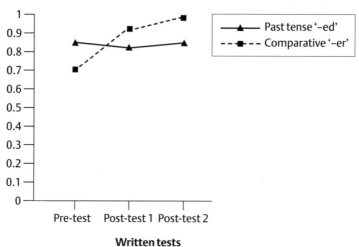

Figure 14.2 Untimed grammaticality judgment test—ungrammatical sentences (metalinguistic groups)

no significant group differences in the grammatical sentences in the oral imitation test ($df = 2$, $F = 2.247$, $p = .123$), in the grammatical sentences in the untimed grammaticality judgment test ($df = 3$, $F = 1.07$, $p = .355$), or in the ungrammatical sentences in the untimed grammaticality judgment test ($df = 2$, $F = 1.067$, $p = .356$). However, the group difference for the ungrammatical sentences in the oral imitation test ($df = 2$, $F = 4.431$, $p = .02$) was statistically significant. The *post hoc* test (least significant difference) showed that the metalinguistic groups outperformed the control group ($p = .006$) but that the differences between the recasts group and the control group ($p = .07$) and also between the experimental groups ($p = .256$) were not statistically significant.

The crucial statistic here, however, is the structure/time/group interaction. This addresses whether the effect of the two types of feedback differed according to structure over time. The results for the multivariate test show that the structure/time/group interaction was not statistically significant in the case of the oral imitation grammatical sentences ($df = 2$, $F = 1.08$, $p = .405$) and in the case of both the untimed grammaticality judgment test grammatical sentences ($df = 2$, $F = 2.105$, $p = .091$) and ungrammatical sentences ($df = 2$, $F = 1.746$, $p = .151$) but that it was significant in the case of the oral imitation test ungrammatical sentences ($df = 2$, $F = 2.565$, $p = .047$).

To interpret these results it is necessary to reconsider the results reported for the effects of the two corrective feedback treatments on the two structures. These show that whereas the recast treatment had a very similar effect for both structures as measured by the oral imitation ungrammatical items, the metalinguistic treatment resulted in much larger initial gains (from pre-test to post-test 1) for the comparative but larger subsequent gains (from post-test 1 to post-test 2) for past tense '–ed'. (See Figure 14.1.)

To sum up, only the metalinguistic feedback was found to be effective in promoting acquisition of both structures but its effect was somewhat different for each structure, with a statistically significant *immediate* effect evident for the comparative but only a *delayed* effect for past tense '–ed'. However, this effect was only evident on the ungrammatical sentences in the oral imitation test.

Discussion

In the introduction, I argued that the comparative presented greater learning difficulty than past tense '–ed'. However, the pre-test scores and the learners' performance in the treatments tasks do not entirely bear out this prediction. The lower-intermediate level learners investigated in this study achieved lower past-tense scores for the grammatical sentences in the oral imitation test than for the comparative and performed the comparative more accurately in the instructional treatment. However, the metalinguistic and control groups' scores (but not the recast group's scores) for the ungrammatical items in the oral imitation test were slightly higher for past-tense '–ed'. Taking the oral imitation test as a test of implicit knowledge, the picture presented, therefore, is a mixed one; the pre-test scores do not convincingly demonstrate that past tense '–ed' was better acquired than comparative '–er'. Nor is the picture much clearer where the scores for the ungrammatical sentences of the untimed grammaticality judgment are concerned; only in the case of the metalinguistic group were the pre-test scores higher for past tense '–ed' than for comparative '–er'. However, in the case of the metalinguistic test, all three groups scored lower on the comparative than on the past tense.

The first research question concerned whether corrective feedback in the form of recasts had a differential effect on the acquisition of the two structures. The answer is clear. It did not. No statistically significant difference on any of the scores for the two structures was found. It is noticeable that the recast group's gains for both structures were only moderate. In the oral imitation test grammatical and ungrammatical sentences the gains for past tense '–ed' from pre-test to post-test 2 were only .236 and .170 respectively. The gains for comparative were very low for the grammatical sentences (only .097) but higher for the ungrammatical sentences (.375). The gains for the control group (a group of ten learners that neither completed the communicative tasks nor received any feedback directed at the target structures) were .093 and .067 for the grammatical and ungrammatical past tense '–ed' sentences and .184 and .183 for the grammatical and ungrammatical comparative sentences. A similar picture emerges from the untimed grammaticality judgment test. The results of the SPANOVA showed that overall there was no difference between the performance of the recasts groups and the control group on the two structures.

The results of this study differ from those of previous studies (for example, Doughty and Varela 1998; Han 2002b), which did find a positive effect for recasts on acquisition. The explanation for these different results may reside in the salience of the recasts. In the case of both Doughty and Varela and Han the recast treatment was provided over several weeks and the recasts were repeatedly directed at the same error. Thus, it is likely that the recasts became salient to the learners. In the case of the present study, there were only 42 recasts directed at past tense '–ed' and 22 at the comparative, all in the course of one hour. Furthermore, the recasts were extremely brief (typically consisting of a single word) and may easily have been overlooked by learners who were likely to have been predominantly focused on meaning as they performed the tasks. If this line of argument is correct, it suggests that recasts will have only a limited effect on *any* grammatical structure unless they are intensive and salient.

The second research question concerned whether corrective feedback in the form of metalinguistic comments had a differential effect on the acquisition of the two structures. The results relevant to this question are summarized in Table 14.7. In this case, differential effects for the two structures were found. Overall, the metalinguistic feedback had a greater effect on the comparative. One might have expected that this was because there were more metalinguistic feedback moves directed at the comparative but as Table 14.3 shows this was not the case (i.e. there were actually more feedback moves directed at past tense).

Test	Result
Oral imitation—grammatical	No difference
Oral imitation—ungrammatical	Different—metalinguistic feedback had greater effect on comparative '-er' initially while its effect on past tense '-ed' was more evident later.
Untimed grammaticality judgment test—grammatical	No difference
Untimed grammaticality judgment test—ungrammatical	Different—the effect was evident on comparative but not past tense '-ed'.
Metalinguistic	Weak effect—effect greater for comparative.

Table 14.7 Effects of metalinguistic feedback on the two structures

Overall, the metalinguistic groups outperformed the control group. In other words, the metalinguistic feedback, even when not intensive and prolonged, appeared to be salient enough to learners to assist acquisition. However, the metalinguistic feedback appears to have assisted the acquisition of the two structures in somewhat different ways. Whereas its effects on past-tense '–ed' were delayed those on the comparative were immediate. The obvious explanation for differences in the two metalinguistic groups' gains in explicit knowledge can be found in the different starting levels of explicit knowledge for the two structures. Pre-test scores on the metalinguistic knowledge test (see Table 14.6) showed that the learners in this study already had well-developed explicit knowledge of past tense '–ed' at the start but not of the comparative. It is therefore hardly surprising that the results for the ungrammatical sentences in the untimed grammaticality judgment test and those for the metalinguistic knowledge test (both designed as tests of explicit knowledge) showed the metalinguistic feedback had a greater effect on the comparative. There was still room to develop explicit knowledge of this structure.

Of greater interest is the result for the ungrammatical sentences in the oral imitation test, designed to measure implicit knowledge. Here, the metalinguistic feedback had a greater impact initially on comparative but a greater delayed impact on past tense '–ed'. To explain this it is necessary to consider how explicit knowledge can facilitate the acquisition of implicit knowledge. N. Ellis (2005) proposes the following learning sequence:

> external scaffolded attention → internally motivated attention → explicit knowledge → explicit memory → implicit learning → implicit memory, automatization, and abstraction

In the case of the comparative, the metalinguistic feedback (constituting 'external scaffolded attention') induced 'internally motivated attention' and the enhancement of 'explicit knowledge' and 'explicit memory'. This had the immediate effect of enabling learners to notice the ungrammatical comparative constructions in the oral imitation test and thus to correct them. Subsequently, the process of implicit learning continues but this is relatively slow as exposure to comparative forms was probably limited given their relative infrequency in input. In the case of past tense '–ed', explicit knowledge and explicit memory are already well-established at the beginning of the study. The effect of the metalinguistic feedback, then, may have been simply that of 'freshening up' their explicit knowledge of this structure, enabling them to attend more closely to the instances of past tense '–ed' in the input they were exposed to between post-test 1 and post-test 2, which were likely to have been plentiful. As a result delayed implicit learning took place. If this explanation is correct, it follows that metalinguistic feedback may work in somewhat different ways for language acquisition depending on two factors: (1) how well-formed learners' existing explicit knowledge of a structure is and (2) the frequency with which learners are subsequently exposed to the structure.

The third research question concerned the differential effects of the two feedback treatments on the two structures. A differential effect was found only on the ungrammatical sentences of the oral imitation test. Whereas the recast treatment resulted in a similar pattern of effect for both structures, the metalinguistic feedback produced varied effects. Again, this suggests that if recasts are not very salient to learners their effect on different structures will be much the same (i.e. they will have minimal effect on acquisition), while metalinguistic feedback, which is salient and provides explicit negative evidence, affects the acquisition of structures differently because of differences in the learners' pre-existing explicit knowledge and differences in the frequency with which the structures appear in subsequent input.

Conclusion

There is increasing evidence (not least from the studies reported in this book) that corrective feedback contributes substantially to L2 acquisition. However, there have been almost no studies that have investigated the effects of different kinds of feedback on different grammatical structures. Yet, there is good reason to believe that the effects of feedback will vary according to the structure being targeted. The study reported in this chapter provides empirical evidence to suggest that this is the case. It found that while the effects of recasts were the same for the two structures investigated (possibly because they were not salient to the learners), the effects of metalinguistic feedback differed, favouring the comparative over the past tense '–ed', especially in the immediate post-test. It would seem, therefore, that the extent to which learners are able to benefit from feedback depends, in part at least, on the structure being targeted and the nature of the feedback. It also suggests that metalinguistic feedback may work for acquisition differently depending on the target structure, sometimes producing immediate effects and sometimes delayed effects.

Metalinguistic feedback has been shown to be effective in promoting acquisition. (See, for example, R. Ellis, Loewen, and Erlam 2006.) However, it cannot be concluded that it will be equally effective for *all* grammatical structures. What is needed is further research to help us identify how linguistic factors determine when different kinds of feedback will work for acquisition. In the meantime, researchers would do well to take care not to generalize from studies that investigate the effects of only one type of feedback on a single target structure.

15

Measuring the effects of oral corrective feedback on L2 knowledge

SHAWN LOEWEN and TOSHIYO NABEI

Introduction

Corrective feedback in meaning-focused second language (L2) lessons is a topic that continues to generate interest. As noted in the Introduction to this book, according to Long's Interaction Hypothesis (1996), feedback provided through verbal interaction can facilitate L2 learning by connecting form and meaning. Pedagogically, corrective feedback is an important component of form-focused instruction, which is advocated as effective for L2 teaching (for example, Long and Robinson 1998). Immediately provided in response to errors during communicative interaction, corrective feedback provides an opportunity for learners to pay attention to form as it relates to their intended meaning (for example, Long 1996; Gass 1997; Doughty 2001).

Previous L2 classroom studies have shown that corrective feedback can and does occur in meaning-focused lessons in both immersion classes (Lyster and Ranta 1997; Lyster 1998b) and ESL/EFL classes (R. Ellis, Basturkmen, and Loewen 2001a; Loewen 2004; Sheen 2004). Feedback provided during conversational interaction varies. It might be given explicitly through direct correction or rule explanation, or it might be provided implicitly through clarification requests or recasts. Chaudron (1977), for example, collected classroom conversation data from three French immersion classrooms and identified complex and detailed feedback moves that the teachers made. More recently, Lyster and Ranta (1997) collected data from six French immersion classrooms. Their analysis of 18.3 hours of classroom interaction identified six typical feedback moves that the immersion teachers made: explicit correction, recasts, clarification requests, metalinguistic feedback, elicitation, and repetition. Using similar categories, R. Ellis *et al.* (2001a), in their study of two ESL classes in New Zealand, identified recasts as being the most frequent type of corrective feedback, followed by the provision of explicit information and then prompts/elicitations.

While various studies have been conducted to identify whether corrective feedback might be effective, there is still debate over what types of corrective feedback might be more or less effective. Based on Lyster and Ranta's (1997) six categories, Figure 15.1 presents some options available in providing feedback. At one level, feedback can be divided according to who performs the repair, either other- or self-repair (Schegloff, Jefferson, and Sacks 1977). In other-repair, the correct form is provided for the learner, generally by the teacher, while in self-repair, the learner is prompted to produce the correct form. In addition, Figure 15.1 illustrates that within each type of repair, the feedback can fall along a continuum of explicitness. Thus, recasts are more towards the implicit side of the continuum for other-repair. Similarly, clarification requests are a more implicit type of feedback prompting self-repair. The present study addresses recasts, metalinguistic feedback, and clarification requests as options which have been proposed as providing potentially differential benefits for learners. These three feedback options were chosen because they (a) occur relatively frequently in L2 classroom interaction, (b) differ in their level of explicitness, and (c) vary in whether they provide other-repair or allow self-repair.

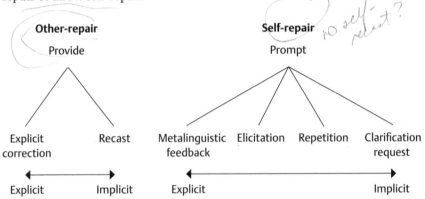

Figure 15.1 Options for corrective feedback

Recasts, as an implicit type of feedback, are argued to be beneficial because they do not disrupt the flow of communication, they are contingent on learners' errors, and they juxtapose the learner's non-targetlike form with the targetlike form (Long 1996; Long and Robinson 1998; Nicholas, Lightbown, and Spada 2001). Furthermore, recasts have been observed to be frequent in meaning-focused classroom interaction (Lyster 1998b; R. Ellis *et al.* 2001a). Nevertheless, doubt has been expressed about learners' ability to notice recasts in classroom interaction, due to their implicitness and similarity to other types of classroom discourse (Lyster 1998a). Furthermore, recasts may vary in their 'implicitness', depending on whether they (a) are segmented or whole, (b) target one or more error, (c) contain additional prosodic emphasis, or (d) occur in conjunction with additional feedback moves (Loewen and Philp 2006).

Metalinguistic feedback, in contrast to recasts, is more explicit by providing an overt indication as to the nature of the learner error (Lyster and Ranta 1997; R. Ellis, Loewen, and Erlam 2006). However, this metalinguistic information does not provide the correct linguistic structure, and thus learners are required to use the information to come up with the correct form on their own. The benefit of such overt correction is that learners are less likely to misconstrue the correctional intent of the feedback; however, such explicit feedback is more likely to disrupt the flow of the interaction.

The third category of feedback to consider is clarification requests, which also involve prompting learners to self-repair (Lyster and Ranta 1997; R. Ellis *et al.* 2001a; Lyster 2004). However, unlike metalinguistic feedback, clarification requests are more implicit and may serve a dual purpose of clarifying meaning as well as prompting self-repair. Consequently, learners may be less likely to notice the corrective intent of such feedback. Nevertheless, prompting, whether through metalinguistic feedback or clarification requests, involves asking learners to correct the error themselves and therefore to process at a deeper level. As a result, prompting may be superior to providing the form—as, for example, in a recast. However, a prompt assumes that learners have the latent knowledge necessary to perform self-repair; consequently, prompts may not work on unknown or novel linguistic items.

Studies investigating the various types of feedback and the impact they have on learning have found different results. Some have found a beneficial effect for recasts. For example, Doughty and Varela (1998) showed corrective recasts, which included a repetition of the learner's non-targetlike utterance and a recast, to be more effective than no feedback. Another study by Mackey and Philp (1998) examined the effects of recasts on learning with respect to L2 learners' acquisition of question forms; they found that the recasts provided to advanced learners had a positive effect on learning higher stages of question forms, whereas other forms of implicit feedback—as, for example, negotiation for meaning—had less effect.

However, other studies have found metalinguistic feedback to be more effective. For example, Carroll and Swain (1993) studied the effects of different feedback strategies on adult ESL learners' ability to recognize verbs which do or do not alternate in dative sentences. They formed four treatment groups. Following participant errors, Group A received metalinguistic explanations, Group B were told they were wrong, Group C received recasts, and Group D were asked if they were sure. A post-treatment recall test showed that the metalinguistic explanation group (Group A) outperformed the other groups. Another study which found evidence of metalinguistic feedback was R. Ellis, Loewen, and Erlam (2006), which investigated the effects of recasts and metalinguistic feedback on L2 learners' use of English regular past tense. They found that, on an elicited imitation test, the metalinguistic feedback group scored significantly higher on a delayed post-test, although there were no differences on the immediate post-test. However, on an untimed grammaticality judgment test, there was no significant improvement for either group on either the immediate or delayed post-tests.

Finally, at least one study has found prompts to be more effective. Lyster (2004) investigated the effects of form-focused instruction and feedback on learners' ability to assign grammatical gender to French articles. Two French immersion classes taught by four teachers received (a) form-focused instruction and prompts, (b) form-focused instruction and recasts, (c) form-focused instruction and no feedback, and (d) no form-focused instruction nor feedback. The results of pre- and post-treatment written and oral production tasks showed that the students who received form-focused instruction out-performed the no form-focused instruction group. Among the form-focused instruction groups, the form-focused instruction and prompts group outper-formed the other form-focused instruction groups.

Clearly these contrasting results suggest that further investigation into the relative effects of different types of feedback is necessary. However, it is also important to consider how to measure the effects of corrective feedback, as there have been recent calls for more rigorous investigation into the construct validity of tests used in SLA research (Douglas 2001; R. Ellis 2004; Purpura 2004). Long (1997: 319) asserts that 'the goal of research on SLA ... is to understand how changes in [learners'] internal mental representation are achieved'. In order to approach this goal, SLA researchers must consider what information their tests provide and what inferences can be made from the test takers' performance (Deville and Chalhoub-Deville 2006).

One criticism of some of the previous research on corrective feedback is that it has often used tests which could be considered better measures of explicit L2 knowledge. (See R. Ellis this volume.) Recent studies into the measurement of implicit and explicit L2 knowledge suggest that tests which focus on discrete linguistic forms and allow unlimited response time may favour the use of learners' explicit L2 knowledge. In contrast, tests which involve spontaneous production, focus on meaning or which allow learners only limited response time may encourage learners to draw on their implicit L2 knowledge (Han 2000; R. Ellis 2004, 2005).

Research questions

In order to address the issues of corrective feedback and testing instruments, the present study investigated the following research questions:

1 Does corrective feedback on English question formation errors during meaning-focused tasks lead to an increase in learners' performance on
   a) a timed grammaticality judgment test,
   b) an untimed grammaticality judgment test,
   c) an oral production task?
2 Is there a difference in the effectiveness of three different types of feedback, that is, metalinguistic feedback, recasts, and clarification requests, for learners' performance on

a) a timed grammaticality judgment test,
b) an untimed grammaticality judgment test,
c) an oral production task?

Method

The study used a quasi-experimental design involving a pre-test, treatment, and post-test. The treatment occurred one day after the pre-test, and the post-test occurred one week after the treatment.

Participants

Two intact English classes, one with 40 students and the other with 35, at a Japanese university provided the participants for the study; however, five participants from the first class and four from the second missed one of the testing or treatment sessions and were consequently excluded from the data set. Of the remaining 66 participants, 45 were male (68 per cent) and 21 were female (32 per cent). All participants were Japanese nationals and all claimed Japanese as their first language and the language they used daily. Ten participants had lived in an English-speaking country (America = 5, Australia = 1, Canada = 1, New Zealand = 3) for time periods ranging from two weeks to five years. Ninety per cent said that their English education had been 'mostly formal', seven per cent said 'mostly informal' and three per cent said a 'mixture'. The average age was 19, the average age at which participants began studying English was 11, and participants had studied English for seven years on average. The participants' self-rated English proficiency, on a scale from one (beginner) to five (native-like), averaged from 1.75 for speaking to 2.2 for reading.

In addition to the student participants, the two authors and an L1 English-speaking research assistant administered the tests and served as interlocutors during the treatment sessions.

Target structure

The linguistic structure chosen as the target for the feedback was English question formation. Question forms were chosen for several reasons: it was a structure that was proven to be problematic for the participants in the study, and therefore would provide opportunities for corrective feedback. Additionally, question forms are relatively easy to elicit in meaning-focused tasks. Several studies have examined the effects of feedback on the development of question forms (for example, Spada and Lightbown 1993; Mackey and Philp 1998; Mackey 1999; McDonough 2005). Finally, learners have been shown to progress through developmental sequences in acquiring question forms (Pienemann, Johnston, and Brindley 1988)—the study could, therefore, employ testing instruments that compared development and accuracy.

Treatment materials and procedures

In order to form the treatment groups, students from one intact class (*n* = 35) were placed into groups of four based on their availability on the day of the treatment. Groupings of four were chosen in order to reflect classroom practices in conducting meaning-focused activities and to allow all learners to complete the tasks within the time allotted for the study. A total of ten groups were formed, and each group was randomly assigned one treatment option. Three groups received recasts (*n* = 10), two received clarification requests (*n* = 8), two received metalinguistic feedback (*n* = 7), and three received no feedback (*n* = 10). Note that the total number of students receiving each type of feedback is not always divisible by four due to the previously mentioned participant attrition. All students in the second class (*n* = 31) were assigned to the control group which received no treatment.

The treatment duration was 30 minutes and the two treatment tasks were a spot-the-difference and a guess-the-storyline task. Each group of four conducted the tasks with either one of the two researchers or the research assistant. The spot-the-difference task (from Mackey 1994) consisted of two sets of picture cards with slightly differing scenes. The students were given one set of cards and the researcher had a slightly differing set. The students were told to ask questions of the researcher in order to elicit information about the pictures. The learners self-nominated to ask the questions and had to discover the ten or so differences between the two cards. In the guess-the-storyline task, learners were shown a series of five picture cards which developed a story. Parts of each picture card were covered, and participants had to ask the researcher questions about the missing items. When participants guessed a missing item, they progressed to the next picture. During the treatment tasks, the researchers provided feedback (according to the designation of each group) when an error in question formation occurred. Definitions and examples of the feedback types from data in the current study are shown in Table 15.1.

The amount of feedback provided to each group varied according to the number of learner errors and therefore differed among the groups. Table 15.2 presents the average frequency and type of feedback provided after question formation errors, and shows that the recast and elicitation groups each received approximately 18 instances of their respective feedback. The metalinguistic groups averaged just over five instances of metalinguistic feedback with an additional four recasts, and finally the no feedback groups received virtually no feedback.

Testing instruments and procedures

In order to use tests which might encourage learners to draw on different types of L2 knowledge, three different instruments were used: a timed grammaticality judgment test, an untimed grammaticality judgment test, and an

	Definition	Example
Recast	A correct reformulation of the error was provided for the participants.	**L** Er how many people in your picture? **R** How many people are there in my picture? Er three people.
Clarification request	An attempt was made to get learners to self-repair the erroneous utterance by asking for clarification. No direct indication of the presence of an error was made.	**L** Why does he taking the flowers? **R** Pardon? **L** Why does he take flowers?
Metalinguistic feedback	The targeted linguistic structure was identified for the learners, and they were asked to correct it.	**L** How many crater on cloud? **R** Um can you think about your question again? It's a good question but think about your form, your grammar form.
No feedback	No attention was given to errors.	

L = Learner, R = Researcher

Table 15.1 Feedback options

	Feedback provided		
Group	**Metalinguistic**	**Recast**	**Clarification**
Recast	0	18.7	.3
Clarification	0	0	18
Metalinguistic	5.6	4	0
No feedback	0	.3	0

Table 15.2 Frequency and type of feedback provided during treatment

oral production task. Both grammaticality judgment tests consisted of 40 items, with 16 distracters (targeting regular past tense '–ed', comparative '–er', plural '–s' and verb complementation) and 24 items related to question formation. The items targeting question formation were designed to cover several stages of question formation development, ranging from stage 3 to 5 (based on Pienemann *et al.* 1988; Mackey and Philp 1998; Mackey 1999; McDonough 2005). Half of the question form items at each stage were grammatical and half were ungrammatical. The appendix provides a list of the test items. The items in both grammaticality judgment tests were the same; the only difference between the tests was the amount of time the participants were allowed in making their judgments. The rationale for using the same sentences in both the timed and untimed grammaticality judgment tests was so that the items themselves would not introduce extra variability into the measurement of implicit and explicit L2 knowledge. Thus, any differences between the timed and untimed grammaticality judgment tests could be attributed to the speeded nature of the learners' responses and potentially to the types of knowledge they could draw on under each condition (R. Ellis 2005). In the untimed grammaticality judgment test, the participants were allowed unlimited time. In the timed grammaticality judgment test, they were given between 1.8 and 5 seconds, depending on the length of the item. The response times for the timed grammaticality judgment test were piloted on 13 L1 English speakers and an additional 20 per cent of the median response time was added to the final allotted time for each item. R. Ellis (2005) recommends such an addition to allow for the extra processing time L2 speakers might need; however, it is acknowledged that 20 per cent is an arbitrary figure and further investigation into the optimal timing would be useful, The test items were placed in a random order. All grammaticality judgment tests were administered on computer, and participants were asked to make their judgment by pressing one of two keys on the keyboard; the enter key was labelled 'correct' and the left-hand shift key was labelled 'incorrect'. One point was awarded for each correct judgment.

The oral production task consisted of two spot-the-difference tasks which were similar in design to the treatment task. Each group of four students received two cards with slightly differing pictures. Two students in each group shared one card, while the other two shared the other card, and in their groups of four, the students had to find around ten differences by asking each other questions about the cards. Two of these tasks were done as a pre-test and two similar tasks were done as a post-test, with each testing session lasting around 25 minutes. Unlike the treatment task, the researchers did not participate in the pre- and post-tests. All group interaction was audio-recorded. Although the control group also participated in the tasks, their data were not available for analysis; therefore, only the data for the treatment groups were analyzed.

Analysis

For the timed and untimed grammaticality judgment tests, average raw scores were calculated for the question items. In addition to overall scores, average scores were calculated separately for the grammatical and ungrammatical items since R. Ellis (2005) found that on grammaticality judgment tests, the grammaticality of the sentence seemed to encourage learners to draw on different types of knowledge, with ungrammatical items being associated more strongly with other measures of explicit second language knowledge (such as a metalinguistic knowledge test) while grammatical items were more closely associated with other measures of implicit second language knowledge (such as an elicited oral imitation test). Such differences in learners' performance on the grammatical and ungrammatical items suggest that it is important to analyze grammatical and ungrammatical items separately. Repeated-measures ANOVAs were performed to determine if there were significant differences among the groups. *Post hoc* analyses were performed when an ANOVA was significant. An alpha level of .05 was set. SPSS *12.1* was used to perform the analyses.

For the oral production tasks, the interaction of the groups was transcribed and all question forms at stages 3, 4, or 5 were identified and coded according to stage. The average frequency of questions at each stage is presented; however, due to low cell counts for certain stages, no inferential statistics were calculated. Fifty per cent of the data were coded by a second rater, and there was a 96 per cent agreement rate for identifying questions in the data and a 98.9 per cent agreement rate for coding the stage of each question.

Results

The answers to the research questions are presented first for the untimed grammaticality judgment test, then for the timed grammaticality judgment test, and finally for the oral production task. Table 15.3 shows the average scores for the untimed grammaticality judgment test. On the pre-test, the groups averaged from 17–20 out of a possible 24 (70 per cent to 84 per cent). On the post-test, the average scores constituted nearly the same range (70 per cent to 82 per cent). A one-way ANOVA on the pre-test scores revealed significant differences among the groups, $F = 2.53$, $df = 4$, $p = .049$, with a *post hoc* Tukey test revealing that the no feedback group differed significantly from the control ($p = .061$) group. Because of the differences among the groups on the pre-test scores, a one-way ANCOVA was performed on the post-test scores, with the pre-test scores as a covariate. This analysis revealed no significant differences among the groups' post-test scores, $F = .537$, $df = 4$, $p = .709$. Thus, the answer to the first research question for the untimed grammaticality judgment test is that there was no significant increase in scores from pre-test to post-test. The answer to the second research question regarding differences among feedback groups is that there were no significant differences among the groups on their post-test scores.

	Pre-test			Post-test		
	μ	SD	Percentage	μ	SD	Percentage
Clarification	20.3	2.05	84.4	19.6	2.83	81.8
Recast	18.8	2.78	78.3	19.7	2.45	82.1
Metalinguistic	18.0	3.83	75.0	18.4	3.36	76.8
No feedback	17.0	2.54	70.8	16.9	3.41	70.4
Control	19.7	2.66	82.1	19.7	3.20	82.2

Effect sizes for post-test: clarification, $d = -.03$, recast, $d = 0.0$, metalinguistic, $d = -.40$, no feedback, $d = -.85$

Table 15.3 Untimed grammaticality judgment test scores

Table 15.4 shows the scores for the timed grammaticality judgment test. On the pre-test, the groups averaged from 6–8 out of a possible 24 (24 per cent to 34 per cent). On the post-test, the average scores ranged between 7 and 12 (31 per cent to 51 per cent). A one-way ANOVA on the pre-test scores revealed no significant differences among the groups, $F = 2.19$, $df = 4$, $p = .080$.

	Pre-test			Post-test		
	μ	SD	Percentage	μ	SD	Percentage
Clarification	7.6	3.11	31.8	12.3	1.83	51.0
Recast	7.2	2.04	30.0	11.8	3.26	49.2
Metalinguistic	6.1	3.08	25.6	10.6	4.04	44.1
No feedback	5.8	2.20	24.2	7.40	2.37	30.8
Control	8.2	2.56	34.1	10.5	3.65	43.7

Effect sizes for gain scores: clarification, $d = .84$, recast, $d = .91$, metalinguistic, $d = .99$, no feedback, $d = -.19$

Table 15.4 Timed grammaticality judgment test scores

A repeated-measures ANOVA was performed to compare the groups' scores on the pre- and post-tests. The results, shown in Table 15.5, revealed a significant main effect for both test and feedback group as well as an interaction effect for test and feedback type. These results indicate that overall there was a significant increase from pre-test to post-test, while the interaction effect indicates that the increase varied among the groups. The results of a one-way ANOVA of the groups' gain scores revealed that the three feedback groups differed from the no feedback and control groups; however, the feedback groups did not differ among themselves, nor did the no feedback and control groups differ from each other. These results indicate that all the groups increased their scores from the pre-test to the post-test; however, the three feedback groups increased at a significantly higher rate than the no feedback and control groups.

Source	df	Mean square	F	Sig.
Test	1	309.373	82.003	.000
Feedback group	4	3.773	2.653	.041
Test * feedback group	4	12.073	3.200	.019

Table 15.5 Repeated-measures ANOVA for timed grammaticality judgment test

Since R. Ellis (2005) recommends examining grammatical and ungrammatical items separately, the next section considers the results for the grammatical and ungrammatical items for both grammaticality judgment tests. Table 15.6 shows the average scores for the grammatical and ungrammatical items on the untimed grammaticality judgment test pre-test and post-test, with grammatical item scores ranging from 8–9.5 (out of 12) on both the pre- and post-tests. Similarly, scores for the ungrammatical items ranged from 9 to almost 11 (out of 12) on both the pre- and post-tests. The results of a repeated-measures ANOVA comparing test, grammaticality, and feedback group are shown in Table 15.7. The main effect for grammaticality was significant, indicating that the scores for the ungrammatical items were significantly higher than for the grammatical items. There was also an interaction effect for grammaticality and test. The mean scores show that while the scores for the grammatical items went up from pre-test to post-test, the scores for the ungrammatical went down.

	Pre-test				Post-test			
	Grammatical		Ungrammatical		Grammatical		Ungrammatical	
	μ	SD	μ	SD	μ	SD	μ	SD
Clarification	9.5	1.60	10.8	1.16	9.25	1.49	10.4	1.77
Recast	8.4	1.84	10.4	1.72	9.6	1.83	10.1	1.91
Metalinguistic	8.0	1.91	10.0	2.24	8.14	1.86	10.3	1.89
No feedback	7.7	2.58	9.3	2.00	9.4	.966	7.5	3.03
Control	9.1	1.77	10.6	1.69	9.5	1.91	10.2	2.49

Table 15.6 Untimed grammaticality judgment test scores for grammatical and ungrammatical items

Source	df	Mean square	F	Sig.
Grammaticality	1	59.290	10.585	.002
Grammaticality *feedback group	4	5.566	.994	.418
Test * grammaticality	1	17.239	13.650	.000

Table 15.7 Repeated-measures ANOVA for untimed grammaticality judgment test (grammatical and ungrammatical items)

Table 15.8 shows the average scores for the grammatical and ungrammatical items on the timed grammaticality judgment test pre-test and post-test, with grammatical scores ranging from 4–6 (out of 12) on the pre-test and 5–8 on the post-test. The scores for the ungrammatical items ranged from 1–2 (out of 12) on the pre-test and from 2–4 on the post-test. The results of a repeated-measures ANOVA comparing test, grammaticality, and feedback group are shown in Table 15.9. As with the untimed grammaticality judgment test, the main effect for grammaticality was significant; however, in this case it is the scores for the grammatical items which were significantly higher than those for the ungrammatical items. Finally, there was no interaction effect for grammaticality and test.

	Pre-test				Post-test			
	Grammatical		Ungrammatical		Grammatical		Ungrammatical	
	μ	SD	μ	SD	μ	SD	μ	SD
Clarification	5.6	2.20	2.0	1.69	8.3	.886	4.0	1.60
Recast	5.8	1.62	1.4	.966	7.8	2.39	4.0	2.58
Metalinguistic	4.6	1.72	1.6	1.72	6.6	2.15	4.0	2.24
No feedback	4.2	1.62	1.6	1.51	5.0	2.49	2.4	2.17
Control	6.3	1.76	1.8	1.46	6.3	2.08	4.2	2.52

Table 15.8 Timed grammaticality judgment test scores for grammatical and ungrammatical items

Source	df	Mean square	F	Sig.
Grammaticality	1	561.601	139.340	.000
Grammaticality * feedback group	4	4.076	1.011	.408
Test * grammaticality	1	3.843	1.533	.220

Table 15.9 Repeated-measures ANOVA for timed grammaticality judgment test (grammatical and ungrammatical items)

The results of the oral production task are analyzed not according to overall accuracy in the use of question forms, but according to the developmental stages proposed by Pienemann *et al.* (1988); in this analysis, any effects for the corrective feedback would be demonstrated by an increase in the number of higher stage question forms from pre-test to post-test. Table 15.10 presents the number of question forms produced at each stage by the various groups; it shows that while all groups produced some questions at stages 3 and 5, the majority of questions were at stage 4. Thus, since the learners are producing stage 4 questions, an increase in the number of stage 5 questions would be evidence of development. While the number of stage 5 questions produced by each group does increase from pre-test to post-test, it does so only by one or two which is not sufficient to demonstrate improvement.

	Stage 3		Stage 4		Stage 5	
	Pre	Post	Pre	Post	Pre	Post
Clarification	1	3	46	33	3	4
Recast	2	11	32	43	0	1
Metalinguistic	4	4	36	48	0	2
No feedback	10	6	37	54	1	2

Table 15.10 Stages of questions in oral production tasks

Table 15.11 summarizes the results, and shows that there was no increase from pre-test to post-test for any of the groups on the untimed grammaticality judgment test; however, on the timed grammaticality judgment test, there was a significant increase for all groups, but the groups which received some type of feedback improved at a greater rate than the groups which did not receive feedback. When considering grammaticality as an additional variable, the results indicate that learners scored significantly higher on the ungrammatical items on the untimed grammaticality judgment test; in contrast, learners scored significantly higher on the grammatical items on the timed grammaticality judgment test. However, there was no interaction effect between grammaticality and type of feedback. Finally, in considering the results of the oral production tests, there was no increase from pre-test to post-tests in the use of higher stage question forms.

Test	Results
Untimed grammaticality judgment test	• No significant differences among the groups on the post-test • Ungrammatical items > grammatical items
Timed grammaticality judgment test	• Significant increase for all groups from pre- to post-test • Significant interaction effect between test and group, with (recast, metalinguistic and clarification) > (no feedback and control)
Oral production	• No apparent increase in higher stage question forms

Table 15.11   Summary of results

Discussion

When answering the first research question regarding the effects of feedback on improving learners' performance, it is important to point out that the answer is contingent on the testing instrument. The untimed grammaticality judgment test and the oral production test did not show any increase, while the timed grammaticality judgment test did. The results for the two grammaticality judgment tests are similar to R. Ellis *et al.*'s (2006) finding of significant effects on their measure of implicit knowledge (in that case, an elicited imitation test) but not on their measure of explicit knowledge (an untimed grammaticality judgment test). One explanation for the difference in results may be that there was a ceiling effect on the untimed grammaticality judgment test, with learners scoring around 80 per cent. Another possible explanation is that the feedback did not provide information which allowed these learners to add to their explicit knowledge which would have been evident on the test. Even the most explicit feedback type provided in the current study, the metalinguistic information, did not provide specific information about the correct formation of questions; instead, the feedback merely indicated that the error was related to question formation. On the timed grammaticality judgment test, there was obviously a practice effect, which is not surprising given the speeded nature of the test, with all groups, including the control, improving on the post-test. Nevertheless, the feedback groups improved at a higher rate than the non-feedback groups; such an increase points to the effectiveness of feedback as measured by the timed grammaticality judgment test, which is largely a measure of implicit L2 knowledge. However, on the oral production test which also provides a measure of learners' implicit L2 knowledge, there was no effect for feedback. Possible reasons for these differing results will be explored below, but these results underscore the importance of employing multiple and varied tests, which may measure improvements in different types of L2 knowledge (supporting claims made by R. Ellis 2005; R. Ellis *et al.* 2006).

When considering the second research question regarding differences in feedback group performance, the results of the timed grammaticality judgment test indicated that all three feedback groups outperformed the non-feedback groups, but did not differ from each other. These results suggest that corrective feedback is beneficial; however, they contrast from other studies which found differences according to feedback type, i.e. prompts over recasts (Lyster 2004) or metalinguistic feedback over recasts (R. Ellis *et al.* 2006). One possible explanation for the present result is that the length of treatment, half an hour, was not sufficient to accentuate the differences among the types of feedback. Other studies ranged from one hour (R. Ellis *et al.* 2006) to five weeks (Lyster 2004). However, it is not clear how much time would be needed to optimize the effects of different feedback options. Related to the issue of length of treatment is the number of feedback responses provided to the learners. Since the feedback was provided in response to learner errors and occurred during unscripted interaction, it was not possible to control the number of times learners received feedback. An analysis of the treatment transcripts indicates that while the recast and elicitation groups averaged 18 feedback responses, the metalinguistic group only averaged five feedback responses. Therefore, the fact that the metalinguistic group performed as well on the post-test as the other two groups suggests that less metalinguistic feedback may be necessary to achieve the same result as compared to recasts or elicitations.

Another possible explanation for the results of the timed grammaticality judgment tests may relate to the explicitness of the feedback. Studies which have found evidence in favor of explicit feedback argue that such feedback is more likely to be noticed by the learners, and in contrast, recasts may be more implicit and therefore less likely to be noticed than other, more explicit, types of feedback. However, in the context of the present study, recasts may have been more explicit due to the nature of the interaction during the treatment. That is to say, the context and interaction patterns in the feedback groups might have drawn learners' attention to any feedback, regardless of the type. For example, the learners were in groups of four rather than in their normal class of 40. Thus, even though their instructor often used group-work activities in the classroom (as advocated by the current Japanese government curriculum, Muranoi, Chiba, and Hatanaka 2001; Ishiguro, Yamauchi, Akamatsu, and

Kitabayashi 2003; Watanabe, Sakai, Shiokawa, and Urano 2003; JACET Educational Problem Study Group 2005), such relatively individualized attention and input from the researchers for Japanese learners who were not used to such conditions could have made the interaction context 'special'. In addition, there were often lengthy pauses during the interaction while the learners self-nominated and decided what questions to ask. As a result, utterances from both the students and researchers were generally produced without overlapping discourse or other distractions, thereby potentially making all researcher input more noticeable. Further investigation into learners' perceptions of feedback could provide further insight into this question.

In regards to the analysis of the grammatical and ungrammatical test items on the grammaticality judgment tests, the results revealed that the learners did better on the ungrammatical items on the untimed grammaticality judgment test; in contrast, they did better on the grammatical items on the timed grammaticality judgment test. These results perhaps speak to the construct validity of the test. If explicit knowledge is most useful (a) when learners have time to draw on it and (b) in identifying ungrammatical sentences (R. Ellis 2004, 2005), then it is reassuring that these learners scored highest on the ungrammatical items on the untimed grammaticality judgment test. Additionally, it is interesting to see that these learners did not seem to be able to bring this explicit L2 knowledge to bear on the timed grammaticality judgment test, as evidenced by the lower scores for the ungrammatical items. Finally, it should be pointed out that there was no interaction between the feedback groups and grammaticality, indicating that feedback or lack thereof, did not improve learners' abilities to judge one type of sentence as opposed to the other.

While the results of the timed grammaticality judgment test indicated an effect for corrective feedback, the results of the oral production test did not. Considering that both tests are argued to provide measures of learners' implicit L2 knowledge, it is important to consider the differing results. One possible explanation is that the type of action taken in each test is responsible for the differing results. In the grammaticality judgment test, learners made decisions about the grammaticality of sentences that were provided for them, while in the oral production test they had to produce question forms on their own. Therefore, the feedback may have impacted the learners' ability to detect grammatical and ungrammatical sentences, but not their ability to produce them. Similarly, it may be that the developmental stages may be too broad to reflect small changes in learners' L2 knowledge. Other studies (for example, Philp 1998) have suggested that stage 4 in the developmental sequence of question formation is a very broad category, and it may be that a more accuracy-based measure of question use, such as targetlike use, might provide additional insights into learners' progress.

It is also possible that the treatment had no effect on development because the treatment was of such a limited nature, consisting of only a handful of instances of corrective feedback. Additionally, learners may not have had enough opportunity to use the stage 5 questions since the post-test was only about 25 minutes in length and the tasks themselves may not have been successful in eliciting questions at higher stages.

It is important to consider some of the limitations of the study. One limitation is the relatively small sample size, particularly in the feedback groups. Another limitation is the lack of a delayed post-test. Given that several studies (Mackey 1999; R. Ellis *et al.* 2006) have found effects for feedback on tests given two or more weeks after the treatment, it would have been desirable to have had a similar delayed post-test in this study. Unfortunately, the learners' academic program prevented such testing; however, a one week post-test was preferable to a post-test immediately following the treatment. Additionally, it would have been interesting to include learners at differing levels of English L2 proficiency given that other studies of feedback on question formation have found greater effects for higher proficiency learners (for example, Mackey and Philp 1998). Finally, it should be pointed out that this study has only looked at the feedback provided to the learners in groups and not at individual learners' production. However, given the small number of stage 5 question forms in the post-test data, it is unlikely that an analysis of individual learner production would provide differing results. Finally, the analysis has not examined learners' incorporation of the feedback into their own production, even though such pushed output may be beneficial for learning (Swain 1995; Loewen 2004; McDonough 2005).

In summary, this study has compared the effectiveness of three different types of corrective feedback on learners' performance on timed and untimed grammaticality judgment tests and an oral production test. The results indicate that, on the timed grammaticality judgment test, all three types of feedback were equally effective and that the feedback groups performed better than the no feedback and control groups. However, no effects for feedback were found on the untimed grammaticality judgment test or the oral production test. In spite of its limitations, this study provides some evidence regarding the effectiveness of corrective feedback and suggests that further investigation into the effects of feedback should continue, using a variety of measures of L2 learning.

Appendix

Grammaticality Judgment Test items

Stage 3

1 Does Motoki live in New Zealand?
2 Does Cathy cook dinner every night?
3 *Is Karou have a new car?
4 *Is John have a blue bicycle?

Stage 4 (Y/N)

5 Is Yuki going to English class today?
6 Is President Bush visiting Japan next year?
7 *Is the teacher is standing next to the window?
8 *Is the girl is holding a balloon?

Stage 4 (*wh-*)

9 What is the best restaurant in Osaka?
10 Who is the best baseball player in Japan?
11 *What the most famous temple in Kyoto is?
12 *Who the new student from England is?

Stage 5 (*is*)

13 What is your brother doing today?
14 When is Keiko going shopping?
15 *What Satomi is thinking about now?
16 *When Mr. Tanaka is going to America?

Stage 5 (*do*)

17 What do you have in the bag?
18 When does Anne return from New Zealand?
19 *Where Koji lives now?
20 *When Paul begins his new job?

Auxiliary Choice

21 Is he thinking about his girlfriend?
22 What is he writing in his letter?
23 *What does he doing tomorrow?
24 *Does she reading a book?

Distractors

Keiko wants to buy a computer this weekend.
Liao stayed at home all day and finished the book.
Mary is taller than her sisters.
*My car is more faster and more powerful than your car.
Martin says he wants to get married next year.
I think that he is nicer and more intelligent than all the other students.
*Keiko bought two present for her children.
*Martin sold a few old coins and stamp to a shop.
Liao left some pens and pencils at school.
Hiroshi received a letter from his father yesterday.
*Martin completed his assignment and print it out.
*This building is more bigger than your house.
Hiroshi found some keys on the ground.
*Joseph miss an interesting party last weekend.
*Liao says he wants buying a car next week.
*Joseph wants finding a new job next month.

16

Interaction-driven L2 learning: characterizing linguistic development

K. SEON JEON

Introduction

Research suggests that interaction is beneficial to language development overall (Mackey, this volume). Yet, whether interaction is beneficial to all aspects of second language acquisition (SLA) is not known. Some SLA theories propose that individual components of language, such as morphosyntax and lexis, may develop in different manners (for example, Fodor 1983; Sharwood Smith 1986, 1993; Schwartz 1993; VanPatten 1994; Ullman 2001, 2005). For instance, Sharwood Smith (1991, 1993) views language learning as a process which involves 'a battery of quite different systems each obeying different principles' (1993: 175). In other words, researchers have suggested there are distinct learning systems, each of which is responsible for a different area of language. In addition, it has been widely claimed that different aspects of grammar may develop in different manners (Eubank 1993/1994, 1996; Vainikka and Young-Scholten 1994, 1998; Larsen-Freeman 1995; Epstein, Flynn, and Martohardjono 1996, 1998; Schwartz and Sprouse 1996; Hawkins 2001; Ullman 2001, 2005). Together, these claims suggest that the unique characteristics of interactive and/or communicative learning environments may promote the development of different linguistic forms.

Within the paradigm of input and interaction in SLA, the importance of the learning target in the relationship between interaction and L2 development has also been acknowledged (Sato 1986; Lyster 1998b; Lyster and Ranta 1997; Mackey, Gass, and McDonough 2000; Carpenter, Jeon, Mac-Gregor, and Mackey 2006; Egi this volume; Long 2006). In a recent review of recast studies, Long (2006) argued that the type of linguistic forms may be an important variable in determining the utility of recasts in facilitating second language learning. In his words, 'among other unresolved issues is the possibility that recasts (or implicit negative feedback of any type) work better for certain classes of target linguistic forms, and less effectively for other classes of items than more explicit treatments of learner error' (Long 2006: 34).

The purpose of this chapter is to report on a study which addressed the issue of whether or not interaction is differentially effective in terms of the development of different areas of language. Forty-one English-speaking learners of Korean as a Foreign Language (KFL) took part in interactive tasks that targeted morphosyntax (Korean object relative clauses and honorific subject–verb agreement) and lexis (20 nouns and verbs). The following question was posed: In which area of language (operationalized as different types of morphosyntax and lexis) does interaction promote L2 development most effectively?

Background

The review of interaction research literature in this section focuses on how interaction-driven L2 development has been characterized in previous studies. Studies conducted with a clear pre-selected linguistic focus are extensively discussed in order to determine the areas of language in which interaction has been found to promote development.

Interaction and L2 morphosyntactic development

Each L2 presents unique morphosyntactic challenges for learners (MacWhinney 1996). Moreover, first language (L1) morphosyntactic knowledge may affect L2 morphosyntactic acquisition (Bley-Vroman 1989; Hawkins 2001; MacWhinney 2005). Therefore, interaction research with pre-selected linguistic targets in languages such as English, French, Spanish, and Japanese is discussed below in order to determine the areas of language in which interaction has been found to promote development.

Many interaction and feedback studies have explored the learning of L2 English morphosyntactic structures. These have included English past tense (for example, Han 2002b; Mackey 2006a), English question forms (for example, Mackey 1999; McDonough 2005), and English articles (for example, Muranoi 2000). Experimental studies suggest that interaction promotes both short- and long-term learning of regular and irregular past tense, whether in the classroom or laboratory. However, there is counterevidence. Sato (1986), in a longitudinal analysis of SLA in a naturalistic setting, did not find a positive relationship between interaction and development of regular and irregular past tense morphology. In addition, Mackey's findings on regular and irregular past tense development through interaction were inconclusive. That is, Mackey did not find support for the possibility that noticing and L2 development may be connected in terms of development of English past tense. Studies that investigated English question form development have demonstrated that interaction facilitated development in English question forms. Muranoi (2000) targeted the English article system in his quasi-experimental study that addressed the question of how 'interaction enhancement' affects EFL learners' restructuring of their interlanguage (IL) article systems. The results indicated that such interaction enhancement had positive effects on L2 learning of English article use and that these effects lasted for at least five weeks. However, the results of this study should not lead to the assumption that the English article system can be learnt via interaction because the interactional treatment in Muranoi's study is artificially enhanced and articles are not usually salient in natural interaction.

Other studies have explored interaction and L2 morphosyntactic development in Romance languages (for example, Long, Inagaki, and Ortega 1998; Ayoun 2001; Leeman 2003; Lyster 2004). These studies suggest that interaction differentially affects morphosyntactic development as a function of the structure that is targeted. For instance, Ayoun (2001) investigated the utility of written recasts in the acquisition of the aspectual distinction between the *passé composé* and the *imparfait* in French. Ayoun found that written recasts were more effective than traditional grammar lessons and than models in promoting L2 development of this aspectual distinction. In addition, Leeman (2003) investigated the development of L2 Spanish agreement features (number and gender) in inanimate nouns and adjectives. Her results suggested that recasts promoted learning of L2 Spanish morphology. Findings by Long, Inagaki, and Ortega (1998) suggest that the effectiveness of recasts may not extend to all components of L2 Spanish morphosyntax. In a comparison of the effect of recasting and modeling, no learning was observed for object topicalization in L2 Spanish. The researchers suggest that the complexity of the targeted rule may have mitigated learning through recasts.

Additional studies have focused on L2 Japanese morphosyntax development (for example, Loschky 1994; Iwashita 2003; Ishida 2004). Using a time-series design, Ishida (2004) examined the effects of recasts on L2 development in the Japanese aspectual form *–te i-(ru)*. The results showed that the overall accuracy rate increased significantly after the recasting treatment began and the high accuracy rate was maintained for at least seven weeks. Loschky (1994) chose both subject-initial and locative-initial locative constructions in Japanese. Loschky found that learners' performance was significantly better on measures of subject-initial and locative-initial locative construction learning when there was an opportunity to negotiate for meaning (as well as when other modifications were present). Iwashita (2003) investigated the effects of both negative and positive evidence on the acquisition of Japanese locative constructions. Iwashita found that implicit negative feedback provided through recasts and interactional moves positively impacted on short-term development of the Japanese locative construction.

Table 16.1 summarizes research on the relationship between interaction and L2 development of morphosyntactic forms in English, French, Spanish, and Japanese. As a whole, this research supports claims that morphosyntactic development may be affected by the learning context. For instance, studies conducted in a controlled laboratory setting (for example, Han 2002b) report positive findings on the relationship between interaction and English past tense but studies conducted in a naturalistic setting (for example, Sato 1986) did not. Moreover, this research also suggests that increased rule complexity may correspond with decreased learning through interaction. That is, learners may find sufficient linguistic information in the input to learn simple rules on their own. However, learning more complex rules may require more than simple exposure to the input. For example, learning some aspects of language may benefit from explicit instruction or feedback. This research suggests that complex syntactic rules might not be most effectively learnt via interaction with a primary focus on meaning. However, it is also possible that some mechanism, which has the effect of making difficult rules salient to the learner, becomes available during the course of interaction.

Interaction and L2 lexical development

A number of studies have investigated the relationship between interaction and vocabulary learning (for example, Loschky 1994; R. Ellis, Tanaka, and Yamazaki 1994; R. Ellis and He 1999; de la Fuente 2002). As summarized in Table 16.2, these studies have shown that interactional modifications and feedback have a positive effect on comprehension and further acquisition of nouns in an L2. For instance, R. Ellis and colleagues have examined how modified input and comprehension can aid the acquisition of L2 English vocabulary. R. Ellis *et al.* (1994) investigated the relative effects of simplified and interactionally modified input on the comprehension of directives containing English nouns. Learners who received the pre-modified input and those who received interactionally modified input outperformed those in the baseline group in a comprehension measure, partially supporting the Interaction Hypothesis. In addition, de la Fuente (2002) examined the differential effects non-negotiated pre-modified input, negotiation without pushed output, and negotiation plus pushed output on the comprehension and acquisition of L2 Spanish nouns whose referents were people or objects in everyday use. The participants were 32 learners of Spanish at an intermediate proficiency level. The results were consistent with the previous finding that learners exposed to input during negotiated interaction attained higher levels of comprehension than those exposed to non-negotiated, pre-modified input.

Other researchers have claimed that learners tend to focus on lexis during interaction in naturalistic classrooms (for example, Pica 1994a; VanPatten 1996; Williams 1999, 2001; R. Ellis, Basturkmen, and Loewen 2001a, 2001b). For instance, Williams (1999), in descriptive research of interaction in a meaning-focused classroom, observed that learners tended to concentrate on lexical features. Williams (1999) found that almost 80 per cent of language-related episodes pertained to lexical items, indicating that learners apparently attended to lexical items rather than to other aspects of language in the communicative classroom. She posited that learning tended to be lexically oriented, especially in meaning-focused classes. In contrast, learners in her study often failed to notice morphosyntactic features. She suggested that these may lack salience or may not be essential for comprehending or creating meaning. Mackey, Gass, and McDonough (2000) also reported that ESL learners recognized feedback on lexis more frequently than feedback on morphosyntax. Finally, Egi (this volume) observed that the benefits of learners' interpretations of recasts as positive evidence were more apparent in lexical than in morphosyntactic learning.

In sum, most of the previous interaction studies suggest interaction promotes lexical development. These may indicate that interaction may be particularly effective in lexical development, especially in learning nouns, because of the high communicative value of lexis. Conversely, previous interaction studies on morphosyntactic development suggest that interaction is not equally beneficial for all aspects of syntactic and morphological development. In this case, the success of interaction may be mediated by variables such as rule complexity. Thus, examining the linguistic targets of interaction should help determine whether or not a given area of language will be benefited via interaction.

Most previous interaction studies have targeted only a small set of linguistic features mainly in Indo-European languages. This trend only allows for the characterization of interaction-driven language development by a particular set of linguistic items. Thus, this study examined the differential utility of interaction across different linguistic targets in L2 Korean. The following research question guided this study:

Research question

In which areas of language (operationalized as different types of morphosyntax and lexis) does interaction promote L2 development most effectively?

Based on the literature review, it was predicted that interaction would promote lexical development more effectively than morphosyntactic development in both the short- and long-term, and within morphosyntax, interaction would be more effective for some forms than others, depending on the level of structural complexity.

Method

Rather than focusing on one interactional feature such as negotiation of meaning, recasts, or pushed output, this study explored the differential effects of conversational interaction in general in promoting linguistic development. The study followed Long's (1996) Interaction Hypothesis in operationalizing interaction. The hypothesis is built upon 'negotiation for meaning', an exchange between interlocutors that occurs when there is a breakdown in comprehension. This process purportedly facilitates language acquisition because it solicits modified input, modified output, and implicit negative feedback such as recasts. In the current research, interaction was task-based rather than naturalistic due to its experimental nature.

Language	Studies	Lx focus	Interactional focus	Study type	Study context	Participants	Treatment	Design/procedure	Method of measuring development	Findings
English	Sato (1986)	Past tense	Interaction/no focus	Longitudinal	Naturalistic	2 adult ESL learners	Naturalistic conversation with a native speaker	Weekly conversational sessions over a 10-month period	Oral production	No development
	Linnell (1995)	Past tense	Interaction/no focus	Experimental	Laboratory	19 adult ESL learners	Communicative task-based interaction (collaborative retelling of picture stories)	Pre-test, post-test and delayed post-test	Written (grammaticality judgment, sentence combination, free writing, cloze test) Oral (sentence imitation and oral interview)	Positive effect on post-test and delayed post-test
	Doughty and Varela (1998)	Past tense	Recast	Quasi-experimental	Classroom	34 adult ESL learners	3 focus-on-form pedagogical labs	Pre-test, post-test, and delayed post-test	Written and oral science reports	Positive effect on post-test and delayed post-test
	Han (2002b)	Past tense	Recast	Experimental	Laboratory	8 adult ESL learners	Communicative task-based interaction	Pre-test, post-test, and delayed post-test	Oral and written narratives	Positive results both on immediate and delayed post-test
	Nobuyoshi and R. Ellis (1993)	Past tense	Modified output	Experimental	Laboratory	6 adult EFL learners	2 picture jigsaw communicative tasks	Pre-test and post-test	Oral production	Positive effect on post-test
	Mackey and Philp (1998)	Questions	Recast	Experimental	Laboratory	35 adult ESL learners	3 sessions of oral interactive tasks	Pre-test, 2 post-tests, and 1 delayed post-test	Oral production	Positive effect on the immediate post-test but no positive effect on delayed post-test

Table 16.1 Summary of research on the relationship between interaction and L2 morphosyntactic development

		focus			context			procedure	development	
English	Silver (2000)	Questions	Interaction/no focus	Experimental	Laboratory	32 adult ESL learners	Structured input/bare-bones output/negotiation treatment	Pre-test, post-test, and delayed post-test	Oral communication test, written word order test, and multiple choice preference test	No greater effect of negotiation on the immediate post-test than input or output condition but greater effect of negotiation found on the delayed post-test
	Philp (2003)	Questions	Recast	Experimental	Laboratory	33 adult ESL learners	Dyadic task-based interaction	5 NS–NNS dyadic interaction over 2 weeks	Cued immediate recall during oral communicative tasks to measure noticing	High level of noticing of recasts. Learners' processing biases may limit noticing
	Mackey and Oliver (2002)	Questions	Recasts/feedback	Experimental	Laboratory	22 child ESL learners	Communicative task-based interaction	Pre-test, post-test and 2 delayed post-tests	Oral production	Positive effect on post-test and delayed post-tests
	Mackey and Silver (2005)	Questions	Recasts/feedback	Experimental	Laboratory	26 child ESL learners	Communicative task-based interaction	Pre-test and 2 post-tests	Oral production	Positive effect of interactional feedback on development of question forms
	McDonough (2005)	Questions/past tense	Modified output	Experimental	Laboratory	60 adult EFL learners	Communicative task-based interaction	Pre-test, post-test and 2 delayed post-tests	Oral production	Clarification requests play an indirect role in ESL question development by facilitating production of modified output
	Mackey (2006a)	Questions/plural/past tense	Interaction/no focus	Quasi-experimental	Classroom	28 ESL learners	Game show activity		Learning journals, oral stimulated recall protocols, written responses to a focused question and written responses on questionnaires	Positive relationship between reports about noticing and L2 development for questions
	Muranoi (2000)	Articles	Enhanced interaction	Quasi-experimental	Laboratory	91 adult EFL learners	Interaction enhancement + formal or meaning-focused debriefing	Pre-test, post-test and delayed post-test	Oral and written picture description, grammaticality judgment	Positive effect of interaction enhancement both on post-test and delayed post-test. Greater effect of interaction enhancement + formal debriefing than interaction + meaning-focused debriefing

Table 16.1 *Summary of studies on the relationship between interaction and L2 morphosyntactic development (continued)*

Language	Studies	Lx focus	Interactional focus	Study type	Study context	Participants	Treatment	Design/procedure	Method of measuring development	Findings
English	Long, Inagaki, and Ortega (1998)	Object topicalization/adverb placement	Recast	Experimental	Laboratory	74 adult learners	Communicative tasks	Pre-test, post-test, and delayed post-test	Oral production	Positive effect of recasts on post-test and delayed post-test
				Experimental	Laboratory	20 adult learners	2 communicative tasks	Pre-test and post-test	Oral production	No learning for object topicalization. Positive effect of recast on the learning of adverb placement
French	Ayoun (2001)	Passé composé and imparfait	Recast	Experimental	Laboratory	145 adult learners	Computerized tasks (written)	Pre-test and post-test (free composition)	Grammaticality judgment task/ correction task and free composition	Written recasts were more effective than modeling and traditional grammar instruction
	Lyster (2004)	Grammatical gender marking	Recast/prompt	Quasi-experimental	Classroom	179 young learners (10–11 years old)	Form-focused instruction	Pre-test-immediate and delayed post-tests	Four production (two oral and two written) tests	Recasts were less effective than prompts in leading to improvements, especially on the written production tasks
Japanese	Ishida (2004)	Aspectual form -te r-(ru)	Recast	Experimental	Laboratory	4 adult learners	Conversation sessions	Time-series design/pre-test-immediate and delayed post-tests	Oral production	Positive effects of recasts. Correlation of number of recasts to accuracy increase
	Iwashita (2003)	-te form verb locative construction	Recast/feedback	Experimental	Laboratory	55 adult learners	Communicative tasks	Pre-test, post-test, and delayed post-test	Oral production	Positive effect on post-test and delayed post-test
	Long, Inagaki, and Ortega (1998)	Locative construction	Recast	Experimental	Laboratory	24 adult learners	Communicative tasks	Pre-test and post-test	Oral production	No positive effect of recasts on the learning of locative construction
	Loschky (1994)	Locative construction	Interaction/no focus	Experimental	Laboratory	41 adult learners	Listening comprehension tasks	Pre-test and post-test	Sentence verification task	No positive effect on the post-test

for L2 morphosyntactic development (continued)

Language	Studies	Lx focus	Interactional focus	Study type	Study context	Participants	Treatment	Design/procedure	Method of measuring development	Findings
English	R. Ellis, Tanaka, and Yamazaki (1994)	Nouns	Negotiation of meaning	Experimental	Laboratory	Study 1: 79 teenaged learners (EFL) Study 2: 127 teenaged learners (EFL)	Listening tasks	Pre-test, post-test, and delayed post-test	Translation task	Both studies found positive effects on immediate and delayed post-test
	R. Ellis and Heimbach (1999)	Nouns	Negotiation of meaning	Experimental	Laboratory	10 ESL child learners	Listening tasks	Pre-test and post-test	Receptive and productive vocabulary tests	Positive effect of negotiation on comprehension
	R. Ellis and He (1999)	Nouns	Modified output	Experimental	Laboratory	50 ESL adult learners	Communicative tasks	Pre-test, post-test and 4 delayed post-tests	Word recognition, picture matching, oral production tests	Immediate and delayed positive effect on comprehension, recognition, and production of words
Spanish	de la Fuente (2002)	Nouns	Negotiation of meaning/output	Experimental	Laboratory	32 adult learners	Listening comprehension tasks	Pre-test, post-test and 2 delayed post-tests	Self-report scale on receptive and productive target vocabulary knowledge	Positive effect on comprehension, receptive, and productive vocabulary knowledge in immediate and delayed post-tests
Japanese	Loschky (1994)	Nouns	Interaction/no focus	Experimental	Laboratory	41 adult learners	Listening comprehension tasks	Pre-test and post-test	Vocabulary recognition test	Positive effect on comprehension but no positive effect on acquisition

Table 16.2 Summary of research on the relationship between interaction and L2 lexical development

Participants

The participants were 41 learners of Korean as a foreign language (KFL) who attended a state university on the west coast of the US. Thirty of them were enrolled in the beginning Korean course and seven in the intermediate course at the time of data collection. The other four participants were undergraduate students who were recruited via flyers and were not currently enrolled in any of the Korean language courses at the university. The learners were randomly assigned to either the experimental (*n* = 32) or control (*n* = 9) group. Participants' ages ranged from 18–29. Most of the participants (*n* = 37) were heritage learners of Korean, and four were non-heritage learners. English was the first language for all of the participants. The native speaker (NS) interlocutor was the researcher.

Target forms

The morphosyntactic targets were object relative clause constructions and honorific subject–verb agreement, and the lexical targets were concrete nouns and action verbs. Each of these will be described next.

Object relative clauses

Korean has a distinct manner of relativizing NPs in a complex sentence. As can be seen in Example 1 (all examples presented in this chapter were collected for the current study), Korean does not have a relative pronoun. Also, any type of relative clause precedes the modified noun. Relativization is indicated by a set of verbal suffixes (*–(u)n, –nun,* and *–(u)l*) called relative markers or relativizers, which are attached to embedded predicates (Sohn 1999).

> *Example 1*   Relative clause constructions in Korean
> Subject relative clause
> [*sakwa–lul mek–nun*]   *namca.*
> Apple–ACC eat–REL.PRE man
> 'The man who is eating an apple.'
>
> Object relative clause
> [*namca–ka mek–nun*]   *sakwa.*
> Man–TOP eat–REL.PRE apple
> 'The apple which a man is eating.'
> (ACC = accusative marker, REL = relative marker, PRE = present tense, TOP = topic marker)

Both L1 and L2 studies on the acquisition of Korean relative clauses have found that subject relative clauses are easier than their direct object counterparts in both comprehension and production (Y.-J. Kim 1987; Cho 1999; O'Grady, Lee, and Choo 2003). For instance, O'Grady *et al.* (2003) conducted an experimental study to examine whether L2 learners of Korean display a preference for one type of relative clause between subject and object relative clauses. In a comprehension test, the participating KFL learners did better on subject relative clauses (73.2 per cent) than object relative clauses (22.6 per cent). It was concluded that the key determinant of relative clause difficulty is the depth of embedding of the gap—that is, its structural distance from the head noun with which it is associated.

Honorific subject–verb agreement

In a broad sense, honorification may be defined as 'direct grammatical encodings of relative social status between participants, or between participants and persons or things referred to in the communicative event' (Brown and Levinson 1987: 179). Korean utilizes highly complex and systematic lexical and morphological honorification as a means to express politeness or deference toward the person being addressed. (See Sohn 1999 for more information.) The focus in this study was on the agreement of the honorific nominative case marker *–kkeyse* and the honorific verbal suffix *–si* in an honorific sentence. The honorific verbal suffix *–si* indicates subject honorification, which is marked by the nominative case marker *–kkeyse*.

> *Example 2*   Honorific subject–verb agreement (*–kkeyse* and *–si*)
> *Halapeci–kkeyse*   *yenghwa–lul po–si–eyo.*
> Grandfather–SUB.HON   movie–ACC   see–HON–DEC.
> 'Grandfather watches a movie.'
> (SUB.HON = subject honorific marker, ACC = accusative marker, HON = honorific verbal suffix, DEC = declarative sentence ender)

Lexical items

The target lexical items were selected from two different parts of speech (nouns and verbs) to explore whether learning outcomes differed for each type. Relatively low frequency concrete nouns and action verbs were chosen in order to minimize the chance of prior exposure. Frequencies of the targeted lexical items were based on the Yonsei Corpora (Seo 1998) and are presented in Figure 16.1. Compared to the frequency of the target nouns, the verbs used had a higher frequency; this was because the target verbs had to be action verbs (as opposed to stative verbs), since action verbs were easier to illustrate in the pictures used in the experiment's testing and treatment materials.

Materials

Treatment materials

Communicative tasks were designed to simultaneously expose learners to the target linguistic forms and to provide contexts where use of these forms was obligatory. To allow learners enough time to process input and feedback, and to provide enough tokens, each task was designed to elicit only one linguistic form. The treatment tasks are briefly described in Figure 16.2.

No.	Noun targets	Frequency counts	Verb targets	Frequency counts
1	Wucheykwuk 'post office'	319	Ssiss-ta 'to wash'	2497
2	Kwangtay 'clown'	298	Ppwuli-ta 'sprinkle'	1947
3	Kyengkicang 'stadium'	256	Cciss-ta 'to tear'	1901
4	chengsopwu 'cleaning person'	178	Tomangci-ta 'run away'	1819
5	Miyongsil 'beauty salon'	110	Calu-ta 'to cut'	1787
6	Yeysikcang 'wedding hall'	87	Hwumci-ta 'to steal'	1553
7	Cemcangi 'fortuneteller'	81	Ttalaka-ta 'to follow'	1449
8	Kyengmacang 'race track'	30	Soksaki-ta 'to whisper'	1014
9	pwunswutay 'water fountain'	29	Cis-ta 'to bark'	793
10	Sopangkwan 'fireman'	14	Maytal-ta 'to hang'	736

Figure 16.1 Frequency counts of the noun and verb targets

Twenty-four treatment tasks were developed for the current study. Two different task types (one-way and two-way) were developed for each linguistic form and each type of task had three different versions (two kinds × four target forms × three versions). Successful completion of all the tasks required the participants to pay attention to meaning rather than to form.

The treatment tasks were administered in two sessions. Amount of exposure was operationalized by time on task, experimental group participants spending 40–45 minutes per target form regardless of the number of tasks they could complete during each session. If learners finished a task sooner than expected, they were asked to conduct another similar task so that the time each learner spent receiving treatment on each targeted form was consistent across learners. During the treatment, learners received feedback from the NS researcher wherever it was appropriate. Such feedback included negotiation for meaning and recasts of the target linguistic forms and other forms that led to communication breakdown. Examples 3 and 4, below, illustrate interaction and feedback in the study.

> *Example 3*   Negotiation over lexical item (noun)
> NS   *Cemcang–nun   eti   isseyo?*
>   Fortuneteller–TOP   where   be–Q?
>   'Where is a fortuneteller?'
> NNS *Cemcang?*

Task	Description	Type	Target forms
Task 1: Draw circles	NS or NNS describes the picture and the location of the circles drawn to their partner who has the picture without the circles. The partner draws circles on the picture based on the description.	One-way	Relative clauses
Task 2: Find the circles	NS and NNS each have a similar picture with circles drawn around different objects and people. They describe the pictures to each other to find out where the circles are drawn in the other's picture.	Two-way	Relative clauses
Task 3: My family	NS describes what each member of the family is doing in the house, based on the picture given, and the NNS partner places the picture cards in the house layout based on the description.	One-way	Honorifics
Task 4: At the park	NS and NNS interlocutors describe people in each other's picture to find out their names.	Two-way	Honorifics
Task 5: Village layout	An interlocutor places pictures of people with different jobs and pictures of different places in a village layout and describes it to the other interlocutor.	One-way	Nouns
Task 6: Street layout	NS and NNS interlocutors are given an incomplete layout of a city. They ask each other questions to fill the empty slots in the layout using picture cards of places and of people with different jobs.	Two-way	Nouns
Task 7: Strange dream	Based on a picture, an interlocutor is asked to narrate a story of a strange dream the night before.	One-way	Verbs
Task 8: What happened?	NS and NNS make up a story of what happened to people based on the pictures given to each other.	Two-way	Verbs

Figure 16.2 Description of treatment tasks

NS *Cemcangi.*
    'Fortuneteller.'
NNS *Cemcangi   mwe–eyyo?*
    Fortuneteller what–Q?
    'What is a fortuneteller?'
NS *Cemcangi   nun milay–lul   malhyecwu–nun salam   i– eyyo.*
    Fortuneteller TOP future–ACC tell–give–REL   person–be–DEC.
    'Cemcangi is the person who tells you the future.'

Example 4   Recast on object relative clause

NNS	*Emma	mek–un	ice cream–ey	iss–eyo.*
	Mother	hold–REL	ice cream–LOC	be–DEC.
NS	*Emma–ka	mek–nun	ice cream–ey	iss–eyo.*
	Mother–SUB eat–REL		ice cream–LOC	be–DEC.

'(It is) around the ice cream that mother is eating.'
(SUB = subject marker, LOC = locative, DEC = declarative
sentence ender, TOP = topic marker, Q = interrogative sentence
ender, REL = relative marker)

Testing materials

A number of oral production tasks involving either picture-naming or one-way communication were used to test learners' knowledge of target forms. No corrective feedback was provided during the tests. Tests for each linguistic target are described next.

1 Object relative clause constructions: knowledge of relative clauses was tested through one-way picture description tasks. In the three different versions of this task that were used as the pre-test, post-test, or delayed post-test, the NNS was instructed to orally describe the locations of the circles drawn in various parts of the picture so that the NS could draw them on the same spots of the picture.

2 Honorific subject–verb agreement: knowledge of honorific subject–verb agreement morphology was tested through a one-way information gap task. In creating a situation that required the learners to use honorifics, special consideration was given to contexts which play an important role in the appropriate use of honorifics in Korean. Participants were given a situation in which they were asked to talk about older family members (for example, grandparents) to those who were also older than the learner (for example, parents) but not older than those being addressed (for example, talking about your grandparents to your parents). Different versions were administered as pre-test, post-test, and delayed post-test.

3 Concrete nouns and verbs: picture-naming tasks were used to assess participants' knowledge about concrete nouns (names of places and occupations) and verbs (action verbs).

Design/procedure

The experimental group (*n* = 31) participated in a pre-test, two treatment sessions, an immediate post-test (post-test 1), and a delayed post-test (post-test 2). The control group (*n* = 9) was administered the pre-test, post-test 1, and post-test 2, but did not participate in the treatment sessions. The control group was included to gauge the extent to which participation in the test tasks led to learning. The independent variable was language area, operationalized by the linguistic forms (i.e. object relative clause constructions, honorific subject–verb agreement, concrete nouns, and verbs), while the dependent variable was learning outcome, operationalized by scores on immediate and delayed post-tests.

The learners in the experimental group participated in two treatment sessions and completed a series of oral production tests over a three-week period. As illustrated in Figure 16.3, on Day 1, four pre-tests were given to assess the participants' existing knowledge of the four target forms. To control for potential ceiling effects, learners were excluded from treatment sessions involving target linguistic forms for which their accuracy rate on a pre-test was higher than 70 per cent. Thus, only those who scored lower than 70 per cent on the pre-test of a particular target proceeded with treatment on that target. Both treatment sessions and the immediate post-test were scheduled in the same week (Week 1). The delayed post-test was administered two weeks after the second treatment session. The order of the tests and the order of the treatment tasks were counterbalanced to control for ordering effects. Finally, an exit questionnaire was administered to ascertain whether the learners had identified the purpose of the study.

Scoring and inter-rater reliability

Object relative clause constructions

All correct and incorrect object relative clauses produced by learners were first identified and coded. Points were given for the use of a nominative subject along with its correct subject particle and correct use of the relative marker along with accurate verbal inflection. One point was awarded for a target-like construction of an object relative clause and 0.5 points for a partially targetlike construction. For instance, in producing an object relative clause, a participant might correctly provide the suffix attached to the embedded predicate but fail to use the nominative case marker for the subject of the embedded sentence (for example, 'woman' in Example 5). A half point was given to such a case. When all elements of a relative clause were incorrect, no points were awarded. Scores were based on the total number of points relative to the total number of attempted uses of object relative clauses.

> *Example 5*   Learner's incorrect formation of an object relative clause
> *Dongkulami–nun   yeca   mi–nun   cacenke–ey   iss–eyo.*
> Circle–   TOP   woman   push–REL   bicycle–LOC   be–DEC.
> 'The circle is on the woman who is pushing the bicycle.'
> (TOP = topic marker, REL = relative marker, LOC = locative, DEC = declarative sentence ender)

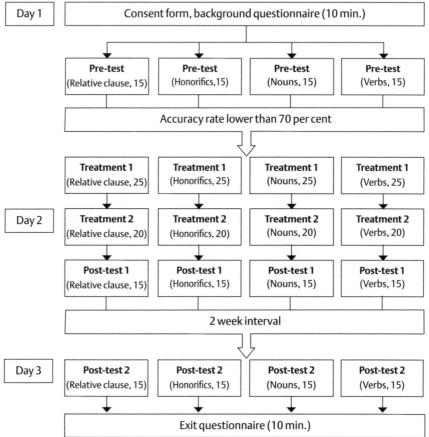

All time in minutes

Figure 16.3 Experimental procedure and approximate times

Honorific subject–verb agreement

In scoring learners' knowledge of honorifics, the first step was to identify obligatory contexts for the use of the honorific subject–verb agreement in each participant's data. Next, learner utterances were scored for accurate use of the honorific nominative case marker *–kkeyse* in the honorific subject and the use of *–si* in the verbal ending with proper inflection. One point was given when a learner correctly used the subject marker *–kkeyse* and correctly conjugated the verb with the honorific suffix *–si*. A score of 0.5 was awarded for a partially accurate honorific agreement. For instance, a learner may have supplied an accurate subject particle but failed to correctly conjugate the verb with the use of honorific verbal suffix *–si*. No points were given if the learner failed to use either *–kkeyse* or *–si*, or if no form of honorific morpheme was produced. Scores were based on the total number of points relative to the total number of obligatory contexts identified for honorific agreement.

Nouns and verbs

For lexical targets, a score of 1 point was awarded for correct production of target items, and 0 points for no answer or partially incorrect production of the target items. Pre-test items for which a learner produced synonyms instead of the target nouns or verbs were excluded from that individual's post-test analyses.

Inter-rater reliability

Inter-rater reliability was calculated on a subset (25 per cent) of the oral production data for each linguistic form. Data from two independent raters were used. Two kinds of statistical tests were performed to assess the consistency in rating of the two scorers: Cohen's Kappa and Pearson's correlations. Cohen's Kappa was used for categorical data and Pearson's correlations were performed for accuracy ratings. The results of inter-rater reliability are shown in Table 16.3. The correlation coefficients indicated that the accuracy scoring that the two raters assigned to four linguistic targets overlap to a significant degree.

Forms/ratings	Statistical tests	Value
Relative clause type identification	Cohen's Kappa	.985
Relative clause accuracy scoring	Pearson correlation	.708*
Honorific subject–verb agreement accuracy scoring	Pearson correlation	.990*
Noun accuracy scoring	Pearson correlation	.967*
Verb accuracy scoring	Pearson correlation	.953*

* $p < .01$

Table 16.3 Inter-rater reliability for each target linguistic form

Results

As mentioned above, the learners received experimental treatments if their accuracy ratings on the pre-test were lower than 70 per cent. Therefore, some learners did not provide data for all four linguistic forms (object relative clause construction, honorific subject–verb agreement, concrete nouns, and verbs). A repeated-measures design was used to accommodate the grouping strategy. Table 16.4 shows the number of participants in each sub-group within the experimental and control groups. This grouping was used for all statistical analyses. Most participants were initially unfamiliar with the honorific subject–verb agreement forms and concrete nouns, leading to a larger data set for analyses of those forms.

	Relative clause	Honorifics	Noun	Verb
Experimental	15	25	30	18
Control	6	9	9	8

Table 16.4 Number of participants for each target linguistic form

Table 16.5 shows descriptive statistics of the mean accuracy scores of the four linguistic forms in the experimental and control groups. Participants demonstrated the least amount of development from pre-test to post-tests on honorific subject–verb agreement forms, whereas they demonstrated the most improvement from the pre-test to the post-tests in their abilities to name the lexical targets.

	Experimental Group							
	Relative clause (*n* = 15)		Honorifics (*n* = 25)		Nouns (*n* = 30)		Verbs (*n* = 18)	
Test	**Mean**	*SD*	**Mean**	*SD*	**Mean**	*SD*	**Mean**	*SD*
Pre-test	29.87	18.35	.88	3.10	13.20	.09	15.22	15.22
Post-test 1	70.86	18.56	12.88	25.81	60.70	28.91	63.61	20.90
Post-test 2	63.73	21.91	15.00	31.82	39.73	27.13	46.72	20.15
	Control Group							
	Relative clause (*n* = 6)		Honorifics (*n* = 9)		Nouns (*n* = 9)		Verbs (*n* = 8)	
Test	**Mean**	*SD*	**Mean**	*SD*	**Mean**	*SD*	**Mean**	*SD*
Pre-test	33.50	28.64	.00	.00	18.78	16.08	36.53	20.91
Post-test 1	38.83	36.87	.00	.00	18.78	16.08	33.58	16.33
Post-test 2	48.83	34.64	.00	.00	28.73	26.28	35.46	22.38

Table 16.5 Descriptive statistics of accuracy rates (experimental and control groups)

Gain scores were used to determine the rank of the targets in terms of the degree of improvement across tests to address the research question, which asked about the differential effects of interaction across language areas. The use of gain scores was enabled by the statistically significant differences across the targets found on the pre-test scores on a general linear model (GLM) repeated-measures analysis for participants in the experimental group (F (3, 24) = 10.692, p = 0.00). Three kinds of gain scores were calculated: difference between the pre-test and post-test 1, difference between the pre-test and post-test 2, and difference between post-test 1 and post-test 2. Table 16.6 and Figure 16.4 illustrate the descriptive statistics of the gain scores for each target on the three tests in both experimental and control groups. In the experimental group, the gain score from the pre-test to post-test 1 was the greatest for verbs (mean gain score: 48.39) and the least for honorifics (mean gain score: 12.00). The rank order of the four targets based on the amount of development which had taken place from the pre-test to the post-test 1 was verb > noun > relative clause > honorifics. This ordering was slightly different when considering pre-test to post-test 2 gains, which was verb > relative clause > noun > honorifics. Learners consistently made gains on learning verbs but were equally consistent in their slow rate of improvement in learning honorific subject–verb agreement.

| | Experimental Group | | | | | | |
| | Relative clause ($n=15$) | | Honorifics ($n=25$) | | Nouns ($n=30$) | | Verbs ($n=18$) | |
Tests compared	Mean	SD	Mean	SD	Mean	SD	Mean	SD
Post-test 1 > pre-test	43.64	22.89	12.00	25.71	47.50	25.77	48.39	18.16
Post-test 2 > pre-test	33.87	26.53	14.12	32.40	26.53	23.63	31.50	13.76
Post-test 1 > post-test 2	-6.71	14.79	2.12	17.22	-20.97	16.85	-16.89	13.45

| | Control Group | | | | | | |
| | Relative clause ($n=6$) | | Honorifics ($n=9$) | | Nouns ($n=9$) | | Verbs ($n=8$) | |
Tests compared	Mean	SD	Mean	SD	Mean	SD	Mean	SD
Post-test 1 > pre-test	5.33	14.60	.00	.00	.00	.00	-3.00	9.84
Post-test 2 > pre-test	15.33	16.21	.00	.00	10.00	20.59	-1.00	9.12
Post-test 1 > post-test 2	-10.00	11.87	.00	.00	-10.00	20.59	-2.00	13.45

Table 16.6 Descriptive statistics of gain scores (experimental and control groups)

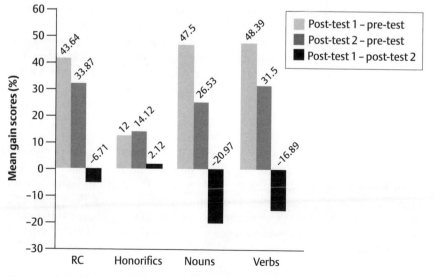

Figure 16.4 Mean gain scores (experimental group)

Based on the gain scores, GLM repeated-measure analysis was conducted to determine whether the improvement of one target significantly differed from that of another targeted form, as well as whether the extent to which the improvement was maintained on post-test 2 differed across targets. Table 16.7 summarizes the results of this statistical test for both groups. The results revealed that in the experimental group, there were statistically significant differences in all gain score categories across all linguistic targets. In contrast, there were no statistically significant differences found for any gain score category for the control group. These results indicate that the degree of improvement from the pre-test to the post-tests differed significantly according to target linguistic form.

Tests compared	df	Experimental Group		
		Mean square	F	p
Post-test 1 > pre-test	3	2822.893	8.277	.00*
Post-test 2 > pre-test	3	1409.940	3.553	.04*
Post-test 1 > post-test 2	3	592.857	5.393	.01*
Tests compared	df	Control Group		
		Mean square	F	p
Post-test 1 > pre-test	3	5.400	.838	.50
Post-test 2 > pre-test	3	244.333	1.231	.34
Post-test 1 > post-test 2	3	209.067	.995	.43

$p < .05$*

Table 16.7 GLM Analysis for gain scores of the four targets (experimental and control groups)

Finally, paired sample *t*-tests were performed *post hoc* to locate the source of the significant differences found in the experimental group. Table 16.8 summarizes the results of this analysis. From pre-test to the post-test 1, significant differences originated in the mean gain score differences between the honorifics and other three forms (relative clause, noun, and verb). Learners accurately produced relative clauses, nouns, and verbs at a significantly higher rate than they produced accurate honorific subject–verb agreement. However, the mean differences between relative clauses and nouns, relative clauses and verbs, and nouns and verbs did not reach statistical significance.

Gain scores from pre-test to post-test 2 indicate that learners performed significantly better on naming verbs than on accurate use of honorific agreement morphology and naming concrete nouns. In addition, learners were significantly more accurate in producing relative clauses than honorific agreement morphology. There were no statistically significant differences found between learners' performance on relative clauses and verbs, relative clauses and nouns, or honorifics and nouns.

Tests compared	Pairs	df	t	p
Post-test 1 > pre-test	Honorifics < relative clause	8	3.91	.00*
	Honorifics < noun	23	-5.06	.00*
	Honorifics < verb	13	-3.77	.00*
	Relative clause < noun	13	.39	.71
	Relative clause < verb	10	-1.06	.31
	Noun < verb	17	-1.99	.06
Post-test 2 > pre-test	Honorifics < relative clause	9	3.10	.01*
	Honorifics < noun	23	-1.79	.09
	Honorifics < verb	13	-2.45	.03*
	Relative clause > noun	14	1.73	.11
	Relative clause > verb	10	-.01	.99
	Noun < verb	17	-2.49	.02*
Post-test 1 > post-test 2	Honorifics < relative clause	8	.57	.58
	Honorifics < noun	23	-5.70	.00*
	Honorifics < verb	13	-4.319	.00*
	Relative clause > noun	13	-1.970	.07
	Relative clause > verb	10	-1.844	.10
	Noun < verb	17	.620	.54

$p < .05*$

Table 16.8 Post hoc *paired sample* t-tests *(experimental group)*

In the comparison between the post-test 1 and post-test 2, the gain score for accurate use of honorific morphology was significantly higher than that for naming nouns and verbs. There was no statistically significant difference in accuracy between the two lexical forms, or between the two morphosyntactic forms (relative clause and honorifics). Also, no statistically significant mean gain score difference was found between the relative clauses and two lexical forms.

Discussion

The research question was 'in which areas of language (operationalized as different types of morphosyntax and lexis) does interaction promote L2 development most effectively?' The results indicated that differential degrees of learning took place across the four different linguistic forms in the short- and the long-term. Results also suggested that interaction promotes L2 learning of nouns, verbs, and object relative clauses more effectively than honorific agreement morphology, at least for the language, forms, learners, and conditions investigated in the current study.

The general prediction was that task-based interaction would facilitate lexical development more effectively than morphosyntactic development in both the short- and the long-term, and that the two targeted morphosyntactic forms would display unequal levels of gain. This was partially supported. Gains between the pre-test and post-test 1 indicated that the learners were significantly more accurate in naming concrete nouns and verbs than in producing honorific agreement morphology. However, the level of gain on object relative clause construction was not significantly different from that on learning lexical items. The largest gain was observed in accurate naming of verbs, while the smallest gain was observed in the accurate production of honorific agreement morphology. In post-test 2, the learners performed significantly better on naming verbs than on producing honorific morphology. However, there were no significant differences in gains from pre-test to post-test 2 between relative clauses and nouns. For morphosyntax, learners showed significantly higher gains in relative clauses than in honorifics, and they also showed significantly higher gains in verbs than in nouns on post-test 2.

To summarize, the results of the empirical study indicated the existence of differential effects of interaction across different linguistic forms in the short- and long-term. In the short-term, the current study showed that the learners improved significantly more in relative clauses, verbs, and nouns than in honorifics. In the long-term, the learners' gain in relative clauses was significantly higher than in honorifics, and the mean gain scores of learners were significantly higher in verbs than in nouns and honorifics.

Explanations for uneven learning gains

The degree of salience of the different linguistic targets may be one possible explanation for the unequal learning outcomes observed across forms. While salience has been operationalized in many ways (Brown 1973; Gass 1980; Bardovi-Harlig 1987; VanPatten 1989, 1996; Harley 1998; Goldschneider and DeKeyser 2001), here only communicative value, perceptual salience, and frequency will be discussed.

First, the communicative value of target linguistic forms may be a crucial factor in the effectiveness of learning through interaction. VanPatten (1989, 1996) has suggested that the relative communicative values of specific forms plays an important role in determining whether the forms will be noticed by learners, particularly in a communicative context. Lexical items, being key to comprehension, might be more likely to be noticed by learners exposed to communicative input. In contrast, other linguistic forms, such as honorific agreement morphology, may be low in communicative value, thus less likely to be noticed. In fact, Pica (1994a) has claimed that when negotiation for meaning occurs, it primarily centers on the meaning of vocabulary items. Thus, the unique communicative value of lexical items may enhance their learnability in communicative contexts.

Secondly, different levels of perceptual salience, 'susceptibility to word and sentence stress and lack of disjuncture caused by a syllable boundary' (Pye 1980: 58), may have affected learning outcomes across different linguistic targets. It has been claimed that the more perceptually salient a grammatical structure is, the earlier it will be learnt (Slobin 1971; Pye 1980). Importantly, in interaction, a form's degree of salience may affect whether a learner notices or ignores it in input (Leeman 2003). In the current study, perceptual salience may be one factor that underlay the difference in mean gain scores between concrete nouns and verbs (gains in naming verbs from the pre-test to post-test 2 were significantly higher than those for nouns, t (17) = 2.49, p = .02). The perceptual salience of Korean verbs may be increased by their sentence-final position (Slobin 1971; Choi 1999).

Frequency may also have affected lexical learning. The higher frequency of Korean verbs over nouns in the discourse might be a related factor in an explanation of the long-term advantage of verbs over nouns. Unlike in English and other Indo-European languages, in Korean, verbs tend to occur more frequently than nouns because verbs can occur as complete utterances without any nouns. Gass and Mackey (2002) argued that interactional modification during conversation can provide ideal opportunities for relating form and function. Thus, it might have been possible that verbs were more frequently repeated and rephrased than nouns during the interactional treatment, thus providing learners a greater likelihood of making appropriate connections between the target verb items and their meanings (Gass and Mackey 2002).

Learner readiness might have also played a role in determining the uneven learning outcomes for morphosyntactic forms. It has been argued that learners who are not ready to acquire a given structure will not be able to acquire that structure regardless of the quantity and quality of the input to which they are exposed (Pienemann 1984, 1998). Research suggests that the effects of various input types are mediated by the learner's developmental stage (for example, Lightbown 1998; Mackey 1999). Learner readiness may explain the greater gains in object relative clauses than in honorifics. According to the Noun Phrase Accessibility Hierarchy (NPAH) (Keenan and Comrie 1977), there is an implicational relationship among different types of relative clauses: Keenan and Comrie claimed that the subject relative clause is acquired earlier than the object relative clause. The participants in the current study were recruited from high beginning and low intermediate level courses and their difference in proficiency level might have contributed to this finding. To explore the possibility that learner readiness played a role, learners' pre-existing knowledge of subject relative clauses was examined. The accuracy of participants' production of subject relative clauses in the pre-test was examined. The mean accuracy rate was 78.06 per cent for the experimental group, compared to below 70 per cent for the sub-group whose data were analyzed for the object relative clause condition. This suggests that the learners in the experimental group had acquired the subject relative clause prior to the onset of the study. This might be related to the participants' greater improvement in the production of the object relative clause. That is, the participants in the experimental group might have been ready to move on to the next structure on the hierarchy, and thus were able to benefit more from the interactional treatment in the experiment.

Finally, low accuracy gains in the learning of the honorific agreement morphology may be related to pragmatic transfer, or the 'transfer of L1 socio-cultural competence in performing L2 speech acts or any other aspects of L2 conversation, where the speaker is trying to achieve a particular function of language' (Beebe, Takahashi, and Uliss-Weltz 1990: 56). The low gains in accurately producing honorific agreement forms may have resulted from the learners' reliance on L1 (English) pragmatic knowledge to understand or carry out speech acts of politeness in Korean. Takahashi (1996) identified the L1 as the primary source of non-native use of speech acts. Interestingly, outside of honorific morphology, very few morphological errors were made by the learners in the study. This may suggest that socio-pragmatic, not morphological, complexity of the Korean honorifics affected their learning. Pragmatically accurate use of honorific morphology required learners to make decisions on the level of politeness necessary in the hypothetical contexts given in the communicative tasks used in the experiment. The successful acquisition of the Korean honorific system requires sociolinguistic and pragmatic knowledge. Along with the pragmatic and sociolinguistic complexity of the Korean honorific system, the negative pragmatic transfer from English speech acts of politeness might be responsible for the relative difficulty of learning the honorifics in Korean. It may be the case that interaction may not be effective in facilitating L2 pragmatic acquisition without careful task design and input.

Limitations

Future research might explore possible variables that were not addressed in the current study such as communicative value, perceptual salience, and learner readiness in relation to linguistic forms when investigating interaction-driven L2 development. To test communicative value as a possible variable, researchers might operationalize the construct as the number of instances of communication breakdown during the treatment session. That is, a study might look at the question of whether there is a correlation between the number of communication breakdowns triggered by learners' incorrect use of the linguistic form and the degree of development within that targeted form. By doing so, the relationship between the communicative value of a particular linguistic form and interaction-driven L2 development can be examined.

As outlined in the section on Methods, the current study investigated the effects of interaction in general, rather than isolating the contributions of different features of interaction (for example, recasts) in promoting L2 development in different language areas. Isolating these components is discussed in several other chapters in this volume. The current study does not address whether specific features of interaction, in isolation or collectively, contributed to L2 development.

As is often the case with any SLA research, the generalizability of the current findings to other learning conditions should not be automatically assumed.

The participants in this study represent a subset of second language learners. Most of the participants were heritage learners of Korean who had previously received both formal and informal Korean instruction. As noted in Gass and Lewis' (this volume) study, heritage language learners are different from non-heritage learners. For instance, one difference Gass and Lewis found was that heritage learners tended to be more focused on semantic feedback than non-heritage learners. As Gass and Lewis suggest, heritage learners' early exposure to their heritage language might affect their language learning later in life. For instance, heritage learners who lived with their grandparents might have more exposure to honorific uses from their parents addressing their grandparents. Thus, they might have less difficulty learning honorifics than non-heritage learners who did not have the similar experience. Additionally, the controlled nature of the experimental study design dictates that learners' exposure to the interactional treatment be intensive and focused only on target structures. Thus, this study may not reflect the effects of the conversational interaction in settings where exposure is less intensive and less controlled.

Finally, some limitations in the design of the treatment tasks can be noted. In the treatment tasks used for honorific agreement, non-use or incorrect use of target morphology did not block the flow of communication during interaction. Thus, it may have been difficult for learners to notice input on the correct use of honorific forms. Also, the nature of these tasks were different from the treatment tasks for the other three linguistic targets in that they evoked a hypothetical situation, possibly increasing the cognitive complexity of the task (Robinson 2001). Had the task required participants to address someone present in the immediate context, the meaning of the honorifics might have been better contextualized and learners' attention might have been better drawn to the honorific forms.

Conclusion

Notwithstanding its limitations, the current study provided some insight into the differential effects of conversational interaction on different language areas. The study investigated whether interaction is equally beneficial for different language areas. Two linguistic targets represented each of the two areas of language, morphosyntax, and lexis. One morphosyntactic target, honorific agreement morphology, was additionally related to pragmatic competence. In this study, interaction did not appear to facilitate the learning of honorific agreement morphology, but did appear to promote the learning of lexis, verbs even more than concrete nouns, and object relative clauses in Korean. These findings, the first that have investigated Korean, may be added to those of prior research on interaction conducted in English, Spanish, and Japanese.

Epilogue

17

Interaction research in SLA: a meta-analysis and research synthesis

ALISON MACKEY and JAEMYUNG GOO

Introduction

This final chapter presents the results of a meta-analysis of research on inter-action. The goal of this chapter is to present and contextualize the current state of the art in interaction research by identifying how specific variables impact the effect of interaction on L2 learning, following suggestions by the editors of the first collection of meta-analyses in second language research (Norris and Ortega 2006).

As discussed in the introduction to the current volume, more than 40 empirical studies have investigated interaction in SLA. While most of the studies have shown generally positive outcomes for interaction, the designs of the research have, of course, differed along a number of interesting dimensions, including settings, sample sizes, learner and interlocutor char-acteristics, and so on. The current meta-analysis focuses on work carried out since the early 1990s, when researchers began to investigate the relationship between interaction and L2 learning. It includes not only research focusing on implicit feedback like recasts, comprehension checks, clarification requests, and confirmation checks, but also more recent studies that have investigated explicit or metalinguistic feedback in interaction. The major question that this meta-analysis seeks to address is how effective interaction is at promoting L2 learning.

As the interaction field moves forward, it is helpful for researchers to gain the sorts of insights that can be obtained by regularly synthesizing and meta-analyzing the studies to date.

In addition to summarizing previous research, a meta-analysis compares the outcomes of a wide range of studies in an effort to gain a better understanding of the area concerned. Second language acquisition researchers are increas-ingly recognizing the importance of research synthesis (for example, Norris and Ortega 2000, 2006; Goldschneider and DeKeyser 2001; Masgoret and Gardner 2003; Keck, Iberri-Shea, Tracy-Ventura, and Wa-Mbaleka 2006; Russell and Spada 2006). The current meta-analysis provides an update in relation to the important and interesting findings reported by Keck *et al.* (2006), who analyzed interaction research up to 2003 and Russell and Spada (2006), who focused on the contribution of corrective feedback to L2 learning up to 2003. Like Keck *et al.*'s meta-analysis of interaction research, our study focuses on the efficacy of interaction in terms of the acquisition of lexical and grammatical target items and investigates a variety of factors that may mediate this relationship. And like Russell and Spada's study, ours includes an investigation of the roles of setting (laboratory versus classroom) and particular feedback characteristics in the efficacy of feedback. The current meta-analysis thus incorporates some of the questions raised by both Keck *et al.* and Russell and Spada, partially replicating, updating, and extending their research. We also examined a number of methodological factors that may impact interaction findings. In this study, we were able to consider the interaction research in the current collection together with all studies reported through June 2006 in order to address the following questions:

1 How effective is interaction at promoting the acquisition of linguistic forms?
2 What are the relationships between interaction-driven L2 development and the following factors?
Theoretical factors
a Type of target feature (lexis versus grammar)
b Occurrence of interactional feedback (presence versus absence)
c Type of feedback (recasts versus negotiation versus metalinguistic feed-back)
d Focus of feedback (general versus specific)
e Opportunity for modified output (encouraged versus discouraged)
Contextual and methodological factors
f Context (second- versus foreign-language)
g Setting (classroom versus laboratory)
h Type of dependent measure (naturalistic production versus open- and closed-ended prompted production versus prompted response)

Factors that have theoretical importance for interaction research include the target feature; the occurrence, type, nature and focus of feedback; and the opportunity for modified output. These have been hypothesized to mediate the relationship between interaction and learning. Contextual and methodological factors such as research context, setting, and type of dependent measure were also included because it is important to gain a better understanding of how these issues might impact the outcomes of interaction studies. We also reviewed a range of factors related to methodology in interaction research, including random assignment, the use of control groups, the timing of post-tests, statistical tools, and reporting conventions.

Method

Identification of analyzable research

In reviewing the available literature, we first searched the Education Resources Information Center (ERIC) database and the Linguistics and Language Behavior Abstracts (LLBA) in order to identify relevant empirical studies and related literature. We used the following key and subject words: interaction, input, output, feedback, corrective feedback, negative evidence, negative feedback, recasts, negotiation, clarification request, tasks, task-based language learning, task-based instruction, second language acquisition, and foreign language acquisition, as well as combinations of these words. Reference sections of interaction-related chapters from textbooks and handbooks of second language acquisition were also checked, including R. Ellis (1994a), Gass (1997), Ritchie and Bhatia (1996), Hall and Verplaetse (2000), Gass and Selinker (2001), Robinson (2001), Doughty and Long (2003a), Davies and Elder (2004), Mitchell and Myles (2004), and Hinkel (2005), as well as two related books by Doughty and Williams (1998) and R. Ellis (2003).

Using the same key and subject words mentioned above, we then replicated and expanded our search in order to ensure that no important journals had been overlooked, exploring one by one the most commonly cited journals in the field of second language acquisition: *Applied Linguistics, Applied Psycholinguistics, Canadian Modern Language Review, Computer Assisted Language Learning, Foreign Language Annals, International Journal of Educational Research, Language Learning, Language Learning & Technology* (online), *Language Teaching Research, The Modern Language Journal, ReCALL, Second Language Research, Studies in Second Language Acquisition, System*, and *TESOL Quarterly*.

As has typically been the practice in other meta-analyses of second language research (for example, the seminal study by Norris and Ortega 2000; Keck *et al.* 2006; Russell and Spada 2006), unpublished research papers, or the so-called 'fugitive literature' (M. C. Rosenthal 1994), were not included in this meta-analysis. The 'file-drawer' problem (as discussed in R. Rosenthal 1991, 1995) suggests that unpublished studies might be tucked away in researchers' filing cabinets due mainly to non-significant results. An important consideration is the fact that research with non-significant findings is less likely to be published and more likely to be part of the fugitive literature, thus creating a potential for bias in any meta-analysis considering only published papers. If this research could be identified and included, it might reveal different patterns to the ones identified here. At the same time, many unpublished studies remain so following editorial decisions to reject the research reports on methodological or theoretical grounds, and it is possible that additional bias might be introduced if only a limited number of unpublished studies were retrieved and analyzed. After encountering logistical difficulties in accessing two frequently cited but unpublished papers in the interaction field, we concluded that it would be an impossible task to retrieve the entire fugitive literature, even following suggested ways to access those unpublished papers (M. C. Rosenthal 1994). Given these considerations and practical matters and notwithstanding the advice of Norris and Ortega (2006), who point out that the consensus among meta-analysts in psychology is to include unpublished work where possible, we excluded all unpublished research papers, and utilized the inclusion and exclusion criteria discussed below.

Inclusion and exclusion criteria

In the initial search stage, more than 150 studies were identified for possible inclusion in this meta-analysis. Below are the inclusion and exclusion criteria used for the final selection.

Inclusion criteria

1 The study was published between 1990 and June 2006 or was included in the current volume.
2 The study was conducted in either an experimental or a quasi-experimental design setting.
3 The study measured either
  a difference(s) in levels of acquisition between the treatment group(s) and the control/comparison group when a control/comparison group was included, or
  b pre-test to post-test gains when a control/comparison group was not included in the design.
4 The study measured the acquisition of specific linguistic forms (lexical or grammatical features) of a second/foreign language by various age groups (children, adolescents, or adults). Child L2 studies were analyzed in an effort to be as inclusive as possible, although, obviously, age may have played an influential role in the results.
5 The study utilized one or more communication tasks, either as the treatment (for example, interaction versus non-interaction) or as a way of providing a context for the treatment(s) in question (for example, studies on feedback).
6 The study involved synchronous interaction. Studies employing synchronous computer-mediated tasks were included since they are similar to face-to-face interactions in terms of temporal immediacy.
7 The study included all necessary information for the coding scheme of this study and for the calculation of effect sizes.

Exclusion criteria

1 The study did not measure the acquisition of specific lexical or grammatical features (for example, descriptive studies, correlational studies, or studies measuring L2 comprehension as opposed to acquisition per se, such as Gass and Varonis 1994; Oliver 1995, 1998, 2000; Shehadeh 1999, 2001; R. Ellis, Basturkmen, and Loewen 2001a, b; Braidi 2002; Philp 2003; Kim and Han this volume; Tocalli-Beller and Swain this volume).

2 The study provided supplementary treatment apart from interaction, often through enhancement techniques, including extra-experimental activities such as out-of-class practice (for example, Doughty and Varela 1998; Izumi 2002; Lyster 2004).

3 The study utilized custom-made tests. Although we believe such tests represent a valuable way to identify and measure the benefits of interaction, they make comparisons unrealistic because the items in a custom-made test differ to varying degrees depending upon each individual learner's errors (for example, Adams this volume; Egi this volume).

4 The study did not manipulate the independent variable (by grouping and providing corresponding treatment) before the dependent variable was measured, but instead based the independent variable on observations of learner behavior during learner activities. In these sorts of studies, the independent variable is not firmly controlled, as compared to studies that manipulate the independent variable before the dependent variable is measured. In other words, the researcher assigned participants to groups as a result of learner behavior during treatment, rather than as a way of examining different types of treatment so grouping occurred not at the beginning of the study, but at the end (for example, McDonough 2004; Smith 2004, 2005).

Coding

A total of 28 unique sample studies from 27 reports on interaction research were identified as suitable for inclusion in the present meta-analysis. The meta-analyses of interaction and feedback research carried out by Keck *et al.* (2006) and Russell and Spada (2006) included 14 and 15 studies, respectively. All 14 of the studies included in Keck *et al.* are included here (though in one case based on a different research report). We included 14 additional studies to Keck *et al.*, 12 that appeared after their cut-off date of 2003, along with two studies published before this date which we included based on different selection criteria (i.e. the ages of the participants and the mode of communication or feedback). Of the 15 studies included in Russell and Spada, only three are included in our study, reflecting a different overall focus and definition of feedback in their meta-analysis. Appendix B lists all of these studies. The ones included only in the current meta-analysis are marked with a single asterisk, those in the current study and also in Keck *et al.*'s meta-analysis are marked with double asterisks, and those in the current study, Keck *et al.*'s study and Russell and Spada's study are marked with triple asterisks.

In addition to doubling the number of primary studies meta-analyzed, the current meta-analysis expands upon both of the previous meta-analyses in that we take a different perspective on some of the factors they examined, (for example, by looking at corrective feedback specifically within the context of interaction) and incorporating additional variables into our analysis.

As is typical in meta-analytic research (see, for example, studies in the edited volume by Norris and Ortega 2006), the effects of substantive features (i.e. factors related to the content of the research area, which are sometimes, but not always, investigated as theoretically important independent variables in the studies included) were examined as independent variables here in order to synthesize findings in ways that individual studies cannot. Methodological practices relevant to interaction research were also examined. Below, the substantive features that this meta-analysis focused on are outlined, followed by a description of the methodological practices. All of the definitions were agreed upon prior to coding, which was independently carried out by two researchers. Appendix A shows coding results and effect sizes for the studies included in the current meta-analysis. Inter-rater reliability scores were calculated using Cohen's Kappa and found to be at an acceptable level ($\kappa = .89$ for substantive features; $\kappa = .96$ for methodological features); disagreements were resolved through a follow-up discussion.

Substantive features

Five substantive features, or factors related to theoretical constructs in interaction research were investigated in this analysis: type of target feature (lexis or grammar), interactional feedback (presence or absence), type of interactional feedback (recasts, negotiation, or metalinguistic feedback), focus of interactional feedback (general versus specific), and modified output (encouragement or discouragement of opportunities to modify).

The decision to investigate the type of target feature as a possible mediator of the relationship between interaction and learning was based on theoretical claims and empirical findings in the interaction literature to the effect that feedback may be more or less beneficial depending on characteristics of the targeted forms (for example, Long 1996; Long, Inagaki, and Ortega 1998; Mackey, Gass, and McDonough 2000). For instance, research by Mackey *et al.* (2000) indicated that learners' perceptions of feedback may differ according to whether the feedback is oriented towards morphosyntax, phonology, lexis, or semantics, and Long (2006) has suggested that implicit feedback may be relatively less effective when it targets non-salient, communicatively redundant forms. This meta-analysis examines lexical and grammatical features.

With regard to interactional feedback more generally, studies were classified according to whether or not the learners were provided with feedback during interactional tasks. Amassing evidence (including Russell and Spada's meta-analysis) indicates that feedback can be facilitative of SLA; however, a few researchers (for example, Truscott 1996, 1999) have argued that the practice of providing feedback is sufficiently problematic and ineffective that it should be abandoned. Thus, the current meta-analysis sought to investigate the effectiveness of feedback in the context of interaction, thereby supplementing Russell and Spada's analysis. Not all studies on task-based interaction necessarily involve the provision of interactional feedback; in fact, some studies were purposely designed so that learners would not receive feedback on their incorrect utterances during negotiation for meaning. For instance, in Loewen and Nabei's study (this volume), the authors set *no interactional feedback* as one of the treatment levels, and thus one of the treatment groups did not receive feedback on their incorrect question forms during interaction. Our coding scheme was intended to reflect this aspect of interaction research, where performance is compared with and without interactional feedback.

Feedback type was also a theoretically important feature. Three types of feedback widely employed in interaction were coded for comparisons of their effects on the acquisition of linguistic structures. These were recasts, negotiation, and metalinguistic feedback. As discussed in the Introduction to this volume, a considerable amount of attention has been drawn to recasts (generally defined as reformulations of learners' ungrammatical or inappropriate utterances which maintain their intended meanings) and their relationship to language learning. As noted earlier, the term is increasingly recognized as being elastic in nature, with researchers specifically examining the length and other characteristics of recasts in relation to their effectiveness. (See Loewen and Philp 2006 for a discussion of the potential effects of various types of recasts on learning.) In the current meta-analysis, however, for practical reasons, we considered recasts as a monolithic construct. Negotiation moves such as clarification requests, comprehension checks, and confirmation checks have also been investigated in several studies which have examined their individual and combined efficacy (for example, Nobuyoshi and Ellis 1993; Takashima and Ellis 1999; Lyster 2004; McDonough 2005; Loewen and Nabei this volume; McDonough this volume), often focusing in particular on clarification requests.

Amidst the recently rekindled debate on implicit and explicit learning, we considered it worthwhile to examine the relative efficacy of different types of feedback falling along the implicit/explicit feedback continuum. Both recasts and negotiation tend to be close to the implicit end of the continuum, whereas metalinguistic feedback is on the explicit side and generally more obtrusive than recasts and negotiation moves. It should be noted that only studies that clearly investigated the efficacy of one or more of these three types of feedback on language learning were included in this particular analysis. That is, studies that simply described interaction without exploring its impact on learning were excluded. Although interaction research has lately begun to explore language-related episodes (LREs), in which learners' attention is drawn to matters of linguistic form as they discuss language (for example, Kowal and Swain 1994; Swain and Lapkin 1998, 2001, 2002; Williams 1999, 2001), these were not examined here since they have thus far been investigated largely through the use of custom-made tests, which, as discussed already, were excluded in the present meta-analysis.

Given arguments to the effect that intensive feedback on particular pre-selected forms may be more effective than more wide-ranging incidental feedback (for example, Lyster 1998c; R. Ellis 2001), we also considered it worthwhile to investigate the effects of feedback focus. This issue is often linked to the question of whether setting impacts the efficacy of feedback, as will be discussed later. Russell and Spada (2006) did not find differences in mean effect sizes according to whether the feedback provided had been general or specific in nature (the effect sizes being large in both cases); however, they noted that the number of studies contributing to the analysis was too few to draw any firm conclusions and that more research should be done.

We also investigated the effect of learners' opportunities for modified output. This distinction was based on whether or not an interactional task promoted the modification of output in some way—in other words, whether the learners were encouraged or required to produce modified output in the course of completing the task (as in studies by Mackey and Oliver 2002; Iwashita 2003; Gass and Alvarez-Torres 2005, R. Ellis *et al.* 2006), or whether the learners were largely relieved of (or prohibited from) any responsibility to do so (as in studies by Loschky 1994; Inagaki and Long 1999; Leeman 2003). Our operationalization differs from Keck *et al.*'s (2006) pushed output category. Our focus was on whether or not learners had an *opportunity* to react to interactional feedback, whereas Keck *et al.*'s pushed output category focused on cases where learners were *required* to produce output, regardless of what sort of output it was. All the groups in Leeman's (2003) study, for example, were categorized as having pushed output by Keck *et al.* because Leeman's learners were required to produce output, or speak, during interaction. However, Leeman's learners did not have the opportunity to modify their original utterances following interactional feedback. We focused on learners' reaction opportunities, the third turn in Oliver's (1995, 2000) three-part coding scheme (initiation–response–reaction), rather than the existence of learners' initial turn which was the main criterion of Keck *et al.*'s pushed output category.

Methodological features

First, we looked at the context of the research, which was classified as being either a second or foreign language context. This was prompted, in part, by our observation that only a few studies have made direct comparisons of the effectiveness of feedback in different communicative classroom environments (for example, Sheen 2004; Lyster and Mori 2006). Sheen's findings in relation to feedback and learner uptake in four instructional contexts (Korean EFL, New Zealand ESL, Canadian ESL, and French immersion) underscored the need to take this factor into account, highlighting the idea that modifications of output may be more likely in contexts where the purpose of feedback is more salient to the learners. Lyster and Mori compared two immersion settings (French and Japanese) in terms of feedback and learner uptake, leading them to propose the counterbalance hypothesis which states that instructional activities and interactional feedback that counterbalance a classroom's predominantly communicative orientation are more effective than those that are consistent with the classroom's orientation.

Related to this distinction are potential differences that have been proposed for laboratory versus classroom research settings, as alluded to above. For instance, based on a study that she argued indicated that negotiation for meaning did not occur in a classroom context, Foster (1998) questioned whether the findings of interaction research are applicable to the classroom. However, research by Gass, Mackey, and Ross-Feldman (2005) did not support Foster's findings, showing instead that negotiation and other forms of interaction were prevalent in the classroom. Other researchers, for example Nicholas, Lightbown, and Spada (2001), have pointed out it is possible that part of the reason behind the positive effects which have been found for recasts may be due to the focused and consistent nature of the feedback provided in laboratory settings. Experimental research often involves dyadic interactions which are arguably free from many of the distractions and the wide variety of linguistic issues which occur in classrooms. This is why researchers have claimed that learners may be more sensitive to corrections in the laboratory, because there, they say, feedback is more clearly interpretable. Russell and Spada (2006) did not find evidence for this in their meta-analysis. (Again, the effect sizes for both classroom and laboratory contexts were equally large.) However, they noted that the small number of studies contributing to the analysis prevented a clear comparison between the effect sizes and suggested that the question merits further investigation, as we are doing here.

The final factor included in our question about methodology and context in the outcomes of interaction research was the type of dependent variable measure employed. Some time ago, as also discussed by Russell and Spada (2006), Krashen (1982) claimed that, while feedback may affect learners' monitored uses of language, it would not directly improve their spontaneous production. Such arguments have been taken up more recently by researchers such as Schwartz (1993) and Truscott (1999). With this in mind, given that interaction often involves feedback, and also considering Norris and Ortega's (2000) meta-analytic finding that studies with free-response measures tend to show smaller effect sizes, we decided to investigate the extent to which measurement decisions might have influenced the strength of the results observed in interaction research. Our coding scheme here was inspired by Chaudron's (2003) exposition of data collection methods on a continuum ranging from naturalistic (contextualized) to elicited production to experimental (decontextualized), utilized by Gass and Mackey's (2007) book on data elicitation, which distinguishes throughout between naturalistic production (for example, spontaneous conversations, which can take place in classrooms), prompted production (for example, sentence-combination tasks, picture-description tasks), and prompted responses (for example, acceptability judgments, multiple-choice questions). These latter three classifications formed the basis for our coding categories. As mentioned above, like Keck *et al.* (2006), we also looked at the following features in order to uncover a sense of the current degree of methodological sophistication in the field of interaction research: (a) use versus non-use of a control or comparison group, (b) total number of participants, (c) number of participants in the treatment group or groups, (d) length of each treatment session, (e) number of treatment sessions, (f) timing of post-tests (immediate, short-term delayed, and longer-term delayed), and (g) L2 proficiency measures employed (impressionistic judgment, institutional status, in-house assessment, standardized test scores, and developmental stage). In addition, we coded studies with respect to the following participant characteristics in order to examine the diversity of learner groups represented: (a) L1, (b) L2, (c) age, (d) L2 proficiency level, and (e) type of school or program from which participants were drawn (university, high school, junior high school, elementary school, or language institute).

As far as statistical methods and reporting conventions are concerned, we coded according to which statistical methods were used for the main analysis (or analyses) and whether the study included details regarding effect size(s) or strength(s) of association, confidence intervals, standard errors of the mean, a preset alpha level, exact *p*-values, and the reliability of any dependent variable measures. This categorization was designed to examine the current reporting conventions overall in this area of SLA.

Calculation of effect sizes

Two main families of effect sizes have been used in much of the research in the social sciences: the *r* family and the *d* family (R. Rosenthal 1994, 1995). In this meta-analysis, we used Cohen's *d* and Cohen's *h* (Cohen 1988, 1992), both of which belong to the *d* family, for the calculation of effect sizes; Cohen's *h* is identical to the arcsine formula (Lipsey and Wilson 2001) which was utilized in Keck *et al.*'s (2006) study as well. There are two reasons for choosing these two methods of calculation. First of all, it is relatively simple to calculate them since they are based on descriptive statistics such as means, standard deviations, and sample sizes (for Cohen's *d*), or simple proportions (for Cohen's *h*), which most studies usually report in one form or another. Secondly, the conventions for interpreting these effect sizes are the same; that is, .2 is considered a small effect size, .5 is medium, and .8 is large for both formulae (Cohen 1988, 1992).

Cohen's *d* is a popular method presumably for the first reason and has been utilized in previous meta-analyses (for example, Norris and Ortega 2000; Keck *et al.* 2006). Some studies, however, do not report the descriptive statistics necessary for the calculation of Cohen's *d*, in which case separate calculations to acquire means and standard deviations have to be conducted, based on the data provided in the report (for example, R. Ellis, Tanaka, and Yamazaki 1994; Inagaki and Long 1999). If a study does not report descriptive statistics, but reports *t*-values or *F*-values ($df = 1$ in the numerator), these can be used in the calculations. Below are the two formulae which were utilized for the calculation of effect sizes when only *t*-values or *F*-values were available (Lipsey and Wilson 2001: 198–9); *n* refers to the sample size of a group.

$$Es_{sm} = t\sqrt{\frac{n_1 + n_2}{n_1 n_2}} \qquad\qquad Es_{sm} = \sqrt{\frac{F(n_1 + n_2)}{n_1 n_2}}$$

Cohen's h (Cohen 1988, 1992; Lipsey and Wilson 2001) was used for studies that reported proportions as evidence for development (for example, Mackey 1999; Mackey and Oliver 2002; Mackey and Silver 2005; McDonough 2005).

$$\text{Cohen's } h = \text{arcsine}_{treatment} - \text{arcsine}_{control/comparison}$$

Contrasts for effect size calculations

If a study used a true control group, effect sizes were calculated by comparing the performance of the treatment group(s) with that of the control group. Some studies, however, used a comparison group rather than a true control group, in which case effect sizes were obtained by comparing the performance of the treatment group(s) with that of the comparison group. As in Norris and Ortega's (2000) and Keck *et al.*'s (2006) meta-analyses, when there was no comparison group, the group that received the least interactive treatment was used as a comparison group. This approach applied to studies in which no pre-test was administered and no control or comparison group was involved, but the post-test scores of multiple groups were available.

Combining and comparing effect sizes

It is not uncommon for researchers to employ a design in which multiple groups are treated under different interactional conditions and later compared (Norris and Ortega 2000; Keck *et al.* 2006). In this meta-analysis, effect sizes were calculated for all of the possible contrasts in each study based on the criteria described in the preceding section. Some meta-analysts (for example, Light and Pillemer 1984) suggest that multiple effect sizes from a single study should be averaged so that each study contributes only one effect size. However, this practice may misrepresent the precise nature of the magnitude of particular treatment effects and blur distinctions related to the constructs of interest in a meta-analysis. We thus decided for the purposes of this meta-analysis that it was permissible to include multiple effect sizes from a single study, where relevant.

To summarize, then, the current meta-analysis was designed to explore the effects of interaction on second language acquisition as well as to better understand the efficacy of specific interactional or contextual features. If a study had multiple dependent variable measures related to a single target item (for example, oral and written tense consistency in Han 2002b), we calculated average effect sizes by dividing the total sum of effect sizes by the number of dependent variable measures in that study; with regard to effect sizes for different dependent variable measures, average effect sizes were calculated only for measures of the same type, whereas multiple effect sizes were calculated for studies in which two or more different types of dependent variable measures were utilized. For an in-depth discussion of these sorts of issues, see Norris and Ortega (2006). However, if a study used multiple treatment groups to investigate different interactional features, we considered the effect sizes separately. R. Ellis *et al.* (2006), for instance, used two treatment groups in their study on the acquisition of English past tense '–ed': a recast group and a metalinguistic feedback group, each of which participated in an interactional treatment. It would have been possible to represent the effects of interaction in a general sense by using a single, averaged effect size for both groups in this study. This approach, however, would not have helped to disentangle the puzzle of what it is in interaction that actually triggers L2 learning; thus, we did not average the multiple effect sizes contributed by a single study in such cases.

In this meta-analysis, we calculated overall effect sizes for each of the following substantive factors:

a interactional treatment,
b pre-test to post-test gains for treatment and control/comparison groups,
c lexical and grammatical target items,
d presence and absence of interactional feedback,
e recasts, negotiation, and metalinguistic types of feedback,
f general and specific focuses of feedback, and
g presence and absence of opportunities for modified output.

In addition, we calculated effect sizes for the following methodologically oriented factors:

h second and foreign language contexts,
i classroom and laboratory research settings, and
j naturalistic, free, and constrained prompted production, and prompted response types of dependent measures.

For the purpose of comparison, we followed the distinctions made by Keck *et al.* (2006) in relation to short-term delayed post-tests (7–29 days after the treatment) and longer-term delayed post-tests (more than 30 days after the treatment). All of the mean effect sizes calculated in the current meta-analysis are presented in a fashion corresponding to this distinction. Confidence intervals were also calculated for the reliability of effect sizes.

We used the inverse variance weight method to calculate mean effect sizes. Statistically, the sampling error (the difference between a statistic and the parameter) decreases as the size of the sample increases, and vice versa. This is also true of effect size estimates with effect sizes calculated from studies with smaller sample sizes being less precise (and reliable) than those calculated from studies with larger sample sizes. To address this issue, we decided to use corrected/unbiased effect sizes and weighted mean effect sizes because some of the studies included in the current meta-analysis had only a small number of participants (for example, Inagaki and Long 1999; Mackey 1999; de la Fuente 2002; Han 2002b; Loewen and Nabei this volume). We obtained corrected (or unbiased) effect size estimates based on the sample sizes and used the inverse variance weight method to get weighted mean effect sizes, a commonly accepted method for weighting in meta-analyses. (See Lipsey and Wilson 2001 for more information on this issue.) Overall, corrected effect sizes and weighted mean effect sizes were smaller than uncorrected effect sizes and unweighted mean effect sizes calculated at the first stage of our quantitative analysis.

Results

Our two research questions, regarding the effectiveness of interaction and the relationships between various interactional processes and L2 outcomes, form the crux of this meta-analysis. However, the results are easier to understand when contextualized within an initial descriptive overview of research design factors, learner characteristics, and statistical approaches used within the interaction approach. Thus, these methodological points will be laid out first, followed by a report of the results for the research questions.

Research synthesis

Research publication

As noted earlier, the 28 sample studies which qualified for inclusion in this analysis are marked with an asterisk in Appendix B and categorized according to their substantive features in Appendix A. Among them, 19 studies (68 per cent) were published in such refereed journals as *Studies in Second Language Acquisition* ($n = 9$), *The Modern Language Journal* ($n = 3$), *Language Learning* ($n = 4$), *System* ($n = 2$), *Canadian Modern Language Review* ($n = 1$), and *TESOL Quarterly* ($n = 1$), while nine studies (32 per cent) appeared as chapters in edited books (R. Ellis 1999; Kanno 1999; Mackey this volume). Figure 17.1 shows the number of empirical studies used in this meta-analysis according to year of publication.

Methodological factors

Research setting and context

As shown in Table 17.1, of the 28 studies that qualified for this analysis, more were laboratory-based than classroom-based. Laboratory-based studies comprised 64 per cent ($n = 18$) of those included, and classroom-based studies 36 per cent ($n = 10$). The majority of the studies, or 71 per cent ($n = 20$), were carried out in foreign-language (FL) contexts, while the remaining 29 per cent ($n = 8$) were conducted in second-language (SL) contexts.

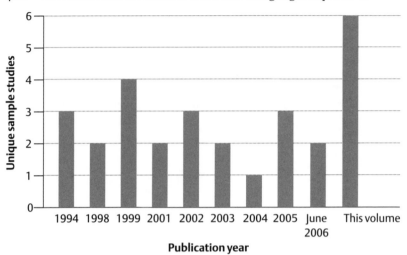

Figure 17.1 Empirical studies qualified for the meta-analysis and their years of publication

Design/context	SL	FL	Total (per cent)
Laboratory	4	14	18 (64)
Classroom	4	6	10 (36)
Total (per cent)	8 (29)	20 (71)	28 (100)

Table 17.1 Research setting and context

Ten studies (36 per cent) of the 28 used a true control group, while the remaining 18 studies (64 per cent) used some sort of comparison group. Table 17.2 illustrates the design characteristics of the 28 sample studies with means and standard deviations. As can be seen from the table, overall sample sizes ranged from 4–145 ($M = 53.46$, $SD = 32.85$); this includes the control/comparison group and the treatment group(s). Sample sizes of the treatment groups ranged from 4–45 ($M = 16.80$, $SD = 10.58$). The length of each interaction treatment session ranged from 5–60 minutes ($M = 31.96$, $SD = 14.36$), and the number of treatment sessions ranged from 1–8 ($M = 2.37$, $SD = 1.50$). Also shown in Table 17.2 is the number of days between the final treatment and each of the post-tests (i.e. the immediate, first delayed, and second delayed post-tests). The types of L2 proficiency measures used are discussed below.

Characteristic	*Mean*	*SD*	Range	n[a]
Sample size	53.46	32.85	4–145	28
Treatment group sample size	16.80	10.58	4–45	28
Length of treatment session (min.)	31.96	14.36	5–60	23 (5 n.r.)
Number of treatments	2.37	1.50	1–8	27 (1 n.r.)
Timing of immediate post-test (days)	1.44	2.31	0–7	27 (1 n.r.)
Timing of delayed post-test 1 (days)	17.00	10.36	7–42	20
Timing of delayed post-test 2 (days)	40.25	19.17	21–75	12

[a] Number of unique sample studies reporting out of 28; n.r. = not reported

Table 17.2 Design characteristics

Of the four types of outcome measures, open-ended prompted productions such as oral production tasks and writing tests (52 per cent) were the most frequently utilized, followed by closed-ended prompted productions such as text reconstructions (30 per cent). Prompted responses such as grammaticality judgment tests and multiple-choice questions (18 per cent) were less frequently used, and naturalistic production was not evidenced in any of the studies included in the present meta-analysis. This indicates that the open-ended prompted production types of outcome measure, especially oral production tasks, were the most preferred means of assessing the impact of interaction on L2 learning in this sample, probably reflecting the fact that the interaction treatment was usually also oral production task-based, and illustrating researchers' preference for testing in the same modality as the treatment (Gass and Mackey 2006).

Learner characteristics

Learner characteristics, including the participants' L1s, L2s, age, and reported proficiency levels are summarized in Table 17.3 along with the proficiency measures employed and the types of schools from which participants were drawn. The mean age of adolescent and adult learners was 20.3 (ranging from 18.3–25) in the nine studies that reported age, and that of child learners 8.5 in the two child language learning studies. Notably, as also found by Keck *et al.* (2006) and Thomas (1994, 2006), institutional status was still the most common type of L2 proficiency measure at 61 per cent ($n = 17$), though a number of studies ($n = 7$, or 25 per cent) classified learners according to developmental stage. Sixty-one per cent of the studies ($n = 17$) used university students (for example, undergraduates learning a non-native language such as Spanish, and so on), while 29 per cent ($n = 8$) obtained their participants from language institutes (for example, learners of English as a second language in an intensive English institute).

n^a L1	n L2	n Proficiency level	n Proficiency measure	n Academic setting
10 English	8 English (SL)	5 Beginner	17 Institutional status	17 University
9 Japanese	8 English (FL)	10 Intermediate	1 In-house assessment	2 High school
7 Chinese	6 Spanish (FL)	7 Multiple	1 Standardized test	1 Elementary school
5 Korean	4 Japanese (FL)	6 Not specified	7 Developmental stage	8 Language institute
5 Thai	1 French (FL)		1 Self-rated	
4 Spanish	1 Korean (FL)		1 Not reported	
2 Swiss-German				
2 French				
2 Czech				
2 Turkish				
2 Indonesian				
2 Russian				
1 Other[b]				

[a] Number of unique sample studies reporting out of N = 28

[b] The following L1s were reported in one study each: Sudanese, Croatian, Bosnian, Farsi, Italian, Serbian, Macedonian, Arabic, Polish, Portuguese, Malay, and Tagalog. One study reported an Ethiopian language. Mackey and Oliver (2002) reported that one of the L1s in their study was an Indian language, and R. Ellis *et al.* (2006) and R. Ellis (this volume) reported L1s of East Asian origin.

Table 17.3 Learner characteristics

Statistical methods and reporting conventions

The most frequently used statistical method for main analyses was ANOVA (50 per cent), followed by ANCOVA (15 per cent), *t*-test (12 per cent), chi-square (12 per cent), Kruskal-Wallis (a nonparametric version of ANOVA, six per cent), MANOVA (three per cent), and logistic regression (three per cent). Effect sizes or strengths of association were reported in four studies (14 per cent), which represents a small improvement in the field of interaction research compared to 2003, when Keck *et al.* (2006) performed their meta-analysis, finding none. No studies reported confidence intervals or standard errors of the mean. Exact *p*-values were reported in 17 (61 per cent) of the 28 studies in which statistical significance was detected. Seven studies (25 per cent) included a statement about a preset alpha level, and the reliability of dependent variable measures was reported in two sample studies (Cronbach's alpha was used in both studies).

Quantitative meta-analysis

Weighted mean effect sizes (the inverse variance weight method was used based on sample sizes and unbiased/corrected effect size estimates adjusted for the sample size) regarding the relationships between interaction and learning were calculated and compared in terms of the target features (lexis versus grammar), the presence or absence of interactional feedback, the feedback type (recasts versus negotiation versus metalinguistic feedback), the feedback focus (general versus specific), and whether opportunities for modified output were encouraged or not. The means of the effect sizes in each comparison category are shown in Table 17.4 along with their standard deviations and 95 per cent confidence intervals. As mentioned above, following Keck *et al.*'s (2006) categorization of delayed post-tests as occurring after a short or a long delay, we compared mean effect sizes based on the amount of time that had elapsed after the final treatment. The results from Table 17.4 relating to the research questions will be discussed next.

Independent variable	n^a	k^b	Weighted		95% CI	
			Mean d	SD d	Lower	Upper
All interactional treatments						
Immediate post-test	22	52	.75	.78	.67	.83
Short delayed post-test	12	28	1.02	.78	.90	1.14
Long delayed post-test	8	13	.99	.61	.89	1.09
Target feature						
Immediate						
Lexis	7	12	1.32	.61	1.19	1.45
Grammar	18	40	.59	.75	.51	.67
Short delay						
Lexis	3	6	.85	.59	.64	1.06
Grammar	10	22	1.07	.82	.93	1.21
Long delay						
Lexis	2	2	.96	.04	.95	.98
Grammar	6	11	.99	.69	.87	1.12
Interactional feedback						
Immediate						
[– Feedback]	6	7	.93	.74	.74	1.12
[+ Feedback]	20	45	.71	.78	.63	.80
Short delay						
[– Feedback]	4	6	.76	.43	.61	.91
[+ Feedback]	12	22	1.09	.84	.95	1.24
Long delay						
[–Feedback]	2	2	.96	.04	.95	.98
[+Feedback]	6	11	.99	.69	.87	1.12
Feedback type						
Immediate						
Recast	10	14	.96	1.04	.75	1.17
Negotiation	3	4	.52	.26	.43	.61
Metalinguistic feedback	3	3	.47	.36	.28	.66

Short delay						
Recast	5	7	1.69	1.13	1.33	2.04
Negotiation	2	3	.58	.18	.51	.65
Metalinguistic feedback	2	2	1.21	.66	.70	1.73
Long delay						
Recast	4	5	1.22	.85	.99	1.44
Negotiation	3	5	.79	.43	.66	.92
Metalinguistic feedback	0	—	—	—	—	—
Feedback focus						
Immediate						
General	5	9	.69	.61	.53	.86
Specific	15	36	.72	.81	.62	.82
Short delay						
General	4	8	.84	.41	.71	.97
Specific	8	14	1.21	.95	1.01	1.41
Long delay						
General	0	—	—	—	—	—
Specific	6	11	.99	.69	.87	1.12
Modified output						
Immediate						
[– Modified output opportunity]	11	21	.90	.94	.76	1.05
[+ Modified output opportunity]	13	31	.63	.61	.55	.71
Short delay						
[–Modified output opportunity]	5	12	1.18	1.01	.95	1.40
[+Modified output opportunity]	10	16	.88	.45	.79	.98
Long delay						
[–Modified output opportunity]	3	5	1.29	.79	1.08	1.50
[+Modified output opportunity]	6	8	.79	.33	.72	.86

[a] Number of unique sample studies contributing to effect sizes
[b] Number of interaction treatments

Table 17.4 Interactional treatment effect sizes

Overall effects of interaction on learning

As mentioned above, and discussed in more detail in Norris and Ortega (2006), an effect size of .8 is considered large, .5 medium, and .2 small (Cohen 1988, 1992). The magnitude of the overall effects of interaction on the acquisition of lexical and grammatical target items at the time of immediate post-tests is large ($M = .75$, $SD = .78$). Half of the studies in the sample employed delayed post-tests. In the short-term delayed post-tests and longer-term delayed post-tests ($M = 1.02$, $SD = .78$ and $M = .99$, $SD = .61$, respectively), the effects of interaction appear to be even greater, indicating a delayed impact of interaction on second language acquisition, as suggested in theoretical claims by Mackey, Gass, and McDonough (2000) and empirically by Mackey (1999) and Keck *et al.* (2006). Figure 17.2 illustrates the effects of interaction on the immediate and delayed post-tests in terms of mean effect sizes (represented by the small horizontal lines) and 95 per cent confidence intervals (represented by the boxes around those lines). The confidence intervals for both short-term delayed and long-term delayed post-tests do not overlap with the confidence interval for the immediate post-tests, clearly indicating that the efficacy of interaction on learner performance in both delayed post-tests is significantly greater than in the immediate post-tests. For the short-term delayed post-tests, the confidence intervals overlap with the confidence intervals of the longer-term delayed post-tests to a great extent. This means that while there is a significant difference between the immediate and any of the delayed post-tests, no significant difference was found between the short-term and the longer-term delayed post-tests, both of which were large, also indicating durable interaction effects on language learning.

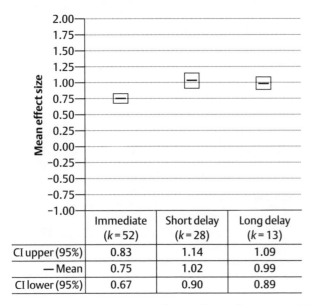

	Immediate (k = 52)	Short delay (k = 28)	Long delay (k = 13)
CI upper (95%)	0.83	1.14	1.09
— Mean	0.75	1.02	0.99
CI lower (95%)	0.67	0.90	0.89

Figure 17.2 Comparison of immediate, short-term delayed, and longer-term delayed post-tests

Pre-test to post-test gains

We also looked at the question of overall effects of interaction from the perspective of within-group change. As can be seen in Table 17.5 and Figure 17.3, the interactional treatment groups showed a considerable change from the pre-test to the immediate post-test in the acquisition of linguistic target items ($M = 1.09$, $SD = .93$), whereas the control/comparison group did not show such a noticeable increase ($M = .44$, $SD = .42$), which is a medium effect size. The difference between these groups in terms of the change in learner performance from the pre-test to the immediate post-test is significant at the alpha level of .05, as indicated by their non-overlapping confidence intervals. Thus, interaction was significantly more effective than little or no interaction by the immediate post-test. At the same time, however, it is important to point out that some improvement was made by the control/comparison group as well, a trend also noted in previous meta-analyses (for example, Norris and Ortega 2000; Keck *et al.* 2006). The mean effect size of .44 for this group indicates that learners who did not participate in interaction or who participated in less interaction nonetheless improved to a certain extent.

Independent variable	n	k	Mean d	SD d	95% CI Lower	95% CI Upper
All interactional treatments	13	41	1.09	.93	.99	1.19
Control/comparison	11	20	.44	.42	.38	.50

Table 17.5 Pre-test to post-test effect sizes

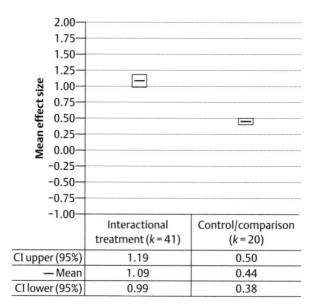

	Interactional treatment ($k = 41$)	Control/comparison ($k = 20$)
CI upper (95%)	1.19	0.50
— Mean	1.09	0.44
CI lower (95%)	0.99	0.38

Figure 17.3. Pre-test to post-test gains by interaction and control/comparison groups

Effects of particular linguistic and interactional features on learning outcomes

Type of target feature

Despite the large overall magnitude of interactional treatment effects on second language acquisition, as evidenced above in learner performance on immediate post-tests, it is noteworthy that these effects appear to be attributable, to a considerable degree, to the positive effects of interaction on the acquisition of lexical items rather than grammatical target structures (M = 1.32, SD = .61 for lexical items and M = .59, SD = .75 for grammatical target structures), at least on the immediate post-tests. This difference is depicted in Figure 17.4. The confidence intervals for the two means do not overlap, indicating a statistically significant difference and suggesting that interaction may initially be more beneficial in the acquisition of lexical items than in the acquisition of grammatical structures. The medium mean effect size (M = .59) for interactional treatments on the acquisition of grammatical features still signifies that interaction is efficacious, although it does not reach the conventional level of the large effect size (d = .8), in promoting the learning of these areas of a target language; it is even better for lexical learning on the immediate post-tests.

What Figure 17.5 indicates is that the positive developmental changes precipitated by interactional treatments remain long enough to show up on short-term delayed post-tests, for both types of target feature (M = .85, SD = .59 for lexical and M = 1.07, SD = .82 for grammatical items). Again, this suggests the efficacy of interaction on the acquisition of grammar may be somewhat delayed in nature, rather than immediate. Having said this, however, we need to keep in mind that only six treatment groups in terms of lexical acquisition were involved in the analysis of the short-term delayed post-tests. Thus, conclusions about the delayed efficacy of interactional treatments with respect to particular types of linguistic targets seem premature despite non-overlapping confidence intervals between the two target types. More studies that administer delayed post-tests would be helpful.

Interactional feedback (occurrence, type, and focus)

The effects of interactional feedback on learner performance on the immediate and short-term delayed post-tests are shown in Figures 17.6 and 17.7. Only two treatment groups in the no feedback condition were involved in the analysis of the longer-term delayed post-tests; therefore, a comparison between the two conditions is not possible. Because interaction is generally accompanied by feedback, however, it was not an easy task to find studies with groups which did not receive feedback during interaction. Accordingly, any claims regarding no feedback conditions would not be legitimate because of the extremely small number of treatment groups involved in this category.

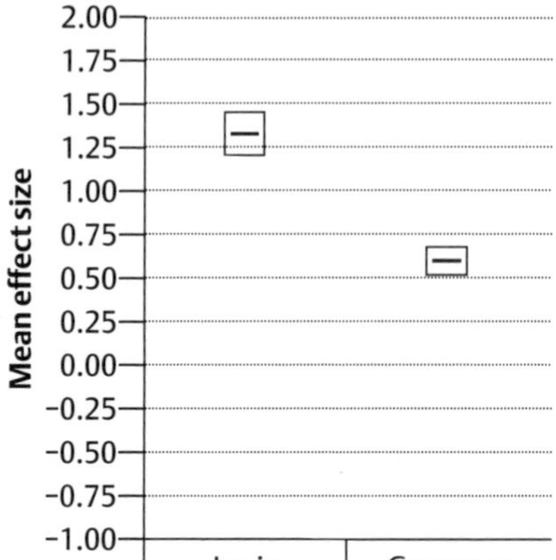

	Lexis (k = 12)	Grammar (k = 40)
CI upper (95%)	1.45	0.67
— Mean	1.32	0.59
CI lower (95%)	1.19	0.51

Figure 17.4 Effect of interaction on lexical and grammatical targets on immediate post-tests

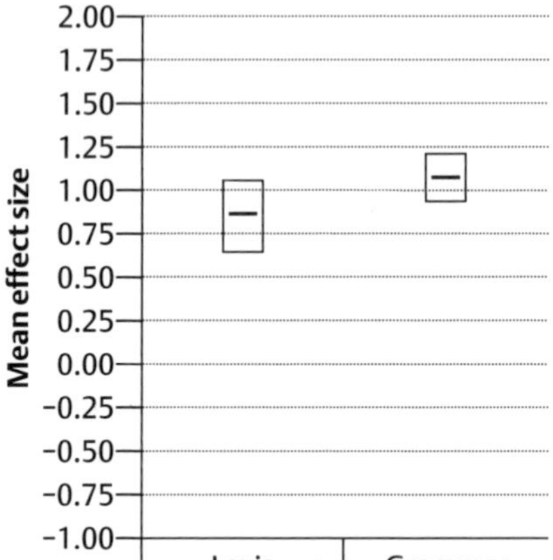

	Lexis (k = 6)	Grammar (k = 22)
CI upper (95%)	1.06	1.21
— Mean	0.85	1.07
CI lower (95%)	0.64	0.93

Figure 17.5 Effect of interaction on lexical and grammatical targets on short-term delayed post-tests

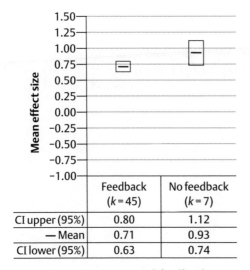

	Feedback (k = 45)	No feedback (k = 7)
CI upper (95%)	0.80	1.12
— Mean	0.71	0.93
CI lower (95%)	0.63	0.74

Figure 17.6 Interactional feedback on immediate post-tests

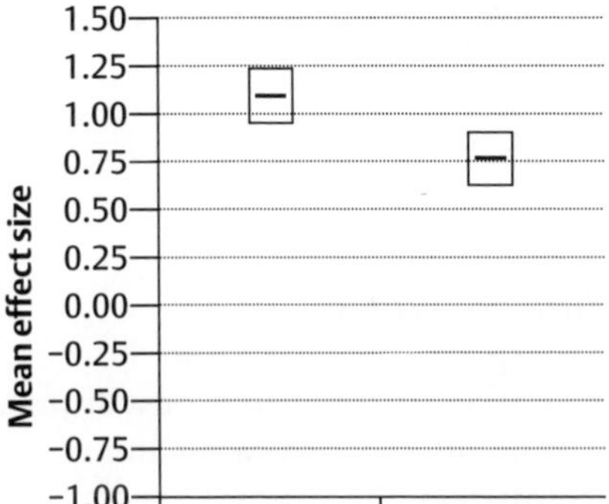

	Feedback (k = 22)	No feedback (k = 6)
CI upper (95%)	1.24	0.91
— Mean	1.09	0.76
CI lower (95%)	0.95	0.61

Figure 17.7 Interactional feedback on short-term delayed post-tests

Similarly, a lack of qualified studies was also observed when we isolated and examined different types of feedback, making conclusions regarding the relative superiority of any of them premature. Interaction research on recasts resulted in large mean effect sizes on all three post-tests ($M = .96$, $SD = 1.04$ for immediate post-tests, $M = 1.69$, $SD = 1.13$ for short-term delayed post-tests, and $M = 1.22$, $SD = .85$ for longer-term delayed post-tests). However, since only four treatment conditions containing negotiation and three treatment conditions containing metalinguistic feedback were available, it is not appropriate to argue that recasts are more or less superior to these other types of feedback. Figure 17.8 shows the results from the immediate post-tests (the lack of qualified studies for the negotiation and metalinguistic feedback conditions made it impossible to make further comparisons of the groups on the delayed post-tests).

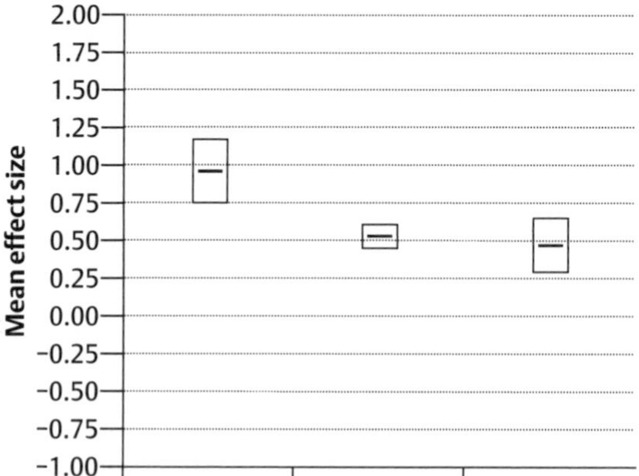

	Recast (k = 14)	Negotiation (k = 4)	Metalinguistic (k = 3)
CI upper (95%)	1.17	0.61	0.66
— Mean	0.96	0.52	0.47
CI lower (95%)	0.75	0.43	0.28

Figure 17.8 Type of feedback on immediate post-tests

Finally, with respect to the distinction between general versus specific focuses of feedback (see Figures 17.9 and 17.10), both types show medium-to-large effect sizes on the immediate post-tests ($M = .69$, $SD = .61$ for general focuses and $M = .72$, $SD = .81$ for specific focuses), confirming Russell and Spada's (2006) findings of nonsignificant differences between the two. However, significantly larger effect sizes for the specific focus conditions on the short-term delayed post-tests than those for the general focus conditions were evidenced ($M = 1.21$, $SD = .95$ for specific focuses and $M = .84$, $SD = .41$ for general focuses conditions). Nine and eight treatment groups with the general focus conditions were involved in the analyses of the immediate and short-term delayed post-tests, respectively, so again conclusions on the issue of feedback focus should be tentative.

Modified output

Interesting results were found in the analyses of the immediate, short-term delayed, and longer-term delayed post-tests. Interaction *without* opportunities for modified output seems to have contributed more to the acquisition of

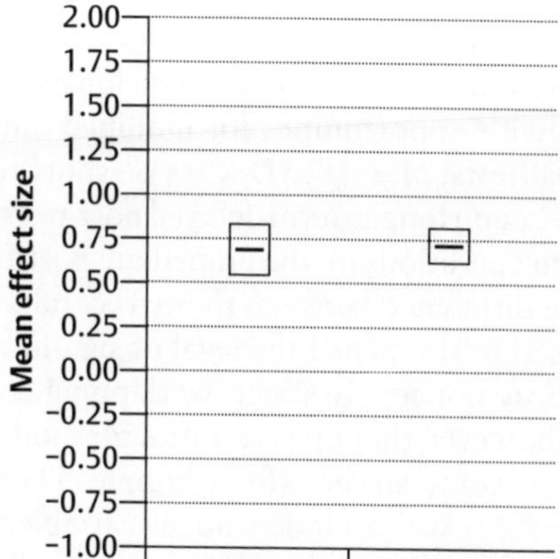

	General (k = 9)	Specific (k = 36)
CI upper (95%)	0.86	0.82
— Mean	0.69	0.72
CI lower (95%)	0.53	0.62

Figure 17.9   Focus of feedback on immediate post-tests

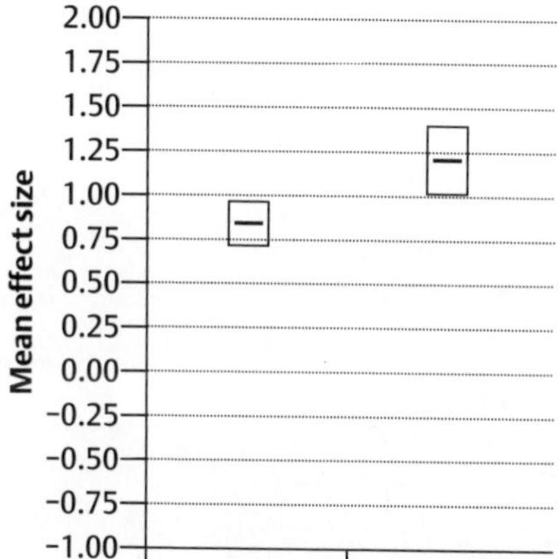

	General (k = 8)	Specific (k = 14)
CI upper (95%)	0.97	1.41
— Mean	0.84	1.21
CI lower (95%)	0.71	1.01

Figure 17.10   Focus of feedback on short-term delayed post-tests

linguistic targets ($M = .90$, $SD = .94$ on immediate post-tests, $M = 1.18$, $SD = 1.01$ on short-term delayed post-tests, and $M = 1.29$, $SD = .79$ on longer-term delayed post-tests) than interaction with opportunities for modified output ($M = .63$, $SD = .61$ on immediate post-tests, $M = .88$, $SD = .45$ on short-term delayed post-tests, and $M = .79$, $SD = .33$ on longer-term delayed post-tests). A significant difference between the two conditions on the immediate post-tests is exhibited in Figure 17.11 and the difference between the two conditions on the short-term delayed post-tests almost reached the level of significance as shown in Figure 17.12 (indicated by noticeably slight overlapping confidence intervals). It should be noted, however, that opportunities for modified output were intentionally blocked in some studies (for example, Leeman 2003; Sagarra this volume) not because it was an independent variable, but for methodological reasons, a design issue, indicating that the comparison between the opportunity and no opportunity conditions may not portray what it is intended to show. This issue will be revisited later in the discussion section. More direct investigations of the role of modified output opportunities are clearly warranted.

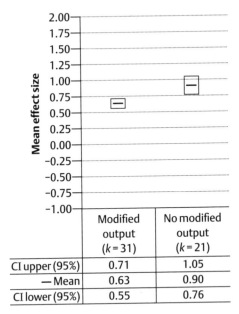

	Modified output ($k = 31$)	No modified output ($k = 21$)
CI upper (95%)	0.71	1.05
— Mean	0.63	0.90
CI lower (95%)	0.55	0.76

Figure 17.11 Effects of opportunities for modified output on immediate post-tests

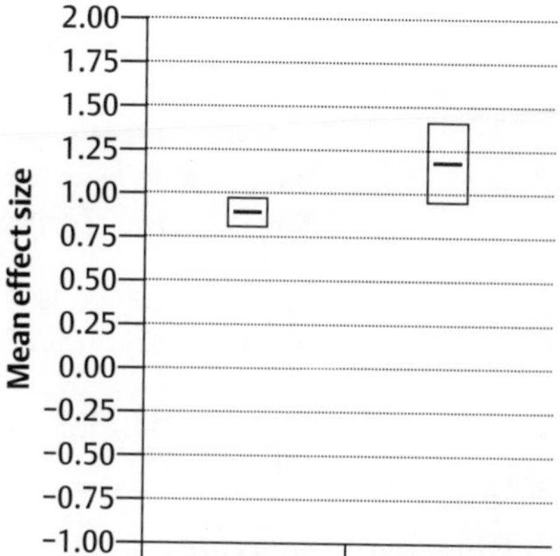

	Modified output (k = 16)	No modified output (k = 12)
CI upper (95%)	0.98	1.40
— Mean	0.88	1.18
CI lower (95%)	0.79	0.95

Figure 17.12 Effects of opportunities for modified output on short-term delayed post-tests

Effects of methodological factors on outcomes

Research context (second language versus foreign language)

This meta-analysis was also designed to investigate whether any effects of interaction would be different depending upon the research context (second language versus foreign language). Large mean effect sizes were consistently found in research conducted in foreign language contexts ($M = .79, SD = .84$ on immediate post-tests, $M = 1.08, SD = .88$ on short-term delayed post-tests, and $M = 1.11, SD = .60$ on longer-term delayed post-tests), as seen in Table 17.6 and Figures 17.13 and 17.14, whereas research implemented in second language contexts showed a large mean effect size only on the short-term delayed post-test ($M = .90, SD = .52$). Two plausible explanations for the increase in effect sizes from the immediate ($M = .55, SD = .38$) to the short-term delayed post-tests ($M = .90, SD = .52$) in second language contexts may illustrate this finding. Firstly, it is likely that in second language contexts such confounding variables as exposure to target linguistic items which can not be controlled for after the treatment may have played a role. Secondly, there were some treatment groups that were included in the analysis of the short-term post-tests, but not in the analysis of the immediate post-tests due to the timing of the first post-tests (for example, Mackey 1999). (Since only two groups from a single study contributed to the calculations of effect sizes for longer-term delayed post-tests, no further discussion of these data seems necessary.)

Independent variable	n	k	Mean d	SD d	95% CI Lower	Upper
Immediate						
Second language	5	10	.55	.38	.46	.64
Foreign language	17	42	.79	.84	.70	.88
Short delay						
Second language	6	12	.90	.52	.76	1.04
Foreign language	6	16	1.08	.88	.92	1.25
Long delay						
Second language	1	2	.44	.29	.32	.56
Foreign language	7	11	1.11	.60	1.00	1.22

Table 17.6 *Effects of interaction in relation to research context*

Independent variable	n	k	Mean d	SD d	95% CI Lower	Upper
Immediate						
Laboratory	12	27	.96	.83	.84	1.09
Classroom	10	25	.57	.68	.47	.66
Short delay						
Laboratory	8	21	1.11	.87	.95	1.28
Classroom	4	7	.81	.45	.68	.94
Long delay						
Laboratory	4	8	1.20	.74	1.03	1.37
Classroom	4	5	.76	.31	.69	.84

Table 17.7 *Effects of interaction in relation to research setting*

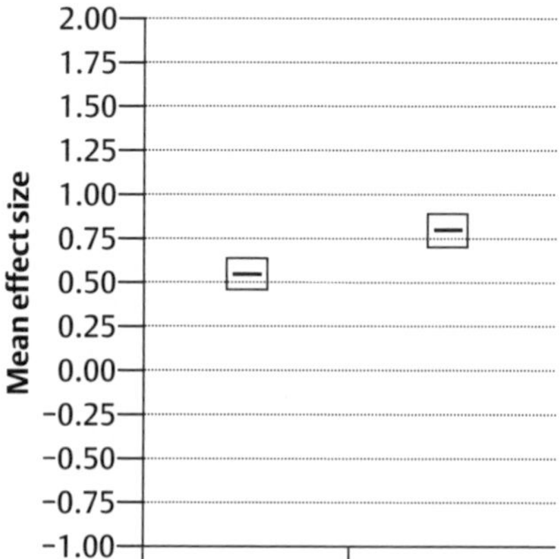

	Second language (k = 10)	Foreign language (k = 42)
CI upper (95%)	0.64	0.88
— Mean	0.55	0.79
CI lower (95%)	0.46	0.70

Figure 17.13 *Efficacy of interaction in different research contexts (immediate post-tests)*

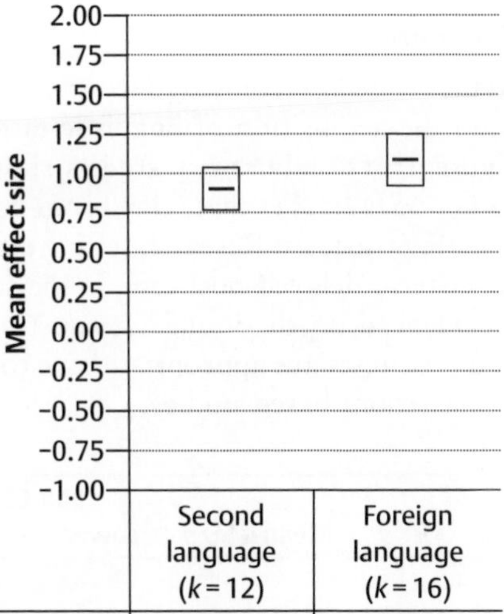

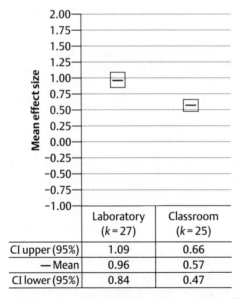

	Second language (k = 12)	Foreign language (k = 16)
CI upper (95%)	1.04	1.25
— Mean	0.90	1.08
CI lower (95%)	0.76	0.92

Figure 17.14 Efficacy of interaction in different research contexts (short-term delayed post-tests)

	Laboratory (k = 27)	Classroom (k = 25)
CI upper (95%)	1.09	0.66
— Mean	0.96	0.57
CI lower (95%)	0.84	0.47

Figure 17.15 Research setting and the efficacy of interaction on immediate post-tests

Research setting (classroom versus laboratory)

Laboratory- and classroom-based studies were also compared in terms of the efficacy of interactional treatments on the acquisition of linguistic targets. As evidenced in Table 17.7 and Figure 17.15, laboratory studies showed significantly larger effect sizes (M = .96, SD = .83) than classroom-based studies (M = .57, SD = .68) on immediate post-tests. Research setting effects also appeared on the short- and longer-term delayed post-tests in the same pattern of significant difference as evidenced on the immediate post-tests; however, no claims about the delayed post-tests are appropriate, due to the small number of treatment groups in classroom-based studies.

Independent variable	n	k	Mean d	SD d	95% CI Lower	95% CI Upper
Dependent measure						
Immediate						
Prompted response	5	16	.24	.56	.13	.34
Closed-ended prompted production	9	18	1.08	.93	.93	1.23
Open-ended prompted production	17	24	.68	.52	.61	.76
Short delay						
Prompted response	2	4	1.35	.66	.98	1.73
Closed-ended prompted production	5	10	1.48	1.13	1.18	1.78
Open-ended prompted production	7	18	.76	.33	.69	.82
Long delay						
Prompted response	0	-	-	-	-	-
Closed-ended prompted production	4	8	1.01	.68	.88	1.15
Open-ended prompted production	5	9	.61	.48	.51	.71

Table 17. 8 Effects of interaction in relation to dependent variable measures

Type of dependent measure

Of four types of dependent measures, adapted from Gass and Mackey's (2007) classification, only three dependent measure types were identified and analyzed: prompted response, closed-ended prompted production, and open-ended prompted production. On the immediate post-tests prompted response (a combination of metalinguistic judgment and selected response in Norris and Ortega's classification) resulted in small effect sizes, and open-ended prompted production measures (equivalent to free-constructed response in Norris and Ortega's classification) showed medium-to-large effect sizes and the difference between the two types is statistically significant. (See Table 17.8 and Figure 17.16.) Closed-ended prompted production (equivalent to Norris and Ortega's constrained constructed response) resulted in the largest mean effect size on the immediate post-tests. Although prompted response measures showed a large mean effect size on the short-term delayed post-tests, considering that only four treatment groups (from two sample studies) were involved in the analysis of the short-term delayed post-tests, any discussion in relation to prompted response measures does not appear appropriate. Closed-ended prompted production measures, however, resulted in significantly larger effect sizes than did open-ended prompted production measures on all three post-tests; nevertheless, more data on short-term and longer-term delayed post-tests seem necessary to make further claims on the role that each type of dependent measure plays in assessing treatment effects in interaction research. Our findings are different from those of Norris and Ortega, probably because the studies included in their meta-analysis are more diverse than those included in the current meta-analysis, as well as because of slightly different classifications of dependent measures.

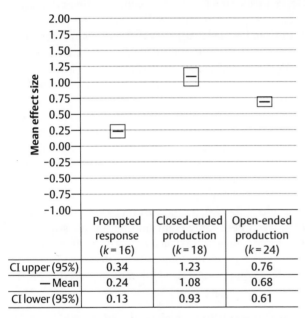

	Prompted response (k = 16)	Closed-ended production (k = 18)	Open-ended production (k = 24)
CI upper (95%)	0.34	1.23	0.76
— Mean	0.24	1.08	0.68
CI lower (95%)	0.13	0.93	0.61

Figure 17.16 Efficacy of interaction in different dependent variable measures (immediate post-tests)

Discussion

A variety of factors have been argued to mediate the relationship between interaction and L2 development. This meta-analysis set out to assess how effective interaction as a whole is , and what influences its efficacy. We wanted to know whether any new conclusions could be drawn regarding the effectiveness of theoretically important variables (i.e. the type of target feature; occurrence, type, and focus of feedback; and opportunities for modified output) in promoting the acquisition of lexical and grammatical target items through interaction. Another goal was to examine some of the methodological factors which may have impacted the findings in this area, many of which may have theoretical implications as well. Below, each of the major variables we considered is discussed in turn. We conclude this chapter, and the book, with an evaluation of the statistical methods and reporting conventions that tend to be employed in the field of interaction research, as well as a few recommendations for the future.

RQ1 How effective is interaction at promoting the acquisition of linguistic forms?

Interaction plays a strong facilitative role in the learning of lexical and grammatical target items. The 28 interaction studies qualified for the present meta-analysis showed large mean effect sizes across immediate and delayed post-tests, providing evidence of short-term as well as longer-term effects on language acquisition. Additional evidence for the effectiveness of interaction was also found in the comparison of interactional treatment conditions with conditions containing little or no interaction; statistically significant differences were found in the magnitude of change from pre-test to immediate post-test, with the interaction groups ($M = 1.09$, $SD = .93$) outperforming the control/comparison groups ($M = .44$, $SD = .42$); of 28 unique sample studies, 18 included comparison groups, which explains the medium mean effect size for the control/comparison group. Another interesting finding was that the delayed effects of interaction may be even stronger than immediate effects, supporting claims to this effect made by some researchers in the past (for example, Gass 1997; Gass, Mackey and Pica 1998; Mackey and Philp 1998). When interpreting these results, however, it is important to keep in mind that, of the 28 studies meta-analyzed here, only eight unique sample studies (13 treatment groups) administered longer-term delayed post-tests. It would thus be helpful for more studies to investigate the longer-term effects of interaction on language acquisition. (See Long 2006 for a different perspective on the value of delayed post-tests.)

RQ2(a) How does the type of target feature mediate the relationship between interaction and L2 developmental outcomes?

Although interaction is beneficial regardless of the linguistic form targeted, learners appear to benefit more on immediate post-tests from interaction targeting lexical items than from interaction targeting grammatical forms. The difference in the magnitude of the effect sizes between the two types of target features was significant at the alpha level of .05. This suggests that the overall large effect sizes found for interactional treatments on the immediate post-tests may be due to the effectiveness of interaction on the acquisition of lexical items, which is not consistent with the findings reported in Keck *et al.* (2006) of no difference in effect sizes between lexis and grammar. Because this is a key issue for interaction research, we investigated further. What we found to explain the difference is that first, our analysis included two new unique sample studies on lexis published after 2003, and the effect sizes calculated from these two studies are large (1.53, 1.96, 2.92 from Gass and Alvarez-Torres's 2005 study and 1.54, 1.48 from Jeon's study in this volume, for example, on the immediate post-tests). Second, four of the ten new sample studies on grammar that we added used comparison groups as opposed to the true control groups used in the two new studies on lexical learning, which we believe may have played a role in widening the gap between the two features. Finally, as shown in Appendix A, Keck *et al.* miscalculated the effect sizes for the treatment group in R. Ellis *et al.*'s (1994) Tokyo study (Casey Keck, personal communication). These factors provide some explanation for our finding that interactional treatments were more effective for lexis than they were for grammar, and that lexis may have been responsible for the large effect sizes on the immediate post-tests.

As many researchers have pointed out (for example, Mackey *et al.* 2000), grammatical feedback provided during interaction may be less immediately usable than lexical feedback. Some interaction researchers have suggested that there may be a delayed effect for interaction on grammar learning. Supporting this suggestion, in this study, we found the impact of interaction on grammar was greater than on lexis in the short-term and longer-term delayed post-tests, and the effect sizes for the treatment groups on lexical learning decreased to a large extent, which indicates that the efficacy of interaction on lexical learning may be strong immediately, but may not be long lasting, unlike the effect of interaction on grammar which takes longer to become effective but is then durable. However, only six treatment groups from three unique sample studies and two treatment groups from two unique sample studies were involved in the calculations of effect sizes for the lexical category on the short- and longer-term delayed post-tests, respectively, and more attention to the longer-term acquisition of lexical items through interaction seems important.

RQ2(b) How does the presence or absence of interactional feedback mediate the relationship between interaction and L2 developmental outcomes?

Interaction researchers have suggested that interactional feedback is one of the key beneficial features of interaction (for example, Long 1996, 2006; Gass 1997). When looking at immediate post-tests, there were no significant differences between feedback and no feedback conditions. However, looking at the short-term post-tests, a significant large effect for feedback was found although this difference was no longer significant in the delayed post-tests. Comparisons of feedback and no feedback conditions, however, are less meaningful when we take into account that since feedback is often an integral part of interaction, only a very small number of no feedback treatment groups were identified. The general lack of interactional treatments without feedback made it unproductive to attempt to draw comparisons. So, while evidence for positive effects of interactional feedback was found, it was not possible at this point in time to unequivocally state that interaction with feedback is more facilitative of L2 development than interaction alone.

In Russell and Spada's (2006) meta-analysis of research on the effectiveness of corrective feedback in a more general sense, the authors were able to apply the positive results they found to a refutation of Truscott's (1996, 1999) arguments against the practice of corrective feedback on both written and oral language. However, in some of the specific areas where their study overlapped with the current meta-analysis, however—for example, in investigating recasts versus other types of feedback, general versus specific focuses of feedback, and laboratory versus classroom contexts—comparisons of the findings (all of which were positive) tended to be inconclusive and demanding of more research. As they put it, 'the wide range of variables examined in CF [corrective feedback] research is spread rather thin' (p. 156). The discussion of these areas below will illustrate how the present study has taken some additional steps within this area. For instance, the inclusion of more studies (15 in their study, 28 in this one) allowed us to compare effect sizes in some cases, as in our investigation of type of target feature, treated above. At the same time, like Russell and Spada's, our meta-analysis also illustrates how much more work needs to be done in order for future meta-analyses to be able to draw firmer conclusions.

RQ2(c) How does the type of feedback which is provided mediate the relationship between interaction and L2 developmental outcomes?

Recasts have become one of the most commonly studied features of interaction. In this meta-analysis, they proved to be successful at generating learning, showing large effect sizes on all post-tests ($M = .96$, $SD = 1.04$ on immediate post-tests, $M = 1.69$, $SD = 1.13$ on short-term delayed post-tests, and $M = 1.22$, $SD = .85$ on longer-term delayed post-tests). Notwithstanding, more studies that investigate delayed post-tests need to be conducted before clear conclusions can be drawn regarding the effects of recasts on delayed post-tests (we used only seven treatment groups for the short-term delayed post-tests and five for the longer-term delayed post-tests). Even fewer empirical studies were found dealing with negotiation and metalinguistic feedback (for example, Takashima and Ellis 1999; McDonough 2005; R. Ellis *et al.* 2006), rendering any arguments for the efficacy of one kind of feedback over another premature. Another issue, discussed in the Introduction to this volume, is the need for greater theoretical specificity or practical motivations in making claims about the superiority of one feedback type over another. Instructors and interlocutors naturally use a range of feedback types, as is appropriate and natural during discourse.

RQ2(d) How does the focus of the feedback provided mediate the relationship between interaction and L2 developmental outcomes?

It has been proposed that feedback is more likely to be effective when it is provided consistently on a narrow set of linguistic forms, as opposed to being used somewhat arbitrarily to deal with whichever errors happen to arise in a communicative situation. As noted above, when Russell and Spada (2006) attempted to examine the relative effects of general versus specific focuses of feedback, they were not able to make any clear determinations due to the large mean effect sizes they found for both types. Similarly, in the present meta-analysis, medium-to-large mean effect sizes were evidenced for both general and specific focus conditions on the immediate post-tests ($M = .69$, $SD = .61$ for the general focus conditions and $M = .72$, $SD = .81$ for the specific conditions), their difference being non-significant. However, the specific focus conditions showed a significantly larger mean effect size than the general focus conditions on the short-term delayed post-tests ($M = .84$, $SD = .41$ for the general focus conditions and $M = 1.21$, $SD = .95$ for the specific focus conditions). Since the present meta-analysis deals with experimental and quasi-experimental studies, predominantly cross-sectional, most of the studies were designed to examine the effects of feedback on specific target features that were predetermined. That is, only a few treatment groups with more diffuse focus conditions were identified. More research on this issue may provide a clearer picture of the role that focus of feedback may play.

RQ2(e) How does the presence or absence of opportunities for modified output mediate the relationship between interaction and L2 developmental outcomes?

Swain (1985, 1995, 2005), in particular, has argued that learners need to be pushed to produce and modify their output for further language development to occur. With the exception of the immediate post-tests, our meta-analysis showed no differences between whether or not learners had opportunities to produce modified output, with both conditions being associated with large effect sizes. At first glance, it may be surprising that receiving interactional feedback but not having the opportunity to produce output resulted in significantly larger mean effect sizes on the immediate and longer-term delayed post-tests than receiving interactional feedback and having an opportunity to produce output. However, as briefly mentioned in the results section, not having any opportunity to produce modified output emerged not as one level of an independent variable, but in the course of controlling the amount of treatment; that is, for methodological reasons. The large effect sizes from Leeman's (2003) and Sagarra's (this volume) studies, for instance, are due to such factors as recasts and enhanced positive evidence, excluding any impact of presence or absence of modified output opportunities on effect sizes; in both studies effect sizes for the treatment groups with no modified output opportunity were calculated in contrast with the control/comparison group with no modified output opportunity, meaning no comparison was made in terms of opportunities for modified output. In other words, our findings regarding this issue do not justify claims about opportunities for modified output. Only one study (McDonough 2005) clearly investigated the efficacy of opportunities for modified output, showing effect sizes of 1.00 for the enhanced opportunity to modify group, .48 for the opportunity to modify group, and .0 for the feedback without opportunity to modify group. More research is necessary before any conclusive claims can be made regarding the effects of opportunities for modified output on language acquisition. For example, McDonough and Mackey (2006) have questioned the term 'modified output' and shown that delayed modified output was associated with learning, whereas immediate modified output was not.

Summary of major results

To summarize the major results related to the theoretically important features of interaction that we investigated, this meta-analysis found large effect sizes for interactional treatments compared with groups engaging in little or no interaction, indicating a facilitative role for interaction in L2 development. Importantly, these results showed up in delayed post-tests, providing empirical support for prior theoretical claims that the effects of interaction might be delayed. We also found that interaction tends to be more beneficial for lexis than grammar in the short-term, but more beneficial and durable for grammar in the longer-term. Recasts seem to be developmentally helpful, with large effect sizes across all post-tests; however, we cannot say they were more or less helpful than other sorts of feedback due to the insufficient number of studies. We need more studies in order to obtain a more clear-cut picture of the effectiveness of different types of feedback.

An important caveat to bear in mind, of course, is that none of these factors are truly independent of one another. For instance, the types of feedback which are provided, as well as the contexts of feedback, have both been linked in primary research studies to the amount of uptake and repair (or modified output) that learners produce (for example, Lyster and Ranta 1997; R. Ellis *et al.* 2001; Panova and Lyster 2002; Sheen 2004). Chaudron (1988) suggested that the amount of corrective feedback provided may be related to the classroom context (second or foreign language), among other things, and a study by Mackey *et al.* (2000) found that different types of linguistic features tend to receive different types of feedback. Another complication already mentioned is the fact that not all of the studies included in this meta-analysis included delayed post-tests; so the claim just made regarding the long-term effects of grammar over lexis must be interpreted with caution. Awareness of this potential circularity in terms of claims about the inter-related factors involved in these sorts of investigations is important for future researchers seeking to tease apart related constructs. It also leads toward a variety of questions regarding the potential influence of contextual and methodological factors, to which we turn next.

RQ2(f, g) What are the relationships between context, setting, and the L2 developmental outcomes that have been found in interaction research?

Foreign and second language contexts were compared. Research by Lyster and Mori (2006) and Sheen (2004) on corrective feedback and learner uptake in different instructional contexts has illustrated the importance of examining context as a potential influence. Research conducted in foreign language contexts appeared to produce stronger evidence for the effects of interaction than research conducted in second language contexts. This difference was statistically significant on the immediate post-tests. Also a large mean effect size for second-language contexts was observed only on the short-term delayed post-tests. Most of the studies meta-analyzed in this chapter (20 out of 28, or 71 per cent) were implemented in foreign language contexts. If more reliable differences were to be found with a greater number of second language contexts included in the analysis, one might speculate that a reason for such differences could be extra-experimental opportunities to interact in the L2 are presumably more readily available in second language contexts. In the absence of sufficient research on the question, however, this remains speculation. Of a total of seven unique sample studies of lexical learning, six were conducted in foreign language contexts. The only second language study is R. Ellis and He's (1999) research. Most of the six studies of lexical learning had large effect sizes, especially on the immediate post-test. In foreign language contexts, studies of grammar showed were much less effective on immediate post-tests. It is possible that interaction may be more effective on lexical learning than on grammar learning in foreign language contexts. We believe that this finding deserves more research attention.

A comparison of laboratory and classroom settings was also made, partially in response to questions that have been raised regarding the generalizability of interactional benefits observed in laboratory settings to the classroom (for example, Foster 1998; Nicholas *et al.* 2001). Researchers have pointed out that differences between laboratory and classroom settings may influence what learners perceive as important and that feedback may be more likely to be perceived as such in laboratory settings, where it is presumably more consistent and focused. A recent study by Gass *et al.* (2005) showed very few differences between the classroom and laboratory settings they studied in terms of the particular interactional features examined (differences corresponding instead to the types of tasks that were carried out), and Russell and Spada's (2006) meta-analysis did not find evidence of differences between the two types of setting, either. In the current meta-analysis, whereas laboratory studies showed large mean effect sizes across all three post-tests in a consistent manner, classroom studies showed large mean effect sizes only on short- and longer-term delayed post-tests (or close-to-large in the case of the longer-term delayed post-tests). The results associated with the two types of setting differed significantly from each other on all three post-tests, with laboratory studies showing larger effects for interaction. It is possible, then, as has been suggested, that the quantity and quality and often dyadic context for the provision of interactional treatments in laboratory settings may have contributed to this significant difference in the efficacy of interactional treatments on learner development between the two settings.

RQ2(h): What is the relationship between the type of dependent measure that is employed and the L2 developmental outcomes that have been found in interaction research?

Considering not only theoretical arguments regarding the types of linguistic knowledge that may be affected by various sorts of language activities (for example, Krashen 1982; Schwartz 1993; Truscott 1996), but also empirical findings suggesting that learners may perform more or less strongly on measures tapping different sorts of knowledge (Norris and Ortega 2000), we investigated the impact of the type of dependent measure employed on the outcomes of interaction studies. We found that the largest mean effect sizes were associated with closed-ended prompted production, followed by open-ended prompted production and prompted response measures. A small mean effect size for prompted response measures (for example, acceptability judgment and selected response) on immediate post-tests was observed in the current meta-analysis. Also, an increasing preference for use of open-ended prompted production measures in interaction research was witnessed, reflecting the focus on authentic language use, and the preference for matching the sort of interaction in the treatment to the test, in an effort to capture any effects in the most effective way.

Limitations and future research

Interaction research has certainly advanced in the sophistication and diversity of its research methodologies from its beginnings in the 1980s. For instance, as with SLA research in general, interaction researchers now pay considerable attention to issues of validity and reliability (Mackey and Gass 2006). However, like other meta-analysts (for example, Norris and Ortega 2000, 2006; Keck *et al.* 2006), we have found that reporting conventions have often not advanced far enough in terms of what is required for the purpose of meta-analyses and other comparisons. This is a limitation which probably reflects the status of interaction research as a relatively new subfield; however, that excuse is fast disappearing.

In following the lead of Norris and Ortega (2000) and evaluating the statistical methods and reporting conventions that have tended so far to be employed in interaction research, we found that none of the studies analyzed here reported confidence intervals or standard errors of the mean. Only seven studies (25 per cent) included a statement of a preset alpha level. The fact that effect sizes or strengths of association were provided in four studies (14 per cent) indicates a gradual improvement in reporting conventions. The journal *Language Learning* now also requires effect sizes to be reported. Only two of our sample studies reported the reliability of dependent variable measures, and both of these had the same first author (R. Ellis *et al.* 2006; R. Ellis this volume). Looking forward, it is clear that interaction research, including, of course, our own, would benefit from including such information. For instance, because effect sizes represent the magnitude of treatment effects, they enable other researchers to better understand research outcomes, which may lead to more constructive theoretical development. Norris and Ortega's (2006) book on meta-analyses will likely achieve a great deal in driving the field of SLA, including interaction research, forward.

As far as the present meta-analysis is concerned, we want to point out that, although we were able to include here about twice as many primary studies as there are in Keck *et al.*'s (2006) meta-analysis of interaction research and in Russell and Spada's (2006) meta-analysis of corrective feedback, like theirs, our analysis also suffered at times from an insufficient amount of data available on the stated constructs of interest. There were several important areas in which firm conclusions could not be drawn, and even the findings which we were able to put forward as reliable may not be applicable to contexts and learners whose characteristics have been relatively under-researched as of yet.

Furthermore, in carrying out this meta-analysis, we identified a variety of additional areas which, despite being theoretically and practically important, have thus far received scant attention. For instance, although it seems logical and has been observed by a number of descriptive studies that the effects of interaction may vary depending on the interlocutor, we found only two meta-analyzable published studies of interaction and L2 development in which the learners interacted with each other (R. Ellis and He 1999; Garcia and Asención 2001). Russell and Spada's (2006) meta-analysis, which included mostly a different set of primary studies due to its particular focus, contained no studies in which the participants provided each other with feedback. Such studies are important given the significant pedagogical value which information regarding the effectiveness of learner-generated feedback would have, as indicated in Keck *et al.*'s (2006) meta-analysis.

We expanded our inclusion criteria, compared to those of Keck *et al.* and Russell and Spada, in order to include studies on synchronous computer-mediated interactions. In practical terms, however, this did not amount to much of an expansion. Learners interacted with a pre-designed computer program providing synchronous interaction in only two computer-based studies which were utilized for this meta-analysis (Ayoun 2001; Sagarra this volume), and it appears to be the case that most computer-mediated communication studies or reports have been asynchronous and/or descriptive as opposed to developmental. More studies in this area would be helpful. Another important area ripe for additional research is the influence of interlocutor age on the effectiveness of interaction for language development. (See, for example, studies by Oliver 2000 and Mackey, Oliver, and Leeman 2003.) In sum, more research is clearly needed to investigate how the type of interlocutor may mediate the relationship between interaction and L2 learning so that future meta-analyses can address this issue.

Conclusion

The meta-analysis reported on in this chapter has investigated the efficacy of interaction in terms of the acquisition of lexical and grammatical target items. We expanded on and updated the research carried out by Keck *et al.* (2006) and Russell and Spada (2006), using their approaches as a point of departure, and combining the sorts of questions asked by each in an attempt to gain an updated and broad view of the state of interaction research. Our main results suggest that interaction facilitates the acquisition of both lexis and grammar to a great extent, with interaction having a stronger immediate effect on lexis, and a delayed and durable effect on grammar. Although feedback (including recasts) and modified output seem to be important interactional features that contribute to the beneficial effects of interaction for language learners on their acquisition of an L2, more research specifically designed to examine the effects of different feedback types and opportunities for modified output is necessary to obtain a clearer understanding of their roles in language learning. Our review of statistical tools and reporting conventions likewise indicates room for growth, but given the increased (and increasing) levels of awareness and methodological training among interaction researchers, we feel there is reason for real optimism in this area. Interaction research is alive and well, and contributing to the big picture of how second languages are learnt.

Appendix A

Summary table of unique sample studies[a]

Study report/treatment groups	n	Feedback type	Feedback focus	Modified output	Target feature	Imm post	Delay (7–29)	Delay (30–75)
Gass & Alvarez-Torres 2005								
Interaction only – vocabulary	26	.	S	+	L	1.53	.	.
Interaction + input – vocabulary	18	.	S	+	L	1.96	.	.
Input + interaction – vocabulary	19	.	S	+	L	2.92	.	.
Interaction only – gender	26	.	S	+	GR	-0.01	.	.
Interaction + input – gender	18	.	S	+	GR	0.19	.	.
Input + interaction – gender	19	.	S	+	GR	0.15	.	.
Interaction only – *estar*	26	.	S	+	GR	0.00	.	.
Interaction + input – *estar*	18	.	S	+	GR	0.33	.	.
Input + interaction – *estar*	19	.	S	+	GR	-0.17	.	.
Iwashita 2003								
Locative word order	41	.	S	+	GR	0.80	.	.
Locative particle use	41	.	S	+	GR	0.86	.	.
Verb morpheme (-*te*)	41	.	S	+	GR	0.66	.	.
Leeman 2003								
Recast – gender	18	Recast	S	–	GR	1.27	0.80	.
Recast – number	14	Recast	S	–	GR	1.82	1.29	.
Negative evidence – gender	18	Negotiation	S	–	GR	0.65	0.31	.
Negative evidence – number	17	Negotiation	S	–	GR	0.03	0.64	.
Enhanced salience – gender	18	.	NA	–	GR	1.44	0.93	.
Enhanced salience – number	18	.	NA	–	GR	0.88	1.00	.
Mackey & Philp 1998b								
Recast ready	9	Recast	S	+	GR	.	.	.
Recast unready	8	Recast	S	+	GR	.	.	.
Interactor ready	6	.	G	–	GR	.	.	.
Interactor unready	6	.	G	–	GR	.	.	.
Han 2002b	4	Recast	S	+	GR	1.17	1.57	.
Inagaki & Long 1999c								
Japanese adjective ordering	8	Recast	S	–	GR	1.23	.	.
Japanese locative construction	8	Recast	S	–	GR	0.37	.	.
R. Ellis, Tanaka, & Yamazaki 1994*								
Saitama study	24	.	NA	–	L	1.35	.	0.92
Tokyo study	42	.	NA	–	L	1.32	.	0.99
Garcia & Asención 2001	18	.	G	–	GR	0.22	.	.
de la Fuente 2002								
Negotiation plus output	11	.	S	+	L	1.68	1.92	.
Negotiation without output	8	.	NA	–	L	1.51	1.51	.

Study report/treatment groups	n	Feedback type	Feedback focus	Modified output	Target feature	Imm post	Delay (7–29)	Delay (30–75)
Ayoun 2001[d]	45	Recast	S	-	GR	0.56	.	.
Mackey & Oliver 2002[e]	11	.	G	+	GR	0.92	1.13	.
Mackey & Silver 2005[e]	14	.	S	+	GR	0.12	0.76	.
McDonough 2005								
Enhanced opp. to modify	15	Negotiation	S	+	GR	.	.	1.00
Opportunity to modify	15	Negotiation	S	+	GR	.	.	0.48
Feedback w/o opp. to modify	15	Negotiation	S	-	GR	.	.	0.00
Ishida 2004[b]	4	Recast	G	+	GR	.	.	.
R. Ellis this volume[f]								
Recast – comparative	12	Recast	S	+	GR	0.49	0.72	.
Metalinguistic – comparative	12	Metaling.	S	+	GR	0.57	0.68	.
McDonough this volume								
Clarification	23	Negotiation	S	+	GR	.	.	1.26
Recast	27	Recast	S	+	GR	.	.	0.81
Loschky 1994								
Vocabulary	13	.	G	-	L	0.06	.	.
Grammar	13	.	G	-	GR	-0.17	.	.
Mackey 1999								
Interactors	7	.	G	+	GR	.	1.16	.
Interactor unreadies	7	.	G	+	GR	.	1.51	.
Observers	7	.	NA	-	GR	.	0.88	.
Scripteds	6	.	NA	-	GR	.	0.06	.
Long, Inagaki, & Ortega 1998[c]								
Spanish object topicalization	12	Recast	S	-	GR	0.00		
Spanish adverb placement	12	Recast	S	-	GR	1.21		
R. Ellis & He 1999								
Negotiated output	16	.	G	+	L	1.24	1.38	.
Interactionally modified input	16	.	NA	-	L	0.48	0.30	.
Jeon this volume								
Interaction – nouns	30	.	G	+	L	1.54	0.40	.
Interaction – verbs	18	.	G	+	L	1.48	0.52	.
Interaction – object RCs	15	.	G	+	GR	1.25	0.56	.
Interaction – honorifics	25	.	G	+	GR	0.57	0.53	.
Loewen & Nabei this volume								
Recast	10	Recast	S	+	GR	0.35	.	.
Elicitation	8	Negotiation	S	+	GR	0.52	.	.
Metalinguistic feedback	7	Metaling.	S	+	GR	0.03	.	.
Interaction with no feedback	10	.	NA	-	GR	-0.89	.	.
Takashima & Ellis 1999*	27	Negotiation	S	+	GR	0.71	0.72	0.94

Study report/treatment groups	n	Feedback type	Feedback focus	Modified output	Target feature	Imm post	Delay (7–29)	Delay (30–75)
Sheen this volume[g]								
Recast	26	Recast	S	+	GR	0.03	.	0.17
Metalinguistic correction	26	.	S	+	GR	0.60	.	0.73
R. Ellis, Loewen, & Erlam 2006[f]								
Recast – past tense	12	Recast	S	+	GR	0.20	0.55	.
Metalinguistic – past tense	12	Metaling.	S	+	GR	0.87	1.95	.
Sagarra this volume[d]								
Spanish gender agreement	35	Recast	S	-	GR	2.52	2.84	2.20
Spanish number agreement	35	Recast	S	-	GR	4.02	3.51	2.38
McDonough & Mackey 2006[h]								
Recast	39	Recast	S	+	GR	.	.	1.06

[a] S = specific focus; G = general focus; NA = not applicable; + = with opportunity for modified output; - = without opportunity for modified output; GR = grammar; L = lexis; Metaling. = metalinguistic feedback; all effect sizes in the table are unbiased/corrected ones adjusted for the sample size.

[b] Only pre-to-post effect sizes were computed for Mackey and Philp (1998) because they did not report descriptive statistics for their control group. Also, we calculated only the pre-to-post effect size for Ishida (2004) as it is a time-series pre-post design without a control group.

[c] Long, Inagaki, and Ortega (1998) did not provide enough information on the Japanese study; thus, we used the Japanese data provided in Inagaki and Long (1999). For the Spanish data, we used Long, Inagaki, and Ortega (1998).

[d] Ayoun (2001) and Sagarra (this volume) are computer-based studies.

[e] Mackey and Oliver (2002) and Mackey and Silver (2005) are child language acquisition studies.

[f] Only the effect sizes for the comparatives in the oral imitation test were computed in R. Ellis (this volume), as participants already had explicit knowledge (their performance was quite high on the pre-tests of the other types). More detailed data on the past tense (oral imitation) are provided in R. Ellis, Loewen, and Erlam (2006).

[g] Since both recasts and metalinguistic feedback were used for the metalinguistic correction group in Sheen (this volume), we did not include the metalinguistic correction group in categorizing for feedback type.

[h] McDonough and Mackey (2006) utilized logistic regression in their study. Although regression analyses are not intended to indicate any causal relationship, this study was included in the present meta-analysis because it provided the necessary information for the calculation of Cohen's *h*. We decided to include this study because it was available to us in an in-press version at the time of our analysis. It has been published in the fourth issue of *Language Learning* 2006.

[*] Keck *et al.*'s miscalculation involved using the unweighted effect size of .64 for the Tokyo study. The corrected/unbiased effect size of 1.32 (the unweighted effect size of 1.33) was obtained in the current meta-analysis. The larger the sample is, the larger the relative weight that a related effect size carries, so the impact of the weighted effect size (1.32) calculated in our meta-analysis is more than twice as large as the unweighted effect size (.64) obtained in Keck *et al.*'s meta-analysis. Because only a small number of lexical studies were included in both meta-analyses, and weighted effect sizes were used in the current meta-analysis, it can be reasonably assumed that their miscalculation contributed, to a large extent, to the difference in terms of the efficacy of interaction on lexical learning between their meta-analysis and the current meta-analysis.

[**] Keck *et al.* misclassified Takashima and Ellis's (1999) study as lexical instead of grammar.

Appendix B

Studies included in the present meta-analysis

*Ayoun, D. 2001. 'The role of negative and positive feedback in the second language acquisition of the *passé composé* and *imparfait*.' *The Modern Language Journal* 85: 226–43.

**de la Fuente, M. J. 2002. 'Negotiation and oral acquisition of L2 vocabulary: The roles of input and output in the receptive and productive acquisition of words.' *Studies in Second Language Acquisition* 24: 81–112.

*Ellis, R. This volume. 'The differential effects of corrective feedback on two grammatical structures' in A. Mackey (ed.). *Conversational Interaction in Second Language Acquisition: A Collection of Empirical Studies*. Oxford: Oxford University Press.

a**Ellis, R. and X. He. 1999. 'The roles of modified input and output in the incidental acquisition of word meanings.' *Studies in Second Language Acquisition* 21: 285–301.

b**Ellis, R., Y. Tanaka, and A. Yamazaki. 1994. 'Classroom interaction, comprehension, and the acquisition of L2 word meanings.' *Language Learning* 44: 449–91.

*Ellis, R., S. Loewen, and R. Erlam. 2006. 'Implicit and explicit corrective feedback and the acquisition of L2 grammar.' *Studies in Second Language Acquisition* 28: 339–68.

**Garcia, P. and Y. Asención. 2001. 'Interlanguage development of Spanish learners: Comprehension, production, and interaction.' *Canadian Modern Language Review* 57: 377–402.

*Gass, S. M. and M. J. Alvarez-Torres. 2005. 'Attention when? An investigation of the ordering effect of input and interaction.' *Studies in Second Language Acquisition* 27: 1–31.

**Han, Z. 2002b. 'A study of the impact of recasts on tense consistency in L2 output.' *TESOL Quarterly* 36: 543–72.

**Inagaki, S. and M. H. Long. 1999. 'Implicit negative feedback' in K. Kanno (ed.). *The Acquisition of Japanese as a Second Language* (pp. 9–30). Philadelphia: John Benjamins.

*Ishida, M. 2004. 'Effects of recasts on the acquisition of the aspectual form *–te i-(ru)* by learners of Japanese as a foreign language.' *Language Learning* 54: 311–94.

**Iwashita, N. 2003. 'Negative feedback and positive evidence in task-based interaction: Differential effects on L2 development.' *Studies in Second Language Acquisition* 25: 1–36.

*Jeon, K. S. This volume. 'Interaction-driven L2 learning: characterizing linguistic development' in A. Mackey (ed.). *Conversational Interaction in Second Language Acquisition: A Collection of Empirical Studies*. Oxford: Oxford University Press.

* * *Leeman, J. 2003. 'Recasts and second language development.' *Studies in Second Language Acquisition* 25: 37–63.

*Loewen, S. and T. Nabei. This volume. 'Measuring the effects of oral corrective feedback on L2 knowledge' in A. Mackey (ed.). *Conversational Interaction in Second Language Acquisition: A Collection of Empirical Studies.* Oxford: Oxford University Press.

* * *Long, M. H., S. Inagaki, and L. Ortega. 1998. 'The role of implicit negative feedback in SLA: Models and recasts in Japanese and Spanish.' *The Modern Language Journal* 82: 357–71.

* *Loschky, L. 1994. 'Comprehensible input and second language acquisition: What is the relationship?' *Studies in Second Language Acquisition* 16: 303–23.

* *Mackey, A. 1999. 'Input, interaction, and second language development: An empirical study of question formation in ESL.' *Studies in Second Language Acquisition* 21: 557–87.

* *Mackey, A. and J. Philp. 1998. 'Conversational interaction and second language development: Recasts, responses, and red herrings?' *The Modern Language Journal* 82: 338–56.

*Mackey, A. and R. Oliver. 2002. 'Interactional feedback and children's L2 development.' *System* 30: 459–77.

*Mackey, A. and R. E. Silver. 2005. 'Interactional tasks and English L2 learning by immigrant children in Singapore.' *System* 33: 239–60.

*McDonough, K. 2005. 'Identifying the impact of negative feedback and learners' responses on ESL question development.' *Studies in Second Language Acquisition* 27: 79–103.

*McDonough, K. This volume. 'Interactional feedback and the emergence of simple past activity verbs in L2 English' in A. Mackey (ed.). *Conversational Interaction in Second Language Acquisition: A Collection of Empirical Studies.* Oxford: Oxford University Press.

*McDonough, K. and A. Mackey. 2006. 'Responses to recasts: Repetitions, primed production and linguistic development.' *Language Learning* 56/4: 693–720.

*Sagarra, N. This volume. 'From CALL to face-to-face interaction: the effect of computer-delivered recasts and working memory on L2 development' in A. Mackey (ed.). *Conversational Interaction in Second Language Acquisition: A Collection of Empirical Studies.* Oxford: Oxford University Press.

*Sheen, Y. This volume. 'The effects of corrective feedback, language aptitude, and learner attitudes on the acquisition of English articles' in A. Mackey (ed.). *Conversational Interaction in Second Language Acquisition: A Collection of Empirical Studies.* Oxford: Oxford University Press.

Takashima, H. and **R. Ellis.** 1999. 'Output enhancement and the acquisition of the past tense' in R. Ellis (ed.). *Learning a Second Language through Interaction* (pp. 173–88). Philadelphia: John Benjamins.

* Studies included only in the present meta-analysis.
** Studies included in both Keck *et al.*'s and the present meta-analyses.
*** Studies included in Keck *et al.*'s, Russell and Spada's, and the present meta-analyses.
   [a] R. Ellis and He's (1999) study is identical to He and Ellis's (1999) used in Keck *et al.*'s (2006) meta-analysis.
   [b] R. Ellis, Tanaka, and Yamazaki's (1994) study is identical to R. Ellis, Tanaka, and Yamazaki's (1995) used in Keck *et al.*'s meta-analysis.

Notes on the contributors

Rebecca Adams is Lecturer in Linguistics and Applied Language Studies at Victoria University of Wellington, New Zealand. Her interests include qualitative research, noticing and feedback, focus on form, and the role of interaction in second language learning.

Ahlem Ammar is Professor in Education at the University of Montreal. Her research interests centre on instructed second language acquisition.

Martha Bigelow is Associate Professor in Second Languages and Cultures Education at the University of Minnesota. Her research interests focus on intersections between literacy, identity, and immigrant education.

Takako Egi is Assistant Professor in Japanese language and linguistics in the Department of African and Asian Languages and Literatures at the University of Florida. Her research interests are input and interaction, attention and awareness, and verbal reports in SLA research methodology.

Rod Ellis is Professor in the Department of Applied Language Studies and Linguistics in the University of Auckland. He has published widely in the field of second language acquisition, focusing on the role of form-focused instruction. His recent books include *Task-based Language Learning and Teaching, Planning in Task-Based Performance*, and *Analysing Learner Language* (with Gary Barkhuizen).

Susan Gass is University Distinguished Professor in the Department of Linguistics and Languages at Michigan State University where she directs the English Language Center and the PhD program in Second Language Studies. She has published widely in the area of input and interaction. In 2006 she was President of the International Association of Applied Linguistics (AILA).

Elizabeth Gatbonton is Associate Professor of Applied Linguistics and is a member of the Center for the Study of Learning and Performance at Concordia University, Montreal. She teaches bilingualism and pedagogy. She has published articles on social issues in bilingualism, the pedagogical knowledge of experienced ESL teachers, and methodological issues in second language teaching and learning.

Jaemyung Goo is a PhD student of Applied Linguistics in the Department of Linguistics at Georgetown University. His research interests include interaction, corrective feedback, and acquisition of L2 syntactic features.

ZhaoHong Han is Associate Professor at Teachers College, Columbia University. Her research pertains to second language learnability and teachability. She has published in journals such as *Applied Linguistics*, *Second Language Research*, and *TESOL Quarterly*, edited volumes, and a monograph entitled *Fossilization in Adult Second Language Acquisition*.

K. Seon Jeon is Assistant Professor of Linguistics in Department of Language and Literature at Columbus State University, Columbus, GA. Her research interests are input and interaction in SLA, the role of language typology in language acquisition, and L2 pragmatics.

Ji-Hyun Kim is a doctoral candidate in TESOL at Teachers College, Columbia University. Her current research interests are learner noticing and corrective feedback in second language acquisition, and the interface of theory and practice in language learning and teaching.

Kim Lewis is a PhD student in Linguistics at Michigan State University where she teaches ESL. Her research interests focus on the effects of input and interaction and the second language acquisition of vocabulary.

Shawn Loewen is Assistant Professor in the Second Language Studies Program at Michigan State University. His research interests include L2 classroom interaction and incidental focus on form.

Roy Lyster is Associate Professor of Second Language Education and Co-Director of graduate programs in the Department of Integrated Studies in Education at McGill University. His research interests include classroom discourse, content-based instruction, and the integration of form-focused instruction and corrective feedback. He is President of the Canadian Association of Applied Linguistics.

Alison Mackey is Associate Professor and head of the Applied Linguistics Programs at Georgetown University where she teaches classes on second language acquisition and research design. She has published widely on her research interests, which include input, interaction and research methodology, and child L2 learning.

Kim McDonough is Assistant Professor of Applied Linguistics in the English Department at Northern Arizona University. Her research and teaching interests include interaction and second language development, syntactic priming, and task-based language teaching.

Toshiyo Nabei is Associate Professor in the Institute of Foreign Language Education and Research at Kansai University, Japan. Her research interests center on English education and language classroom interaction in Japanese context.

Lauren Ross-Feldman is a recent graduate of Georgetown University with a PhD in Applied Linguistics. Her research interests are focused on interaction in SLA, task-based language teaching, and the influence of learner gender on language learning.

Rebecca Sachs is a PhD candidate in Applied Linguistics at Georgetown University. Her interests include L2 learners' attentional processes and aptitudes, CALL, interaction, research methodology, and language testing. She is currently conducting research on awareness constraints on the effectiveness of corrective feedback.

Nuria Sagarra is Assistant Professor of Spanish/Linguistics at Penn State University. She investigates the effect of working memory on L2 morphosyntactic processing. She also examines how input simplification and enhancement, computer-delivered recasts, and simple tasks help reduce cognitive load and raise grammar consciousness.

Masatoshi Sato is an instructor of EFL in the Human International Universities and Colleges Consortium in Japan and a graduate of McGill University. His research interests include second language acquisition, interaction, and the procedualization of grammatical knowledge, especially with EFL learners.

Younghee Sheen is Assistant Professor in TESOL at American University, Washington DC. Her main area of interest is the role of corrective feedback and individual differences in instructed second language acquisition and she has published several articles on these topics.

Bo-Ram Suh is a PhD candidate in Applied Linguistics at Georgetown University. Her research interests include second language acquisition, attention and awareness, the effects of input, interaction and output, implicit and explicit learning, and second language acquisition research methodology.

Merrill Swain is Professor in the Second Language Education Program at OISE/UT. Her interests include bilingual education (particularly French immersion education) and communicative second language learning, teaching and testing. Her present research focuses on the role of 'languaging' in second language learning. She has published extensively in these areas. She is a past President of the American Association for Applied Linguistics.

Elaine Tarone is Distinguished Teaching Professor of English as a Second Language, and Director of the Center for Advanced Research on Language Acquisition, at the University of Minnesota. She has published widely on interlanguage development and variation theory in second language acquisition.

Agustina Tocalli-Beller completed her PhD in the Second Language Education Program at the Ontario Institute for Studies in Education of the University of Toronto. Her interests include bilingual education, conflict in collaborative activities, and language-play. She and her family have recently moved to Peru.

Pavel Trofimovich is Assistant Professor of Applied Linguistics at the TESL Centre in the Department of Education at Concordia University in Montreal and a member of the Centre for Study of Learning and Performance. His research and teaching focus on cognitive aspects of second language processing, second language phonology, sociolinguistic aspects of second language acquisition, and computer-assisted language learning.

Bibliography

Abu-Rabia, S. 2003. 'The influence of working memory on reading and creative writing processes in a second language.' *Educational Psychology* 23/2: 209–22.

Adams, R. This volume. 'Do second language learners benefit from interacting with each other?' in A. Mackey (ed.). *Conversational Interaction in Second Language Acquisition: A Collection of Empirical Studies.* Oxford: Oxford University Press.

Adams, R. 2006. 'L2 tasks and orientation to form: a role for modality?' *I.T.L. Review of Applied Linguistics* 152: 7–34.

Adrian, J. A., J. Alegría, and J. Morais. 1995. 'Metaphonological abilities of Spanish illiterate adults.' *International Journal of Psychology* 30: 329–53.

Alanen, R. 1995. 'Input enhancement and rule presentation in second language acquisition' in R. Schmidt (ed.). *Attention and Awareness in Foreign Language Learning.* Honolulu: University of Hawai'i Press.

America Online®. 2004. *AOL Instant Messenger*™ (computer web-based chat program). http://www.aim.com.

Ammar, A. and N. Spada. 2006. 'One size fits all? Recasts, prompts, and L2 learning.' *Studies in Second Language Acquisition* 28/4: 543–74.

Ammar, A., P. Trofimovich, and E. Gatbonton. 2006. 'What makes recasts noticeable? Contributions of learner proficiency and error type.' Manuscript in preparation.

Anderson, R. 1991. 'Developmental sequences: the emergence of aspect marking in second language acquisition' in T. Huebner and C. Ferguson (eds.). *Crosscurrents in Second Language Acquisition and Linguistic Theories.* Amsterdam: John Benjamins.

Anderson, R. and Y. Shirai. 1996. 'The primacy of aspect in first and second language acquisition: the pidgin-creole connection' in W. Ritchie and T. Bhatia (eds.). *Handbook of Second Language Acquisition.* San Diego, Calif.: Academic Press.

Arbuthnott, K. and J. Frank. 2000. 'Trail Making Test, Part B as a measure of executive control: validation using a set-switching paradigm.' *Journal of Clinical and Experimental Neuropsychology* 22: 518–28.

Aries, E. J. 1976. 'Interaction patterns and themes of male, female, and mixed groups.' *Small Group Behavior* 7/1: 7–18.

Aries, E. J. 1996. *Men and Women in Interaction: Reconsidering the Differences.* New York: Oxford University Press.

Ayoun, D. 2001. 'The role of negative and positive feedback in the second language acquisition of *passé composé* and *imparfait*.' *The Modern Language Journal* 85/2: 226–43.

Ayoun, D. 2004. 'The effectiveness of written recasts in the second language acquisition of aspectual distinctions in French: a follow-up study.' *The Modern Language Journal* 88/1: 31–55.

Baddeley, A. 2003. 'Working memory and language: an overview.' *Journal of Communication Disorders* 36/3: 189–208.

Baddeley, A., S. Gathercole, and C. Papagno. 1998. 'The phonological loop as a language learning device.' *Psychological Review* 105: 158–73.

Baddeley, A., C. Papagno, and G. Vallar. 1988. 'When long-term learning depends on short-term storage.' *Journal of Memory and Language* 27/5: 586–95.

Baker, W. and P. Trofimovich. 2006. 'Perceptual paths to accurate production of L2 vowels: the role of individual differences.' *International Review of Applied Linguistics* 44: 231–50.

Barcroft, J. 2003. 'Distinctiveness and bidirectional effects in input enhancement for vocabulary learning.' *Applied Language Learning* 13/2: 47–73.

Bardovi-Harlig, K. 1987. 'Markedness and salience in second language acquisition.' *Language Learning* 37/3: 385–407.

Bardovi-Harlig, K. 1992. 'The relationship of form and meaning: a cross-sectional study of tense and aspect in the interlanguage of learners of English as a second language.' *Applied Psycholinguistics* 13/2: 253–78.

Bardovi-Harlig, K. 1998. 'Narrative structure and lexical aspect: conspiring factors in the second language acquisition of tense-aspect morphology.' *Studies in Second Language Acquisition* 20/4: 471–508.

Bardovi-Harlig, K. 1999. 'From morpheme studies to temporal semantics: tense-aspect research in SLA.' *Studies in Second Language Acquisition* 21/3: 341–82.

Bardovi-Harlig, K. 2000. *Tense and Aspect in Second Language Acquisition: Form, Meaning and Use*. Oxford: Blackwell.

Bardovi-Harlig, K. and A. Bergström. 1996. 'The acquisition of tense and aspect in SLA and FLL: a study of learner narratives in English (SL) and French (FL).' *The Canadian Modern Language Review* 52/3: 308–30.

Bardovi-Harlig, K. and D. Reynolds. 1995. 'The role of lexical aspect in the acquisition of tense and aspect.' *TESOL Quarterly* 29/1: 107–31.

Basturkmen, H., S. Loewen, and R. Ellis. 2002. 'Metalanguage in focus on form in the communicative classroom.' *Language Awareness* 11/1: 1–13.

Beebe, L. M., T. Takahashi, and R. Uliss-Weltz. 1990. 'Pragmatic transfer in ESL refusals' in R. Scarcella, E. Andersen, and S. Krashen (eds.). *Developing Communicative Competence in a Second Language*. New York: Newbury House.

Bell, N. 2002. *Using and Understanding Humor in a Second Language: A Case Study*. Unpublished doctoral dissertation. University of Pennsylvania.

Beltz, J. 2002. 'Second language as a representation of the multicompetent self in foreign language study.' *Journal of Language, Identity, and Education* 1/1: 13–39.

Berns, M. 1990. '"Second" and "foreign" in second language acquisition/foreign language learning: a sociolinguistic perspective' in B. VanPatten and J. Lee (eds.). *Second Language Acquisition, Foreign-language Learning*. Clevedon, UK: Multilingual Matters.

Biber, D. 1988. *Variation Across Spoken and Written English*. Cambridge: Cambridge University Press.

Biber, D., R. Reppen, and S. Conrad. 2002. 'Developing linguistic literacy: perspectives from corpus linguistics and multi-dimensional analysis.' *Journal of Child Language* 29: 458–62.

Bigelow, M., B. delMas, K. Hansen, and E. Tarone. 2006. 'Literacy and the processing of oral recasts in SLA.' *TESOL Quarterly* 40: 665–89.

Blake, R. 2000. 'Computer mediated communication: a window on L2 Spanish interlanguage.' *Language Learning and Technology* 4: 120–36.

Bley-Vroman, R. 1989. 'What is the logical problem of foreign language learning?' in S. M. Gass and J. Schachter (eds.). *Linguistic Perspectives on Second Language Acquisition*. Cambridge: Cambridge University Press.

Block, D. 2003. *The Social Turn in Second Language Acquisition*. Washington, D.C.: Georgetown University Press.

Bohn, E. and R. Stutman. 1983. 'Sex-role differences in the relational control dimension of dyadic interaction.' *Women's Studies in Communication* 6/Fall: 96–104.

Bowles, M. A. and R. P. Leow. 2005. 'Reactivity and type of verbal report in SLA research methodology: expanding the scope of investigation.' *Studies in Second Language Acquisition* 27/3: 415–40.

Boxer, D. and F. Cortés-Conde. 1997. 'From bonding to biting: conversational joking and identity display.' *Journal of Pragmatics* 27/3: 257–94.

Braidi, S. M. 2002. 'Reexamining the role of recasts in native-speaker/nonnative-speaker interaction.' *Language Learning* 52: 1–42.

Brock, C., G. Crookes, R. Day, and M. Long. 1986. 'The differential effects of corrective feedback in native speaker–nonnative speaker conversation' in R. Day (ed.). *Talking to Learn: Conversation in Second Language Acquisition*. Rowley, Mass.: Newbury House.

Broner, M. and E. Tarone. 2001. 'Is it fun? Language play in a fifth-grade Spanish immersion classroom.' *The Modern Language Journal* 85/3: 363–79.

Brown, J. D. 1988. *Understanding Research in Second Language Learning*. New York: Cambridge University Press.

Brown, P. and S. Levinson. 1987. *Politeness: Some Universals in Language Usage*. Cambridge: Cambridge University Press.

Brown, R. 1973. *A First Language*. Cambridge, Mass.: Harvard University Press.

Bruton, A. and V. Samuda. 1980. 'Learner and teacher roles in the treatment of oral error ingroup work.' *RELC Journal* 11/2: 49–63.

Butler, Y. 2002. 'Second language learners' theories on the use of English articles.' *Studies in Second Language Acquisition* 24: 451–80.

Bygate, M., P. Skehan, and M. Swain. (eds.). 2001. *Researching Pedagogic Tasks: Second Language Learning, Teaching and Testing*. Harlow, UK: Pearson Education.

Cameron, D. 2003. 'Gender issues in language change.' *Annual Review of Applied Linguistics* 23: 187–201.

Campbell, R. and J. Rosenthal. 2000. 'Heritage languages' in J. Rosenthal (ed.). *Handbook of Undergraduate Second Language Education*. Mahwah, N.J.: Lawrence Erlbaum Associates.

Camps, J. 2003. 'Concurrent and retrospective verbal reports as tools to better understand the role of attention in second language tasks.' *International Journal of Applied Linguistics* 13/2: 201–21.

Carpenter, H., S. Jeon, D. MacGregor, and A. Mackey. 2006. 'Recasts as repetitions: learners' interpretations of native speaker responses.' *Studies in Second Language Acquisition* 28/2: 209–36.

Carreira, M. 2002. 'A Connectionist approach to enhancing the phonological competence of heritage language speakers of Spanish' in J. Sullivan (ed.). *Literacy and the Second Language Learner*. Greenwich, CT: Information Age Publishing.

Carroll, J. B. 1990. 'Cognitive abilities in foreign language aptitude: then and now' in T. Parry and C. Stansfield (eds.). *Language Aptitude Reconsidered*. Englewood Cliffs, N.J.: Prentice Hall.

Carroll, J. B. and S. M. Sapon. 1958. *Modern Language Aptitude Test*. New York: The Psychological Corporation.

Carroll, S. 1995. 'The irrelevance of verbal feedback to language learning' in L. Eubank, L. Selinker, and M. Sharwood Smith (eds.). *The Current State of Interlanguage*. Amsterdam: John Benjamins.

Carroll, S. 1999. 'Putting "input" in its proper place.' *Second Language Research* 15/4: 337–88.

Carroll, S. 2001. *Input and Evidence: The Raw Material of Second Language Acquisition*. Amsterdam: John Benjamins.

Carroll, S. and M. Swain. 1993. 'Explicit and implicit negative feedback: An empirical study of the learning of linguistic generalizations.' *Studies in Second Language Acquisition* 15: 357–86.

Carter, R. 2004. *Language and Creativity. The Art of Common Talk*. London: Routledge.

Carter, R. and M. McCarthy. 2004. 'Talking, creating: interactional language, creativity, and context.' *Applied Linguistics* 25/1: 62–88.

Castañeda, M. E. 2005. *Corrective Feedback in Online Asynchronous and Synchronous Environments in Spanish as a Foreign Language Classes*. Unpublished doctoral dissertation. University of South Florida.

Castro-Caldas, A., K. M. Petersson, A. Reis, S. Stone-Elander, and M. Ingvar. 1998. 'The illiterate brain: learning to read and write during childhood influences the functional organization of the adult brain.' *Brain* 121: 1053–63.

Cathcart, R. and J. Olsen. 1976. 'Teachers' and students' preferences for correction of classroom conversation errors' in J. E. Fanselow and R. Crymes (eds.). *On TESOL 76*. Washington, D.C.: TESOL

Celce-Murcia, M. and D. Larsen-Freeman. 1999. *The Grammar Book: An ESL/EFL Teacher's Course (Second edition)*. Boston: Heinle and Heinle.

Chant, S. and N. Craske. 2003. *Gender in Latin America*. New Brunswick, N.J.: Rutgers University Press.

Chapelle, C. 1998. 'Research on the use of technology in TESOL: analysis of interaction sequences in computer-assisted language learning.' *TESOL Quarterly*, 32/4: 753–7.

Chapelle, C. 2001. *Computer Applications in Second Language Acquisition: Foundations for Teaching, Testing, and Research*. Cambridge: Cambridge University Press.

Chaudron, C. 1977. 'A descriptive model of discourse in the corrective treatment of learners' errors.' *Language Learning* 27: 29–46.

Chaudron, C. 1988. *Second Language Classrooms: Research on Teaching and Learning*. Cambridge: Cambridge University Press.

Chaudron, C. 2003. 'Data collection in SLA research' in C. Doughty and M. H. Long (eds.). *Handbook of Second Language Acquisition*. Malden, Mass.: Blackwell.

Chenoweth, A., R. Day, A. Chun, and S. Luppescu. 1983. 'Attitudes and preferences of ESL students to error correction.' *Studies in Second Language Acquisition* 6: 79–87.

Cho, S. 1999. *The Acquisition of Relative Clauses: Experimental Studies on Korean*. Unpublished doctoral dissertation. University of Hawai'i.

Choi, M-Y. 2000. *Effects of Recasts on Irregular Past Tense Verb Morphology in Web-Chat*. Unpublished MA thesis. University of Hawai'i.

Choi, S. 1999. 'Acquisition of Korean' in O. L. Taylor and L. Leonard (eds.). *Language Acquisition Across North America: Cross-cultural Perspectives*. San Diego, Calif.: Singular Publishing Group, Inc.

Chun, D.M. 1994. 'Using computer networking to facilitate the acquisition of interactive competence.' *System* 22/1: 17–31.

Cicogna, C., M. Danesi, and A. Mollica. 1992. *Problem-solving in Second-language Teaching*. Welland, Ont.: Éditions Soleil Publishing Inc.

Coates, J. 1993. *Women, Men and Language: A Sociolinguistic Account of Gender Differences in Language*. London: Longman.

Cohen, J. 1988. *Statistical Power Analysis for the Behavioral Sciences* (Second edition). Hillsdale, N.J.: Lawrence Erlbaum Associates.

Cohen, J. 1992. 'Quantitative methods in psychology: A power primer.' *Psychological Bulletin* 112: 155–9.

Cook, G. 1996. 'Language play in English' in J. Maybin and N. Mercer (eds.). *Using English from Conversation to Canon*. London: Routledge.

Cook, G. 1997. 'Language play, language learning.' *ELT Journal* 51/3: 224–31.

Cook, G. 2000. *Language Play, Language Learning*. Oxford: Oxford University Press.

Corrigan, J. and N. Hinkeldey. 1987. 'Relationships between Parts A and B of the Trail Making Test'. *Journal of Clinical Psychology* 43: 402–09.

Coupland, J. 2000. *Small Talk*. London: Longman.

Cowan, N. 1988. 'Evolving conceptions of memory storage, selective attention, and their mutual constraints within the human information processing system.' *Psychological Bulletin* 104/2: 163–91.

Crookes, G. and S. M. Gass (eds.). 1993a. *Tasks in a Pedagogical Context: Integrating Theory and Practice*. Clevedon, UK: Multilingual Matters.

Crookes, G. and S. M. Gass (eds.). 1993b. *Tasks and Language Leaning: Integrating Theory and Practice*. Clevedon, UK: Multilingual Matters.

Crystal, D. 1998. *Language Play*. London: Penguin Books Ltd.

Danesi, M. 1989. *Puzzles and Games in Language Teaching*. Lincolnwood, Ill.: National Textbook.

Danesi, M. 2002. *The Puzzle Instinct: The Meaning of Puzzles in Human Life*. Bloomington, Ind.: Indiana University Press.

Danesi, M. 2003. *Second Language Teaching: A View from the Right Side of the Brain*. Dordrecht, Boston: Kluwer Academic.

Danesi, M. and A. Mollica. 1994. 'Games and puzzles in the second language classroom: a second look.' *Mosaic* 2/2: 13–22.

Davies, A., A. Brown, C. Elder, K. Hill, T. Lumley, and T. McNamara. 1999. *Dictionary of Language Testing*. Cambridge: University of Cambridge Local Examinations Syndicate.

Davies, A. and C. Elder. 2004. *The Handbook of Applied Linguistics*. Malden, Mass.: Blackwell.

de Graaff, R. 1997. *Differential Effects of Explicit Instruction on Second Language Acquisition*. Netherlands: Holland Institute of Generative Linguistics.

DeKeyser, R. 1993. 'The effect of error correction on L2 grammar knowledge and oral proficiency.' *The Modern Language Journal* 77: 501–14.

DeKeyser, R. 1995. 'Learning second language grammar rules: an experiment with a miniature linguistic system.' *Studies in Second Language Acquisition* 17: 379–410.

DeKeyser, R. 1998. 'Beyond focus on form: cognitive perspective on learning and practicing second language grammar' in C. Doughty and J. Williams (eds.). *Focus on Form in Classroom Second Language Acquisition*. New York: Cambridge University Press.

DeKeyser, R. 2000. 'The robustness of critical period effects in second language acquisition.' *Studies in Second Language Acquisition* 22: 499–533.

DeKeyser, R. 2005. 'What makes learning second language grammar difficult? A review of issues.' *Language Learning* 55/S1: 1–25.

de la Fuente, M. J. 2002. 'Negotiation and oral acquisition of L2 vocabulary: the roles of input and output in the receptive and productive acquisition of words.' *Studies in Second Language Acquisition* 24: 81–112.

de la Fuente, M. J. 2003. 'Is SLA interactionist theory relevant to CALL? A study on the effects of computer-mediated interaction in L2 vocabulary acquisition.' *Computer Assisted Language Learning* 16/1: 47–81.

Demetras, M., K. Post, and C. Snow. 1986. 'Feedback to first language learners: the role of repetition and clarification requests.' *Journal of Child Language* 13: 275–92.

Deville, C. and M. Chalhoub-Deville. 2006. 'Old and new thoughts on test score variability: implications for reliability and validity' in M. Chalhoub-Deville, C. Chapelle, and P. Duff (eds.). *Inference and Generalizability in Applied Linguistics: Multiple Perspectives*. Amsterdam: John Benjamins.

Dewaele, J. M. and D. Véronique. 2001. 'Gender assignments and gender agreement in advanced French interlanguage: a cross-sectional study.' *Bilingualism: Language and Cognition* 4: 275–97.

Donato, R. 1994. 'Collective scaffolding in second language learning' in J. Lantolf and G. Appel (eds.). *Vygotskian Approaches to Second Language Research*. Norwood, N.J.: Ablex.

Donato, R. 2000. 'Sociocultural contributions to understanding a foreign and second language classroom' in J. Lantolf (ed.). *Sociocultural Theory and Second Language Learning*. Oxford: Oxford University Press.

Donders, J., D. S. Tulsky, and J. J. Zhu. 2001. 'Criterion validity of new WAIS-III subtest scores after traumatic brain injury.' *Journal of the International Neuropsychological Society* 7: 892–98.

Dörnyei, Z. 2005. *The Psychology of the Language Learner*. Mahwah, N.J.: Lawrence Erlbaum Associates.

Doughty, C. 2001. 'The cognitive underpinnings of focus on form' in P. Robinson (ed.). *Cognition and Second Language Instruction*. Cambridge: Cambridge University Press.

Doughty, C. 2003. 'Effects of instruction on learning a second language: a critique of instructed SLA research' in B. VanPatten, J. Williams, and S. Rott (eds.). *Form-Meaning Connections in Second Language Acquisition*. Mahwah, N.J.: Lawrence Erlbaum Associates.

Doughty, C. and **M. H. Long** (eds.). 2003a. *Handbook of Second Language Acquisition.* Oxford: Blackwell Publishing.

Doughty, C. and **M. H. Long**. 2003b. 'Optimal psycholinguistic environments for distance foreign language learning.' *Language Learning and Technology* 7: 50–80.

Doughty, C. and **E. Varela**. 1998. 'Communicative focus on form' in C. Doughty and J. Williams (eds.). *Focus on Form in Classroom Second Language Acquisition.* New York: Cambridge University Press.

Doughty, C. and **J. Williams** (eds.). 1998. *Focus on Form in Classroom Second Language Acquisition.* New York: Cambridge University Press.

Douglas, D. 2001. 'Performance consistency in second language acquisition and language testing research: A conceptual gap.' *Second Language Research* 17: 442–56.

Dulay, H., **M. Burt**, and **S. Krashen**. 1982. *Language Two.* New York: Oxford University Press.

Eckert, P. 1998. 'Gender and sociolinguistic variation' in J. Coates (ed.). *Language and Gender: A Reader.* Oxford: Blackwell.

Efron, B. and **R. J. Tibshirani**. 1993. *An Introduction to the Bootstrap* (Monographs on Statistics and Applied Probability 57). New York: Chapman and Hall.

Eggins, S. and **D. Slade**. 1997. *Analysing Casual Conversation.* London New York: Cassell.

Egi, T. 2004. 'Verbal reports, noticing, and SLA research.' *Language Awareness* 13/4: 243–64.

Egi, T. 2005. 'Interpreting recasts as linguistic evidence: the modularity role of length and degree of change.' Unpublished manuscript. Georgetown University.

Egi, T. This volume. 'Recasts, learners' interpretations, and L2 development' in A. Mackey (ed.). *Conversational Interaction in Second Language Acquisition: A Collection of Empirical Studies.* Oxford: Oxford University Press.

Ehrman, M. and **R. Oxford**. 1995. 'Cognition plus: correlates of language learning success.' *The Modern Language Journal* 79: 67–89.

Ellis, N. C. 1996. 'Sequencing in SLA: phonological memory, chunking and points of order.' *Studies in Second Language Acquisition* 18/1: 91–126.

Ellis, N. C. 1998. 'Emergentism, connectionism and language learning.' *Language Learning* 48/4: 631–64.

Ellis, N. C. 1999. 'Cognitive approaches to SLA.' *Annual Review of Applied Linguistics* 19: 22–42.

Ellis, N. C. 2002. 'Frequency effects in language processing.' *Studies in Second Language Acquisition* 24/2: 143–88.

Ellis, N. C. 2005. 'At the interface: dynamic interactions of explicit and implicit language knowledge.' *Studies in Second Language Acquisition* 27/2: 305–52.

Ellis, N. C. and **S. G. Sinclair**. 1996. 'Working memory and the acquisition of vocabulary and syntax: putting language in good order.' *Quarterly Journal of Experimental Psychology* 49/A: 234–50.

Ellis, R. 1994a. *The Study of Second Language Acquisition.* Oxford University Press.

Ellis, R. 1994b. 'A theory of instructed second language acquisition' in N. Ellis (ed.). *Implicit and Explicit Learning of Languages.* London: Academic Press.

Ellis, R. 1999. *Learning a Second Language through Interaction.* Philadelphia: John Benjamins.

Ellis, R. 2000. 'Task-based research and language pedagogy.' *Language Teaching Research* 4/3: 193–220.

Ellis, R. 2001. 'Non-reciprocal tasks, comprehension, and second language acquisition' in M. Bygate, P. Skehan, and M. Swain (eds.). *Researching Pedagogic Tasks: Second Language Learning, Teaching, and Testing.* Harlow: Pearson.

Ellis, R. 2003. *Task-Based Language Learning and Teaching.* Oxford: Oxford University Press.

Ellis, R. 2004. 'The definition and measurement of L2 explicit knowledge.' *Language Learning* 54: 227–75.

Ellis, R. 2005. 'Measuring implicit and explicit knowledge of a second language: a psychometric study.' *Studies in Second Language Acquisition* 27/2: 141–72.

Ellis, R. 2006. 'Researching the effects of form-focussed instruction on L2 acquisition.' *AILA Review* 19: 18–41.

Ellis, R. This volume. 'The differential effects of corrective feedback on two grammatical structures' in A. Mackey (ed.). *Conversational Interaction in Second Language Acquisition: A Collection of Empirical Studies.* Oxford: Oxford University Press.

Ellis, R. and G. Barkhuizen. 2005. *Analysing Learner Language.* Oxford: Oxford University Press.

Ellis, R., H. Basturkmen, and S. Loewen. 2001a. 'Learner uptake in communicative ESL lessons.' *Language Learning* 51/2: 281–318.

Ellis, R., H. Basturkmen, and S. Loewen. 2001b. 'Preemptive focus on form in the ESL classroom.' *TESOL Quarterly* 35/3: 407–32.

Ellis, R., H. Basturkmen, and S. Loewen. 2002. 'Doing focus on form.' System 30/4: 419–32.

Ellis, R. and X. He. 1999. 'The roles of modified input and output in the incidental acquisition of word meanings.' *Studies in Second Language Acquisition* 21/2: 285–301.

Ellis, R. and R. Heimbach. 1997. 'Bugs and birds: children's acquisition of second language vocabulary through interaction.' *System* 25/2: 247–59.

Ellis, R., S. Loewen, and R. Erlam. 2006. 'Implicit and explicit corrective feedback and the acquisition of L2 grammar.' *Studies in Second Language Acquisition* 28: 339–68.

Ellis, R. and Y. Sheen. 2006. 'Re-examining the role of recasts in second language acquisition.' *Studies in Second Language Acquisition* 28: 575–600.

Ellis, R., Y. Tanaka, and A. Yamazaki. 1994. 'Classroom interaction, comprehension and the acquisition of L2 word meanings.' *Language Learning* 44/3: 449–491.

Epstein, S. D., S. Flynn, and G. Martohardjono. 1996. 'Second language acquisition: theoretical and experimental issues in contemporary research.' *Behavioral and Brain Sciences* 19: 677–714.

Epstein, S. D., S. Flynn, and G. Martohardjono. 1998. 'The strong continuity hypothesis: some evidence concerning functional categories in adult SLA' in S. Flynn, G. Martohardjono, and G. O'Neil (eds.). *The Generative Study of Second Language Acquisition.* Mahwah, N.J.: Lawrence Erlbaum Associates.

Ericsson, K. and N. Charness. 1994. 'Expert performance: its structure and acquisition.' *American Psychologist* 49/8: 725–47.

Ericsson, K. and H. Simon. 1984. *Protocol Analysis: Verbal Report as Data.* Cambridge, Mass.: MIT Press.

Ericsson, K. and H, Simon. 1993. *Protocol Analysis: Verbal Reports as Data* (Second edition). Boston: MIT Press.

Erlam, R. 2006. 'Elicited imitation as a measure of L2 implicit knowledge: an empirical validation study.' *Applied Linguistics* 27/3: 464–91.

Eubank, L. 1993/94. 'On the transfer of parametric values in L2 development.' *Language Acquisition* 3/3: 183–208.

Eubank, L. 1996. 'Negation in early German-English interlanguage: more valueless features in the L2 initial stage.' *Second Language Research* 12: 73–106.

Eviatar, Z. 1998. 'Attention as a psychological entity and its effects on language and communication' in B. Stemmer and H. A. Whitaker (eds.). *Handbook of Neurolinguistics.* New York: Academic Press.

Farrar, M. 1992. 'Negative evidence and grammatical morpheme acquisition.' *Developmental Psychology* 28/1: 90–8.

Finnemann, M. D. 1992. 'Learning agreement in the noun phrase: the strategies of three first-year Spanish students.' *International Review of Applied Linguistics in Language Teaching* 30: 121–36.

Fishman, J. 2001. '300-plus years of heritage language education in the United States' in J. Peyton, D. Ranard, and S. McGinnis (eds.). *Heritage Languages in America: Preserving a National Resource.* Washington, D.C.: Center for Applied Linguistics.

Fishman, P. M. 1978. 'Interaction: the work women do.' *Social Problems* 25/4: 397–406.

Fodor, J. A. 1983. *Modularity of Mind*. Cambridge, Mass.: MIT Press.

Foster, P. 1998. 'A classroom perspective on the negotiation of meaning.' *Applied Linguistics* 19/1: 1–23.

Foster, P. and A. Ohta. 2005. 'Negotiation for meaning and peer assistance in second language classrooms.' *Applied Linguistics* 26: 402–30.

Futaba, T. 2001. 'A task works for negotiation of meaning' in *JALT Applied Materials*. Tokyo: Japan Association for Language Teaching.

Galliano, G. 2003. *Gender: Crossing Boundaries*. Belmont, Calif.: Wadsworth/Thomson Learning.

Garcia, P. and Y. Asención. 2001. 'Interlanguage development of Spanish learners: comprehension, production, and interaction.' *Canadian Modern Language Review* 57: 377–402.

García-Mayo, M. P. 2005. 'Interactional strategies for interlanguage communication: do they provide evidence for attention to form?' in A. Housen and M. Pierrard (eds.). *Investigations in Instructed Second Language Acquisition. Studies on Language Acquisition Series*. Berlin: Mouton de Gruyter.

García-Mayo, M. P. and T. Pica. 2000. 'L2 learner interaction in a foreign language setting: are learning needs addressed?' *International Review of Applied Linguistics* 38/1: 35–58.

Gass, S. M. 1980. 'An investigation of language transfer in adult second language learners' in R. Scarcella and S. Krashen (eds.). *Research in Second Language Acquisition*. Rowley, Mass.: Newbury House.

Gass, S. M. 1997. *Input, Interaction, and the Second Language Learner*. Mahwah, N.J.: Lawrence Erlbaum Associates.

Gass, S. M. 2003. 'Input and interaction' in C. Doughty and M. H. Long (eds.). *The Handbook of Second Language Acquisition*. Oxford: Blackwell.

Gass, S. M. and M. J. Alvarez Torres. 2005. 'Attention when? An investigation of the ordering effect of input and interaction.' *Studies in Second Language Acquisition* 27/1: 1–31.

Gass, S. M. and Lewis, K. This volume. 'Perceptions of interactional feedback: differences between heritage language learners and non-heritage language learners' in A. Mackey (ed.). *Conversational Interaction in Second Language Acquisition: A Collection of Empirical Studies*. Oxford: Oxford University Press.

Gass, S. M. and A. Mackey. 2000. *Stimulated Recall Methodology in Second Language Research*. Mahwah, N.J.: Lawrence Erlbaum Associates.

Gass, S. M. and A. Mackey. 2002. 'Frequency effects and second language acquisition.' *Studies in Second Language Acquisition* 24/2: 249–60.

Gass, S. M. and A. Mackey. 2006. 'Input, interaction and output in SLA' in B. VanPatten and J. Williams (eds.). *Theories in Second Language Acquisition: An Introduction*. Mahwah, N.J.: Lawrence Erlbaum Associates.

Gass, S. M. and A. Mackey. 2007. *Data Elicitation for Second and Foreign Language Research*. Mahwah, N.J.: Lawrence Erlbaum Associates.

Gass, S. M., A. Mackey, and T. Pica. 1998. 'The role of input and interaction in second language acquisition: Introduction to the special issue.' *The Modern Language Journal* 82/3: 299–307.

Gass, S. M., A. Mackey, and L. Ross-Feldman. 2005. 'Task-based interactions in classroom and laboratory settings.' *Language Learning* 55/4: 575–611.

Gass, S. M. and L. Selinker. 2001. *Second Language Acquisition: An Introductory Course*. Mahwah, N.J.: Lawrence Erlbaum Associates.

Gass, S. M., I. Svetics, and S. Lemelin. 2003. 'Differential effects of attention.' *Language Learning* 53/3: 497–546.

Gass, S. M. and E. Varonis. 1984. 'The effect of familiarity on the comprehensibility of nonnative speech.' *Language Learning* 34/1: 65–89.

Gass, S. M. and E. Varonis. 1985a. 'Task variation and nonnative/nonnative negotiation of meaning' in S. M. Gass and C. Madden (eds.). *Input in Second Language Acquisition*. Rowley, Mass.: Newbury House.

Gass, S. M. and E. Varonis. 1985b. 'Variation in native speaker speech modification to nonnative speakers.' *Studies in Second Language Acquisition* 7/1: 37–58.

Gass, S. M. and E. Varonis. 1986. 'Sex differences in NNS/NNS interactions' in R. Day (ed.). *Talking to Learn: Conversation in Second Language Acquisition.* Rowley, Mass.: Newbury House.

Gass, S. M. and E. Varonis. 1989. 'Incorporated repairs in nonnative discourse' in M. Eisenstein (ed.). *The Dynamic Interlanguage.* New York: Plenum Press.

Gass, S. M. and E. Varonis. 1994. 'Input, interaction, and second language production.' *Studies in Second Language Acquisition* 16: 283–302.

Gathercole, S. E. and A. D. Baddeley. 1990. 'The role of phonological memory in vocabulary acquisition: a study of young children learning new names.' *British Journal of Psychology* 81: 439–54.

Gathercole, S. E., S. J. Pickering, M. Hall, and S. M. Peaker. 2001. 'Dissociable lexical and phonological influences on serial recognition and serial recall.' *Quarterly Journal of Experimental Psychology* 54/A: 1–30.

Geva, E. and E. B. Ryan. 1993. 'Linguistic and cognitive correlates of academic skills in first and second languages.' *Language Learning* 43: 5–42.

Goldschneider, J. M. and R. M. DeKeyser. 2001. 'Explaining the "natural order of L2 morpheme acquisition" in English: a meta-analysis of multiple determinants.' *Language Learning* 51/1: 1–50.

Gonzalez Velasquez, M. D. 1995. 'Sometimes Spanish, sometimes English: language use among rural New Mexican Chicanas' in K. Hall and M. Bucholtz (eds.). *Gender Articulated: Language and the Socially Constructed Self.* New York: Routledge.

Good, P. I. 2001. *Resampling Methods: A Practical Guide to Data Analysis.* Boston: Birkhauser.

Grevisse, M. 1993. *Le bon usage* (Treizième édition). Paris: Duculot.

Gutmann, M. C. 1997a. 'The meanings of macho: changing Mexican male identities' in L. Lamphere, L. H. Ragone, and P. Zavella (eds.). *Situated Lives: Gender and Culture in Everyday Life.* New York: Routledge.

Gutmann, M. C. 1997b. 'Seed of the nation: men's sex and potency in Mexico' in R. N. Lancaster and M. di Leonardo (eds.). *The Gender/Sexuality Reader: Culture, History, Political Economy.* New York: Routledge.

Hall, J. K. and L. S. Verplaetse (eds.). 2000. *Second and Foreign Language Learning through Classroom Interaction.* Mahwah, N.J.: Lawrence Erlbaum Associates.

Han, Y. 2000. Grammaticality judgment tests: how reliable and valid are they? *Applied Language Learning* 11: 177–204.

Han, Z-H. 2001. 'Fine-tuning corrective feedback.' *Foreign Language Annals* 34/6: 582–99.

Han, Z-H. 2002a. 'Rethinking corrective feedback in communicative language teaching.' *RELC Journal* 33/1: 1–33.

Han, Z-H. 2002b. 'A study of the impact of recasts on tense consistency in L2 output.' *TESOL Quarterly* 36/4: 543–72.

Han, Z-H. 2004. *Fossilization in Adult Second Language Acquisition.* Clevedon: Multilingual Matters.

Han, Z-H. and S. Peverly. 2007. 'Input processing: a study of *ab initio* learners with multilingual backgrounds.' *The International Journal of Multilingualism* 4/1: 17–37.

Hansen, K. 2005. *Impact of Literacy Level and Task Type on Oral L2 Recall Accuracy.* Unpublished MA thesis. University of Minnesota.

Harley, B. 1993. 'Instructional strategies and SLA in early French immersion.' *Studies in Second Language Acquisition* 15/2: 245–59.

Harley, B. 1998. 'The role of focus-on-form tasks in promoting child L2 acquisition' in C. Doughty and J. Williams (eds.). *Focus on Form in Classroom Second Language Acquisition.* Cambridge: Cambridge University Press.

Harley, B. and D. Hart. 1997. 'Language aptitude and second language proficiency in classroom learners of different starting ages.' *Studies in Second Language Acquisition* 19: 379–400.

Harrington. M. and M. Sawyer. 1992. 'L2 working memory capacity and L2 reading skill.' *Studies in Second Language Acquisition* 14: 25–38.

Hatch, E. 1978. 'Acquisition of syntax in a second language' in J. C. Richards (ed.). *Understanding Second and Foreign Language Learning.* Rowley, Mass.: Newbury House.

Hauser, E. 2005. 'Coding "corrective recasts": the maintenance of meaning and more fundamental problems.' *Applied Linguistics* 26: 293–316.

Havranek, G. 2002. 'When is corrective feedback most likely to succeed?' *International Journal of Educational Research* 37: 255–70.

Havranek, G. and H. Cesnik. 2001. 'Factors affecting the success of corrective feedback' in S. Foster-Cohen and A. Nizegorodzew (eds.). *EUROSLA Yearbook, Volume 1.* Amsterdam: John Benjamins.

Hawkins, R. 2001. *Second Language Syntax: A Generative Introduction.* Oxford: Blackwell.

Hedgcock, J. 1993. 'Well-formed vs. ill-formed strings in L2 metalingual tasks: specifying features of grammaticality judgements.' *Second Language Research* 9/1: 1–21.

Heift, T. 2001. 'Error-specific and individualized feedback in a web-based language tutoring system: do they read it?' *ReCALL* 13/2: 129–42.

Heift, T. 2004. 'Corrective feedback and learner uptake in CALL.' *ReCALL* 16/2: 416–31.

Henley, N. M. 1995. 'Ethnicity and gender issues in language' in H. Landrine (ed.). *Bringing Cultural Diversity to Feminist Psychology: Theory, Research, and Practice.* Washington, D.C.: American Psychological Association.

Hinkel, E. (ed.). 2005. *Handbook of Research in Second Language Teaching and Learning.* Mahwah, N.J.: Lawrence Erlbaum Associates.

Hirsh-Pasek, K. R. Treiman, and **M. Schneiderman.** 1984. 'Brown and Hanlon revisited: Mothers' sensitivity to ungrammatical forms.' *Journal of Child Language* 11: 81–8.

Holmes, J. 1994. 'Improving the lot of female language learners' in J. Sunderland (ed.). *Exploring Gender: Questions and Implications for English Language Education.* London: Prentice Hall.

Holmes, J. 1998. 'Complimenting—a positive politeness strategy' in J. Coates (ed.). *Language and Gender: A Reader.* Oxford: Blackwell.

Holmes, J. and M. Marra. 2004. 'Relational practice in the workplace: women's talk or gendered discourse?' *Language in Society* 33/3: 377–98.

Holmes, J. and M. Meyerhoff. 2003. 'Different voices, different views: an introduction to current research in language and gender' in J. Holmes and M. Meyerhoff (eds.). *Handbook of Language and Gender.* Oxford: Blackwell.

Howell, D. 1992. *Statistical Methods for Psychology.* Belmont, Calif.: Duxbury Press.

Hulstijn, J. H. 2002. 'Towards a unified account of the representation, processing, and acquisition of second language knowledge.' *Second Language Research* 18/3: 193–223.

Hulstijn, J. and R. de Graaff. 1994. 'Under what conditions does explicit knowledge of a second language facilitate the acquisition of implicit knowledge? A research proposal.' *AILA Review* 11: 97–112.

Inagaki, S. and M. H. Long. 1999. 'Implicit negative feedback' in K. Kanno (ed.). *The Acquisition of Japanese as a Second Language.* Philadelphia: John Benjamins.

Ishida, M. 2004. 'Effects of recasts on the acquisition of the aspectual form of *-te i (ru)* by learners of Japanese as a foreign language.' *Language Learning* 54: 311–94.

Ishiguro, T., N. Yamauchi, N. Akamatsu, and **T. Kitabayashi.** 2003. *Gendai-no eigoka kyouikuhou (Contemporary English Teaching Methods).* Tokyo: Eihousha.

Itakura, H. 2001. *Conversational Dominance and Gender: A Study of Japanese Speakers in First and Second Language Contexts.* Philadelphia: John Benjamins.

Iwashita, N. 2001. 'The effect of learner proficiency on interactional moves and modified output in nonnative–nonnative interaction in Japanese as a foreign language.' *System* 29: 267–87.

Iwashita, N. 2003. 'Negative feedback and positive evidence in task-based interaction: differential effects on L2 development.' *Studies in Second Language Acquisition* 25: 1–36.

Izumi, S. 2002. 'Output, input enhancement, and the noticing hypothesis: an experimental study on ESL relativization.' *Studies in Second Language Acquisition* 24: 541–77.

JACET Educational Problem Study Group. 2005. *Shin eigoka kyouiku-no kiso-to jissen (New foundation and practice of English education).* Tokyo: Sanshusha.

Jeon, S. This volume. 'Interaction-driven L2 learning: characterizing linguistic development' in A. Mackey (ed.). *Conversational Interaction in Second Language Acquisition: A Collection of Empirical Studies.* Oxford: Oxford University Press.

Jourdenais, R. 2001. 'Cognition, instruction and protocol analysis' in P. Robinson (ed.). *Cognition and Second Language Instruction.* Cambridge: Cambridge University Press.

Jourdenais, R., M. Ota, S. Stauffer, B. Boyson, and C. Doughty. 1995. 'Does textual enhancement promote noticing? A think-aloud protocol analysis' in R. Schmidt (ed.). *Attention and Awareness in Foreign Language Learning.* Honolulu: University of Hawai'i Press.

Just, M. A. and P. A. Carpenter. 1992. 'A capacity theory of comprehension: individual differences in working memory.' *Psychological Review* 99: 122–49.

Kanno, K. (ed.). 1999. *The Acquisition of Japanese as a Second Language.* Philadelphia: John Benjamins.

Kasanga, L. A. 1996. 'Effect of gender on the rate of interaction: some implications for second language acquisition and classroom practice.' *I.T.L. Review of Applied Linguistics* 111–2: 155–92.

Ke, C. 1998. 'Effects of language background on the learning of Chinese characters among foreign language students.' *Foreign Language Annals* 31: 91–100.

Keck, C. M., G. Iberri-Shea, N. Tracy-Ventura, and S. Wa-Mbaleka. 2006. 'Investigating the empirical link between task-based interaction and acquisition: a quantitative meta-analysis' in J. M. Norris and L. Ortega (eds.). *Synthesizing Research on Language Learning and Teaching.* Amsterdam: John Benjamins.

Keenan, E. and B. Comrie. 1977. 'Noun Phrase Accessibility and Universal Grammar.' *Linguistic Inquiry* 8: 63–99.

Kess, A. 1996. 'Predictable problems of Japanese students: in-group belonging and saving face.' *Intensive English Program Newsletter* 12: 8–9.

Kim, H. and G. Mathes. 2001. 'Explicit versus implicit corrective feedback.' *The Korea TESOL Journal* 4: 1–15.

Kim, J-H. and Z-H. Han. This volume. 'Recasts in communicative EFL classes: do teacher intent and learner interpretation overlap?' in A. Mackey (ed.). *Conversational Interaction in Second Language Acquisition: A Collection of Empirical Studies.* Oxford: Oxford University Press.

Kim, Y.-J. 1987. *The Acquisition of Relative Clauses in English and Korean:Development in Spontaneous Production.* Unpublished doctoral dissertation. Harvard University.

Kimmel, M. S. 2004. 'Introduction' in M. S. Kimmel (ed.). *The Gendered Society Reader.* New York: Oxford University Press.

Kitade, K. 2000. 'L2 learners' discourse and SLA theories in CMC: collaborative interaction in internet chat.' *Computer Assisted Language Learning* 13/2: 143–66.

Klein, W. and C. Perdue. 1992. *Utterance Structure: Developing Grammars Again.* Amsterdam: John Benjamins.

Kowal, M. and M. Swain. 1994. 'Using collaborative language production tasks to promote students' language awareness.' *Language Awareness* 3/2: 73–93.

Kowal, M. and M. Swain. 1997. 'From semantic to syntactic processing: how can we promote metalinguistic awareness in the French immersion classroom?' in R. Johnson and M. Swain (eds.). *Immersion Education: International Perspectives.* Cambridge: Cambridge University Press.

Krashen, S. 1978. 'Second language acquisition' in W. Dingwall (ed.). *A Survey of Linguistic Science*. Stamford, Conn.: Greylock.

Krashen, S. 1982. *Principles and Practice in Second Language Acquisition*. New York: Pergamon Institute of English.

Kroll, J. F., E. Michael, N. Tokowicz, and R. Dufour. 2002. 'The development of lexical fluency in a second language.' *Second Language Research* 18/2: 137–71.

Lantolf, J. 1997. 'The function of language play in the acquisition of L2 Spanish' in W. Glass and A. Perez-Leroux (eds.). *Contemporary Perspectives on the Acquisition of Spanish*. Somerville, Mass.: Cascadilla Press.

Lantolf, J. 2000a. 'Second language learning as a mediated process.' *Language Teaching: The International Abstracting Journal for Language Teachers and Applied Linguists* 33/2, 79–96.

Lantolf, J. 2000b. *Sociocultural Theory and Second Language Learning*. Oxford: Oxford University Press.

Lantolf, J. and G. Appel. 1994. *Vygotskian Approaches to Second Language Research*. Norwood, N.J.: Ablex Pub. Corp.

Lapkin, S., M. Swain, and M. Smith. 2002. 'Reformulation and the learning of French pronominal verbs in a Canadian French immersion context.' *The Modern Language Journal* 86/4: 485–507.

Lardiere, D. 1998. 'Case and tense in "fossilized" steady state.' *Second Language Research* 14/1: 1–26.

Larsen-Freeman, D. 1995. 'On the teaching and learning of grammar: challenging the myths' in D. H. F. Eckman, P. W. Lee, J. Mileham, and R. R. Weber (eds.). *Second Language Acquisition Theory and Pedagogy*. Mahwah, N.J.: Lawrence Erlbaum Associates.

Lee, E. 2001. 'Interlanguage development by two Korean speakers of English with a focus on temporality.' *Language Learning* 51/4: 591–633.

Lee, G. 1999. 'Positively interdependent: developing oral fluency via task design' in D. Kluge, S. McGuire, D. Johnson, and R. Johnson (eds.), *JALT Applied Materials: Cooperative Learning*. Tokyo: Japan Association for Language Teaching.

Lee, T. M. C., C. C. Y. Cheung, J. K. P. Chan, and C. C. H. Chan. 2000. 'Trail making across languages.' *Journal of Clinical and Experimental Neuropsychology* 22: 772–8.

Leeman, J. 2003. 'Recasts and second language development: beyond negative evidence.' *Studies in Second Language Acquisition* 25/1: 37–63.

Leow, R. P. 1997a. 'Attention, awareness, and foreign language behavior.' *Language Learning* 47: 467–506.

Leow, R. P. 1997b. 'The effects of input enhancement and text length on adult L2 readers' comprehension and intake in second language acquisition.' *Applied Language Learning* 8/2: 151–82.

Leow, R. P. 1998. 'Toward operationalizing the process of attention in SLA: evidence for Tomlin and Villa's (1994) fine-grained analysis of attention.' *Applied Psycholinguistics* 19: 133–59.

Leow, R. P. 1999. 'The role of attention in second/foreign language classroom research: methodological issues' in J. Gutierrez-Rexach and F. Martinez-Gil (eds.). *Advances in Hispanic Linguistics*. Somerville: Cascadilla Press.

Leow, R. P. 2000. 'A study of the role of awareness in foreign language behavior: aware vs. unaware learners.' *Studies in Second Language Acquisition* 22/4: 557–84.

Leow, R. P. 2001. 'Do learners notice enhanced forms while interacting with the L2? An online and offline study of the role of written input enhancement in L2 reading.' *Hispania* 84/3: 496–509.

Leow, R. P., T. Egi, A. M. Nuevo, and Y-C. Tsai. 2003. 'The roles of textual enhancement and type of linguistic item in adult L2 learners' comprehension and intake.' *Applied Language Learning* 13/2: 1–16.

Leow, R. P. and K. Morgan-Short. 2004. 'To think aloud or not to think aloud: the issue of reactivity in SLA research methodology.' *Studies in Second Language Acquisition* 26/1: 35–57.

Levelt, W. 1989. *Speaking: From Intention to Articulation*. Cambridge, Mass.: The MIT Press.

Levelt, W. 1992. 'Accessing words in speech productions: Stages, processes, and presentations.' *Cognition* 42: 1–22.

Light, R. and D. Pillemer. 1984. *Summing Up: The Science of Reviewing Research*. Cambridge: Harvard University Press.

Lightbown, P. M. 1998. 'The importance of timing in focus on form' in C. Doughty and J. Williams (eds.). *Focus on Form in Classroom Second Language Acquisition*. New York: Cambridge University Press.

Lightbown, P. M. and N. Spada. 1990. 'Focus-on-form and corrective feedback in communicative language teaching: effects on second language learning.' *Studies in Second Language Acquisition* 12: 429–48.

Lightbown, P. M. and N. Spada. 1994. 'An innovative program for primary ESL in Quebec.' *TESOL Quarterly* 28: 563–73.

Lin, H. and J. Hedgcock. 1996. 'Negative feedback incorporation among high-proficiency and low-proficiency Chinese speaking learners of Spanish.' *Language Learning* 46: 567–611.

Linnell, J. 1995. 'Can negotiation provide a context for learning syntax in a second language?' *Working Papers in Educational Linguistics* 11/2: 83–103.

Lipsey, M. and D. Wilson. 2001. *Practical Meta-analysis*. Thousand Oaks, Calif.: Sage.

Liu, D. and J. Gleason. 2002. 'Acquisition of the article *the* by nonnative speakers of English.' *Studies in Second Language Acquisition* 24: 1–26.

Lochtman, K. 2002. 'Oral corrective feedback in the foreign language classroom: How it affects interaction in analytic foreign language teaching.' *International Journal of Educational Research* 37: 271–83.

Loewen, S. 2003a. 'The effectiveness of incidental focus on form in meaning-focused ESL lessons.' *New Zealand Studies in Applied Linguistics* 9/1: 63–83.

Loewen, S. 2003b. 'Variation in the frequency and characteristics of incidental focus on form.' *Language Teaching Research* 7/3: 315–45.

Loewen, S. 2004. 'Uptake in incidental focus on form in meaning-focused ESL lessons.' *Language Learning* 54/1: 153–88.

Loewen, S. 2005. 'Incidental focus on form and second language learning.' *Studies in Second Language Acquisition* 27/3: 361–86.

Loewen, S. and T. Nabei. This volume. 'Measuring the effects of oral corrective feedback on L2 knowledge' in A. Mackey (ed.). *Conversational Interaction in Second Language Acquisition: A Collection of Empirical Studies*. Oxford. Oxford University Press.

Loewen, S. and J. Philp. 2006. 'Recasts in the adult English L2 classroom: characteristics, explicitness, and effectiveness.' *The Modern Language Journal* 90/4: 536–56.

Long, M. H. 1977. 'Teacher feedback on learner error: mapping cognitions' in H. D. Brown, C. A. Yorio, and R. H. Crymes (eds.). *On TESOL '77*. Washington, D.C.: TESOL.

Long, M. H. 1981. 'Input, interaction and second language' in H. Winitz (ed.). *Native Language and Foreign Language Acquisition*. New York: Annals of the New York Academy of Sciences.

Long, M. H. 1983. 'Native speaker/non-native speaker conversation and the negotiation of comprehensible input.' *Applied Linguistics* 4/2: 126–41.

Long, M. H. 1985. 'Input and second-language acquisition theory' in S. M. Gass (ed.). *Input in Second Language Acquisition*. Rowley, Mass.: Newbury House.

Long, M. H. 1991. 'Focus on form: a design feature in language teaching methodology' in K. de Bot, R. B. Ginsberg, and C. Kramsch (eds.). *Foreign Language Research in Cross-cultural Perspectives*. Amsterdam: John Benjamins.

Long, M. H. 1996. 'The role of the linguistic environment in second language acquisition' in W. C. Ritchie and T. K. Bhatia (eds.). *Handbook of Second Language Acquisition*. New York: Academic Press.

Long, M. H. 1997. 'Construct validity in SLA research: a response to Firth and Wagner.' *The Modern Language Journal* 81: 318–23.

Long, M. H. 2006. *Problems in SLA*. Mahwah, N.J.: Lawrence Erlbaum Associates.

Long, M. H., S. Inagaki, and L. Ortega. 1998. 'The role of implicit negative feedback in SLA: models and recasts in Japanese and Spanish.' *The Modern language Journal* 82: 357–71.

Long, M. H. and P. Porter. 1985. 'Group work, interlanguage talk and second language acquisition.' *TESOL Quarterly* 19/2: 207–28.

Long, M. H. and P. Robinson. 1998. 'Focus on form: theory, research and practice' in C. Doughty and J. Williams (eds.). *Focus on Form in Classroom Second Language Acquisition*. Cambridge: Cambridge University Press.

Loschky, L. 1994. 'Comprehensible input and second language acquisition: what is the relationship?' *Studies in Second Language Acquisition* 16/3: 303–25.

Lucas, T. 2005. 'Language awareness and comprehension through puns among ESL learners.' *Language Awareness* 14/4: 221–38

Lyons, J. 1996. 'On competence and performance and related notions' in G. Brown, K. Malmkjaer, and J. Williams (eds.). *Performance and Competence in Second Language Acquisition*. Cambridge: Cambridge University Press.

Lyster, R. 1998a. 'Form in immersion classroom discourse: in or out of focus?' *Canadian Journal of Applied Linguistics* 1: 53–82.

Lyster, R. 1998b. 'Recasts, repetition and ambiguity in L2 classroom discourse.' *Studies in Second Language Acquisition* 20/1: 51–80.

Lyster, R. 1998c. 'Negotiation of form, recasts, and explicit error correction in relation to error types and learner repair in immersion classrooms.' *Language Learning* 48: 183–218.

Lyster, R. 2004. 'Differential effects of prompts and recasts in form-focused instruction.' *Studies in Second Language Acquisition* 26: 399–432.

Lyster, R. and H. Mori. 2005. 'Comparing interactional feedback across instructional contexts'. Paper presented at the 28th Second Language Research Forum. New York, New York.

Lyster, R. and H. Mori. 2006. 'Interactional feedback and instructional counterbalance.' *Studies in Second Language Acquisition* 28: 269–300.

Lyster, R. and L. Ranta. 1997. 'Corrective feedback and learner uptake: negotiation of form in communicative classrooms.' *Studies in Second Language Acquisition* 19: 37–66.

Mackey, A. 1994. *Using Communicative Tasks to Target Grammatical Structures: A Handbook of Tasks and Instructions for their Use*. Sydney: Language Acquisition Research Centre.

Mackey, A. 1995. *Stepping up the Pace: Input, Interaction and Interlanguage Development. An Empirical Study of Questions in ESL*. Unpublished doctoral dissertation. University of Sydney.

Mackey, A. 1999. 'Input, interaction, and second language development: an empirical study of question formation in ESL.' *Studies in Second Language Acquisition* 21/4: 557–87.

Mackey, A. 2002. 'Beyond production: learners' perceptions about interactional processes.' *International Journal of Educational Research* 37: 379–94.

Mackey, A. 2006a. 'Feedback, noticing and second language development: an empirical study of L2 classroom interaction.' *Applied Linguistics* 27: 405–30.

Mackey, A. 2006b. 'From introspections, brain scans, and memory tests to the role of social context: advancing research on learning and interaction.' *Studies in Second Language Acquisition* 28: 369–79.

Mackey, A. 2007. 'Interaction as practice' in R. DeKeyser (ed.). *Practice in a Second Language: Perspectives from Applied Linguistics and Cognitive Psychology*. Cambridge: Cambridge University Press.

Mackey, A. This volume. 'Introduction to the relationship between conversation and second language acquisition' in A. Mackey (ed.). *Conversational Interaction in Second Language Acquisition: A Collection of Empirical Studies*. Oxford: Oxford University Press.

Mackey, A., R. Adams, C. Stafford, and P. Winke. April 2002. 'Exploring the relationship between modified output and working memory capacity.' Paper presented at the American Association for Applied Linguistics conference. Salt Lake City, Utah.

Mackey, A. and S. M. Gass. 2006. 'Pushing the methodological boundaries in interaction research: Introduction.' *Studies in Second Language Acquisition* 28: 169–78.

Mackey, A., S. M. Gass, and K. McDonough. 2000. 'How do learners perceive interactional feedback?' *Studies in Second Language Acquisition* 22/4: 471–97.

Mackey, A. and J. Goo. This volume. 'Interaction in SLA: a research synthesis and meta-analysis' in A. Mackey (ed.). *Conversational Interaction in Second Language Acquisition: A Collection of Empirical Studies*. Oxford: Oxford University Press.

Mackey, A. and R. Oliver. 2002. 'Interactional feedback and children's L2 development.' *System* 30/4: 459–77.

Mackey, A., R. Oliver, and J. Leeman. 2003. 'Interactional input and the incorporation of feedback: an exploration of NS–NNS and NNS–NNS adult and child dyads.' *Language Learning* 53/1: 35–66.

Mackey, A. and J. Philp. 1998. 'Conversational interaction and second language development: recasts, responses, and red herrings?' *The Modern Language Journal* 82/3: 338–56.

Mackey, A., J. Philp, T. Egi, A. Fujii, and T. Tatsumi. 2002. 'Individual differences in working memory, noticing of interactional feedback, and L2 development' in P. Robinson (ed.). *Individual Differences and Instructed Language Learning*. Amsterdam: John Benjamins.

Mackey, A. and R. E. Silver. 2005. 'Interactional tasks and English L2 learning by immigrant children in Singapore.' *System* 33: 239–60.

MacWhinney, B. 1996. 'Language specific prediction in foreign language acquisition.' *Language Testing* 11: 292–320.

MacWhinney, B. 2005. 'A unified model of language acquisition' in J. Kroll and A. De Groot (eds.) *Handbook of Bilingualism: Psycholinguistic Approaches*. Oxford: Oxford University Press.

Markee, N. 2000. *Conversation Analysis*. Mahwah, N.J.: Lawrence Erlbaum Associates.

Masgoret, A.-M. and R. C. Gardner. 2003. 'Attitude, motivation, and second language learning: a meta-analysis of studies conducted by Gardner and associates.' *Language Learning* 53: 123–63.

Master, P. 2002. 'Information structure and English article pedagogy.' *System* 30: 331–48.

McDonough, K. 2004. 'Learner-learner interaction during pair and small group activities in a Thai EFL context.' *System* 32: 207–24.

McDonough, K. 2005. 'Identifying the impact of negative feedback and learners' responses on ESL question development.' *Studies in Second Language Acquisition* 27/1: 79–103.

McDonough, K. 2006. 'Interaction and syntactic priming: English L2 speakers' production of dative constructions.' *Studies in Second Language Acquisition* 28: 179–207.

McDonough, K. This volume. 'Interactional feedback and the emergence of simple past activity verbs in L2 English' in A. Mackey (ed.). *Conversational Interaction in Second Language Acquisition: A Collection of Empirical Studies*. Oxford: Oxford University Press.

McDonough, K. and A. Mackey. 2000. 'Communicative tasks, conversational interaction and linguistic form: an empirical study of Thai.' *Foreign Language Annals* 33: 82–91.

McDonough, K. and A. Mackey. 2006. 'Responses to recasts: repetitions, primed production and linguistic development.' *Language Learning* 56/4: 693–720.

McLaughlin, B. 1987. *Theories of Second Language Learning*. London: Arnold.

Medgyes, P. 2002. *Laughing Matters: Humor in the Language Classroom*. Cambridge: Cambridge University Press.

Mehnert, U. 1998. 'The effects of different lengths of time for planning on second language performance.' *Studies in Second Language Acquisition* 20: 83–108.

Meisel, J., H. Clahsen, and M. Pienemann. 1981. 'On determining developmental stages in natural second language acquisition.' *Studies in Second Language Acquisition* 3/1: 109–35.

Melzi, G. and C. Fernandez. 2004. 'Talking about past emotions: conversations between Peruvian mothers and their preschool children.' *Sex Roles* 50/9–10: 641–57.

Microsoft Corporation. 2005. *MSN Messenger Version 7.0.* (Computer web-based chat program). http://messenger.msn.com.

Mitchell, R. and F. Myles. 1998. *Second Language Learning Theories* (First edition). London: Arnold.

Mitchell, R. and F. Myles. 2004. *Second Language Learning Theories* (Second edition). London: Arnold.

Miyake, A. and N. Friedman. 1998. 'Individual differences in second language proficiency: working memory as language aptitude' in A. F. Healy and L. E. Bourne (eds.). *Foreign Language Learning: Psycholinguistic Studies on Training and Retention.* Mahwah, N.J.: Lawrence Erlbaum Associates.

Mollica, A. 1976. 'Cartoons in the language classroom.' *The Canadian Modern Language Review* 32/4: 424–44.

Mollica, A. 1979. 'Games and language activities in the Italian high school classroom.' *Foreign Language Annals* 12/5: 347–54.

Montrul, S. 2002. 'Incomplete acquisition and attrition of Spanish tense/aspect distinctions in adult bilinguals.' *Bilingualism: Language and Cognition* 5: 39–68.

Montrul, S. 2004. 'Subject and object expression in Spanish heritage speakers: a case of morphosyntactic convergence.' *Bilingualism: Language and Cognition* 7:125–142.

Morais, J., L. Cary, J. Alegría, and P. Bertelson. 1979. 'Does awareness of speech as a sequence of phones arise spontaneously?' *Cognition* 7/4: 323–31.

Morgan, J., K. Bonamo, and L. Travis. 1995. 'Negative evidence on negative evidence.' *Developmental Psychology* 31/2: 180–97.

Morgan, J. and L. Travis. 1989. 'Limits on negative information in language input.' *Journal of Child Language* 16/3: 531–52.

Mori, H. 2000. 'Error treatment at different grade levels in Japanese immersion classroom interaction.' *Studies in Language Sciences* 1: 171–80.

Morreall, J. 1989. 'Enjoying incongruity.' *Humor* 2/1: 1–18.

Muranoi, H. 2000. 'Focus on form through interaction enhancement: integrating formal instruction into a communicative task in EFL classrooms.' *Language Learning* 50: 617–73.

Muranoi, H., M. Chiba, and T. Hatanaka. 2001. *Jissen-teki eigoka kyouikuhou (Practical English language teaching method).* Tokyo: Seibido.

Musumeci, D. 1996. 'Teacher-learner negotiation in content-based instruction: communication at cross-purposes?' *Applied Linguistics* 17: 286–325.

Myerson, J., L. Emery, D. A. White, and S. Hale. 2003. 'Effects of age, domain, and processing demands on memory span: evidence for differential decline.' *Aging Neuropsychology and Cognition* 10: 20–7.

Nabei, T. and M. Swain. 2002. 'Learner awareness of recasts in classroom interaction: a case study of an adult EFL student's second language learning.' *Language Awareness* 11/1: 43–63.

Nagasawa, F. 1995. 'L1, L2, bairinguru no nihongo bunpoo nooryoku (Comparative grammatical competence among L1, L2, and bilingual speakers of Japanese).' *Nihongo kyooiku* 86: 173–89.

Nagata, N. 1993. 'Intelligent computer feedback for second language instruction.' *The Modern Language Journal* 77/3: 330–39.

Nagata, N. 1997. 'An experimental comparison of deductive and inductive feedback generated by a simple parser.' *System* 25/4: 515–34.

Nash, R. 1997. *NTC's Dictionary of Spanish Cognates.* Lincolnwood, Ill.: NTC Publishing Group.

Nash, W. 1985. *The Language of Humor.* New York: Longman.

Nelson, K. E. 1987. 'Some observations from the perspective of the rare event cognitive comparison theory of language acquisition' in K. E. Nelson and A. V. Kleek (eds.). *Children's Language.* Hillsdale, N.J.: Lawrence Erlbaum Associates.

Nerlich, B. and D. Clarke. 2001. 'Ambiguities we live by: towards pragmatics of polysemy.' *Journal of Pragmatics* 33/1: 1–20.

Nicholas, H., P. M. Lightbown, and N. Spada. 2001. 'Recasts as feedback to language learners.' *Language Learning* 51: 719–58.

Nobuyoshi, J. and R. Ellis. 1993. 'Focused communication tasks and second language acquisition.' *ELT Journal* 47: 203–10.

Norrick, N. 1993. *Conversational Joking: Humor in Everyday Talk.* Bloomington: Indiana University Press.

Norris, J. and L. Ortega. 2000. 'Effectiveness of L2 instruction: a research synthesis and quantitative meta-analysis.' *Language Learning* 50: 417–528.

Norris, J. and L. Ortega. 2003. 'Defining and measuring SLA.' in C. Doughty and M. Long (eds.). *The Handbook of Second Language Acquisition.* Malden, Mass.: Blackwell.

Norris, J. M. and L. Ortega. 2006. *Synthesizing Research on Language Learning and Teaching.* Philadelphia: John Benjamins.

Nunan, D. 1989. *Designing Tasks for the Communicative Classroom.* Cambridge: Cambridge University Press.

O'Brien, I., N. Segalowitz, J. Collentine, and B. Freed. 2006. 'Phonological memory and lexical, narrative and grammatical skills in second-language oral production by adult learners.' *Applied Psycholinguistics* 27: 377–402.

O'Grady, W., M. Lee, and M. Choo. 2003. 'A subject-object asymmetry in the acquisition of relative clauses in Korean as a second language.' *Studies in Second Language Acquisition* 25: 433–48.

Ohta, A. S. 2000. 'Rethinking recasts: a learner-centered examination of corrective feedback in the Japanese classroom' in J. K. Hall and L. Verplaetse (eds.). *Second and Foreign Language Learning through Classroom Interaction.* Mahwah, N.J.: Lawrence Erlbaum Associates.

Ohta, A. S. 2001. *Second Language Acquisition Processes in the Classroom: Learning Japanese.* Mahwah, N.J.: Lawrence Erlbaum Associates.

Oliver, R. 1995. 'Negative feedback in child NS–NNS conversation.' *Studies in Second Language Acquisition* 17/4: 459–81.

Oliver, R. 1998. 'Negotiation of meaning in child interactions.' *The Modern Language Journal* 82/3: 372–86.

Oliver, R. 2000. 'Age differences in negotiation and feedback in classroom and pairwork.' *Language Learning* 50/1: 119–51.

Oliver, R. 2002. 'The patterns of negotiation for meaning in child interactions.' *The Modern Language Journal* 86/1: 97–111.

Oliver, R. and A. Mackey. 2003. 'Interactional context and feedback in child ESL classrooms.' *The Modern Language Journal* 87/4: 519–33.

Olson, D. 2002. 'What writing does to the mind' in E. Amsel and J. E. Byrnes (eds.). *Language, Literacy, and Cognitive Development: The Development and Consequences of Symbolic Communication.* Mahwah, N.J.: Lawrence Erlbaum Associates.

Omaggio, A. 1982. 'Using games and interaction activities for the development of functional proficiency in a second language.' *The Canadian Modern Language Review* 38/3: 517–46.

Ortega, L. 1999. 'Planning and focus on form in L2 oral performance.' *Studies in Second Language Acquisition* 21/1: 109–48.

Orwin, R. 1994. 'Evaluating coding decision' in H. Cooper and L. Hedge (eds.). *The Handbook of Research Synthesis.* New York: Russell Sage Foundation.

Osaka, M. *and* N. Osaka. 1992. 'Language-independent working memory as measured by Japanese and English reading span tests.' *Bulletin of the Psychonomic Society* 30: 287–9.

Osaka, M., N. Osaka, and R. Groner. 1993. 'Language independent working memory: Evidence from German and French reading span tests.' *Bulletin of the Psychonomic Society* 31: 117–8.

Overstreet, M. 1998. 'Text enhancement and content familiarity: the focus of learner attention.' *Spanish Applied Linguistics* 2/2: 229–58.

Panova, I. and R. Lyster. 2002. 'Patterns of corrective feedback and uptake in an adult ESL classroom.' *TESOL Quarterly* 36: 573–95.

Park, E. S. 2004. 'Constraints of implicit focus on form: Insights from a study of input enhancement.' *Teachers College, Columbia University Working Papers in TESOL and Applied Linguistics* 4/2.

Pavlenko, A. 2002. 'Poststructural approaches to the study of social factors in second language learning and use' in V. Cook (ed.). *Portraits of the L2 User*. Clevedon, UK: Multilingual Matters.

Payne, J. S. and B. Ross. 2005. 'Working memory, synchronous CMC, and L2 oral proficiency development.' *Language Learning and Technology* 9/3: 35–54.

Peirce, B. N. 1995. 'Social identity, investment, and language learning.' *TESOL Quarterly* 29: 9–31.

Pelletieri, J. L. 2000. 'Negotiation in cyberspace: the role of chatting in the development of grammatical competence' in M. Warschauer and R. Kern (eds.). *Network-based Language Teaching: Concepts and Practice*. Cambridge: Cambridge University Press.

Philp, J. 1998. 'Interaction, noticing, and second language acquisition.' Unpublished doctoral dissertation. University of Tasmania.

Philp, J. 2003. 'Constraints on "noticing the gap": nonnative speakers' noticing of recasts in NS–NNS interaction.' *Studies in Second Language Acquisition* 25/1: 99–126.

Pica, T. 1984a. 'Methods of morpheme quantification: their effect on the interpretation of second language data.' *Studies in Second Language Acquisition* 6/1: 69–78.

Pica, T. 1984b. 'L1 transfer and L2 complexity as factors in syllabus design.' *TESOL Quarterly* 18/4: 689–704.

Pica, T. 1991. 'Foreign language classrooms: making them research-ready and researchable' in B. Freed (ed.). *Foreign Language Acquisition Research and Classroom*. Lexington, Mass.: D.C. Heath.

Pica, T. 1992. 'Communication with second language learners: what does it reveal about the social and linguistic processes of second language learning?' in J. Alatis (ed.). *Georgetown University Round Table on Languages and Linguistics*. Washington D.C.: Georgetown University Press.

Pica, T. 1994a. 'Research on negotiation: what does it reveal about second-language learning conditions, processes, and outcomes?' *Language Learning* 44/3: 493–527.

Pica, T. 1994b. 'Questions from the language classroom: research perspectives.' *TESOL Quarterly* 28/1: 49–79.

Pica, T. 1996. 'Second language learning through interaction: multiple perspectives.' *University of Pennsylvania Working Papers in Educational Linguistics* 12: 1–22.

Pica, T. 2002. 'Subject-matter content: how does it assist the interactional and linguistic needs of classroom language learners?' *The Modern Language Journal* 86: 1–19.

Pica, T., L. Holliday, N. E. Lewis, D. Berducci, and J. Newman. 1991. 'Language learning through interaction: what role does gender play?' *Studies in Second Language Acquisition* 13/3: 343–76.

Pica, T., L. Holliday, N. E. Lewis, and L. Morgenthaler. 1989. 'Comprehensible output as an outcome of linguistic demands on the learner.' *Studies in Second Language Acquisition* 11/1: 63–90.

Pica, T., R. Kanagy, and J. Falodun. 1993. 'Choosing and using communication tasks for second language instruction and research' in G. Crookes and S. Gass (eds.). *Tasks and Language Learning: Integrating Theory and Practice*. Clevedon, UK: Multilingual Matters.

Pica, T., H-S. Kang, and S. Sauro. 2006. 'Information gap tasks: their multiple roles and contributions to interaction research methodology.' *Studies in Second Language Acquisition* 28: 301–38.

Pica, T., F. Lincoln-Porter, D. Paninos, and J. Linnell. 1996. 'Language learners' interaction: how does it address the input, output, and feedback needs of L2 learners?' *TESOL Quarterly* 30/1: 59–84.

Pica, T., R. Young, and C. Doughty. 1987. 'The impact of interaction on comprehension.' *TESOL Quarterly* 21: 737–58.

Pienemann, M. 1984. 'Psychological constraints on the teachability of languages.' *Studies in Second Language Acquisition* 6: 186–214.

Pienemann, M. 1998. *Language Processing and Second Language Development: Processability Theory.* Amsterdam: John Benjamins.

Pienemann, M. and M. Johnston. 1987. 'Factors influencing the development of language proficiency' in D. Nunan (ed.). *Applying Second Language Acquisition Research.* Adelaide, Australia: National Curriculum Resource Centre, Adult Migrant Education Program.

Pienemann, M., M. Johnston, and G. Brindley. 1988. 'Constructing an acquisition-based procedure for second language assessment.' *Studies in Second Language Acquisition* 10/2: 217–43.

Piller, I. and A. Pavlenko. 2001. 'Introduction: Multilingualism, second language learning, and gender' in A. Pavlenko, A. Blackledge, I. Piller, and M. Teutsch-Dwyer (eds.). *Multilingualism, Second Language Learning, and Gender.* New York: Mouton de Gruyter.

Pinker, S. 1989. *Learnability and Cognition: The Acquisition of Argument Structure.* Cambridge, Mass.: MIT Press.

Platt, E. and F. Brooks. 2002. 'Task engagement: a turning point in foreign language development.' *Language Learning* 52/2: 365–400.

Polinsky, M. 1995. 'Cross-linguistic parallels in language loss.' *Southwest Journal of Linguistics* 14:87–124.

Polinsky, M. 2000. 'A composite linguistic profile of a speaker of Russian in the USA' in O. Kagan and B. Rifkin (eds.). *The Learning and Teaching of Slavic Languages and Cultures.* Bloomington, Ind.: Slavica.

Polinsky, M. In press. 'Heritage language narratives' in O. Kagan and D. Brinton (eds.). *Heritage Languages: A New Field Emerging.* Mahwah, N.J.: Lawrence Erlbaum Associates.

Polio, C., S. Gass, and L. Chapin. 2006. 'Using stimulated recall to investigate native speaker perceptions in native-nonnative speaker interaction.' *Studies in Second Language Acquisition* 28: 237–67.

Porter, P. 1986. 'How learners talk to each other: input and interaction in task-centered discussions' in R. Day (ed.). *Talking to Learn: Conversation in Second Language Acquisition.* Rowley, Mass.: Newbury House.

Posner, M. I. 1995. 'Attention in cognitive neuroscience: an overview' in M. S. Gazzaniga (ed.). *The Cognitive Neurosciences.* Cambridge, Mass.: MIT Press.

Preston, D. 2002. 'A variationist perspective on SLA: Psycholinguistic concerns' in R. Kaplan (ed.). *Oxford Handbook of Applied Linguistics.* Oxford: Oxford University Press.

Psychological Corporation. 1997. *WAIS-III – WMS-III Technical Manual.* San Antonio: Harcourt.

Purpura, J. 2004. *Assessing Grammar.* Cambridge: Cambridge University Press.

Pye, C. 1980. 'The acquisition of person markers in Quiche Mayan.' *Papers and Reports on Child Language Development* 19: 53–9.

Pynte, J. and S. Colonna. 2002. 'Competition between primary and non-primary relations during sentence comprehension.' *Journal of Psycholinguistic Research* 30: 569–99.

Quirk, R., S. Greenbaum, G. Leech, and J. Svarvik. 1972. *A Grammar of Contemporary English.* London: Longman.

Ranta, L. 2002. 'The role of learners' language analytic ability in the communicative classroom' in P. Robinson (ed.). *Individual Differences and Instructed Language Learning.* Amsterdam: John Benjamins.

Raskin, V. 1985. *Semantic Mechanisms of Humor.* Hingham, Mass.: D. Reidel Pub. Co.

Ravid, D. and L. Tolchinsky. 2002. 'Developing linguistic literacy: a comprehensive model.' *Journal of Child Language* 29: 417–47.

Rayner, K. and A. Pollatsek. 1989. *The Psychology of Reading.* Hillsdale, N.J.: Lawrence Erlbaum Associates.

Read, C., Y. Zhang, H. Nie, and B. Ding. 1986. 'The ability to manipulate speech sounds depends on knowing alphabetic spelling.' *Cognition* 24: 31–44.

Reid, P. T., C. Haritos, E. Kelly, and N. E. Holland. 1995. 'Socialization of girls: issues of ethnicity in gender development' in H. Landrine (ed.). *Bringing Cultural Diversity to Feminist Psychology: Theory, Research, and Practice*. Washington, D.C.: American Psychological Association.

Reis, A. and A. Castro-Caldas. 1997. 'Illiteracy: a cause for biased cognitive development.' *Journal of the International Neuropsychological Society* 3: 444–50.

Révész, A. and Z-H. Han. 2006. 'Task content familiarity, task type, and efficacy of recasts.' *Language Awareness* 15/3: 160–79.

Richards, J. C. 1990. *The Language Teaching Matrix*. Cambridge: Cambridge University Press.

Richards, J. C. and T. S. Rodgers. 2001. *Approaches and Methods in Language Teaching*. Cambridge: Cambridge University Press.

Ritchie, W. and T. Bhatia (eds.). 1996. *Handbook of Second Language Acquisition*. New York: Academic Press.

Roberts, M. 1995. 'Awareness and the efficacy of error correction' in R. W. Schmidt (ed.). *Attention and Awareness in Foreign Language Learning*. Honolulu: University of Hawai'i Press.

Robinson, P. 1995. 'Attention, memory, and the "Noticing" Hypothesis.' *Language Learning* 45/2: 283–331.

Robinson, P. 1996. 'Learning simple and complex second language rules under implicit, incidental, rule-search, and instructed conditions.' *Studies in Second Language Acquisition* 18: 27–67.

Robinson, P. 1997. 'Individual differences and the fundamental similarity of implicit and explicit adult second language learning.' *Language Learning* 47/1: 45–99.

Robinson, P. 2001. 'Individual differences, cognitive abilities, aptitude complexes and learning conditions in second language acquisition.' *Second Language Research* 17: 368–92.

Robinson, P. (ed.). 2002a. *Individual Differences and Instructed Language Learning*. Amsterdam: John Benjamins.

Robinson, P. 2002b. 'Learning conditions, aptitude complexes, and SLA: a framework for research and pedagogy' in P. Robinson (ed.). *Individual Differences and Instructed Language Learning*. Philadelphia: John Benjamins.

Robinson, P. 2003. 'Attention and memory during SLA' in C. Doughty and M. Long (eds.). *The Handbook of Second Language Acquisition*. Oxford: Blackwell.

Robinson, P. 2005. 'Aptitude and second language acquisition.' *Annual Review of Applied Linguistics* 25/1: 45–73.

Robinson, P., M. Sawyer, and S. Ross. 2001. 'Second language acquisition research in Japan: theoretical issues' in *JALT Applied Materials*. Tokyo: Japan Association for Language Teaching.

Robison, R. 1995. 'The aspect hypothesis revisited: a cross-sectional study of tense and aspect marking in interlanguage.' *Applied Linguistics* 16/3: 344–70.

Rosa, E. M. and R. P. Leow. 2004a. 'Awareness, different learning conditions, and second language development.' *Applied Psycholinguistics* 25/2: 269–92.

Rosa, E. M. and R. P. Leow. 2004b. 'Computerized task-based instruction in the L2 classroom: the effects of explicitness and type of feedback on L2 development.' *The Modern Language Journal* 88: 192–217.

Rosa, E. and M. D. O'Neill. 1999. 'Explicitness, intake, and the issue of awareness: another piece to the puzzle.' *Studies in Second Language Acquisition* 21/4: 511–56.

Rosenthal, M. C. 1994. 'The fugitive literature' in H. Cooper and L. Hedges (eds.). *Handbook of Research Synthesis*. New York: Russell Sage Foundation.

Rosenthal, R. 1991. *Meta-analytic Procedures for Social Research*. Newbury Park, Calif: Sage.

Rosenthal, R. 1994. 'Parametric measures of effect size' in H. Cooper and L. Hedges (eds.). *Handbook of Research Synthesis*. New York: Russell Sage Foundation.

Rosenthal, R. 1995. 'Writing meta-analytic reviews.' *Psychological Bulletin* 118: 183–92.

Ross-Feldman, L. This volume. 'Interaction in the L2 classroom: does gender influence learning opportunities?' in A. Mackey (ed.). *Conversational Interaction in Second Language Acquisition: A Collection of Empirical Studies.* Oxford: Oxford University Press.

Rumelhart, D. and J. McClelland. 1986. *Parallel Distributed Processing: Explorations in the Microstructures of Cognition.* Cambridge: Cambridge University Press.

Rutherford, W. and M. Sharwood Smith. 1985. 'Consciousness-raising and universal grammar.' *Applied Linguistics* 6: 274–82.

Russell, J. and N. Spada. 2006. 'The effectiveness of corrective feedback for the acquisition of L2 grammar' in J. M. Norris and L. Ortega (eds.). *Synthesizing Research on Language Learning and Teaching.* Amsterdam: John Benjamins.

Sachs, R. and C. Polio. 2007. 'Learners' uses of two types of written feedback on a L2 writing revision task.' *Studies in Second Language Acquisition* 29/1: 67–100.

Sachs, R. and B. R. Suh. This volume. 'Textually enhanced recasts, learner awareness, and L2 outcomes in synchronous computer-mediated interaction' in A. Mackey (ed.). *Conversational Interaction in Second Language Acquisition: A Collection of Empirical Studies.* Oxford: Oxford University Press.

Sadker, M. and D. Sadker. 1994. *Failing at Fairness: How Our Schools Cheat Girls.* New York: Charles Scribner's Sons.

Sagarra, N. May 2004. 'Reformulating the error in CALL: does metalinguistic knowledge matter?' Paper presented at the annual American Association of Applied Linguistics. Portland, Oregon.

Sagarra, N. This volume. 'From CALL to face-to-face interaction: the effect of computer-delivered recasts and working memory on L2 development' in A. Mackey (ed.). *Conversational Interaction in Second Language Acquisition: A Collection of Empirical Studies.* Oxford: Oxford University Press.

Salaberry, M. R. 2000. 'L2 morphosyntactic development in text-based computer-mediated communication.' *Computer Assisted Language Learning* 13/1: 5–27.

Samuda, V. 2001. 'Guiding relationships between form and meaning during task performance: the role of the teacher' in M. Bygate, P. Skehan, and M. Swain (eds.). *Researching Pedagogic Tasks: Second Language Learning, Teaching and Testing.* Harlow, UK: Pearson Education.

Sanz, C. 2003. 'Computer delivered implicit vs. explicit feedback in processing instruction' in B. VanPatten (ed.). *Processing Instruction: Theory, Research, and Commentary (Second Language Acquisition Research).* Mahwah, N.J.: Lawrence Erlbaum.

Sato, C. 1986. 'Conversation and interlanguage development: rethinking the connection' in R. Day (ed.). *"Talking to Learn": Conversation in Second Language Acquisition.* Rowley, Mass.: Newbury House.

Sato, M. and R. Lyster. This volume. 'Modified output of Japanese EFL learners: variable effects of interlocutor versus feedback types' in A. Mackey (ed.). *Conversational Interaction in Second Language Acquisition: A Collection of Empirical Studies.* Oxford: Oxford University Press.

Saville-Troike, M. 1988. 'Private speech: evidence for second language learning strategies during the "silent" period.' *Journal of Child Language* 15/3: 567–90.

Saxton, M. 1997. 'The contrast theory of negative input.' *Journal of Child Language* 24: 139–61.

Schegloff, E., G. Jefferson, and H. Sacks. 1977. 'The preference for self-correction in the organization of repair in conversation.' *Language* 53: 361–82.

Schmidt, R. 1990. 'The role of consciousness in second language learning.' *Applied Linguistics* 11: 129–58.

Schmidt, R. 1993. 'Awareness and second language acquisition.' *Annual Review of Applied Linguistics* 13: 206–26.

Schmidt, R. 1994. 'Deconstructing consciousness in search of useful definitions for applied linguistics.' *AILA Review* 11: 11–26.

Schmidt, R. 1995. 'Consciousness and foreign language learning. A tutorial on the role of attention and awareness in learning' in R. Schmidt (ed.). *Attention and Awareness in Foreign Language Learning*. Honolulu: University of Hawai'i Press.

Schmidt, R. 2001. 'Attention' in P. Robinson (ed.). *Cognition and Second Language Instruction*. Cambridge: Cambridge University Press.

Schmidt, R. and S. Frota. 1986. 'Developing basic conversational ability in a second language: a case study of an adult learner of Portuguese' in R. Day (ed.). *Talking to Learn: Conversation in Second Language Acquisition*. Rowley, Mass.: Newbury House.

Schmitt, N., Z. Dörnyei, S. Adolphs, and V. Durow. 2003. 'Knowledge and acquisition of formulaic sequences: a longitudinal study' in Schimitt, N. (ed.). *The Acquisition, Processing, and Use of Formulaic Sequences*. Amsterdam: John Benjamins.

Schmitz, J. 2002. 'Humor as a pedagogical tool in foreign language and translation courses.' *Humor* 15/1: 89–113.

Schwartz, B. D. 1993. 'On explicit and negative data effecting and affecting competence and linguistic behavior.' *Studies in Second Language Acquisition*, 15: 147–63.

Schwartz, B. and R. Sprouse. 1996. 'L2 cognitive states and the Full Transfer/Full Access model.' *Second Language Research* 12/1: 40–72.

Scott, V. 1989. 'An empirical study of explicit and implicit teaching strategies in French.' *The Modern Language Journal* 73: 14–22.

Sebastián-Gallés, N., M. A. Martí, M. F. Carreiras, and F. Cuetos. 2000. *LEXESP, Léxico Informatizado del Español*. Barcelona: Ediciones de la Universitat de Barcelona.

Segalowitz, N. 1997. 'Individual differences in second language acquisition' in A. M. B. de Groot and J. Kroll (eds.). *Tutorials in Bilingualism: Psycholinguistic Perspectives*. Hillsdale, N.J.: Lawrence Erlbaum Associates.

Segalowitz, N. and S. Frenkiel-Fishman. 2005. 'Attention control and ability level in a complex cognitive skill: attention-shifting and second language proficiency.' *Memory and Cognition* 33: 644–53.

Selinker, L. and U. Lakshmanan. 1992. 'Language transfer and fossilization: the multiple effects principle' in S. M. Gass and L. Selinker (eds.). *Language Transfer in Language Learning*. Philadelphia: John Benjamins.

Seo, S.-K. 1998. *Frequency Analysis of Modern Korean Usage*. Seoul, Korea: Yonsei Language Information Institute.

Service, E. 1992. 'Phonology, working memory, and foreign-language learning.' *Quarterly Journal of Experimental Psychology* 45/A: 21–50.

Sharwood Smith, M. 1986. 'The competence/control model, cross-linguistic influence and the creation of new grammars' in E. Kellerman and M. S. Smith (eds.). *Crosslinguistic Influence in Second Language Acquisition*. Oxford: Pergamon Press.

Sharwood Smith, M. 1991. 'Speaking to many minds: on the relevance of different types of language information for the L2 learner.' *Second Language Research* 7/2: 118–32.

Sharwood Smith, M. 1993. 'Input enhancement in instructed SLA: theoretical bases.' *Studies in Second Language Acquisition* 15: 165–79.

Sheen, Y. 2004. 'Corrective feedback and learner uptake in communicative classrooms across instructional settings.' *Language Teaching Research* 8/3: 263–300.

Sheen, Y. 2006. 'Exploring the relationship between characteristics of recasts and learner uptake.' *Language Teaching Research* 10/4: 361–92.

Sheen, Y. This volume. 'The effects of corrective feedback, language aptitude, and learner attitudes on the acquisition of English articles' in A. Mackey (ed.). *Conversational Interaction in Second Language Acquisition: A Collection of Empirical Studies*. Oxford: Oxford University Press.

Shehadeh, A. 1999. 'Non-native speakers' production of modified comprehensible output and second language learning.' *Language Learning* 49: 627–75.

Shehadeh, A. 2001. 'Self- and other-initiated modified output during task-based interaction.' *TESOL Quarterly* 35: 433–57.

Shehadeh, A. 2003. 'Learner output, hypothesis testing, and internalizing linguistic knowledge.' *System* 31: 155–71.

Shook, D. J. 1994. 'FL/L2 reading, grammatical information, and the input-to-intake phenomenon.' *Applied Language Learning* 5/1: 57–93.

Shook, D. J. 1999. 'What foreign language reading recalls reveal about the input-to-intake phenomenon.' *Applied Language Learning* 10/1: 39–76.

Silver, R. E. 2000. 'Input, output, and negotiation: conditions for second language development' in B. Swierzbin, F. Morris, M. E. Anderson, C. A. Klee, and E. Tarone (eds.). *Social and Cognitive Factors in Second Language Acquisition: Selected Proceedings of the 1999 Second Language Research Forum*. Somerville, Mass.: Cascadilla Press.

Simard, D. and W. Wong. 2001. 'Alertness, orientation, and detection.' *Studies in Second Language Acquisition* 23: 103–24.

Sinclair, J. 1991. *Corpus, Concordance, Collocation*. Oxford: Oxford University Press.

Skehan, P. 1998. *A Cognitive Approach to Language Learning*. Oxford: Oxford University Press.

Skehan, P. 2002. 'Theorising and updating aptitude' in P. Robinson (ed.). *Individual Differences and Instructed Language Learning*. Amsterdam: John Benjamins.

Slabakova, R. 2003. 'Semantic and morphological reflexes of functional categories: the case of telicity marking in L2 Russian' in J. Liceras *et al.* (eds.). *Proceeding of the 6th Generative Approaches to Language Acquisition* (GASLA 2002). Somerville, Mass.: Cascadilla Proceedings Project.

Slimani-Rolls, A. 2005. 'Practitioner research: rethinking task-based language learning: what we can learn from the learners.' *Language Teaching Research* 9/2: 195–218.

Slobin, D. 1971. 'Data for the symposium' in D. Slobin (ed.). *The Ontogenesis of Grammar* New York: Academic Press.

Slobin, D. 1973. 'Cognitive prerequisites for the development of grammar' in C. Ferguson and D. Slobin (eds.). *Studies of Child Language Development*. New York: Holt, Rinehart and Winson.

Smith, S. C. 1997. *UAB Software*. Department of Rehabilitation Sciences: University of Alabama at Birmingham.

Smith, B. 2004. 'Computer-mediated negotiated interaction and lexical acquisition.' *Studies in Second Language Acquisition* 26: 365–98.

Smith, B. 2005. 'The relationship between negotiated interaction, learner uptake, and lexical acquisition in task-based computer-mediated communication.' *TESOL Quarterly* 39: 33–58.

Sohn, H.-M. 1999. *The Korean Language*. Cambridge: Cambridge University Press.

Soler, E. A. 2002. 'Relationship between teacher-led versus learners' interaction and the development of pragmatics in the EFL classroom.' *International Journal of Educational Research* 37: 359–77.

Sorace, A. 1996. 'The use of acceptability judgements in second language acquisition research' in W. Ritchie and T. Bhatia (eds.). *Handbook of Second Language Acquisition*. San Diego: Academic Press.

Sotillo, S. 2000. 'Discourse functions and syntactic complexity in synchronous and asynchronous communication.' *Language Learning and Technology* 4/1: 82–119.

Spada, N. and P. M. Lightbown. 1993. 'Instruction and the development of questions in L2 classrooms.' *Studies in Second Language Acquisition* 15: 205–24.

Spada, N. and P. M. Lightbown. 1999. 'Instruction, first language influence, and developmental readiness in second language acquisition.' *The Modern Language Journal* 83/1: 1–22.

Storch, N. 1998. 'Comparing second language learners' attention to form across tasks.' *Language Awareness* 7/4: 176–91.

Storch, N. 2001. 'How collaborative is pair work? ESL tertiary students composing in pairs.' *Language Teaching Research* 5/1: 29–53.

Storch, N. 2002. 'Patterns of interaction in ESL pair work.' *Language Learning* 52: 119–58.

Stratman, J. F. and L. Hamp-Lyons. 1994. 'Reactivity in concurrent think-aloud protocols: issues for research' in P. Smagorinsky (ed.). *Speaking about Writing: Reflections on Research Methodology.* Thousand Oaks, Calif.: Sage.

Sullivan, P. 2000a. 'Language play and communicative language teaching in a Vietnamese classroom' in J. Lantolf (ed.). *Sociocultural Theory and Second Language Learning.* Oxford: Oxford University Press.

Sullivan, P. 2000b. 'Spoken artistry: performance in a foreign language classroom' in J. K. Hall, and L. S. Verplaetse (eds.). *Second and Foreign Language Learning through Classroom Interaction.* Mahwah, N.J.: Lawrence Erlbaum Associates.

Suls, J. 1983. 'Cognitive processes in humor appreciation' in P. McGhee and J. Goldstein (eds.). *Handbook of Humor Research* (Vol. 1). New York: Springer Verlag.

Swain, M. 1985. 'Communicative competence: some roles of comprehensible input and comprehensible output in its development' in S. M. Gass and C. Madden (eds.). *Input in Second Language Acquisition.* Rowley, Mass.: Newbury House.

Swain, M. 1995. 'Three functions of output in second language learning' in G. Cook and B. Seidlhofer (eds.). *Principle and Practice in Applied Linguistics: Studies in Honour of H.G. Widdowson.* Oxford: Oxford University Press.

Swain, M. 1997. 'Collaborative dialogue: its contribution to second language learning.' *Revista Canaria de Estudios Ingleses* 34: 115–32.

Swain, M. 1998. 'Focus on form through conscious reflection' in C. Doughty and J. Williams (eds.). *Focus on Form in Classroom Second Language Acquisition.* Cambridge: Cambridge University Press.

Swain, M. 2000a. 'French immersion research in Canada: recent contributions to SLA and applied linguistics.' *Annual Review of Applied Linguistics* 20: 199–212.

Swain, M. 2000b. 'The output hypothesis and beyond: mediating acquisition through collaborative dialogue' in J. Lantolf (ed.). *Sociocultural Theory and Second Language Learning.* Oxford: Oxford University Press.

Swain, M. 2001a. 'Examining dialogue: another approach to content specification and to validating inferences drawn from test scores.' *Language Testing* 18/3: 275–302.

Swain, M. 2001b. 'Integrating language and content teaching through collaborative tasks.' *The Canadian Modern Language Review* 58/1: 44–63.

Swain, M. 2005. 'The output hypothesis: theory and research' in E. Hinkel (ed.). *Handbook of Research in Second Language Teaching and Learning.* Mahwah, N.J.: Lawrence Erlbaum.

Swain, M. 2006. 'Verbal protocols: what does it mean for research to use speaking as a data collection tool?' in M. Chaloub-Deville, C. Chapelle, and P. Duff (eds.). *Inference and Generalizability in Applied Linguistics: Multiple Research Perspectives.* Amsterdam: John Benjamins.

Swain, M. In press. 'Languaging, agency and collaboration in advanced language proficiency' in H. Byrnes (ed.). *Advanced Language Learning: The Contributions of Halliday and Vygotsky.* London: Continuum.

Swain, M., L. Brooks, and A. Tocalli-Beller. 2002. 'Peer–peer dialogue as a means of second language learning.' *Annual Review of Applied Linguistics* 22: 171–85.

Swain, M. and S. Lapkin. 1998. 'Interaction and second language learning: two adolescent French immersion students working together.' *The Modern Language Journal* 82/3: 320–37.

Swain, M. and S. Lapkin. 2001. 'Focus on form through collaborative dialogue: exploring task effects' in M. Bygate, P. Skehan, and M. Swain (eds.). *Researching Pedagogic Tasks: Second Language Learning, Teaching, and Testing.* London: Longman.

Swain, M. and S. Lapkin. 2002. 'Talking it through: two French immersion learners' response to reformulation.' *International Journal of Educational Research* 37/3–4: 285–304.

Takahashi, S. 1996. 'Pragmatic transferability.' *Studies in Second Language Acquisition* 18: 189–223.

Takashima, H. and R. Ellis. 1999. 'Output enhancement and the acquisition of the past tense' in R. Ellis (ed.). *Learning a Second Language through Interaction*. Amsterdam: John Benjamins.

Talmy, L. 1996. 'The windowing of attention' in M. Shibatani and S. A. Thompson (eds.). *Grammatical Constructions*. Oxford: Oxford University Press.

Tannen, D. 1990. 'Gender differences in topical coherence: creating involvement in best friends' talk.' *Discourse Processes* 13/1: 73–90.

Tarone, E. 1980. 'Communication strategies, foreigner talk and repair in interlanguage.' *Language Learning* 30: 417–32.

Tarone, E. 2000. 'Getting serious about language play: language play, interlanguage variation and second language acquisition' in B. Swierzbin, F. Morris, M. Anderson, C. Klee, and E. Tarone (eds.). *Social and Cognitive Factors in SLA: Proceedings of the 1999 Second Language Research Forum*. Somerville, Mass.: Cascadilla Press.

Tarone, E. 2002. 'Frequency effects, noticing, and creativity: factors in a variationist interlanguage framework.' *Studies in Second Language Acquisition* 24/2: 287–96.

Tarone, E. and M. Bigelow. 2005. 'Impact of literacy on oral language processing: implications for SLA research.' *Annual Review of Applied Linguistics* 25: 77–97.

Tarone, E. and M. Bigelow. This volume. 'Alphabetic print literacy and oral language processing in SLA' in A. Mackey (ed.). *Conversational Interaction in Second Language Acquisition: A Collection of Empirical Studies*. Oxford: Oxford University Press.

Tarone, E., M. Bigelow, and K. Hansen. Forthcoming. 'The impact of alphabetic print literacy on oral second language acquisition' in L. Condelli and N. Faux (eds.). *Research, Practice and Policy for Low-Educated Second Language and Literacy Acquisition – for Adults*. Richmond, V.A.: Literacy Institute at Virginia Commonwealth University.

Tarone, E., M. Bigelow, and B. Swierzbin. Forthcoming. 'Impact of literacy level on features of interlanguage in oral narratives' in T. Baldwin and L. Selinker (guest eds.). *Rivista di Psicolinguistica Applicata, Special Issue on Interlanguage*.

Taube-Schiff, M. and N. Segalowitz. 2005. 'Within-language attention control in second language processing.' *Bilingualism: Language and Cognition* 8: 195–206.

Thomas, M. 1994. 'Assessment of L2 proficiency in second language acquisition research.' *Language Learning* 44: 307–36.

Thomas, M. 2006. 'Research synthesis and historiography: the case of assessment of second language proficiency' in J. Norris and L. Ortega (eds.). *Synthesizing Research on Language Learning and Teaching*. Philadelphia: John Benjamins.

Tocalli-Beller, A. 2005. *Peer–peer Dialogue: Bringing Second Language Learning into Play*. Unpublished doctoral thesis. Ontario Institute for Studies in Education, University of Toronto.

Tocalli-Beller, A. and M. Swain. 2005. 'Reformulation: the cognitive conflict and L2 learning it generates.' *International Journal of Applied Linguistics* 15/1: 5–28.

Tocalli-Beller, A. and M. Swain. This volume. 'Riddles and puns in the ESL classroom: adults talk to learn' in A. Mackey (ed.). *Conversational Interaction in Second Language Acquisition: A Collection of Empirical Studies*. Oxford: Oxford University Press.

Tomasello, M. (ed.). 1998. *The New Psychology of Language: Cognitive and Functional Approaches to Language Structure*. Mahwah, N.J.: Lawrence Erlbaum Associates.

Tomlin, R. S. and V. Villa. 1994. '*Attention in cognitive science and second language acquisition*.' *Studies in Second Language Acquisition* 16/2: 183–203.

Trahey, M. and L. White. 1993. 'Positive evidence and preemption in second language classrooms.' *Studies in Second Language Acquisition* 15/2: 181–204.

Trofimovich, P., A. Ammar, and E. Gatbonton. This volume. 'How effective are recasts? The role of attention, memory, and analytic ability' in A. Mackey (ed.). *Conversational Interaction in Second Language Acquisition: A Collection of Empirical Studies*. Oxford: Oxford University Press.

Truscott, J. 1996. 'The case against grammar correction in L2 writing classes.' *Language Learning* 46: 327–69.

Truscott, J. 1998. 'Noticing in second language acquisition: a critical review.' *Second Language Research* 14: 103–35.

Truscott, J. 1999. 'What's wrong with oral grammar correction.' *The Canadian Modern Language Review* 55: 437–55.

Tsang, W. 2004. 'Feedback and uptake in teacher–student interaction: an analysis of 18 English lessons in Hong Kong secondary classrooms.' *Regional Language Centre Journal* 35: 187–209.

Ullman, M. T. 2001. 'The neural basis of lexicon and grammar in first and second language: the declarative/procedural model.' *Bilingualism: Language and Cognition* 4/1:105–22.

Ullman, M. T. 2005. 'A cognitive neuroscience perspective on second language acquisition: the declarative/procedural model' in C. Sanz (ed.). *Processing Approaches to Adult SLA: Theory and Practice*. Washington D.C.: Georgetown University Press.

Ur, P. 1981. *Discussions that Work: Task-centered Fluency Practice*. New York: Cambridge University Press.

Ur, P. 1988. *Grammar Practice Activities: A Practical Guide for Teachers*. New York: Cambridge University Press.

US Army Individual Test Battery. 1944. *Manual of Directions and Scoring*. Washington, D.C.: War Department, Adjutant General's Office.

Vainikka, A. and M. Young-Scholten. 1994. 'Direct access to X' — Theory: evidence from Korean and Turkish adults learning German' in T. Hoekstra and B. Schwartz (eds.). *Language Acquisition Studies in Generative Grammar*. Amsterdam: John Benjamins.

Vainikka, A. and M. Young-Scholten. 1998. 'The initial state in the L2 acquisition of phrase structure' in S. Flynn, G. Martohardjono, and W. O'Neil (eds.). *The Generative Study of Second Language Acquisition*. Mahwah, N.J.: Lawrence Erlbaum Associates.

Valdés, G. 1995. 'The teaching of minority languages as academic subjects: Pedagogical and theoretical challenges.' *The Modern Language Journal* 79: 299–328.

Valdés, G. 2001a. 'Heritage language students: Profiles and possibilities' in. J. Peyton, D. Ranard and S. McGinnis (eds.). *Heritage Languages in America: Preserving a National Resource*. Washington, D.C.: Center for Applied Linguistics.

Valdés, G. 2001b. *Learning and not Learning English: Latino Students in American Schools*. New York: Teachers College Press.

Van den Branden, K. 1997. 'Effects on negotiation on language learners' output.' *Language Learning* 47: 589–636.

VanPatten, B. 1989. 'Can learners attend to form and content while processing input?' *Hispania* 72/2: 409–17.

VanPatten, B. 1994. 'Evaluating the role of consciousness in second language acquisition: Terms, linguistic features and research methodology.' *AILA Review* 11: 27–36.

VanPatten, B. 1996. *Input Processing and Grammar Instruction: Theory and Research*. Norwood, N.J.: Ablex.

VanPatten, B. 2000. 'Processing instruction as form-meaning connections: issues in theory and research' in J. Lee and A. Valdman (eds.). *Form and Meaning: Multiple Perspectives*. Boston: Heinle and Heinle.

VanPatten, B. 2004. *Processing Instruction*. Mahwah: Lawrence Erlbaum Associates.

VanPatten, B. and J. Williams (eds.). 2006. *Theories in Second Language Acquisition: An Introduction*. Mahwah, NJ: Lawrence Erlbaum Associates.

Varonis, E. and S. M. Gass. 1985a. 'Miscommunication in native/nonnative conversation.' *Language in Society* 14/3: 327–43.

Varonis, E. and S. M. Gass. 1985b. 'Non-native/non-native conversations: a model for negotiation of meaning.' *Applied Linguistics* 6/1: 71–90.

Vendler, Z. 1967. 'Verbs and times.' in Z. Vendler (ed.). *Linguistics and Philosophy*. Ithaca, N.Y.: Cornell University Press. Reprinted from *Philosophical Review* (1957) 66/1: 143–60.

Vizmuller-Zocco, J. 1992. 'Critical thinking and verbal humor in textbooks of Italian as a second language' in C. Cicogna, M. Danesi, and A. Mollica (eds.). *Problem-solving in Second-language Teaching*. Welland, Ont.: Éditions Soleil Publishing Inc.

Vos, S. H., T. C. Gunter, H. Schriefers, and A. D. Friederici. 2001. 'Syntactic parsing and working memory: the effects of syntactic complexity, reading span and concurrent load.' *Language and Cognitive Processes* 16: 65–103.

Vygotsky, L. 1978. *Mind in Society*. Cambridge, Mass.: MIT Press.

Vygotsky, L. 1986. *Thought and Word*. Cambridge, Mass.: MIT Press.

Vygotsky, L. 1987. *The Collected Works of L. S. Vygotsky* (Vol. 1). New York: Plenum.

Walter, C. 2004. 'Transfer of reading comprehension skills to L2 is linked to mental representations of text and to L2 working memory.' *Applied Linguistics* 25/3: 315–39.

Warschauer, M. 1995. 'Comparing face-to-face and electronic discussion in the second language classroom.' *CALICO Journal* 13/1: 7–25.

Warschauer, M. and R. Kern. 2000. *Network-Based Language Teaching: Concepts and Practice*. Cambridge: Cambridge University Press.

Watanabe, T., H. Sakai, H. Shiokawa, and K. Urano. 2003. *Eigo-ga tsukaeru nihonnjin-no ikusei (Cultivating Japanese with English abilities)*. Tokyo: Sanseido.

Waters, G. S. and D. Caplan. 1996. 'The measurement of verbal working memory capacity and its relation to reading comprehension.' *Quarterly Journal of Experimental Psychology* 49: 51–79.

Wertsch, J. 1985. *Culture, Communication and Cognition: Vygotskian Perspectives*. New York: Cambridge University Press.

Wesche, M. and T. Paribakht. 1996. 'Assessing L2 vocabulary knowledge: depth versus breadth.' *The Canadian Modern Language Review* 53/1: 13–40.

West, C. and A. Garcia. 1988. 'Conversational shift work: a study of topical transitions between women and men.' *Social Problems* 35/5: 551–75.

White, J. 1998. 'Getting the learners' attention: a typographical input enhancement study' in C. Doughty and J. Williams (eds.). *Focus on Form in Classroom Second Language Acquisition*. New York: Cambridge University Press.

White, L. 1987. 'Against comprehensible input: the input hypothesis and the development of second-language competence.' *Applied Linguistics* 8: 95–110.

White, L. 1991. 'Adverb placement in second language acquisition: some effects of positive and negative evidence in the classroom.' *Second Language Research* 7/2: 133–61.

White, L., E. Valenzuela, M. Kozlowska-Macgregor, and I. L. Yan-Kit. 2004. 'Gender and number agreement in nonnative Spanish.' *Applied Psycholinguistics* 25/1: 105–33.

Williams, J. 1999. 'Learner-generated attention to form.' *Language Learning* 49/4: 583–625.

Williams, J. 2001. 'The effectiveness of spontaneous attention to form.' *System* 29/3: 325–40.

Williams, J. and J. Evans. 1998. 'What kind of focus and on which forms?' in C. Doughty and J. Williams (eds.). *Focus on Form in Classroom Second Language Acquisition*. Cambridge: Cambridge University Press.

Wong, W. 2001. 'Modality and attention to meaning and form in the input.' *Studies in Second Language Acquisition* 23: 345–68.

Wong, W. 2003. 'Textual enhancement and simplified input: effects on L2 comprehension and acquisition of non-meaningful grammatical form.' *Applied Language Learning* 13/2: 17–45.

Young-Scholten, M., C. Ijuin, and A. Vainikka. 2005. 'Organic Grammar as a measurement of development.' Paper presented at TESOL Conference, San Antonio, Texas.

Index

Entries referring to tables or figures are in italics, e.g. *258*